THE MAKING OF MODERN MEXICO

THE MAKING OF

MODERN MEXICO

FRANK BRANDENBURG

INTRODUCTION BY
FRANK TANNENBAUM
COLUMBIA UNIVERSITY

PRENTICE-HALL, INC. · **ENGLEWOOD CLIFFS, N. J.**

The Making of Modern Mexico, by Frank Brandenburg

PRENTICE-HALL INTERNATIONAL, INC., *London*
PRENTICE-HALL OF AUSTRALIA, PTY., LTD., *Sydney*
PRENTICE-HALL OF CANADA, LTD., *Toronto*
PRENTICE-HALL OF INDIA (PRIVATE) LTD., *New Delhi*
PRENTICE-HALL OF JAPAN, INC., *Tokyo*
PRENTICE-HALL DE MEXICO, S.A., *Mexico City*

Printed in the United States of America

Dedicated to the visionaries of the Revolutionary Family who elevated Mexico to an exemplary position among Latin American nations and to Rachel and Joan Brandenburg, who patiently lived with the book page by page.

INTRODUCTION

Dr. Brandenburg has written an interesting and broadly based book that seeks to explain how an undeveloped nation with a troubled and revolution-ridden history moved into the modern world. The changeover in the years that span 1910 to 1964, the period with which the author is primarily concerned, is dramatic. The Mexican story as told here suggests what a revolution can and can not do, and at what cost. The price in Mexico was high. The revolution took a million lives. It destroyed a ruling society; the "upper classes," from which the governors, generals, diplomats, landowners, intellectuals were drawn, were impoverished, expropriated, exiled, or killed. The government, the constitutional system, the army, the courts, the landholding system, peonage, and many things besides were swept away by the revolutionary tide. The people who came to replace those who were driven out were newcomers. Neither they nor their parents before them (in most cases) had ever appeared on the political stage. Many of them came from the peasantry—Zapata, Villa, Amaro, most of them were poor with little formal education and no political experience—Obregón, Calles, Cárdenas, Mújica, and many, many others. These made the revolution, learned their military art, and acquired their political experience while fighting to stay alive. For the revolution was incoherent, unorganized, directionless, coalescing one moment into a seeming unity only to splinter again into factional rebellion where friends of yesterday killed each other for personal rather than for political reasons.

Dr. Brandenburg explores how this directionless and bloody upheaval grew into a coherent social movement he describes as the "Mexican Proposition." There is very considerable distance between Pancho Villa and Díaz Ordaz, who has been selected to be the president of Mexico for the term beginning in December 1964. How this distance was traversed and the present "Mexican Proposition" achieved is the story related in this volume. In between Pancho Villa and Díaz Ordaz is the transition from a primitive agricultural society to one increasingly industrial, and from a purely military dictatorship to a government resting on popular consensus.

The significance of the story told here lies more in the moral and spiritual changes that have occurred than in the striking economic or even the political spheres, though these are challenging. In the political sphere, true enough, there has developed a government that rests upon a broad consensus. But the government itself is embodied in the chief executive to a greater extent than before, if for no other reason than that the power of the president is more widely based both in the law and custom than in the past. The single party system has served to make the president omnipotent as long as he is the visible embodiment of the "Permanent Revolution." It has also killed off all political activities and eliminated all politicians. There are no longer visible candidates for president; no one has a party that he can claim. The candidate for the succession, *El Tapado*, remains covered over until he is revealed by the magic touch of the president. The next executive, who may be an unknown figure, is suddenly thrown into the political arena and given some six months to capture the imagination and affection of the people before he catapulted into the presidential chair by an almost unanimous vote and becomes incarnate as the embodiment of the "Permanent Revolution."

As president he will for six years shape the political fortunes of all other Mexicans. No one will be elected as governor, member of the Senate or House of Representatives, or mayor of even a medium-size city without his consent. This is an improvement upon the politics of Díaz, but it is not a durable political system for a large and growing nation. Political leadership can not be manufactured.

Dr. Brandenburg is kinder to the political machinery than he need be. The important gain of the Mexican Revolution, as the author makes evident, is the changed moral environment. Cárdenas established the principle that Mexico can be governed without violence. For the first time in its history a president had ruled for six years without killing anybody. That was an example which every executive since had to follow. Mexicans for the first time in their history have stopped being afraid of each other and of their government. This, primarily, as well as agrarian reform, an independent foreign policy, and the amalgam produced by the revolution has given to the people a sense of freedom and pride which they never had before. Mexicans no longer want to be either Europeans or Americans. They look upon themselves and what they have done and are content with being Mexicans. The Renaissance which is visible in Mexico—the only place one can speak of it as existing in our day—is, if one can draw such causal relation, the fruit of the people's sudden discovery of themselves and of their past. They have for the first time in four hundred years identified themselves with their ancient history, and one can see the results in the work of their great artists, architects, and more recently in their music, poetry, and fiction. The Mexicans, like the ancient Greeks, now look upon all people beyond their own borders as barbarians. This self-awakening is the real fruit of their bitter, cruel, and bloody revolution. But it is a fruit no one fought for, and no one expected. And yet the gift that Mexico has given to mankind, not just to itself, is this unlooked-for flowering of the human spirit. This volume will help the reader to an understanding of the puzzling and contradictory elements out of which the "Mexican Proposition" has grown.

Frank Tannenbaum
Columbia University

PRELUDE

^^

With underdeveloped countries everywhere pushed by their masses into modernization schemes that promise the arrival of tomorrow today, recent Mexican experiences have much to offer the world. The legacies that form the issues in today's freedom struggles in Africa, Asia, and Latin America have striking counterparts in the Mexican record: brutality, militarism, racism, poverty, privileged foreigners, feudalism, ignorance. A half-century before President Kennedy launched his Alliance for Progress, a bearded mystic from the northern plains of Mexico led his compatriots against the invincible dictator Porfirio Díaz and unleashed forces that would make Mexico one of the first nations to undergo a national social revolution. Transforming Mexico into a modern nation meant undertaking a permanent revolution—the most sweeping transformation of Mexican life since the impact of Cortés and the Spaniards who followed him.

This book is an interpretation of the causes and effects of this revolution, the Mexican Revolution, and of the present health and probable direction of the Mexican nation. It is a timely reminder of the urgency of discovering practical solutions to the problems imposed on the emerging nations by economic backwardness, social estrangement, and authoritarianism.

Yet this is not the definitive book on Mexico; that will never be written. Examining the country's long past, colored by contradiction, is a no less formidable task than probing her complex, elusive present or the promises of her challenging future. The burden of Mexico's complexity is unduly heavy on a writer attempting to analyze present-day Mexico, the aim of this book. Without curiosity, extensive residence, and personal involvement in that country, he cannot hope to interpret modern Mexico— certainly not if he seeks to supply answers to the major questions of Mexican political, economic, religious, and social life. On the other hand, a clear and objective analysis of Mexican society as a whole becomes more and more difficult as an observer becomes more deeply enmeshed in Mexican realities and potentialities and finds himself in previously unexplored depths.

xi

The late ambassador Francis J. White alerted me a decade ago to an ageless instruction for foreign writers coming to Mexico. "Any book on Mexico," he said, "should be written from the impressions the foreigner receives during his first month here. A more prolonged investigation will devour the writer and will never end." In writing the pages that follow I learned well the truth of his words. For almost a decade I was devoured by Mexico, often wondering whether my investigations would ever produce the evidence I sought. My travels around Mexico took me through the lands of the Mayas, Quetzals, and Zapotecs, from the picturesque island of Cozumel near British Honduras and the rolling coasts of Veracruz, Guerrero, and Sinaloa to the beautiful valleys of Guanajuato, Michoacán, and Morelos and the desolate expanses of Baja California, Sonora, and Chihuahua. My investigations led me for extended periods into the head-quarters of Mexico's official political party, into academic life at the National University, National Polytechnic Institute, and the University of the Americas, and into Mexican business and government. I talked to the leaders of Mexico's political, economic, religious, and educational life, as well as to the humblest peasants of Chiapas, Colima, and Oaxaca and the poorest slum-dwellers of Mexico City, Monterrey, and Guadalajara. I spoke with presidents, cabinet ministers, governors, municipal presidents, diplomats, political refugees, secret police, military commanders, regional political bosses, local Indian rulers, wealthy entrepreneurs, managers of state industries, street vendors, fascists, socialists, anarchists, Communists, great *hacendados*, small ranchers, communal *ejidatarios*, academicians, economists, sociologists, intellectuals visiting from abroad, Freemasons, Catholics, village priests, bishops, Jewish Catholics, Catholic Freemasons, trade unionists, doctors, engineers, and many, many students.

Although not a few Mexicans may resent my wisdom in analyzing their nation by presenting its liabilities as well as its assets, this approach is both sympathetic and necessary. Pointing out authoritarian customs and shortcomings—and Mexico has its share of them—is just as indispensable to an understanding of Mexican society as identifying Mexico's achievements and promises and placing them in historical perspective. Hence, I have noted constructive and destructive forces alike in seeking a synthesis of recent Mexican history that would explain the making of modern Mexico.

This dual approach also emerged from the very nature of the questions I have tried to answer: Who rules Mexico? How do they govern? What is the essence of the ideological image driving Mexico forward? What is the nature, influence, and promise of religion in Mexico? How do Catholicism and Freemasonry influence and interact in Mexican society? Is it possible for free enterprise to flourish when ownership of the elements of production and distribution is increasingly lodging in the state? Can Mexico feed its rapidly growing population and simultaneously do justice to agrarian reform, industrialization, and social justice? What is the relationship of liberty and equality in Mexico? Of freedom and order? What explains Mexican foreign policy? I have attempted to present selected themes that together might offer insight into the way in which five decades of revolution have transformed Mexico from a resentful, backward, and inharmonious society into an apparently dynamic nation gaining unity and forward momentum from planned economic, social, and political programs.

During the long time given to research and writing I have accumulated unusually heavy obligations of an intellectual nature. Although most of those who generously and patiently gave their time to help, guide, and encourage must necessarily remain nameless here, including everyone in the active ranks of Mexican political life, I should like to acknowledge my long-outstanding debts to the late Miron Burgin and to professors Robert N. Burr, Russell H. Fitzgibbon, Howard C. Perkins, Ben Stephansky, and Arthur P. Whitaker. In Mexico, in addition to my students whose field research over a six-year period contributed greatly to the pages that follow, I owe a special debt of gratitude to Anita Brenner, Edmundo Flores, Pablo González Casanova, Richard Greenleaf, Gilberto Loyo, Gustavo Romero Kolbeck, Paul Murray, John Paddock, Victor Urquidi, Ramón Xirau, and Luis Yáñez-Pérez. Several intellectuals who resided in Mexico for extended stays contributed fresh insights to my research: Harold E. Davis of American University; Richard Dettering of San Francisco State University; John Elmendorf of Brown University; Joseph Kahl of Washington University; Oscar Lewis of the University of Illinois; Edwin Lieuwen of the University of New Mexico; David McClelland and Raymond Vernon of Harvard University; the late C. Wright Mills; and Allen Whiting, now of the Department of State. I also wish to acknowledge suggestions received from Howard F. Cline of the Library of Congress after his reading of the first draft of Chapters 1 and 2. Above all, I wish to express my deepest gratitude to seven scholars in the United States—Harold E. Davis, Russell Fitzgibbon, Oscar Lewis, Edwin Lieuwen, Stanley Ross, Frank Tannenbaum, and Bryce Wood—who kindly read drafts of my manuscript and offered many constructive suggestions for its improvement. Words could never voice my indebtedness to the persons named and to those who remain nameless. I can merely hope that this book lives up to their expectations and partially reflects my obligations to them.

Years consumed in research also create obligations of a financial nature. The Doherty Foundation at Princeton and the Penfield Committee at the University of Pennsylvania awarded funds permitting twelve months of research during 1953–54. A Ford Foundation postdoctoral seminar at the State University of Iowa in the summer of 1955 provided an opportunity to scrutinize materials on Latin America in world politics. The Committee on Comparative Politics of the Social Science Research Council awarded liberal funds for pursuing fifteen months of research in Mexico during 1957–58. The same committee underwrote my expenses to attend two conferences held under its auspices, from which I gained valuable insights into the politics of the developing areas. Since 1955, several business firms have permitted me to go beyond usual consultant assignments and probe, at their expense, topics largely of personal interest to me. Finally, with considerable financial sacrifice, Charles Stone, now of the University of California at Berkeley, supplied valuable research assistance, and Elvira Nistal typed the manuscript.

CONTENTS

	Introduction	vii
	Prelude	xi
ONE	The Revolutionary Family and the Mexican Proposition	1
TWO	Before the Revolution	19
THREE	Fifty Years of Revolution (1)	47
FOUR	Fifty Years of Revolution (2)	79
FIVE	The Mexican Publics	119
SIX	The Liberal Machiavellian	141
SEVEN	Religion	166
EIGHT	Economic Progress: The Big Look	205
NINE	Mexico Versus Malthus	234
TEN	Industrial Revolution	264
ELEVEN	Commercial Revolution	293
TWELVE	Foreign Policy and International Affairs	318
	Postlude: Mexico Tomorrow	341
	A Note on Sources	348
	Index	369

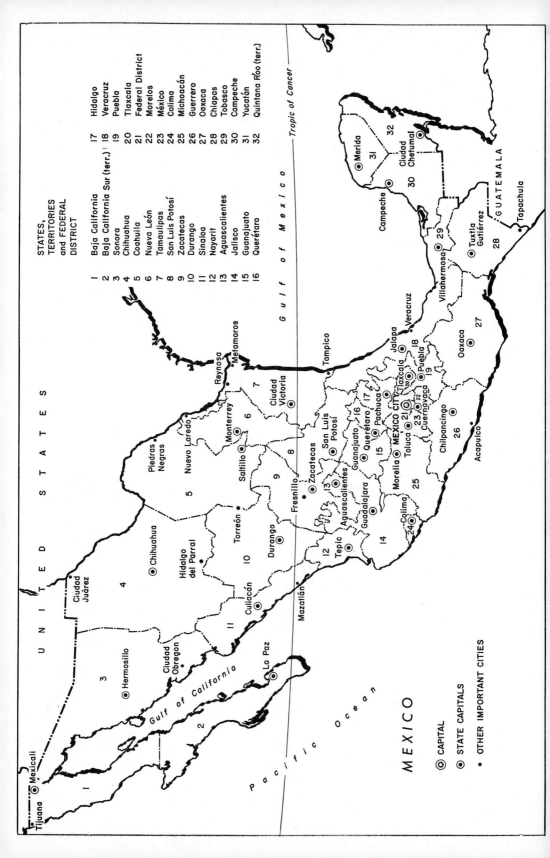

STATES,
TERRITORIES
and FEDERAL
DISTRICT

1	Baja California
2	Baja California Sur (terr.)
3	Sonora
4	Chihuahua
5	Coahuila
6	Nueva León
7	Tamaulipas
8	San Luis Potosí
9	Zacatecas
10	Durango
11	Sinaloa
12	Nayarit
13	Aguascalientes
14	Jalisco
15	Guanajuato
16	Querétaro
17	Hidalgo
18	Veracruz
19	Puebla
20	Tlaxcala
21	Federal District
22	Morelos
23	México
24	Colima
25	Michoacán
26	Guerrero
27	Oaxaca
28	Chiapas
29	Tabasco
30	Campeche
31	Yucatán
32	Quintana Róo (terr.)

MEXICO

◎ CAPITAL

◉ STATE CAPITALS

• OTHER IMPORTANT CITIES

ONE

THE REVOLUTIONARY FAMILY
AND THE MEXICAN PROPOSITION

Revolution in Mexico, the permanent revolution, is a dynamic political, social, and economic fact. First unleashed in 1910, its perennial goal is inspiring in its simplicity: Social justice for all Mexicans. Many routes have been tried, some followed, some expanded, some abandoned, but all have been directed toward achieving the over-all goal.

This Revolution has been the quest of tens of millions of human beings striving to make a particular and private version of democracy meaningful. More exactly, it has been the quest of a mere handful of Mexicans, the elite, who have literally determined how the millions will live. Philosophically, the Revolution may have embraced contradictions and inconsistencies, but the Mexican is not troubled by this; he is quite willing to admit fallacy in some of yesterday's aspects of the Revolution. Yet he is forcefully certain that self-determination, not adherence to foreign credos, is the path of wisdom. In fact, the Mexican often finds himself puzzled in this era of superpowers contesting whether the ends of freedom and human dignity are best attained in institutions flaunting the banner of Karl Marx or of Adam Smith. In his own country, the Mexican can observe some nationalized industries giving workers more respect and higher real wages than enterprises conducted by private owners. And he knows that social and economic improvement and greater political freedom have come about without the "blessings" of a multiple-party political system. Yet he also sees private businesses flourishing and making a substantial contribution to the well-being of the people.

Revolution for this modern Mexican is more than an ideal: It is the continuing struggle to transform his society into the shape of an ideological image. The Mexican sees himself as part of this struggle.

The overwhelming majority of persons in the United States probably see Mexico and the Mexican quite differently. The time is long overdue for a refinement of our ideas. True, some Mexicans are illiterate "wetbacks." Some live on the border to exploit U.S. tourists. Some are irresponsible, carefree peons. Yet these Mexican types constitute an in-

1

significant portion of Mexican society. Industrialists, merchants, bankers, teachers, engineers, doctors, factory workers, farm laborers, bus drivers—all are making their imprint on the society emerging below the Rio Grande. Illiteracy and poverty are losing ground to universal public education and rising living standards. Few Americans realize that thousands of Mexicans are graduates of American universities, and even these thousands represent a small minority beside the tens of thousands graduated from institutions of higher learning in Mexico.

As the number of educated Mexicans rises, so does the population in general. By the end of the century, according to United Nations estimates, Mexico will reach the astonishing population of 110 million inhabitants. In Europe (excluding Russia), Africa, and the entire Western Hemisphere, only the United States and Brazil will be more populous.

The Mexicans believe they understand Americans better than we do them. They are anxious to learn from us, despite the presumption in many quarters north of the Rio Grande that we have nothing to learn from Mexico. Russians and Chinese make no such presumption. They want to know how the Mexicans have transformed their society through a revolution directed against foreigners and capitalism without becoming Communist. They know that the Mexican Revolution is an object lesson for the Americas as well as for the entire underdeveloped world. Beyond this, and far more important in the long haul, they realize that revolution in the Mexican way constitutes an alternative to revolution in the Communist way. This realization, no less than their desire to establish a beachhead on the mainland of North America, is the reason the Communists keep hammering at Mexican institutions.

It is within this larger context of Cold War and developmental politics that we must acknowledge the importance of the Mexican Revolution. To influence the content of popular movements today, we must present acceptable alternatives to Marxism-Leninism—and by itself, the example of the United States has proven inapplicable. Nor is a "good-neighbor policy" adequate, because taking friendship for granted carries with it the danger of misunderstanding and alienation, as Mexican–U.S. relations in the thirties and after proved. By studying the problems and progress of the people and institutions of our immediate neighbor to the south, we can learn what we need to know to inject new life into our global policy.

WHO RULES MEXICO?

From the outset of any study of modern Mexico, there are compelling reasons for understanding that patterns of government there differ radically from American notions on democracy. The precise scope and nature of these divergencies will be clear only after studying the Mexican Revolution in its totality, which is the aim of this book. Chapters 5 and 6 bear particularly on these differing concepts of democracy. Reserved for later discussion are such important themes as how Mexico is run, the limitations on arbitrary use of power, the manner in which the political selection process works, the interplay and influence of interest groups, the institutionalization of opposition forces, and the big themes of democracy versus dictatorship and capitalism versus socialism. But here at the beginning, brief attention to the question of who runs Mexico is appropriate to set the stage on which the Mexican panorama will unfold.

Mexico is ruled by an elite. For the sake of convenience, and to suggest the nature of this leadership group, it will be assigned the label of "Revolutionary Family," or simply "Family." The Revolutionary Family is composed of the men who have run Mexico for over half a century, who have laid the policy-lines of the Revolution, and who today hold effective decision-making power.

On September 6, 1961, in a moment of domestic political controversy, Senator Manuel Moreno Sánchez, intimate collaborator of President López Mateos of Mexico, offered some insight into the nature of this Revolutionary Family. On the floor of the senate, he made two statements of note in unequivocal terms: First, he said, "I wish to affirm vigorously and courageously that an oligarchy supported by the people governs in Mexico, an oligarchy that has made possible the leading of the nation into development." Second, to make it clear that the Mexican elite is not the usual type of Latin American oligarchy, Moreno Sánchez observed that "the difference between the Mexican elite and others is that ours is a revolutionary minority, while others in Latin America are of a military, clerical, large agricultural, or of a simple industrial-financial type, and [as] conservative minorities they hold back from becoming revolutionary minorities." The shortcoming of other Latin American oligarchies, he said, is that they "do not think [seriously] about the problem of transforming their people, but merely about development of properties and of their own businesses."

Working to keep the Revolutionary Family together are five major forces that might be identified as the psychological dynamics of the elite: (1) *dedication* to the Revolutionary past, present, and future, and to the proposition of building a better nation; (2) *friendship* forged on the battlefields and sports fields, in the halls of government and in army service, in the public schools, technical institutes, and universities, in Masonic lodges, in the business community, in civic affairs, and in the intermarriages among Revolutionary families; (3) *self-interest* in accumulating and retaining power, prestige, and wealth; (4) *fear* of political defeat, of anti-Revolutionaries coming into power, of losing everything gained, and in the last instance, of actual physical elimination; and (5) the *inertia* of being an integral part of a working mechanism, of going along with what exists, and of not wishing to risk disturbing the Revolutionary setup.

Revolutionary Family affairs are conducted on three separate levels. At the top, an inner council, in which the final word belongs to the Family head alone, is composed of about twenty favorite sons—the incumbent President of Mexico and, one year out of every six, the president-elect; former presidents (although several presidents failed to become head of the Family, every sole head has served as president); a few powerful national and regional political leaders, usually including the ministers of government (*gobernación*) and national defense and other outstanding cabinet members; and, depending on the orientation of the Family head, a few extremely wealthy individuals or labor union leaders, or both. Formal meetings of this kitchen cabinet rarely occur. Instead, the Family head consults each individual member to arrive at a consensus, which he may or may not choose to respect when he declares his disposition—the final word. This is the level where decisions made at lower levels are reversed or sustained, where one Family head passes his power on to another, where the prestige and power accumulation of Mexicans on the inside and the outside are discussed, where the over-all economic and political orientation of the nation is set, and where the father and favorite sons of the Revolutionary Family determine the fate and future of Mexico.

The inner council keeps the Revolution intact and rolling forward by understanding the relative power of the major vested interests—the economic, political, social, governmental, religious, educational, and military sides of Mexico. Although it is not always necessary, interest groups can best make their demands heeded by personal consultation with the head of the Family. Anyone on the fringes of power who is requested to offer "advice" in this way, and who enjoys in the process an intimacy with the Family head, is admitted to the second level of the Family structure. Since 1952, this level has been occupied by approximately two hundred spokesmen from finance, commerce, private industry, and agriculture; from cabinet ministries, state-owned industries, federal agencies, and provincial governments; from educational, religious, professional, and social organizations; from the armed forces and veterans' groups; from labor unions, cooperatives, communal agricultural groups, and civil-servant federations; and from the judiciary, political groupings (official party and "opposition" parties), and the press. To the degree that the Family has institutionalized the Revolution, its successors come from this level of operation and not, as so many foreign observers are inclined to write, from the ranks of the proletariat-oriented official political party.[1] This official party, originally organized by Calles as a gambit to institutionalize Family leadership of

---

[1] This contention receives detailed consideration in Chapters 5 and 6.

the nation, has for two decades remained on the fringe of Mexican development, in terms of both its principles and the influence of its rank-and-file membership.

The third level of the Family hierarchy is the formal political apparatus headed by the President of Mexico in his immediate capacity as president. It embraces the national bureaucracy (the executive, legislative, judicial, and administrative branches), the armed forces, the official political party, captive opposition parties, and state and local public administrations. All these segments owe ultimate loyalty to the chief of state, and the orientation and timing of policies and programs under their charge depend on instructions received from the President of Mexico. Failure to observe his dictates means an eclipse of prestige, discharge from position, or an even worse fate. Although policy may be originated anywhere on the bureaucratic ladder, every significant policy change must clear with the president. Similarly, the official party may conduct intraorganizational primaries without presidential intervention, but the president reserves the right to veto any nomination offered and to substitute his own choice. The official party is merely an appendage of the bureaucratic apparatus. Nominations for the office of president and governor are out of reach of not only the official party organization, but the entire third rung of Revolutionary Family authority. The last, if not always the first, word on these matters belongs to the President of Mexico or, in his stead, the Family head.

The Family is thus directed by the undisputed head of the clan. He inherits Hidalgo and Morelos, leaders of Mexican independence, as godparents. He acquires Benito Juárez, nineteenth-century liberal, as his grandfather. He joins the line of successors to the first father of the Revolution, Francisco I. Madero. He usually, but not necessarily, holds the office of President of Mexico. The head of the clan exercises all power— or no power. He either delivers the definitive word on every matter, or someone else rises to take his place. Aggregation of interests can happen both inside and outside the Family, but in the last instance, all demands are judged by the head of the Family. When he does not also hold the office of President of Mexico, presidential authority is regularly questioned and often ignored in favor of the Family head. When no single leader is capable of gaining undisputed recognition as head of the Family, or when a leader, on gaining it, proves incapable of being a truly strong father, multiple leadership temporarily results. But only temporarily.

Once elevated to the high lordship of Mexico, the Family head constantly must prove that he, and he alone, runs the nation. Carranza had to prove his first chieftainship against Pancho Villa, Emiliano Zapata, and Álvaro Obregón. Failing against the last, Carranza ceded to Obregón. Calles, who had the title of "Supreme Chief of the Revolution" bestowed upon him by the National Congress, asserted his dominium by eliminating General Escobar and cohorts, by removing the puppet President Pascual

Ortiz Rubio, and by setting up an official political party whose president answered to Calles for all political nominations. Once Cárdenas wrested Family leadership from Calles and dramatized his assumption of power by expelling Calles from Mexican territory, he still had to prove his undisputed leadership when it was questioned by different interests: by Saturnino Cedillo in San Luis Potosí; by Tomás Garrido Canabal in Tabasco; the Monterrey factionalists in Nuevo León; and by Vicente Lombardo Toledano and organized labor. Miguel Alemán seized Family leadership from Cárdenas and Manuel Ávila Camacho eleven months before he entered the presidency, but had to share it with Cárdenas during the last months of his own presidential term. Adolfo Ruiz Cortines needed sixteen months of his presidential term to consolidate his hegemony; then, while still Family head and President of Mexico, Ruiz decided in mid-1958 to share with President-elect Adolfo López Mateos the final word on Mexican affairs.

Leadership of the Revolutionary Family has been possessed by eleven men; only eight of these, however, managed to become sole head. Beginning with Francisco Madero (1910–13), Family leadership passed to the triumvirate of Zapata, Villa, and Carranza (1913–15), next to Carranza alone (1916–19), and to Carranza together with Álvaro Obregón (late 1919 to early 1920). Obregón then ruled alone (1920–24) and subsequently shared leadership with Plutarco Elías Calles (1924–28). After the assassination of Obregón, Calles became the "Supreme Chief" (1928–35), but was squeezed into sharing Family leadership with Cárdenas (until June 1935), then lost the role completely to Cárdenas (1935–40). Cárdenas prolonged his Family leadership in conjunction with Manuel Ávila Camacho (1940–46), but both lost out to Miguel Alemán (1946–51). When Alemán attempted to impose a successor unacceptable to other members of the Family inner circle, he was forced into dividing Family control with Cárdenas (1952); nonetheless, the new president, Adolfo Ruiz Cortines, had to share Family leadership with both Alemán and Cárdenas (1952–54) until the serious political crisis splitting the Family was overcome by the consolidation of Ruiz's position as sole head of the Family (1954–58). Ruiz, in turn, shared the fathership with President-elect Adolfo López Mateos for six months, then bowed out in favor of López Mateos alone (1958–64). At the time when these respective leaders took over control of the Family elite, seven were army generals and two were lawyers, one was a political reformer and intellectual mystic, and one was a politician from the ranks of the career civil service.

Judged on a scale of power possessed, four men stand out: Calles, Cárdenas, Obregón, and Alemán. The first two managed to stay at the top for periods totaling more than a decade and each of the last two remained in power for only slightly less time. The combined popularity, prestige, and power of each of these Family heads reached such heights that, on penalty of expulsion from the country or some even worse fate, no one—including former Presidents of Mexico—ventured to question his overlordship unless he were invited to do so by the Family head himself. None of these four held such absolute dominion during his entire regime, but at the high point in his career: Calles was in this position for six years, Obregón, Cárdenas, and Alemán for five years each. Francisco I. Madero, the "Apostle" and first father, never enjoyed comparable power, nor did he seem desirous of acquiring it. And even though Carranza was knighted "First Chief of the Constitutionalist Army," and wielded fairly absolute power from 1917 to 1919, there were too many favorite sons on the scene for him to completely consolidate Family forces. The two other sole heads, Ruiz Cortines and López Mateos, have had no need and probably no desire to amass the kind of crude power wielded by earlier heads. Yet this should not imply that the position of Family head has recently become less powerful; on the contrary, as we shall observe in Chapter 6, power is seemingly concentrating more and more in the Family head.

THE REVOLUTIONARY CREED

The ruling elite in Mexico derives no less strength from its presumed and real dedication to acceptable social ideals than from its ability to walk with its feet on firm political ground. Aware of its direction and its moment in history, the Family cannot long ignore pressures coming from deeply rooted national aspirations. The members of the Family, along with Mexican society in general, see themselves as part of the continuing struggle to transform the society into the shape of an ideological image. This image is decidedly not an exclusive possession of the elite. If not always democratically governed, Mexicans are generally democratically minded. And though the elite usually publicizes the great progress of the Revolution and underplays the serious problems that remain, the ideological image in which Mexican leaders are trying to reshape society has not been imposed by any notable brainwashing of the proletariat. The extent to which specific Revolutionary policies are presumably acceptable to the majority of Mexicans and to various interest groups is analyzed in subsequent chapters. Suffice it to observe here that, even though there are weighty arguments against the proposition that the realities of Mexico today are manifestations of the beliefs of the people as a whole, the Revolutionary Family's dedication to building a better Mexico is, in day-to-day practice, virtually tantamount to this very proposition.

The essence of this motivating ideological image combines basic aspirations with various strands and policies of the Revolution itself. For this reason, "fundamental objectives guiding Mexico under Revolutionary leadership" or simply "Revolutionary Creed" seem proper alternative terms for "image." The Revolutionary Creed, of course, contains both constants and dynamics—the one because of its recognition of presumably constant characteristics of human behavior, the other because of its incorporation of beliefs that form the will to action. It is also constant in the sense that every objective in the Creed can be given justification under the broad provisions of Mexico's Constitution of 1917. And it is additionally dynamic in that every objective can be interpreted differently by one president after another.

An over-all synthesis would reveal the Revolutionary Creed's insistence that reason govern tradition, that secular authority supersede divine right, that nationalism transcend particularism, and that the state perform welfare functions that historically depended on religious charity. The basic objectives further hold that state intervention is indispensable to economic growth; that social, political, and economic integrations on a national scale are intrinsically good; and that international stature is gained and held by adherence to recognized principles of diplomatic conduct.

In analyzing the basic objectives that guide Mexico under its Revolutionary leadership, no observer of Mexican life can fully escape the dangers of sinning by omission, false interpretation, or incorrect emphases. Yet the need for specificity cannot be disowned if we are to attempt an understanding of what has happened in Mexico since 1910, what is happening there today, and what is likely to happen there tomorrow. Against this background, then, the Revolutionary Creed will be dissected into its interrelated components.

1. *Mexicanism.*   The first objective of the Revolutionary Creed, that of Mexicanism, involves patriotism, nationalism, and pride in being Mexican. Mexicanism implies first and foremost building a Mexico by and for Mexicans. The average Mexican is encouraged to believe that he is just as important as a foreigner, priest, or big landowner, and that Mexican works, especially in art, architecture, drama, music, literature, and philosophy, are as good as any in the world. The foreigner and his ideas and things are not to be excluded, but they are always to be subjected to a different set of rules; they must prove themselves pragmatically. The conduct of foreigners must be exemplary. Foreign ownership, foreign employees, foreign textbooks, foreign professionals, and foreign educational philosophy have all been able to abide by the rules and have become intertwined with part of the concept of Mexicanism.

Patriotism is glorified in Revolutionary ideology through a set of symbolic examples taken (with the facts sometimes colored or juggled a bit) from Mexican history. The Mexican is urged to find a personal counterpart in one of the nation's past glorious heroes. These object-lessons, frequently selected to justify the Revolution itself, are carefully injected with sound Revolutionary interpretations. The strong Indian character, with its anti-imperialism and its refusal to be compromised, are symbolized in the heroic last-ditch defense of the Aztec civilization by the youthful chieftain Cuauhtémoc. Magnanimity in the Mexican is inspired by the admirable Bartolomé de las Casas, Vasco de Quiroga, and Sahagún, all of them Spaniards who undertook the task of protecting, educating, and otherwise elevating the status of the downtrodden Indian; these models inspire young Mexican schoolteachers and medical doctors to leave the city and administer to the needy of rural Mexico. Patriotism and nationalism draw much fuel from the self-sacrifices of Hidalgo and Morelos, the excommunicated priests who initiated the independence movement in Mexico. And lauded conspicuously is the bravery of the young military cadets who gave up their lives in the battle against the seasoned soldiers of General Winfield Scott: A monument to their memory stands at the entrance to Chapultepec Park, where it is used to give Mexican schoolchildren inspiring lessons at least once each year.

Many other examples of heroism, bravery, sacrifice, and patriotism are touted with Revolutionary zeal. Neglect of Benito Juárez would be unforgivable. His authorship of progressive legislation and his indomitable resistance to the imperial forces of Maximilian make Juárez the greatest liberal in nineteenth-century Mexico and, from our present vantage point, the leading precursor of the Revolution itself. He is the *benemérito* (worthy one) of Mexican liberals. The trade-union movement has its own heroes in the martyrs of Rio Blanco (Veracruz) and Cananea (Sonora), who sacrificed themselves in the name of labor syndicalism—so say official Revolutionary historians—against the brutality of the Rio Blanco textile factory system and the William Greene copper mining management in strikes that broke out during the first decade of this century. There were other martyrs, thousands of them: Aquiles Serdán, who died for his part in the abortive beginning of the Madero Rebellion; Francisco Madero and José María Pino Suárez, first Revolutionary president and vice-president, who were assassinated in 1913 by the regime of the "usurper" Victoriano Huerta; Emiliano Zapata, the sincere, sad, yet single-minded champion of the landless and of agrarian reform, who was murdered in 1919 by a "treasonous" turncoat; Pancho Villa, generous, idealistic, and colorful on the one hand, cruel, cynical, and sadistic on the other, who met a violent death (the one value of Villa in Revolutionary annals, which may draw from fiction as well as fact, is his personification of the Mexican's ability to outwit representatives of powerful, advanced nations—in this case, General Pershing and the United States); Álvaro Obregón, army general and former president, whose assassination at the hands of a Catholic fanatic occurred when Church and State had not resolved their outstanding differences, thus elevating him to a martyrdom that he probably would not have attained otherwise.

Bearing solidly on the Mexicanism theme is the example of the unprecedented courage of Lázaro Cárdenas: Cárdenas the poor boy who rose to the presidency of his country; Cárdenas the chief of state who expelled the number-one strongman of Mexico and became president in fact as well as in name; Cárdenas the humble Mexican who nationalized the petroleum industry, the railroads, and the telegraph; Cárdenas the lover of Mexican peasantry, who turned over millions of acres of agricultural land to the rural masses. Unquestionably, Cárdenas reanimated the drive for social justice inherent in the Revolution and, in the process, made his fellow countrymen proud to be Mexican. Today, Cárdenas, as the expropriatory president, vies with Cárdenas, the private citizen, for popular acclaim: He is a Revolutionary symbol, and he is still a powerful force in Revolutionary councils.

Some intellectuals claim to perceive a trend away from Mexicanism in favor of a more universal image. It is true that the chauvinism and xenophobia of the 1930's have been moderated. Yet the relative absence of radicalism does not imply a rejection of the symbols of patriotism and nationalism to which the 1930's gave birth. Nor should it hide the intro-spective philosophical movement among certain Mexican intellectuals seeking to discover what constitutes the Mexican personality. Some uni-versalism enters into the writings of a few intellectuals, philosophers, and international politicians, but Mexicanism, based on sound patriotism and nationalism, remains at the heart of the Mexican Creed. Furthermore, there are no clear signs pointing to its disappearance for some years to come.

2. *Constitutionalism.* Every Revolutionary leader bestows an aura of sanctity on the Constitution of 1917. Statements like the following are commonplace:

"The Revolutionary banner is our Constitution."

"The program of the Revolution is that outlined in the Magna Carta."

"Solutions to our common problems will be found in the Constitution."

Inasmuch as the Constitution of Mexico is one of the longest and most self-contradictory charters governing any nation, a president can find constitutional justification for just about anything he wishes to do. Be that as it may, the Creed does gain a number of specific objectives from the Revolutionary reverence for constitutionalism: a federal, republican, and presidential form of government; free, universal, and secular education; freedom of religion, as modified by prohibitions on clericalism and property ownership by religious institutions; exclusive national possession of subsoil rights; restriction of the title of agricultural lands to small private farms, cooperatives, and communal farms; state responsibility for the defense of labor rights; judicial and penal systems operated to control civil and crimi-nal acts against the law; establishment of Mexican birth as a requisite for eligibility for high political office; an "open-door" policy for political refugees seeking asylum; finally, all kinds of ownership and initiative—private, public, cooperative, communal—necessary for economic development. This listing does not imply that the Constitution has no other worthy provisions. But it does mean that many constitutional provisos are not stressed by Revolutionaries because the realities of Mexican life simply do not permit application of them now or in the foreseeable future. When the Revolutionary asserts constitutionalism, therefore, he is ignoring more than a few provisions to which the Revolution can give little or no attention at the moment.

3. *Social Justice.* Everywhere in Mexico—in national, state, and local governmental organs, in official political party literature, in schools and universities, in newspapers and periodicals, on radio, television, and the motion-picture screen—one observes the national obsession with *justicia social.* Translated into simplest terms, social justice means that today and tomorrow are worth living for their promise of a better life than yesterday's. Implementations of this proposition show the state establishing and extending social security; building public clinics, hospitals, schools, libraries, and reading rooms; erecting large public housing developments; laying out athletic fields; redistributing agricultural lands; allotting part of the government budget to poor, indigenous communities; making available basic foodstuffs at reduced prices to the Mexican masses; enforcing rent controls, low transportation rates, and labor rights; and constructing sanitary public markets, slaughterhouses, drainage systems, and water supplies. Finally, redistribution of national income and the improvement of the living standards of all Mexicans are important factors in the translation of *justicia social.*

4. *Political Liberalism.* Political liberalism in Mexico has traditionally encompassed such doctrines as federalism, republicanism, separation of powers, anticlericalism, local self-government, and a prohibition on immediate re-election to public office. These concepts lie on the surface of the Revolutionary's avowed political liberalism today, often obscuring other noteworthy planks: freedom of speech, thought, press, religion, and assembly; effective universal suffrage; an independent judiciary; political stability; a career civil service; an independent national legislature and autonomous state and local governments; and civilian supremacy.

Nowhere has the Revolutionary elite been criticized more severely than for its failure to implement its self-styled political "liberalism." To deal honestly with the critics, the Revolutionary Family must admit a division of all the glittering generalities on liberalism into long-range and short-range objectives. For realization in the far future are effective suffrage, political opposition, local autonomy, a stronger judiciary and legislature, and real freedom of speech, press, and assembly. Each successive Revolutionary regime asserts that Mexico comes nearer to the realization of these long-range goals with the passage of every six-year administration. This is probably true. In the category of more urgent objectives are a career civil service, political stability, civilian supremacy, open political criticism, peaceful elections, universal adult suffrage, prohibition of re-election to the presidency or governorships and immediate re-election to other high elective offices, freedom of religion.

The Family is not immediately concerned with those liberties which are considered requisite by conventional Western federalism. Translated into everyday Revolutionary practice, political "liberalism" has come to mean tolerant rule, guided by the general wisdom of the Revolutionary Creed. Propping up the leader (or leaders, as the case may be) is an authoritarian, official party that serves as a clearinghouse in seating dependable "revolutionaries" in impotent legislative bodies. No effective opposition parties are permitted. An aspirant to political office either operates within the official party or faces the prospect of political demise. The only elected officials who possess any real power to make decisions are the president, the governors, and the municipal presidents—but significantly, all of these are selected outside the regular, official-party organization. The president is chosen by the inner council of the Revolutionary Family, governors by the President of Mexico, and municipal presidents by these hand-picked governors. Elections, whether internal to the official party or external and open to the general public, are hardly more than travesties. Political liberalism, therefore, really means respect for the Revolutionary Family ("which after all is exceedingly liberal and tolerant"), as well as submission to Family interpretation of its many facets. Within this context, Mexicans enjoy what political freedom they do have for the simple reason that the Revolutionary elite heading the nation is itself composed of moderate, forward-looking individuals, however skeptical they may be about the wisdom of doing away with six-year authoritative patterns of national and state governance.

5. Racial Tolerance.   Strains from all great races of mankind run through the Mexican population. Red, white, black, brown, or yellow—none enjoys any special privilege. More often than not, the Mexican cannot be sure of his own racial origin. The muralist Diego Rivera theorized that Mongoloid features predominated. And in the 1920's, José Vasconcelos propounded a theory of the "Cosmic Race" in which he submitted that the Mexican is racially superior because of his intermixture of Mongoloid, Negroid, and Caucasian blood. If any racial group holds an edge, it is the mestizo (mixed-blood). Up and down the social ladder, leadership of the nation resides preponderantly with the mixed-bloods. Is there any wonder, therefore, that racial intolerance in the United States and in Africa evokes revulsion in the Mexican?

6. *Religious Tolerance.*   The Revolutionary religious ethic has been compounded from tenets of Christianity, indigenous paganisms, Freemasonry, Judaism, mysticism, agnosticism, and atheism. Although Mexico is nominally Catholic, some Catholics in Mexico are simultaneously Freemasons, Jews, and mystics. We find orthodox Catholics who are equally devout mystics and fanatical indigenous Catholics who worship their own dark-skinned Virgin of Guadalupe or some local patroness saint; there are Jewish Catholics and Catholic Jews, anticlerical Masonic Catholics and proclerical Catholic institutionalists, Catholics who care little for devotion to the Virgin of Guadalupe and Catholics who know nothing of the Virgin Mary; and there are Hebrew-speaking Indian communities and Spanish-speaking idolatrous worshippers.

Although the Revolutionary Creed underwrites freedom of religion, that freedom is circumscribed substantially when applied to Roman Catholicism. One of the major crises in modern Mexico arises from divergencies within the Catholic credo on the one hand, and the proclaimed anticlericalism, at times even antireligion of Revolutionary programs on the other. As we shall see in Chapters 6 and 7, pragmatism, rationalism, and mysticism constitute too weak a triumvirate to overcome the spiritual hunger of the popular masses.

7. *Intellectual Freedom and Public Education.*   The edifice of Revolutionary intellectual attitudes dates back to those who first laid a foundation for a Mexican nationality based on racial equality, economic progress, and the enhancement of civil liberties. For in spite of their selfishness, arrogance, and greed, their blind faith in the Spanish crown, and their practice of enslaving the indigenous population, the Spaniards could count in their ranks not a few champions of toleration and intellectual freedom. To the teaching and deeds of liberal colonial churchmen, governors, and soldiers, today's Revolutionaries owe a sizable intellectual debt. The Revolutionaries have also incorporated much from the teachings of Rousseau, Jefferson, Bergson, Mill, and James into their Creed. Of all the "worldly" philosophers who pop up in theoretical justifications advanced for one Revolutionary proposal or another, Karl Marx holds a decided edge. What Marx lacks, the Creed finds in Adam Smith, Malthus, and Ricardo; in Owen, Rochedale, and the Webbs; in Veblen, Marshall, and Keynes; and in Schumpeter, Hansen, and Harrod. This does not mean that the Mexicans have overlooked their own statesmen or intellectuals: Contributions in statesmanship are lauded from Benito Juárez, Francisco Madero, Álvaro Obregón, and Lázaro Cárdenas; for the intellectual area, there are Andrés

Molina Enríquez, Luis Cabrera, José Vasconcelos, Manuel Gamio, Alfonso and Antonio Caso, Samuel Ramos, Alfonso Reyes, and Jesús Silva Herzog. Nevertheless, the Revolution has yet to produce an outstanding philosopher on political economy, political sociology, or Mexican ethics.

Intellectual freedom is accompanied by the Revolutionary emphasis on free, secular, public education. Lack of education, say the Revolutionaries, must be attacked on all fronts: by building educational institutions, by providing textbooks gratuitously, by sending cultural missions into the rural countryside, by making education truly free and secular, by sending Mexicans abroad for technical and higher education, by training tens of thousands of young Mexicans to become good teachers. In fact, there is no end to the proposals on expanding and improving public education in Mexico.

8. *Economic Growth.*   An eighth objective is sustained economic growth. A myth about being a perpetual mineral and foodstuff supplier for world markets hung heavy on early Revolutionary regimes. Essentially, Mexico is still a producer of basic commodities, but growth on all fronts of economic activity—industry, commerce, agriculture, mining, and the services—is the goal that Revolutionaries have set for Mexican economic development. Such "balanced" economic growth demands steady industrialization, constant agricultural reform, expansion of electricity generation and other power resources, availability of sufficient credit for all sectors, forced capital accumulation, and a growing reservoir of entrepreneurial and manpower skills. Ownership of the means of production is merely one side of the economic coin. Its other face is stamped with higher output and efficient land utilization. Therefore, "who owns" is tied together with "how much is produced." To the economist, this boils down to an axiom: Higher output from factories, mines, and farms is an intrinsic good, indispensable to an ever-greater gross national product, to a higher per capita national income, and hence, to over-all economic growth.

9. *Economic Integration.*   The ninth objective of the Creed—economic integration—is based on a desire for interdependence. It recognizes that Mexico must be built by all Mexicans in all parts of Mexico: by the industrious northerner and the indolent southerner; by the isolated *yucateco* and carefree *veracruzano*; by people from the mountains, valleys, deserts, plateaus, jungles, plains, and coasts; by the inhabitants of cities, towns, villages, indigenous communities, small farms, communal agricultural settlements, and haciendas; and, of course, by bankers, civil servants, industrialists, merchants, and teachers. Mexicans are to become interdependent through the exchange of goods and services, each region buying from and selling to other regions. Encompassed in the idea of integration are both industrial concentration and decentralization—the concentration of

enough industry in one center to make it economically sound, and the decentralization of industry into new centers to provide jobs in widespread locations and to prevent population pressures from building up in any one area. The major problem in this respect is to de-emphasize the Monterrey and Valley of Mexico industrial complexes. Revolutionaries conceive a three-pronged solution: (1) encouraging industry to locate in the older urban centers of Querétaro, Guadalajara, Morelia, Toluca, Puebla, and Orizaba; (2) opening new settlement areas in Quintana Roo, Tabasco, Baja California, and the Isthmus of Tehuantepec; and (3) regional development of the Papaloapan Basin, the Balsas River system, the coal and steel complex of Palau and Monclova, the new industrial city of Ciudad Sahagún, the Torreón–La Laguna area, and the Grijalva River basin.

Mexicans are also to become interdependent through the extension of a national transportation and communication network. Implementation of this goal requires the building and maintenance of roads, railroads, ports, and airfields, of oil and gas pipelines, of lines for power transmission, telephone, and telegraph, and of radio, television, and telex facilities. It means that Mexico must build a fleet of coastal boats to gather in the food of the seas and to transport goods up and down the coasts, and also build up its fleet of trucks to service inland areas. Above all, artificial barriers to the free movement of people and goods must be removed.

10. *Public and Private Ownership and Initiative.* A tenth objective is the encouragement of all forms of ownership to utilize the initiative of private, public, communal, and cooperatist sectors. This objective makes it crystal clear that the Revolutionary Family and the Mexican government are not identical, since many Family members oppose government proposals to extend public ownership into new sectors. Reserved exclusively for public ownership and exploitation are such realms of economic activity as the oil industry, the electric-power industry, railroads, and telegraph. Conversely, other realms find public and private ownership in competition; this is the case in steel, chemicals, paper, shipbuilding, banking, construction, aviation, mining, publishing, and textiles. In this group of businesses, the Mexican government sometimes owns an entire enterprise outright or sometimes holds majority control; it may enter a fifty-fifty arrangement or even take a minority equity. Additional realms are reserved almost exclusively for nongoverment ownership, which is the pattern in the canning of fruits and vegetables, the bottling of beer and soft drinks, the hotel industry, and the manufacture of office equipment. Cooperatives are strong in trucking, bus lines, mining, cement, sugar, bananas, and consumer purchasing. Communal ownership characterizes more than one-half of all arable land in Mexico, and yet private farms and cooperatives still possess a substantial share. Foreign ownership is not regarded as good or bad per se, but is totally dependent on conduct, business performance, and the

specific business activity in which the foreigner has invested or wishes to invest. The Mexican government, however, has favored majority owner-ship by nationals over foreign control. In any case, foreign capital becomes subject to Mexican law.

As Mexican economic development goes forward, more and more at-tention is directed toward productivity in both a quantitative and qualita-tive sense. If private enterprise falls short in keeping pace with the needs of the Mexican economy, as in the 1960 cases of Consolidated Steel and the electric-power companies, the Mexican government intervenes to assume equity and managerial interest. Many Revolutionaries do not want state intervention to become so pronounced as to take the privacy out of private enterprise, for many Revolutionaries are capitalists themselves. One con-sequence is that the Mexican government is expected to encourage new investments through protective tariffs and tax concessions. Many Revolu-tionaries hope that, in time, the traditional concept of "property is not inviolate" will make room for a new concept of "some property is in-violate."

11. *Defense of Labor Rights.* The objective of defending and ad-vancing the rights of labor is clearly defined in the Constitution and in numerous decrees. Each of the three houses of labor—trade, agriculture, and civil service—has had its heyday. The agricultural laborer obtained his own land, or at least formal recognition of his right to obtain land when-ever the government sees fit to expropriate additional acreage. The govern-ment worker acquired full bargaining status in the statute covering "Workers in the Service of the State," which has served to provide the bureaucrat with regular pay increases, low-cost housing, vacations with pay, and multiple fringe benefits. The worker in industry and commerce was permitted to organize strong trade unions, participate in political decision-making, and in some instances, to take over the ownership and management of enterprises. Viewed globally, the government worker has prospered most appreciably since Cárdenas left the presidency in 1940. Agricultural labor, especially the two million families in communal agriculture and the million families on privately owned *minifundia* plots, has received credit and some price supports, but only a political demagogue can contend that the preponderant majority of these three million families are much better off today than they were twenty years ago. The same goes for the trade unionist: Brute industrialization, forced capital accumulation, and at-tempts to balance international payments have left little room for higher real wages.

The objective of defending and advancing the rights of labor thus re-mains a long-range goal in the over-all Revolutionary timetable of develop-ment. The immediate objective is to industrialize and commercialize the nation; redistribution of income and placing greater purchasing power in the hands of labor can come later. Meanwhile, trade unionists are to enjoy a minimum wage, job security, and minimal collective-bargaining rights, and agricultural labor will have to satisfy itself with credit on more favorable terms and with some benefits from instruction in scientific farming. On the bigger issue of equitable income distribution, urban and rural labor have shown unusual forbearance in accepting their place on the economic margin of Mexican life with only few relative improvements in the form of price-setting, state distribution of basic foodstuffs, rent controls, social security, and other manifestations of social justice.

12. *Financial Stability.*   A twelfth objective, intertwined with economic growth, economic integration, entrepreneurial patterns, and income distribution, is the preservation of financial stability. Economic growth becomes meaningful, say many Revolutionary economists, whenever inflation is kept in bounds and savings are transformed into investment. Too-rapid circulation of money is undesirable, despite the chronic shortage of credit and the accompanying high interest rates. For these reasons, a central banking system is invested with authority to set monetary policy, and other public agencies are charged with responsibility for establishing over-all fiscal policy. Foreign loans, commodity exchanges, and the balance of payments are supervised. The tourist trade is encouraged. Migratory labor is permitted to work on farms across the border. Foreign capital is invited to share in the investment complex. Price-setting and rent controls are also utilized. All in all, financial stability appears high on the list of Revolutionary objectives.

13. *A Share in World Leadership.*   The Revolutionary bid for regional stature is reflected in its objective of grabbing traditional leadership of the Spanish-speaking world from Spain, and of the Spanish-American nations from Argentina. Beyond these spheres of influence, Mexico keeps more silent about its longer-range goal of vying triumphantly with Brazil for the undisputed leadership of Latin America. For demographic reasons alone, these three groupings can hardly be ignored in international councils.

Mexico is already the most populous Spanish-speaking nation in the world. Revolutionaries contend that decades of the reactionary authoritarianism of Franco have squelched whatever promise Spain held of ever again holding the cultural leadership of the Spanish-speaking world. Measuring in terms of belles-lettres, technology, basic education, agronomy, publishing, medicine, and motion pictures, Revolutionaries claim that Mexico now surpasses Spain. Their belief in the eventual attainment of leadership of Spanish and Latin America largely rests on the same arguments, plus two others: First, Argentina's population is merely about half that of Mexico today, and demographers estimate that by the turn of the century Mexico's 110 million population will be two and one-half times the population of Argentina; second, political geography and an increasingly intimate contact with the United States indicate the important middle role that Mexico can play in interpreting the United States to its southern neighbors and Latin America to the United States. More important than the objectives themselves are the trials and tribulations that striving for them will make an integral part of hemispheric politics in the decades ahead.

14. *International Prestige.*   A final goal is Mexican prestige in the international community. Most Revolutionaries prefer to avoid upsetting Mexican stature before the world, even to the point of shelving, if necessary, the threefold objective identified in the preceding paragraph. Mexican foreign policy is to follow the accepted principles leading to meritorious acclaim in international affairs: universalism, regionalism, the juridical equality of states, collective security, peaceful settlement of disputes, political asylum, payment of foreign debts, limitations of armaments, nonintervention, and the application of sanctions on aggressors.

The Mexican policy of relative aloofness from bipolar politics permits condemnation of all pernicious actions, whether of Soviet, American, or some other national origin. Mexico realizes fully that getting along with its powerful neighbor to the north is indispensable for its economic growth; income is essential from American investments, imports, tourists, and, possibly, the remittances of migratory labor. At the same time, Mexico sees no reason for turning away Russia or China.

Finally, the Revolutionaries seek an enhancement of prestige by building Mexico City into the most beautiful metropolis in the world, by shipping Mexican culture abroad, and by extending international airlines bearing the Mexican flag.

These, then, are the objectives that guide Mexico under Revolutionary leadership. More will be said about them in subsequent chapters for, by and large, they are the blueprint of the nation's future. Even if the moment in history arrives for a new elite to assume command of Mexico, the Revolutionary Creed will probably undergo few major changes, for its adaptability and self-contained dynamism have enabled the country to move toward fulfillment of the aspirations of the Mexican people. So far, pushing forward in the context of dedication to the fourteen objectives, the Revolutionary Family has proved capable of leading Mexico into greener pastures. Yet it is reasonable to predict that new groupings will arise and successfully challenge the long hold that the Revolutionary Family has enjoyed. Because Mexico's present and future are so intimately connected with its past, with its character and traditions, the following chapter will briefly survey the long period before the Revolution.

TWO

BEFORE THE REVOLUTION

Even though the Revolutionary Creed began to be spelled out clearly only after the armed uprisings of 1910, the fuse that was lighted then had been laid throughout the Mexican past. It is true that the Revolutionaries' experience of governing the nation for more than five decades—witnessing two world wars, a major economic depression, the emergence of the United States as a superpower, and the rampant search by Americans for foreign markets and investments—contributed much to the annealing of the objectives. It is equally true that determination of Revolutionary principles drew much from pre-1910 experience. By dividing Mexican history into five distinct epochs, of which the Revolutionary period itself is the last, we may discover the historical bases on which the Creed took form.

PRE-CONQUEST EPOCH

The first and longest epoch dates from deep in antiquity up to the arrival of Hernán Cortés and his Spanish *conquistadores* in 1519. This longest period is the one about which we know least; only in recent years have anthropologists and archeologists pieced together a reasonably consistent reconstruction of parts of the period. Of course, these after-the-fact reconstructions must depend on fragmentary, inconclusive data and on the hypotheses of the experts, which are not infrequently challenged, occasionally modified, and sometimes reversed. Nevertheless, it is safe to assert that pre-Conquest Mexico did deposit the basic Indian heritage of modern times, and that it was not—contrary to some demagogic chroniclers of a regeneration of Indian patterns—an idyllic paradise for the Indian masses. The land, the terrain itself, has always been a hard taskmaster: Great territorial expanses were arid, others mountainous, both types of little productive value. Uncontrolled disease and extremes of weather hampered civilizations then as they do today. Relatively advanced cultures and fairly advanced cultivation accompanied by commercial interchange had been achieved, in fact, by a mere handful of the many "tribes," "states," "nations," and "empires" spotting the territory now comprised by

19

Mexico. A living for the individual depended on primitive agriculture, hunting, or gathering fruits and nuts.

Wherever one Indian civilization rose above the norms, however, its accomplishments in some realms—notably in architecture, in the engineering of great pyramids and other monuments, in astronomy, in sculpture, and in the creation of finely-wrought jewelry—challenge the imagination of our contemporaries who view them. As much as six centuries before the Pilgrims landed at Plymouth Rock, the Mayas, Toltecs, and Zapotecs could well have boasted of their "advanced" cultures across extensive regions of central and southeastern Mexico. During the first post-Christ millennium, the Mayas had already abandoned the older cities of their First Empire—Tikal, Palenque, Copán, Piedras Negras—in favor of resettlement in what is now the Yucatán peninsula of Mexico, where they erected other cities that remain for us as glorious archeological gems—Uxmal, Chichén Itzá, Mayapán, Tulum, and Coba. By the same period, or perhaps earlier, the culture of the Toltecs in central Mexico had reached its zenith, and they had emigrated away to the southeast and, to a lesser extent, to the southwest.

The Aztec civilization—whose empire was the one to receive and eventually be crushed by Cortés—founded a city and a culture regarded by conquistadores and moderns alike as remarkable. The Aztec nation had expanded its militant culture in every direction, finally stabilizing supreme authority over the Valley of Mexico by alliance with the neighboring cities of Texcoco and Tlacopán. By their own lights, the Aztecs were a godfearing people. In honor of their greatest god, Huitzilopochtli, they made innumerable human sacrifices, including one of 20,000 prisoners of war in dedicating a temple pyramid to the god in 1487. It is no mere coincidence that the Cathedral of Mexico stands on the very spot today. At the time of Cortés' arrival, the Aztec domain reached eastward to the Gulf, west into the state of Michoacán, and south into Oaxaca. Through all this expanse of territory, only the Tarascans and Tlaxcalans had maintained a sort of independence, albeit hard pressed; it was, in fact, the latter group that provided indispensable manpower and supplies in assisting Cortés to overpower the Aztec empire.

But while Moctezuma II, who reached the throne in 1502, struggled with the affairs of the doomed empire, other Indian peoples were continuing their primitive ways. In the southeast, the Mayas were in numerical ascendancy, but other quasi-autonomous groups held on, including those who spoke Tzotzil, Tzeltal, Chontal, Huave, Zoque, and Lacondón. In the central region, the already-mentioned Tarascans and Tlaxcalans enjoyed a relatively independent status along with the Totonacs, Huastecas, Pames, Guamares, and Jomars. Also present in the central region were the Mixtecs. In the northeast, where making a living demanded a more rigorous life, the Tamaulipecs and Coahuiltecs constituted the major language groupings.

(These, at least, are the conclusions of the linguists, whose theories find supporting evidence in the present-day language habits of the peoples in the various areas. The linguists identify, for example, the Guachichils, Laguneros, Cacxte, Tobasco, Concho, Tepehuán, Tarahumara, and Sumajumana as separable culture groups in the north-central region.) Finally, in the northwest, which embraces the present states of Sinaloa, Sonora, Baja California, and the territory of Baja California Sur, the most accepted language units (hence family units) were the Pima, Joya, Cahita, Guesave, Papagó, Kikime, Diegueño, Cochimi, Layomon, and Guaicua.

This multiplicity of Indian units (anthropologists identify at least 150 distinct languages, and tell us that at least forty of these are still the first tongues of at least three million indigenous souls) points up an often forgotten truth of pre-Conquest times: Several million Indians were never brought together under a single central authority. Had Moctezuma, for example, somehow managed to spread his authority over the entire territory, the simple task of communication would have presented formidable barriers.

Other forces besides the language-culture divisions worked against integration of the Indians. No single form of government seems to have established itself, although clan, tribe, and "empire" alike bore the stamp of authoritarianism. Similarly, no single form of religion found universal acceptance, although polytheism, mysticism, and belief in an omnipotent, benevolent Father of white skin, the great Quetzalcoatl, who presumably once walked among the Indians and had promised that one day he would return to guide the destinies of "his" people, prevailed among the civilizations in the central, south, and southeastern regions. No particular urban center achieved political, economic, or social hegemony, although the Valley of Mexico exerted great influence by the time of Cortés' arrival.

There were still other elements of diversity, multiplicity, and fragmentation, for the various Indian peoples seem to have embraced a variety of psychological and philosophical differences. There was no single theory of landownership or land usage; communal agriculture existed, but the broad, arid expanses in the north and certain other agricultural zones did not lend themselves to community patterning. Little belief in the preciousness of human life had taken hold; human sacrifices made on behalf of the gods were commonplace. Some cultures were warlike, some peace-loving; some extroverted, others introverted; some authoritarian, others democratic-minded. And even though the Indians constructed magnificent architectural monuments, there is doubt that they employed the wheel in practical problems. In fact, about all that the people of pre-Conquest Mexico had in common—and even here minor exceptions occurred—was an appetite for corn.

From this evidence, it is easy to understand why the conquest of Indian cultures was facilitated and why those cultures laid the foundation for innumerable problems with which the Revolutionary Family is today contending.

What the pre-Conquest epoch contributes most to the Revolutionary Creed is an awareness of continuity: On the very terrain that today belongs to Mexico, there once stood elaborate cultures, in their day the most advanced anywhere in North America.

THE COLONIAL EPOCH

The second epoch of Mexican history, though of shorter duration than its predecessor, prevailed almost twice as long as the three epochs that have followed it. Dating from 1519 to 1810, the Spanish colonial period injected enduring ideas and values into the Mexican complex.

In the historical museum in Mexico City's Chapultepec castle is a gallery of the 61 viceroys who ruled over New Spain. (A striking comment on the stability of the period!) The paintings are all done in a similar flattering "salon" style, but with brutal realism in the actual features of the faces. These faces—the Mendozas, the Velascos, Revillagigedo, Bucareli—reflect determination and refinement. They show strength, shrewdness, occasionally cupidity, rarely weakness. Above all else, these are faces of men of vision, whatever their motives. Nowhere is there more eloquent testimony of the spirit that welded Mexico out of a wilderness.

But the entire period comes to us through a historian's haze. On one side, there is what some historians term the "black legend" of Spanish administration—rigid class distinctions, religious inquisitions, greed, suppression, racial intolerance, cruelty, rapacious economic exploitation, and involuntary servitude. On the more laudable side, there are practicing Christianity, urbanization, deep sympathy for the Indian, intermarriage of the races, political integration, new manual skills, public administration, and a common language. The truth of the matter, then, is that the good existed side by side with the bad. Once Mexican historians grasped this characteristic of the social-cultural complex of colonial days, their preoccupation with past evils shifted to a meaningful analysis of Mexico and the Mexicans—of the values, institutions, and practices that were indispensable for the modernization and integration of their nation, whether they were of Spanish origin or not.

A common misconception about the colonial epoch arises out of exaggerated accounts of the "omnipotent" Spanish *conquistadores*. The fallacy lies in depreciating the transcendental part that the Indians played in bringing about their own downfall. Cortés displayed extraordinary wisdom, courage, and faith—but he also stumbled into unbelievably favorable circumstances. All the horses, guns, mistresses, and intrigue that Cortés pulled out of his Spanish bag of tricks were minor contributions compared to those of the indigenous population. To begin with, Indians held the conviction, injected into religious beliefs by the high priests of Indian astrology, of an imminent downfall of Indian civilization at the hands of "white gods" who would arrive from the East. The Spaniards were also helped by the hatred, envy, and unruliness of non-Aztec vassals of Moctezuma II, who suffered from his exacting demands for tribute and sacrificial victims, as well as by the jealousies within the Aztec ruling house itself. Most important of all, the Spaniards enjoyed military, material, and fraternal assistance of tens of thousands of Tlaxcalans and other Indians who despised the Aztecs. The simple truth is that Cortés' mission was converted into a crusade when legions of Indians joined in the common cause to overthrow the Aztecs. Obviously, Cortés and his few hundred Spanish companions did not single-handedly overthrow tens of thousands of militant warriors; the decisive battles of the Conquest saw Indian pitted against Indian. The decisive military value of the Indians opposed to the Aztecs was ultimately recognized even by that old despot Charles I, King of Spain, who granted the Tlaxcalans—who formed the major phalanxes in Cortés' army—perpetual exemption from tribute to the Spanish crown.

Once the Aztecs fell, the new "gods" of Tenochtitlán looked in all directions for more conquests. Of high priority were conquests of the soul, for the cross invariably accompanied the sword. But conquest of land, mines, and seas remained uppermost. Some of the Spaniards, like the aggressive Alvarado, who was the greatest of Cortés' lieutenants, headed south and southeast into the lands which today comprise Central America and the Yucatán peninsula. Others, led by the vengeful, despicable Núñez, turned westward and explored lands between the Valley of Mexico and the Pacific coast. Still others, and particularly Nuño de Guzmán and Coronado, pushed northward, where they encountered little gold but, aided by expeditions that originated from other points in the New World, did annex millions of square miles of new territory to the glory of Spain. When surveys of all expeditions were finally tallied and approved by the King of Spain, Mexico City had become the center of a New World empire that stretched from northern South America to the Oregon Territory, from the Pacific to the Mississippi River, and from there into Florida and over the entire Caribbean. Appropriately, New Spain was the name bestowed on this vast empire, which remained virtually intact for almost 300 years. Ironically, when the hour for splitting up this extensive imperial holding arrived, neither Spain nor its colonial subjects were directly responsible for carving off the biggest slice; the villain in that drama was none other than Napoleon Bonaparte. What the present Revolutionary Creed draws from colonial political geography is the knowledge that Mexico City once represented the center of a great colonial empire—perhaps the greatest of all New World cities in the greatest of all New World colonial holdings.

Cortés and the Spanish men of the sword are not the only conquerors who deserve acclaim. Their glory must be shared with the devoted men of the cross. For in the long run, adding souls to the Catholic faith made a more enduring mark on Mexico than any other single action of Spain. Tens of millions of Mexicans adhere to some form of Catholicism today. Their faith largely stems from the benevolent works of dedicated friars—Dominicans, Franciscans, Augustinians, Mercedarians, and Jesuits—who came to New Spain to search out man, Christianize him, and in this way save his soul.

Unfortunately, the missionary zeal of the friar gave way to Catholic institutionalism and the whims of the Spanish crown. The Church became an all-encompassing State-Church, exercising omnipotent secular authority. "Spain in America," as Professor Clarence Haring tells us, "reflected the indissoluble union of the altar and the throne." Clerics assumed high position in public office, and because conflicting loyalties to Rome and the king were usually resolved in favor of the king, the State became a Church-State. New Spain prospered, vegetated, or retroceded according to the authoritarian doctrine of the divine right of kings. And divinity, in the form of royal prerogative and unilateral Catholic action, brought innumerable benefits to the Church: exclusivity in religious matters, privileged positions for the clergy, broad powers of raising and spending tribute, tax exemption, and ownership of extensive tracts of lands. No wonder that in later years the Church, as Hubert Herring observes, "remained a thoroughly Spanish institution in days when the great majority of the people she served were thinking of themselves as Americans."

The Catholic Church in New Spain was thus a Spanish Church, and being intimately bound up with the destiny of Spain in America, it contained for the masses and liberal-minded colonists little promise of better things to come. The Church placed many understanding clerics among the inhabitants of New Spain, but its close alliance with the crown, the colonial administrator, and propertied interests in general befuddled native minds taught to look upon the Church as merely a spiritual body. And it was precisely the secular sins of the Church that, after national independence was achieved, provoked liberal Mexicans into fighting for the adoption of anti-Church and anticlerical legislation. When the question of religion and the Revolution is discussed at length in Chapter 7, it will be clear that the role of religion in the colonial epoch had much to do with the incorporation of anticlericalism into the Revolutionary Creed.

The concept of indisputable authority implicit in the theory of the divine right of kings infected all political institutions and actions in the colonial government. If the king required more gold to fight his imperial wars in Europe and on the high seas, his governors in New Spain had to produce it. If the king wished the Inquisition applied less vigorously in New Spain than in Spain itself, his agents were informed accordingly. If the king found high officials no longer suited to his royal taste, he simply removed them. The king commanded, his agents and subjects obeyed.

The highest authority in New Spain was a viceroy (vice-king); can a king be questioned by anyone less than another king? Authoritarianism, whether it followed the normal administrative channel of king to viceroy to president to captain-general or the channel of king directly to any of these three major officials who ran the show in New Spain through most of its existence, was the order of the day. The king himself appointed all viceroys, presidents, and captains-general.

But speaking of authoritarianism should not conjure up a vision of omnipresent ruthlessness. New Spain may have been ruled over by more-or-less autocratic kings who accepted or rejected the advice of a more-or-less autocratic Council of the Indies and who appointed more-or-less autocratic administrators to assume posts in the colonies; nevertheless, in view of the medieval concepts of imperial rule over a conquered people, Spain deserves credit for its comparatively benevolent governance. In fact, during the last half of the 1700's, enlightened Bourbon monarchs injected a decidedly humanitarian note into colonial rule. And as early as the sixteenth century, abusive exercise of power was partially curbed by *audiencias*, city councils (*cabildos*), and occasionally by open town meetings (*cabildos abiertos*); by court judges appointed by the king; by royal auditors; by special Indian courts; and by the right at all levels of colonial administration to send petitions directly to the king. Besides these checks, relatively slow and cumbersome communication impeded the execution of excessively arbitrary dictates passed from one level to another. (Conversely, of course, this extra impediment also delayed cognizance and removal of tyrannical officers.)

The Spanish king in all his omnipotence found it expedient to authorize one infringement on his authority for the sake of political stability: He conferred the right of self-government on Indian villages, where "ancient custom" was permitted to control the political system. Thus, while the government of larger towns, mining cities, and commercial centers roughly emulated urban political forms in Spain, many Indian communities had their own political institutions, which the Indians themselves ran to a considerable degree. Aside from this local autonomy and various checks devised from time to time to contain authoritarianism, the making, enforcement, and adjudication of law centered overpoweringly in the executive arm of government.

What the Revolution finds unacceptable in Spanish political administration, as well as in much of nineteenth-century government, is precisely this authoritarianism, centralism, and executive dominance. In reaction to this, the Revolutionary Creed incorporated specific defenses: effective suffrage, no re-election, separation of powers, checks and balances, federalism. But as subsequent chapters will show, there is a tremendous gap between the written law and cold reality—an indication that the old authoritarian legacies still shackle modern Mexico.

Besides the political, religious, and geographical remnants of New Spain, present-day Mexico also bears the heritage of colonial economic and social systems. The economic substance of Spain rested squarely on the doctrine of mercantilism, a philosophy that relegated New Spain to the subordinate position of supplier of silver, gold, and other commodities to the mother country and, at the same time, buyer of processed goods sent from Spain.

Commerce in its broadest sense—laying down import and export prohibitions, designation of exclusive ports from and to which goods were sent (Veracruz became the monopoly port on the east coast, and trade with the Orient was conducted through the port of Acapulco), setting of tariffs and import duties, selection of vessels in which goods were transported, and government intervention in numerous other aspects of commerce—rested on the monopolistic dictates of the chief commercial agent of the Spanish crown, the House of Trade. Little wonder that an entrepreneurial mind in New Spain had minimal room for creative expression in the arena of world trade.

But to the early Spanish colonial, a career in commerce, industry, or farming appeared dull alongside the glamorous search for gold. First by plunder and later by mining, seizure of the precious metal preoccupied colonist and crown alike. Silver soon assumed the pre-eminent place in colonial exploitation for the two-way trade between Spain and her coveted viceroyalty. This exaggerated attention to precious metals warped the very personality of many colonists who arrived in New Spain. Prepossessed with the notion of making great fortunes overnight, they cared little for settling down on the land and, if forced into this relatively plebeian alternative, they regarded the Indians as slightly more than sources of cheap labor. "Gold fever" became a disease more deadly than smallpox. Too many colonists awaiting the discovery of their own mines applied the get-rich-quick philosophy to other activities. Grandiose schemes abounded. This tendency to plan beyond sensible limits by no means disappeared with colonial rule. On the contrary, *proyectismo* is one of the lasting burdens of Mexican character.

The fast-profit dreams of mining extended into agricultural production, encouraged by the virtually unlimited land supply and cheap labor. The abundant and servile native labor force that awaited the colonist was ready-made for Spanish-style feudalism. For here, too, the king never relinquished the reins. Land and labor, like Church and government, were his domain. It was the crown who granted land concessions and laid down rights and obligations for colonists and natives alike. Even Cortés, who presumably had all of Mexico from which to pick and choose, received his 25,000 square miles of land from the king.

In the latter years of the colony, agriculture and stock-raising became the primary economic activities of New Spain; there were simply not enough precious-metal mines to go around. Through the crown's jealously guarded controls, Spain continued to exploit New Spain, but it would be shortsighted to ignore the many contributions that the Spanish made to New World agriculture. The list of commercially valuable products of Spanish origin is impressive by itself: fruits (bananas, oranges, limes, apples, peaches, pears); grains (wheat, barley, rye, oats); livestock (horses, hogs, sheep, goats, mules, cattle, oxen); chickens; and sugar. In addition, many farming techniques, methods of irrigation and fertilization of crops, and adaptations of the precious wheel were introduced by Spain.

Any Mexican public grade-school student can reel off the abuses of Spain, but it would be difficult to find one who realizes that Spaniards brought anything more than horses, guns, suppression, and heartaches.

Growing up from the base of a rigid Spanish mercantilism, manufacturing in New Spain naturally lagged miserably, even though it came to occupy the third rank behind agriculture and mining among income producers. Regulated, forbidden, and taxed for the benefit of the Spanish crown and Spanish businessmen, New World industry produced little more than a class of arrogant and embittered capitalists. The exorbitant prices normally charged in the European-controlled economy could hardly endear the local businessmen to the rest of society. When the eighteenth-century Bourbon monarchs attempted an enlightened policy by opening colonial trade to other parts of the world and by lifting many onerous regulations and taxes, new elements were attracted into the business world. But the change was too late. The basic commercial psychology, values, and practices were too fixed in the colony to undergo any transformation. *Laissez-faire* economics simply never had a fair chance.

A cheap labor force was perhaps the greatest single element of wealth in New Spain, and the Spanish colonists in the New World wielded special weapons in the realm of labor employment. Land and labor were inextricably bound together. Historian Silvio Zavala points out that the usual pattern of the *conquistadores* was to seize the land they wanted, to obtain permission from the king of Spain to have natives entrusted to their charge in order to acquire the labor needed, and to solicit the Spanish crown for title to the land. Throughout the colonial epoch, Spain devised comprehensive regulations on land and labor. At times these legal procedures permitted the collection of certain taxes or tribute, which the Indian might pay in the form of personal service. At times the natives were temporarily assigned to Spanish landowners under a system of forced labor for wages. For most of the colonial period, though, whatever the land-labor policies in effect, Indians enjoyed specific legal recourses in case of abuses. Abuses there were, of course, as nearly three hundred years of sworn testimony confirms. Some *conquistadores* and later colonists seized Indians willy-nilly and virtually enslaved them on the land and in the mines. The fact remains that the Indian was given a position in the economy with some measure of rights and a degree of human dignity, however low the measure and degree compared with the status of his overlords.

Inequitable ownership patterns and labor practices deserve condemnation not only for the many evils they contained for labor, but also for the adverse consequences they had on productivity. Since land and mines belonged to the king, he disposed of them as he saw fit. As mine owner, the crown throughout much of the colonial epoch took a fifth share (*quinta real*) of all precious metals. The theory of property and subsoils incorporated in the Constitution of Mexico today is a direct inheritance from colonial Spanish laws. But ownership is one thing, productivity or the lack of it another. In the colonial epoch, and in the pre-Revolution independence period as well, agricultural productivity was overly retarded by underemployment of labor, lack of managerial skills, disinterest of owners, and forced levels of low consumption. The land baron too frequently earned enough from inefficient farming methods to support him in knightly fashion. The Indian had little incentive to produce more. In mining operations, however, entrepreneurs gradually came to grasp the wisdom of raising output through improved labor conditions. The demand for skilled workers in mining operations grew, and by the end of the eighteenth century Indians working in the silver mines had achieved a relatively free bargaining status vis-à-vis the mine operators.

Although the rural masses in the Revolutionary epoch won the battle of landownership when large estates were split up and the land was redistributed, present-day leaders ponder the merits of emphasizing landownership over land use. Many of the more than three million peons who are heads of families today have their own land. Political sociologists probably would deem this desirable. But Mexico cannot eat the fruits of land distribution unless higher productivity results. To the degree that archaic, unproductive methods of agriculture survive, the agrarian-reform process of splitting up lands hardly assists in raising output. Agricultural backwardness survives more than the Revolutionary Family normally admits.

A final major influence from the colonial epoch comes through the social system. Rigid class lines demarcated society. The top of the social ladder was reserved for two sets of whites: the *gachupín*, or Spaniard born in Spain, and below him, the creole, or Spaniard born in New Spain. Friction between the two was great, since the *gachupines* kept most political and economic plums to themselves.

The next rung down the social ladder belonged to the mestizo, with special subranks for the quarter-, eighth-, and sixteenth-part white. The mixed-blood was regarded as outcast by white and Indian alike. Rejected on both sides, the mestizo nonetheless came to constitute the class if not the caste of the middle sector. Many mestizos were really little if anything more than Europeanized Indians. In time, the culture mixture was much more significant than the race mixture.

The third rung of the social ladder was occupied by the Indian—the "Christianized" Indian only, for many Indians never were "civilized" and brought into New Spain society. And at the bottom of the social ladder were the *zambo*, additional offspring of miscegenation of the races, and the Negro.

Although this social structuring was not inflexible—a few Indians, Negroes, and mixed-bloods managed to accumulate more economic power than some whites—a few hundred *gachupín* and creole families dominated the economic and social life of New Spain.

All classes suffered from the absence of good schools. Education was left in the hands of religious orders, both at lower levels and at the University of Mexico, which was founded in 1551 and two years later became the first institution of higher learning in the New World to offer courses. The Church saw to it that New Spain remained a Church-State, and churches, cathedrals, and monasteries flourished. Native imagination was permitted little expression in architecture and painting; these arts invariably reflected the colonial preference for European techniques and tastes. Belles-lettres wore the intellectual straightjacket of Spanish formalism, and although the Inquisition was not totally effective in keeping out "censored" books from France, Great Britain, and other foreign sources, the rigor of censorship, lack of stimulation for intellectual works, and minimal intellectual intercourse with the outside world combined with clerical control of education to make their mark. The rise of rationalism and pragmatic thought, which characterized much of northern Europe, France, and the British colonies, was stopped virtually dead in its tracks in New Spain.

The concise portrait of the liberal Mexican's view of colonial history that has been presented here could not take into detailed account differences in political, economic, and social institutions and policies from one century to the next. Rule in New Spain, of course, changed in many respects over the long period of almost three centuries. To a substantial degree, policies and institutions in the latter part of the 1700's, when Spanish rule was drawing to an end, reflected many constructive lessons that the Spaniards and the indigenous population had learned from living with one another. Ideas of the Enlightenment also reached eighteenth-century New Spain. No reader of the history of New Spain should be left with the incorrect impression of a Spanish rule oblivious to the need for adjustments once the Conquest and initial political consolidation had been consummated. Outlook, policy, and implementation naturally changed.

Yet there was a certain unity and continuity in Spanish colonial rule. Over-all balance sheets of Spanish rule have been drawn up by many historians and demand no refinement here. But identification of the colonial legacies that seem to have influenced the Revolutionary Creed most strongly may provide some insight into the permanent Revolution. Ten legacies of various importance seem to stand out:

1. Introduction and use of the Spanish language.
2. Establishment of an economic system in accord with Spanish concepts of private property and of the power of the state over subsoil rights.
3. Government according to the divine right of kings, incorporating authoritarianism, censorship, centralism, and personalism.
4. Imposition of Catholicism (Spanish in character) as an official state religion.
5. Claims to the superiority of the white foreigner and European values; degradation of indigenous values.
6. Miscegenation of races and the development of a class stratification with ethnic aspects.
7. A low estimation of physical labor, especially a disrespect for manual employment, and a high estimation of leisure, nobility, and power.
8. Imposition of a "gold rush" psychology, seeking fortune just beyond the horizon, projecting grandiose schemes improbable of practical realization.
9. Suspicion of the "outside world."
10. The firm establishment of Mexico City as the political, economic, and social center of New Spain.

INDEPENDENCE AND EARLY NATIONALISM, 1810–1876

Three centuries of peace and political stability is an enviable accomplishment in almost any historical period. Spain bestowed these luxuries on her colony. But mere orderliness provided little in the way of political freedom. Perhaps it was natural, therefore, that when the colonists finally rose against Spanish rule, liberty took precedence over stability. Freedom-lovers soon learned that liberty unbridled by authority can be difficult to live with. Monarchists and democrats, Catholics and Masons, centralists and federalists, conservatives and liberals—no matter what the stripe of Mexican leadership from 1810 forward, none proved itself capable of giving Mexico genuine political stability until Porfirio Díaz assumed the presidency in 1876. Lawlessness, civil strife, insurrections, complicity, ambivalence, and corruption were some of the growing pains during Mexico's coming of age. Anarchy was the primary symptom.

The search for a national identification introduced all kinds of dilemmas. Who should run Mexico? What should be its mission? How should the new nation be governed? Could Mexico effectively answer these questions in accord with the multiple features cut deeply into her character? For it was true that Mexico suffered a split personality: Two basically incompatible cultures, the European and the Indian, lived side by side, and neither came to grips with reality. The first seemed to feel that it could not risk doing so without committing political and economic suicide; the second, illiterate and apathetic, never truly understood what was happening, and when on rare occasions an Indian who grasped political realities came forward, the Indian masses instinctively turned away, still suspicious of the "outside world."

Cultural duality was reflected in innumerable unresolved tensions. The creoles early asserted their supremacy over the mestizos and Indians. Even when preaching racial equality, the creole had no intention of relinquishing his power, prestige, or property to the Indian or mestizo. There were two Catholic churches: The sophisticated European and creole honored the white-skinned Virgin Mary, the dark-skinned Lady of Guadalupe served as the religious matron of the Indian. Religion became further complicated by the rise of several competing Masonic orders which, despite conventional Catholic opposition, housed Catholics along with Jews, Protestants, and spiritualists. The economy was also organized on two differing concepts: feudalism and capitalism. There were two major political groupings—conservatives and liberals—split over the specific issues of monarchy versus republicanism, centralism versus federalism, and a state church versus freedom of religion. More often than not, the closest resemblance to political parties was found in the Masonic orders. Essentially, the whole record of 1810–76 points up the human fear of confronting political reality, as Mexicans failed to unite to overcome the basic social and economic polarity of their country.

In the Revolutionary archives of today, the leading personalities of 1810–76 are neatly filed under the two obviously oversimplified labels of "good" and "bad." "Good" contains those who were liberal Masons, small bourgeoisie, federalists, republicans, anticlericals, and with notable exceptions, Indians, mestizos, and unyielding defenders of nationalism. "Bad" refers to those who supported the clergy, a strong Church, large landholders, monarchy, centralism, and a large army, as well as those who, like Santa Anna, stood for little except demagoguery, self-interest, betrayal of the masses, and intrigue. The "good" are credited with unbelievable purity, and the "bad" are maligned or ignored. Assigned to oblivion along with the Spanish colonial overlords, the "bad" are represented more as traitors than as the reactionaries and conservatives that most of them really were. Even today, the Revolutionary Family refuses to see public good in the politically bad (the opposition); adversaries of the Revolution are equally steadfast in closing their eyes to the good works of the Family.

Heralded today as the greatest of the "good" are Hidalgo, Morelos, and Juárez. It was Miguel Costilla de Hidalgo who called together his parishioners in the small village of Dolores, Guanajuato, on the night of September 15, 1810, where he first raised the cry of independence—"Death to the Spanish-born, long live Our Lady of Guadalupe!" Assuming the title of "Captain-General of America," Hidalgo led an army of the masses against established colonial authority. The second of the heroes, José María Morelos, another priest and comrade-in-arms of Hidalgo, kept up the fight against the Spanish for two years after his former teacher had been captured and executed; his plan for molding a nation, issued in 1813, proposed such sweeping social and economic reforms as racial equality, land redistribution, and anticlerical measures—all of which even today are in keeping with permanent Revolutionary goals. The third nineteenth-century saint, Benito Juárez, authored anticlerical and anti-large-landholding legislation and promulgated the liberal Constitution of 1857. During his tenancy in the presidency, he championed the mestizo and bourgeoisie forces in the period known in Mexican history as the Reform (1855–76). Juárez's inspirational leadership of elements opposed to Maximilian and the French occupation make him a patriot par excellence.

This triumvirate of nineteenth-century liberals represents the gamut of Mexican racial and social composition. All three knew poverty: Morelos and Juárez by birth, Hidalgo by choice of profession. Taken together, all major racial strains ran through their veins. Hidalgo was a creole, Morelos a mestizo with Negro blood, and Juárez an Indian. None of them was outstandingly successful in raising the immediate economic well-being of the Indian masses. Revolutionaries contend that Hidalgo was a liberal who had solid ideas on social reform, that he questioned papal infallibility, and that he identified himself with the masses, all in addition to his efforts on behalf of independence. In reality, Hidalgo's hard-core solution to colonialism was ruthless extermination of the Spanish-born—a solution that left much to be desired when we remember the Mexican cultural complex of that day. On the other hand, despite the inability of Morelos and Juárez to translate ideals into realities, they unequivocably advocated profound social and economic reforms.

Early in life, these three heroes adhered to Catholicism; later, all sympathized with Freemasonry. All received their early education from churchmen. Although Mexican independence was inspired by two priests and "consummated on the altar," the Church condemned their escapades. Excommunicated and stripped of their clerical garb, both were executed by arrangement of the Church-State and State-Church, Hidalgo in 1811 and Morelos in 1815. Mexican history might have been a different story if Church had broken with State, hailed Hidalgo and Morelos as Catholic heroes, and encouraged them to lead the masses against an offensive State. By the time Juárez came along, political lines had drawn so taut that a leader was, plain and simple, either for or against the Church. Juárez was dead set against it. As high chief of liberal Freemasonry and the anticlerical camp, he probably cared little about the perpetual condemnation issued upon him by the Church. While Juárez actively participated in Freemasonic ranks for years, Hidalgo and Morelos probably never became formal Freemasons, although there is evidence that they maintained contacts with Freemasons. The powerful role of Freemasonry in shaping nine-teenth-century society in Mexico is discussed in Chapter 7.

Today, a conglomerate array of other nineteenth-century personalities appear among the ranks of the "good" leaders. Let us content ourselves with comment on five of the more important figures. (1) *Ignacio Allende.* A young creole army captain, Allende rode Paul Revere fashion to warn Hidalgo that Spanish authorities planned to seize him and suppress all revolutionary schemers. Joining Hidalgo in his military campaign, Allende won the signal honor of being shot in the back as a traitor, having his head severed, and for ten years (1811–21) having it hung alongside Hidalgo's head on a fortress wall in Guanajuato as a warning to liberal elements in the general public. (2) *Vicente Guerrero.* Like Morelos, whom he followed, Guerrero was a mestizo with Negro blood. Unwilling to lay down his arms after the execution of Morelos, this illiterate soldier kept fighting against the Spanish and the creole monarchists and centralists. Becoming grand master of the Masonic York Rite, which harbored the federalists and republicans, he aided in the overthrow of Emperor Iturbide, the promulgation of the Constitution of 1824, and the seating of Guadalupe Victoria as first President of Mexico. Guerrero himself became President in 1829, and proceeded to outlaw slavery and expel many Spaniards from Mexico. Such radicalism provoked his unseating after a matter of months by the opportunistic Santa Anna. In 1833, with the centralists controlling the nation, Guerrero was captured and executed as a traitor. (3) *Miguel Ramos Arizpe.* Renouncing the priesthood in favor of a political career, Ramos Arizpe became an outstanding federalist republican. In 1812, he was sent as one of New Spain's delegates to the Cádiz parliament, which drafted a new liberal Constitution for Spain. Such subversive activity got him jailed when King Ferdinand returned from exile bent on suppressing liberalism. Released from prison, Ramos Arizpe returned to New Spain, where he took up the fight for independence. He opposed the pompous Iturbide and, through the high councils of the Masonic York Rite, worked ardently on behalf of forces trying to depose the monarchists. His fame comes chiefly from his authorship of Mexico's liberal Constitution of 1824, a rough copy of the U.S. Constitution. Assuming a cabinet post in the first republican government Mexico ever knew, Ramos Arizpe labored for the cause of federalism-republicanism until his death in 1831. (4) *Valentín Gómez Farías.* Gómez Farías left the profession of medicine to become a politician. In his second profession he distinguished himself among federalists, republicans, and liberal Masons. In fact, for three decades he held the recognized leadership of the liberals. Elected vice-president in 1833, he assumed presidential powers when Santa Anna deserted the highest office. Ousted in 1834 by Santa Anna, Gómez did not re-enter the presidency until 1846, when once again Santa Anna rode onto the scene and deposed him. Valentín Gómez Farías is acclaimed today for his liberal ideas on public education, clericalism, special privileges, and militarism. (5) *Juan Álvarez*. Like Morelos and Guerrero, Álvarez was a mixed-blood with Negro strains. Like Guerrero, he was a military *caudillo*, a York Rite Mason, highly patriotic, and a liberal who became president of his country. The inclusion of his name in a list of the "good" personalities derives principally from his leadership of the "Revolution of Ayutla," which culminated in 1855 in overthrowing the hated Santa Anna, in seating Álvarez in the presidential chair, and in the passage of anticlerical laws of Juárez and Lerdo. All in all, the "Revolution of Ayutla" accomplished much more, for it really initiated the period known as the Reform (1855–76), which gave birth to the anticlerical, federalist, small bourgeoisie, and republican Constitution of 1857.

Now for the "bad" characters. This file bulges over with names of churchmen, monarchists, centralists, large landowners, intriguing foreigners, foreign military leaders, traitors, anti-Masons, religious fanatics, insurrectionists, and racial supremacists. Retrospectively, anyone not measuring up to the present Revolutionary standards can be found here. Relegated to oblivion as a class, their constructive works notwithstanding, are Spanish and U.S. generals, Catholic bishops, and *hacendados*. Specifically condemned are the Spanish militarist of independence fame, General Urrea; Joel Poinsett, first U.S. diplomatic minister accredited to Mexico; the brilliant intellectual, centralist statesman, and writer, Lucas Alamán; the army generals Miramón and Mejía, who in the 1860's commanded royalist forces against federalist troops; the two emperors, Iturbide and Maximilian; the *caudillo* Antonio López de Santa Anna; and the American generals Zachary Taylor and Winfield Scott. Let us concentrate attention on four of the "worst": Iturbide, Santa Anna, Winfield Scott, and Maximilian.

Iturbide betrayed the cause of independence, not once, but on virtually every opportunity presented. As a soldier in the pay of Spain, he helped destroy the great patriot Morelos. Sent against Vicente Guerrero and his republican army, he saved his own head by pretending to join Guerrero. His vicious treatment of enemies, including the shooting of all prisoners, hardly gained him much respect among his adversaries. Although Iturbide did eventually fight for independence from Spain, his monarchical principles ran counter to the hopes of those who saw independence as the catalyst for social revolution. To Iturbide, independence came to mean simply exchanging a foreign king for a creole king—and when the proper time arrived, he manipulated sentiments so that the creole king turned out to be none other than Iturbide himself, who was crowned as Emperor Agustín I. After a constitutional monarchy was established as the form of government under which Mexico was to be ruled, Iturbide even betrayed this: He first imprisoned fifty members of Congress and later dissolved the entire Congress. Overthrown by republican forces in which Guerrero, Guadalupe Victoria, and Santa Anna were conspicuous, Iturbide's dominance over Mexican politics, which had lasted from September, 1821, to March, 1823, ended in exile. Returning from Europe in 1824, Iturbide earned the reward of being shot as a traitor.

But in the annals of intrigue, treachery, and betrayal, Iturbide deserves an amateur rating alongside Santa Anna. This colorful demagogue amassed an unbelievable record. He betrayed, successively: the Spanish in 1821; Iturbide in 1823 (by turning on his commander in chief and assisting in his overthrow); the liberal cause and Vicente Guerrero in 1829 (by marching on Mexico City and deposing the illiterate general); the conservative cause and President Bustamante in 1832 (by unseating him); his own vice-president Gómez Farías and the federalists in 1834 (by summarily dismissing him and instituting centralist reforms); the Texans and Mexicans in 1836 (by duplicity and intrigue); Bustamante and the conservatives again, this time in 1841 (by forcing him out of the presidency and making himself provisional president); U.S. President Polk in 1847 (who had permitted Santa Anna safe conduct from his exile in Cuba in order to conciliate anti-U.S. forces in Mexico); Zachary Taylor and the Mexicans in 1847 (by promising one thing to Taylor and telling the Mexican Congress the reverse); Gómez Farías and the liberals again, in 1847 (by overthrowing the established government); the whole Mexican nation (with the Gadsden Purchase of 1853); and finally, Lucas Alamán and the centralists from 1853 to 1855 (by governing Mexico contrary to conservative expectations). Whatever may be said for his sporadic appearances to restore order, Santa Anna symbolized chaos and anarchy. Always posing as the savior of his country, he mutilated, corrupted, and betrayed his nation more than any other Mexican or foreigner before him or since.

Santa Anna, along with Zachary Taylor, Winfield Scott, and John Charles Frémont, are the principal figures of the Mexican War (1846–48). All are culprits from the Mexican point of view. Quite aside from the real issues involved and the comparative fighting qualities of the American and Mexican forces, Texas was really lost to Mexico long before the war broke out. From the moment Sam Houston defeated and captured Santa Anna at San Jacinto—an event that occurred after the Mexican attack on the Alamo and the massacre of more than three hundred prisoners at Goliad—we should remember that the Texans had no intention of ever returning to the Mexican union. Inasmuch as Frémont and Taylor had entered central Mexico (Frémont occupied California; Taylor went only as far south as Saltillo, where he engaged Santa Anna in the indecisive Battle of Buena Vista in 1847, returning from there to the United States with his presidential ambitions inflated by what he had reported as an "overwhelming American victory"), they represented a more remote threat than the forces commanded by Winfield Scott. Scott came into direct contact with the mass citizenry in Mexico. He landed an expeditionary force at Veracruz and captured that important seaport, then moved inland to Cerro Gordo, where he defeated Santa Anna, and from there marched through Puebla and finally took Mexico City. (Inspiring to the Mexicans were the several young military cadets who jumped to their deaths—and martyrdom—from Chapultepec Hill rather than surrender to the Americans.) Once Scott had occupied Mexico City, the residents complained of the general disorderliness of the American troops, which reportedly included firing into crowds. The Mexicans were forced to their knees in a contest that later evoked sentiments of dissatisfaction with the unfairness of the whole episode from three great Americans— Abraham Lincoln, Ulysses S. Grant, and Robert E. Lee—and the Mexican War formally ended on February 2, 1848, with the Treaty of Guadalupe Hidalgo. The indisputable loss of Texas alone would have shaken Mexican pride. Imagine their shock when they discovered that not only Texas had been signed away but also the territory now comprising California, Nevada, Utah, part of Colorado, New Mexico, and Arizona as well. All in all, Mexico lost half of her national territory, receiving in return little more than a paltry fifteen million dollars. Who can deny that Mexico paid dearly for losing a couple of battles to a few soldiers from her supposedly friendly neighbor "who unfairly invaded Mexico"?

A fourth undesirable is Maximilian. As could be expected, the second and last of Mexico's experiments with monarchy resulted from the same old formula: A minority imposed an unwanted government on the majority. Indubitably, Maximilian's empire would not have materialized without both heavy support from influential Mexicans and the desire of Napoleon III of France to take advantage of the Civil War raging in the United States. The *cause célèbre* was the arrival of French, English, and Spanish vessels at Veracruz in early 1862 to force the payment of debts. Though they failed to collect, only the French marched inland, where on May 5, 1862, they met and were soundly defeated by Mexican troops. Reinforced, the French tried again and this time succeeded, entering Mexico City in June, 1863. The new Emperor and Empress, Maximilian and Carlota, arrived from Europe the next year, completely unaware of the feeble, precarious position of the monarchists and of the over-all popularity of Benito Juárez, number-one enemy of monarchy and centralism. Maximilian sincerely tried to understand Mexico and do something about its problems, but he was, after all, a foreigner, and Mexicans resented a benevolent foreigner, even more than a ruthless national, taking over the government. As soon as the emperor's troops met with a first serious defeat at the hands of federalist forces, even the monarchists deserted Maximilian. Alone, he personally assumed field command of troops remaining loyal to him. But the time had arrived to end monarchy forever. Maximilian lived long enough to see his troops destroyed before he himself faced a firing squad on an early morning in June, 1867, in the hills over-looking the provincial city of Querétaro.

After the collapse of this last adventure in monarchy, the glory of "liberalism" was brief, for the last decade of the period continued to be typified by fratricidal jealousy and chaos. Juárez's death in 1872, before the end of his second term as president, helped set the stage.

So the third period of Mexican history, the struggle for independence lasting from 1810 to 1876, closed as it had started—with the bickerings of idealistic federalist republicans. The special emphasis still given to the "bad" figures of the period is no accident: Few people have suffered as miserably as the Mexicans during their first years of independence. The Mexican balance sheet of 1876 carried shocking debits for each of the asset entries: Liberty—one sure path to anarchy and chaos! Political sta-bility—a brief episode when a strongman imposed his will! Leadership—cunning, not skill, was most often the determinant! Property rights and life itself—unassessed integers! National property—a pie for booty-bar-gaining giveaway! Economic development—an investment for the insane! Constitutional government—the written word, paper thin, was no test for the strong! Communication—hazardous travel over miserable roads! Land reforms—feudalism persisted despite the breakup of some Church lands! In short, the big, fundamental problems continued to menace the country. Only one of the new national assets, in fact, was not outweighed by its negative corollary: the action against the Church's economic strangle-hold on the nation. Enforcement of legislation from the 1850's and the constitutional amendment of 1874 went far toward canceling forever that reactionary strangulation of the economy and toward removing the Church from official favor. By word, if not precisely by deed, subsequent governments have been committed to anticlericalism and to freedom of religion.

THE PORFIRIAN EPOCH

The fourth epoch of Mexican history belongs to one man: Porfirio Díaz. His "military Díaz-potism" managed to amputate the cancerous political instability that had been eating away at the country since 1810. Out of chaos and civil strife, Díaz brought law and order, though both largely of his own personal brand. He virtually eliminated banditry and brigandage. Solid material progress ensued in commercial, industrial, and mineral development. Property, at least that of big landholders and foreign holders, became secure. Mexico's credit rating soared in foreign exchanges. Investment capital entered freely and willingly. The new society so im-pressed diplomats that they placed Díaz on the highest international pedestal. All in all, the outside world credited Don Porfirio with extraordinary wisdom. Mexico was fortunate indeed in having such a great, benevolent leader!

But whatever its international reputation, the Díaz regime ultimately provoked the Mexican Revolution and instilled in the Revolutionary Family a permanent disgust for Díaz himself and for things bearing his stamp. Why, may we ask, is discredit heaped on the one Mexican who succeeded in consolidating the country where others before him had failed?

The Revolutionary indictment bears powerful charges on this count. In the political realm, Díaz gave only lip-service to the liberal, federalist Constitution of 1857 while building a highly authoritarian, centralist police state. Effective suffrage was a meaningless notion from a disregarded Constitution. The tenure of Díaz and his governors in the states challenges the record of American city bosses such as Crump, Hague, and Curley. Judges, legislators, army men, and local officials did precisely what he ordered, or they lost their posts. His rural police guaranteed the big landholder a cheap labor supply. The peasant had to accept debt peonage and involuntary servitude because his alternative was a beating, imprisonment, or the firing squad. Similarly, industrial peace came to mean government intervention on behalf of ownership; strikes were treason. Freedom of press, assembly, and speech constituted doctrines "unsuited to Mexican political life," as did regionalism, localism, popularism, and judicial review. The political system was a textbook demonstration of despotism. Díaz prevailed, and he was omnipotent.

In the economic realm, the Revolutionary indictment bears equally harsh terms. The existence of enormous haciendas and "colonization" tracts in the hands of a few persons of a mentality similar to the feudal lords of sixteenth-century Europe had emerged in part from the nineteenth-century liberal formula (not conceived by Díaz) of basing Mexican agriculture on small private properties instead of on the communal *ejido*. Though of noble purpose, the agrarian reforms begun in the 1850's ended in the fortification of the *latifundio* and a still greater concentration of agrarian property. The 1856 law of disamortization directed against properties of the clergy succeeded in wresting away the bulk of Church-owned lands, but failed to create a nation of small, privately owned farms. Then, through colonization schemes under Díaz, foreigners managed to gain title to tens of millions of acres of forest, grazing, and agricultural land; eight foreigners became proprietors of more than 55 million acres, much of it along the United States border. When the Revolution initiated agrarian reform in earnest and land-reclamation claims dominated American-Mexican troubles, much of the land under question was precisely those large tracts whose old titles had been taken away from the Indians and given away by Díaz for practically nothing. Of the strictly Mexican landlord class, fifteen *hacendados* owned more than 100,000 acres each;

the Hacienda of San Blas in the state of Coahuila alone had almost a million acres.

But the peon hungered for more than his own parcel of land; he also wanted food and justice. The income of the peon in 1910 was about the same as it had been a century earlier, despite the higher prices of basic necessities he bought from the hacienda store. His diet was composed of corn, beans, chile, and, too frequently, of the intoxicating *pulque*. Bread, rice, milk, and meat were luxuries that he enjoyed rarely, if ever.

A typical large hacienda centered on the *hacendado*'s mansion—composed frequently of an enormous dining room, numerous bedrooms and bathrooms, a study, a giant kitchen, a luxuriously furnished living room, a billiards room. Ample lighting, hot and cold running water, and beautiful flower gardens were among its features. Nearby was a modestly furnished house for the general manager, smaller houses for employees of confidence, a general office-supply-equipment shed, a church, a jail, a "tienda de raya" (hacienda store) that sold basic necessities to the peon and kept him in perpetual debt peonage, and at a distance of a quarter or a half mile from the rest of the buildings, the huts of the peons. The huts were usually one-room shacks made of adobe, without windows, lamps, beds, or running water; the peon and his big family cooked, ate, and slept in one small, dirt-floored room. In addition, some haciendas provided a small shack to be used as a schoolroom and for the conduct of civic affairs. The contrast between mansion and hut—between the life of the *hacendado* and administrator on the one hand and the peon on the other—bore heavily on the peasant as he daily entered the fields before sunrise and returned at sunset. To the peon, justice meant the unquestioned word of *hacendado*, administrator, jailor, and priest. And if the overlord needed assistance in keeping his peons in line, he simply called upon Díaz's rural shock-troopers. The poverty-stricken peasant had no hope of a better tomorrow, no promise of somehow raising himself from his deplorable status.

Along with this unequitable landownership pattern and the deplorable living conditions of the peon came unproductive use of the land. What the *hacendado* did with his property was left to his own discretion, which often meant that much land stood idle and that uneconomical methods of cultivation were used on the rest. "Colonization" companies grabbed title to tremendous tracts of land, then left millions of acres untouched. Too frequently, the landlord looked upon his domain as a never-ending source of wealth to keep himself in high style in a provincial capital, in Mexico City, or abroad. Reinvestment or changes in ageless patterns of cultivation were seldom considered—raising corn year after year for centuries on the same land was good enough!

The Revolutionaries also indict Díaz for turning over much of the productive machine to foreigners, for making Mexico the "father of foreigners and stepfather of Mexicans." Besides the powerful hold that they held over rural lands, foreigners dominated mining, utilities, industry, and commerce. Americans seized the cement industry. The French monopolized large department stores. The Germans controlled the hardware business. The Spanish took over foodstores and, together with the French, controlled the textile industry. The Canadians, aided by Americans and Englishmen, concentrated on electric power, trolley lines, and water companies. The Belgians, Americans, and English invested heavily in the railroads. And what ultimately shook the roots of Revolutionary ideology was the American and British exploitation of minerals, especially oil. Doheny, Guggenheim, Cooke, Cowdray, and other foreigners operated in Mexico within an economic context not much unlike that of the Manifest Destiny and Robber Baron epoch in the United States. Some made great fortunes; others lost millions. Unfortunately for foreign investment, in the early years of Revolution Mexicans looked upon foreign capital and Díaz's whole undesirable political rule as inextricable twins. Foreign capital as such bothered the nascent Mexican capitalist as much as it did the rank and file.

The latter had still another gripe, which Díaz and foreign companies ignored: Being Mexican precluded them from the better jobs in industry and commerce. Professor Silva Herzog relates an account of an American and Mexican applying during the late years of the Díaz regime for the job of railroad machinist.[1]

Supervisor:	"Are you an American?"
American:	"Yes, sir."
Supervisor:	"Come in and sit down. What are wheels?"
American:	"Round things."
Supervisor:	"Where is the stove?"
American:	"In the caboose."
Supervisor:	"Where are the wheels taking the trains?"
American:	"Forward."
Supervisor:	"Good enough; you can be a machinist."
Supervisor:	"What are you?"
Mexican:	"Mexican."
Supervisor:	"Oh, all the time giving us trouble! Do you understand English?"
Mexican:	"No, sir."
Supervisor:	"What quantity of fuel will a locomotive burn running twelve leagues per hour and with a pressure of one hundred pounds? How many calories will be developed? What is the consumption of water and oil? What is the friction on

[1] Jesús Silva Herzog, *Breve historia de la revolución mexicana: los antecedentes y la etapa maderista* (México: Fondo de Cultura Económica, 1960), p. 44.

the rails? What is the work of the pistons and the number of revolutions of the wheels? What is the amount of steam consumed in a 4 per cent decline of two leagues? . . ."

Mexican: "Sir, I do not know because you are asking me many things at the same time."

Supervisor: "Ah! You are a Mexican, you do not know anything. You are very stupid, you still have to ride many miles of track. You will not do as a machinist. You will not do for anything more than a guard with a club on a freight train. You cannot become a machinist because you could not answer my question."

The peculiarities of life in the cities also militated against social justice. A pseudoaristocratic society prevailed in which the rich, the foreigner, and the select politician denigrated the lower classes. The middle-class professional and intellectual were little better off unless they worked for a foreign concern, where they also felt shackled by a superiority-conscious employer. Ideas incongruous with positivism were not permitted to circulate. To justify racial superiority, Díaz's brain trust infected education and society at large with the doctrine of white supremacy. Indians, claimed the positivists, were inferior because nature willed it! "Salvation lay in transforming Mexico into a white man's country oriented by European values and customs." Díaz handled the proverbial question of Church and State relations inconsistently but realistically. Church properties were confiscated one day, the Church permitted to buy new property the next; anticlerical legislation was enforced by his left hand, retracted by his right. These apparently contradictory actions might be attributed to a desire to conciliate sources of friction. They certainly underscored his own religious predicament, for like thousands of Mexicans before him and since, Díaz was a Freemason married to a devout Catholic.

Some men make their place in history through their actual achievements. Díaz belongs to this group, for he began the material buildup of Mexico. The ends to which he dedicated power may have contradicted man's very nature, but he opened sleepy eyes to what man could erect through physical labor, even in a backward nation. Railroads, electric-power facilities, a steel mill, cement plants, textile mills, and an oil industry became solid realities. By leaving the land to work on the railroads, in the mines, and elsewhere, a few Mexican laborers shook off their provincialism and found a new world unfolding before them, even though social and geographical mobility remained much too low for the dynamic economic development that Mexico required. And although innovation, entrepreneurship, and promotion never became part of the mass vocabulary, they did take root among a select group of foreigners and privileged Mexicans who ran some financial risks, governmental assurances notwithstanding. Excessively feudalistic, exploitative, paternalistic, and foreign-dominated, the material progress introduced by Díaz was not entirely without benefits for Mexico and the Mexican. However harsh the Revolutionary indictment of Díaz may be for not implanting in the popular mind the promise of a better life ahead, it cannot justify exclusion of the fact that Mexico really began its economic progress under the aegis of the old autocrat.

The last decade of the Age of Díaz coincided with the first decade of the emergence of the United States as a world power. In the eyes of survival-of-the-fittest doctrinaires in Mexico there was no mistaking the implications of the United States victory over Spain. The Roosevelt Corollary to the Monroe Doctrine, following the United States' gobbling up of Panama, produced a new fear among the Mexicans: Their country was also part of Latin America and, worse still, it was located dangerously near to the United States—much closer than Panama. U.S. interventionism and its growing naval strength thus represented imminent threats. True, Díaz was not anti-American, yet how much leeway would Washington have permitted him had he preferred a different line? Central American and Caribbean nations experienced sad fates whenever they forgot that anti-Americanism was a luxury that weak nations could ill afford. In Mexico, U.S. mining, lumber, and oil interests became increasingly more confident, more aggressive, more powerful. Some Mexicans who opposed Díaz on many counts hesitated to shift any blame for his regime's shortcomings to undesirable foreigners or to crude American foreign policy. The impact of foreign influence before 1910 therefore played a decisive role in shaping things to come after 1910, when Woodrow Wilson first began to rectify certain tenets of American foreign policy.

Other circumstances of the last decade of the gestation period of the Mexican Revolution sprang more directly from uniquely Mexican sources. There were the general problems of peonage and *hacendadismo*, which retarded economic development of the land, forestalled the creation of markets that were indispensable for the rise of industrialization and commercialization, and perhaps most important, banished hope and instilled fear into the rural masses. There were also problems related to the arbitrary rule of Díaz and his military governors and local *caciques*; problems exacerbated by the lack of educational facilities and opportunities; problems flowing from the absence of a stable, propertied middle class and the depreciation of existent middle-class elements; problems associated with long-harbored regional grievances, especially those of the northern and western states, who resented the exaggerated preference given Mexico City and the port of Veracruz; problems imposed by the neatly demarcated class structure and underscored by the doctrine of the survival of the fittest and tremendous gaps between the rich and the poor, between the governors and the governed, between the pseudoaristocracy and the Indian masses; and problems created by government resistance to the presentation of new ideas in educational institutions, in publishing and journalism, in Freemason councils, political groupings, and intellectual circles wishing to toss off the stranglehold of positivism, and in Catholic Church groups desirous of spreading the Christian social doctrines of Pope Leo XIII.

But the omnipotent Díaz himself could not entirely stop the encroachment of new ideas. The humanism of his own onetime minister of education, Justo Sierra, inspired an intellectual revival of ideas opposed to positivism. Two of Sierra's students, José Vasconcelos and Alfonso Caso, were destined to become great Revolutionary intellectuals. As early as the 1890's, Ricardo Flores Magón began his attack on the Díaz regime. Ringing through the appeals of the Mexican Liberal Party that he and others organized in 1906 to declare political warfare on the Díaz regime was his insistence that political freedom without bread was no freedom at all and that economic equality was an imperative. Liberal "clubs," some inspired by the writings of Flores Magón, sprang up in several parts of Mexico and asserted that Díaz was betraying the Constitution of 1857. Filomeno Mata and a few other brave journalists who were in and out of jail regularly, published liberal ideas in bold periodicals that Díaz rarely permitted to exist for more than a few issues. Freemasons began to challenge the content and organization of the whole Masonic apparatus in Mexico; this provoked the schismatic movement of 1909, led by English-speaking lodges, and culminated in the Mexicanization of the dominant core of Freemasonry. Pablo Macedo published a book on economic and financial development, in which he identified many shortcomings of Porfirian fiscal and monetary policy. Andrés Molina Enríquez published a powerful indictment of the Mexican social and economic system in his book entitled *Great National Problems* (1909). In advocating effective suffrage and observance of the principle of no re-election in his book, *The Presidential Succession in 1910* (published in 1908 and released to the public in the following year), Francisco Madero first came to the attention of political liberals and simultaneously initiated a political career that ultimately swept him into the presidency. A small group of young students destined to become leaders in their respective professions— among them, José Vasconcelos in education, philosophy, and literature, Diego Rivera in art, Jesús Acevedo in architecture, and Alfonso Caso in philosophy—regularly discussed philosophies in a humanist-oriented forum. Furthermore, there were other groupings of diverse ideological molds that appeared on the scene to challenge Díaz's political and intellectual monopoly.

Ideas from these new schools of thought spilled over into practical action. In 1906, miners at the Cananea Consolidated Copper Company properties in the state of Sonora took the unprecedented step of striking for higher wages, better working and living conditions, and equal treatment regardless of nationality. Of course, the state governor and federal troops combined with company strongmen to put down the strike and, under threat of sending them to fight against the militant Yaqui Indians, to force the workers back to the mines without redress of their grievances. A few months later, and more than a thousand miles to the southeast, textile workers at Rio Blanco, Veracruz, raised the strike banner. The results were more than two hundred dead and wounded at the hands of federal troops, the firing squad for two leaders, deportation of other leaders to forced labor in Quintana Roo, and absolutely no redress of grievances. Díaz fully intended to suppress labor on any and all accounts. Besides these two cracks in the Porfirian wall, there were several minor armed uprisings in diverse localities during the years 1908, 1909, and 1910, some of them inspired by the Flores Magón group; without exception, Díaz quickly and ruthlessly put down these rebellions. As long as Díaz could keep opposition elements disorganized and his own military and political machine well oiled, discontent, hunger, and misery could be kept in line. And hunger and misery became deeply critical problems in consequence of an economic crisis in 1908, which followed in the wake of the 1907 financial panic in the United States and was aggravated by an exceedingly bad harvest in 1909.

The specific and immediate political *cause célèbre* leading to Díaz's ouster was the reprinting in Mexico of the celebrated "Creelman Interview" of February 17, 1908. James Creelman, a reporter for *Pearson's Magazine,* credited Díaz with having told him in a private interview that the old dictator was determined to retire at the end of his present term, and that under no circumstances would he accept re-election. Díaz reportedly pointed out that despite his misgivings about what someone else would do if given a chance to rule, personal magnanimity and patriotism prompted his decision to welcome any and all political elements to organize for the coming election. Regardless of Díaz's sincerity or lack of it, or for that matter the validity of Creelman's account of the interview to begin with, the appearance of the article in the Mexico City *El Imparcial,* on March 3, 1908, was taken by some leaders at face value. And why not? Díaz had long ago passed the normal age of senility and would actually reach his eightieth birthday before election time. Intimate collaborators no less than bitter enemies viewed the announcement as an invitation to install themselves in public offices. Proven Porfirians, among them Vice-President Ramón Corral and Gen. Bernardo Reyes, as well as proven opponents immediately began to group their forces.

To the dismay of these ambitious politicians, Díaz informed his cabinet some months after publication of the *El Imparcial* article that he *would* seek another term. He had no intention of stepping down because of old age, patriotism, or any other motive. Nonetheless, some political groupings taking form believed that they could still gain control if, acting on the supposition that the aging dictator would not live through another six-year term, they concentrated on winning the vice-presidency, legislative posts, and governorships. Others took an all-or-nothing approach in the belief that with a free election and effective suffrage, Díaz could be defeated for the presidency. In addition to concentrating on winning different public offices, political groups soon divided on the selection of candidates and on the content of platforms. Sporadic organization brought fragmentation. Pro-Díaz forces split on governmental policy and on the vice-presidential nomination. Liberals disagreed on the issues of clericalism and re-election. Members of all groups were afflicted with the opportunism inherent in politics.

Once Díaz had made the official ticket of Díaz and Corral public, he tried to strengthen his slate by "exiling" General Reyes, Corral's leading opponent—and, of course, he rejected the principles of no re-election and effective suffrage. It was precisely on these points that effective suffragists chose to concentrate their campaign. As election time drew near, only the re-electionist ballot of Díaz and Corral and the Anti Re-electionist ticket of Francisco Madero and Francisco Vásquez Gómez carried substantial backing. Madero was young and dynamic; Díaz, old and senile. Madero campaigned vigorously; Díaz made no effort to reach the people directly. Madero favored political liberalism; Díaz stuck to positivism and re-election. Madero received endorsement from some articulate individuals, among them Filomeno Mata, Toribio Esquivel Obregón, Félix F. Palavicini, Federico González Garza, and José Vasconcelos, but he lacked support of the monied and military interests; Díaz drew his organizational strength from the Mexican army, the bureaucracy, the *hacendados*, clergymen, and from the plutocracy in general. Never one to waver in his authoritarianism, Díaz ordered Madero and other Anti Re-electionists imprisoned—and particularly in the case of Madero, this act led to a growing popular sympathy for the "victims of a despotic regime."

Nobody will ever know the true results of the balloting on June 26, 1910, for honest vote-tallying had ceased long ago in Mexico. Whatever the real vote may have been, the government announced that Díaz and Corral had won handily. Madero supporters then petitioned for a nullification of the election, which the chamber of deputies denied, and, on September 11, Díaz added insult to injury by dissolving a public manifestation of Anti Re-electionists in Mexico City. Only one course for justice remained open: armed rebellion. Madero, who escaped from his guards and fled across the border to San Antonio, supplied the indispensable spark. On October 5, 1910, he issued his "Plan of San Luis," which declared the July elections null and void, affirmed the adhesion of the revolutionaries to the principle of no re-election, and proclaimed Francisco Madero provisional president of Mexico on the thesis that Madero would undoubtedly have won a free and honest election. In addition, the "Plan" declared the need for revising agrarian titles and, most important, designated November 20, 1910, for a nationwide uprising to overthrow the Díaz regime. At the same time, Madero issued a manifesto inviting members of the Mexican army to defect and join forces with the revolutionary movement he directed. When Aquiles Serdán, leader of the Madero cause in Puebla, and his family were provoked into fighting against federal troops on November 18, when Pancho Villa, Pascual Orozco, and José de la Luz Blanco revolted in Chihuahua on November 20 according to Madero's plan, and when small groups in numerous localities rose in arms against Díaz, the Mexican Revolution was forcefully underway.

THREE

FIFTY YEARS OF REVOLUTION (1)

The outbreak of uprisings in accord with Madero's plan marked an end to the incubation period of the Mexican Revolution. Yet right up to May 25, 1911, when the senile autocrat formally resigned and two days later set sail for Europe, the upheaval assumed the character of a simple revolt—of toppling Díaz and installing Madero. Everything became subordinate to getting rid of Díaz. While Madero himself remained in Texas from November 20 to early 1911, Pascual Orozco, Emiliano Zapata, Pancho Villa, and a host of other underdogs risked their lives in guerrilla tactics against Díaz's troops. Poorly trained and meagerly equipped for warfare, the insurrectionists engaged federal troops in only one contest worthy of the designation "battle," and this, the Battle of the City of Juárez, simultaneously terminated hostilities.

One force apparently influencing the downfall of Díaz was not mentioned in the previous chapter: the uncalculable response of the United States to events of 1910–11. U.S. Army forces had been mobilized along the Mexican northern border, assertedly in response to the danger posed by Flores Magón and his international anarchists, who had seized several towns in Baja California and hinted that they would spread their base northward. In May, 1911, when Madero, Villa, and Orozco commanded rebel contingents moving on the border town of Ciudad Juárez, members of the Díaz brain trust feared the United States might intervene. The ever-present danger of Uncle Sam's disposition changing in favor of armed intervention prompted several *científicos* to urge Díaz to resign in order to "save Mexico." Of course, other motives entered into his decision to resign, but with the federal army still intact, the force of rebel arms alone could hardly have brought about Díaz's resignation. Ciudad Juárez was the only metropolis in the nation actually under Madero's full control, although a considerable area outside of the urban centers was under Revolutionary control. Public opinion—indeed, public disgust —and not force of arms overturned Díaz. Madero's victory in a border city 1,200 miles from Mexico City was the drop that overflowed the barrel.

THE MADERO PHASE, 1911–1913

As Madero moved southward from Chihuahua, the masses paid little attention to the fact that Díaz's military machine was virtually untouched. They wholeheartedly hailed Madero as their long-awaited deliverer from the ruthless Díaz. No Mexican had ever before received such an enthusiastic, moving, and sincere welcome as did Madero when he triumphantly entered Mexico City on June 7, 1911. The masses naturally could not have anticipated the bloody upheavals that would come in his wake, but they did realize that the presence of Madero meant the end of Díaz, and this alone was cause for rejoicing.

The City of Juárez Treaty provided for a provisional governing arrangement concluding with general elections, but as subsequent events proved, the masses wanted more than the simple political reform measures contained in the Treaty—much more than the "effective suffrage and no re-election" program under which Madero set about to reconstruct Mexico. Despite his claim that "nobody can accuse me of promoting the revolution for personal ambitions," Madero committed a series of errors tinged with personalism. While waiting to be duly elected and installed, Madero permitted Francisco León de la Barra, minister of foreign affairs under Díaz, to serve as provisional president during the crucial days from May 26 to November 6. In the De la Barra cabinet of eight members, chosen in accord with Madero, were only three social Revolutionaries, and two of the remaining five were conservative relatives of Madero. In addition to exposing himself in this way to charges of selling out the Revolution and of nepotism, Madero subverted the principle of "effective suffrage" by employing arbitrary tactics to have Pino Suárez chosen as his vice-presidential running mate. And though Madero generally observed effective suffrage in the election of congressmen to the memorable XXVI Federal Legislature, he thus condoned the seating of many legislators who opposed reform and despised him personally. Furthermore, although Madero placed Revolutionaries in high posts in the national and state governments, he left the Porfirian-oriented army and civil service largely intact. Worst of all, Madero sanctioned the sending of troops under command of Gen. Victoriano Huerta to combat Zapata and his agrarian reformers. All in all, for five long months the interregnum government prolonged the reactionary tendencies of the Díaz regime.

On November 6, 1911, Madero became president of a Mexico in which his popularity, already reduced since he first entered Mexico City, was to suffer markedly. He added fuel to critical liberal fires when he named only two outspoken Revolutionaries to his own cabinet. He had made up his mind, as one journalist wrote, "to govern with his enemies and against his friends." A week before he took office, a faction of one-time supporters had weakened his position by issuing the "Plan of Tacubaya," in which they accused Madero of nepotism and of having imposed Pino Suárez and several governors on the electorate. They declared that the election of Madero and Pino Suárez was null and void and that Congress should be dissolved. Once in office and still procrastinating on agrarian reform, Madero was denounced by the peasant leader Emiliano Zapata, in his now-famous "Plan of Ayala" (November 25, 1911), for treason, imposing officeholders, joining forces with Díaz politicians and rich *hacendados,* and being unfit to govern. Zapata and his aides withdrew recognition of Madero as first chief of the Revolution and as President of Mexico. When Madero still failed to take any positive steps to encourage social reforms, Pascual Orozco revolted in the north. Although the Orozco movement was strongly colored by its leader's personal ambitions and by conservative encouragement and support, it did contain popular social-reform objectives. Under the banner of a "Plan Orozco," dated March 25, 1912—which demanded fulfillment of measures in the Plans of San Luis, Tacubaya, and Ayala, and went beyond all three in calling for comprehensive social and economic reforms—Orozco's forces were ready to move in Chihuahua. The forces Zapata and Orozco headed were more than crude outlaw bands, which was what Madero labeled them; they dramatically characterized all the elements demanding that Madero fulfill his pledge to carry out agrarian reform. Early in the Revolution, therefore, land reform became a central issue dividing the Revolutionary Family, which had already divided on the alternatives of following Madero, Zapata, Orozco, or the authors of the Tacubaya Plan. Zapata and Orozco, in the tradition of the Tacubaya faction, unwittingly had set the precedent for a transcendental feature of Mexican governance: The President of Mexico is either head of the Revolutionary Family and ruler—or else he does not last. From the outset, the Revolutionary Family demanded a head who could unite and rule, who had all power or no power.

Zapata and Orozco put social reform first and political reform second, while Madero favored the reverse of this combination. To Zapata and Orozco, Madero's brand of nineteenth-century political liberalism was meaningless; it did not lead to the building of an electorate that was fed, clothed, educated, and respected. Their conception attracted many followers. Meanwhile, Madero experienced little success with his much-heralded political liberalism. Mexico was less prepared for effective federalism, separation of powers, and judicial review in 1911 than it is today— and the country today is far from practical realization of these concepts. Mexican history taught that a President of Mexico must circumscribe the legislature and provincial governments or fall prey to political instability; yet Madero believed that power should be shared. Probably for this reason, and for the only time in the past five decades, the legislature truly fulfilled the Revolutionary Creed objectives on political democracy. The

XXVI Legislature represented a brilliant period in the history of Mexican parliamentarianism. There were true oratorical duels. Legislators opposing Madero or his cabinet ministers spoke openly and frankly. Díaz reactionaries, Zapata radicals, Madero moderates—the views of all factions were heard in debates. A formidable speech justifying the reconstitution of *ejidos*, delivered by Deputy Luis Cabrera to the chamber of deputies on December 3, 1912, represents a classical assertion of agrarian rights no less than a highpoint in parliamentary debate. Some legislators, nominally behind Madero, split with him in supporting Zapata's claim that "those who fight for the welfare of the people are not bandits." They disagreed with Madero's narrow perspective on Zapata, Orozco, Villa, and the thousands like them "who were moved in the first instance to take arms against Díaz because of the misery and injustice which they suffered, because of their deep-rooted desire for social and economic reform." Counterrevolutionaries also expressed dissatisfaction, thereby contributing to the regrouping of the Porfirian elite and to the preparation of the counterrevolution soon to explode. Not since Madero has the Revolution witnessed (or permitted) a truly independent legislature, as this concept is understood in American political life.

By February, 1913, the prestige of Madero had fallen to low depths. He could not re-establish order. Orozco had been crushed in the north, but government forces could do no better than reach a draw with the indomitable Zapata. Every day, Mexicans were abandoning homes and jobs to follow leaders opposed to Madero. In the eyes of many liberals, Madero had not demonstrated qualities of liberal statesmanship. Some, with mixed emotions, doubted his sincerity on effective suffrage. Many journalists were against him. Madero, born and reared a conservative, simply could not comprehend and begin to resolve the basic problems of Mexico pointed out by Zapata, Orozco, and other popular heroes. Resident English-speaking foreigners in independent Masonic lodges were challenging the pro-Madero Mexican lodges. In Mexico City, traditionally a stronghold of conservative elements, Porfirians were regrouping. Above all, the professional military class, career civil servants, and the U.S. ambassador to Mexico, to say nothing of the high Catholic clergy and many foreigners, *hacendados*, factory owners, mine operators, and electric power, railroad, and petroleum entrepreneurs, were never won over to the Madero cause. From radically different motives, Revolutionaries and reactionaries alike wanted Madero out of the way.

His actual downfall came at the hands of three non-Revolutionaries who wished him deposed in order to end all talk of "the Revolution" and kill any social movement that he might be pressured into undertaking. These villains of the counterrevolution—Gen. Victoriano Huerta, Gen. Félix Díaz, and U.S. Ambassador Henry Lane Wilson—served the very groups who had enjoyed pre-eminence under Díaz. Huerta's claim to fame was based on his command of federal troops sent against Zapata and Orozco, on his barroom orgies, and on his extraordinary appetite for gambling. Félix Díaz, nephew of the recently deposed autocrat, was an opportunist pure and simple; Madero personally saved him from the firing squad after a court-martial had condemned him to death for an abortive revolt in Veracruz in late 1912. The third man of the triumvirate, Henry Lane Wilson, escapes easy description. A product of the Big Business and Dollar Diplomacy clique of Taft, he misadvised Washington on the Mexican state of affairs, interfered in Mexican domestic politics, and falsely led Mexicans to believe that his actions were variously sanctioned by President Taft, the Department of State, or the American people. At best, Ambassador Wilson may be accused of greatly overstepping his authority; at worst, he may be charged with direct complicity in the assassination of Madero, Pino Suárez, and other Revolutionaries.

Félix Díaz and Gen. Bernardo Reyes (the latter, a leading pre-candidate in the election of 1910, had returned from "exile" only to be imprisoned when his *reyista* rebellion against Madero failed) bribed prison guards into releasing them to attack the presidential palace—an attack that cost Reyes his life. Following the attack, Díaz and Huerta, whom Madero foolishly appointed commander in chief to crush Díaz's insurgents, kept Mexico City terrified for nine days with a put-up show of arms, and Ambassador Wilson "intervened to protect American lives." He collaborated with Díaz and Huerta in drawing up a pact calling for a truce, the deposition of Madero, the seating of Huerta as provisional president, and the convoking of elections in which Díaz could be a candidate. Madero was duly deposed on February 19, 1913.

Everything might have moved along as scheduled, except for three unpredictable events: the tremendous public indignation that arose when Madero and Pino Suárez were assassinated while being transported from one prison to another, the stubborn refusal of Woodrow Wilson to recognize the Huerta government, and the revolt of the masses under the leadership of Carranza, Obregón, Villa, and Zapata. The Revolutionary Family dramatically served notice on Huerta that its internal squabbles might lead Revolutionary factions to oppose one of their own seated in the presidency, but that under no circumstances would they condone the intervention of outsiders (Huerta and Díaz were nothing more than "usurpers"). The assassination of Madero succeeded in making him something he was never quite capable of becoming in real life: the undisputed first head of the Revolutionary Family, the Apostle of Modern Mexico.

CARRANZA, OBREGÓN, VILLA, AND ZAPATA, 1913–1919

For the next seven years, the Mexican Revolution engulfed the nation in civil war, first to rid Mexico of Huerta and other counterrevolutionaries, then to decide on the content of the Revolutionary Creed and on Madero's successor as head of the Revolutionary Family. These were years of common men following a variety of chieftains into battle. Peasants, workers, and students left their homes, sometimes alone, other times with wives and mistresses stringing along. Few understood for what they were fighting. As Mariano Azuela, one of the great Revolutionary novelists, saw it, the rank and file knew "enthusiasm, hopes, ideals, happiness . . . nothing!" To Azuela, the Revolution was "a hurricane, and the man who enters it is no longer a man, but merely a miserable dry leaf beaten by the wind." Perhaps these insurgents unconsciously were seeking identification with a larger Mexico in which they would have a respected place. Whatever their motives, they provided the rank-and-file military strength of the Revolutionaries, who drew support from labor unionists, intellectuals, middle-class elements, and deposed Madero governors. Huerta early supplied them with dozens of martyrs, among them Madero, Pino Suárez, Governor Abraham González of Chihuahua, Deputy Serapio Rendón, and Senator Belisario Domínguez. For his own strength, Huerta counted on the federal army, career bureaucrats, the high clergy, rich merchants and industrialists, bankers, and foreigners.

As had been the case 28 months before, preoccupation with ridding the nation of a reactionary dictator closed Revolutionary ranks. The first Madero governor who refused to give fealty to Huerta, Venustiano Carranza of the northern state of Coahuila, named himself First Chief of the Constitutionalist Forces dedicated to overthrowing Huerta. Unlike the 1910–11 uprising, this revolution was intended to crush the professional army and other political holdovers of the Díaz regime. For nineteen months, the Revolutionary Family accepted Carranza as its new head. Four regional chieftains in command of military divisions enjoyed favorite-son status—Emiliano Zapata (southern army), Álvaro Obregón (northwestern army), Pancho Villa (northern army), and Pablo González (northeastern army). Other local chieftains also rallied to the Revolutionary cause. By and large, the Constitutionalist Army was a middle- and lower-class army headed by middle- and lower-class generals.

Within five months after he seized the presidency, Huerta had substituted military men for every Madero-elected governor in the states. On October 10, 1913, he swept the vestiges of the honest elections of the Madero epoch completely aside by dissolving both houses of Congress.

With the dissolution of Congress and seating of puppet governors in the states, the Revolutionaries could concentrate their fire on the government itself and, with some oversimplification, on the high clergy, foreigners, rural land barons, and wealthy urban interests. Wealth became punishable by death. Factories, mines, haciendas, and whole villages were ravaged. Railroads were dismantled. Libraries, schools, and great works of art were burned. Mexico ripped herself apart. No simple revolt this time, the first truly popular national social revolution in Latin American history was becoming fact. Within six months—that is, by April, 1914—assisted materially by Woodrow Wilson's lifting of the U.S. embargo on arms to Mexico, the Revolutionaries had gained control of virtually the entire north—Baja California, Sonora, Sinaloa, Chihuahua, Coahuila, Nuevo León, and Tamaulipas—plus the central states of Michoacán, Morelos, and Guerrero, and parts of Puebla, San Luis Potosí, and Veracruz. Determined to bring about the fall of Huerta by preventing the landing of a cargo of German arms, Woodrow Wilson then ordered the U.S. Navy to take and occupy the vital port of Veracruz, a task it accomplished on April 27 with the loss of 19 Americans and more than 300 Mexicans. The U.S. Navy stranglehold on the Veracruz customhouse denied Huerta a powerful source of income, and this, coupled with the growing worthlessness of his paper currency, brought about the financial collapse of his government. Further Revolutionary military victories led to the complete collapse of his regime, which terminated with his resignation on July 14, 1914, and his departure for France the next day. General Obregón entered Mexico City one month later, followed five days afterwards by Carranza. The dictator was dead, long live the Revolution!

But which Revolutionary should assume command? Carranza presumed that he was the legitimate heir of Madero, and his greatest strategist, Obregón, supported his claim. But Villa and Zapata had other ideas. In September, Villa formally notified Carranza that he, Villa, no longer recognized Carranza as First Chief. The Big Four somehow agreed to call a convention in the provincial capital of Aguascalientes in October, 1914, for purposes of selecting a provisional president; but when the choice of Villa and Zapata—Gen. Eulalio Gutiérrez—was elected president, Carranza and Obregón repudiated the whole proceeding. By November, Villa and Zapata had driven Carranza out of Mexico City and established their own conventionist government in the capital city. Whatever may be said for the military genius of Villa and Zapata, little can be said in their favor on statesmanship: They could neither unite the nation, nor crush Carranza and Obregón, nor assume undisputed leadership of the Revolutionary Family. The Carranza-Obregón combination, on the other hand, regrouped their forces in Veracruz and appealed for general popular support through a series of decrees promising satisfaction of the economic, social, and political needs of the country—agrarian reform, labor legislation, nullification of foreign monopolies, judicial independence, municipal self-government—in short, the promise of a real social and political transformation. The nascent trade-union organization, the IWW-oriented "House of the World's

Workers," joined the Carranza-Obregón cause and contributed six "Red Battalions" of workers to Constitutionalist forces. Peasants and students joined the cause. With renewed manpower, Obregón took to the field of battle once again, first driving Zapata back to the hill country of Morelos and Guerrero, then pushing Villa out of Mexico City. In February, 1915, Carranza re-entered the nation's capital to remain there for five more years. Meanwhile, Obregón won encounter after encounter as he pushed Villa farther and farther northward; he won a decisive battle at Celaya, and by October he had reduced his former comrade-in-arms to little more than the local chieftain of Villa's home state of Chihuahua. By the end of 1915, the Carranza-Obregón team had reunited the hard core of the Revolutionary Family, with Zapata, Villa, and a few other local strongmen on the outside looking in. If they wished to rejoin Family ranks this time, they would have to acknowledge Carranza as undisputed chief. Carranza had proven his legitimacy in ancient Mexican fashion—by crushing opponents who doubted his claim to rule.

Once the question of who should head the Revolutionary Family was answered in favor of Carranza, there remained the formidable problem of keeping the Family intact and supported by the nation at large. Carranza avoided one error made by Madero: He replaced what was left of the old career bureaucracy and professional soldiery with Revolutionaries. From Carranza's time forward, the civil service and army never again defected in favor of the traditional conservatives. But politics, politicians, and the generals had to contend with other problems—ponderous ones of a financial and economic nature. Unlike other Latin American nations that profited from the exigencies of World War I, Mexico found her productive machine torn apart and beset by poverty, famine, disease, and inflation. Foreign investors found the new Mexican order unattractive, and Mexican private capital preferred the security of U.S. banks to the insecurity of Mexican popularism. To make matters worse, Pancho Villa crossed the U.S. border in 1916 and killed enough Americans to provoke President Wilson into ordering a punitive expedition, under the command of Gen. John Pershing, to track down the elusive Mexican general. Economically bankrupt, militarily overstaffed, politically weak, and diplomatically in trouble with the United States, Mexico nonetheless chose this moment to undertake the long-overdue constitutional reorganization of her society. The medium was a convention of nominally pro-Carranza sympathizers selected by the general populace in areas under the control of Carranza-Obregón forces. The convention met in the centrally located provincial city of Querétaro from late November, 1916, to early February, 1917.

The central problem was the specific content of a new and, as the delegates soon indicated, a revolutionary constitution. Beginning with the Mexican Liberal Party plan of 1906, a voluminous amount of literature had poured forth on "revolutionary" reorganization of Mexican society:

Flores Magón, Madero, Zapata, Orozco, Villa, Carranza, and other liberals emphasized different points, but collectively they represented the voice of the common man crying out against the traditionally vested interests of the ruthless politicians, the high clergy, the *hacendados*, the foreigners, the army, and the local *caciques*. Nevertheless, Carranza's closest intimates in the government, excluding his secretary of war, Álvaro Obregón, favored a moderate approach in accord with the Constitution of 1857. In the Madero tradition, they prepared a working draft of a new constitution in which nineteenth-century political concepts outweighed twentieth-century economic-welfare considerations—although it was precisely the latter that Obregón and a majority of the convention delegates wanted incorporated. The Revolutionary generals, intellectuals, and labor leaders gathered at Querétaro felt that inertia and disinterest could not be overcome, nor could a nation activated by popular vitality be created, with the hacienda system, or with labor dispossessed, or with social welfare ignored, or with foreigners in possession of the subsoil, or with Mexicans controlled by foreign capital, foreign ideas, or foreigners themselves.

The convention rubber-stamped about 70 per cent of Carranza's working model—including effective suffrage, no re-election to the presidency, a bicameral legislature, federalism, municipal liberty, division of powers, an independent judiciary, presidential form of government, separation of church and state, free compulsory public education, and universal male suffrage—but it went far beyond the First Chief on the substantive matters of economic and social welfare. The heart of these reforms was put into Articles 3 and 130 on religion and education,[1] and in Articles 27 and 123 on ownership of natural resources, agrarian reform, and labor rights. Largely the intellectual product of delegate Pastor Rouaix and his chief advisor Andrés Molina Enríquez (author of the classic *Great National Problems*, published in 1909), agrarian-reform measures provided for restitution of lands to peasants illegally dispossessed, for rotation of lands to those without them but who required land in order to subsist, for recognition of existing small private farms and encouragement of the creation of more, for the creation of new agricultural centers in order to bring about widespread distribution of the rural population, for the limitation of the size of rural property holdings to avoid land concentration, and, in general, for the forced breakup of the hacienda system. The Constitution thus made unequivocally clear that the semicollective *ejido* and small private farm were to exist side by side. In this way the precolonial-oriented peasant living in the central and southern states could return to ancient landholding patterns, while the more capitalistically inclined northerner could possess his individual plot. In either event, the dreaded hacienda system was doomed for what it had done to the Mexican soul and soil—

[1] See Chapter 7.

for its power concentration and marginal productivity. Convention debates show that land use was mentioned with land ownership; the Revolutionary intellectuals wanted to satisfy the landless peon's appetite for land, but contrary to the claims of modern critics, they did not believe that breaking up the hacienda would necessarily lower production.

The Constitution extended the state's dominion over property beyond the agricultural sphere. Subsoil deposits were declared the property of the nation, and their exploitation by private interests was made subject to prior approval of the state. Since original ownership of resources belonged to the state, the rights of private enterprise in mining, petroleum, and related industries became subordinate to the public interest. Privateness in agricultural land as well as subsoil exploitation was made a social function correlated to the responsibility of the state to conserve natural resources, bring about equitable income distribution, and in general, to protect the economically weak rural and urban classes. Trade unions were recognized as legal entities to be encouraged by the state, even to the point of direct labor participation in profits. This series of measures on economic welfare represented the first comprehensive codification of social law anywhere in the twentieth century, predating the Soviet and German Weimar constitutions.

Contradictory yet flexible, the Constitution in final form was to permit Revolutionary governments tremendous latitude. The central government could be strengthened at the expense of the states—through taxation and the right to declare a "disappearance of powers" in any state, following up this action by appointing provisional authorities to replace ousted state officials—or it could be kept in bounds by preserving federalism. The executive could circumscribe other branches of government—especially through the president's power to issue decrees without congressional approval—or the legislature and judiciary could be encouraged to become truly independent powers. The civil liberties of the individual could come first, or trade unions and *ejido* associations could be made intermediaries between the personal liberties of their members and the state. Private property could be enhanced or destroyed; for that matter, either private, public, communal, cooperative, or trade-union ownership could be advanced or discouraged. Distribution, including corporate profits, could rest in private hands or become a principal function of the state. By allowing for such multiple interpretations, the Revolutionary constitution-makers produced a document that was well suited to the Mexican character and the complexities of Mexico itself. True to his pledge, on February 5, 1917, Carranza decreed the new Constitution the supreme law of the land.

The first major application of the Revolutionary charter came a few months later in putting "effective suffrage" to the test in national elections. Although specific mention of political parties had been omitted in the

Constitution, Carranza supporters managed to put together a "constitutional party" to back his candidacy for the presidency and the candidacies of Carranza sympathizers for congressional and state offices. Regardless of the meaning of "effective suffrage" elsewhere in the world, Carranza interpreted this concept in traditional Mexican fashion by approving nominations and permitting only "Constitutionalists" to be elected. The First Chief had no intention of repeating Madero's electoral mistakes. Carranza encountered little difficulty in being elected for a four-year term, yet despite his great popularity, less than 18 per cent of the Mexicans legally qualified to vote actually went to the polls. Apathy and disinterest could no more be legislated out of existence in 1917 than it can today. The mandate was clear: Carranza and his immediate successors would have to rely on army generals for major governmental support. When Carranza took office, two generals—Zapata and Villa—were still in revolt and there was some doubt whether the rest looked in the first instance to Obregón, who had become Carranza's secretary of war, or to the president himself.

Once installed in the presidency, Carranza, the first chief of state constitutionally elected since Madero, governed the nation according to a conservative interpretation of the Constitution: little land reform, suppression or at best passive protection of trade unions, marginal enforcement of mandates on clericalism and education (although Carranza had suggested certain modifications of Articles 3 and 130 of the Constitution to make them more workable), and minimal efforts to replace private Mexican or foreign ownership with communal or state ownership. In foreign affairs, Carranza refused to join Germany in declaring war on the United States, whether or not Mexico would, as the Zimmermann note sent by the German Foreign Office so enticingly put it, regain territory lost to its northern neighbor in the 1800's. While proving himself adroit in international affairs, which brought Mexico full diplomatic recognition from Washington, Carranza failed miserably in domestic matters concerning land reform.

One of Carranza's major problems was the peasant leader Emiliano Zapata. As *zapatistas* persisted in revolt, demanding "Land and Liberty," Carranza resolved to put Zapata out of the way once and for all. Liquidating the "Attila of the south" was indispensable for eliminating the agrarian agitation that was embarrassing his government and for achieving domestic tranquility. Carranza tried all kinds of trickery to capture the rebel leader. Finally, in April, 1919, a presumed turncoat of the federal militia, seeking the fifty thousand pesos put on Zapata's head, maneuvered the agrarian leader into entering an ambush. Although the corpse of Zapata was hung in the public square of Cuautla in the state of Morelos, many of his followers contend to this day that the body put on display was not that of Zapata, "because Zapata had sent his double to be assassinated while he sailed from Acapulco to self-exile in Arabia," while others contend that "mounted on his favorite white horse, Zapata still reappears from time to time in the hill country of Morelos to see that his people are receiving just treatment."

THE REVOLUTIONARY FAMILY UNDER OBREGÓN AND CALLES, 1919–1935

The liquidation of Zapata crystallized popular sentiment against Carranza, whose hold on the nation began to slip measurably during the rest of 1919. The old First Chief had decreed the Constitution effective, yet he had failed to carry out its liberal provisions. He had emerged victorious from civil war only to lose battles over education, religion, foreign ownership, land reform, the position of labor, political reform, and social welfare. Pancho Villa went on the warpath again, naming himself provisional president. Outlaw bands became bolder. Some tension arose with Washington over a "kidnapping" of the American consular agent in Puebla, William O. Jenkins. Interest-group leaders joined the generals in asserting that Carranza would never have become president in the first place without the military genius and support of Obregón. Since the devastation of Villa's forces at Celaya in 1915, a majority of the Revolutionary generals had made no bones about idolizing Obregón. Disillusionment with Carranza made one thing clear: The Revolutionary Family was switching its loyalty from the president to the one-armed hero of Celaya.

The Rise of the Sonoran Dynasty

Obregón had broadened popular sentiment in his favor by supporting a newly organized national trade union confederation set up in 1918— the Regional Confederation of Mexican Labor or, from its Spanish initials, the CROM—as well as various agrarian organizations, the cooperatives movement, and numerous civic groupings. Solid support came from his home state of Sonora, where Obregón had returned to become a chickpea merchant after his voluntary retirement from the post of secretary of war. Besides, many former Sonoran comrades were commanding important posts in the federal army and in government ministries. Who else could succeed the "First Chief," with the shadow of Obregón spreading over the nation? Of Carranza's top four zone commanders in the old Constitutionalist army, Zapata was dead, Villa had become a notorious bandit in the desert country of Chihuahua, and Pablo González was on active duty in the federal army, where he enjoyed the singular honor of being known as the "general who had never won a battle"—and there was Obregón. Obregón had in fact become head of the Revolutionary Family while someone else held the office of President of Mexico.

Power could not be shared. Carranza or Obregón, or both, had to be eliminated. Intending to finish his term of office and then impose Ignacio Bonillas, Mexican ambassador to Washington, as his successor, Carranza was holding a losing hand. He stubbornly refused to name Obregón as his successor. After Obregón narrowly escaped from the clutches of Carranza's agents, he wasted no time in issuing a call to rebellion against the legally constituted government. His "Plan of Agua Prieta," named for the border town where Pancho Villa's forces had been routed by Plutarco Elías Calles, represented the beginning of the Sonoran Dynasty in national politics. Supported by virtually every Revolutionary of this border state, the plan carried hopes of much more than change for the sake of change. It embodied the resentment of the entire north both against the long-time commercial monopoly of Mexico City and Veracruz and against inefficiency in government. Carranza now learned the iron law of Mexican politics: The President of Mexico must keep the army loyal or, failing in this, retain overwhelming popular support to be used as a bargaining wedge to bring generals into line. Carranza enjoyed neither.

Abandoning the capital in twenty railroad cars loaded with an entourage of faithful followers and the national treasury as well, Carranza set out for Veracruz, purportedly to move the Mexican government to a safer site until the Obregón rebellion could be suppressed. He never made it to Veracruz. Soldiers loyal to Obregón forced the Carranza troops to abandon their train and take to the hills. Deserted at the end by all but a very few loyal individuals, Carranza was murdered on May 21, 1920, as he lay asleep in a mud hut in the mountain village of Tlaxcalantongo. The Revolution's second constitutionally elected president had met the same fate as the first. But this time the murderer could not be condemned as a treasonous reactionary: Carranza's demise had occurred at the hands of Revolutionaries. What had happened to the beautiful new Constitution? To democratic promise? To government by law and order? Fortunately for Constitutionalism, this was the last time that an armed uprising succeeded in unseating a legally elected chief of state.

From the death of Carranza until the effective power assumption by Lázaro Cárdenas in June, 1935, two Revolutionary generals from Sonora brilliantly juggled multiple factional interests to maintain leadership of the Revolutionary Family. These two northerners, Álvaro Obregón and Plutarco Elías Calles, resolved the battle of personalities by demanding that unqualified, ultimate fealty be given the head of the Family. Beyond resolving this vital problem of who should command, they laid down the ground rules for how to govern, backing up their formulas with the creation of uniquely Mexican political institutions. Their leadership was challenged more than once, but for fifteen years all challengers fell by the wayside. For the first eight years of their rule, until mid-1928, national patronage flowed directly from the president in Mexico City to "loyal" Revolutionaries—to the governors, military zone commanders, and local *caciques,* to labor bosses, agrarian leaders, and spokesmen for cooperatives, to old friends and new acquaintances, and to merchants, bankers, miners, and industrialists. When patronage failed, Obregón and Calles resorted to bribes, blackmail, and purges.

The Generals, the Politicians, and Elections

To reduce the incidence of armed rebellion by "disloyal" army generals who throughout this period constituted the biggest threat to political stability—but also to assuage other sectors—these two northerners regularly put pragmatism and the sword ahead of idealism and liberty. Wavering militarists were bought off, transferred, or dismissed. Whenever politically expedient, the size of the military establishment was cut back. And solid steps were taken to professionalize the military, particularly by Calles from 1926 on, through measures supervised by the career soldier, Gen. Joaquín Amaro. Revolutionary politicians were permitted to build national and regional political "parties" enjoying official favor; but whenever a dominant party criticized Family direction of the nation or backed an opponent of the regime, it was headed for oblivion. This made for shifting majorities in the virtually impotent national legislature: The majority of the Constitutional Liberal Party (1920 to 1922 legislatures) gave way to the Cooperativist Party (1922–23 legislature), which in turn was replaced by a coalition of the Mexican Labor Party, the National Agrarian Party, and the Socialist Party of the Southeast (1923–24), and then by the Mexican Labor Party alone (1924–28). By 1925, a tally of political parties showed that the Constitutionalists and Cooperativists hardly existed, that the Agrarians had come to identify themselves closely with Obregón, and that the Laborites and Socialists found their champion in Calles. In these early years, state political "parties," under the tutelage of popular local leaders, also appeared on the scene. Those in Michoacán, Tamaulipas, Veracruz, and Yucatán came forth with ideological programs of some note.

But with power traveling along personalistic lines, normally from the President of Mexico downward and rarely as an aggregation of interests from the grass-roots level upward, there was little residual power for which political coalitions could bid. On the national scene, political "parties" became pawns used by the president against other parties or the military. Authoritarian as they were, however, Obregón and Calles hardly deserve the entire blame for the failure of "his majesty's loyal opposition" to materialize. True, the ambitions, suspicions, and fears of these two northerners went far to preclude effective criticism and grass-roots democracy. Still, the all-or-nothing mentality of those not part of the inner elite combined with other factors to forestall the growth of republicanism: insufficient patronage, lack of promising job opportunities, an absence of experience in self-government, the difficulty of reducing the size of the large and hungry standing army, the encumbrances of Mexican geography, and opportunism.

Politicking against the central government carried fatal consequences. Opposition was considered a challenge that had to be eliminated sooner or later, and preferably sooner, for if left unmolested too long it might acquire formidable military support—enough perhaps to dethrone and replace the Family head himself. Many questionable elements, among them Carranza holdovers who resented the manner in which Obregón had seized power and the suspicion with which they were regarded by both Obregón and Calles, were provoked into premature revolt and eliminated forthwith. Such was the fate of generals Lucio Blanco and Francisco Murguía in 1922 and generals Arnulfo Gómez and Francisco Serrano in 1927. When a real military rebellion arose, Obregón and Calles would take personal command of loyal troops and lead them into battle. This happened in 1923, when Adolfo de la Huerta—a Sonoran henchman who had served as interim president from the fall of Carranza until Obregón had been duly elected and then formally installed in the presidency on December 1, 1920—challenged Obregón's wisdom in picking Calles to become president in 1924. Actually, De la Huerta and Calles had been vying for the second position behind Obregón ever since the one-armed hero first became president—De la Huerta from his cabinet post of treasury minister, Calles from that of government (*gobernación*) minister. When Obregón made it known that Calles would receive official support, diverse factions, including conservative elements, cooperativists, and military chiefs who commanded about 50 per cent of the Mexican army, put forth the candidacy of De la Huerta in full awareness that they would either defeat Obregón and Calles on the battlefield or be crushed by them. The result was thousands dead, including the young socialist governor of Yucatán, Felipe Carrillo Puerto, and an equally young Revolutionary general, Fortunato Maycotte; the complete collapse of the Cooperativist Party, whose leaders had preferred De la Huerta to Calles; the firing squad for many soldiers who went astray; the labeling of De la Huerta's supporters as "reactionaries" (the fate in those days of all opponents); the elevating of dozens of "loyal" officers to army generalships, from which position they would soon prey on the public treasuries; the forced exile of De la Huerta to the United States; and, of course, the ultimate undisputed election of Calles to the four-year term beginning December 1, 1924.

Revolutionary Family influentials were disappearing from the scene quickly. Fortuitous for the Obregón-Calles team was the assassination in 1923 of their old foe and former Revolutionary great, Pancho Villa. His demise snuffed out another of the great Revolutionary figures of the decade 1910–20. Of the five outstanding personalities of that first decade, four had been killed: Madero in 1913, Zapata in 1919, Carranza in 1920, and, now, Villa in 1923. Only Obregón remained, and he had just found that eliminating De la Huerta, one of his most intimate collaborators in overturning Carranza and ushering in the Sonoran Dynasty, was indispensable to the survival of his hold over the Revolutionary Family. Few of those who were members of the Revolutionary Family's inner circle at the time Obregón became head or who had been added shortly after he entered the presidency still enjoyed that status when Obregón left the presidency: General Hill and Felipe Carrillo Puerto were dead; Adolfo de la Huerta and Jorge Prieto Laurens lost out in the 1923 uprising; Luis Morones had become temporarily discredited by an affair involving the cold-blooded murder of a senator; José Vasconcelos, Obregón's brilliant education minister, had left the cabinet in 1923 disgusted with Obregonism. Still around were Calles, the two agrarian leaders, Aurelio Manrique and Antonio Díaz Soto y Gama, and a long list of generals, headed by Serrano, Amaro, Almazán, Cedillo, Sáenz, and Cárdenas.

The next serious challenge to the Revolutionary machine driven by the northerners involved determination of Calles' successor. The two mighty generals thought they had the problem neatly resolved: They amended the Constitution to provide for re-election. They assuaged sentiment against re-election by prohibiting *immediate* re-election—that is, at least one term had to elapse before a former president could become eligible once again. They extended the term of office to six years and made Obregón the official candidate. But the two Sonorans miscalculated somewhat, for a number of generals and civilians did not look favorably on what appeared to be the beginning of an alternation of the presidency between Calles and Obregón or, conceivably, in light of the ease with which the Constitution had been changed, of a long era of Obregón alone. When those opposing re-election centered their hopes on two army generals, Arnulfo Gómez and Francisco Serrano, the two of them had had their death warrants signed. Neither lived long enough to have his name put on a ballot. White crosses on one side of the old Cuernavaca highway long marked the spot where Serrano and thirteen followers met death at the hands of Calles' soldiers; Gómez was trapped in Veracruz and executed forthwith. Additional purges of army ranks facilitated Obregón's re-election, but on July 18, 1928, several months before he was to take office, a young religious fanatic murdered the president-elect. Obregón thus departed as he had lived, violently, and by the same technique of premeditated murder that had claimed the lives of Madero, Zapata, Carranza, and Villa before him.

Calles now stood alone. His benefactor, the president-elect, was dead. The Constitution prohibited immediate re-election to the presidency.

The leaders of one of the two major props of his government, the mighty CROM national trade union, were in ill-repute for their corruptness and, though the charge was later proven false, for accusations of complicity in the murder of Obregón. Elements of his other major prop, the Mexican army, began politicking anew and talked of plotting against him. Much of their loyalty to Calles accrued from respect for Obregón, and with the hero of Celaya dead, army generals who had served under Obregón began re-examining the requisites of Calles. Leaders of the National Agrarian Party, who had waited four years for the return of their favorite to the presidency, were agitating and, on the least provocation, pouncing on Calles. Anti Re-electionists were demanding strict respect for constitutionalism. Carranza holdovers, still bearing a grudge against those they deemed responsible for the downfall of their "First Chief" in 1920, wanted Calles out of the way. De la Huerta sympathizers had little love for the man who had grabbed the presidency out of the hands of their idol. State and local strongmen sought assurances that their power would continue inviolate. To make matters worse, Calles was in the midst of his nation-wide attack on the Catholic Church, a policy that had provoked an armed "Christian uprising" (the *cristero* rebellion) that was still raging in several central states. Finally, his inner circle of Family favorites—Luis Morones, J. M. Puig Casauranc, Aarón Sáenz, Melchor Ortega, Luis León, his son Rodolfo Elías Calles, Adalberto Tejeda, Carlos and Manuel Riva Palacio, Emilio Portes Gil, Luis Montes de Oca, and generals Amaro, Almazán, Cedillo, Cárdenas, Aguirre, Pérez Treviño, and Escobar—were themselves divided on the biggest issue, that of selecting a provisional president.

A lesser figure might have resigned and retired from political life, but Calles rose to the occasion and displayed brilliant statesmanship. As provisional president, he installed a young lawyer who, as governor of Tamaulipas, had enforced radical measures on agrarian reform, the rights of labor, education, and clericalism, and who at the moment was holding down the important post of minister of government. This man, Emilio Portes Gil, was not a soldier, but the army had no special grudge against him. His favorable record on agrarian reform elevated his stature among the nation's agrarians. His outspoken criticism of CROM leaders attracted those Revolutionaries who had come to despise Luis Morones, the CROM's secretary-general and a member of Calles' cabinet. And Portes Gil's active participation in the Frontier Socialist Party of Tamaulipas assured him of favorable treatment by radical reformers. The selection of Portes Gil, plus Calles' promises to army generals and other factions, saved the day.

Calles next faced the problem of how to keep the army intact and the state governors and local *caciques* pacified. He resolved it in two ways: First, he set up an official national party, the Partido Nacional

Revolucionario (the National Revolutionary Party, or PNR), into which both military and nonmilitary elements were henceforth to channel their political ambitions. As far as nonmilitary elements were concerned, the PNR was conceived along the lines of a confederation, grouping state political parties and regional political associations into a single national machine. The generals held individual memberships. Second, Calles himself took to the field of battle to crush those generals who wanted to rid the country of him and his solutions to the common problems facing the nation. This uprising, the last rebellion of regular army contingents against the central government down to the present day, assumed major proportions, but Calles and his celebrated "CACA" (generals Cedillo, Amaro, Cárdenas, and Almazán) settled the issue definitely in favor of Calles, the PNR, and constitutionalism. Among the generals eliminated from the scene were several outstanding personalities: Escobar, Manzo, Topete, and Caraveo went into exile; Miguel Alemán (father of a later president), Francisco Aguirre, and Brígido Escobedo lost their lives.

With the passing of the politico-military crisis, Calles and the PNR concentrated on the election of their candidate for the presidency, Pascual Ortiz Rubio, one-time general, engineer, and governor of Michoacán, who was serving as diplomatic envoy to Brazil when Portes Gil recalled him at Calles' request. His absence from Mexico actually constituted his major qualification, for he never would have obtained the nomination in the first place had the "CACA" concurred with Calles on his first choice, the middle-of-the-road Obregón-Calles disciple, Aarón Sáenz. Since Calles had no desire to split PNR ranks unnecessarily or to run the risk of retaining his own power without the "CACA" behind him, he abandoned Sáenz and picked the colorless Ortiz Rubio, against whom the "CACA" had no grudge. The presidential election, held on November 17, 1929, offered the Mexican electorate three choices: Ortiz Rubio (and Calles and the PNR); José Vasconcelos, educator, former cabinet minister, philosopher, and prolific scholar, running under the banner of an Anti Re-electionist party; or Gen. Pedro Rodríguez Triana, the Communist Party candidate. Although many Mexicans believed that Vasconcelos really won the election, the legislature, as expected, announced that Ortiz Rubio had been elected by an overwhelming majority. Vasconcelos' call to rebellion failed to bring about the desired effects and accomplished little more than forcing the renowned scholar to spend much of the next seven years in exile in the United States.

From the inauguration of Ortiz Rubio on February 5, 1930, until Cárdenas took charge five years later, Calles made the final decisions affecting the destinies of the Revolutionary Family, despite the fact that someone else was President of Mexico. Public policy was laid down in cabinet meetings in which the President of Mexico had little more to say than his ministers; cabinets continued loyal to Calles or had their composition changed. Undecisive, timid, and hamstrung on all sides by Calles, and amid a growing power struggle between his own few supporters and those, like the "CACA" generals, loyal to Calles alone, Ortiz Rubio resigned the presidency on September 4, 1932, and left Mexico. The man formally selected by Congress to replace him—with the explicit approval of Calles, of course—was the former professional baseball player, one-time governor of Baja California, and cabinet minister in the Ortiz Rubio administration, Gen. Abelardo Rodríguez.

The new substitute president made no attempt to accumulate political power or to checkmate Calles and the PNR. The official party became a highly authoritative mechanism, with political patronage flowing directly from Calles to the PNR to worthy Revolutionaries, conveniently bypassing the president. Calles' original conception of the PNR as an aggregation of the interests of the generals, state political "parties," and regional coalitions, empowered to articulate uniform political policy for the nation as a whole, underwent two modifications: (1) The programs that the PNR announced were simply never translated into action, for Calles had become more conservative than the hard core of the Revolutionary Family; and (2) the party's organizational base shifted to emphasize individual membership, in order to reduce the autonomy of state groupings—which, Calles believed, had overly enhanced the personal reputations of such regional bosses as Garrido Canabal in Tabasco, Tejeda in Veracruz, and Cedillo in San Luis Potosí. Calles and the PNR imposed candidates simply by notifying the cabinet minister in charge of electoral matters how to tally votes.

Many criticize Calles for his dictatorial ways. Without doubt he was highly authoritarian, and he retained leadership of the Revolutionary Family long after he left the presidency. Yet Obregón's death, exacerbating tensions in the nation's factories, fields, and halls of government, required strong, definitive leadership from some quarter. Inertia, dedication, and friendship, no less than self-interest, convinced the northern general to stay at the helm. Well-wishing inner-circle intimates not under Calles' instructions—men such as Luis León and Melchor Ortega—publicized him as the "supreme chief" and the "chief of chiefs" of the Mexican Revolution. In fact, the members of the Revolutionary Family's inner circle, who during some or all of this period included Portes Gil, Ortiz Rubio, Rodríguez, León, Ortega, the Riva Palacio brothers, Garrido Canabal, Cedillo, Amaro, Puig Casauranc, Alberto Pani, Luis Montes de Oca, Cárdenas, Almazán, Rodolfo Calles, Fernando Torreblanca, Manuel Pérez Treviño, Aarón Sáenz, and Narciso Bassols, all looked to Calles first and the president later without apparent discomfort.

During the temporary absences of Calles from Mexico, the presidents of the PNR, General Amaro (the watchdog of the army), the respective constitutional presidents of the nation, and the cabinet ministers somehow managed to keep the country running. But as soon as Calles returned to Mexico, foreigners and Mexicans alike besieged the Sonoran general for promotions, concessions, and advice—in short, for the "final word." Whether residing at his Anzures home in Mexico City, his ranch on the Puebla highway, his Cuernavaca cottage, or his farm in Sinaloa, Calles could not escape. He helped shape political habits, but basic Mexican behavior long antedated Calles. Detractors often exaggerated the extent of his interference, and corrupt or inept subordinates found the omnipotence of the *jefe supremo* a convenient shield behind which to hide their sins. Mexico demanded a final arbiter, and Calles was willing and able. If he had not filled the role, someone else would have seized the position.

Calles as President of Mexico (1924–28), sharing leadership with Obregón, and Calles as sole head of the Revolutionary Family (1928–35) carried out decidedly different policies. President Calles was anticlerical, prolabor, pro-public works, and nominally proagrarian. In contrast, governments of the *callista* period (1928–34) by and large dropped the anti-Church crusade, favored foreign capital, virtually abandoned progressive labor and agrarian programs, and sought a *rapprochement* with the United States. Abandonment of the progressive measures of his own governmental administration, far more than the personality of Calles, led to his ultimate downfall. To understand why the Northern Dynasty came tumbling down, we must turn over the political, military, and electoral face of the 1919–35 coin to examine its other side: governmental policy on additional objectives of the Revolutionary Creed.

The Social Order and Interest Groups

The social order imposed on Obregón and Calles by the Constitution of 1917 assumed the presence of a social system that simply did not exist in 1919 and, in fundamental respects, does not exist today. The elimination of clericalism, of foreign ownership of mineral rights, and of large agricultural holdings would necessitate encouragement of public-school teachers, native capitalists, small farmers, communal farmers, and cooperatives. But transforming the social order that Obregón and Calles inherited to one that would make the fulfillment of the constitutional mandates possible presented extremely complex problems. How was such a transformation to be implemented and coordinated? Which interests were paramount? Which were subject to rationalization? Could a new regime overturn powerful traditional vested interests without first integrating the numerous military elements and militant groups roaming the Mexican countryside and awaiting their rewards for sacrifices made during the recent civil war? Were excessive constraint and coercion morally justi-fiable tactics in a society pledged to defend freedom of choice?

Powerful forces early intervened to complicate and restrict the crea-tion of a social order in harmony with constitutional mandates. First of all, the Revolution was seriously restricted by fragmented and incomplete incorporation of its basic principles into Family ideology and government programs. At best, this shortcoming was a manifestation of the shift from the traditional order of things to a new Revolutionary social structure; at worst, it was a product of Family opportunism. Second, and no less important, socialization was limited by the desire of interest groups to attain a highly favorable status for themselves and by the quest of influ-ential leaders for power, prestige, and wealth. The ascendancy of particu-lar and private interests over universal and socialized goals was nowhere more marked than in the demands of the armed elements of the society. Predatory militarism kept the incidence of violence high and the pros-pect of civil war ever present. Obregón could only counter this threat by going onto the field of battle himself. Preoccupied always with poten-tial military opposition, therefore, and with no nonmilitary aggregation of power to describe and prescribe universally applicable programs, is it any wonder that Obregón and Calles established authoritarian regimes depending heavily on armed might?

The pre-eminence of the military does much to explain the slow progress toward political liberalism during the period 1919–35, when ef-fective suffrage, free and peaceful elections, and the prohibition on re-election remained largely unfulfilled promises. The politicians that emerged were not willing or able to coordinate the various national in-terests, and as president, both Obregón and Calles were too busy crushing their opposition to be able to seek a national consensus. Throughout the period, soldiers were prominent in public posts. Obregón and Calles, of course, were army generals, as were six of the eight cabinet ministers under De la Huerta, five ministers under Obregón, three under Calles, two under Portes Gil, four under Ortiz Rubio, and three under Rodríguez, to say nothing of the monopolistic hold of military leaders over state and local governments. Federalism and autonomous state and local govern-ments fared relatively well until 1929, when Calles and the PNR began the effective centralization of politics. Separation of power—the operation of independent legislative and judicial branches—made little progress. Apathy and low cultural levels did nothing to further the cause of civil liberty, but freedom of speech, thought, press, assembly, and—if Catholi-cism is excluded—of religion were more in evidence than in previous periods. Toward the goal of political stability, notwithstanding the revolts in 1920, 1923, 1927, and 1929, plus that of the *cristeros*, the rule of the Northern Dynasty made obvious advances over the decade 1910–20. Fi-nally, on the goal of creating a career civil service, a great deal was accomplished by the removal of the old Porfirian bureaucrats and, in the Calles presidency, by the establishment of an office of retirement pensions for civil servants.

Constitutionalism, Mexicanism, and Social Justice

How did the northerners regard constitutionalism? In comparison with the Cárdenas regime that followed, relatively little was done to implement the agrarian, labor, subsoil, and electoral provisions. The Constitution was amended on petroleum (which worked to the favor of foreign petroleum interests), on education (to give public instruction a more "socialistic" bent), on electric energy (which empowered the legislature to make laws on this matter), on mining, commerce, credit, and on presidential elections (first to provide for no immediate re-election, then to return to the original absolute prohibition), and on increasing the presidential term of office to six years. Constitutionalism was probably best observed in the areas of anticlericalism and public education, although the Labor Code of 1931 also represents a high point in the implementation of constitutional mandates on workingmen's rights.

During this period, Mexicanism was prominent. New Revolution-oriented educational institutions, described in Chapter 7, came into being, and in art, the muralists Rivera, Siqueiros, and Orozco were commissioned to depict their unique visions of Revolutionary values on the nation's public buildings. Painting, music, architecture, and literature all reflected the Revolution. In politics, Obregón evinced a strong feeling of Mexicanism in his insistence that diplomatic recognition by the United States must come before the resolution of economic issues outstanding between the two nations. (On the other hand, after 1928, Calles seemed more concerned with friendly U.S.–Mexican relations than with Mexicanism and constitutionalism.)

Social justice, another objective in the Revolutionary Creed, took a back seat during this period. Aside from Calles' well-intentioned but unimplemented program on behalf of the proletariat, redistribution of national income made little headway. Whatever permanent advances organized labor might have accomplished, Morones and his CROM henchmen negated. Both Obregón and Calles encouraged and protected the mighty CROM, but they permitted its leaders far too much leeway to abuse the rank and file and other unions in general. Calles permitted strikes and seated laborites in important public offices. The period 1925–27 might well have become years of great advancement for Mexican workers—if the labor movement had been directed by dedicated unionists. Social justice was advanced by the Labor Code of 1931, which even today constitutes the basic labor law of Mexico. Little progress ensued in the way of constructing public markets, public housing developments, or a social security program. The poor indigenous communities remained poor, although under Vasconcelos and his successors in the ministry of education, a challenging program of rural cultural missions got underway.

A vital component of social justice in these early years was agrarian reform. To the impoverished peasant, the Revolution meant land distribution. Yet Obregón and Calles concurred in the opinion that military instability and recovery from civil war damages precluded the initiation of a vast agrarian-reform program. Both had lived on farms and knew rural Mexico at first hand, but they also knew that feeding the nation was as important as satisfying the peon's appetite for land. Being from the north, where private farms predominated, Obregón and Calles understandably favored the small, privately owned plot over the communal *ejido*. Constitutionalists could not object to this preference, because the supreme law of the land condoned small private farms as well as communal ownership, but they could (and did) object to the failure to take action to split up the large farms. Obregón believed that the rural masses should be trained in the responsibilities of farm management first and receive lands later. Despite this belief, however, he distributed much more land than did Carranza before him. The program was stepped up considerably by Calles and by Portes Gil, who followed him, then slowed down—indeed, virtually came to a halt—with the arrival of the PNR, Ortiz Rubio, and the Great Depression.

The Northern Dynasty, fifteen long years of it, distributed less than half the amount of land that Cárdenas turned over to the peasants during a crowded four years following Calles' fall. To ardent Cárdenas supporters, this difference makes Obregón and Calles "reactionaries," but on the basis of what Obregón accomplished in the milieu of the early 1920's, Antonio Díaz Soto y Gama and other *zapatistas* still hail Obregón as the greatest statesman the Revolution has produced.

By emphasizing the problem of feeding Mexico, the northerners accented productivity and getting the most from the land. Output, land use, and the creation of a strong, independent rural class characterized their thinking, whereas communal living itself and the right to lands per se constituted the central theme of Cárdenas' philosophy. In view of the weighty problems Cárdenas' programs caused the nation at large as well as the *ejidatarios*—uneconomical land size, labor underemployment, and insufficient credit, irrigation, fertilizers, and equipment—Obregón and Calles may have possessed a truer vision of what rural Mexico needed. They were not blind to the fact that some regions demanded communal ownership. But for the two northern generals, and for many economists, agronomists, and political leaders looking at the agrarian reform in retrospect, the key question was whether Mexico really required so many communal holdings of such unproductive size. The Ruiz Cortines and López Mateos administrations (December 1, 1952, forward) in particular have been wrestling with this dilemma.

Race, Religion, and Education

Although over-all judgment on the Obregón and Calles contribution to social justice must be equivocal, the Northern Dynasty clearly gave solid content to Creed objectives on racial equality, intellectual freedom, public education, and religious equality. The positivist doctrine of superiors and inferiors lost its footing: Race no longer determined one's fate, however much meaning "blanco" and "indio" continued to have socially. As the mestizo came into prominence, a search for identification with the Indian past began. For the first time since Cortés, the Indian was exalted, perhaps overly so, in murals, paintings, literature, and education. Obregón and Calles became possessed with the idea of building a nation of all races, or rather, a nation of no races. The principal instrument for carrying out this mission was public education. Primary, secondary, technical, and normal schools, universities, literacy schemes, and the rural cultural missions reflected the northerner's sincerity in attempting to bring Mexicans everywhere into the mainstream of national life.

The intellectual freedom permitted by Obregón and Calles gave birth to new ideas drawn from Mexico and the Mexican—to a true spiritual transformation of the nation. The impact of the Revolution on the intellectual life of Mexico, and simultaneously, the influence of intellectuals on the Revolution, profoundly altered old habits. In 1921, the department of education was raised to the rank of a cabinet ministry, and in 1929, the National University of Mexico became autonomous. When promising minds were revealed, the state encouraged their free expression. Emerging in this epoch were the educators José Vasconcelos and Manuel Gamio, muralists Rivera, Siqueiros, and Orozco, architects Jesús Acevedo and Federico Mariscal, composers Manuel Ponce and Carlos Chávez, the poet Jaime Torres Bodet (who later became secretary-general of UNESCO), and a host of new philosophers headed by Vasconcelos, Alfonso Reyes, and Alfonso Caso. These men and thousands like them were living testimony to the Revolution's dedication to freedom of thought, speech, and press. Collectively, they gave expression to a new Mexico.

This fervent introduction of Revolutionary ideals constituted a direct attack on Catholicism. Though Obregón believed that Church education was better than no education and, hence, that parochial schools should be tolerated until public schools could displace Church schools, Calles wanted nothing to do with anything Catholic, including parochial education. Their divergence on this point caused varying treatment of the

Church during the rule of the Northern Dynasty: a period of minimal enforcement of anticlerical provisions of the Constitution (1920–26), followed by a period of rabid, intolerant, and probably excessive enforcement of constitutional mandates (1926–29), and a period of relative letdown in the central government's attack on churches and priests (1929–35), although many state governors were unwilling to discontinue the harsh policies of the preceding period. Even after the central government in 1929 relaxed its direct attack on the priests and the Church as such, parochial education continued to be subject to comprehensive surveillance of the state right down to 1937. State governors, who under the Constitution could determine the number of priests that would officiate in their states, continued to keep a tight rein on this aspect of Catholicism.

Calles' assault on the Church produced radical consequences. On the one hand, Calles expelled many priests from the country, took over Church properties, restricted priests to the churches proper, prohibited the wearing of clerical garb in public, scrutinized the instruction in parochial schools, established (though with virtually no success) a "National Catholic Church," and fostered the growth of Freemasonry and Protestantism. On the other hand, the Catholic Church retaliated by closing the nation's churches, by calling upon all Catholics to resist the Calles government, and by inspiring a series of armed uprisings known as the *Cristero* Rebellion. The *cristeros* had hoped that the religious issue would become so intense that Washington would intervene to help topple Calles and end radical enforcement of the Constitution once and for all. When Washington did not intervene and added insult to injury by sending Dwight Morrow, a "Protestant tool of a Protestant White House," to be its ambassador to Mexico, the more intense fanatics became anti–United States. Some Catholic historians condemn Morrow for intervening to resolve the religious issue along "Protestant" lines. They may not be entirely wrong, but what Morrow really wished was a termination of persecution and an end to fanaticism, whether Church or State inspired. Calles acceded to his desires to bring religious peace to Mexico, but the armistice hardly deserves inclusion in the annals of pro-Church actions, since the consensus reached by Church and State represented a clear-cut victory for the government. When state governors refused to honor the spirit of the conciliatory arrangement, this, the central government kept informing Church officials, was outside its control and in perfect harmony with federalism.

But if state governors were the nemesis of the Church from 1929 to 1935, they ultimately became the nemesis of Calles as well. Many of the governors had been lifted to power within the context of Calles' "socialist" administration, and they considered his abandonment of radical anticlericalism tantamount to selling out the Revolution. Their suspicions were confirmed when Calles, running the show from behind the scenes, also abandoned land and labor reforms, restrictions of foreign capital, and public works programs. The idealism and dedication of these state governors, and of the cabinet ministers and some army generals, enjoyed little room for concrete expression after Calles finished his own administration. The governors could exhibit their radicalism only in the one realm where the Constitution gave them exclusive decision-making powers, by limiting the number of priests officiating in the respective states. This, in turn, provoked a second *Cristero* Rebellion which, though by no means assuming the dangerous proportions of the 1926–29 revolt, persisted sporadically from 1932 to 1937. Little by little, Calles' abandonment of agrarian reform, public works, labor advancement, native capitalism, popular credit institutions, irrigation programs, and petroleum regulation alienated many of his intimates, although they recognized him as head of the Revolutionary Family because their immediate survival depended on keeping in the good graces of *el que manda* (the one who gives orders).

United States–Mexican Relations

Meanwhile, what was happening in U.S.–Mexican relations? The Northern Dynasty began, we should remember, with the assassination of Carranza, an incident that confronted Washington with the question of recognition of the new regime. For three years, feelers emanating from both sides of the border sought ways and means of re-establishing diplomatic relations, with the United States insisting that agreement should be reached on the bonded debt, on war reparations, and on petroleum legislation before the United States could seriously consider full diplomatic recognition. Obregón, with international law generally on his side, contended that acceptance of the American approach would condone the meddling of a foreign power in Mexican domestic affairs. Denied recognition for three years, however, Obregón finally agreed to a meeting of representatives of the two nations in order to attempt to iron out economic and financial problems. The deliberations of this meeting, held in Mexico City during 1923 and popularly referred to as the Bucareli Conference, were only partially made public, largely because Mexico as well as the United States made some concessions. Nonetheless, anti-U.S. intellectuals in Mexico still assert that it was not until Mexico had toed the Washington line, had humiliated herself sufficiently to show that she knew who was the boss, that the United States formally resumed diplomatic relations in 1923.

The three big issues of American-Mexican relations during the 1920–35 period were payment of the external debt, petroleum legislation, and reparations for property damaged or destroyed in the civil war or confiscated under the name of agrarian reform. Progress on the American position was slow until Dwight Morrow, onetime senior associate of the Wall Street firm of J. P. Morgan, assumed the ambassadorship in 1927. His impact was profound. His accomplishments, according to Lord Nicolson's official biography, came about because "Morrow arrived at the precise stage in Calles' own evolution when the latter was most receptive of experience, encouragement, and advice. Had Morrow arrived a year earlier or three years later, his Mexican mission would not have been the dramatic triumph that it became." [2] Morrow's presence, often cited as "one of the most constructive episodes in modern diplomatic history," and Calles' own growing conservatism, which saw his puppet presidents abandon virtually every major economic measure favoring popular reform, coincided neatly. Morrow and conservatism generally won, and popular Mexican aspirations for economic reforms lost.

The Depression and the change of personalities in the White House, Department of State, and American embassy in Mexico from 1933 forward brought deeper understanding of the true planks in the Revolutionary Creed. The arrival of Josephus Daniels, Franklin Roosevelt's choice as U.S. ambassador to Mexico, roughly coincided with the beginning of a new phase of the Revolution, which began during the Rodríguez presidency and reached its apex a few years later under Cárdenas. In the last half of the Sonoran Dynasty, the Mexican masses rarely encountered sympathetic response from either their own governors or from Washington to their aspirations for social reform. The years 1928–32, which were free of overt tensions and generally considered an epoch of friendly U.S.–Mexican relations, were also years of regressive economic policies in Mexico. The Depression contributed; yet up to 1933, as Chapter 8 will point out in some detail, doing the things that Washington wanted usually meant shelving the things that Mexicans desired.

The different perspective on international relations assumed by the United States and Mexico during the Sonoran Dynasty is seen in their respective postures on Communism and the Soviet Union. The Third International first entered Mexico in 1919, making some inroads among intellectuals, artists, labor unionists, and peasants. At the time, sincere Revolutionaries in Mexico sympathized with Communism in Russia, which they frequently described as "the only other truly social revolution in the world." And while Washington refused the Soviet Union recognition, Mexico entered into full diplomatic intercourse with Moscow in 1924. Russian ideology often paralleled Mexican Revolutionary goals. The Mexican Constitution of 1917 permitted numerous social-welfare and state-socialism projects. On the matter of landownership, for example, the Constitution condoned *ejido* collectives. The document also incorporated ad-

[2] Harold Nicolson, *Dwight Morrow* (New York: Harcourt, Brace, 1935), p. 304.

vanced provisions on workingmen's rights, including worker ownership of the means of production. Additionally, it bestowed broad regulatory powers on the state, especially over subsoil exploitation and public utilities. A generation before Franklin Roosevelt introduced his New Deal, therefore, the Mexican expected far more from the state than did his counterpart across the Rio Grande. Yet Mexico learned its lesson on the true nature of Communism from Moscow agents in the 1920's. Moscow wanted things its way, and nationalism had no place in its plans. Mexico broke diplomatic relations in 1930, when Calles decided that Communist agents were carrying their enthusiasm for the Mexican Revolution too far by instructing peasants, workers, and teachers to "improve conditions immediately." Formal diplomatic intercourse between the two nations was not resumed until November 19, 1942.

Economic Advances and Retreats

In terms of five objectives in the Revolutionary Creed—those on economic integration, financial stability, economic growth, public and private ownership and initiative, and the defense of labor rights—the achievements of the Northern Dynasty were spotty. Obregón accomplished little in the way of solid economic growth or of building the economy's infrastructure, although he did introduce measures designed to keep inflation in bounds and to stabilize the Mexican peso. He promoted trade unions and cooperatives (until 1923) and initiated a modest program of taxation and agrarian reform. But there were too many soldiers preying on the public treasury to make room for much reform. In contrast, the achievements of Calles in the short span from 1925 to 1927 were truly remarkable. Entering office on December 1, 1924, with the assertion that Mexico would have to put its economic house in order and live off its own resources and effort, Calles backed up his pledge by a series of measures.

These are some of Calles' more important achievements: (1) Direction of the national fiscal and monetary system was put firmly in the hands of the state, which gave birth to the central Bank of Mexico, to efforts to resolve the differences outstanding on Mexico's external debt and reparations claims, to sounder taxation, and to the establishment of a general controller's office for overseeing national budgetary matters; (2) for the first time since Díaz, Mexico achieved the semblance of financial stability; (3) public road construction was undertaken in earnest and placed under the direction of a new agency, the National Road Commission; (4) the desire of Mexican farmers for irrigation found real hope of fulfillment for the first time in Mexican history when Calles established a National Irrigation Commission; (5) public ownership of subsoil rights was reasserted in the promulgation of a new Law on Petroleum; (6) the electric power industry became subject to strict governmental regulations with the passage of the National Electricity Code; (7) cognizance of the urgent need to help in the financing of agriculture led to the founding of a National Bank of Agricultural Credit; and (8) the first real steps were taken to profession-alize the army and reduce its numbers to sensible proportions, under the able direction of Gen. Joaquín Amaro, Calles' secretary of war. Besides these revolutionary innovations, Calles set about to consolidate agricultural and labor organizations, to construct a nationwide system of schools, and to make a career in the civil service more attractive. Banking and financial interests, industrialists, real estate developers, and mining groups had enough confidence in Calles and his "new economic policy" to invest in Revolutionary Mexico. Calles had behind him trade unionists and agrari-ans, plus a stockpile of anxious local entrepreneurs prepared to develop the nation's business. He had grasped the urgent need for pushing forward with the expansion of the economy's infrastructure. And he possessed the rare qualities of leadership indispensable for the task that he seemed to have set for himself. Properly speaking, it was Calles, not Cárdenas and his successors, who first injected the state into economic life on a broad scale. Under his leadership, Mexico was ready for its "take-off" into sustained economic growth.

Yet Cárdenas and his successors, not Calles, properly deserve credit for actually generating the "take-off." Why did Calles so abruptly halt his dynamic program? This is one of the greatest enigmas of the entire Mexi-can Revolution. Largely on the basis of Calles' subsequent actions, some Mexicans are prone to assert that Calles was really a reactionary all along —that had it not been for his anticlericalism, he would deserve no recog-nition as a liberal. Others contend that the corruptness and corruptibility of Calles' underlings sidetracked the vast program—yet a decade later, when graft and corruption were no less prevalent, Cárdenas succeeded where Calles failed. Calles' failure to carry out the program that he had so admirably laid out is explainable only in terms of a basic change in Calles' philosophy. Calles had a strong character. He had built his own solid faction in the Revolutionary Family from among socialists, trade unionists, agrarians, and radical-minded military men. To swing 180 de-grees required a truly basic conversion to new principles—a shift Dwight Morrow probably influenced. After Morrow arrived on the scene, foreign ownership was encouraged, local capitalists depreciated, labor unionism suppressed, anticlericalism abandoned, and the agrarian reform stopped dead in its tracks.

After 1927, not a few generals, governors, cabinet ministers, and in-tellectuals hoped that Calles would reaffirm his previous Revolutionary zeal on economic reform. Right down to 1935 this never happened, though Calles was surely not blind to liberal pressures within the Revolutionary Family. These pressures, intensified by the Depression, the new Good Neighbor Policy, and the world-wide battle of political ideologies, became very strong during the last years in which Calles held power. Following on the heels of the liberal Federal Labor Code of 1931, the passage of banking laws in 1931 and 1932 strengthened the position of the Bank of Mexico. Then, in late 1933, 1934, and early 1935, the revival of trade unionism received little adverse treatment from Calles. Furthermore, in 1934 alone, new laws empowered the President of Mexico to create a Federal Electricity Commission that could own and distribute electric power; created the ministry of national economy, and placed under its jurisdiction strict regulation of electric power; converted the National Agrarian Commission into a cabinet-level agrarian department, with broad powers that eliminated much red tape in the redistributing of lands; and established what was to become a powerful state financial institution, the Nacional Financiera. These measures were a victory for those who believed that Calles had been wrong in following conservative policies. The consensus of opinion within Revolutionary Family councils favored radical enforcement of the Constitution—promoting and defending labor unions, carrying out agrarian reforms, strengthening the state's role in economic life, keeping foreign capital in bounds, "socialistic" education, and anticlericalism. Calles bowed to the group of Revolutionaries who never abandoned these ideals or their continuous loyalty to Calles by assenting to the nomination of Lázaro Cárdenas for the presidency for the six-year term beginning December 1, 1934. Although Calles personally believed that his own conservative approach, not radical action, was best for the nation, he was willing to permit a partial radical comeback. At its national nominating convention held in Querétaro in 1933, the PNR adopted a six-year plan to guide its candidate once he assumed the presidency. The plan incorporated the hard core of programs initiated in Calles' own earlier administration and went beyond them in calling for enforcement of constitutional mandates on other economic and educational matters.

Though Calles may have assented to the nomination of Cárdenas and the six-year plan under false pretenses—in the expectation that he would be around to supervise things and keep radicalism in bounds—he was not wholly blind to the strength of the social-reform wing of the Revolutionary Family. Furthermore, there is room to ponder whether the faction that Cárdenas represented, the authors of the six-year plan, itself expected the degree of radicalism that Cárdenas later brought. Calles was amenable to some changes, but not to the point where his personal philosophy of what was best for Mexico would be mutilated.

The Fall of the Sonoran Dynasty

Cárdenas campaigned vigorously. The masses, unaware of the swing within the Revolutionary Family itself, regarded him as just another hand-picked candidate of Calles. They wanted the reforms that Cárdenas and his new six-year plan promised, but all politicians since Madero had been making more or less the same pledges. The chamber of deputies faithfully announced that Cárdenas had swept the election. Assuming the presidency on December 1, 1934, he entered office with a Calles-approved cabinet whose membership reflected Calles' partial, albeit passive, acceptance of growing liberal pressures. The former "socialistic" education minister and self-styled liberal, Narciso Bassols, became finance minister; the former provisional president, Emilio Portes Gil, who stood for agrarian reform and liberalism, was appointed minister of foreign affairs; the non-Communist, independent leftist agrarian reformer, Gen. Francisco Múgica, assumed the post of national economy minister; and the liberal Silvano Barba González took over the labor department. But to keep these four ministers and Cárdenas from proceeding too rapidly in carrying out the PNR's six-year plan, proven conservative *callistas* were seated in other ministries—Rodolfo Elías Calles (communications and public works), Tomás Garrido Canabal, hater of Catholicism but a conservative on other matters (agriculture), Juan de Dios Bojórquez (government), and Aarón Sáenz (Federal District governor). Gen. Matías Ramos remained PNR president. From the experience of preceding administrations and of "institutional life" à la *callismo*, both Cárdenas and Calles realized that the make up of the cabinet was vitally significant in finding a workable formula governing relations between president and *jefe supremo*.

But Calles overemphasized the role that the cabinet would play under Cárdenas. He similarly underestimated the influence of forces beyond his absolute control. There was the posture of the new trade unions and peasant leagues that had come to life during the Rodríguez administration. There was the attitude of the U.S. embassy and Franklin Delano Roosevelt. There was the policy of the Catholic Church and the second *Cristero* Rebellion. There was the position of the army, particularly generals Almazán, Amaro, and Cedillo. And, though long latent, there was public opinion. Calles probably intended to keep hands off as long as the conditions that evolved were not far removed from his own conservative philosophy. Cárdenas probably intended to work closely with Calles as long as the Revolutionary Family head adapted himself to the six-year plan, to which both Cárdenas and Calles had pledged the new administration. To Cárdenas, the survival of Revolutionary Mexico depended on keeping faith with the masses, which he felt the PNR leadership had done in laying down the six-year plan and in selecting him, Cárdenas, to be its standard-bearer.

This philosophy guided the first months of Cárdenas' public administration: Conspicuous consumption by politicos had to end—Cárdenas closed the gambling casinos and moved the presidential residence from the palatial Chapultepec Castle to modest quarters at "Los Pinos." The army had to reflect the new order of things—he dismissed or reassigned predatory militarists. The rank and file of organized labor deserved respect and better living standards—he condoned strikes, which in turn grew in geometric proportions. Agrarian reform was imperative—he drastically stepped up land redistribution. The courts should uphold the new reforms—he rescinded the law prohibiting the executive from removing federal judges, then removed all of them and appointed his own slate.

While Cárdenas assumed that the *jefe supremo* would go along with his conscientious reform government, perhaps only half-heartedly, Calles expected the new president to introduce changes gradually, only when indispensable. But radicalism brought more radicalism. To Calles, the new president appeared to be leading Mexico inevitably to the brink of open civil strife. Calles wavered for six months, and then, on June 12, 1935, the *jefe supremo* issued an unpropitious open message to the nation—a "patriotic declaration," he called it—reaffirming his faith in conservative solutions and hinting at what had happened to Ortiz Rubio under similar conditions. Calles thus challenged Cárdenas before the entire nation; Cárdenas had to accept the challenge or face the prospect of a political future stripped of prestige and dignity. Cárdenas, no less than Calles, grasped the "all power or no power" psychology of Mexicans which Calles attempted to utilize by notifying the nation that Cárdenas was no longer his obedient son. The trinity consisting of Family head, President of Mexico, and public policy was disunited. Worse still, the nation at large knew about it.

If Cárdenas himself was to rule, then he and he alone had to correct things. To achieve this, however, he had to become head of the Revolutionary Family as well as President of Mexico. This meant relegating Calles to political oblivion, dismissing die-hard *callistas* and anyone else who refused to carry out orders, and keeping the army loyal. As for the army, zone commanders now appeared loyal to Cárdenas; General Cedillo would stay in line if given more authority; General Almazán could be placated by giving him more government contracts for his roadbuilding firm; and General Amaro could be isolated and watched. So the immediate problem reduced itself to Calles and the die-hard *callistas*. Without consulting Calles, Cárdenas dissolved his cabinet, appointed a new one firmly committed to economic reform and to Cárdenas personally, and informed intermediaries that the hour had arrived for the retirement of Calles. The new cabinet took office on the same day that a government plane flew Calles to Mazatlán and retirement. On that day, June 19, 1935, having delivered a fatal blow to the Sonoran Dynasty, Lázaro Cárdenas became sole head of the Revolutionary Family.

FOUR

FIFTY YEARS OF REVOLUTION (2)

The second twenty-five years of the Mexican Revolution—or the period from June, 1935, into the six-year administration of Adolfo López Mateos that began December 1, 1958—brought striking reforms and solid advances on many fronts, yet it did not, and perhaps could not in such a short time, eliminate poverty, ignorance, and authoritarianism. Military revolts ended, peaceful elections ensued, political stability emerged, and basic freedoms were enlarged. Social justice found expression in national literacy campaigns, respect for certain labor rights, strengthening of educational facilities, agrarian reform, and in many social-welfare measures. Interest-group structure became defined and institutionalized. Church and State discovered mutually satisfactory relationships. The middle sectors of society grew. Economic nationalism intensified; new ownership patterns, large-scale public works, and industrial, commercial, and agricultural revolutions were introduced. Mexico also played new roles on the international stage. These impressive accomplishments should not, however, obscure the older problems that the Revolutionary Family failed to solve or the unresolved newer problems that arose during the period: economic backwardness, population pressures, forced savings, low per capita income, low agricultural efficiency, inadequate housing, urban slums, rural poverty, illiteracy, political authoritarianism, and popular unrest. Primary responsibility for the advances and retreats of the epoch belongs to the few men at the top, the heads of the Revolutionary Family: Lázaro Cárdenas, Manuel Ávila Camacho, Miguel Alemán, Adolfo Ruiz Cortines, and Adolfo López Mateos.

THE CÁRDENAS AND ÁVILA CAMACHO EPOCH

The Cárdenas and Ávila Camacho leadership of the Revolutionary Family stretched across a decade, precisely from June, 1935, to January, 1946. It approximated the presidential terms of Cárdenas (December 1, 1934, to November 30, 1940) and Ávila Camacho (December 1, 1940, to November 30, 1946). Cárdenas remained the exclusive Family leader until

Ávila Camacho became President of Mexico, after which the two shared leadership, Cárdenas largely outside public cognizance. During some or all of this epoch, the inner circle of the Revolutionary Family included, besides Cárdenas and Ávila Camacho, army generals Saturnino Cedillo, Gildardo Magaña, Francisco Múgica, Juan Andreu Almazán, Rafael Sánchez Tapia, Maximino Ávila Camacho, Heriberto Jara, and José Siurob; lawyers Emilio Portes Gil, Silvano Barba González, Luis I. Rodríguez, Vicente Lombardo Toledano, Javier Rojo Gómez, and Ezequiel Padilla; and Marte R. Gómez, Gustavo Baz, Jaime Torres Bodet, Fidel Velázquez, Graciano Sánchez, and Antonio Villalobos. The powerful governors of the epoch, those enjoying most-favored status, were Enrique Fernández Martínez and Luis Rodríguez (Guanajuato), Javier Rojo Gómez (Hidalgo), Marte R. Gómez (Tamaulipas), generals Anacleto Guerrero and Bonifacio Salinas Leal (Nuevo León), Pedro V. Rodríguez Triana (Coahuila), Silvano Barba González (Jalisco), Wenceslao Labra (México), Héctor Pérez Martínez and Eduardo Lavalle Urbina (Campeche), Gildardo Magaña (Michoacán), Gonzalo Santos (San Luis Potosí), Leobardo Reynoso (Zacatecas), and Rodolfo Sánchez Taboada (Baja California Norte).

Like Calles before him, Cárdenas' primordial task was to consolidate his power—to elevate himself to such a powerful stature in the Revolutionary Family that no one could question his leadership. Though Calles had departed, first to Sinaloa and from there to Los Angeles and Hawaii, certain holdovers could be expected to plot for his return. Cárdenas wished to avoid another clash, and by eliminating scheming *callistas* and conservative-minded generals, governors, politicians, and self-styled agrarian and labor bosses, he would reduce this prospect and fortify his own position. The announcement of new cabinet ministers had already enhanced the president's prestige: The agrarian reformer, religious moderate Gen. Saturnino Cedillo, replaced the fascist-oriented, fanatically anti-Catholic Tomás Garrido Canabal as agriculture minister; the independent liberal, agrarian reformer, Gen. Francisco Múgica, replaced Calles' son Rodolfo in the communications and public works ministry; Cárdenas' close friend, Silvano Barba González, took over the important post of government minister from Juan de Dios Bojórquez; the nominally Communist, long-discredited, onetime minister of "socialist" education, Narciso Bassols, handed over the finance ministry to the noncontroversial Eduardo Suárez; and Cárdenas' comrade in the high councils of the schismatic "Cárdenas Masonic Lodge," Gen. Rafael Sánchez, also joined the inner circle. Cárdenas placed Emilio Portes Gil, the former provisional president who carried a grudge against Calles for the highhanded way in which the *jefe supremo* had treated him, in command of the PNR, with instructions to purge the official party of *callista* sentiment, organize peasant leagues loyal to Cárdenas, and topple governors out of tune with the new regime.

What purges did the new team deem indispensable? First of all,

General Amaro lost his over-all influence in the army, some zone commanders were transferred (without their troops), and a few old soldiers saw the wisdom of leaving military life permanently. Second, Cárdenas encouraged new labor leaders to organize militant trade and peasant unions as counterweights against the army. Third, the PNR purged from its ranks many die-hard *callistas*, including, in December, 1935, Rodolfo Elías Calles and Fernando Torreblanca (Calles' son and son-in-law, respectively), the Riva Palacio brothers, Luis León, and Melchor Ortega. And fourth, Portes Gil proceeded with a vengeance to unseat *callista*-oriented governors, sometimes by having a state legislature toss the governor out of office (Colima, Durango, Guanajuato, Guerrero, Sinaloa, Sonora, and Tabasco in 1935, Chiapas in 1936, and Morelos in 1938) or grant the governor permission to leave office (Tamaulipas, Veracruz, and Yucatán, all in 1935), and other times by inducing the governor to renounce his post unilaterally (Durango and Veracruz, both in 1936). He permitted a few governors to remain in office only because their term of office would end shortly (Aguascalientes, Campeche, Chihuahua, Nuevo León, Oaxaca, and Zacatecas). When Calles returned to Mexico City in December, 1935, intent on reinstating himself at the head of the Revolutionary Family by attacking Cárdenas, the trade unions, and the PNR, he learned the hard way that Cárdenas alone ruled and reigned. On April 10, 1936, Cárdenas forced Calles, Luis León, Luis Morones, and Melchor Ortega into involuntary exile by having them escorted by plane to Brownsville, Texas.

Cárdenas had acquired transcendent authority and consolidated his leadership. He exercised his power on behalf of and in the name of the worker and peasant. He had long attracted the humble and poor. From his presidential campaign, if not earlier, the nation had learned that Cárdenas was one of eight children born and raised in the village of Jiquilpan, state of Michoacán, located in the heart of the communal-minded Tarascan country. The masses knew that at one time or another Cárdenas had fought under Zapata, Villa, Carranza, Obregón, and Calles; that by 1920, at the age of 25, he was a brigadier general and provisional governor of Michoacán, earning himself a reputation for integrity, industriousness, and support of agrarian reform. More important than the masses knowing Cárdenas, however, was his own deep insight into the masses and his knowledge of the ways officials manipulated public funds to thwart popular ambitions. Having served as war minister and PNR president, he knew the background and personality of the individual army generals and politicians —knew them all for what they really were. His knowledge of people, institutions, and character had grown in proportion to his own dedicated participation in the strictly national schismatic Masonic lodge, which he helped found in 1927 and once served as grand master. By the same token, long before Cárdenas received Calles' nod for the presidency, soldiers, liberal politicians, teachers, peasants, and workers in the "Cárdenas lodges" had become acquainted with their liberal brother. More details on Free-masonry are reserved for Chapter 7.

Insight into the nature of the power elite in Mexico is provided by Cárdenas' handling of three men—Emilio Portes Gil, Saturnino Cedillo, and Vicente Lombardo Toledano—upon whom he relied heavily in destroying Calles and what he represented. Once the issues dividing Calles and Cárdenas became clear, Cárdenas himself had no other choice but to topple Calles. This was not the case with Portes Gil and Cedillo, whose stature when Cárdenas entered office was no less than his, and who added their prestige when Cárdenas most needed it. Portes Gil joined the Cárdenas band wagon partly out of belief in what the new president represented, but partly to build himself up within the PNR. Vicente Lombardo Toledano, despite this labor leader's continuing claims that the Mexican labor movement itself put him at its head, was a Cárdenas creation. Lombardo knew that a return to Calles-ism would bring the longtime boss of the CROM, Luis Morones, back to power. Lombardo, by this time pro-Communist, conceived the Cárdenas scheme of things as being conducive to the development of a popular-front movement with none other than Lombardo himself at the head.

Despite their early help, Cárdenas ultimately eliminated all three. Figuratively speaking, each dug his own grave: Portes Gil was fired from the PNR presidency after Cárdenas realized that this power-hungry lawyer had tricked him into approving too many candidates for public office who were loyal to Portes Gil first and Cárdenas second. Cárdenas also frustrated Cedillo's ambitions to become president by reducing the functions of the agriculture ministry. Then, when Cedillo attempted a direct showdown by resigning his cabinet post and building up a private army of his own, the old *caudillo* was killed in action after losing a rebellion. Two of the triumvirate thus disappeared from the scene by 1938.

Lombardo Toledano's star shone brilliantly until his blind addiction to international Communist strategy meant that a 180-degree switch, "to turn on the democracies," became necessary to keep abreast of Moscow directives after the signing of the Stalin-Hitler pact in 1939. As long as Moscow policy coincided with Cárdenas policy, which by and large was the case in the 1935–39 period, President Cárdenas cared little about Lombardo's international connections. But turning on the Cárdenas institutions was a horse of a different color. Cárdenas had clipped Lombardo's wings from time to time since 1935: by splitting the agrarians, civil servants, bank employees, and teachers away from his giant labor central; by fostering a peasant militia officered by regular army men to balance Lombardo's militant industrial proletariat; by permitting Leon Trotsky, over the strong objections of Lombardo, to assume political exile in Mexico; by encouraging sectors of the independent left to swing away from Lombardo and group around General Múgica; and by blasting the hopes of a Lombardo-led popular front by establishing a uniquely Mexican popular front centered in the official party. Cárdenas never forgave Lombardo or Stalin for their anti-Mexican tactics of 1939–41. Not until Stalin died and Khrushchev liberalized international Communism did Cárdenas again speak in terms sympathetic to the Kremlin. Lombardo's incorrigible Communism alienated Cárdenas, a big wing of Mexican trade unionism, and much of the Mexican general public. Kept under close surveillance until his secretary-generalship term of the CTM labor central ended in 1941, Lombardo lost his inner-circle status forever.

Interest Groups

Cárdenas' disillusionment with these and other personalities strengthened his resolve to create a series of functionally specific interest groups. His tremendous faith in his fellow Mexican stemmed from a deep conviction that, given institutional means by which to express themselves, all Mexicans would actively participate in decision-making processes. He recognized in his people a deficiency of civic spirit and a lack of awareness of the difference between liberty and license, but he believed that these obstacles would be overcome in time if the masses as well as the elite groups in society possessed strong, permanent organizational mechanisms through which their demands would reach the government directly. What Cárdenas accomplished on this score, by merely setting up the organs to institutionalize all significant economic interests, was truly remarkable. Since the general organizational structures of these interest groups remain intact today, though the influence of one group or another has varied considerably from one year to the next, the actions of Cárdenas in this realm are indispensable for understanding the basic interest-group system in Mexico. How did his vision affect the structuring of the most important economic publics?

1. *Trade Unionists.*   The trade-union movement allied with the government and entered the mainstream of Mexican political life twice before 1935. Both times, the rank and file became disillusioned. The first pact occurred during the heat of civil war, when the anarcho-syndicalist House of the World Workers (the Casa) sublimated their anarchistic ideals and contributed six "Red Battalions" to the Carranza-Obregón forces in return for Carranza's pledge that labor would enjoy special benefits once hostilities ceased. But Carranza broke his promise and, worse still, ordered government officials to close Casa headquarters. To add insult to injury, the Mexican labor movement was placed under a new central (the CROM) in 1918, which completely dispossessed the Casa. The CROM, in turn, was called upon to back Obregón in his showdown with Carranza. By joining forces with Obregón, the new central irrevocably

committed itself to politicking. It organized a Mexican Labor Party that managed to obtain a majority of the federal congressional seats during the Calles administration. Luis Morones, CROM secretary-general, and other CROM leaders took over major public offices. CROM membership probably rose to more than a million laborers, which included peasants along with trade unionists, yet the rank and file enjoyed fewer benefits than expected from the possession of such apparent strength. Union bosses used membership statistics in bargaining for personal political privileges and abused rank-and-file confidence to amass personal fortunes. Rank-and-file unionists came to believe that CROM leaders had sold them out completely—obviously, not an unwarranted belief—and that the "decade of organized labor," 1918–28, had really amounted to little more than ten years of predatory unionism, boss opportunism, and extremely meager advances for laborers. One of the dilemmas, probably unobserved by most workers, was that labor had organized before Mexico industrialized; short of taking over society and imposing a worker's state, organized labor could not obtain high rewards in a nation shackled by economic backwardness. Nonetheless, few tears were shed by the rank and file when Morones and his henchmen appeared implicated in Obregón's assassination and Calles removed them from high public posts.

Cárdenas rejuvenated the hopes of older labor centrals and nascent unions that had begun activities in the early 1930's. Although his promises of future rewards in return for support against Calles failed to impress some unionists, others considered whether the long-range interests of the labor movement would best be served by political activity or by remaining aloof from politics. This question is still raised today. But young leaders in 1935, spurred on by the fiery oratory of the former CROM intellectual, Vicente Lombardo Toledano, stepped into the political frying pan; Lombardo's worker-democracy speeches held strong appeal. Cárdenas kept his word on one point: He backed labor in organizing a giant, national central. This labor confederation, set up in 1936 with Stalinists and Trotskyites on its first executive council along with non-Marxists, took the name of Confederación de Trabajadores de México (Workers' Confederation of Mexico or CTM). With the president's explicit approval, Lombardo became secretary-general and virtual dictator of the new organization.

From the outset, the CTM included peasants, civil servants, bank employees, teachers, and miners, plus laborers in commerce and industry. But Lombardo's personal ambitions soon engendered jurisdictional disputes among various Communist factions and between the Communist and non-Communist trade unionists, which gave Cárdenas a pretext for backing the autonomy of several occupational groupings and in the process reducing the CTM membership base to laborers in industry and commerce. Expropriation of the railroads and oil industry also reduced the

CTM hold on these industries, for their workers now found that contesting management's terms of work meant nothing less than criticizing the government. The Trotskyite-led miners and metallurgical workers' union split away from the CTM and Stalinist-oriented Lombardo in 1938, setting up an autonomous central of its own. Peasants, bank employees, civil servants, and teachers likewise obtained independence from the CTM in 1938. These splits have been lasting. Although Communism no longer divides the leadership of the miners and of the CTM, the miners never returned to the ranks of the CTM. Nonetheless, despite all these and other break-offs from the CTM, despite subsequent jurisdictional squabbles that led to the creation of new centrals, and despite two decades of rapid industrialization, almost three decades after its founding the CTM remained the largest labor central in Mexican commerce and industry.

2. *Ejidatarios.* Unlike Obregón and Calles before him, who both preferred small private farms, Cárdenas favored the semicollective *ejido.* He conceived agrarian reform as a means of rejuvenating ageless Indian cultural patterns, of relating the land to the small universe of each locality, and of making the peasant lord and master of Mexican agriculture. By redistributing land in the form of *ejidos,* whose title would be held in perpetuity by the nation, Cárdenas thought to make these communal units the effective base of a meaningful grass-roots democracy. Encouraging Portes Gil in mid-1935 to organize peasant leagues and bring them into the PNR, Cárdenas simultaneously permitted trade unions to enlist *ejidatarios* and small independent farmers in their ranks. But the sheer scope of his land-redistribution program soon created more *ejidatarios* than there were workers in the entire industrial labor force. These communal farmers hardly belonged under the tutelage of Lombardo, thought Cárdenas, and besides, they deserved an autonomous labor confederation of their own. Based on state agrarian leagues that had become a pillar of the redesigned official party in March, 1938, the new *ejidatario* central was officially baptized in August, 1938, with the name of Confederación Nacional Campesina (National Campesino Confederation or CNC). Membership in the CNC became obligatory for every *ejidatario* in the nation. In practice, the three-man local *ejidal* commissariats, state agrarian leagues, and CNC national executive committee were expected to aggregate interests and guide the CNC secretary-general. The CNC immediately became an intimate bed fellow of the CTM in the official party and highly independent on the national and state governments. In time, this close tieup with the whole political system made CNC officials subject to the not always unjustified charge of abusing membership trust by intervening with government banks to obtain financial credit for CNC officialdom. Nevertheless, a quarter of a century after Cárdenas established the *ejidatario* central it persisted, with

only minor alterations in its original structure, as the largest labor confederation in Mexican agriculture, possessing a membership of more than
two million.

3. *Civil Servants.*   Eliminating the Porfirian bureaucracy did not
eliminate the spoils system. Successive administrations paid off personal
and political debts by pushing out previous appointees or by creating offices
to make room for new "civil servants." Longevity, job security, and set pay
scales meant little. To correct these abuses and establish civil service on
a sound career basis, Cárdenas encouraged civil servants to unionize, first
in CTM ranks and then, by virtue of a decree law on the "juridical statute
of civil servants" in 1938, by giving the civil servants an autonomous union
of their own. This new central, the FSTSE (Federación de Sindicatos de
Trabajadores en el Servicio del Estado), excluded the upper 10 per cent
of the bureaucracy but encompassed all other civil servants. Cárdenas
thereby cleared the haze of status identification so frequently surrounding
civil servants by unequivocally asserting that they were workers, not professionals or a special white-collar class, and workers who deserved the
protection of the state in unionizing.

By its very nature in Mexican political life, the FSTSE was solidly
committed to membership in the official party. It became, and remains,
the pillar of the party's "popular sector," and selects civil servants to be
congressmen. Yet the greatest strength of the FSTSE lay in its role as a
vested-interest group negotiating directly with the President of Mexico
and cabinet ministers for the economic and social advancement of civil
servants. Since possessing their own autonomous union, the civil servants
have unquestionably prospered more than any other single "labor" union
in Mexico, obtaining higher wages, job security, seniority, fringe benefits,
vacation hotels, large clinics, discount houses, and above all, giant low-rent
housing developments. By 1964, the FSTSE had grown into a tightly knit,
highly disciplined organization of 310,000 members. As in the case of the
CTM and CNC, few structural changes in FSTSE organization have taken
place since Cárdenas first introduced the federation.

4. *Teachers.*   An unusual feature of the FSTSE is its inclusion of
public-school teachers paid by the national government, who are considered
civil servants because they receive their pay envelopes from the ministry
of public education and legally fall under its supervision. Other motives,
however, originally convinced Cárdenas that these "workers" should enter
the bureaucrats union. Public schooling was dear to Cárdenas; he sought
to release the people from superstition, fanaticism, and fear by making a
"socialistic" education compulsory. His crusade stretched beyond public
schools into privately owned educational institutions, where inspectors

were sent to insure that constitutional mandates were fulfilled. His vast public schooling program required many more teachers, thus necessitating the construction and expansion of normal schools. Cárdenas would not risk placing the future of public education in the hands of the Communist-riddled CTM, with which the majority of teachers had affiliated; nor did he feel that the teachers, who tended to confuse "socialistic" with "Communistic," should possess an independent union. The solution was to unite the teachers with other public employees—a plan often regretted since, but nonetheless still in effect today. Although the teachers were left the task of settling the differences separating primary- and secondary-school instructors, which culminated in the appearance of a unified teachers syndicate in 1942, the basic affiliation of teachers with the FSTSE remains intact. Of total FSTSE membership in 1964 approximately one-third, or 100,000 members, were teachers or other employees paid by the education ministry.

5. Bank Employees. Apprehensive of potential Communist inroads into financial institutions, Cárdenas removed bank employees from Lombardo's tutelage. By prohibiting the CTM and other trade unions from organizing this occupational group, Cárdenas gave bank employees (and bankers) immunity from union organizers. But he made clear that other provisions of the labor code, such as job security, maximum hours, and minimum wages, should apply to bank employees, and these stipulations regulate bank employment today.

6. Small Independent Farmers. Although Cárdenas emphatically singled out the semicollective *ejido* for the base of Mexican agriculture, he did not neglect small, privately owned farms. Some small farms antedated the Revolution; others, thousands of them, had come into existence during the Sonoran Dynasty. The Cárdenas blueprint outlined a special status for small farmers by barring them from the CNC and assisting them in setting up a permanent, quasi-official vested-interest grouping, the National Confederation of Small Agricultural Property. The government's emphasis on private farms since 1946 has firmly established the small farm in Mexican agriculture, though it has not produced the desired effect of uniting this group of farmers into one giant federation. Other agricultural organizations compete for recognition with the original Cárdenas grouping, yet by 1964 this group claimed a membership of 750,000 small farmers, of whom approximately one-third were *ejidatarios* possessing small farms of their own.

7. Cooperativists. On a political scale of values, cooperatives suffered miserably after Jorge Prieto Laurens placed the National Cooperativist Party behind the De la Huerta uprising of 1923–24. Once Obregón and Calles crushed this rebellion, they removed cooperativists from public offices, and the Sonoran Dynasty gave cooperatives no further opportunity to enter politics. Cárdenas, on the other hand, bore no grudge against cooperatives. He passed a general law of cooperative societies, spelling out in detail the rights, obligations, and functions of the four types of cooperatives permitted in Mexico: producer, consumer, state-participating, and state intervention. Lodging the power of granting permits to organize cooperatives in the ministry of national economy, Cárdenas made it obligatory for all cooperatives to enter a new semiofficial National Cooperativist Confederation. A cooperative society automatically became a member of the new confederation. From the late 1930's, when the national cooperativist organ first saw the light of day, it has grown into a powerful spokesman for thousands of cooperatives, which in Mexico are concentrated in the fishing, bus lines, mining, trucking, forestry products, banana, coffee, cacao, and sugar industries. The structure of the National Cooperativist Confederation, though modified in 1947, remains essentially the same today as in the Cárdenas administration.

   8. *Businessmen: Commerce.*   Although Cárdenas visualized a transformed Mexican society centering on workers and the state, he did not ignore private business interests. But instead of setting up new organizations for this sector, as he did for the various occupational groups, he simply restructured existing chambers of commerce and industry. In 1936, he replaced the antiquated law of chambers of commerce that dated back to the pre-Revolutionary year of 1908 with a new Law of Chambers of Commerce and Industry, under whose terms the separate National Confederation of Chambers of Commerce (CONCANACO) and Confederation of Industrial Chambers of Mexico (CONCAMIN) were combined into one large semiofficial association, which set the stage for the modern evolution of both chambers. In the case of the CONCANACO, full-fledged membership became obligatory for all nonindustrial businesses whose equity capital exceeded a set minimum (four hundred U.S. dollars today) and junior membership was obligatory for nonindustrial businesses whose equity capital was less than the minimum required for full-fledged membership but above an unusually low minimum equity capital (forty U.S. dollars today). In essence, the Cárdenas law exempted from membership in the CONCANACO only the small independent artisans and street vendors.

   Obligatory membership in the CONCANACO had several purposes. Cárdenas wanted the chambers of commerce brought under state supervision in order to provide the entire private commercial sector—not just the biggest capitalists—with a voice before the government, as well as to provide the government with a representative source of business attitudes on public policy. Besides, in a united commercial chamber, Mexican composed and managed, the members might in time discover that Mexicanism superseded capitalism—that Mexican capitalists had less in common with foreign capitalists than they did with other sectors of Mexican society— and the CONCANACO might then support the displacement of foreign owners in Mexico.

Local chambers of commerce formed the CONCANACO and elected its president. By 1964, the number of individual businesses belonging to the national federation exceeded 20,000 (all members of local chambers simultaneously belong to the national). And though few of the entrepreneurs heading these businesses probably had anything praiseworthy to say about Lázaro Cárdenas—and Cárdenas would no doubt have been happier to have fewer private businessmen—it was he who institutionalized private business interests in Mexico.

9. Businessmen: Industry. Industrialists, like their associates in commerce, also were provided with a permanent institutional means to express themselves. In line with the 1936 law, Cárdenas rejected the notion of a division of business into commerce and industry, joining the major industrial chamber into the CONCANACO. By 1941, however, the industrialists had recaptured their independence, though the legal obligation to belong to a chamber remained. The chamber for industrialists was the Confederation of Industrial Chambers of Mexico (CONCAMIN). Unlike the CONCANACO, where membership in the locals was based on geographical location, membership in the CONCAMIN chambers was based on types of industrial activity. Fifty industrialists engaged in a similar activity, such as the manufacture of chemicals or electrical products, could apply to the government for permission to split off from their existing chamber to form a new one. Invariably, the split-off would find industrialists leaving the National Chamber of Manufacturing Industries, largest single chamber in the CONCAMIN. Voting strength within a chamber is apportioned according to the amount of dues paid—and dues are calculated on the capitalization of a member firm's business. Voting by chambers in CONCAMIN organs also follows a weighted system, prorated on financial contribution. Therefore, some chambers have become strong because of the heavy capitalization required in their industries, such as the National Chamber of Iron and Steel; others have gained their strength from the sheer number of industrialists who belong, which is the case with the National Chamber of Manufacturing Industries. By 1964, the CONCAMIN incorporated 46 full-fledged national chambers of industry, plus five affiliated associations representing industrial activities like brewing that showed little promise of achieving a fifty-company minimum. Paralleling

CONCANACO growth and economic development in general, the industrialist group has grown far larger than Cárdenas could possibly have foreseen.

Functional Democracy?

Through this multiple institutionalization of occupational groups, Cárdenas anticipated the emergence of a functional democracy headed by the CTM and CNC, but incorporating the other interest groups as well. In pushing forward in this direction, Cárdenas faced some formidable obstructions. He had assumed office amidst a clash of personalities and ideologies within the Revolutionary Family, and by deposing the *callistas*, he had opened positions for which a new set of power-hungry personalities could aspire. Cedillo, Portes Gil, Lombardo Toledano, Almazán, Múgica, and a host of other power aspirants had to be watched and balanced one against the other. Meanwhile, personal ambitions soon became intermeshed with strong differences of opinion on the nature and pace of public policy in Mexico and on international ideologies. Opposition political groupings, not wholly divorced from foreign creeds, came into vogue. United States–Mexican relations entered the picture, as did the Spanish Civil War, Hitler, Stalin, Mussolini, Trotsky, Salazar of Portugal, and the British Foreign Office. Thus, both domestic politics and pressures and foreign ideologies and events outside Mexico helped shape and qualify the Cárdenas programs. Cárdenas generally sympathized with the Spanish Republicans (he permitted thousands of Spanish refugees to come to Mexico), with Moscow (until 1939), and with the New Deal of Franklin Roosevelt (although for a time he sold Mexican oil to Nazi Germany). Cárdenas was regularly raked over the coals for pursuing a pro-Communist line, yet the bulk of criticism leveled against him on this point would apply equally to Franklin D. Roosevelt.

The outside world and agents on the spot in Mexico did not forestall Cárdenas from completely overhauling the official party in line with his philosophy of functional democracy. To Cárdenas, the major catalysts that would bring about the advancement of the masses were the new interest-group organizations that would form and control the official party. Yet, as we have already observed, Cárdenas encouraged the institutionalization of other interest groups that obviously would play a marginal role at best in his new functional democracy. Cárdenas preferred a classless society, but he doubted that Mexico was ready for it, at least not until public education and the new unions overcame the hold of the Catholic Church and other legacies of the Mexican past. Fostering the CONCANACO and CONCAMIN hardly bespoke an absolute lack of confidence in the eventual emergence of a responsible group of Mexican private entrepreneurs. Turning over the management of the national railways to the railroad workers showed his faith in rank-and-file abilities, although when the workers failed to provide the minimum management necessary, they lost control and direction passed to the state.

Cárdenas believed that the political system demanded in the first instance a strong President of Mexico, backed up by an official party run by trade unionists, *ejidatarios*, civil servants, and professional soldiers. Outside the official party, the president could consult all interest groups directly. His scheme was put to the practical test of reality in the congressional elections of 1937. Satisfied with the result, Cárdenas convoked a national convention of the PNR in March, 1938, with one purpose in mind: to have the PNR commit suicide. Dutifully, the delegates rubber-stamped the statutes establishing the PNR's successor, the *Partido de la Revolución Mexicana* (the PRM). Organization of the new party rested on a functional, job-occupational concept. The old geographical and individual membership structure of the PNR gave way to an organization of four sectors—labor, agrarian, military, and popular. The first sector was turned over to the trade unionists, the second to the *ejidatarios*, the third to the soldiers, and the fourth to civil servants and miscellaneous elements. These four sectors collectively decided which among them should be allotted specific public offices to fill, then turned over the actual nominating process to the designated sector. Once this sector announced its nomination, all four sectors were pledged to support the candidate at the polls.

Over-all direction of PRM affairs lodged in a national executive committee composed of a president, a secretary-general, and four secretaries heading the respective sectors. This pattern prevailed at the state, district, and local levels, although there was no agrarian sector in urban districts and no labor and popular sectors in exclusively *ejidal* regions. Aside from the fact that several significant occupational and other socioeconomic interests had no voice nor place in the PRM, the sector nominating arrangement proved workable in electing state congressmen and federal deputies and senators. But a serious loophole in the Cárdenas scheme soon appeared in candidate selection for executive offices. In the 1937 trial elections, sectors had proven themselves willing to horse-trade, because a legislator really did not possess any power once elected. Election simply meant a little prestige and adding a few thousand pesos a month to the regular income of sector leaders. However, grabbing the presidency, a governorship, or a municipal presidency meant access to real power—to the setting of policy, to control over the legislative and judicial bodies, and not the least, to the final word on how tax monies were to be spent. PRM statutes provided that three of the four sectors had to concur on a given nomination, but with such high goals at stake, the numerically strongest agrarian and labor sectors thought that they deserved more say in the nominations for executive offices than the relatively weak military and popular sectors. On the basis of sheer numbers, logic was on their side.

But what would happen when the orientation of the proletariat did not coincide with the public policies of the president, governors, and municipal presidents? If the labor movement was captured by Communists, should the president permit all governorships and municipal presidencies in areas where labor predominated to fall into their hands? The solution reached was clearly observable in the selection of Ávila Camacho to succeed Cárdenas: The head of the Revolutionary Family chose his successor after consulting sector leaders, strong interests outside the PRM, and powerful individuals in their own right; he informed the PRM president of his choice, and then permitted the respective sectors to announce him as "their" candidate to the general public. The rank and file of unions affiliated with the official party had every reason to go along with the powerful political machine when they were led to believe that their leaders had really chosen the president-elect. Similarly, governors were selected by the President of Mexico after nominal consultation with party leaders and other interests in a respective state; the selection of municipal presidents was left to the discretion of the respective state governors.

The presidential election of 1940 brought out another inadequacy in Cárdenas' functional democracy. According to the new rules of the game, the millions of workers and peasants in unions affiliated with the PRM, along with their union bosses, should be counted upon to support all PRM candidates. But Lombardo Toledano and the CTM, putting the Communist International ahead of Mexico, had become caught up in the policy changes brought about by the Stalin-Hitler pact of 1939. In addition, a substantial segment of the army, without Cedillo and Amaro, had only two great generals to choose from—Cárdenas and Almazán—and one of them was barred from re-election. To make matters worse, many agrarians favored the liberal Gen. Francisco Múgica. With the PRM in such a predicament, with Cárdenas sensitive to divisions created by his own radical programs, and with the popular sector still in an amorphous state, Cárdenas overlooked all sectors and decided that his rather colorless defense minister, Manuel Ávila Camacho, should be the candidate of the official party. Needless to say, Ávila Camacho was a bitter pill for the labor and agrarian sectors to swallow, because they failed to recognize in him the liberal qualities they sought in a candidate. And many soldiers preferred Almazán or another general with a more distinguished record in the annals of Revolution.

Cárdenas argued that the time had come for consolidating the gains of his administration and for averting reaction identified with the rising tide of fascism. At the same time, he convinced the military that international Communism had to be stopped dead in its tracks, and that Communist leaders in the CTM and CNC had to Mexicanize their outlooks.

To accomplish this and keep the Revolutionary Family intact, Cárdenas maintained, the presidency should pass into the hands of an individual known for moderation and fair play. Cárdenas promised the CTM and CNC that he personally would guarantee the new administration's respect for their organizations, thus convincing the sector leaders to remain in a united front behind the Ávila Camacho candidacy. But the sector leaders encountered considerable opposition from their own rank and file. Many workers and peasants wanted a more radical candidate, others a more conservative one. Ávila Camacho simultaneously helped and harmed his candidacy by declaring during the campaign that "*Yo soy creyente*" (I am a believer), for it conciliated some Catholics but drove radicals further into the leftist camp. The army also divided when General Almazán announced that he would enter his own candidacy on a platform opposed to socialist education and Communism, and favoring business.

The presidential election in 1940 was one of the bloodiest election days in Mexican history. Ávila Camacho was declared the winner over General Almazán and the independent leftist General Múgica. These two generals had attracted tens of thousands of PRM rank-and-file members to their candidacies, and to this day not a few impartial observers insist that Almazán really won the election. But Almazán deserted his followers by going abroad after the election instead of leading an armed revolt as he had promised to do "in the event that the will of the electorate is not respected." His departure eased tensions considerably between election day and the day when Ávila Camacho took office five months later. The whole electoral fiasco strengthened Cárdenas' conviction that the official party had to become clearly subordinate to the authority of the President of Mexico and the state governors.

But the subordination of vested interests within the official party did not imply a policy of reducing the influence of these vested interests in society as a whole. Cárdenas kept his pledge to the CTM and CNC by defending these unions whenever and as often as feasible. Outside the public purview, his task became easier when the Nazi attack on Russia brought a new, more moderate policy from Moscow on international Communism. Still, Cárdenas had learned his lesson about die-hard Communists, and for the good of the Mexican labor movement, he concurred with non-Communist union leaders in deposing Lombardo Toledano. To succeed him, the CTM selected Fidel Velázquez, a onetime milkman who, like Lombardo, had abandoned the CROM to become an original member of the CTM's national executive committee. Organized labor, including the CTM and CNC, had no major complaints against the Ávila Camacho administration. Their headaches began with Miguel Alemán.

Two major changes altered the PRM structure. First, the military sector was dropped from the official party in order to place the Mexican army into the real power structure of the Mexican political system, which focused on the President of Mexico without the intermediary of the official party, and to stop officers from slighting their military duties to take seats in impotent legislative bodies. Thenceforth, the armed forces played politics through the ministries of national defense and the navy, whose cabinet ministers enjoyed direct contact with the president. The fact that Cárdenas himself headed the ministry of national defense during much of the Ávila Camacho administration eased the transition—indeed, it guaranteed it. And the fact that an army general has held the official party presidency uninterruptedly since 1946 while dozens of military men have become governors refutes the contention that Cárdenas permanently removed the military from politics.

The second change saw the creation of the National Confederation of Popular Organizations (*Confederación Nacional de Organizaciones Populares* or CNOP), which served to institutionalize certain elements within the official party structure. Grouped into the CNOP were civil servants, cooperativists, small farmers, intellectuals and professionals, artisans, nonsalaried workers (such as taxi drivers), small merchants (those outside the CONCANACO), small industrialists (those outside the CONCAMIN), women, youths, and virtually anyone else who wished to join the party. This modification gave the President of Mexico a pretext for reducing or eliminating the number of individuals not in the labor or agrarian sectors who kept pestering him for a legislative seat, while permitting him to retain the final word on the selection of deputies and senators. The broadened base of the popular sector also offered the president and the state governors an opportunity to rationalize their handpicked candidates as "members of the popular sector."

The functional-democracy formulas of Cárdenas, which looked so attractive on paper, thus gave way to Mexican realities and traditions that favored the omnipotent executive. Cárdenas himself was one of Mexico's strongest chiefs of state, and in making Ávila Camacho president he negated his own principle of functional democracy. Throughout the 1940–45 period, Cárdenas underplayed his own popularity with the Mexican masses in an effort to strengthen Ávila Camacho and the prestige of the presidency. Revolutionary Family leadership could not lodge in Ávila Camacho alone, because the millions of agrarian and trade unionists and the hard core of the Mexican army looked first to Cárdenas. Cárdenas kept labor and the military in bounds, checked Communism and fascism, and headed the national defense ministry during World War II. Mexican entrance into the war, on the side of the United States and the Soviet Union, itself contributed to raising Ávila Camacho's stature, since it justified granting him the extraordinary emergency powers that he retained until the Japanese surrendered. Cárdenas and Ávila Camacho so succeeded in weakening functional democracy, by the time-proven policy of divide and rule under the label of national unity, that when the question of presidential succession once again rolled around, they had no trouble whatsoever in hand-picking a new Family leader and in assuring a peaceful transfer of power.

Race, Religion, and Education

Racial equality, religious tolerance, intellectual freedom, and public education had their ups and downs, but on the whole, these propositions received favorable treatment during the Cárdenas–Ávila Camacho period. Like the Northern Dynasty, these leaders encouraged the indigenous Indian communities to toss off their fanaticisms, superstitions, and poverty. Mexicans increasingly thought of themselves less and less in terms of skin color, more and more as one people. Although Cárdenas initiated his rule with an intense anticlericalism and strict regulation of private schools, he had toned down this policy considerably by 1938. High churchmen also desisted from open attack on the government; the second *Cristero* Rebellion, which dated back to 1932, terminated. But churchmen never desisted from lobbying for constitutional reform until "socialistic" education was dropped in 1945. Cárdenas did not guarantee that "socialistic" education, which he advanced partly out of his deep distaste for fanaticism, would not in many schoolhouses become Communistic. Indeed, Cárdenas had no particular quarrel with the Communists as long as their beliefs coincided with Mexican socialism, which he believed to be the case until the Third International adapted itself to the Nazi-Soviet pact. Finding teachers willing to go into the rural areas was difficult enough without setting up additional ideological barriers. After 1939, however, Cárdenas parted with the Communists. The slow, painful task of training new teachers, eliminating rampant Communists, and reshuffling officials in the education ministry began. In the meantime, Cárdenas relied on the Cárdenas lodges and other Masonic groups, army zone commanders, and state governors to be watchdogs against fanaticism.

As pressures from the right increased, as well as those from the popular masses who wanted an end to "anti-God" instruction, education received a new definition in a constitutional amendment of 1945. "Socialistic" education gave way to patriotic Mexican education, greater tolerance of private schools, and the revision of textbooks. (Revision of texts proceeded slowly, however; some public-school textbooks are still basically as they were in 1935). Constitutional revision did not sell out Revolutionary Creed objectives on religious equality, as some would maintain; on the contrary, it helped fulfill this proposition. Catholics, no less than adherents to other creeds, now enjoyed freedom, and fanatical priests gave way to new, Mexican-born priests who accepted the broad policies of the new Mexico. In case some priests forgot their civic responsibilities, they would have to contend with Masonic lodges, the army, governors, and public schools. The construction of schools and other educational institutions pushed forward throughout the Cárdenas–Ávila Camacho decade. This, combined with rural cultural missions and the "each one teach one" literacy campaign begun in 1942, reduced illiteracy notably from 1935 to 1945. Education provided the talent that Alemán and his successors drew upon to extend the nation's development.

Economic Development and Economic Nationalism

A release of creativeness also stemmed from Cárdenas' assertion of economic nationalism. In addition to giving every major occupational class its own institutional means for expressing itself before government, Cárdenas tried to correct the causes of the socio-economic diseases plaguing Mexico. This required overcoming the country's instilled fear of the United States, as well as the fear of one Mexican for another. By 1945 Mexico had overcome both fears: The Good Neighbor Policy and World War II contributed substantially to uniting the Mexicans, but economic nationalism contributed more. When Cárdenas entered office, the nation was overwhelmingly rural, illiterate, and poor; industrialization was largely an aspiration; and the principal means of production were foreign-owned. Mexico is still more rural than urban, illiteracy is high, and per capita income is low, but great progress has been made. By resuming and expanding the public works and other social overhead programs first laid down by Calles, Cárdenas started Mexico on its "takeoff" into sustained growth. Raising per capita income, industrializing Mexico, and making the country something more than a mere supplier of minerals and foodstuffs were by-products of the new character of Mexicans.

The peasants learned that land reform meant receiving land: Distribution of land under the Cárdenas administration surpassed twofold the amount distributed up to 1934. The net effect of his breakup of big estates, a program continued by Ávila Camacho and subsequent presidents, though slowed down until López Mateos took office, was to break the back of the large *hacendados* once and for all. Agricultural land thenceforth belonged to those who live on it and, through recent modifications in the agrarian reform, those who worked it. Cárdenas knew that communal farmers could expect little financial assistance from private banks, so he set up a new National Bank of *Ejidal* Credit in 1935 to assist *ejidatarios* in financing of their crops. He tried to make the land and the living it provided more attractive by accelerating irrigation programs and by creating the Comisión Federal de Electricidad (Federal Electricity Commission), a wholly state-owned enterprise empowered to enter the business of generating and distributing electricity to areas that private companies found unattractive. He set up special agricultural schools to train peasants to become more efficient farmers. He sent rural cultural missions to reduce illiteracy and initiate community projects. He began the military training of Mexican peasants, a program greatly expanded by Ávila Camacho under the compulsory military-service program.

Cárdenas changed the basic landownership pattern in many regions of Mexico, and to the degree that he succeeded in crushing the *latifundio*, later regimes have been plagued with the problem of *minifundia*. The peasants now "owned" much of the land, but too often the parcels given them were uneconomically small. In stressing ownership of the land rather than its use, Cárdenas partially resolved an ageless problem only by creating a serious new problem.

The theories of Cárdenas on ownership of the means of production were not acquired from Moscow or from local Communists, but from Mexican experience. If a responsible rural landlord class had treated the Mexican better, there would have been no need for agrarian reform to begin with. Having large tracts of farming, grazing, and timber lands in the hands of foreigners had produced undesirable effects; Cárdenas wanted the land owned by Mexicans—responsible Mexicans. He did not do away with or try to do away with private Mexican ownership of the land; he did reduce the size of Mexican-owned lands. He knew rural Mexico for what it was: distinct regions holding distinct philosophies of agricultural development. To Cárdenas, the large landholder had pushed the government and masses around long enough. The economic sin of Cárdenas was not taking lands away from unproductive land barons, but redistributing lands into small unproductive parcels; not favoring *ejidos* over private farms, but making the communal units uneconomically small.

Cárdenas' philosophy on industrial and commercial ownership coincided with his outlook on agriculture. He was not against foreign capital per se; on the contrary, he repeatedly invited foreign capital to assist in financing economic development. What he wanted, however, was not just any kind of foreign capital, but the kind that was willing to help build Mexico on Mexican terms. He deplored 100 per cent foreign-owned subsidiaries intent on exploiting the mineral wealth of Mexico, which is the way he viewed the three Big A's—American Metal, Anaconda, and American Smelting and Refining. But foreign capital willing to invest in enterprises under Mexican majority ownership, foreign capital granting loans to Mexican industrialists and merchants, foreign capital setting up businesses oriented toward the Mexican domestic market, and foreign capital making loans to the Mexican government—these were welcomed. In reality, Cárdenas left much Mexican-owned and foreign-owned business untouched. Foreigners and first-generation Mexican capitalists such as William Jenkins, Harry Wright, Carlos Prieto, Carlos Trouyet, Raúl Bailleres, the Legorretas, the Azcárragas, the Garza Sadas, the Salinas and Rocha families, Antonio Ruiz Galindo, and Luis Aguilar—none of them politicians—kept building their private businesses. And whenever a cement plant, sugar mill, or textile factory was taken out of private Mexican hands and turned over to the workers, the financial and organizational structure of the companies that had owned them was generally weak in the first place.

Two cases of Cárdenas' intervention deserve special comment: the railroads and the oil industry. Cárdenas did not nationalize the railroads; that had been completed, as far as more than half of the nation's railroad mileage was concerned, before the Mexican Revolution began. What he actually did was expropriate the National Railways System, a property already government-owned, in order to remove the voice that foreign creditors had maintained in their management; in financial terms, he added the railroad debt to the over-all public debt. Once the foreign creditors lost all say, Cárdenas first placed the management of the railroads in the hands of the railroad workers' union and then, when this arrangement proved unworkable, brought the railroads under the direct authority of an autonomous government agency. Not all the nation's railways became publicly owned—the Southern Pacific holdings on the west coast of Mexico and other lines remained untouched. Considering the ownership status of the railroad lines that Cárdenas did expropriate, the only real change he made was to remove private creditors, who had no prospect of or desire to resume ownership, from a voice in management, and actually to raise the prospects of retiring the debt.

The case of the petroleum industry is somewhat more complex. Oilmen, politicians, and union bosses had long terrorized the workers in the oil fields, defiantly broken laws, and juggled deeds and leases. For twenty years, Washington and London, backing up their nationals who controlled the industry, had persistently wrangled with the Mexican government on questions of constitutionality, title to subsoil rights, and taxes. Therefore, in May, 1937, when representative union leaders spurred the oil workers to strike for higher wages, for better living and working conditions, and for fringe benefits, the Mexican government and general public understandably sympathized with the workers. After Cárdenas promised the oil workers that their demands would be submitted to an economic investigation, they returned to their jobs. The findings of the economic investigation, which upheld the major contentions of the oil workers, served as the basis of a labor board's August, 1937, decision to award wage increases and fringe benefits. The oil companies then appealed this decision to the Mexican supreme court, but lost. Foolishly, they then appealed the decision over the head of President Cárdenas and the courts in full-page advertisements in the Mexican press. This proved to be the last time that the oil companies tried to circumvent Mexican institutions, for when the court deadline for compliance was not met and last-minute efforts at reconciliation proved futile, Cárdenas decreed the expropriation of oil properties on March 18, 1938. The overwhelming majority of Mexicans, including fervent Catholics and businessmen, enthusiastically supported Cárdenas. The oil expropriation represented a transcendental assertion of economic nationalism: Cárdenas had stood up against the giants of "international piracy" and won. Again, expropriation— a technique embodying repayment, not confiscation—characterized the action of Cárdenas. The foreign capital behind the oil industry was precisely the kind that Cárdenas did not want for Mexico.

The Cárdenas formula for ownership of the means of production carried over into the years of World War II. Many "undesirable" companies were left untouched, for the moment, while arrangements for payment of external creditors, including the railroad and expropriated oil companies, were completed. Isolated by the war, which precluded heavy investment by giant American or European corporations, Mexico found for the first time since independence that its domestic market had been left to the Mexicans and to a new clique of foreigners—draft dodgers, gamblers, racketeers, flight capitalists, black marketeers, and others who preferred a haven in Mexico. Unattractive as this new group of foreign capitalists may have appeared, they helped finance the expansion of older industries and the establishment of new ones. Perhaps the most outstanding and wealthiest figure in the entire foreign lot was the multimillionaire Axel Wenner-Gren, who invested heavily. These individuals could hardly invoke the protection of their home government if the sledding got rough. The same applied to the sizable group of Spanish refugees who brought some money and more important, the skills of entrepreneurship and a driving urge to succeed. The seizure of properties owned by nationals of the Axis countries brought additional revenues, and, above all, Mexico acquired substantial financial reserves from her exports, direct assistance from the Export-Import Bank in Washington, and remittances from her agricultural labor force that migrated to the United States. Unmolested by competition from foreign manufactures, Mexican business grew.

A central question for Ávila Camacho, as for the Cárdenas administration before him and others to follow, was to choose between private enterprise and state socialism. Public, private, joint public-private, cooperative, communal, and worker ownership were all permissible. The key problem involved determining what the state should own and what sectors of the economy—whether owned privately, cooperatively, communally, jointly with the government, jointly with foreigners, or by workers—should be controlled by Mexicans alone. July, 1944, brought the first explicit public announcement on the "ownership by nationals" theme:

The ministry of foreign affairs had been authorized to require Mexican ownership to the degree of at least 51 per cent in companies where foreign interests were involved. Though partly a war measure, the ruling that a minority equity interest is the best position allowable to foreign capital in specific industries holds true today. What the Ávila Camacho administration never made public, but nonetheless used as a guide in granting permits for new businesses and other concessions, was that in order to be permitted to remain private, at least 51 per cent had to lodge in the hands of nationals in the following industries: radio broadcasting, truck and bus transportation, national air transport, production, distribution and exhibition of motion pictures, fishing, publishing, and the production and marketing of carbonated beverages. Not until 1959 and 1960, however, did the state move in earnest against firms that had not abided by the Mexican ownership formula.

The decade of Cárdenas and Ávila Camacho resembled the reign of the Sonoran Dynasty before it. Both epochs started with dramatic elimination of the preceding Revolutionary Family head, and both professed radical reform but ended with conservative leanings. Yet there was one real difference: After Calles left the presidency, his puppet presidents largely abandoned basic economic reforms, while the Ávila Camacho administration consolidated Cárdenas' economic advances. And consolidation in this case was tantamount to a basic transformation of Mexican economic life.

The Cárdenas–Ávila Camacho leadership of the Revolutionary Family ended almost a year before the latter's presidential term formally ended. This happened for one reason: Cárdenas and Ávila Camacho wanted Family headship to lodge in the president-elect in order to permit him to accumulate the great popular strength that the two generals realized was indispensable for leading the nation. They wanted no serious factionalism, no splits at the top. Cárdenas and Ávila Camacho insisted that if political stability and economic progress were to continue free of internecine strife, final word must reside in one person. That one person for the immediate years ahead was Miguel Alemán.

THE MIGUEL ALEMÁN EPOCH

Alemán's assumption of power took place in the context of the events of late 1945 and early 1946. Mexico had emerged from World War II a creditor nation. Her industry was operating, her peasants producing, her miners extracting, and prospects of dollar income from American tourists and Mexican migratory labor were high. Mexico had committed herself to the internationalism of the United Nations and the regionalism of the inter-American system. Constitutional revision had abolished "socialistic" instruction in favor of patriotic, moderate education, and the

Catholic Church appeared satisfied. A new electoral law adopted in 1945 called for the creation of a system of national political parties. Cárdenas and Ávila Camacho had accomplished the miracle of eliminating the ever-present fear of armed revolt.

Alemán faced minimal opposition. The sudden and dramatic deaths of the Soviet czar in Mexico, Russian Ambassador Oumansky, and the self-styled leader of the Revolutionary Family's right wing, Maximino Ávila Camacho, improved the political climate. And though the CTM had pushed the candidacy of Javier Rojo Gómez and the CNC favored Gen. Miguel Henríquez Guzmán, Cárdenas and Ávila Camacho let union leaders know that Family leadership and the presidency would lodge in Alemán alone; whatever advances the CTM, CNC, and other unions would make (for the unions had no special complaints against Cárdenas or Ávila Camacho), depended squarely on the disposition of Alemán. Finally, there was an unwritten agreement with the army that while a civilian was in the nation's presidency, army generals would take over the presidency of the official party; in short, a civilian would run the nation while a general headed the official party. Sticky problems of the past—religion, education, foreign relations, militarism, factionalism, and unionism—somehow appeared less troublesome.

In this promising context, Miguel Alemán achieved peacefully what many ambitious Revolutionaries before him had sought vainly on the battlefield: undisputed leadership of the Revolutionary Family. His meteoric ascendancy had been aided by the reputation of his father, a popular, liberal-minded general killed by Calles' men in 1929. Alemán started with a law degree, assumed the governorship of Veracruz in 1936, and moved to the national scene as campaign manager and minister of government (*gobernación*) for Ávila Camacho. When Cárdenas and Ávila Camacho made the young *veracruzano* omnipotent, he was only 43 years of age. Alemán's grand debut in January 19, 1946, dramatically redesigned the official party in the image of Alemanism: the PRM became the PRI (*Partido Revolucionario Institucional*, or the Party of the Institutionalized Revolution—and how can revolution remain revolution if institutionalized?) and the old party theme "For a Democracy of Workers" gave way to the PRI theme of "Democracy and Social Justice." Alemán exercised his new power by arbitrarily informing party leaders that he had selected Rafael Gamboa, his personal campaign manager, to be first president of the new PRI. After December, the post belonged to a general, so Gamboa became the last civilian party president. Gamboa launched a whirlwind campaign, enhancing his mentor's popularity tremendously. When election day rolled around in July, Alemán overwhelmed his leading opponent, Ezequiel Padilla. No bloodshed, no threats of rebellion, no trouble: Alemán was popular and respected as well as powerful. When he formally assumed the presidency on December 1,

1946, his occupancy of this highest public office coincided with his real status as Revolutionary Family potentate.

Alemán's inner circle also enjoyed high status in the Revolutionary Family. It included, besides Cárdenas and Ávila Camacho, specific public officials, businessmen, and regional leaders. Among the thirteen cabinet members were two military men—those in charge of national defense and the navy—and the favorites Ramón Beteta (finance), Rafael Gamboa (health), Fernando Casas Alemán (Federal District), Antonio Ruiz Galindo [1] (national economy), Héctor Pérez Martínez [2] (government), and Jaime Torres Bodet (foreign affairs). When the hydraulic resources and agrarian affairs departments achieved an autonomous status in 1947, the civilians Adolfo Oribe Alba and Alfonso Caso took charge of them. Gen. Rodolfo Sánchez Taboada became PRI president. Other officials enjoying intimacy with Alemán included Rogerio de la Selva (presidential secretary), Antonio Díaz Lombardo (Social Security Institute), and Antonio Carrillo Flores (Nacional Financiera). Without official portfolios, but enjoying inner-circle status, were the political-business intermediaries Carlos Serrano, Jorge Pasquel, and Enrique Parra Hernández. The most-favored businessmen were Carlos Trouyet, Bruno Pagliai, Eloy Vallina, and Luis Aguilar. And the regional strongmen of the Alemán epoch were Lázaro Cárdenas (Michoacán), Manuel Ávila Camacho (Puebla), Abelardo Rodríguez (Sonora and Baja California Norte), Gen. Margarito Ramírez (Quintana Roo), Gen. Agustín Olachea (Baja California Sur), Gonzalo Santos (San Luis Potosí), and Gilberto Flores Muñoz (Nayarit).

Alemán's philosophy of labor contained overtones of Díaz and Carranza, and his philosophy of politics elements of *callismo*. Governmental defense of strikes was nonsense: The courts would settle labor disputes peacefully and in accord with the promotion of constructive relations with management. Company unions were protected, promoted, and given immunity from mandatory membership in a big central. Rapid industrialization, an Alemán fetish, required low wages and the sacrifice of the labor force to capital accumulation. Alemán insisted that Communists had no place inside or outside the labor movement. His intimate knowledge of Communists, acquired while holding the post of government minister under Ávila Camacho, was based on personally compiled biographical records of all labor and peasant leaders. Perhaps nobody in Mexico knew the Communists better than Alemán, and he maintained close surveillance over them. He also knew the reactionary rightists, who for more than a decade had been conspiring through the fascist-minded *sinarquistas*. Alemán took pleasure in canceling the legal registration of the *sinarquista* party in 1948. Organized labor, in the absence of Communist and *sinarquista* parties, could play politics inside the PRI, competing with *ejida-*

[1] Until 1948, when he resigned.
[2] Pérez Martínez died in office and was replaced by Adolfo Ruiz Cortines.

tarios and the popular sector for legislative posts leading to a regular monthly paycheck, or they could join forces with Lombardo Toledano's new opposition Popular Party.

Continuous protests from organized labor made no perceptible change in Alemán's philosophy or conduct. His own peculiar genius prevailed. Cárdenas and Ávila Camacho refused to intervene nationally. They suggested, encouraged, and urged, but never demanded; the final word was left to Alemán. To support organized labor, Alemán kept insisting, would split the Revolutionary Family and the government wide open. Without Cárdenas, the army, the bureaucrats, and dynamic union leadership, organized labor capitulated—and with them the *ejidatarios*, whom Alemán relegated to a back seat behind private agricultural interests. For Alemán, the sacrifice of a generation of workers and peasants was a small price for making his nation materially strong, industrialized, modernized, advanced. He ran roughshod over his redesigned official party. Effective suffrage lost all meaning. Alemán picked governors without the courtesy of consulting sector leaders and, except where regional strongmen controlled, without consideration of local sentiment. At least thirteen governors took office over the serious protests of responsible provincial leaders. Flagrant abuses of public opinion were involved in the seating of Gen. Raúl Gárate (Tamaulipas), Alejandro Gómez Maganda (Guerrero), Manuel Mayoral Heredia (Oaxaca), and Tomás Marentes Miranda (Yucatán). (Ruiz Cortines—Alemán's successor—removed the last three after assuming the presidency.) Revolutionary Creed objectives on political liberalism retrogressed.

Alemán's unbounded energy, matching that of Cárdenas, was injected into industrializing Mexico, whatever the costs. Production superseded consumption. Capital accumulation, forced savings, and foreign capital became the new gods. Agriculture was squeezed, driven harder, and crudely exploited to provide surpluses for export. The passage of hundreds of thousands of persons across the Rio Grande was stimulated—American tourists spending dollars in Mexico, and Mexican migrant farmhands remitting dollars earned in the United States. Mexicans with a high propensity to save and invest displaced their fellow countrymen with a high propensity to consume. Alemán somehow found the wherewithal to fulfill many of his dreams. Taxation, tariffs, foreign credits, and national savings bonds provided hundreds of millions of dollars. Meanwhile prices soared and denied the popular masses milk, meat, and fresh fruits—everything, in fact, but corn and beans. Conspicuous consumption by these new "Revolutionary Conservatives" and others exacerbated critical balance-of-payments problems. Alemán temporarily held back the rising tide of inflation by devaluation of the peso and enforcement of rent controls.

Alemán is frequently accused of selling out the national interest to capitalism. Although he favored private over communal agriculture, the accusation ignores the realities of what was the biggest public spending spree up to that moment in Mexican history. The building of roads, dams, ports, docks, and airfields, of universities, technical institutes, schools, and hospitals, and of government-owned and state-participating enterprises placed the public sector more firmly than ever in economic life. The government purchased the Mexican subsidiary of the Southern Pacific Railways; acquisition of new rolling stock and the extension of existing rail lines rejuvenated the national railways. Street railways were also modernized and extended. The government-owned petroleum industry (Pemex) seriously began the slow process of rebuilding, expanding, and modernizing the oil industry to provide Mexico with its petroleum and gas needs. The Federal Electricity Commission worked side by side with the ministries of hydraulic resources, communications and public works, and agriculture in expanding government activity (and ownership) in the electric-power field. The government-controlled steel mill, Altos Hornos, received huge sums to increase iron and steel output and improve the quality of its products. The government-controlled fertilizer company, Guanos y Fertilizantes, acquired new financing to step up production and reduce costly fertilizer imports. The National Lottery and the Social Security Institute employed their funds to construct hospitals, clinics, and playgrounds. Regional economic development projects rolled forward in the Tepalcatepec and Papaloapan basins. Modernization of Acapulco and the city of Veracruz became solid realities. Many new government commissions—stock exchange (1946), insurance (1946), corn (1946), etc.—were established. Cabinet ministries and government agencies moved into large new office buildings. New specialized government banks appeared. The role of the Central Development Bank (Nacional Financiera), was expanded to facilitate government equity participation in many nominally private enterprises; through this financial institution the state acquired minority ownership in scores of large companies. The central Bank of Mexico, National Bank of Foreign Commerce, and Nacional Financiera collaborated in attracting foreign loans. And, in collaboration with the United States, a nationwide campaign to eliminate hoof-and-mouth disease proved immeasurably successful, as did the joint Mexican government–Rockefeller Foundation project for improving seeds.

This grandiose program created new needs and new jobs. It led to the formation of a stockpile of public entrepreneurs, men who learned what it meant to direct and manage relatively big businesses. The public sector required an increasing number of competent technical and administrative personnel, a need Alemán attempted to fill by building a giant national university, a polytechnic institute, and regional universities, by sending civil servants abroad to acquire advanced instruction, and by bringing foreign specialists into government consultative posts. Meanwhile, the private sector was building its own crew of entrepreneurs. The vigor and dynamism of government policies imparted an upward thrust to private enterprise. Flight capital, both American and Mexican, entered from the United States. Large American and European corporations established Mexican operations. Alemán encouraged private investment not only by his vast public spending but also by setting up high protective tariffs, extending tax concessions, and by largely overlooking the 51 per cent Mexican-ownership formula. Foreign companies brought highly coveted entrepreneurial and technical skills, which shortly were transmitted to Mexican nationals. For the long haul, the Alemán regime provided the environment for the growth of a strong Mexican private capitalist class. Older businessmen, such as the Garza Sadas, the Legorretas, the Rochas, Raúl Bailleres, Carlos Trouyet, Antonio Ruiz Galindo, Carlos Prieto, and Pablo Díaz, expanded their operations, which in turn encouraged younger entrepreneurs. The truth of the matter, therefore, is that the Alemán regime gave birth to a dual class of socially conscious managers—some heading private companies, others in charge of government-owned enterprises.

By inviting both foreign and domestic investment to build Mexican industry and commerce, the Alemán economic policy brought quick rewards. Mining expanded, agriculture diversified, the sugar, cotton, and cacao industries grew, and commerce flourished. Foreign capital developed newly discovered sulfur deposits. Construction spurred the establishment of new cement plants, metallurgical enterprises, and the expansion of existing steel and cement concerns. The electrical appliance, chemical, pharmaceutical, paper, textiles, publishing, food canning, beer and carbonated beverage, radio and television, and shrimp industries rapidly expanded. Alemán, however distasteful his means and ways, succeeded in pushing the sustained growth of the Mexican economy.

Alemán furthered agriculture too, although in the process he substantially changed the nature of agrarian reform. At the beginning of his administration, in December, 1946, the Constitution was amended to legalize the program that he had in mind for agriculture. (In Mexico, large agricultural property is incompatible with agrarian politics, and therefore illegal.) Alemán's preference for the private farm over the communal *ejido* was acceptable in itself, but the Alemán amendment defining the size of "small" agricultural property evoked much criticism from political leaders, who pointed out that there were still millions of impoverished peasants without land. The reform of Article 27 of the Constitution defined small property as an agricultural holding not exceeding one hundred *hectáreas* (247 acres) of irrigated or otherwise choice land, or its equivalent. Its equivalent was twice the amount in temporal rainfall lands, four times the amount in relative drought lands, or eight times the amount in arid, mountainous lands. Of special importance were the specific provisions for lands dedicated to growing Mexico's choice crops: 370.5 acres of irrigated land were permitted for growing cotton, and 741 acres for raising bananas, sugar cane, coffee, henequen, olives, vanilla, cacao, rubber plants, and fruit trees. Alemán thus augmented the size of small properties in precisely the most remunerative crops. Dedicated agrarian reformers pointed out that legalizing 741 acres of choice land as a "small farm" to all intents and purposes ended the agrarian reform. Inasmuch as the minimum size of agricultural property was to be not less than ten *hectáreas* (24.7 acres) of irrigated land or its equivalent, land was allotted under two sets of standards: about 25 acres for a peon, and up to 741 acres for Alemán's friends. The new law also defined "small" stock-raising land as that necessary to maintain up to five hundred head of major stock or the equivalent in minor stock.

Thus, Alemán virtually neglected rural as well as urban labor. Yet his policy paid off in attracting new investments into agriculture and effectively breaking the long-time monopoly of a corn economy. The northwest zone (Sonora and Sinaloa) in particular became the breadbasket of the nation as well as a rich center of fruit and vegetable raising. The fundamental changes that Alemán brought into agriculture, which included large-scale irrigation (primarily for the new "small" farms), helped to solve Mexico's problem of food supply and to provide exports to pay for imports of capital goods and industrial raw materials. Simultaneously, it shifted the weighty political problem of how to satisfy the minimum needs of millions of poor peasants (with or without land) to subsequent administrations.

Alemán's undisputed leadership of the Revolutionary Family ended a year before he left the presidency. Forced savings, capital accumulation, and his new agricultural policy, plus inflation and conspicuous graft, had alienated the masses. Many others—such as private capitalists, middle-class professionals, and higher career civil servants—accepted and understood his economic policies, but condemned his personal conduct and that of his inner-circle intimates. Dedicated Revolutionaries everywhere deplored the conspicuous consumption, graft, and highhandedness of Alemán and his clique. Many governors, probably most governors, experienced the same lack of popular support. In late 1951, Alemán went through the motions of soliciting opinions of Cárdenas, Ávila Camacho, national and state political leaders, and certain interest-group representatives on the big question of who should succeed him, then privately announced that the "consensus" of opinion favored Fernando Casas Alemán, erstwhile governor of the Federal District who symbolized many undesirable features of Alemán's rule and who was identified as a clericalist. At this point, Cárdenas and Ávila Camacho forcefully stepped back into Revolutionary Family leadership. Toppling Alemán required the firm action of these two senior members of the inner circle, since by now the

Family had split into *cardenistas, avilacamachistas,* and *alemanistas,* plus marginal factions of *carrancistas, obregonistas, callistas,* and *portesgilistas.*

Meeting the crisis was uppermost. If Cárdenas had openly broken with Alemán, he probably could have counted on the support of a majority of the nation's teachers, soldiers, trade unionists, civil servants, and *ejidatarios.* On the other hand, Alemán probably could have found strong backing from many bankers, industrialists, merchants, foreign capitalists, and "small" farmers. Through a process of back-scratching and log-rolling that involved former presidents, military men, regional strongmen, and other individuals, a modus vivendi emerged: Alemán would remain president (long live constitutionalism); all factions, including the *alemanistas,* would lend support to the candidacy of Adolfo Ruiz Cortines, a noncontroversial career civil servant; the major economic programs of the Alemán administration would continue into the new regime; and the masses would receive greater attention.

THE EPOCH OF THE TWO ADOLFOS

Adolfo Ruiz Cortines. The price of upholding constitutionalism and permitting Alemán to finish his term was high. Some top officials and Alemán himself, grasping the sad truth that the concluding months of his term provided them the last opportunity to become rich at public expense, ran wild with public treasuries. Contrary to the expectations of Ruiz Cortines and anti-*alemanistas,* Alemán preserved a relatively tight hold on political machinery and prevented the kind of dynamic campaign that had introduced his own administration. Thus on election day Ruiz Cortines encountered strong popular opposition in the candidacies of Gen. Miguel Henríquez Guzmán (favorite of the *ejidatarios* and miners), Vicente Lombardo Toledano (former CTM boss who ran as an independent leftist), and Efrain González Luna (candidate of the traditional conservatives). Even the official ballot tally conceded the opposition almost one-fourth of all votes cast. On entering office, then, Ruiz Cortines enjoyed few assets comparable to Alemán's advantages six years earlier, and in addition faced the prospect of running the government under a divided Revolutionary Family.

Adolfo Ruiz Cortines inherited a disrupted machine under adverse circumstances. Dissension was rampant: *alemanistas* versus *cardenistas; ejidatarios* versus "small" farmers; trade unionists versus businessmen; public ownership versus private enterprise; industry versus agriculture; the people versus state governors. In addition, he inherited inflation, corruption, an empty government treasury, unfinished giant public works, balance-of-payments problems, and an amorphous Family leadership. Adolfo Ruiz Cortines combated this adversity with the weapons he possessed: stamina, intelligence, integrity, patience, and political acumen. The new

President of Mexico slowly yet surely governed his way into leadership of the Revolutionary Family. In the process, he became a statesman.

National expectations for a competent, honorable administration capable of restoring dignity to Mexican government were raised by the cabinet Ruiz Cortines selected to guide public affairs. Industrious career bureaucrats filled several posts: Antonio Carrillo Flores (finance), Luis Padilla Nervo (foreign affairs), Gilberto Loyo (national economy), Ernesto Uruchurtu (Federal District), Adolfo López Mateos (labor), José López Lira (national properties), Ángel Carvajal (government), and generals Rodolfo Sánchez Taboada (marine) and Matias Ramos Santos (national defense). Two *cardenistas*, Eduardo Chávez and Castulo Villaseñor, took charge of hydraulic resources and agrarian affairs, respectively. José Ángel Ceniceros, a *portesgilista*, became minister of education. Dr. Ignacio Morones Prieto, an Alemán designate for the governorship of Nuevo León, resigned this position to head the ministry of health; the popular, energetic architect of University City, Carlos Lazo, was rewarded with the ministry of communications and public works; and the regional strongman, Gilberto Flores Muñoz, became agriculture minister. The always important presidential secretaryship went to Benito Coquet. Backing up the first team were Antonio Ortiz Mena (Social Security Institute), Rodrigo Gómez (Bank of Mexico), Ricardo Zevada (National Bank of Foreign Commerce), José Hernández Delgado (Nacional Financiera), Pascual Gutiérrez Roldán (Altos Hornos), Raúl Salinas (National Investment Commission), and Roberto Amorós (national railways). General Gabriel Leyva Velázquez, the son of an early martyr of the Revolution, moved into the presidency of the PRI. Ruiz Cortines' administrators were on the whole moderate, patriotic, honest, and intelligent—men much like the president himself.

Once these implementors of policy assumed office, the new president concentrated on policy itself. Of highest priority were economic matters. To place the national treasury back on its feet, no mean task in itself, and to inject confidence and dynamism into the economy, Ruiz Cortines undertook the completion of Alemán's worthy public projects: roads, dams, airfields, bridges, superhighways, ports and docks, electric-power installations, University City and other schools, public housing developments, the regional complexes of the Tepalcatepec and Papaloapan basins, public buildings, streets, and public markets. The government-owned railroads, oil industry, electricity commission, and street railways as well as the state-controlled steel mills, fertilizer plants, textile mills, and the railroad rolling-stock factory passed into improved management that consolidated, modernized, and expanded these concerns. The new administration emphasized "balanced" economic growth that contributed to resolving the political issue of industry (*alemanistas*) versus agriculture (*cardenistas*); Mexico obviously needed both industry and agriculture, plus a good number of other economic components. The "march to the sea" program (fish for food and fertilizer, emigration to coastal regions, and development of fluvial transportation) pushed forward. Slum clearance, state distribution of basic commodities to the poor, and the construction of public markets, water and sewerage systems, playgrounds, slaughterhouses, schools, clinics, and hospitals continued. As Alemán had favored Acapulco, Ruiz Cortines loved Mexico City, and he instructed Federal District Governor Ernesto Uruchurtu to transform the capital into a modern, beautiful metropolis. Governmental emphasis on industrial decentralization (encouraging factories to locate outside metropolitan Mexico City and Monterrey) resulted in important new industries situating in Ciudad Chihuahua, Guadalajara, Morelia, Orizaba, Querétaro, Salamanca, Toluca, and Torreón. Water, gas, and oil pipelines stretched across the nation. Cities, towns, and villages all over the country formed local committees on moral, civic, and material betterment for purposes of appraising municipal needs and doing something about filling them. Special public works authorities concentrated on improving the principal border and coastal towns. Public buildings continued apace.

Meanwhile, the debate on extending public ownership into new industries was momentarily tabled. This does not mean that existing state-owned enterprises did not expand; on the contrary, virtually all of them did precisely that. Notable exceptions were the failures of the government-controlled Diesel Nacional (an automobile assembly plant, then in league with Fiat of Italy) and Toyoda (a textile-machinery manufacturer using Japanese patents). Tuxtepec Paper Mills, another state promotion, succeeded in manufacturing newsprint for the first time in Mexico, and other state-owned businesses opened in the meat packing and canning, fertilizer, insecticide, and petrochemical industries. When the specialized steel manufacturer Acero Ecatepec went into bankruptcy, the state assumed ownership of it; the government also took a majority equity in La Consolidada steel mills by purchasing stock from some of its owners. Thus, while tabling the debate on ownership of the means of production being carried on between CONCAMIN and CONCANACO on the one hand and the Mexican government on the other, Ruiz Cortines quietly added new industries to the public domain.

Yet the private-business sector had an abundance of opportunities of its own. Private enterprise flourished. Foreign capital poured into Mexico—flight capital, corporation funds, government and private bank loans, tourist dollars, *bracero* remittances, and promotion capital of all sorts. Most concerns, foreign and Mexican alike, reinvested a substantial share of their earnings. But aside from the workers in the Monterrey industrial complex, those in the Ruiz Galindo industries outside Mexico City, and those employed by a few other industrialists who gave real content to "fringe benefits," workers in Mexican factories lost much of whatever wage increases they received to inflation. The big companies grew and, joined by thousands of new firms, pushed industry and commerce upward, notably so in the construction and construction material, synthetic textile, chemical, pharmaceutical, auto assembly and parts manufacture, food canning and beverage, office equipment and furniture, home appliance, and electronics industries, and in real estate, merchandising, and transport. Mining as a whole lagged behind, but copper, manganese, and nonmetallic minerals, notably sulfur, prospered.

In agriculture, the Ruiz Cortines administration emphasized "agricultural reform" instead of the traditional "agrarian reform." Land redistribution continued at about the same annual pace as the earlier Ávila Camacho and Alemán governments, with use of the land accented instead of mere ownership of land. Many communal farmers profited for the first time from irrigation, insecticides, fertilizers, farm machinery, and better seeds, financed directly by the central government or made available through agricultural credit banks. Crop rotation and diversification programs helped alleviate the ageless problem of a "corn economy." Purified water, beer, and carbonated beverages effected a telling blow on agriculturalists growing maguey (the plant from which the intoxicating pulque is made). But agrarian politicians kept asserting that there was little relief for several million peasants with insufficient land or with none at all. (It is quite possible that the landless peasants, though relatively poorly fed by modern standards, are not quite so unhappy as many politicians indicate.)

Five shocks hit Mexico during the Ruiz Cortines administration. The first, in 1953, was the granting of universal adult suffrage, which forced many males to swallow a good deal of traditional pride by permitting women the right to vote in all federal, gubernatorial, and local elections. Woman suffrage in federal elections (some states had permitted women to vote in local elections for some decades) was first exercised in the gubernatorial contest in the new state of Baja California, which became the twenty-ninth state of the Mexican union in 1953. A second shock occurred the following year with the devaluation of the peso (making it worth eight cents in U.S. currency), an action only partially and temporarily successful in retaining inflation; prices soon outstripped wages, leaving the popular masses worse off than before. The third and fourth shocks were physical. The third came in 1957: a major earthquake that caused heavy property damage, particularly in the coastal state of Guerrero and in Mexico City. The fourth, in 1958, was a series of hurricanes that lashed eastern and western coastal towns, destroying property and claiming lives. The final shock—really a series of shocks occurring at different times—was caused by the death notices of some outstanding Revolutionaries: Manuel Ávila Camacho, Francisco Múgica, Carlos Lazo, Luis Cabrera, Rodolfo Sánchez Taboada, and Diego Rivera.

Besides developments in the economic sphere, Ruiz Cortines advanced other planks in the Revolutionary Creed: those on racial and religious tolerance, constitutionalism, Mexicanism, education, a share in regional leadership, and internationalism. Against the background of adverse Family politics, Ruiz Cortines slowly reunited the Family by placing himself between *alemanistas* and *cardenistas*. In the process he appointed moderates, neither *alemanistas* nor *cardenistas*, to governorships, and he approved nominally nonpolitical appointments for other public posts. Unlike the older groups, the *ruizcortinistas* played down personalism. Their raison d'être was to be a buffer between the right (*alemanistas*) and the left (*cardenistas*). It was in this sense that Adolfo Ruiz Cortines "governed" his way into Revolutionary Family leadership, a position he achieved by early 1954.

Backed by the central moderates, who appealed to reason and fair play, Ruiz Cortines moved into the big game of Family politics. He had earlier informed Gen. Leyva Velázquez, president of the official party, that the soft-spoken novelist and professor Agustín Yáñez, and not the front-running *cardenista* or *alemanista*, would be the PRI's candidate for the governorship of Jalisco. He outlawed the party of Gen. Henríquez Guzmán, whose nominally *cardenista* and Trotskyite followers had been persistently agitating since election day in 1952. He informed *alemanistas* who had pilfered the public treasury that exchanging any more of their "investments" into dollars for purposes of taking capital out of Mexico would prove extremely unwise; this capital was to remain in Mexico and contribute to economic development. He openly challenged Alemán by having the *alemanista* governors of Oaxaca, Yucatán, and Guerrero removed from office, replacing them with his own men. Aside from a few elections, he delicately handled gubernatorial nominations with PRI sector leaders, particularly those of the popular sector, and with state organizations and regional strongmen. He cleared political matters concerning key states where authority of regional strongmen prevailed with Gonzalo Santos in San Luis Potosí, Abelardo Rodríguez in Baja California, Leobardo Reynoso in Zacatecas, Gilberto Flores Muñoz in Nayarit, the Ávila Camacho family in Puebla, and Lázaro Cárdenas in Michoacán. By the time he turned over the reins of power to Adolfo López Mateos in 1958, Adolfo Ruiz Cortines had forged a third force in the Revolutionary Family.

The first Adolfo deserves a high place among Revolutionary strategists. He not only survived the crisis of 1951–54 but introduced a new type of relationship between the administration and the Revolutionary Family —one in which a president had to earn leadership, placing respect above iron rule. Whether Mexican political life was ready for this kind of direction appears dubious, not the least because politicians regard the leader who refuses to make, apply, and interpret the law as weak, incapable, and inviting danger. Ruiz Cortines succeeded partly because circumstances forced him to do so, and partly because he placed such a high premium on honesty, intelligence, and moderation. The day-by-day politician—and Mexico needs them, too—thrives on other qualities. In the quarrel over industry versus agriculture Ruiz Cortines pacified all except the *ejidatarios*, the farmers working very small plots, and the landless—which collectively represented rather crucial exceptions. On the production versus consumption issue he sided with the *alemanistas*. Living standards of the masses were to be improved less through direct pay raises than through "fringe benefits"—social security, clinics, job security, education, and distribution of basic necessities at low prices. His posture on Communism amounted to a policy of watchful waiting. All considered, Ruiz Cortines gave Mexico an indispensable breathing spell and seated moderates on the powder keg filled with *alemanistas* and *cardenistas*. To his successor, the second Adolfo, fell the responsibility of defining and firmly establishing the political public of the center, or else losing the battle of policies and personalities to Alemán, to Cárdenas, or to both.

Choosing a successor to govern the nation from December 1, 1958, to November 30, 1964, devolved in the first instance on Ruiz Cortines. The "consensus" of Revolutionary greats, according to Ruiz Cortines, sustained none of the four precandidates: the professional politician, Nayarit strongman, and incumbent agriculture minister, Gilberto Flores Muñoz, whose nomination would have represented a victory for Cardenism; the career civil servant, intellectual, and finance minister, Antonio Carrillo Flores, who favored foreign capital and industrialization—in other words, Alemanism; the moderate, career bureaucrat, and government minister, Ángel Carvajal; and the Federal District governor, one of the foremost public administrators in Mexico, Ernesto Uruchurtu. Overlooking the four of them, Ruiz Cortines announced to the inner circle of the Revolutionary Family that the "consensus" of opinion really centered on his young minister of labor, Adolfo López Mateos, sometime professor, college rector, secretary-general of the PRI, legislator, lawyer, and labor arbitrator. Ruiz Cortines prevailed, and unions affiliated with the official party jumped on the band wagon by announcing the candidacy as their very own. On his part, Ruiz Cortines assisted his young disciple in every way possible, convincing three "opposition" parties—the independent leftist Popular Party of Lombardo Toledano, the Authentic Party of the Mexican Revolution headed by the old Carranza-ite Gen. Jacinto Treviño, and the moderate rightist Mexican Nationalist Party—to join forces with the official party in support of the López candidacy. The organized legal opposition, mild as it was, came only from Luis H. Álvarez, candidate of the traditional conservatives in the National Action Party. Of the 7.5 million votes cast, the ministry of government reported that López Mateos was given an overwhelming 90 per cent.

Adolfo López Mateos.   The mandate of López Mateos was not so clear as his popularity, however. All sectors of Mexican society—except the Communists, whose agitation temporarily went unchecked—sat back from election day in July until his inauguration in order to discover what philosophy he would inject into public policy. The general public found little indication of just what his six-year regime would bring from his appointment of cabinet ministers. The new ministry was highlighted by young, intellectual, professionally minded holdovers of the Ruiz Cortines regime. With high popular acclaim, Ernesto Uruchurtu remained Federal District governor; Jaime Torres Bodet was recalled from diplomatic assignment to become education minister; and Manuel Tello returned from his ambassadorship in Washington to take charge of foreign affairs. Streamlining the administrative setup of the executive branch shortly after he entered office, López Mateos created a Ministry of the Presidency; enlarged the functions of the old national properties ministry and gave it the new title of National Patrimony Ministry; split up the old communications and public works ministry to form a separate Ministry of Communications and Transport and a Ministry of Public Works; changed the name of the old national economy ministry to Ministry of Industry and Commerce, enlarging its functions in the process; raised the tourism bureau to the status of autonomous department; and suggested new frontiers for the old agrarian department by renaming it the Agrarian and Colonization Department. Walter Buchanan was promoted to head the new communications and transport ministry, and Javier Barros Sierra became minister of public works. The former undersecretary of labor, Salomón Blanco, moved upstairs to succeed his former chief, now in the presidency. Antonio Ortiz Mena moved from the Social Security Institute to the finance ministership, Raúl Salinas from the national investment commission to the new industry and commerce ministership, and Gen. Agustín Olachea from PRI presidency to national defense ministership. The top-level government bank direction continued untouched—Rodrigo Gómez at the Bank of Mexico, José Hernández Delgado at Nacional Financiera, and Ricardo Zevada at the National Bank of Foreign Commerce. Ruiz Cortines' former presidential secretary, Benito Coquet, took charge of the Social Security Institute, while Donato Mirando Fonseca became the first head of the ministry of the presidency. Four highly qualified individuals were placed in charge of the ministries of government (Gustavo Díaz Ordaz), agriculture (Julian Rodríguez Adame), national patrimony (Eduardo Bustamante), and hydraulic resources (Alfredo del Mazo). Fernando López Arias became attorney general. The navy ministry went to an admiral and the health ministry to a medical doctor. The final posts of top influence were given to Pascual Gutiérrez Roldán (Pemex), Gen. Alfonso Corona del Rosal (PRI presidency), and to Manuel Moreno Sánchez (leadership of the legislature).

The López Mateos administration provided no neat classifications, no ironclad definition of the Revolutionary center that was begun by Ruiz Cortines.

Policy had to be made in a complicated context: After twenty years of being sacrificed to capital accumulation, organized labor and the *ejidatarios* wanted higher real wages, a bigger share of national income. Under the new pacifist line from Moscow, which some Revolutionaries contended coincided with Mexican national interest, the Communist sector was agitating for reforms, "functional democracy," and closer relations with Castro's Cuba. Direct foreign investment, fearful of a Castro repeat in Mexico, dwindled to a trickle, then slowly reappeared. Catholic Action groups resurged against the "outrages of Communism," particularly in the states of Guanajuato, Jalisco, and Puebla. Student politics became a major problem, sometimes because of its pro-Communist, pro-Castro, anti-American appeals, other times because of its anti-Communist, pro–Catholic Church, and anti–"atheistic" education appeals. Young army officers were pressing for more pay and benefits. The official party fell under constant fire for being little more than an empty shell in which the true desires of the rank-and-file Mexican found virtually no expression. Private business sought assurances that the administration would not swing to the left, that private investment would appear sound, and that state socialism would, at its worst, only creep forward. Several million landless or otherwise impoverished peasants were listening to political demagogues telling them that they deserved more from life than the prospect of having their names drawn from a hat to determine whether they would cross the Rio Grande as migratory laborers. The indispensability of setting up a comprehensive petrochemical industry was recognized by Revolutionary elite; yet there was disagreement on who should own the many plants still required and, if they were to be government-owned, where would it obtain the capital investment to transform this urgent need into reality. Finally, the nation was placed in a quandary over American foreign policy and Cuban developments.

Faced by these problems, Adolfo López Mateos emphasized Mexicanism. He consecutively purged the teachers' union of Communist leadership, firing the militant Othón Salazar who directed the secondary-school syndicate; jailed the number-one Communist leader in the railroad workers' union, Demetrio Vallejo; suppressed Communist-inspired riots among normal school and university students; and, in 1960, imprisoned David Siqueiros, long-time Communist and internationally known muralist and painter, when he forgot that Mexico comes before Moscow. López Mateos' policy on Cuba, an extremely delicate subject in view of Cárdenas' generally sympathetic attitude toward Castro, incorporated his conviction that no revolution in the hemisphere should surge ahead of or surplant the Mexican Revolution. U.S. indecisiveness frequently complicated the formulation of Mexican foreign policy, although Washington's transfer of hundreds of thousands of tons of sugar from the Cuban quota to the Mexican quota made few Mexicans unhappy. Finally, overaggressiveness on the part of Communist elements in the relatively wealthy electrical workers' unions, though by no means the principal reason, led to López Mateos' nationalization of the electric-power industry.

A public resurgence of Lázaro Cárdenas, with or without its Communist overtones, appeared to challenge the President of Mexico's power and policy. Cárdenas initiated an open propaganda campaign designed to influence the general public into demanding that Mexico side with Castro and adopt the over-all policy of the Revolutionary left faction that he headed, including nationalization of certain economic activities and an increase in the real wages of labor. López Mateos countered this apparent challenge by announcing that his administration was pursuing a policy not merely of "the left" but, within constitutional bounds, of "extreme left." This apparent attempt to take some of the wind out of Cárdenas' sails accomplished the desired ends of keeping Mexico on relatively friendly terms with the United States, restraining Mexico from taking any rash action on Cuba and, in general, restoring faith in Mexican institutions. It also permitted López Mateos to shift official policy to the left under the pretext of countering Cardenism.

Mexico opposed resolutions sponsored by Washington to oust Castro Cuba from inter-American regional organizations, although she did condemn the presence of Marxism-Leninism in the hemisphere. López Mateos set a record for meetings of a Mexican chief of state with presidents of the United States, holding three with Dwight D. Eisenhower, one with John F. Kennedy, and one with Lyndon B. Johnson. Ticklish electoral problems in Sonora and San Luis Potosí resulted in bloodshed and accusations of presidential imposition of gubernatorial candidates. Unpopular state government in Guerrero also led to bloodshed, causing the removal of the incumbent governor and designation of a substitute. The assassination of peasant leader Jaramillo and his family in the state of Morelos shocked the agrarian elements. And the appearance of Revolutionary extremist organizations reflecting domestic and foreign-policy cleavages influenced López Mateos' decision to appoint seven ex-Presidents of Mexico to formal government positions.

When the second Adolfo took office, all political publics had speculated on whether state ownership would be extended. (A substantial sector of economic activity was already in public hands.) The new president asserted that performance and output of all major plants was most important, and that as long as private enterprises delivered the goods and re-invested earnings when the market justified expansion, his administration would have no reason to intervene. In June, 1962, the presidential office published a list of five hundred new industrial promotions desired before 1965, inviting private capital to participate.

In the case of the electric-power industry, which at the time López Mateos entered office was about 70 per cent privately owned and the rest totally government owned and managed, controversies over rates and re-investment of earnings had colored government–private power relations off and on since 1926. In 1960, therefore, when Electric Bond & Share's foreign holding company, American & Foreign Power, approached the president with an offer to sell its Mexican holdings to the government, there was nothing particularly "Communistic" in his accepting the offer. Purchasing the electric-power holdings in private hands meant an end to frictions with an important foreign investor and, furthermore, brought the pro-Communist unions controlling electrical workers under direct government control. On its part, American & Foreign Power drove a hard bargain— perhaps, in light of impartial accountings of what they had invested, too hard a bargain. At any rate, this particular American company has made no public complaint: They offered their company for sale at a handsome price, and the Mexican government accepted. Purchase of another major power concern, the Mexican Light and Power Company of Sofina of Belgium and of Canadian and American investors, was transacted a short time later through stock purchase by the government. By the end of 1961, after the government had acquired some smaller companies, public owner-ship, which Cárdenas had begun more than two decades earlier with the creation of the Federal Electricity Commission, was complete, and electric power was a state-owned and state-operated enterprise. If American private enterprises in Mexico were worried by the government purchase of the electric-power industry, they might have advised their parent corporations in the United States to pay closer attention to what their banks and in-surance agents were doing, for it was loans made by Prudential Insurance Company and other U.S. financial institutions to the Mexican industrial development bank that helped make possible the purchase of electric companies.

Control of another major industry, motion-picture distribution and exhibition, also passed from the private sector into public hands. Purchased were two companies—both controlled by the long-resident American multi-millionaire, William Jenkins—which for years had wielded a virtual mo-nopoly in determining which pictures would play in their affiliated Mexi-can theaters. This sector of commercial activity had been pinpointed as early as 1944 as one in which foreigners should not have majority control. Involved in the state's decision to purchase was its desire to keep theater prices low, regardless of overhead, and to exhibit more Mexican-made films.

The giant foreign petroleum companies were dismayed when López Mateos announced that 18 of the 21 largest petrochemical complexes being planned would be state-owned and state-managed. Mexicans will retain a majority equity in the other three petrochemical plants. The second largest private mining complex in Mexico, that owned by American Metal Climax, sold much of its equity to private Mexican investors.

Automobile assembly was seriously affected by a presidential decree that raised duties on eight-cylinder cars and lowered duties on four-cylinder automobiles. López Mateos wanted to lower prices on the cheaper models in order to permit more Mexicans to become car-owners and, at the same time, to price luxury models out of the market. The president later informed assemblers that they must decide once and for all to manufacture in Mexico or lose their markets by default. Eight assemblers received government approval on this basis. Private meat packers and canners complained when the state-owned Industrial de Abastos plant began placing its products on the market, but the superb quality of its cold meats and canned foods met no objections from the Mexican consumer. Also bearing on industrial ownership were the enlarged activities of ANDSA (the governmental builder and operator of warehouses), CONASUPO (the state agency distributing basic commodities at reduced prices), and Pemex (petroleum industry). Pemex undertook the building of new pipelines carrying oil or natural gas, of expanding exploration and drilling operations, and of constructing additional petrochemical plants.

In the agricultural sphere, López Mateos accelerated land redistribution so much that only the Cárdenas government, of all preceding regimes, surpassed his performance on this count. He paid relatively close attention to making the size of plot economical, emphasizing small private farms over communal *ejidos*. Much of the land distributed, however, was not of high quality: There simply is insufficient expropriable good land left. Largely for this reason, the López Mateos regime began pushing the opening of new lands in the Grijalva River basin and Quintana Roo territory. To reduce the politics and graft long characteristic of agricultural banks, the president consolidated the small-farm and communal-farm banks under one director and simultaneously decentralized agricultural credit at state and local levels.

López Mateos left his imprint on other activities. He attacked the inflationary spiral at several points, enlarged the distribution of basic commodities at reduced prices, made a concerted effort to collect taxes, obtained new legislation to prevent interest rates from rising, retired old external debts, and paid other foreign indebtedness promptly. He sponsored a constitutional amendment ordering the participation of labor in business profits. He reached a settlement with Washington on the century-old "Chamizal" boundary dispute between the United States and Mexico, as well as a consensus on distribution of waters of the lower Colorado

River. He inaugurated the long-dreamed-of railway line linking Chihuahua with the Pacific. He put into effect a comprehensive eleven-year plan for expanding Mexico's educational facilities. He encouraged closer ties with the rest of Latin America, sponsoring Mexican participation in the Latin American Free Trade Area. He initiated a multimillion-dollar cleanup campaign of cities on the U.S.–Mexican border. He directed his government to purchase two Mexican airlines. And he stimulated the formation of stronger regional economies in the Balsas and Grijalva river basins and in the Ciudad Sahagún, Torreón, and Irapuato areas. The first President of Mexico to enjoy a billion-dollar annual government budget, López Mateos employed this increased public revenue in so many projects that economists were asking how he managed to accomplish so much.

A big part of the answer is furnished by national development planning and substantial financial assistance from abroad. In December, 1958, the new ministry of the presidency assumed direction of "planning and execution of programs leading to the economic and social development of the nation." By late 1962, Mexico had formulated a comprehensive three-year "immediate action plan" for economic and social development in 1963–65. An intragovernmental commission appointed in March, 1962, was assigned the task of preparing a development plan for 1965–70 by projecting policies and programs in Mexico's immediate action plan. But attempts at implementation encountered such disarray in the vast empire of state enterprises that in December, 1962, López Mateos decreed a new law designed to centralize financing of all state enterprises. Planning also signaled the need for extensive foreign assistance in order to finance state investments beyond the hundreds of millions of dollars supplied the López Mateos government by outside financial sources. In July, 1963, Mexico offered its first government dollar bonds in the United States market since the days of Porfirio Díaz. The combination of development planning and dollar bonds restored memories of Díaz's measures in implementing his scientific policy of "order and progress."

The successors of the second Adolfo will surely confront many crises. As his immediate successor for the 6-year presidential term beginning December 1, 1964, López Mateos selected his minister of government, Gustavo Díaz Ordaz, to become the candidate of Mexico's official party. No projection of probable new directions can ignore the composition of the several Mexican publics, the detailed political apparatus in the hands of the "liberal Machiavellian," and the nature and force of religion in Mexico. The next three chapters are concerned with these themes.

FIVE

THE MEXICAN PUBLICS

Not all Mexicans accept their present lot or agree on the shape their society should assume in the future. Although the hard core of most interest groups probably respects the essence of the Revolutionary Creed, interest-group leadership and rank-and-file membership often divide on objective implementation. Moreover, some interest groups—leadership and rank and file alike—openly reject certain planks in the Revolutionary Creed and disagree with Revolutionary Family preferences on public policy. It is this departure from conformity and uniformity, compounded by the absence of reliable measuring rods of public opinion, that makes analyses of the Mexican Revolution elusive. The public is not united, despite the claim that a majority of Mexican voters belong to the official political party, one organ among several charged with carrying out the directives of the head of the Revolutionary Family and regional and local political bosses.

Extensive conversations with politicians and interest-group leaders, first-hand observations of political rallies and elections, a study of statutes and action programs, and a perusal of the files of several political groups, plus a decade of reading Mexico's daily newspapers and of carrying on a dialogue with Mexicans from many walks of life has provided strong evidence that Mexico is divided into several political publics that entertain distinct views of the role of government in economic activity, foreign policy, religious and educational matters, and political life itself. A slight swing in the political pendulum caused by one of many domestic and external forces brings one political public into prominence and obscures another. To grasp where Mexico is today and where it might be tomorrow, we should understand the ideologies and composition of these publics, which may be categorized as the Radical Left, the Independent Left, the Traditional Conservatives, the Reactionary Conservatives, and the Revolutionary Publics—Left, Right, and Center.

THE RADICAL LEFT

The Radical Left of Mexican society houses the anarchists, the Communists, and the Trotskyites. All three drew their original inspiration from foreign sources. All share the belief that present society should be replaced by another. All are likely to employ violence as a means to their goal of seizing government. And all three put forth the class struggle and the inevitable downfall of capitalism as their unique interpretations of history. But here similarities end.

1. *Anarchists.* The first faction dates back in Mexico to the turn of the century. Led by the clique that centered around the Flores Magón brothers and the Mexican Liberal Party formed in 1906, even though the anarchist program of Ricardo Flores Magón was not fully evolved and proclaimed until 1911, the anarchists preached violent overthrow of the triumvirate of Díaz dictatorship, capitalism, and foreign property. The anarchists' creed of direct action by workers was embodied in their slogan, "Union unites, politics divides." By 1912, the dominant strain of anarchism—inspired by the example and urged onward by the actual assistance of the radical wing of American labor, the IWW—united to form an anarcho-syndicalist union. This labor central, the House of the World Worker (*Casa del Obrero Mundial*), constituted the first truly national syndicalist grouping ever organized in Mexico. Its strategy and tactics, which rested squarely on giving government no quarter, swung a full 180 degrees in 1915 when, facing the exigencies of civil war, the Casa joined the Revolutionary chieftain Venustiano Carranza and placed under his command several "Red battalions" of workers. The price for these contingents was a promise that the Casa would receive most-favored union status, including labor organization privileges in zones controlled by the Constitutionalists, and that the post-Revolutionary government would incorporate into basic law provisions guaranteeing to labor a legal identity and the right to organize and bargain collectively. Although legal recognition of labor became part and parcel of the Constitution of 1917, the Casa itself became lost somewhere along the wayside. This neglect, compounded by the official favor bestowed on a rival union, drove Casa leadership back to rugged anarcho-syndicalism, then into an ideologically incongruous alliance with Third International Communists. From the factious squabbles between anarcho-syndicalists and Communists emerged the successor to the Casa, the General Confederation of Labor (*Confederación General de Trabajadores*, or CGT), founded in 1921 and soon to become firmly anti-Communist. Rough treatment from its officially-backed rival as well as from the Mexican government directly strengthened CGT preference for aloofness from politics.

The decade 1918–28, which witnessed the sad consequences of tying a labor movement inextricably to the government, was followed by seven years of relatively high popularity for syndico-anarchism, within an overall environment of labor repression. From 1935, when the CGT first formally joined forces with government and other trade unions to form a mighty popular force, to the present day, the CGT has found itself in the rather schizophrenic position of preaching a qualified sort of syndico-anarchism while retaining membership in the government's official political party. Anarchism as a political public ideology in Mexico is syndico-anarchism centering on the CGT. Its continuing importance for the Mexican labor movement is found in its ambivalent pleas for an independent labor movement, free of government domination.

2. *Communists.* The Communists are the only truly militant, disciplined, and financially strong faction in the Radical Left. Nothing would serve their purposes better than oversimplification and exaggeration of Communist strength by lumping all groups left of center into the Red camp. If the Left were in fact united, there is little likelihood that the Mexican economic system would adopt the Communist policy of abolition of private enterprise. The truth of the matter is that responsibility for driving Mexican labor into a less militant grouping rests squarely upon the Communists.

Communists, unless indicated otherwise, are persons who follow the dictates of Soviet-export Communism, who blindly subordinate patriotism to obedience to orders from Moscow. Their inflexibility indicates the discipline of their organizations—a quality the Kremlin can utilize. From the outset of Comintern agitation in Mexico, which can be dated to 1919, the inflexible, rigid, unwavering loyalty demanded by the Soviet overlords has provoked many intraparty squabbles that frequently provoked resignations from and denunciation of Communist organs in Mexico.

As hopes for rapid social revolution gave way in the mid-1920's to a policy of infiltration and cautious agitation, Mexican liberals early felt the impact of the true nature of Communism. The incompatibility of Red designs and Mexican social nationalism did much to vitiate legitimate Mexican radicalism. Since the first rupture of diplomatic relations with Communist Russia in 1930 (relations were not renewed until 1942), Mexico has experienced five distinct phases of Communist strategy: (1) agitation, extremism, and isolation, until mid-1934; (2) popular front, until the Hitler-Stalin pact of 1939; (3) alignment with profascist forces and condemnation of the democracies, until Germany's attack on Russia in June, 1941; (4) suspension of anticapitalist attacks and support of pro-Allied parties and governments, until 1946; and, since 1946, (5) renewed attacks on capitalism, support of the U.S.S.R. in the Cold War, cautious agitation, and arousal of intense nationalism. How, in the face of such policy gymnastics, thousands of Mexicans held Communist memberships remains a mystery.

Communist appeals since the advent of the Cold War have centered on the themes of defense of the national economy before imperialism, abuse of Mexican aspiration to support the Cold War designs of the United States, the high cost of living, worker ownership of the means of production, and agrarian reform. Finding themselves outside the mainstream of the Mexican labor movement, which since 1939 has advocated the Communist heresy of business unionism, the Communists have attacked low wages, low living standards, labor leadership sellout to the bourgeoisie, and government vacillation on land reform. These appeals naturally held attraction for the urban proletariat and for the several million peasant families still without land.

For decades, Communist strategy in Mexico has centered on the peasantry and agrarian reform. "Agrarian reform," in Communist semantics, has usually meant confiscation rather than expropriation and repartition of private farms in order to extend the pattern of the collective-type *ejidal* farms. Today, the Communists assail the Mexican government for its "surrender to private capital" in permitting private farms to exist and its "betrayal of the needs of rural Mexico." Communist strength in rural Mexico centers in the large collective farms of the Laguna region—which is the home of Dionisio Encinas, Communist party boss since 1940—and in smaller *ejidos* located elsewhere.

City life is also subject to Communist disturbances, provoked by powerful cliques in important sectors of Mexican life. At the top of the list are trade union elements, headed by the UGOCM (General Union of Mexican Workers and Peasants) and the CTAL (the pro-Communist labor central for Latin America). It appears that the CTAL was superseded by the new hemispheric trade union organization set up at the congress of delegates of CTAL affiliates in Latin America and of delegates from Communist countries, held at Brasilia, Brazil, in late January 1964. Given the name *Confederación Única de Trabajadores de América Latina* (CUTAL), the new organization will establish its headquarters in Santiago, Chile. From time to time, Moscow-inspired extremism erupts in significant sections and locals of the railroad and petroleum workers' unions, the actors' and motion-picture workers' unions, the telephone workers' union, and electrical workers' unions. These union elements have their counterparts in certain student federations, especially at the National University, the National Polytechnical Institute, and the national normal school, in provincial normal schools, and in several sections of the teachers' federation. Beyond this, a few intellectuals, artists, and professionals are always ready to come to the aid of their comrades.

Communist influence in the unions thrives on rank-and-file desires for more vigorous labor leadership. There is no doubt that the Communists view labor unions simply as instruments for attaining Russian objectives, but the proletariat is bothered little by this tactical aspect of Communist strategy when it sees no other political grouping as boldly and openly demanding higher wages and better working conditions. For this reason, Communist popularity with both the industrial and agricultural laboring masses is directly proportionate to the degree to which the Revolutionary Left fails to assume militant leadership of the Mexican Revolution.

The Communist team in Mexico finds the Russian embassy alternating at quarterback with other Communist satellite diplomatic legations. Filling out the backfield are the Mexican Communist Party (PCM), the UGOCM, and the Mexican Labor-Campesino Party (POCM). The Confederation of Workers of Latin America (CTAL) holds down the center slot. At the ends, the Moscow-coached team displays great depth, with students and teachers competing against certain artists, journalists, intellectuals, bureaucrats, and professional men for regular berths. Rounding out the line posts are proven candidates from one section of the railroad, electrical, telephone, and petroleum workers' unions.

While the major Communist thrust in Mexico is thus engineered by Moscow, Castro Communism and Chinese Communism are present nonetheless. Castro's initial policies and strategies in Mexico emphasized relative independence from Moscow, glorifying at times Cuban Communism as an alternative to Russian Communism. This approach seemed to give way during 1962 in favor of policies minimizing differences in Russian and Cuban outlook. Precious little information is made public on Chinese Communist policy and organization in Mexico. It is common knowledge, however, that hundreds of Mexican teachers, students, unionists, and professionals have journeyed to Peiping, all expenses paid. One repeatedly hears the rumor that Red Chinese agents enter Mexico by illegal ship landings on the Pacific coast and from there disperse among the Mexican peasantry.

3. Trotskyites. Unlike the Moscow-oriented Communists, who have an outside source for final dogmatic decision-making and financial assistance, the Trotskyites exercise their militancy unguided and unaided by a central world authority. Absence of a higher authority, however, has not vitiated the dedicated and visionary nature of hard-core Trotskyites. Although they despise the Moscow-led Communists, "who diverted world Communism from its true revolutionary course," Trotskyites also advocate the overthrow of capitalism and the establishment of a working-class socialism. They view union rank and file as the potential base of revolutionary action; all that is required, say the Trotskyites, is to place real leaders in command of the labor movement—leaders who will engage in radical political activity and train the rank and file of trade unionism to take over society.

The Communist-Trotskyite split runs deep into the fissure opened decades ago by the death of Lenin. As Leon Trotsky (pseudonym of Leo Davidovich Bronstein) became the subject of Stalin's uncontrollable wrath, the famous Mexican muralist Diego Rivera prevailed on President Cárdenas to grant the world revolutionist political exile in Mexico. From the day of his arrival until his assassination three years later (August 20, 1940) at the hands of Jacques Mornard,[1] Leon Trotsky became the whipping-boy for ideological conflicts in Mexican politics. Few political pronouncements appearing in local newspapers from 1938 to mid-1940 failed to mention his presence, and after his death until the release and expulsion from Mexico of his assassin, the newspapers kept his memory alive by reports on Mornard.

The Trotskyite movement or, as it is known in Marxian schools of thought, the Fourth International, finds its strongest Mexican cadres in the Miners and Metal Workers' Union. This labor central, which militantly and aggressively injected the Fourth International into Mexican politics and trade unionism in the late 1930's, has preserved a relatively independent status in the labor movement since its breakoff in 1938 from the CTM, largest trade-union federation in Mexico. From time to time, several teacher and student federations have also declared themselves to be Trotskyites. The death of the sometime Trotskyite Diego Rivera, lack of funds, and absence of a central high command have combined to preclude continuing any undivided rank-and-file support. The major significance of Trotskyite elements in Mexico today is seen in their crusading vigilance against Communist activities and in their agitation for a return of the Revolutionary Left to public power.

THE INDEPENDENT LEFT

Although divided on strategies and tactics, members of the Independent Left agree on the basic features of the ultimate society required in Mexico. These fundamental characteristics can be identified quite specifically:

1. Since ownership of property is the only true cause of class stratification, private property and economic liberty must give way to economic equality and to state or at least worker ownership of the means of production.

2. The exploited class of today, the wage workers, must be converted into a class-conscious proletariat in order to prepare for its role as the architect of tomorrow's society.

3. Labor leadership must constantly and militantly fight capital and even state-owned industries for ever-higher wages, better working con-

[1] Also known as Jacques Mornard Vandendrasched, José Mercador, Frank Jackson, Jaime Ramón Mercader del Río Hernández; on his release from Mexican prison on May 6, 1960, his Cuban passport was issued in the name of Jacques van Dendresch.

ditions, and profit-sharing. The right to strike is an indispensable weapon. Immediate material rewards are no more important than the example set by leaders to overcome rank-and-file political apathy and indifference.

4. All private capital opposes the true interest of labor and, therefore, should be abolished. Although the domestic capitalist is bad, the foreign investor is worse; inherently imperialistic, foreign capital is always repugnant to national pride and to labor's sense of national destiny.

The Independents are conspicuously absent from official-party ranks whenever the Revolutionary Left is not setting over-all policy for the government. In the face of centralist and rightist domination since 1945, the Independents accuse the Revolutionary Left of being asleep, of selling out to foreigners, and of failing to fulfill the Revolution's promises of social justice. Outside official-party ranks, the Independents stand up against, and sometimes openly fight, the bureaucracy. They find anarchist and Trotskyite programs too unrealistic, too radical. They may collaborate with the Communists, but their excessive Mexican nationalism guides them into directions that Moscow-oriented elements are frequently prohibited from taking. In the 1952 presidential elections, the Independent Leftists divided over Gen. Henríquez Guzmán, candidate of the major opposition party, and Vicente Lombardo Toledano, standard-bearer of the Popular Party. Despite usual consensus among Latin American experts that Lombardo Toledano has been one of the Kremlin's foremost agents in Latin America, Lombardo Toledano has tried hard to be accepted inside Mexico as the intellectual and political leader of the Independent Left.

Divergencies in strategies and tactics characterize the Independent Left. Some elements consider the general strike and the secondary boycott the best means to reach their goals. Others propose immediate expropriation of the means of production and total replacement of private entrepreneurship with state socialism. Still others, in the Fabian tradition, consider slower, evolutionary, and nonviolent tactics the proper approach to nationalization or to workers' socialism. Some Independents believe participation in an opposition party indispensable, others hold to the conviction that direct action is the sole effective strategy. What appears to be the greatest single intellectual shortcoming in all Independent strategy is that, contrary to their over-all view, Mexican society has not stabilized into two classes. Nonetheless, say some Independents, any inconsistencies in theory are counteracted by the respect from union rank and file that has accrued to Independent Leftist trade-union leaders because of their persistent demands on management and government.

The record of wage increases and fringe benefits won by individual trade unions during the decade 1950–60 shows clearly that the unions that received more on both counts were under Independent Leftist leadership.

Unions tied to and supporting the government face a bewildering paradox: Their hundreds of thousands of laborers constitute a formidable army of potential opposition, yet a relatively small number of workers outside official ranks—at most, several tens of thousands—constantly challenge the government and receive the greatest material benefits. Brute industrialization has crudely exploited all labor in Mexico, but its effects have touched the Independent Leftist unions more lightly than others. After the rank and file recognizes the captive status of the union leadership "guiding" the dominant core of the Mexican labor movement, the leaders of the Independent Left may be favored to head the labor movement when the political pendulum again swings to the left.

In the meantime, however, lack of organizational machinery is the great weakness of the diversity of elements composing the Independent Left. Intellectuals, journalists, professionals, artists, and teachers who fancy themselves a part of this group are virtually unorganized; informal get-togethers of intimate friends are the usual media through which they express their independent theories. Of course, they may choose to express their liberalism collectively through active participation in the Popular Party (now bearing the name of Popular Socialist Party), which since 1949, has been the sole permanent political outlet of the Independent Left. In addition, two relatively obscure trade unions, the CROC and the CRT, are usually headed by Independent Leftists; both shun the officially supported Labor Unity Bloc. Of all elements in the Independent Left, only three militantly active trade unions contain real organizational strength: the telephone workers' union, the Mexican Electricians' Union (SME), and another independent electrical workers' union. Early in 1961, these three syndicates joined forces with the CROC, CRT, and several other unions to establish a new labor bloc—the National Workers Confederation (CNT). The fact that the great majority of workers in the electric-power industry now work for the Mexican government (the private interests of Electric Bond & Share and the Sofina consortium were purchased by the government in 1960) places the traditionally militant electrical workers in a new occupational relationship to management. Undoubtedly, complete public ownership of the electric-power industry came about partly out of disgust with relatively excessive union demands. Under public ownership, a new set of rules will govern the conduct of these two trade-union groups.

Frequently pro-Communist, invariably Marxist and anti-American, unions in the Independent Left have provided about the only bold leadership in the entire ranks of organized labor. But this leadership has brought concrete material advances for the rank and file of Independent Left unions alone, not for the entire Mexican trade-union movement. The sharp contrast with relatively weak progovernment union leadership has not passed unnoticed by the rank-and-file.

TRADITIONAL CONSERVATIVES

The Traditional Conservatives advocate a concoction of Spanish colonial values intermixed with corporate state designs. Its elite, who are not troubled by feelings of inferiority, still view society as founded on caste-like racial distinctions and composed of inferiors and superiors, with the latter (themselves)—selected from among large landowners, wealthy bankers and industrialists, the upper hierarchy of the Catholic clergy, and the "educated" foreigners, particularly from pro-Franco constituents within the long-resident Spanish colony—filling the role of overlords. Despite similarities in the economic tenets of this political public and the Revolutionary Right, notably their mutual preference for private foreign capital over public foreign capital and for crude forced savings over wage increases, Traditional Conservatives divide sharply with the Revolutionary Right on the issues of religion and education. It is the Traditionalists' views on these subjects that underlie their insistence on extricating Mexican society from the "socialistic" mandates imposed by the Mexican Constitution.

The Traditional Conservatives' attack on specific constitutional provisions is methodical, fervent, and persistent. Tradition-directed in the Latin American sense, they perceive the basic issue in society as that of State versus Church. If the Church is not permitted free rein in secular as well as temporal affairs, say the Traditionalists, the State is *ipso facto* against it both spiritually and politically. In other words, if the Catholic hierarchy wishes to become the biggest landowner, the largest real estate owner, the sole word in educational matters, and the selector of political leadership, the State has no legitimate right to oppose it. To this end, the Traditional Conservatives would release the Church from legal mandates prohibiting its ownership of property, restricting the number of priests in proportion to population, and forbidding priests and nuns from wearing clerical garb in public and participating in politics. Instead, they would require "explicit recognition of Catholicism as the sole religion" and permit the Church directly to fulfill the imperative need for "Christian principles to replace atheistic socialism" in public educational instruction. Catholic private schools should operate "unconstrained" by government. Surrender of any Revolutionary government to these constitutional revisions would constitute an outright betrayal of the Revolutionary creed. Yet, the Traditionalists put forth several more demands inimical to the twentieth-century revolution.

The agrarian-reform provisions of the Constitution, of cardinal importance to the Revolutionary Left, are anathema to the Traditional Conservatives. They want the whole project overhauled, communal property ownership seriously qualified, and the Mexican countryside placed once again under the tutelage of rural land barons. Centuries earlier, their Spanish prototypes could rationalize the feudal-like hacienda system as an indispensable institution for saving the souls of the illiterate and inferior Indian; Traditionalists of today are more likely to sustain their theories on the argument that Mexico's food-supply shortages can only be overcome by replacing the inefficient communal *ejido* and small farm with the efficient, mechanized, large-scale, privately owned unit. Whatever the economic soundness of this plan, it runs directly counter to some four decades of Revolutionary preaching on the social justice of collective landownership, and any serious attempt to undo *ejidos* and subjugate the peasant to the feudalism of Traditional Conservative schemes probably would provoke an impassioned uprising.

In the sphere of ownership of the means of production, similarly explosive consequences could be anticipated from the implementation of Traditionalist projections. Counter to the growth of Mexican nationalism and the social and economic developments of the Revolution, Traditional Conservatives contrive to remove the newly developing petrochemical industry from government control and supervision and to induce the government to relinquish a substantial part of its holdings. In short, they preach an economy governed by the price mechanism, by supply and demand, and by free competition, even though they reveal themselves in the semiofficial business chambers of commerce as desirous of corporate monopolies (which they would head) and little competition. There is, therefore, little promise that, if they ever reach power, they would set about to create the kind of economic system they advocate.

Under a Conservative Traditional regime, it appears likely that trade unions would amount to little more than paternalistic mutualist societies. First of all, the essence of their proposals suggests that labor legislation should relegate the worker to his given place in society, at the bottom of the economic ladder. Second, the Traditionalists would perform a major operation on Article 123 of the Constitution and remove present "socialist" provisions on worker participation in profits, worker ownership, and the right to organize freely, bargain collectively, and strike. Government protection, union participation in politics, and efforts to create a unified national trade movement should, say the Traditionalists, give way to paternalism, the establishment of company unions unaffiliated with nationals, a prohibition on strikes, and the complete removal of unions from the political decision-making process. They insist that unions be cleared of all radicals, liberals, socialists, anarchists, Communists, and Trotskyites.

Traditionalist philosophy probably holds greater appeal than this brief review of its beliefs might indicate. The elite of this political public includes some old families of wealth antedating the Revolution, whose offspring are prominent in agriculture, banking, commerce, insurance, and real estate, as well as elements of the proclerical *nouveau riche*, foreign interests, professional men, and Franco enthusiasts in the Spanish colony. Geographically, Traditionalist strength is concentrated in Mexico City, Guadalajara, Monterrey, the states of Baja California, Chihuahua, and Sonora, and among certain Catholic youth groups, women's organizations, and the peasantry in regions of Guanajuato, Michoacán, Oaxaca, Puebla, Querétaro, and San Luis Potosí. For more than two decades, the intellectual leader of the Traditional Conservatives has been Manuel Gómez Morín, onetime professor, Marxist, and counselor to the Russian embassy, who turned financier in the early 1930's and became a pillar of the private banking community.

The political embodiment of Traditional Conservatism is the National Action Party, or as it is popularly known in Mexico, the PAN. Originally established as a pro-Axis political movement, the PAN even today espouses a pseudo-McCarthyism: It would have the public believe that Communism is synonymous with leftist political views, radicalism, state ownership, public education, land reform, progressive taxation, Protestantism, and Freemasonry. This is also the general approach of the less-prominent group of Traditionalists who head the relatively obscure Mexican Nationalist Party (PNM).

REACTIONARY CONSERVATIVES

The Reactionary Conservatives center on the fascistic doctrines of *sinarquismo*—the opposite of anarchy. They exalt the Spanish inheritance of intense Catholicism and militarism and advocate the establishment of a true "Christian Order" based on home and village life, a corporate state, and military order. Like Franco Spain and Salazar Portugal, a *sinarquista* Mexico would probably find itself without free speech and a free press, with rigorous suppression of the Radical Left, the Independent Left, and all Revolutionary elites, and with the Roman Catholic faith installed as an official state religion.

Arising in the 1930's largely as the Mexican counterpart of Franco, Salazar, Hitler, and Mussolini, the *sinarquistas* were anti–United States during World War II because of "the U.S. alliance with Russia" and continued their antipathy after the global conflict because "the United States is a Protestant nation." The stormy decade of the thirties, coming as it did shortly after the bloody uprising of the fanatic *cristeros* against the Mexican government's efforts to separate Church and State, attracted hundreds of thousands of Mexicans to the banner of Christian Order. They denounced the "socialist" education taught in public schools, condemned the "Masonic plot" to convert Mexico into a Protestant bailiwick, and attacked non-Catholics as heathens and atheists. Fortunately for liberalism in Mexico, *sinarquismo* never drew to its banner more than a handful of educated lay Mexicans and probably never enlisted the official support of the Catholic hierarchy.

Sinarquismo, we should understand, is not the projection of the Catholic Church into Mexican political life. True, some members of the clergy guide this rightist movement and even inject *sinarquista* ideology into Catholic youth groups and adult fraternal orders. But the Catholic hierarchy wisely sits on the sidelines unwilling to upset the acceptable *modus vivendi* governing Church-State relations. And if high churchmen did change their approach to favor support of the *sinarquistas*, there is reason to expect that the vast majority of priests, who are Mexican-born, usually of lower-class or lower-middle-class origins, and Mexican-educated, would hesitate to implement orders directly challenging Revolutionary policies. Those who deplore clerics who interfere in secular matters overlook the real support that the Revolution has received from clergymen since the *modus vivendi* became effective. By contrast with pre-1937 Mexico, the average cleric today, perhaps because he is a creature of the Revolution as well as of Rome, identifies himself more closely with the papal encyclicals Rerum Novarum, Quadragésimo Anno, and Mater et Magistra, epistles directed toward social and economic improvement of the working masses. Christian Socialism and Catholic Social Action as distinct political movements have failed to attract much attention because the Mexican government itself has sponsored programs closely analogous to the designs of Pope Leo XIII, Pope John XXIII, and Pope Paul VI. For this reason, too, Christian Socialism in Mexico does not stand out as a clear-cut political force, as it does in other Latin American societies. Too often the importance of the clerical fanatic is exaggerated while the priest who expresses Christian liberalism day by day in working conjointly with officials and semigovernmental agencies is overlooked. In short, Catholic Church ties with the Reactionary Conservatives are at best informal and limited to the independent clericalism of some churchmen.

The Reactionary Conservatives draw their following from among the same classes that support the Traditional Conservatives and, also like the Traditionalists, lack organizational machinery. Prominent spokesmen include the heads of old land-owning families, pro-Franco elements, a small minority of the Catholic clergy, and a few foreigners, intellectuals, and professionals. Backing up this elite are certain Catholic youth groups, intense lay Catholics, a few company unions, and finally, illiterate peasants, predominantly from specific regions of Guanajuato, Jalisco, Michoacán, Querétaro, Puebla, and San Luis Potosí. The major political arm of the Reactionaries, of course, is the *sinarquistas*. Various men from the ranks have been elevated to headship of the *sinarquistas*. A rumor current in the 1940's, which proved impossible to substantiate, had it that the closely concealed top-level leadership resided in José Vasconcelos. Since 1949, when the Mexican government withdrew their legal status as a political party (which was named "Fuerza Popular"), the *sinarquistas* have enjoyed no legally recognized organization of their own. For this reason, the Reactionary Conservatives frequently have lent electoral support to and had dealings with the PAN.

THE REVOLUTIONARY PUBLICS

The Revolutionary publics differ substantially from other publics in one striking respect: They have been the only ones in over twoscore years to have actually exercised public power—the only groups from which presidents, state governors, supreme court justices, and senators have been selected. The elite of the Revolutionary publics comprises the oligarchy ruling Mexico, the Revolutionary Family responsible for realizing the basic objectives of Mexican society. Homogeneity and common adherence of the Revolutionary publics are indispensable for assuring continuance of Family leadership.

Why talk of Revolutionary publics, therefore, when the elite ruling Mexico seems backed by one unified public? Despite the unity and similarity of belief of all Revolutionaries, they have divergent viewpoints on the timing and emphasis of public policy, on the precedence to be given one objective over another, and on the substance of government programs at a given moment. So broad are these differences that their unconstrained expression might tear apart the Revolutionary alliance. From these divergent viewpoints, we can identify three separate Revolutionary publics—the Revolutionary Left, Right, and Center.

1. The Revolutionary Left. The Revolutionary Left centers on the person and personality of Lázaro Cárdenas. For decades, Cárdenas has been glorified, exalted—indeed, virtually deified by the masses. And why should they regard him with less esteem? He expropriated the petroleum industry, railroads, and millions of acres of land. He distributed among the landless peasants more agricultural land than all chiefs of state before him. He redesigned the entire interest-group structure by setting up a broadly democratic official political party (the PRM), a vast communal agriculturalist federation (the CNC), a virtually unified national trade-union confederation (the CTM), an all-inclusive civil servants' union (the FSTSE), and a host of other private, semiofficial groups, organizations, unions, chambers, and agencies. His highly nationalistic administration emphasized class-consciousness. Urban proletarian, peasant, and teacher; bureaucrat, technician, and soldier; artisan, intellectual, and clerk—all joined hands with the government to bring fulfillment to the hopes and aspirations of the Mexican masses. Cárdenas defied Wall Street, condemned Hitler and Franco, expelled from Mexican soil the powerful dictator Calles, crushed local strongmen, and attacked frontally the rural land barons and bourgeois aristocracy. Here was a real

Mexican, humble yet monumental, human yet powerful. To the masses, Cárdenas became one of the greatest of Mexicans, living or dead. This is the man who wields the leadership of the Revolutionary Left.

The Revolutionary Left steadily lost ground after the late 1930's. Lombardo Toledano's sellout of the labor movement to Third International directives and the unworkableness of Cárdenas' "functional democracy" were major contributing causes. Before 1946, this public had no special grudge against the Mexican government, since they realized that Mexico's declaration of war on the Axis powers and preoccupation with supplying the Allies with strategic raw materials would have to place in abeyance their earlier demands for economic, political, and social reform. The fact that Cárdenas continued to share leadership of the Revolutionary Family, even though Manuel Ávila Camacho served as titular head by virtue of being President of Mexico, also augured well for postwar developments. But Miguel Alemán's ideas on the role of organized labor and the peasantry ran counter to Revolutionary Left sentiment, and Ruiz Cortines pursued his forced-savings policy at the immediate expense of higher real wages for the laboring classes. From 1946 to 1959, therefore, Revolutionary Leftists were clearly relegated to a back seat and usually confined the voicing of their objections on public policy to closed meetings of the oligarchy running the nation. Then, from 1959 to 1964, Cárdenas himself became more vociferous in public and openly expressed his dissatisfaction with the course of affairs since the end of World War II, especially in the realm of foreign policy. (Some believe that Cárdenas was merely testing public reaction on behalf of the Revolutionary elite as a whole.) Of course, not all Revolutionary Leftists agreed with everything Cárdenas had to say, yet this public as a whole seemed enlivened by the mere return of their leader to public forums. Certain policy shifts of the López Mateos regime seemed clearly attributable to this new militancy of the Revolutionary Left.

Class-consciousness is the key to Revolutionary Left proposals for reform. The industrial proletarian and peasant, according to this public, must in the long run win over the upper classes, the big capitalist, and even the white-collar class. To the Revolutionary Left, it is not the structure of the official party that requires change but its leadership. In other words, a Revolutionary Leftist should be President of Mexico. Peasant and labor associations should remain under government tutelage, but encouragement and assistance should replace suppression and passive opposition in official public policy. Thus, the Revolutionary Left advocates a more popular, class-conscious government than those the Revolutionary Family have given Mexico since 1940.

Should a popular Revolutionary Left government be reinstalled, it is likely that the Mexican economic system would undergo several basic changes. State ownership and control would certainly extend further into mining, transport, iron and steel, chemicals, and auto assembly. The state would tend to enlarge its role in the distribution of basic foodstuffs. Through higher taxation, higher wages, and price controls, the government would probably attempt a more equitable distribution of national income. At the same time, communal agriculture, producer and consumer cooperatives, and "local" economies would receive emphatic support. Along with these transformations would conceivably come greater respect for labor's right to strike and associate freely, better working conditions, and attempts to unify the trade-union movement. Forced savings for industrialization ends would undoubtedly be slowed up in favor of an immediate material improvement of the living standards of the Mexican masses. Although private foreign capital would still find a minor place in national economic development, the Revolutionary Left would clearly prefer loans from such international public sources as the World Bank.

In foreign affairs, the Cardenist wing displays an intense nationalism and equally pronounced anticolonialism. Retaining great admiration for Franklin Roosevelt and New Deal policies, the Revolutionary Leftists have exhibited little enthusiasm for the Republican Party or its conduct of American foreign relations, emphatically condemning the "pseudo good-neighborliness" contained in Eisenhower's "Good Partner Policy." Antifascist, anti-imperialist, pro–Republican Spain, and pro–Castro Cuba, this political public places responsibility for the overthrow of the Arbenz Guzmán regime in Guatemala and the Bosch regime in the Dominican Republic squarely on the U.S. Department of State. They also take issue with United States strategy in the Cold War and, once returned to power, would probably push for recognition of Communist China and its seating in the United Nations.

A return to dominant power presumes organizational strength, and in this realm the Revolutionary Left is not lacking. Its support comes from all social and economic classes and from all geographical regions of the nation. The great bulk of the urban masses, peasants, cooperatives, union rank and file, artisans, and rural schoolteachers seem more sympathetic to the Revolutionary Left than to any other political public in Mexico. This is probably equally true of the civil servants, the military, the small businessmen, many intellectuals, and most political exiles resident in Mexico. In terms of sympathetic response from specific governmental enterprises, the Revolutionary Left counts on employees in the ministry of public education, the ministry of hydraulic resources, the department of agrarian affairs, Pemex, the National Bank of *Ejidal* Credit, the National Railways, the Federal Electricity Commission, and the state-owned and managed insecticide, fertilizer, iron and steel, and petrochemical industries. Beyond this, Revolutionary Leftists usually retain the administrative and surely the intellectual leadership of the National University, the national normal school, the National Polytechnical Institute, the several agricultural colleges, and some of the regional univer-sities. Indigenous communities, small towns and villages, and perhaps even some of the army of rural unemployed that periodically migrates across the U.S. border ideologically belong in the Revolutionary Left camp. Geographically, the *cardenistas* are strongest in industrial centers, in Michoacán (the home state of Cárdenas) and other states of central Mexico, in Yucatán, and in the Laguna region.

Why, then, with what is apparently a preponderant majority of Mexicans behind it, has the Revolutionary Left failed to seize public power? A leading *cardenista* several years ago gave this explanation: "Ob-viously, because Don Lázaro does not as yet wish it. But never forget that ever since the expulsion of Calles in 1935 Cárdenas has remained the *mero mero* [Number One]. Foreign capitalists who have come to Mexico these last years will learn soon enough that Don Lázaro has outsmarted them." Needless to say, the apparent unwillingness of Cárdenas is a transcendent factor, but there are others. Although popular sympathies generally lie with the Revolutionary Left, it does not follow necessarily that the masses will respond automatically to their beck and call on any and all issues. Mexican and foreign capitalist alike fear Cárdenas' return to power, and not a few leading bankers and industrialists have financial reserves abroad for just such a contingency. Many educated Mexicans oppose him because he is "too popular, too plebeian, too irrational, too outdated." Many professionals, top-level bureaucrats, and middle-class elements favor a more moderate approach to economic development than that which Cárdenas symbolizes. *Alemanistas* oppose him on other grounds. Some *cardenistas* say that they must await the return of a real social democrat to the White House in Washington, which they believed John F. Kennedy was becoming. Finally, popular respect for constitutional-ism and for peaceful transfer of political power has grown immeasurably in recent years. This will be discussed more fully in Chapter 6.

From all this, one thing seems certain: Unless job opportunities materialize more rapidly than in the last decades, unless economic de-velopment gives way at least temporarily to wage increases, unless im-pending agrarian problems are resolved, then quite aside from U.S. politi-cal leadership (or the lack of it) and world economic vacillations, the return of the Revolutionary Left to power will be accelerated.

2. *The Revolutionary Right (New Conservatives).* The New Conservatives are led by wealthy, influential, and markedly elusive Revo-lutionary businessmen. Precise observation of the moguls as a group is diffi-cult. My own research on several hundred businessmen, while still incon-clusive, has produced several findings that should stand the test of future scholarly endeavor.

By country of birth, the moguls are divided into approximately

80 per cent Mexican-born and 20 per cent foreign-born. The foreign category itself is split rather evenly into naturalized citizens (Bruno Pagliai, César Balsa, Antonio Sacristán, Harry Steele, et al.) and long-resident foreigners who never acquired Mexican citizenship (the late William Jenkins, Julio Serrano, et al.) Their place of birth notwithstanding, most of them entered the world as offspring of lower-middle-class families. With a few notable exceptions—e.g., Jenkins, the Macedo and Rocha families, and Raúl Bailleres—they were barely scratching out an existence as late as two decades after the Revolution began. Less than one-fifth of the top echelon of the Revolutionary wealthy began their sustained capital accumulation while holding public office. (Conspicuous among the *político* moguls are Miguel Alemán, Antonio Díaz Lombardo, Aarón Sáenz, and Abelardo Rodríguez.)

Not every Mexican or resident foreigner of wealth belongs to a Revolutionary elite. Many lend their support to the Traditional Conservatives and Reactionaries; a few back the Communists or the Independent Left. And among wealthy Revolutionaries, not all are found in New Conservative ranks: Antonio Sacristán and some rich Spanish refugees, for example, identify themselves with a sound, middle-of-the-road position. But these few exceptions aside, the rich Revolutionary is usually a Revolutionary Rightist. To him, only two individuals since 1920 have truly led Mexico in the proper direction: Calles (while *jefe máximo* in the years 1929–35) and Alemán. The latter, himself a wealthy man, has been the titular head of the New Conservatives from 1945 onward. But it is really those who truly enriched themselves while Alemán sat in the presidential chair—some cabinet ministers and ministers without portfolio, some private Mexican capitalists, and even some foreigners—who keep the former chief as their symbolic leader. In this way, they can continue to rationalize their accumulation of wealth with the assertion, "Not I, but Alemán; he led, I followed."

Rank-and-file support comes from several quarters. Thousands of industrialists, real estate owners, merchants, and promoters seeking a place nearer the top see the private-enterprise appeal of the New Conservatives appropriately fitted to their own aspirations. The traveling salesman—and Mexico has thousands of them—tends to support the *alemanistas*. Many professionals—doctors, dentists, architects, engineers, and others—carry on practices geared to the high fees collected from other New Conservatives. The professional in Mexico often equates the *cardenista* with socialized medicine and other social-welfare programs. Additional backing comes from local and state politicians who held office through the good graces of Alemán. Finally, intellectual underpinning is provided by the philosophy of some professors and top-level career civil servants, many of whom studied at universities in the United States.

The New Conservatives visualize the Revolution reaching its greatest heights under private initiative and large-scale foreign investment. The special brand of free enterprise that this group advances does not, however, subsume free competition or an open-market mechanism. In the matter of state ownership of the means of production, they join with the Revolutionary Left in defending government ownership and administration of the oil industry, railroads, telegraph services, electric-power industry, and international aviation. Beyond this, the New Conservatives argue that the state should stay out of business and concentrate on helping Mexican capitalists to attract ever more foreign funds into Mexican economic development. Tax exemption, tariff protection, government contracts, and access to development bank credit are some of the measures that the Revolutionary Right advances as stimulants to Mexican-style free enterprise. Whenever they begin the manufacture of a new article in Mexico, the New Conservatives will appear and reappear before governmental agencies charged with tariff protection. The "infant industry" argument has rarely, if ever, received a more vociferous defense anywhere in the world. As with ownership, so with distribution: The Revolutionary moguls would restrict the scope of CONASUPO, the state agency responsible for the distribution of basic foodstuffs at regulated prices to the masses, and encourage private merchants to fill the gap.

There are other planks in the New Conservative platform. They place economic liberty before economic equality, industrialization before communal agriculture, forced savings before political equality. They prefer Mexican control of industry and commerce to foreign ownership, large-scale industries to artisans' shops and craft industries, production to strikes. They make a distinction between union leadership and union rank and file, because "management can work with union leaders, especially to limit and regulate labor activities." Although they oppose worker ownership and wish to minimize class-consciousness, they uphold the right of labor association, because "unions represent a counterforce against radicalism." They believe that a just distribution of national income must await the completion of a solid industrial base for the Mexican economy. They do not, in principle, oppose corporate taxation, which is the source of a great deal of government revenue and which most foreign-owned companies pay according to the letter of the law, but they do find old friends in the government convenient for avoiding payment of taxes by the firms that they themselves own.

On the type of economic system best suited to Mexican needs, the New Conservative outlook coincides with Traditional Conservative sentiment on several basic considerations. Both share the belief in the intrinsic goodness of free enterprise, notwithstanding the wide gap separating their uniquely Mexican interpretations of the true philosophy of Adam Smith. Both take issue with Leftist agricultural policy and prefer privately owned farms. And both deplore state intervention in private banking, insurance, and real estate development. With a common meeting ground on these and other economic policies, these two political publics have tended to modify certain of their incompatible views. On the one hand, Traditionalist antipathy toward Revolutionary agricultural, religious, and educational programs has declined notably during the post–World War II years. This moderation, brought on partly by governmental laxity in enforcement of pertinent constitutional provisions, has permitted recent regimes to devote less effort to pacifying the popular masses, more to productivity. On the other hand, the Revolutionary Right seems more amenable to Traditional Conservative agricultural, religious, and educational programs, to a point. The New Conservatives say: "Why oppose large rural estates, when a few haciendas won't hurt the agrarian-reform program and may help alleviate food shortages? Why not permit the Church greater freedom, as long as clericalism is kept in bounds? Why not encourage parochial schools, which are really needed for the children of better families (including wealthy Revolutionary families), because a public education simply does not provide the disciplined, learned scholasticism desired?"

New Conservative outlook on international affairs emphasizes universalism, regionalism, and nationalism. In general principles, therefore, they concur with the Revolutionary Left. Where they differ is in the New Conservative's pronounced respect for the United States, Germany, and Japan, all of them societies that made the industrialization grade without Communism; in their approval of American foreign policy in the Cold War; and in their deprecation of the Soviet Union and Red China. They agree with all Revolutionary publics in opposing Franco Spain and foreign influence in Mexican politics. Finally, the New Conservatives seem to prefer Republicans or Democrats of the Lyndon Johnson mold to radical New Dealers. All in all, the moguls of the Mexican Revolution are not far removed from certain big businessmen in the United States.

3. *The Revolutionary Center.*   A third Revolutionary elite emerged about 1950 from the ideological split on the issues of industrialization, agricultural reform, and foreign investment. While New Conservatives were overstating the need for rapid industrialization—a characteristic that was to become one of their distinguishing features—and Revolutionary Leftists were exaggerating agrarianism, elements from both of these publics joined career bureaucrats, intellectuals, and political leaders who owed no special allegiance to Alemán or Cárdenas to form a relatively amorphous grouping favoring "balanced economic growth." There is little evidence to suggest that a third force was consciously put together at that time. Certain Mexicans simply analyzed the Mexican scene, assisted by foreign critics such as professors Frank Tannenbaum and the late Sanford Mosk, and concluded that industry versus agriculture was an inappropriate statement of the issue —that national development required many *ad hoc* arrangements in both

agriculture and industry. If development programs demanded large-scale investment capital and domestic sources were unable to meet the financial burden imposed, this new elite grouping concluded, there was nothing unconstitutional or unpatriotic in permitting foreign capital to assist.

Its ideology, abstracted from the epoch of the two Adolfos, shows clearly that the Revolutionary Center is more middle-class-oriented than the Left or the Right. But this, too, is paradoxical, since individuals in the Left and Center rarely hide their desire to become wealthier, and the sooner the better; actually, it is the Right that seems to push hardest for the creation of a solid middle class. This probably results from Rightist conviction that a propertied middle class will defend private property against Leftist radicalism. To claim that the Revolutionary Center represents the "middle class" is to overlook the philosophy of rapid social mobility that marks virtually all Mexican middle-sector thinking. Middle-class elements waste no time in pushing upward and, failing once, twice, or even more often, they nonetheless hold to the belief that a place still remains for them in the wealthy class. The subtle social process by which a middle class in Mexico will ultimately come to identify itself as such and be proud of its status is probably going on, but as yet this sense of identity still remains elusive.

An analysis of the composition of the Revolutionary Center does not seem to be advanced by the several theories of "balancing interests" any more than by class stratification. The Center may choose to mediate between *alemanistas* and *cardenistas*, but this is quite different from seeking a balance of all socio-economic interests in Mexico. The government, under predominantly Central direction since 1952, seems to have adopted unbalance as an implicit plank in its platform. Subordination of workers to rapid economic development, which essentially was Ruiz Cortines' policy, hardly constituted the preservation of a balance of socio-economic interests.

Briefly, then, what identifies the Revolutionary Center is its dedication to industry *and* agriculture, to higher productivity, and to "balanced economic growth." But another goal intervenes in making the task of Center economic objectives unusually complex: This Revolutionary public also advocates greater social justice, including higher wages. The Revolutionary Center, as economist Alfredo Navarrete of Nacional Financiera has pointed out on several occasions, seeks to attain a rate of economic growth that exceeds population increase, to accomplish this with reasonable price and financial stability, and, in the process, to enlarge social-welfare services and increase labor's share of productivity. Yet it is precisely here where Center plans become incongruous. Pushing for a greater marginal propensity to save and invest, they also advocate a redistribution of income that can only raise marginal propensity to consume. Mexico is finding great difficulty in doing much about income redistribution. Indeed, the decade of the fifties witnessed a relatively emphatic policy favoring savings and investment—of course, at the short-run expense of lower-income groups.

On agricultural policy, the Revolutionary Center accents the use rather than the ownership of land. In this concept there is no room for the Right-versus-Left argument over private or collective farms; productivity alone should determine the merits of one form of landownership or another. Agrarian reform must give way to agricultural reform: Simple redistribution of land and rural credit are replaced by farm mechanization, irrigation, better seeds, fertilizers, insecticides, crop rotation—in short, by higher productivity. Within this context, *ejidos* and private farms are to receive maximum financial and technical assistance from the Mexican government.

By contrast with the Revolutionary Left and Right, the Center determines ownership of the means of production by a pragmatic, industry-by-industry test. Centralist policy is unequivocally clear: Neither state nor private control represents a pattern of ownership for all basic industries. As long as privately owned enterprises produce and expand facilities according to societal needs—i.e., to requirements interpreted by governmental estimates of what the Mexican economy demands—there is no reason for the state to take over. But when an industry whose output of goods or services is indispensable to the over-all economy repeatedly fails to keep abreast of expectations or serves notice that profits no longer justify new investment, government should intervene and, if necessary, *purchase* the enterprise. Such conditions prevailed, say the Revolutionary Centralists, when the government purchased control of American & Foreign Power interests, the Mexican Light and Power Company, and the La Consolidada steel mills. Although no case is yet on record, the Revolutionary Center advocates a return of some companies to private hands as soon as state management has pulled them back to the productive levels required.

The practical nationalism of the Revolutionary Center is prominently disclosed in its foreign-policy perspectives. Toward the United States, there should be no alternative to good neighborliness: American tourist dollars are indispensable to avoid serious balance-of-payments disequilibria. Provoking the U.S. into lowering commodity prices on Mexican exports could also jeopardize the Mexican economy. And if the Export-Import Bank, Prudential Insurance Company, and other large American financial institutions stopped their big loans to Nacional Financiera, the state would have to locate capital elsewhere to finance state-operated industries. Unlike the New Conservatives, who openly express their pro–United States sympathies in Mexico as well as abroad, the Revolutionary Center limits expression of friendship to more formal diplomatic intercourse, rarely engaging in enthusiastic praise for Uncle Sam in Mexico. The Revolutionary Center favors close identification of Mexico with underdeveloped nations everywhere, with popular social movements, and with all liberal govern-ments in Latin America. International stature and leadership in Latin America are vital components of this elite's foreign-policy objectives.

Understanding the ideology of these several publics prepares the way for an appreciation of how the political system really operates below the Rio Grande; how each public receives its due, or fails to receive it; how the Revolutionary Family manages to remain in power decade after dec-ade—in short, the realities and dynamics of the Mexican political system. Accordingly, the next chapter deals with these themes.

SIX

THE LIBERAL MACHIAVELLIAN

Good, bad, or indifferent, the means and ends of public policy under Revolutionary Family leadership depend squarely on the executive branch of government. When the President of Mexico simultaneously controls the Family, "the power of a President of Mexico has no limit but that of time, his six years in office." [1] All political publics uphold executive dominance. The publics not on the extremes—Revolutionary (Left, Center, and Right), Independent Left, and Traditional Conservatives—adhere to the principle of no re-election for the presidency and governorships, which in accord with Mexican constitutionalism means a change in executive leadership every six years. On the other hand, the political theories of the Radical Left and the Reactionary Conservatives suggest that if these groups were to capture the government, the principle of no re-election would be abandoned in favor of unlimited tenure. There are virtually no restraints by legislative and judicial agents. Checks and balances, separation of powers, pressure groups, effective federalism—all the elements of the United States system—have little more than paper counterparts in Mexico. Dictatorship of the Díaz variety has slowly given way to six-year authoritarianism of the Revolutionary variety, directed by executives of relatively liberal mold dedicated to the broad lines of the Revolutionary Creed. Within the Mexican milieu, the political sun rises and sets every six years on the presidency, and in identical cycles on gubernatorial offices. Mexicans avoid personal dictatorship by retiring their dictators every six years.

Such executive supremacy may cause Americans to think that the political system of Mexico, like its economy, is underdeveloped and backward. But trying to judge Mexico by American standards—presuming that interest groups support political parties which in turn compete for public power—engages an observer in a fascinating game of mental gymnastics that invariably terminates in a victory for irrationality, partial truths, and falsehoods. U.S.-style democracy is not willed into existence anywhere in the world unless some sturdy requisites are present, and many of them

[1] Statement made in 1953 by Enrique Parra Hernández, an inner-circle politician in the Alemán epoch. Quoted in *The New York Times*, July 23, 1953.

141

were absent in the Mexico of 1910, 1935, and 1964. Mexican political realities are radically different from those north of the Rio Grande. The Mexican system is equally underdeveloped as regards the Revolutionary Creed objective on political liberalism. We know it; the Mexicans know it. But we and the Mexicans look on democracy in different ways. The perfect system for Americans would have marginal utility for Mexicans, and vice versa. Because of the insuperable differences, it is well to reject comparability scales and concentrate on precisely how and why the Mexican system operates the way it does. Behind the whole complex subject looms the impact of preceding centuries which, coupled with the nature of Mexican temperament, presents an inheritance that in all probability neither the Revolutionary Family nor another elite will ever overcome.

MEXICO'S OFFICIAL PARTY: THEORY AND REALITY

The President of Mexico and state governors must walk with their feet on the ground, with a firm sense of the direction they are taking in time and space. Doomed is the leader who loses sight of the urgency to rule and reign in the context of yesterday's and today's as well as tomorrow's stage of development. Both Cárdenas and Calles possessed transcendent power, but the latter fell from the Revolutionary throne because his sense of the direction of the nation's development proved completely outdated. Both men were strong presidents, powerful heads of the Revolutionary Family. Both believed in executive dominance. Both arbitrarily unseated governors and hand-picked officeholders. In the interests of legitimizing government, Calles propounded a theory of "institutionalizing" Mexican politics which, stripped of its pragmatic aura, meant that Calles would pass his orders on public policy through the President of Mexico and his selection of presidents, governors, senators, and deputies through an official party. The political ambitions of poor and rich, of lawyers and intellectuals, of militarists, regional chiefs, and politicians were to be channeled through central party headquarters, where the aspirants were to flex their political muscles before a trusted Calles lieutenant presiding over the PNR. The high point of official-party domination was reached in 1933 under Gen. Carlos Riva Palacio; not before or since has the official party wielded such supreme authority over the nomination process.

Cárdenas, on the other hand, conceived of public policy and selection of officeholders as centering in an official party based on a four-part elite of trade unionists, communal agriculturists, military men, and "politicians". In Cárdenas' plan, these four sectors would "democratically" select candidates whose nomination assured election. Both theories, those of Calles and Cárdenas, subsumed governance by partial and fragmented incorporation of important social groups into the active decision-making process. Cárdenas, however, came closest to constructing a broadly based political mechanism—one that might have succeeded if Moscow had not raised havoc with trade unionism, if Mexico had been prepared for a popular-front democracy, if the general populace had subordinated other interests to supremacy of the proletariat, if literacy had been higher, if . . .

Despite Cárdenas' own rejection of the principal features of his model, as we have observed in Chapter 4, the paper outlines of his design persist today. The theory of the official party in the 1960's varies slightly from the Cárdenas conception, even though several structural changes in the 1940's altered sector alignment. Today there is an official party composed of three sectors—organized labor, communal agriculture, and "popular" elements—which theoretically nominate candidates to public offices through a functional, proportional-representation, intraparty process structured from local to national levels. Unions, federations, and associations formally affiliated with the official party purportedly take over the sectors and appoint party officialdom. A number of local "ward" committees are subject to district committees, which in turn fall under the jurisdiction of state executive committees that answer to national organs of the official party. At all levels, party-affiliated interest groups are to assume control of the party's three sectors. Theoretically, the sectors then decide among themselves which elective offices are to be apportioned to each sector, each sector selects the candidates for its designated offices, and all three sectors collectively support the nominations in the name of the official party. National organs presumably take direct charge of nominating a candidate for the office of President of Mexico, while state-level party organs select governors and senators, district organs select federal and state deputies, and local organs select municipal presidents and councilmen. In the Cárdenas plan, this kind of institutionalization was to assure "majority rule," since sector leaders during his administration represented an absolute majority of the Mexican electorate.

Cárdenas wanted interests outside official-party ranks to channel political demands through organized chambers, associations, leagues, political parties, and similar groups. As we have seen in Chapter 4, he created a series of semiofficial groupings corresponding to specific socio-economic interests, and he permitted the establishment of the National Action Party (the PAN), spokesman for the Traditional Conservatives. Yet in Cárdenas' view, all the interest groups and political parties outside the official organization would play a minor role in Mexican politics, because the government itself would be run by the majority inside the official party. What opposition, thought Cárdenas, what combination of interests outside the official party could possibly render the official party ineffective once it had entrenched itself in public power? An official party oriented toward and directed by the proletariat would guarantee perpetual control by selecting officeholders and by formulating public policy.

That the official party never fulfilled the role originally or subsequently assigned it frequently misleads observers of Mexican electoral patterns. Accepting party propaganda at near face value, one study of Mexican politics contended: "As long as the present official party continues to work out a formula for satisfying a majority of the strongest influence associations, dissatisfying as few as possible, not only the aggregating function but the decision-making process itself will reside in it and not in the formal government." [2] Contrary to this line of thought, however, the official party cannot "continue" interest satisfaction, since this role in the Mexican political system has always been performed elsewhere, whether under Cárdenas, Ávila Camacho, Miguel Alemán, or under the two Adolfos. And as for "the decision-making process," if this had actually resided in the official party instead of in the Revolutionary Family inner council and in the formal government, Mexico probably would have become a workers' state long ago. Such contentions regarding an omnipotent official party prompted the author of this book to make the following comment in *The Annals of the American Academy of Political and Social Science:* [3]

> Organized industrial and communal agricultural labor wish . . . [the claim of official-party omnipotence] were true. Party leadership dreams of it, indeed, even speaks of it once a week on its regular television program. But, once again, this time at the party's third national assembly, held the last week of March, 1960, party membership was restricted by and large to the laboring classes and popular masses. Industry and commerce, banking and insurance, top-level bureaucrats, university and normal school administrators, and military men—in short, the interests which really prospered since 1939—are still excluded from official-party ranks. Are we to believe . . . that a proletarian oriented and staffed party would sponsor two decades of government favoring its adversaries . . . ?

Belief in official-party control of Mexico is clearly fallacious. It is an idea that observant Mexicans shrug off philosophically. Not until the official party works out a formula for satisfying a majority of the strongest influence associations—and perhaps not even then—is there the slightest possibility that the political decision-making process will reside in the party instead of in the Revolutionary inner circle and the formal governmental apparatus. This does not imply that Mexico's political system as a whole does not or cannot approach majority rule or "functional democracy" through other channels. Nor does it necessarily mean that Mexican leadership has been unresponsive to basic popular needs and demands. It merely indicates that misleading, partial explanations of Mexican politics and government—including measurements of majority rule, elections, rulemaking, and the responsibility of governors to the governed—will emerge

[2] Robert E. Scott, *Mexican Government in Transition* (Urbana, Illinois: University of Illinois Press, 1960), p. 29.
[3] July 1960, pp. 188–89.

from studies that credit too much of what happens in the Mexican political system to its official party.

One of the biggest discrepancies between what the official party claims and what happens in reality involves transfer of presidential power. Therefore, let us examine this subject in some detail.

PRESIDENTIAL SUCCESSION

The Revolutionary Family has advanced certain tenets of political liberalism by lodging the real political power, the effective decision-making power, in a small elite directed by the President of Mexico or, in his stead, by the head of the Revolutionary Family. Improvement of the political climate flows directly from limiting a given "administrative team" to six years of total power. Political recruitment and political advancement operate on the principle of opening up many thousands of bureaucratic positions every six years. And everything else is subordinated to the president-designate, for it is he, in concert with the Family's inner council, who decides on the next administrative team. Superseding other presidential responsibilities is that of designating a successor according to a power formula of liberal authoritarianism in six-year doses.

The transfer of power from one president to the next—that is, the entire process of the presidential succession—involves nine steps. The first three are known in Mexican parlance as (1) *el tapado*, (2) *el verdadero tapado*, and (3) *irse a la cargada*. These initial steps collectively represent the designation and band-wagon stages. The show begins unfolding when the president (or Family head) inquires of the Revolutionary Family's inner circle, of vested interests outside the official party, and sometimes of sector leaders inside the official party what their dispositions are toward Señor X, General Y, or Lawyer Z. Aspirants are circumscribed by several constitutional provisions of which the most compelling are age (at least 35 years of age at the time of election), birth ("a Mexican by birth of Mexicans by birth"), residence (one year in the country before becoming president), and an absolute prohibition on re-election to the presidency. (The proviso that both parents must have been born in Mexico eliminates such competent men as Jaime Torres Bodet and Manuel Gómez Morin.) In reality, the narrowing-down process rarely concerns more than a half-dozen cabinet officers, with the final nod in earlier decades favoring the incumbent defense minister (Calles, Cárdenas, and Ávila Camacho) and of late the *gobernación* minister (Alemán, Ruiz Cortines, and Díaz Ordaz). The ring today seems to be widening, so that virtually any cabinet post or directorship of a major autonomous agency or government-owned industry can qualify a man for stepping upward.

Insofar as the theory of the official party is concerned, it seems pertinent to note that not a single president ever headed a labor union or the *ejidatario* confederation, the two kingpins of official-party organization. Although Alemán and López Mateos served as campaign managers for their predecessors, Cárdenas, Ávila Camacho, and Ruiz Cortines did not. Only in the 1946 election did an official-party president, Pascacio Gamboa, simultaneously serve a president-designate as campaign manager; in 1940, Gen. Heriberto Jara made room for Miguel Alemán; in 1952, Gen. Rodolfo Sánchez Taboada stepped aside for Adolfo López Mateos; and in 1958, Gen. Agustín Olachea gave way to Alfredo del Mazo. It is interesting to note that from 1940 forward, both the party president and the campaign manager became cabinet members in the new administration. And although Cárdenas, Alemán, and Ruiz Cortines once served as state governors, Ávila Camacho and López Mateos never held a governorship, although the latter did serve one term in the senate. Only two of the five last presidents distinguished themselves in formal party officialdom—Cárdenas as PNR president and López Mateos as PRI secretary-general, both for a short period of time.

In terms of place of birth, presidents since the Sonoran Dynasty have been selected from the populous entities of central Mexico: Cárdenas from Michoacán, Ávila Camacho from Puebla, Alemán and Ruiz Cortines from Veracruz, and López Mateos from the state of México. In the 1960 census, these four entities, plus the Federal District and Jalisco, comprised the most populous in the republic. There is good reason to suspect that regional pressures for seating a native son of Jalisco, third in population, or of Guanajuato or Oaxaca, seventh and eighth entities, respectively, in the presidency may prove convincing in future elections. About the only rule of thumb that seems pertinent is that those born in a heavily populated entity of central Mexico enjoy a decided edge over those born elsewhere.

The Revolutionary Family has placed less emphasis on the religion of presidential candidates than the casual observer may suspect. At one time or another in his life, every president seems to have dabbled in Catholicism, although Ávila Camacho is considered to be the only Revolutionary who became a "Catholic" president. Some Presidents of Mexico never became Freemasons, but others achieved high prominence in Masonic councils. Five attained the highest, or thirty-third, degree in Scottish Rite: Francisco Madero, Emilio Portes Gil, Pascual Ortiz Rubio, Abelardo Rodríguez, and Miguel Alemán. Two others were associated with the Mexican or Cárdenas Rite (Lázaro Cárdenas, one of the lodge's founders and grand masters, and Manuel Ávila Camacho), and two other chief executives entered orthodox Freemasonry but took little interest in the rite (Victoriano Huerta and Plutarco Elías Calles). There is no evidence suggesting that Venustiano Carranza, Alvaro Obregón, Adolfo Ruiz Cortines, or Adolfo López Mateos entered Freemasonry. To compound the religious question, mysticism constituted a strong element in the religious thinking of Madero and Calles. Divorce did not prevent Cárdenas and

Ruiz Cortines from winning the nomination, nor did the notorious atten-
tions of Calles, López Mateos and Alemán, to the fairer sex affect their
presidential ambitions adversely. The record of fifty years of Revolution
suggests that religious moderation and opposition to fanaticism probably
comprise the two "religious" qualities sought after in presidential candidates.

For every politician and high-ranking career bureaucrat, the months
leading up to the designation are full of anxiety. All are trying to out-
guess the next man on who will be named, on the identity of *el tapado*
(the hidden one). Guessing his identity early or wrongly identifying
him can mean the difference between remaining or arriving at the top
and falling into political oblivion. Uncovering *el tapado* too soon encour-
ages the taking of advanced positions and may produce mass exodus
away from the incumbent president. When the Family head finally arrives at the "correct" consensus, when the propitious moment arrives for
revealing *el tapado*, the candidate becomes *el verdadero tapado* (the one
and only true candidate). The first officials apprised of the identity of
el verdadero tapado after the inner circle of the Family has concurred
on the designation are the government minister and official-party president. Revelation to the general public comes shortly thereafter in the
form of an announcement of support by the largest trade union, the
CTM, or by the communal agricultural union, the CNC or by the FSTSE
civil servants federation. Having one of these large organizations declare
itself in favor of *el verdadero tapado* provides an aura of popularism not
otherwise available. Whether the CTM, CNC or FSTSE will enjoy the
privilege of being the first to announce the candidacy is determined by
el verdadero tapado himself. The public announcement simultaneously sets
in motion the *irse a la cargada*, or band-wagon stage. Unions, federations,
associations, agencies, regional strongmen, artificial groupings—everyone
everywhere proclaims that the only man who can continue the Revolution
is the proposed candidate. All manner of virtues are ascribed to him, and
complete silence shrouds his defects. There is no mention of his mistresses,
of his divorces, of his mistakes, or of his shortcomings. Everyone expatiates,
everyone promises submission.

The stage is now set for making the candidacy legal and for the
president-designate to "campaign." A giant outdoor rally in Mexico City
takes care of the formalities of making Señor X the candidate of the
official party. With this out of the way, the official-party president sits
back to await orders from his new chieftain, provided that the head of
the Revolutionary Family (generally the incumbent President of Mexico) sanctions the passage of total political power to the president-
designate. In actual practice, then, not only does the official party fail to
select the candidate on a sector basis, according to the theoretical plan,
but it is relegated to the position of simply rubber-stamping the choice

handed it from above. One president-designate may incorporate the official party into his program just as he finds it; another may relegate it to the role of a minor formalism, borrowing the name of the party for his own personally directed propaganda apparatus.

The presidential "campaign" in Mexico differs substantially from its counterpart in the United States. Although the foreign observer is led to believe that the candidate is seeking votes to overwhelm the opposition, this aspect never enters into the candidate's "campaign," for by this point all Mexico knows that, barring an armed revolt, the president-designate will in fact become president. In this context, the heir apparent is not a candidate in the American sense; he is the favorite son of the Revolutionary Family. The president-designate utilizes the campaign to permit people to see him in person, to size up regional strongmen on their own terrain, to examine the credentials of aspirants to the posts of senator, federal deputy, and governor, to bargain with opposition elements, and to satisfy the hundreds of friends and relatives who pop up everywhere. At this stage in the presidential succession, it counts for one to be a friend of a friend of the president-designate. The "campaign" also affords those state and local elements that wish to retain, enhance, or acquire power their big opportunity to impress the president-designate by organizing meetings, by spending money, by oratory, by unfolding economic-development schemes, and by any other means they believe will pay off. Aided by the incumbent president and government minister, "opposition parties" horse-trade for concessions in return for supporting the official candidacy or, as the case may be, for not supporting it. For his usual opposition, Vicente Lombardo Toledano traditionally receives the right to name several deputies, ambassadors, or second-level bureaucrats; Lombardo himself is permitted to retain a diplomatic passport. For his opposition in the 1950's, Gen. Jacinto Treviño of the PARM party was given the powerful directorship of the governmental agency controlling free ports and, additionally, was permitted to seat some of his people in legislative bodies. The president-designate must become president: the whole Revolutionary apparatus depends on it. Bankers, industrialists, merchants, union leaders, intellectuals, foreigners, large farmers—everyone who wishes something in the coming administration has the "campaign" period to prove himself. Spokesmen for the several Mexican publics establish their worthiness by direct consultation with the president-designate.

Although the president-designate never need worry about his own election, he does face one pressing duty at this time. Deciding on 60 senatorships, almost three times as many federal deputyships, and, if gubernatorial terms are expiring, on several governorships is a mighty task involving the ingratiation of friends, relatives, official-party affiliates, regional strongmen, and opposition elements. Hasty decisions in the case of federal deputyships can be corrected after election day by giving these seats to "opposition" candidates. But Family prestige and the unquestioned leadership of the President of Mexico demand that all senators and governors come from the official slate. However, since nominations for senators, deputies, and governors are made months before election day, the immediate months before election day are free of appeals from office-seekers for these posts.

These last few months find the president-designate working in unison with the defense minister, the government minister, and his campaign manager (who may simultaneously be official-party president) to assure that the masses and classes will stay in line before, after, and especially on election day. The major task of this concerted effort is the judicious stationing of trusted election officials, government-ministry agents, secret police, and army troops.

The sixth and seventh steps in the presidential succession are the general election and legalization of the vote tally. These steps produce invariable results: The official candidate and his senatorial team receive overwhelming majorities, opposition elements cry fraud and point out electoral illegalities, and the chamber of deputies verifies the vote tally sent it by the Federal Election Commission through the government minister. Accusations of fraud are intended to suggest the authenticity of an organized opposition, of free and effective suffrage, and of a give-and-take electoral contest in which the official slate truly won by an overwhelming majority, even though a few minor electoral manipulations occurred.

Ever since *el verdadero tapado* was revealed, an eighth step has been unfolding—that of choosing the new administrative team. Unlike a senatorship or deputyship, the offices of cabinet minister, military chief of staff, military zone commander, or director of an autonomous agency or state-owned enterprise carry access to public monies, to patronage, and to real economic and political power. For politicians and interest groups alike, these are the designations that really count. Now that the "elective" posts are filled, the various elites engage in a new guessing game: speculating on who will become treasury minister, director of Pemex, director of the Nacional Financiera, and so on. When private secretaries, undersecretaries, bureau chiefs, ambassadors, diplomatic ministers, consuls general, assistant directors and agency heads, military zone commanders and chiefs of staff, official-party officers down to the local level, special assignments, and several assistants per position are added to ministry-level appointments, then more than fifteen thousand political plums are at stake. The process of *el tapado* and *el verdadero tapado* begins anew. Revealing a minister-designate too far in advance introduces numerous dangers, such as the probability of undermining the authority of the incumbent minister or the possibility of giving an enterprising fellow a chance to set up a construction company to do business with his uncle who is slated to become public works minister. The residual patronage accruing to cabinet ministers and directors of autonomous agencies and state industries is so great that merely being a friend of their relatives and close friends means enjoying an inside track. For these and other reasons, the president-designate normally awaits inauguration day, the final step in the presidential succession, to reveal the identity of the top-level bureaucrats who will rule under him.

GUBERNATORIAL SUCCESSION

Power transfer from a state governor to his successor follows the presidential pattern. The final word belongs to the head of the Revolutionary Family, although in several instances he merely rubber-stamps the selection by a regional strongman. Under optimum "effective suffrage" procedures, the President of Mexico consults with the Family's inner circle, "opposition" factions, military zone commanders, incumbent governors, regional strongmen, and vested interests outside and inside the official party to reach the "consensus" of the important people in a given state. A senatorship, federal deputyship, military zone command, or cabinet post in the national government normally qualifies a man for consideration. *El tapado* becomes *el verdadero tapado* when the President of Mexico informs the government minister, official-party president, incumbent governor, and military zone commander of his choice, and when one of the vested interests affiliated with the official party formally announces that General X and only General X can carry on the Revolution in X's state. All important interests in the state then *irse a la cargada*, the official party legalizes the nomination, the governor-designate "campaigns," selects state legislators, and reaches a modus vivendi to govern his relationship with local *caciques* and municipal authorities. He subjects himself to the formalities of a general election whose results are verified by the state legislature, appoints his administrative team, and finally, has himself duly inaugurated.

From prenomination to inauguration, the gubernatorial succession is controlled from Mexico City. The President of Mexico selects, the government minister oversees, and the defense minister enforces. The theory of official-party sector nomination simply never enters the picture. The party's president and secretary-general may assist the President of Mexico in reaching his "consensus," but this depends on the president, not on convention. The pattern varies slightly in states where a regional strongman is permitted to call the plays; there, the president sanctions the puppet-designate of the strongman and makes the latter personally answer for government in that entity. Since López Mateos removed the holds of Gonzalo Santos over San Luis Potosí and Margarito Ramírez over Quintana Roo Territory (an appointed post), four states continue subject to strongmen: Michoacán (Lázaro Cárdenas), Puebla (the Ávila Camacho family), Nayarit (Gilberto Flores Muñoz), and Baja California (Abelardo Rodríguez). In seven additional entities, a commanding role is played by Javier Rojo Gómez (Hidalgo), Adolfo López Mateos (state of México), Gen. Gabriel Leyva Velázquez (Sinaloa), Marte R. Gómez and Emilio Portes Gil (Tamaulipas), Gen. Alfonso Corona del Rosal (Tlaxcala), Adolfo Ruiz Cortines (Veracruz), and Leobardo Reynoso (Zacatecas). Yet by 1964, of all regional chieftains only Lázaro Cárdenas in Michoacán and incumbent president Adolfo López Mateos enjoyed extraordinary power, with the latter choosing to share it in his home state with Dr. Gustavo Baz. (The regional *cacique* persists because keeping him constitutes less of a problem than removing him. At times, not removing a regional chief, such as Gonzalo Santos in San Luis Potosí, can also produce serious political tensions.) In completely ignoring Javier Rojo Gómez and Marte R. Gómez, Miguel Alemán caused serious political tensions in Hidalgo and Tamaulipas, which the two Adolfos resolved by bringing Rojo and R. Gómez back into prominence.

Miguel Alemán also illustrated another characteristic of executive succession in the states: A very strong personality in the presidency may not consult anyone on gubernatorial nominations—and, further, he may impose his personal choice over multiple objections. Alemán's treatment of labor unions was extremely harsh. Placing Sánchez Colín in the state of México governorship, for example, constituted an outright refutation of CTM leadership. Alemán ran counter to intense local antipathy toward Dr. Ignacio Morones Prieto by making this nonresident of Nuevo León governor of that important northern entity; Ruiz Cortines reduced tension there by bringing Morones Prieto into his own national cabinet. Alemán also reversed two decades of civilianism in Tamaulipas, overriding the personal objections of Marte R. Gómez and Emilio Portes Gil, by making Gen. Raúl Gárate governor. Alemán further selected unpopular governors for Guerrero, Oaxaca, and Yucatán, all of whom Ruiz Cortines subsequently removed. And Alemán highlighted the fact that the army had not been removed from politics by running the nation at one time or another during his six-year regime with fifteen military men in gubernatorial posts, including those of Baja California Sur and Quintana Roo. In short, the "consensus" may and frequently does reflect the disposition of important vested interests in a given federative entity, but it always reflects the prevailing attitude of the Revolutionary Family head (normally the President of Mexico)—and for Michoacán, Puebla, and Nayarit, the desire of regional strongmen.

Local government is based on the *municipio*, roughly analogous to a county, governed by a *presidente municipal* and *regidores*, or councilmen. In electing municipal presidents, the "consensus" is normally determined by the respective state governors or, as the case may be, governors-designate. Nonetheless, the national government minister, acting under instructions of the President of Mexico or president-designate, can intervene, overrule a governor, and impose an alternate for the official-party nomination. A state governor can never forget that regular army, navy, and air force contingents in his state are commanded from Mexico City. The national government often intervenes when a governor becomes *persona non grata* with the President of Mexico—not an unusual situation under the system of staggered gubernatorial elections. Although the Constitution provides six-year terms for both the presidency and governorships, election dates do not coincide. Thus the new president inherits state governors from his predecessor, and he rarely sees eye-to-eye on policy with all governors during the initial years of his administration—unless, of course, he legally removes uncongenial governors before their constitutional terms end. This drastic alternative may complicate yet improve state politics; it may upset political equilibrium in the inner circle of the Revolutionary Family or re-establish it. Nonetheless, except for those few states in which regional strongmen prevail, it is not difficult for the President of Mexico to unseat a governor; in the last instance, the military zone commander can insure the acquiescence of the governor. Lázaro Cárdenas removed a majority of the state governors by forced resignations, which he ordered through the national legislature, state legislatures, or achieved by direct pressure on governors to renounce their offices. Ruiz Cortines removed four governors, replacing them with politicians less enthusiastic about Miguel Alemán. A state governor in the Mexican political system either stands in the shadow of Mexico City or loses his position. *Gobernación* agents, military zone commanders, Masonic lodges, business chambers, labor, cooperativist, and agrarian unionists, Catholic prelates, and official-party representatives are continually reporting on a governor's conduct to their corresponding higher councils in Mexico City. Senators and federal deputies, themselves frequently competing for prestige with the governor of their home state, also exert an influence that keeps a governor loyal to the president. These multiple checks on a governor, plus his own normal ambitions to proceed up the bureaucratic ladder, mean that nominations for *presidente municipal* and *regidores* preferred by the national government minister in Mexico City will prevail. In general, however, the President of Mexico usually permits a governor in good standing to designate municipal presidents, who in turn select their own *regidores*. Local official-party organs finally proclaim these choices to be the party's very own candidates.

THE LEGISLATORS

By now, the reader should anticipate the "consensus" patterns marking the election of legislators. Aside from *regidores*, who theoretically fulfill the legislative function at the local level, there are three sets of legislators in Mexico: state deputies, federal deputies, and (federal) senators. Deputies to unicameral state legislatures represent electoral districts mapped out on the basis of population. Who will sit in a state legislature depends on the whims of the governor, governor-designate, or regional strongman, who determines the "consensus" of a given electoral district. He passes the nomination of a deputy-designate along to the state minister of government and to the official-party state president, who in turn picks an interest group affiliated with the official party to make the candidacy known publicly. Finally, the official party legalizes the candidacy. Though official-party nomination resolves the succession question then and there, the fiction of effective suffrage is upheld by a general election, accusations of fraud, and the seating of official candidates, who invariably win thumping majorities. Some governors arbitrarily select all state legislators; others turn over the entire nomination apparatus to regional strongmen, and still others permit union bosses, *ejidatario* leaders, local *caciques*, and politicians in the official party to designate candidates. The last procedure results in local labor and *ejido* bosses grabbing as many seats as they can for themselves. Whether official-party sectors cut up the electoral pie or someone outside the party does it for them, no effective power is at stake anyway: a state legislature obsequiously follows the state leader, be he governor, regional strongman, or governor-designate.

Under these circumstances, why does anyone seek a state deputyship in the first place? For additional salary, for the privileges and immunities that the office bestows, and in the peculiar Mexican sense, to rise above the masses—to no longer be like the average man-in-the-street or peasant-in-the-field. A union boss or a peasant leader hardly looks upon his "election" to a deputyship as a mandate for representing the electorate or his own rank and file—he and everybody else knows that the legislature is an impotent branch of government. The material benefits that accrue to the interest groups whose leaders sit in legislative bodies come from the executive branch, completely independent of these deputies. Groups never bring their claims before a legislature unless they are putting on a show for the executive or for visiting foreign dignitaries. It is the executive who answers to Mexico City for the conduct of his legislature. Inside or outside the official party, groups seek and obtain governmental benevolence from the executive branch directly, not through the powerless legislature or official party. When union leaders become state deputies, they add a few thousand pesos to their regular monthly incomes and acquire fringe benefits in the form of immunity from the application of certain laws and the privilege of importing certain items tariff-free; union rank and file receive nothing. The leaders use the new prestige and extra money to live better and to facilitate their upward mobility in the Mexican political system and captive union network. For two decades, the union boss has kept the rank and file in line, loyal to Revolutionary regimes. His reward, besides the permanence of his tenure, sometimes comes in the form of a legislative office.

The practice of rewarding labor bosses in this fashion is nowhere more pronounced than in the designation and composition of the national senate and chamber of deputies. For more than two decades, the big bosses of the biggest labor union, the CTM, have regularly sat in both chambers, yet the proletariat which they avowedly represented gained few notable advances in real income. Since 1940, the CTM bosses have conveniently alternated from senate to chamber of deputies. (Immediate re-election to either house is prohibited constitutionally). This kind of deal originated in 1940, when Cárdenas decided that Lombardo Toledano would relinquish his leadership of the CTM on terminating his secretary-generalship in 1941. To replace him came four of the "five little wolves" who had deserted Luis Morones and the CROM in the early 1930's to back Cárdenas and ultimately form a part of the CTM core: Fidel Velázquez, Fernando Amilpa, Alfonso Sánchez Madariaga, and Jesús Yurén. Division of the spoils resulted in Amilpa and Sánchez Madariaga becoming senators in 1940, Velázquez becoming CTM secretary-general in 1941, and Yurén becoming secretary-general of the biggest "state" federation, that of the Federal District. Six years later, Velázquez and Amilpa switched places—the former became a senator, the latter CTM secretary-general for three years. In 1949, Velázquez reassumed the CTM secretary-generalship, a post that he had not relinquished by 1964. In 1952, Yurén took a senate seat, and in 1958, Fidel Velázquez was back once again in the senate. Meanwhile, Amilpa died and Sánchez Madariaga became secretary-general of the hemisphere-wide Inter-American Labor Organization (the ORIT), of which the AFL-CIO is a member. Throughout this score of years, the CTM chieftains also took federal deputyships; in addition to his senatorship during 1940–46, Sánchez Madariaga became a deputy in 1937–40, 1946–49, and 1955–58. In the states and, to a lesser degree, in the Federal District, other CTM and railroad, petroleum, and mining union bosses have followed an identical pattern. Whenever the labor sector is awarded the right to designate official-party candidates for legislative offices, the labor bosses nominate themselves. And why not? There is no real power involved in the federal legislature, and the President of Mexico keeps his captive labor leaders placated by permitting them to acquire the extra money, privileges, immunities, and prestige of an office that other labor leaders are denied.

Division of the spoils of the federal legislature is a principal responsibility of the president-designate during his presidential campaign; three years later, as President of Mexico, he again decides on the membership composition of the chamber of deputies. In all, 60 senators (two from each state and from the Federal District) enter the upper house for a six-year term, and 178 deputies (based on total population proportioned among the states) enter the lower house for a three-year term.[4]

The "consensus" for a senator depends on the president-designate who, after insisting on his personal choices, usually permits sector leaders to name the rest. Since 1940, labor bosses, CNC spokesmen, and other known regulars of the official party account for approximately two-thirds of total senatorial seats awarded. Translated into other terms this means that interest-group leaders in the official party were permitted to name about two-thirds of the senators, while the president-designate, with or without the advice and consent of governors, regional strongmen, factional leaders of the Revolutionary Family, or the incumbent President of Mexico, personally named the rest. But no single *tapado* from the official party becomes *el verdadero tapado*, whether he is a party regular or not, unless the president-designate gives his final approval. Once candidates are approved by the president-designate, the official party holds intraparty primaries to nominate these same candidates by "democratic process," after which the party's president makes the candidacies public. Thus formally and legally proclaimed the senatorial candidates of the official party, all senators-designate share the comfort of knowing that 32 years of precedent will not be reversed to seat any opposing candidates. Furthermore, the government minister, election commission, President of Mexico, president-designate, and Mexican army are at hand to guarantee their election. Regardless of what happens on election day, official-party nomination guarantees a seat in the senate.

With federal deputies as well, the "will of the people" is what the president-designate and President of Mexico say it is. Since 1940, the Revolutionary Family head, President of Mexico, and president-designate have hand-picked about 20 per cent of the deputies; governors and regional *caciques* have selected approximately 15 per cent; opposition parties have been given almost 5 per cent; and the remaining 60 per cent has emerged from sectors in the official party. Invariably, candidates picked outside the official-party sector arrangement have been conveniently made

---

[4] The new election law of December, 1962, provides that any political party winning 2.5 per cent of the national vote, whether five of its candidates actually win or not, will automatically obtain at least five deputy seats. Any party will acquire another seat for each additional one-half of 1 per cent of the total national vote. The new formula, to be applied for the first time in the 1964 federal elections, will prevail up to a maximum of twenty deputy seats. No similar provision was written into the new law on senatorial elections.

the choices of the popular sector. This means that every three years about 35 labor leaders and 40-odd *ejidatario* spokesmen become federal deputies, while the remaining seats in the lower house ostensibly go to the "popular sector." The nominations from the three sectors and those of governors and regional *caciques* reach the president-designate or President of Mexico or both, where they are approved or disapproved, other choices are added, and the final definitive slate is given to the official-party president. Intraparty primaries then "democratize" all nominations, and the candidates are legally registered with the government minister. A meaningless campaign culminates on election day with victory for 95 per cent of the official slate. The official party runs candidates for every federal deputy district in the republic, and a few official candidates lose to "opposition" standard-bearers. Not one instance of complaint from a "defeated" official-party candidate is on record. Opposition parties, on the other hand, variously accuse the official party, governors, electoral officials, and military men of manifold sins of omission and commission. These post-election-day antics are supposed to suggest that although the election was not entirely free, "effective suffrage" did materialize because opposition parties "participated vigorously" in the election. The token seats awarded to opposition parties are usually from election districts in which the official-party organization for historical causes is in fact weak— districts in Durango, the Federal District, Guerrero, Jalisco, Nuevo León, Oaxaca, and Puebla. But sometimes the president or president-designate hands over a deputyship to the opposition in order to discipline an official candidate who has fallen from official grace between the time of his nomination and election day.

A chief executive who wishes to strengthen the legislative branch into a real power factor faces insuperable problems. Mexican tradition expects, virtually demands, an omnipotent president. Official-party composition and electoral procedures further combine to seat legislators who are unrepresentative of Mexican interests as a whole. Few interest-group leaders who reach the legislature are truly dedicated to their respective interest groups; they merely authoritatively manage the interest group in their charge. In this context, magnanimous presidents who sincerely attempt to build up the legislature invariably run into trouble.

POLITICAL PRESTIGE AND POLITICAL MOBILITY

If new jobs made available through electoral procedures comprised the entirety of bureaucratic patronage, there is little doubt that a sad fate would befall Revolutionary Mexico. Recruitment of new elements in sufficient numbers to give the political system continuous vitality would become impossible, and ambitious, politically conscious young men, denied hope of ingratiating themselves before the ruling elite, would be forced to look outside the Revolutionary mechanism for opportunities to enter public offices. Periodic access to all top jobs constitutes the Revolutionary formula for avoiding political stagnation. The price of permanent revolution is bureaucratic job turnover and the creation of new jobs. Top wages for loyal public service come in the form of six years of golden opportunity at the head of a cabinet ministry, autonomous agency, government-owned enterprise, or state government. Even when the change amounts to little more than switching jobs among a certain set of individuals (as occurred during the switchover from Ruiz Cortines to López Mateos), whereby managers of state enterprises move to other state enterprises, directors of autonomous agencies become cabinet ministers, and some cabinet ministers remain but bring new undersecretaries and bureau chiefs into their ministries—even then, the principle of change for the sake of patronage and vitality is upheld. Old elements entering different offices are permitted a relatively free hand in selecting a new team to serve under them.

Providing an ever-increasing number of public jobs, if not in government service proper, then in government-owned enterprises, thus comprises a major ingredient of the permanent revolution. Some idea of pressures for jobs in the public sector is gleaned from the growing number of sons, grandsons, brothers, nephews, and cousins of big and near-big Revolutionaries who have appeared on the scene since 1910. Of course, many of these descendants forgo a political career for private business and the professions, but thousands of new Revolutionary offspring come of age every six years. More imposing is the increasing number of university graduates who prefer the security and promise of public service to private pursuits. Satisfying all Mexicans, or even a majority of Mexicans, is not the *sine qua non* of permanent revolution. Finding jobs for enough Revolutionary descendants and college graduates is an important matter, however—one in which the Revolutionary Family has been successful so far, either by providing posts in the public quarter or through public policies that have stimulated new and bigger opportunities in private industry, commerce, and the professions. Gearing continuance of the Revolution to job satisfaction for Mexicans in the twenty-to-thirty-year age bracket may never have comprised a conscious Revolutionary Family policy, but it is precisely one achievement of the past two decades that checked praetorianism and permitted a generation of Mexicans to enjoy greater political liberalism and a life free from ruthless suppression.

From the presidential office down to municipal governmental organs, from giant state industries to small regulatory agencies, from the official party to captive opposition parties, every six-year administration witnesses a turnover of approximately 18,000 elective offices and 25,000 appointive posts. Discounting most of the 12,000-odd local councilmen and the 8,000 appointive jobs in the official party because of the relatively low pay involved leaves some 6,000 elective and 17,000 appointive positions for which the politicians compete in full knowledge that success will bring higher income. The politically ambitious enter anyplace along the line—as private secretaries of ministers, as technicians in a state industry, as normal school teachers, or in one of hundreds of ways. The general tendency is for the educated, technically prepared young men, including the usual host of young lawyers, to enter the political system through the civil service, and for the less-educated to initiate a political career through the lower elective offices. Of course, there is a fair amount of crossover, with onetime career bureaucrats becoming senators, federal deputies, or governors. The president of the official party (since 1946, an army general) moves on to the national defense ministership. Local *caciques*, whose power position lies outside the normal pattern, usually grab off state legislative posts. Since Alemán, the bureaucratic machine has favored placing technically qualified individuals in high appointive positions as well as in the thousands of middle-rank positions in cabinet ministries, autonomous agencies, boards, and commissions, and in state industries, banks, and related business enterprises. Captive leaders of communal agriculture, civil service, trade, and other unions enter politics through the official party; their future rarely holds the promise of anything beyond a senatorship.

From this complex patronage structure, a hierarchy of political prestige has slowly emerged. Does a state cabinet office carry more prestige than a federal deputyship? A supreme court justice more than a state governor? A manager of a big state industry less than a senator? Does the Mexican ambassador to Washington deserve higher prestige than the private secretary to the President of Mexico? What is the relationship of members of the Family's inner circle to cabinet members? That of a big trade-union boss to an official-party president? The answers to these questions can be found in the scale of political prestige that applies to the Mexican political system as a whole. Excluding business elements, which exert political influence but rarely wish for "political" prestige, and understanding that some persons through special talents or influences are able to enjoy prestige and power beyond that expected from their specific posts, the ladder of political prestige has twelve rungs:

12. Local party officials and municipal councilmen.
11. Municipal presidents, local military commanders, and state and federal officials at the local level.
10. State deputies, state judges, district official-party officials, federal officials in the states, and local *caciques*.
 9. Federal deputies; federal judges; the president and members of regional executive councils of the official party; leaders of minor opposition parties; labor, agrarian, and federal credit bank bosses at the state level; and state cabinet officers.

8. Municipal presidents in large cities.
7. Directors and managers of medium-size state industries; directors of secondary federal boards, commissions, and agencies; governors of medium and small states; ambassadors, ministers, and consuls general.
6. Supreme court justices; senators; undersecretaries of cabinet ministries and assistant directors of large state industries, commissions, boards, and dependencies; the secretary-general and sector heads of the official party, leaders of major opposition parties; and the secretaries-general of the CTM, CNC, and FSTSE.
5. Governors of the big states and the federal territories, ambassadors in prestige posts, regional strongmen not in the inner circle, the two presidential legislative spokesmen in the respective houses of congress, military zone commanders, and the official-party president.
4. Cabinet members, including the governor of the Federal District; the military chief of staff; the private secretary of the president; managers of major state industries; and directors of large semiautonomous agencies, commissions, banks, and boards.
3. Members of the inner circle and factional leaders of the Revolutionary Family.
2. The President of Mexico.
1. The head of the Revolutionary Family.

Permanent revolution thus depends on a political system that opens top bureaucratic positions every three years at the local level and every six years at the state and national levels. Bright, competent individuals who miss the patronage boat with one administration know that the next regime will offer them another opportunity to hop aboard. For example, a Marxist economist in an advisory capacity to the president may not remain or obtain a better position when an avid pro-private-enterprise Revolutionary becomes president. What does he do? He returns to his classes at the National University, writes a few treatises on aspects of political economy, and participates in special research projects while awaiting the next administration.

Two notable exceptions to general mobility, both of them potential monkey wrenches in the Revolutionary mechanism, have occurred in trade unions and the Mexican army. Bosses of the largest labor central, the CTM, have not relinquished their control of the labor movement for more than two decades, not the least because no president since Cárdenas has emphatically supported syndicalism, hence no president has dared risk upsetting economic development by removing these captive leaders. But big troubles lie ahead for CTM leadership; the rank and file despise their opportunistic conduct and, permitted a free, honest vote, would unload the whole leadership forthwith. The blockade to mobility in the military is raised by the old Revolutionary generals who have run the army since 1940. Though near or over seventy years of age, they refuse to step down. Becoming a general has been denied virtually all officers who are not veterans of civil war days. With an estimated 11,000 "auxiliary" officers—officers who draw full pay but engage in private pursuits—the military today, as in the past, is top-heavy with officers. What will happen when the younger officer crew, professional soldiers by vocation, finally move into zone commanderships, cabinet posts, and governorships is anybody's guess. Defense ministers obviously will have to come from among those officers without active service in the 1920's. The army as an institution, instead of simply a means by which several thousand old military men drain from the public treasury enough to keep themselves personally content, has prospects of regaining a bigger voice in Mexican political life. The stockpile of several thousand younger officers probably constitutes the most concentrated force of highly educated and surely best-disciplined men in the entire nation. For many years they have observed as their senior officers shared in the allocations of contracts let in their respective military zones, or obtained low-interest loans from government banks. And they have noted that accountants, engineers, small businessmen, and even full-time university professors receive higher salaries than theirs. Without this officer core behind it, the Revolutionary elite cannot continue to direct the destiny of Mexico—and of late, much of the younger officer corps seems noticeably impatient for more authority and higher income.

It is doubtful whether the Revolution could continue if the individual bureaucrat, in addition to being socially responsible, were not also self-seeking and opportunistic. A bureaucrat helps himself from the public till—sometimes more, like the *alemanistas*, sometimes less, like the *ruizcortinistas*. But graft there is, and undoubtedly, graft there always will be. Reduction of grafting? Possible. Elimination of graft? A contradiction of human nature. Many Mexican career civil servants live almost solely on their biweekly paychecks from the government. Aside from picking up a few pesos here and there by expediting papers, temporarily borrowing minor papers in their charge, and accepting gifts at Christmas and before Easter week from middlemen regularly engaged in government work—all in all, totaling less than four hundred U.S. dollars annually—perhaps 90 per cent of the bureaucrats are "honest," and thus persons of modest incomes. Even if tempted by grafting on a grandiose scale, civil servants below the upper 10 per cent bracket rarely hold positions important enough to realize their dream. In case the American tourist suffers from the illusion that customs officials at the border pocket the ten or twenty pesos that they politely fleece from the American, let us make clear that the lion's share goes to higher officialdom. It is these higher positions to which ambitious bureaucrats aspire. The prospect of $120 monthly and, after forty years, retirement with a modest pension is not their goal. Some of the presumed career bureaucrats who possess high political acumen (and usually technical competence as well) rise to the top, take what they can, retire from public service forever, and engage in more pleasant, less painstaking pursuits. What truly keeps a large stockpile of bureaucrats loyal to the Revolution is the prospect of someday satisfying their personal appetites—the hope that through dedicated service they too can rise to the top, make a fortune, and retire, not at 62, but at 42.

The bureaucracy as an interest group seeking benefits for itself in return for loyal, continuous services by and large encompasses only those civil servants up to the top 10 per cent—the "policy-making" level. Government financing of low-cost housing projects for civil servants, government dispensing of foodstuffs, clothing, and medicines at reduced prices to civil servants, government-financed vacation hotels for civil servants, vacations with pay, pay bonuses, shorter work hours, all manner of fringe benefits—every advancement of this nature holds little attraction for the top 10 per cent of the bureaucracy. For this bureaucratic elite, a fashionable home in the Lomas or San Angel districts of Mexico City, a weekend cottage in Cuernavaca, Cuautla, or Acapulco, and vacations in the United States or Europe for their families—all achievements beyond the reach of the career civil service—are the awards worth striving for. Social prestige, and particularly the snobbishness of the high bureaucrat's wife, precludes his living in a mass-style housing development or vacationing in the same hotel with the bureaucratic rank and file. While the 90 per cent are thinking of working a lifetime for the government, the 10 per cent are usually thinking of ways to boost their incomes high enough to permit them to get out of government work—or out of work in general.

It is the spokesmen of the FSTSE (the civil servants' union) who proclaim the rights of civil servants before the President of Mexico and the upper 10 per cent of the bureaucracy. In the final instance, it is the president who rules on FSTSE requests for higher benefits and on the union leaders' ambitions for extra income. Seating a few civil-service union leaders in legislative chambers, which adds to their regular pay, takes care of the leadership; the vast majority of Mexican civil servants, perhaps like career civil servants elsewhere, are not very ambitious. Thus it is that the FSTSE, which avowedly speaks for the 90 per cent, manages to gain a few deputy and senator seats for men who are usually technically unprepared for ever reaching the higher positions in public administration.

The ambitious Mexican who rises to the top of the politico-bureaucratic heap, whether through the career civil service, the military, state industries, or state governments, by faithful political militancy in political parties, or merely by virtue of being a descendant of a great Revolutionary, rarely needs more than six years to accumulate sufficient capital to retire for life. Of course, many officials continue to serve in successive administrations. But unlike the first eight rungs of the political prestige ladder, the top four rungs provide the bureaucratic wherewithal to earn a comfortable retirement. A cabinet minister, for example, begins with his base pay and his privilege of importing certain commodities tariff-free; his salary is then greatly augmented by service on the boards of directors of government banks, agencies, dependencies, and state industries. For the finance minister, these extra "duties" on boards of directors pay handsomely: as much as $60,000 annually for six years. Even a minor cabinet minister will sit on ten or twelve boards and earn $15,000 yearly. Besides these sources of income, a cabinet minister can usually invest in companies doing business with his ministry and in other ways "honestly" increment his income by taking advantage of public works, changes in tariff schedules, new laws, etc. When all "honest" paths come to an end and a cabinet minister still lacks desired capital, he will find suppliers to his ministry anxious to kick back 10 per cent on large sales, more on small sales. The precise amount a cabinet minister or state-industry manager finally accumulates by the end of six years largely depends on himself, although when grafting becomes excessive and injurious to his rule, the President of Mexico may step in and close some sources of a subordinate's income. The average minister or director finishes his term with two or three houses, a good library, two or three automobiles, a ranch, and $100,000 cash; about 25 directors and ministers hold posts from which they can leave office with fifty times that amount in cash. In this perspective, it is clear why six years in a top office is long enough, why the politically conscious Mexican is willing to serve faithful apprenticeships, or why the indefinite terms of office characterizing pre-Revolutionary days have been replaced by firm adherence to the principle of no re-election.

POLITICAL SECURITY

Why have Mexicans condoned the manner in which their Revolution has developed over the past two decades? The privileged, forming the top 20 per cent, naturally accept the present direction. Most of the rest probably do not accept it, but they are led by men from the privileged class. University graduates and politically ambitious youths find opportunities inside and outside the bureaucracy and soon join the top 20 per cent. Periodic opening of the bureaucratic machine absorbs substantial new elements every six years at the national and state levels, every three years at the local level. There is some doubt whether private enterprise is doing the same—that is, providing attractive jobs in sufficient number to satisfy the job appetites of college and technical school graduates. Meanwhile, what can the masses do about their plight? They may be conscious of long-range benefits brought by the Revolution—political stability; relative freedom of speech, press, religion, and assembly; education; roads; the promise of electrification; irrigation; sanitation—all of which tends to soothe day-by-day poverty. They may even think that they are contributing to the building of a greater Mexico, to national integration, and to other planks in the Revolutionary Creed. But if they chose to force the issue of real-wage increases now, of easier access to credit, and of a bigger share in national income, how would they proceed? Would the central government order the army, navy, and air force to repress an armed rebellion of the peasantry and proletariat? Would they choose to shoot down the very elements that the Revolution purportedly represents? So far the government has snuffed out armed factions founded on basic discontent before they could grow into serious threats. A look at the permanent channels of political security offers insight into the small chances of success internal rebellion holds so long as control points remain loyal to the President of Mexico.

In addition to the regular cabinet ministries, federal agencies and banks, government-owned industries, and the federal court system, the President of Mexico relies on dozens of other permanent channels of political communication and sanction application. Captive labor-union and agricultural-federation leaders report on their rank-and-file membership and on outside powers making attempts to divert the labor movement from Mexicanism. Senators, federal deputies, and state governors keep the chief executive advised on affairs in their respective constituencies. The official party and "opposition" political groupings loyally communicate information to party headquarters and the *gobernación* ministry. Masonic lodges serve as watchdogs over religious tolerance; the Catholic Church reports on Communist abuses. Foreign embassies and legations stalemate one another. Vested private interests, including the press, radio, and television industries, offer information voluntarily. To bring the security picture into sharper focus, the President of Mexico relies on seventeen principal agents: (1) the minister of the presidency and special presidential aides; (2) the military chief of staff, the presidential guards, the ministers of defense and navy, and the army and navy zone commanders; (3) *gobernación* agents; (4) agents of the Federal Security Commission (*Comisión Federal de Seguridad*); (5) treasury agents; (6) the attorneys general; (7) judicial police; (8) federal judges; (9) labor conciliators; (10) federal credit bank officials; (11) the minister of foreign affairs and the diplomatic and consular corps; (12) state governors; (13) official-party officials; (14) regional and local strongmen; (15) teachers, agricultural agents, and public-health officials; (16) telegraph and railroad agents; and (17) private bankers. The three essential, continuous key agents of the security apparatus are the armed forces, *gobernación* and secret police agents, and state governors. The armed forces, in turn, are watched by state governors and *gobernación* agents, who themselves are reported upon by military zone commanders. In comparison with the federal security system, the security apparatus of governors is relatively restricted. The whole mechanism draws heavily on the principle of divide and rule.

To say the least, the Revolutionary Family is in a strong position to meet opposition. The loyalty of the armed forces is buttressed by a variety of factors: professional status, the prohibition on military zone commanders taking their troops with them when transferred to another zone, faith in the continuance of the Revolution, the privilege of generals to graft on government contracts. The danger of any cabinet minister or other favorite building up sufficient personal power to challenge Family leadership is reduced by the changeover of the administrative team every six years. All in all, the success of liberal authoritarianism in six-year doses owes much to the security apparatus of the Revolutionary elite heading Mexico.

POLITICS AND THE PEOPLE

Little by little, the gap between the President of Mexico and the people of Mexico is closing. Presidents have become less fearful of the people and the people less afraid of their presidents. This encouraging state of affairs improves tolerance and extends freedom. Violence is rarely employed by a president to sustain himself in power—although, on the other hand, opposition elements have never been permitted to acquire enough power to be in a position to challenge the Revolutionary elite. Personalism persists, however, and the President of Mexico still *gives* public works to the nation—"el señor presidente da a los mexicanos." The president, as final arbiter, must appear to be just and impartial and always "take from the rich (the bad) and give to the poor (the good)." When questioned on abuses of the ruling elite, the Mexican usually replies with a stock answer: Politics is that way; anyway, we have more freedom today, and we do not like the thought of returning to the cruelty and destruction of the first decade of the Revolution. Besides, Mexicans today have the good fortune of a turnover in dictators every six years.

The actual Mexican political system is far removed from theory and legality. The presidential, gubernatorial, and legislative nominating process varies greatly from the theory of official-party operation, effective political opposition, and legal norms. Significant interest groups affiliated with the official party are captives of the ruling elite, and the several interests that have really prospered since 1939 are outside the official party. Tradition, the expectation (and perhaps dire necessity) of a strong executive, civic apathy, illiteracy, an entrenched bureaucracy, and a host of other factors accentuate gaps between constitutionalism and practice. Fifty years of Revolution suggest that the appearance of effective interest groups and political parties unimpeded by constant governmental intervention is wishful thinking. In working toward the fulfillment of ideals in the Revolutionary Creed, the Revolutionary Family has brought a fair measure of political liberalism into Mexican life. It has also shown itself sensitive and responsive to many popular needs. But the future, like the past five decades, holds little promise of improving democratic goals beyond the expectation of placing in the presidential office a tolerant, powerful chief executive—of retaining the "liberal Machiavellian."

SEVEN

RELIGION

~~~~~~

Some observers believe that the vested interest of greatest potential danger to the permanent Revolution, especially to Family control over it, is the Catholic hierarchy. As we have discovered in earlier chapters, clericalism has purportedly been checked by countervailing planks in the Revolutionary Creed. But how effective are these planks? Is the government unwittingly encouraging a resurgence of clericalism? Does the Revolutionary Family rely solely on public education and Freemasonry to prevent fanaticism and clericalism?

From the outset, we should recognize that the Church in Mexico is simultaneously Roman and Mexican: So much Mexicanism enters the spiritual content of religion and prompts the Church's temporal activities that Catholicism in Mexico bears but slight resemblance to the Catholic Church in the United States. In fact, Mexican religious institutions are unique to Mexico. This chapter focuses on Catholicism and Freemasonry, the two most important religious institutions in Mexico, but also discusses Judaism, Protestantism, and education.

CATHOLICS, PROTESTANTS, JEWS, AND FREEMASONS

The ethical and moral values held by most Mexicans stem from both Indian and Western European sources. But this gives little definition, since there were hundreds of separate Indian "nations" in Mexico and a number of nation-states in Western Europe, each giving a special twist to Catholicism, Protestantism, Judaism, and Freemasonry. Catholicism originally entered Mexico through Spanish clerics who, by virtue of papal extension of the royal prerogative (*real patronato*) and recognition of the "divine right of kings," answered first to the Spanish crown and then, if at all, to the Vatican. New Spain was a State-Church and a Church-State in which a cleric often held office as viceroy or governor. The obligation of the general citizenry to pay certain tithes to the Church was a legal requirement as well as a moral duty. The state energetically back-scratched and log-rolled on behalf of the Church, and vice versa. Any meaningful "God and Caesar" division of society was impossible. Why, reasoned high clerics, should the Church not acquire real estate and engage in banking, industry, and commerce? After all, the Church was the king's most loyal ally.

When Napoleon upset the Spanish imperial applecart, the prospect of Mexican independence raised crucial questions on the role of the Catholic Church. Would the royal prerogative naturally devolve upon the government of a former Spanish colony? Should the new governors work hand-in-hand with churchmen, just as Spanish overlords had done in the past? Or, contrary to the old order of things and to the accepted dictates of wisdom, had the time arrived for reducing the Church's temporal power? Clerics themselves were divided, with high clergymen tending in one direction and parish priests in another. Beyond jurisdictional problems involving temporal matters, there also existed a duality of beliefs and dogma: The Europe-oriented Catholic, for example, had little if anything to do with the Indian's dark-skinned Virgin of Guadalupe, the so-called "Empress of America."

The powerful Church-State, aided by the Inquisition and other censorship devices, succeeded in shutting out virtually all non-Catholic creeds. At the very time when Protestantism was making decided inroads into northern European societies, Catholicism flowered into a militant, all-pervasive religion in Spain. This resurgence of Catholicism in Spain intensified the missionary zeal of priests newly arrived in the Spanish colonies to save the Indian soul at all cost. It was only after national independence that Protestant missionaries could begin to think of large-scale, open proselytizing in Mexico. When they arrived, and even then on a small scale, they brought special brands of Protestantism from the United States, a nation in which Catholicism had never approached a status of the religion of the majority, much less become officially established. American missionaries had to deal with a society in which other institutionalized religions stood like David before the mighty Catholic Goliath.

If the Reformation ever reached Mexico, it did so in the backhanded form of Freemasonry. The inference should not be drawn, however, that Freemasonry is a reformed Christianity. It is not. Nor should it be concluded that Catholics are prohibited from entering Freemasonry by virtue of Freemasonry itself. What precludes the devout Catholic from entering Freemasonry are papal encyclicals prohibiting the Catholic from becoming a Freemason. To the degree that Catholics in Mexico (including not a few priests) did in fact enter Masonic lodges, they questioned papal infallibility and were no longer Roman Catholics. Few Protestant missionaries coming to Mexico even today understand how a Mexican can be baptized a Catholic, abandon Catholicism in favor of Freemasonry during his entire adulthood, and, in some cases, return to the Church for the final sacrament of extreme unction. Not that a more enlightened Protestant approach would have produced different results: Nineteenth-century Mexico was profoundly "Catholic," a condition that 150 years of Protestant proselytizing has not altered perceptibly. Today, Protestant religions still hold little promise of making large-scale inroads: The percentage of Protestants rose from 1.28 per cent of Mexico's total population in 1950 to 1.60 per cent in 1960, when the number of Protestants amounted to just under 579,000.

We should also understand that Judaism blends uniquely into Mexican society. Except for World War II refugees, old resident Americans, and new resident foreign businessmen and diplomats, Judaism in Mexico assumes its fundamental characteristics from Sephardism, particularly in the case of the anomalous "Catholic Jews" and "Jewish Catholics." The Sephardic Jew, who follows the Spanish Jewish rituals, accents mysticism and Messianic tendencies, not the least because it was in Spain of the thirteenth century that Jewish mysticism reached its highest point of development. After the reconquest of Granada in 1492, Jews were ordered to accept Christianity or leave Aragon and Castile. Spanish monarchs even attempted to exclude Jews from the Spanish colonies by requiring immigrants to prove "purity of blood." When confronted by the Inquisition, not a few Jews saved their lives by assuming new names and seeking refuge in baptism. Sephardic Jews probably predominated among Jews coming to the American colonies, but they ceased to emigrate to the United States after 1800. The Yiddish-speaking German and Eastern European Jew who came to dominate American Jewry professed different spiritual beliefs. In short, Sephardic became a distinct minority factor in American Jewry. But the Sephardic Jews kept coming to New Spain and independent Mexico, "Catholicized" or not.

The most notorious case of anti-Judaism in Mexico on record goes back to New Spain of the late sixteenth century. At the center of the whole affair was one Luis de Carvajal, a Portuguese convert to Christianity, who led the conquerors into the northern province of Nuevo León in which Monterrey became and still remains the principal city. Under Governor Carvajal's guidance, this remote, desert-ridden province became a prosperous, orderly community. Helping Carvajal in his settlement venture were a hundred Portuguese families brought to Nuevo León by virtue of King Philip II's royal permission. Ecclesiastical authorities entered the picture when Carvajal was denounced to the Holy Office. His crime? Simply that most of the Portuguese turned out to be Jews—not "Catholic Jews" or "Jewish Catholics," either, but fervent, unrepentant Sephardic Jews. The Inquisition turned first upon Carvajal and, in 1590, despite his own affirmation of Catholicism, condemned this enlightened colonial official to a six-year exile for not having informed the Holy Office of the existence of Jews in Nuevo León.

The Inquisition next moved against the entire Carvajal family and other victims, impounding 120 "heretics" in all. Unapprised of the charges brought against them and never confronted by their accusers, a niece, a young nephew, and several other relatives of Carvajal were subjected to judicial torture, strangled, and burned in the public "burning house" of Mexico City. Ironically, the Palace of Fine Arts stands today on the very spot where the Carvajal clan went up in flames.

How deeply the conversion of Sephardic Jews to Catholicism took root with the passage of time is a moot question. We do know, however, that some former Sephardic Jews completely ignored Judaism, came to Mexico, and gave birth to outstanding Catholic families, and that others gave lip-service to Catholicism while maintaining their old faith. And there is evidence, particularly since 1910, that some families divided on religion. There is the case of the "first-generation Jew"—the Sephardic Jew who marries a Jewess and renounces Catholicism, while his own parents remain Catholics. Some Jewish families have remained nominal Catholics, which gives rise to the anomaly of Catholic Jews and Jewish Catholics, depending on first preferences.

Another unusual manifestation of Judaism in Mexico is the Jewish Indian who speaks Hebrew and attends the synagogue. The initial shock of the American Jew who by chance enters the poorer synagogue while vacationing in Mexico is profound. Who taught the Indian this ancient language? Who converted him to Judaism? Why does he ostracize himself from the Catholics of his village? Indian Jewish families are dispersed throughout the states of Puebla, México, Veracruz, Nuevo León, and in the Federal District. Once again, the mysteries of Mexico run deeply into the past.

Instances of anti-Semitism are recorded during both the colonial era and the national independence period. In the present century—although some violence against the so-called "Syrians" has flared up from time to time, and although the Nazi organization in Mexico whipped up some racial tensions before and after Mexico entered World War II and a surreptitious neo-Nazi group caused ill-will in 1959 and 1960—the first fifty years of Revolution were relatively free of religious and ethnic intolerance, save of course that directed against Catholics and the Catholic Church. The relative absence of anti-Semitism is reflected in the numerical growth of Judaism between 1950 and 1960: The number of *Israelitas*, as recorded in official censuses, increased during the decade from 17,572 to 100,750. Yet even such a remarkable percentage growth failed to make Jews more than 0.3 per cent of the total Mexican population.

CATHOLICISM AND CHURCH–STATE RELATIONS

Like every ruling clique before it, the Revolutionary Family must tackle the problem of Church and State relations. The Revolutionaries attempted to resolve the problem—at least on paper—by incorporating into the Constitution provisions forbidding clericalism, religious education, and Church ownership of property. Enforcement of these provisions has depended primarily on the disposition of the president and the state governors on the one hand, and on the high clergy and educational institutions on the other. Viewed administratively, the ministries of government (*gobernación*) and public education and the attorney general are the legal organs charged with enforcement of laws pertaining to religion. In the states, this responsibility falls on the shoulders of state governors. Masonic lodges all over the country voluntarily maintain a close vigilance of Church conduct, and in this sense, Freemasons are a watchdog of religious freedom. Masonic lodges, together with public-school teachers and local army garrisons (the teacher and soldier are in many instances Masons as well), serve as informants to municipal, state, and national government officials.

But the last word in law enforcement resides in the head of the Revolutionary Family. Carranza and Obregón opposed the Church in principle, yet both discovered a modus vivendi acceptable to the Church hierarchy. Calles exercised his Family authority by viciously turning upon the Church while president and then, out of public view in 1929–35, condoning state governors who all but eliminated Catholic institutions and influence in many provinces of Mexico. The Cárdenas–Ávila Camacho leadership of the Revolutionary Family (1935–45) witnessed a direct assault on religious instruction in the schools, on fanaticism, and on the presence of foreign priests in Mexico, but Cárdenas, like many other statesmen before him, recognized the validity of Carlos Bustamante's words: "All nations have their character, and that of Mexico is Catholic." President-elect Ávila Camacho's statement in 1940 that "I am a believer" was designed to bring about the effect it did: reconciliation of Catholics and the State. Cárdenas reached the peasant through the "Cárdenas lodge," the "Cultural Sundays," and rural cultural missions, but he respected churchmen who taught Catholicism stripped of its traditional Spanish flavor. Where Calles had been flatly against the Church, Cárdenas was not anti-Catholic, but opposed to the religious abuses of the clergy. Leadership of the Family devolved upon Miguel Alemán in 1946, and his policy, as well as that of the Ruiz Cortines–López Mateos leadership since, was to "live and let live." Strict legalists say that the Church has regained too much influence since 1939, and despite circumscription of the Church on many sides, this claim is not unfounded.

In a deeper sense, the religious question in Mexico arises from far more transcendent considerations than Church and State relation per se, or from enforcement of laws restricting clerical activities, or even from strict observance of prohibitions on property ownership by the Church. By reducing the whole subject of religion to restraining clerics and clericalism, the Revolutionary Family comes up with a Church policy that seems too incomplete and too incongruous for a nominally Catholic nation. What frequently baffles the American Catholic is how Mexico, a nation 90 per cent composed of Catholics, became so intensely anti-Catholic. There seems little reason to doubt the numerical preponderance of Catholics; all non-Catholics combined have probably never exceeded 10 per cent of the total Mexican population at any time during the entire fifty years of Revolution. Taking the Protestants, Jews, Freemasons, Quakers, orientalists, spiritualists, agnostics, and atheists, adding to this the anomalous Catholic Jew, Protestant Catholic, and Catholic Freemason, and even including all resident foreigners and all tourists coming to the interior of Mexico in any given year, Catholics still comprise a vast majority of the Mexican people. Mexico is a Latin American nation and, as Professor Mecham of the University of Texas maintains, "There is no substitute for Roman Catholicism in Latin America—it is a case of the Catholic faith or none at all."

Confronting such odds, how did the handful of liberals who drafted the anticlerical Constitution of 1917 possess any confidence whatsoever that their product would enjoy respect or lasting value in a Catholic nation? Why did these statesmen, so intent on molding a nation, proceed by weakening what the conservative Mexican statesman Lucas Alamán has described as the "only common link which joins all Mexicans"? Four centuries of clericalism and a century and a half of Freemason activity supply much of the answer. But there is more, much more, that deserves consideration. Foremost are the forces of anticlericalism and anti-Catholicism that derive from the Mexican's own perception of Catholicism—or, strictly speaking, from the psychology and psychopathology of the Catholic in Mexico.

The psychopathology of Catholicism is just beginning to interest Mexican psychologists. Few in number, and seldom bold enough to publish findings that may undermine the standing of their profession with either Church or State, Mexican psychologists have traditionally ignored this subject. For this reason, I am particularly indebted to Santiago Ramírez and Francisco González Pineda of the Mexican Psychoanalytical Association for their pioneering studies on religion and the Mexican character.[1] Frequently based on clinical psychoanalyses, their findings by and large substantiate my own judgments, although I have reached my conclusions from living alongside Catholicism in Mexico and from empirical sources quite independent of these studies.

A first distinction to be made in understanding Catholicism in Mexico concerns the spiritual content of beliefs. The vast majority of Mexicans know little and care little about the Roman Catholic doctrines of the Trinity, the Incarnation, and the redemption, of heaven and hell, or of papal infallibility. They look for inspiration neither to the universal Ro-

[1] See "A Note on Sources" in the Appendix.

man Catholic Church nor to the Virgin Mary. More often than not, the Virgin Mary is supplanted by the dark-skinned Virgin (or "Our Lady") of Guadalupe. Saint Joseph is virtually unknown to the Mexican masses, and even Christ is frequently supplanted in popular devotion by some local patron saint. The Crucifixion enjoys local and partial primacy at best. The highest religious symbols for the Mexican are usually a local saint and the Virgin of Guadalupe.

Within Mexican Catholicism, the Virgin of Guadalupe variously occupies the place of the Virgin Mary, mother of Jesus, or of God "herself," or of "Goddess of the gods." As a Mexican characterization and as a feminine image with maternal value, the Virgin of Guadalupe makes Jesus a secondary figure. Incorporation of the dark-skinned virgin into the Catholicism of Mexico took place early after the first Spanish churchmen reached Mexico. Professor Hubert Herring has vividly described the miraculous apparition in the following way:

> On December 9, 1531, an Indian, Juan Diego, was passing the hill of Tepeyac on the northern outskirts of the Mexican capital when an Indian maiden appeared in a half-moon of dazzling light, announced herself as the Mother of God and the mother of all Indians, and bade Juan Diego carry a message to the bishop begging that a shrine be built upon the spot. [Bishop] Zumárraga was properly cautious. The virgin appeared to the Indian a second and a third time. On the third occasion she gave him a miraculous sign: roses suddenly appeared on the slopes of barren Tepeyac. Juan Diego wrapped the flowers into his mantle and hurried to the bishop. When he unfolded his mantle, the roses had disappeared, leaving in their place the painting of the Virgin of Guadalupe, which now hangs over the high altar of the basilica near Tepeyac. The story, long debated by churchmen, conveyed the dramatic message that the religion of the Spaniard was not an alien faith, that it belonged to Indian Mexico, that the Mother of God could rightfully appear with the dark hair, golden skin, and somber eyes of a Mexican maiden.[2]

The miraculous apparition occurred precisely on the hill of Tepeyac where the Aztecs had built a temple to the goddess Tonantzin ("Our Mother"). Professor Richard Greenleaf in his recent study of Bishop Zumárraga observes that this popular churchman and the Franciscans "were able to transfer this allegiance paid to Tonantzin to the Virgin of Guadalupe and to her shrine at Tepeyac, which was built on top of the earlier native shrine to Tonantzin." Yet the apparition introduced new problems for the Church, for "the Indian thought Mary and God to be the same person, and tended to call God and all of the images they saw Santa María."

Some Mexicans claim that Guadalupe was the creation of Bishop Zumárraga's imagination—that Juan Diego never experienced any "mar-

[2] Hubert Herring, *A History of Latin America from the Beginnings to the Present* (New York: Alfred Knopf, Inc., 1955), p. 178.

velous apparition," that the Virgin of Guadalupe first "appeared" to the artist who produced the controversial mantle picture, and that the Mexican popular masses have been led into believing in a complete fraud. Whatever the truth or fiction of the marvelous apparition, two considerations invariably escape the attention of Catholic detractors. One is that the Vatican has never elevated belief in the Virgin of Guadalupe to the stature of Church dogma. The other is that the popular masses worship the Virgin of Guadalupe so deeply, so profoundly, and so intensely that removing her presence from popular belief would be as unthinkable as removing Christ from American Christianity. To millions of Mexicans, the Virgin of Guadalupe is the holiest of the holy.

The spiritual content of the Roman Catholicism that converted millions of Indians varied substantially from community to community, region to region, and, as miscegenation gave birth to the mestizo, mulatto, and other mixed-bloods, from one caste and social class to another. With the passage of time, variances from orthodox Roman Catholicism, especially in the form of local saints and the Virgin of Guadalupe, became more and more important, even to the point where these "extras" frequently assumed a central role while many Roman Catholic concepts were discarded. Viewed in this way, Catholicism in Mexico is merely a catch-all label for multiple religious beliefs often bearing little resemblance to Roman Catholicism, yet all brought together under the administration and nominal authority of the Catholic Church hierarchy in Mexico. Some anthropologists contend that substitution of Catholicism for Indian creeds proceeded so rapidly because at the time of the Conquest the basic religious beliefs of the Indian coincided with certain Catholic doctrines. Building churches over Indian ceremonial altars may have assisted in transferring old beliefs to Catholicism, but apparently in the process the Indian did not discard his former religion completely. Human sacrifices ended, yet it is mere conjecture whether the beliefs underlying this symbolism also disappeared.

Catholic men and women alike look to the priest for fulfilling the three indispensable tasks of baptism, marriage, and extreme unction. For many "Catholics," even a Church marriage has become less a religious obligation than a social affair. Rare indeed is the priest who succeeds in instilling into the Mexican mind the doctrine of the Trinity, the Incarnation, and the redemption. The Mexican has a peculiar awareness of the idea that religion is primarily a matter of individual conscience; besides, how could the unsophisticated Mexican be brought to understand the Virgin of Guadalupe as less than "God" and thereby reconciled with the basic dogma of orthodox Roman Catholicism? Orthodoxy characterizes beliefs of the upper classes in Mexico City, Cuernavaca, Monterrey, Guadalajara, Chihuahua, Puebla, and other provincial towns where foreign priests traditionally predominated. By geographical regions, Roman Catholicism remains purest in the north, most diluted in the central and southern rural regions. By social classes, acceptance of universal Roman Catholic dogma is largely confined to the upper and upper-middle classes in the metropolitan centers.

As these characteristics suggest, the incidence of practicing Catholics varies greatly from one social class to another. Those who display the fewest modern tendencies—the rural communal Indians of all ages and of both sexes—attend Church from baptism to extreme unction. Outside the Indian community and in the central stream of modern Mexico, the picture becomes increasingly complex. Men of all social classes generally refrain from formal, outward religious manifestations. In the middle-middle class and the upper-middle class (roughly, families with an income range of $150 to $650 a month) the highest percentage of men remain active, practicing Catholics during an entire lifetime. A smaller percentage of lower-middle-class men remain active in the Church, and the percentage in the lower class is still smaller, though the absolute number of practicing males is highest in this class. In the upper class, by and large, the Revolution has destroyed the common symbol that the Church represented for the older aristocratic families—so much so that the percentage of male descendants of the old, wealthy families of Mexico attending Catholic churches today is negligible indeed. At the same time, their wives and daughters usually attend church regularly. The upper-class Catholic families who maintain continuous lifetime contact with the Church, both as a family and as individuals, are usually families of foreign birth (excluding Spanish- and Italian-born) and those headed by an American-born father. One exception to this general pattern is observable in certain regions of Jalisco, Michoacán, Oaxaca, and the Bajío, where relatively higher percentages of the men in all social classes regularly attend church services. Even in these regions, however, the percentage of men who are practicing Catholics is always much lower than the number of women who adhere to Catholic formalism.

Distinctions according to sex are profound. Regardless of what type of religion she professes, from orthodox Roman Catholicism to idolatrous indigenous creeds, and regardless of her education, the Mexican female is intensely religious. Women in Mexico live their religion, not the least because men expect their wives, mothers, aunts, sisters, and daughters to attend church regularly. The male is guilty of extended absences from home and irresponsibility in assuming his family duties as a husband and father. This, according to the clinical analyses of González Pineda, explains the frequency of the Mexican female's visits to the priest. For the women of Mexico, the priest represents far more than a confessor: Taking the place of father and husband, he is the source of counsel, compassion, and psychological treatment. This role of the priest, whose counsel is quoted by women to their husbands, often antagonizes the male and may give substance to his anticlericalism. The mother demands that her daughter attend church regularly, live an exemplary "Catholic" life, and conduct herself according to high moral principles—and on these points, she enjoys the full approval of her husband.

Perhaps the greatest crisis in Catholicism in Mexico arises from the great number of adolescent boys who abandon practicing Catholicism. At the age of twelve or thirteen, many Mexican boys stop attending Church services altogether and give up other external manifestations of Catholicism. Seeking an explanation for this phenomenon, González Pineda suggests that the adolescent who continues to practice the Catholic religion becomes subject to the teasing of his buddies for being "a mommy's boy," "still not a man," or "feminine or homosexual." In the eyes of the Mexican youth, leaving the Church thus symbolizes an affirmation of masculinity. Beyond that, it is also a rebellion against his mother—an impulse "to get out from under the subjection of his mother," an expression of his disapproval of her submissive and obsequious character. A boy is encouraged by the secret and unconscious complicity of his mother who tries to make her son "more masculine than either he or she really considers necessary in order to become masculine—she permits him to go out alone, return home late, and absent himself from family affairs at home," to take trips alone, to play in the streets, and to have unreproved fist-fights, all because "men are like that," or because "he is a man," or because "he is *my* son." The boy is sent to church but goes elsewhere in full knowledge of his mother. Thus it is that the Mexican mother condones the development of traits that will inevitably cause her son to make another woman the victim of the same circumstances that she herself suffers as wife and mother.

A youth's abandonment of practicing Catholicism is also a rebellion against his father—the father who abandons, brutalizes, deprecates, cheats, and shows little or no respect for his mother. González Pineda contends that the resentment of a boy against his real father is transferred to his symbolic father, the priest, "who during his infancy has been the source of many fears, many admonitions . . . many repressions, much blame. Such a father is, in the last instance, perceived as being more frustrating, more severe than his real father." To go to church means confession and chastisement for immoral sexual behavior. In Mexico, the adolescent boy experiences sexual intercourse early (usually in a house of prostitution) in order to prove his masculinity, to prove that he is *muy macho*. In his pathology of sex and religion, González Pineda goes so far as to suggest that the hypersexuality of the Mexican male arises in part from his reaction against the Church.

What happens to the Mexican male who, on entering adolescence, abandons his external respect for religion? His first communion may become his last until he marries, and the marriage mass in turn may truly constitute his last communion. His religion becomes secret and exclusively internal. He continues to invoke the Virgin of Guadalupe. Although he may retain a profound respect for "Catholicism," he cannot express any religious sentiments out of fear of losing his masculine identity. He may wear a saint's medal around his neck, but he carefully guards against exposing it in public. He may come to think that his masculinity will be recognized more quickly by others if he speaks against the Church and becomes anticlerical or even anti-Catholic. He will participate in collective religious acts, such as the annual peregrination that his union or community group makes to the Basilica of Guadalupe, but usually does so when his presence will not carry the threat of criticism from his friends.

Paradoxically, therefore, most detractors of the Church come from Catholic families. They were baptized, raised, and married in the Church, and they expect their wives, mother, sisters, and children to remain devout, practicing Catholics while they join forces with the small, nonreligious, antireligious, and non-Catholic minority who lead the open attack on Catholicism. In viewing Catholicism as a thing of women, the Mexican male's own attitude toward Catholicism is at best one of indifference, at worst one of outright contempt. While such multiple peculiarities characterize Catholicism in Mexico, is it any wonder that from time to time the nation becomes intensely anticlerical or even anti-Catholic?

The major shortcomings of Mexican religion cannot be laid at the doorstep of Freemasons, Protestants, Jews, or atheists. Nor should all the blame be placed on the priest, or on clericalism, or on Church ownership of property, or on the teaching of Catholicism in the schools. All these enter the picture, but the first and foremost shortcoming lies in Mexican family life: In the father and son who must unceasingly prove their masculinity; in the irresponsible father who neglects his wife and family; in the submissive, passive mother who condones her son's abandonment of religion; in the childish manner in which adult men look upon church attendance. Perhaps the Church itself has contributed to this state of affairs. Is it possible that the Church in Mexico overstresses feminine values? The symbolism of the Virgin of Guadalupe? The role of the local patroness saint? Is it possible that Catholicism there has not adjusted itself to the demands of social modernization? That it too frequently overlooks the instructions of Pope Leo XIII? That it excessively concentrates upon defending and protecting itself from the government, instead of exerting more effort to improve its image before the people of Mexico?

The saddest aspect of the whole matter is that neither the Revolutionary Family nor the Catholic Church seems to be producing in the Mexican a meaningful identification with his society. Women live in a world of illusion too far removed from reality. Men live in a world of delusion fraught with complexes and frustrations. Freemasonry provides a workable alternative for some Mexicans, but promises no solution for most Mexicans. The modus vivendi marking Church and State relations since 1937 has not eliminated the key problem of how to mold a basically "Catholic" nation in the image of Revolutionary propositions that run counter to Mexican Catholic traditions, and at the same time enhance the spiritual values of the Mexican. Unfortunately, most Mexican factory hands, storekeepers, and heads of family in the popular mass have no moral sanction for their actions, no equivalent of the Protestant, Catholic, and Judaic ethics upon which American society was forged.

That these considerations have been neglected is less an indictment of Revolutionary leadership than a natural effect of the Mexican passion to launch reforms in negative terms. The planks in the Revolutionary platform opposing clericalism, property ownership, and Church education were workable policy directives; the effects on religion itself were unplanned by-products. Too frequently, often unconsciously, the fight against the clergy became a direct assault on religion. On its part, the high clergy did not help the situation by persistently opposing the entire Revolution.

CHURCH AND STATE

For government officials and clerics alike, Church and State relations have involved five basic issues: education, freedom of religion, clerics in politics, church ownership and the churches proper, and the number and nationality of priests. First of all, let us examine the issue of education.

Issue No. 1: Education. Broadly conceived in Revolutionary terms, the Church-State issue of education in Mexico involves a dispute over removal of all traces of religious education in the schools versus the right of private and primarily Church-operated educational institutions to impart religious instruction in the classroom. Article 3 of the Constitution originally provided that education was to be "free," that attendance at public schools was to be gratuitous, that only lay instructors were permitted to teach in the nation's schools, that no religious corporation or minister could establish or direct schools of primary instruction, and finally, that private primary schools could only be established subject to the approval and vigilance of public officials. Modification of Article 3 came in December, 1934, just after Cárdenas entered the presidency, when education was changed to read "socialistic education" and its teaching made mandatory. Most teachers did not have the vaguest notion what "socialistic education" was, let alone how to establish it in a country that was obviously not "socialistic." All manner of problems followed.

The current definition of education was promulgated in December, 1945, when Miguel Alemán was just beginning his leadership of the Revolutionary Family by virtue of his nomination as the official party's presidential candidate. Primarily the brain-child of Jaime Torres Bodet, then minister of public education and soon to become director-general of UNESCO, the new and revised Article 3 defined the subject in considerable detail. Education was to develop in the Mexican a love for his country and a consciousness of internationalism, independence, and justice. It was to remain completely removed from any and all religious doctrines and, instead, be based on the results of scientific progress, "always fighting against ignorance, prejudice, and fanaticism." Education also was to be democratic ("in the sense that democracy is a system of life founded on continual economic, social, and cultural improvement") and to be national ("attending to the solution of Mexican problems, including the defense of Mexican political and economic independence"). In addition, education was to avoid privileges based on race, sect, group interest, sex, and the individual. What really counted was the "dignity of the individual" and the "integrity of the family." Beyond these provisions, the revised version of Article 3 explicitly grants the right of private individuals to impart education of "all types and at all levels," as long as they obtain prior permission of the government and orient education along the lines described above. To keep private institutions in line, however, the government reserves the right to close any privately owned educational institution. A final section prohibits groups or individuals associated with any religious creed from intervening in primary, secondary, or normal school education or in education imparted to workers or campesinos.

Compared with nineteenth-century laws on Church education, the Revolutionary elite introduced nothing particularly repressive. As early as 1833, the Santa Anna–Gómez Farías administration had ordered the complete exclusion of the clergy from public instruction, and Dr. Mora was informing his Masonic brothers in the Mexican National Rite that a way had to be found to expedite the "diffusion of public education, absolutely independent of the clergy, into the popular classes." By mid-century, Benito Juárez and his coterie of Reformers saw to it that anti-Church education mandates were incorporated into the Constitution of 1857. The Lerdo de Tejada laws of the 1870's prohibited the teaching of religion in any governmental establishment. Díaz permitted the reopening of Church schools, yet his own positivist brain trust and Masonic lodges saw to it that the ecclesiastics did not move into public education.

The ironic twist to nineteenth-century legislation on the Church is that to the degree it succeeded in removing clerics from education it also removed many of the most competent educators willing and able to teach. Ardent Freemasons and fervent anti-Catholics who contended that "no schooling was better than Catholic schools" had their day in court, but the education of the Mexican nation suffered by default. Not until the last third of the nineteenth century did construction of public schools and training of public-school teachers get under way in any meaningful style.

By 1910, probably no more than one-fourth of the Mexican nation was literate in any language, and even fewer had enjoyed an "education."

Accompanying the Revolution was the firm conviction that education demanded new content, new schools, and new teachers. But a poor nation, leveled by civil war, had meager resources for carrying out the large-scale program required. Carranza and Obregón accepted Church schools as being "better than no schools," and permitted these educational institutions to operate. Meanwhile, José Vasconcelos had taken command of the National University and, in 1921, of the newly created Department of Education. It was Vasconcelos who really initiated the long-overdue job of establishing public education on a national scale, without caste or class distinction. Classes and classrooms were improvised in many parts of the nation. Missionary teachers were sent to the provinces. Public libraries were established. Diego Rivera, Orozco, and Siqueiros were commissioned to translate the story of the Revolution through murals painted on the walls of public buildings. For the first time in Mexican history, education was beginning to take on a true national character.

Just when it appeared that the new public-education system was beginning to work side by side with private schools, Calles intervened. In rapid succession, orders were issued to close all schools, convents, and asylums where religious instruction was given. Priests were forbidden to teach school. Foreign priests were expelled from Mexico. Once again, the government found itself unprepared to supply teachers to take the place of ousted priests. High churchmen counterattacked with admonitions against Catholic parents sending their children to the "atheist" public schools. The battle spread from the question of who would teach school to the question of what would be taught. The result was "socialistic education."

The debate on what the new direction of education meant in terms of classroom instruction raged for more than a decade. In the meantime, the education ministry, other governmental dependencies, and private institutions undertook the task of building schools, reducing illiteracy, and introducing civilized modes of living that made sense within the specific physical setting in which the Mexican lived. Cultural missions, which Frank Tannenbaum once characterized as "traveling normal schools," ventured into every region. Rural schoolhouses began to dot the countryside. All manner of schools were set up—technical, agricultural, and normal schools, early morning and evening schools for the workingman, primary and secondary schools, fine arts institutes, regional universities, new military educational institutions, and language centers. A big medical center and a huge teachers college were established in Mexico City. Public libraries, museums, and reading rooms came into vogue. If anti-Church education in the Calles image accomplished anything constructive, it was the impetus given to public-school construction and teacher training. In addition to these many changes in public education, a nationwide literacy campaign was undertaken during the war years, based on the proposition that "every literate Mexican should teach the ABC's to at least one illiterate"—further testimony of the Revolutionary zeal in preparing the Mexican to comprehend wider horizons.

The "university crowd" moved in with Alemán. Qualitativeness became the byword in official thinking on education. The Torres Bodet reform of Article 3 gave constitutional sanction to this new approach, to the intellectual maturity of the Revolution. The erudite brain trust propping up the Revolutionary high command had no fear of Church education or, for that matter, of any other private education. Let the Church and religious orders open schools, if not in their own names, then in the names of lay corporations. Let lay Roman Catholics from the United States become principals and teachers. Public education would stand on its own two feet, as long as the phalanx of Mexican intellectuals simultaneously in government posts and professorships at the National University of Mexico (*Universidad Nacional Autónoma de México*, or UNAM), the normal school, and National Polytechnical Institute joined with the thousands of Spanish refugee intellectuals in giving Mexico sound academic direction. Fulfillment of this new plan depended squarely on supplying continuous, scholarly services at the National University and elsewhere. With top intellectuals dedicated to teaching, scholarly investigations, and publishing, and every year producing more and more bright young students, the sheer weight of competently trained youths (and not in scholasticism) would always overpower the Church-school educated. Besides, virtually all good career jobs in the government would be reserved for public-education graduates.

Change became the mode at Mexico's oldest and most prestigious institution of higher learning, the National University of Mexico. Financed by the Mexican government, UNAM moved from antiquated quarters in downtown Mexico City to a majestic new "University City" campus in the suburbs. Career professorships were established in every faculty, degree programs were enlarged, and new schools of academic specialization were set up. Enrollment mushroomed: The number of students tripled between 1945 and 1961, with a great increase in absolute terms occurring in the short eight-year period of 1954–61. The number of degrees granted also increased but, at the regular university level, at a much slower pace than enrollment.

A word of explanation is in order on enrollment and degrees at UNAM. While popular U.S. journals print widely divergent and often misleading estimates of its number of students, UNAM annually publishes generally reliable statistics on its total enrollment and on enrollment apportioned among the five levels of instruction available there. As the following chart indicates, less than two-thirds of UNAM's 68,492 students in 1961 pursued courses of instruction corresponding to offerings that universities in the United States would designate regular, orthodox, university-level courses.

NATIONAL UNIVERSITY OF MEXICO ENROLLMENT, 1925–1961

	Secondary level [a]	Prepara-tory [b]	Special programs [c]	Quasi-pro-fessional [d]	Regular	TOTAL
1925	—	2,810	555	1,698	6,068	11,131
1930	—	1,528	772	1,156	6,105	9,561
1935	1,416	2,065	464	554	5,614	10,113
1940	1,086	3,379	1,955	782	9,888	17,090
1945	1,500	4,387	1,906	1,037	14,470	23,300
1950	1,978	4,805	764	993	16,389	24,929
1952	2,390	6,510	495	1,019	18,685	29,099
1954	3,121	7,277	563	1,173	21,294	33,428
1956	2,718	7,885	771	1,063	25,322	37,759
1958	3,291	9,883	870	1,185	29,565	44,794
1960	2,850	16,642	1,007	1,961	37,510	59,970
1961	3,833	20,076	1,400 [e]	2,197	40,986	68,492

[a] Initiation of university-accredited courses at the secondary-school level (grades 7–9).
[b] Preparatory-level (tenth and eleventh years of education) institutions under direct supervision of UNAM.
[c] Includes special summer instruction for foreign students, pedagogical experimentation, and special capacitation centers for laborers.
[d] Includes schools of nursing, physical education, social work, and plastic arts.
[e] Not verified.

SOURCE: Annual reports of the Rector of the National University and Porfirio Muñoz Ledo, "La educación superior," in México: 50 años de revolución, Vol. IV, La cultura (México: Fondo de Cultura Económica, 1962), p. 120.

Enrollment in special university initiation courses at the secondary (ninth grade) and preparatory (tenth and eleventh grade) level accounted for over one-third of UNAM's total number of students in 1961. Yet, after subtracting the number of students at these lower levels, UNAM still had in excess of 40,000 regular students above the preparatory level—a formidable university student body. Unfortunately, UNAM is having little success in keeping the tens of thousands of students who enroll there in school long enough to finish their education. During the fifties, less than 2,000 students graduated from UNAM at the university level, and not until 1961 did it manage to graduate more than 2,000 in a single year. By then, however, as noted above, more than 40,000 students were enrolled.

Of course, graduates from other institutions of higher learning in Mexico considerably boost the total number of college graduates. The Mexican government finances the National Polytechnic Institute, the military and naval academies, and agricultural, normal, and nursing schools. State governments finance provincial universities, schools of technology, and normal schools. In addition, Mexico has private universities, colleges, and institutes. While an educator in Mexico is deeply impressed by the tremendous strides made, particularly by the National University, the National Polytechnical Institute, and the provincial universities of Nuevo León and Veracruz, he is equally impressed by private educational institutions—the Colegio de México, the University of the Americas, and Ibero-American University in Mexico City, the Technological Institute in Monterrey, and other private institutions. Indicative of optimistic Church views on the future of Catholic education was the reinstallation in 1961, after more than a century's absence from Mexico, of the Dominican Province of Mexico with an initial staff of sixty Dominican friars, as well as the establishment by American priests of a Catholic institute of superior studies in Cuernavaca. An over-all picture of Mexican higher education enrollment in 1961 showed that, including preparatory and quasi-professional school attendance, more than 200,000 students were registered, that more students were enrolled in the National University than in all provincial state universities combined, and that enrollment in private institutions ran a distant second place behind that in public institutions.

The Mexican government intends to accelerate its literacy program and its primary-school construction program. With Jaime Torres Bodet once again at the head of the education ministry, the López Mateos administration announced an "eleven-year education plan" intended to make 80 per cent of all Mexicans literate by 1973. As the accompanying statistics indicate, illiteracy has been reduced one-half over the first six decades of the twentieth century, from 77.5 per cent in 1900 to 38 per cent in 1960.

LITERACY IN MEXICO, 1900–1960 [a]

Year	Population 6 years of age or over	Literate	Illiterate	Literacy (%)	Illiteracy (%)
1900	11,260,920	2,536,139	8,724,781	22.5	77.5
1910	12,527,201	3,271,676	9,255,525	26.1	73.9
1921	12,460,880	3,564,767	8,896,113	28.6	71.4
1930	13,542,305	4,786,419	8,755,886	35.3	64.7
1940	16,220,316	7,263,504	8,956,812	44.8	55.2
1950	21,038,742	11,766,258	9,272,484	55.9	44.1
1960	28,245,802	17,884,397	10,361,405	62.0	38.0
1973 (estimate)	—	—	—	80.0	20.0

[a] From data supplied by the ministry of public education.

The construction of public schools has been pushed markedly, yet since 1940 the growth rate in private elementary schools has been equally impressive. By the beginning of 1960, the number of public primary schools had increased 4,551 over 1940, while private schools increased

2,957. In 1910, 78 per cent of all elementary schools were public; in 1960, more than 85 per cent were public. Nevertheless, after fifty years of Revolution the percentage of elementary students attending public schools had risen only 4 per cent, from 78.5 in 1910 to 82.6 in 1960. The number of students per school varied substantially: 679 students per public school; only 55 students per private school. As relatively overcrowded as the public grade schools of the nation appeared by 1964, an estimated 1.6 million children of primary-school age were still not in school. This represented a heartening improvement over 1950, when more than two million children of primary-school age were denied an education, but indicated the urgency of building more schools immediately.

Incorporated in the "education plan" is provision for increasing financial allotments to education. Allocations for education occupied first place in the 1963 federal budget, representing over one-fifth of total federal expenditures which permitted the ministry of education to make expenditures at a daily rate in excess of $650,000. By 1962, the 5.6 million students enrolled in public schools were receiving millions of free textbooks, and the government also planned to extend the provision of free textbooks to secondary schools. In the first four years of the López Mateos regime, more than 16,000 new classrooms had been built. Despite this bold, new effort to secularize education, and all previous efforts, Professor Jesús Silva Herzog, a senior Revolutionary intellectual and trustee of the National University, expressed the sentiment of many Revolutionaries and Independent Leftists by advancing his judgment that "neither the letter nor the spirit of Article 3 is enforced, simply because the ministry of public education permits religious education to be imparted in private primary and secondary schools as well as the participation of the clergy in such establishments." [3] One thing is certain: Religious education is not a dead letter.

Issue No. 2: Freedom of Religion. Few founders of a nation lacked more insight into the future course that the ship of state would steer on the waters of religion than the framers of Mexico's first constitution. The Charter of 1824 confidently asserted that the religion of the Mexican nation "will be *perpetually* the Roman Catholic Apostolic" and, furthermore, that the nation "will *protect* it by wise and just laws and will *prohibit* the exercise of any other." Before the ink had dried, Freemasons were sniping at the law. And long before the outbreak of Revolution in 1910, Vicente Guerrero, Guadalupe Victoria, Lorenzo Zavala, Juan Alvarez, Melchor Ocampo, Benito Juárez, the Lerdos, and a host of other nineteenth-century "liberals" had shattered papal hopes of estab-

---

[3] Jesús Silva Herzog, *Breve historia de la revolución mexicana: la etapa constitucionalista y la lucha de facciones* (México: Fondo de Cultura Económica, 1960), p. 257.

lishing Roman Catholicism as the official, exclusive religion of the land. For a few Catholics, who certainly did not speak for the majority of Roman Catholics in Mexico, disestablishment of the Church meant keeping faith with the divine character of a Church "which neither desired nor required any special protection."

Freedom of religion normally embodies the dual concept of an individual's freedom of choice in matters of religious belief and the right of any religious institution to proselytize. To the degree that any human being has freedom of choice, the Mexican today enjoys freedom of religion. The extraordinary nature of Mexican Catholicism in the matter of sexes was noted earlier (the male Catholic tends to exercise his freedom by ceasing to observe the basic doctrines and practices of Roman Catholicism). Another uniqueness of Mexican Catholicism is the apparent freedom from restriction in holding a diversity of belief: Thousands of individual communities in Mexico view Catholicism in their own peculiar local manner. So many superstitions and prejudices color nominal Roman Catholicism that for millions, little if any Romanism remains—and at times, not much Catholicism, either.

Freedom of choice is also observable in the existence of Masonic temples, of synagogues, and of Protestant churches, and in the periodic announcements of clerics that "Protestant influence is becoming strong." The atheist and agnostic also enjoy freedom of expression, which has brought some Mexicans of this mold considerable prestige in certain education and literary circles. All in all, freedom of religion in the sense of the Mexican's right to choose his own faith has not been a point of friction in Church-State relations for some decades.

What does constitute a major point of contention is the claim of the Church that the ways in which the State enforces anticlerical laws too frequently prevent the Church from reaching the Mexican people and carrying out services indispensable for the maintenance of Catholicism as a living religion. The Church often has a legitimate complaint in this respect, for the vindictiveness of some public officials is appalling. A few state governors still represent the apotheosis of the anti-Christ; under the façade of freedom of religion, they seem intent on destroying Catholicism as a religion. Yet very few Revolutionaries go this far, and the spirit of the Constitution and its amendments does not support the actions of the governors who do. At the national level, Revolutionary policy on Catholicism and freedom of religion has followed a relatively persistent direction for two decades now: Restrain clericalism, but do not weaken Catholicism.

Issue No. 3: Clerics in Politics.   Facets of the preceding issue point up the importance of anticlericalism in determining the boundaries of freedom of religion. In its broadest sense, clericalism suggests the participation of Church organization and individual churchmen in temporal affairs. Here we shall be concerned with one temporal affair—politics—in the full realization that isolating political activity from other mundane considerations is quite impossible. When Mexican priests go into the countryside preaching land-reform measures according to Pope Leo XIII's social Christianity, are they guilty of political intervention—even when such instruction coincides with Revolutionary policy on agrarian reform? If a hundred clerics instead of a mere handful of priests were permitted to proselytize in the state of Tabasco, would this, as a former governor maintained, constitute a challenge to the government and, hence, excessive influence in politics? If decidedly pro-Catholic political programs of such basically religion-oriented societies as the Knights of Columbus stem directly or indirectly from churchmen, should the government forbid meetings of these lay groups on the grounds of clericalism?

To suppose that priests are merely holy men living and instructing in a political vacuum is to ignore reality. Nor would the Church sustain the doctrine that priests cannot err in taking sides on a political issue. In fact, the Catholic hierarchy excommunicated Hidalgo and Morelos for joining forces with the "wrong" side and denied the sacraments to not a few other former priests. In the early independence period, leaders of both the federalists and centralists were churchmen, although some in the former camp earned designations of "disgraced priest," "defamer of his benefactress, the Church," and "antipapal, nonrepentant Freemason." As the nineteenth century unfolded, priests who supported a given lay interest were considered "good," while those who opposed were "bad." Good or bad, archbishops, bishops, governors of bishoprics, provisors, and vicars were constitutionally prohibited from becoming members of the chamber of deputies as early as 1824. (This does not imply that the higher clergy sought the right to assume seats in legislative bodies; they did not.) The Constitution of 1857 declared clergymen ineligible for election to the presidency as well as to the national legislature; at the same time, their right of suffrage was restored. So far as eligibility for popular office enters the issue of clericalism, there has been no noteworthy friction for scores of years.

Alienation of "liberals" in the 1830's and Reform years was influenced by the liberals' relative economic impotence before the Church hierarchy. The financial power of the Church permitted it to grant loans to friendly presidents and withhold them from unfriendly politicos, although in one way or another the Church was even compelled to underwrite financially several anticlerical administrations. The Church always loomed politically powerful because its extensive properties alone provided more income than total government revenue; cut off from all donations, gifts, and collections in the churches, the Church could still go on living indefinitely. Anticlerical forces contended that the Church participated in politics whether it interfered directly or not: The mere fact that high churchmen turned down a request for money became intervention. The Constitution of 1857, its amendments of the 1870's, and the Revolutionary Constitution of 1917 all rested on the proposition that to render the Church politically impotent first of all required depriving it of wealth. Under this general policy directive, the Church in Mexico has lived for more than a century.

Clerical plotting toward the establishment of a medieval theocracy by and large ended with the execution of Maximilian. This event dramatized the issue of keeping clerics out of politics, for only a few years before the high clergy had forbad government officials on pain of deprivation of the sacraments to take any oath of allegiance to the Constitution of 1857 and, by supporting the centralists financially, had converted the War of Reform into a holy war. Freemasonry and positivism ganged up with Díaz's "divide and rule" policies to check clericalism in politics during the long *porfiriato*. The high clergy had still not learned its lesson, however, and the overthrow of Madero and seating of Huerta evoked clerical reassertion of the temporal rights of the Church. The demise of Huerta again brought cries of "down with clericalism" and demands to "confine churchmen to strictly spiritual matters." The Constitution of 1917 attempted to answer these cries.

The Constitution left no doubt where the Revolution stood on clerics in politics. Ministers were prohibited from criticizing the laws of Mexico and public authorities. Churchmen were denied suffrage, made ineligible to hold public office, and banned from assembling for political purposes. Political associations were prohibited from adopting names that made reference to religious belief. Assemblies of a political nature could never be held in places of worship. And no publication of a religious nature was permitted to comment on the political affairs of the nation or give any information regarding the acts of officials or private individuals insofar as such acts concerned public affairs. Infractions of constitutional mandates on religion *ipso facto* negated the right of the accused to trial by jury. All these provisions, enforced by the denial of juridical personality to the Church, by severe limitations placed on the property rights of individual members of the clergy, and by the "nationalization" of the priesthood, established the juridical bases for the actions of Calles.

To the anticlerical faction in Mexico, the counterattack of churchmen against Calles was treasonous: The Church had no right whatsoever to question the State, even if that State became opposed to the Catholic religion. The stubbornness of the Church in removing the sacraments from the nation's churches and in "provoking the *Cristero* Rebellion" only proved the claim of anticlerics who insisted that the Church had been working to stamp out the Revolution ever since its inception.

The bishops nonetheless fought back by announcing publicly that all Catholics should organize to change the Constitution and that they, the high clergy, personally opposed Articles 3, 5, 24, 27, and 130 of the Constitution. Calles in turn made all priests register with the government, which probably made little difference to members of the high clergy, who had already lost their citizenship by virtue of refusing to obey the Constitution. From its clash with Calles, the high clergy learned another basic lesson about Catholicism in Mexico: Few churchgoers in rural Mexico know or care much about Roman Catholicism, and millions of peasants will not rise up in rebellion simply because a priest urges them onward. On the other hand, the Revolutionary claim that the masses do not revolt against an anticlerical government because they understand the difference between Catholic Church as a spiritual institution and Catholic Church in its temporal capacities seems unfounded. As we have seen, the great majority of "Catholics" in Mexico are not "Roman," and they do not fear that their local saint is in danger whenever high churchmen say the Church is threatened.

Realization of their lack of authoritative command and the impact of Revolutionary programs brought about a fundamental change in the thinking of the high clergy. Stripped of the more worldly-minded foreign-born priests—whom Calles and his successors saw fit to expel from the country in line with the constitutional provision that "to exercise in Mexico the ministry of any cult, it is necessary to be Mexican by birth"—Catholic organs began to take on a more democratic form. Mexican-born priests were elevated to the highest posts in the Church hierarchy. From top to bottom, from archbishop to parish priest, Mexico could say for the first time that Catholicism was becoming more than a religion *for* Mexicans; its basic organization began to be structured by, for, and of Mexicans. Assuming posts of high authority were priests who fully understood that the little peasant could not be "brought into line" by the threat of excommunication, any more than could the government official, Freemason, or professional soldier. Utmost misery and lavish luxury no longer characterized disparities between rural priest and bishop. By "democratizing" their own ranks, the Catholic hierarchy could put forward a cleaner face in public. It is this new Church, more democratic and more Mexican, that is growing up alongside the Revolution. It is this same new Church, not the older royalist, medieval, Spanish-oriented Church, that has worked hand-in-hand with the State to keep Church and State relations on a cordial plane for the past two decades. Whenever a clergyman enters politics today, he proceeds in a Mexican way and under Revolutionary rules of the game. Church and State understand each other politically, despite the general failure of both to resolve the tremendous gap separating "Catholic" beliefs and Revolutionary realities.

Issue No. 4: Church Ownership and the Churches Proper. This issue centers on the broad theme of the Church and churchmen owning property, including the very church buildings in which religious ceremonies take place. Americans have never had the experience of a single private institution holding a stranglehold on an economic system by virtue of its overwhelming control of the nation's means of production and national income. Even the "Robber Barons" left much of the American economy, particularly in the field of agriculture, free of capricious cartelization. Mexico, on the other hand, entered nationhood with the property of the Church consisting of one-half of the total value of all productive real estate in the nation, according to the conservative Lucas Alamán. The economic development of Mexico is as much a story of confiscation of Church properties as it is of attracting and controlling foreign capital.

To private entrepreneurs, the tremendous economic power of the Church posed two alternatives: work in concert with the Church, or work to destroy its powerful holdings and influence in order to make room for greater private growth. Anticlerical forces thus included some businessmen who were nominally devout Roman Catholics. Had the wealth of the Church been shared up and down the ecclesiastical ladder, the Church organization might have become a tightly knit power. But the property of the Church was by and large the property of the bishops. Carlota, the Catholic wife of Maximilian, observed in a letter to a close friend in Europe that the "village priests were dying of hunger" while the bishops were living in unbelievable luxury and splendor. And too often the foreign-born priest sent from Europe to Mexico regarded himself as superior to the native-born, worthy of higher material rewards by virtue of his education, breeding, nationality, and separation from Europe.

In the matter of Church ownership, the Constitution of 1917 strengthened nineteenth-century liberal outlook. As early as 1828, the buildings of the College of Jesuits had been handed over to the state of Chihuahua. The next year the properties of all monastic orders, as well as those of the Jesuits, the Hospitalers, and the Inquisition, were declared national property. In 1833, mission lands and buildings in California were confiscated and divided among natives and settlers. In 1834, missions everywhere in Mexico were ordered secularized and their properties nationalized. From these beginnings, the State clearly asserted its right to take over Church properties, notwithstanding conservative regimes that saw fit to return properties to the Church.

When Juárez and his cohorts lashed out at Catholicism in the 1850's, the Church probably still owned one-third of the entire land in Mexico. It is no wonder that not a few capitalists of economic and ideological mold alike joined anticlericals in support of Juárez and the prohibitions of the Constitution of 1857 on the acquisition and administration by religious corporations of any real estate not destined immediately and directly for the purpose of worship. The so-called Juárez Laws had earlier empowered state governors to designate any and all buildings to be used for religious services. In 1859, Juárez issued another decree, this time declaring all property of the regular and secular clergy nationalized. And in 1868, with Maximilian dead and the Empire demolished, Juárez' offer of liberal rewards to all who denounced property concealed by clericals brought about the liquidation of a considerable amount of Church holdings from 1869 to 1879. In the early 1870's, the State further restricted Church interests by prohibiting religious institutions from acquiring real property and lending money on mortgages, by denying priests the right to be heirs or legatees, and by abolishing the Church's special juridical status. Nevertheless, the takeover of Church lands did not create legions of small farmers, as envisaged by Juárez, but simply further enriched some already rich men and made way in some instances for Church ownership by proxy. Once Díaz became solidly entrenched in office, his divide-and-rule policy brought ups and downs for the Church, although there were more ups than downs. By the Revolution's outbreak, the Catholic Church and individual churchmen in most parts of Mexico—not all parts, because Díaz left enforcement of religious legislation to local authorities—had found ways and means to circumvent most legal restrictions on their ownership of property, despite the general uncertainty of such titles.

Although the Constitution of 1917 strengthened nineteenth-century liberal reforms on Church ownership, it is not peculiarly "revolutionary" on this subject. Perhaps, as one scholar contends, the new charter "exceeded in severity all prior legislation on ecclesiastical matters," but it clearly does not outstrip the spirit of all previous laws on the specific point of property ownership. The Constitution denies both religious institutions and individual churchmen the right to property ownership, and specifically prohibits religious associations from acquiring, possessing, or administering real estate or income from property. The Constitution precludes the possibility of proxy ownership, for another article prohibits any religious institution from acquiring juridic personality. After declaring all places of public worship national property, the Revolutionary *magna carta* invests the government with the right to determine which properties may be devoted to religion. It further provides that no new places of worship may be dedicated without prior governmental consent, and that once created, they too will become national property. An official caretaker is to be legally responsible for the faithful performance of the laws within each place of worship and for all objects used in religious worship. Finally, the Constitution charges municipal authorities, sub-

ject to fines and dismissal, with responsibility in their respective provinces for keeping a register of all churches and of their caretakers and for
reporting on the opening of any new places of public worship.

Taken together, these mandates effectively exclude the Church and
individual prelates from property ownership. Hamstrung on all sides,
priests also must suffer humiliation before official custodians of church
buildings proper. Without legal right of petition, the priest depends exclusively on the whims of public officials. The Church has few problems
in obtaining legal clearance for the construction of new churches in some
localities, but in others, the government has seen fit to deny petitions.
All in all, high clerics look forward to a time when religious institutions
can own real property and invest in the economic development of Mexico. They believe that a constitutional amendment should at the least
provide for Church ownership of new church buildings used exclusively
for purposes of worship. Meanwhile, they live under Revolutionary interpretations of present laws and, at the same time, hope that law enforcement will never again return to the excessive applications of Calles.

Issue No. 5: The Number and Nationality of Priests. A final
major issue in Church-State relations concerns the number and nationality of priests. An absence of serious friction on this issue is symptomatic
of laxity in law enforcement and not, as some Protestant missionaries
resident in Mexico would have it, of a basic change in Catholic disposition on the subject. The issue stems principally from two constitutional
mandates. One prohibits foreign clergymen from administering religious
functions in Mexico ("To exercise in Mexico the ministry of any cult, it
is necessary to be Mexican by birth"). The other lodges in the state legislatures' exclusive power to determine the maximum number of ministers
of religious creeds according to the needs of each state. (In the Federal
District and two territories, this function devolves on the national government.) This means that the Catholic Church may not call on any
foreign-born priest to minister in Mexico and, further, that the maximum
number of Mexican-born priests who may conduct religious services is
determined by the respective states, not by the Church itself.

The high clergy does not, and probably never will, accept the second provision, and with good reason: There is an ever-present danger that
a state will arbitrarily decide that its maximum number of priests "according to need" is zero. This is precisely what happened in 1931 in the
state of Tabasco. Such an eventuality, say high clergymen, blatantly con-
tradicts the constitutional guarantee of religious liberty. Since the content of Catholic practice varies so markedly from one locality to another,
there is something to be said in favor of decentralizing authority over
this matter. On the other hand, however, permitting a handful of legislators, who almost invariably are under the iron hand of a governor,

to exercise the legal right to keep all priests out of their entity violates the principle of religious freedom.

There is no ready-made solution to the dilemma, but a look at the record indicates the shortcomings in present constitutional provisions. Enforcement in the states has run from one extreme to another. In addition to the action of Tabasco in 1931, another state once maintained that, since all priests owe allegiance to a foreign prince, the Pope, they are by definition enemies of the state. Yet another state decreed that priests had to marry in order to exercise the duties of their office. Over the last four decades, the most oppressive, intolerant policies of all have emanated from Tabasco and Veracruz. At the other extreme, leniency in setting the number of priests and enforcing established maximums has characterized policy in other states—Jalisco and Puebla in particular.

The exclusion of foreign priests has several implications. First of all, the generally better-educated priests from abroad can no longer match wits with the Revolutionary brain trust; Church and State problems are to be resolved among Mexicans of the State and Mexican-born priests of the Church. Second, the exclusion of foreign-born priests tends to discourage the intellectually inclined and socially-minded Catholic family from encouraging a son to enter the priesthood. Prestige, wealth, and power are acquired much faster in other pursuits. The result is a Mexican clergy recruited from the poorer, rural families, some of whom probably chose the priesthood for their sons because no alternative career was in the offing. The presence of rural-born priests in urban churches may indicate a high degree of democratization in the Catholic Church, but it does antagonize the snobbish *damas* of the middle and upper classes, who want advice from a *caballero* (gentleman) priest, not from an *indio*. Finally, exclusion of mendicant religious orders, coupled with nationality provisos, was designed to reduce prospects of elite religious orders developing in Mexico. Nonetheless, foreign-born priests and particularly American-born Jesuits are in evidence in several parts of Mexico, despite the letter and spirit of the law. Although successive governments may overlook such violations, the fact remains that churchmen are still vulnerable before the law.

FREEMASONRY

Though the mysteries of Judaism, Protestantism, and Catholicism are profound, they hardly challenge the obscurities of Freemasonry. The powerful impact of Freemasonry on Mexican development makes a critical analysis of Masonic influence imperative.

The long history of Masonic influence in Mexican life dates back to the eighteenth century. The first appearance of Freemasonry in Mexico recorded in official Masonic histories tells of a lodge set up as early as 1753 by two Dominican friars in the region that today comprises the state of Durango. If such a lodge actually existed, it antedated other lodges established in New Spain by several decades. The existence of "Masonic groupings" during the late eighteenth and early nineteenth centuries is reported in several Masonic histories; these "lodges" supposedly followed rituals adopted by Spanish lodges under original patents from Great Britain. But it was not until after Napoleon invaded Spain in 1808 that regular lodges began to mushroom in New Spain—first in Mexico City, Yucatán, and Veracruz, and later spreading into many regions. Some of these lodges followed Spanish rituals; others drew their patents from Cuba, France, New Orleans, and from lodges in the United States. Despite Revolutionary mythology, it is impossible to substantiate the claim that the fathers of Mexican independence, Morelos and Hidalgo, were Freemasons. The fact that some of their ideas coincided with orthodox Masonic principles, or "landmarks," hardly makes them *ipso facto* Freemasons.

The important York ritual [4] entered Mexico with the assistance of Joel Poinsett, first American diplomatic minister accredited to Mexico, who in 1825 was instrumental in obtaining credentials from the Grand Lodge of New York. By this time, "Scottish" or Ramsay rituals—not to be confused with the Ancient & Accepted Scottish Rite—had become the vogue in Mexican Masonry, so much so that the *escoceses* became the prime object of Yorkist attack. Within three years after its introduction in Mexico, the York Rite had lodges all over the country—ten in Mexico City, eight in Puebla, thirteen in Veracruz, six in the state of México— reportedly, 102 lodges in all. Generals Guadalupe Victoria and Vicente Guerrero, first and second Presidents of Mexico, became *yorkinos*, as did many liberal-minded federalists. Nonetheless, within five years the Yorkists had heaped discredit on their rite by exerting greater effort in displacing *escoceses* from public office than in giving the new nation a truly liberal government. To top things off, leading Yorkist Gen. Anastasio Bustamente turned against the grand chieftain of the York Rite, Vicente Guerrero, and helped unseat him from the presidency. Thus, the first attempts to establish Freemasonry in Mexico were chaotic, disorganized, and generally divorced from the true "landmarks." Mexican Freemasonry became sick and deformed in early youth. But let us not forget that politics and religions in Mexico, quite aside from their origins, invariably acquire a unique Mexican flavor.

The next stage in Masonic development, roughly encompassing the years 1830–60, was characterized by the hegemony of the Mexican National Rite (*Rito Nacional Mexicano*, or RNM). Properly credited with playing a foremost role in nineteenth-century attacks on Church and

---

[4] Specific characteristics of the several rites of Freemasonry are explained later.

army privileges, on religious education and property ownership by the Church, and on fanaticism and clerical participation in politics, the RNM was first of all a Mexican institution. It did little to hide its political and religious nature; in fact, the avowed purpose of the five *escoceses* and four Yorkists who founded the rite in 1825 was to eliminate interjurisdictional squabbles then dividing Masonry by uniting all men "distinguished for their righteousness, patriotism, and liberal ideas" into a "party of political progress." Organizationally, the RNM patterned itself partly after York rituals followed in the United States, partly along French Masonic lines, and partly in the shadow of Indianism. Authority over the first three degrees (individual ratings) was vested in a Mexican National Grand Lodge, while supervision of the next six degrees accrued to a Supreme Grand Orient. Mexicanism crept into the structure of the orders themselves—upon completion of the sixth degree, a Mason earned the title of Knight of the Mexican Eagle (*Caballero del Águila Mexicana*).

A re-examination of Mexican political life in the nineteenth century leads to the conclusion that the Mexican National Rite represented beliefs more closely akin to political liberalism than to orthodox Freemasonry. For example, at a general assembly of sixth to ninth degree RNM members held in Mexico City in the early 1830's, Dr. José María Luis Mora, one of its outstanding leaders, informed his brothers of the true program of action to be followed: (1) absolute freedom of expression, including opposition to all repressive laws against the press; (2) abolition of special privileges of the clergy and the military; (3) suppression of the monastic orders and of all laws that attribute knowledge of civil affairs, such as the marriage contract, to the clergy; (4) improvement of the general moral state by the destruction of the clerical monopoly over public education, the diffusion of learning, and the inculcation of social responsibility through the establishment of museums, art centers, and public libraries, and through the creation of centers of instruction devoted to the classical literature of the sciences and morality; (5) abolition of capital punishment for all political crimes except those involving premeditated murder; and (6) guarantee of territorial integrity through the creation of settlements based on the Mexican language, practices, and customs. Although aspects of orthodox Freemasonry are contained in this program, the basically political makeup of the RNM cannot be easily ignored. The fact that many "free and accepted" organizations outside Mexico abhorred the avowed Masonry of the RNM (apart from formal recognition from a few grand lodges in the United States and elsewhere) is evidence for accepting the RNM as one "political party," if not the foremost of the 1830 to 1860 epoch. Not even the official historian of the RNM denied its aggressive policy of working on behalf of the election of RNM members to political office. All in all, the RNM program reached its culmination in the promulgation of the anticlerical legislation of the 1850's, the liberal Constitution of 1857, and the decidedly anti-Church laws of 1874. The same might be said of the Liberal Party of the mid-1800's headed by Dr. Mora. Unfortunately, no documentary evidence is available to suggest whether the RNM worked harder for the election of its own lodge members than it did for election of Liberal Party candidates as such, or for that matter, to what degree membership in these two groups overlapped.

Two transcendental events in the development of Mexican Masonry occurred in the 1860's: establishment of the Valley of Mexico Grand Lodge, whose jurisdiction and membership became the largest in "blue lodge" organization, and the founding of the Ancient and Accepted Scottish Rite, destined to become the most influential, enduring branch of philosophical Masonry. At the center of both organizations was the businessman James Lohse, a Pennsylvanian who had come to Mexico in 1853. Lohse (known in Mexico as Santiago Lohse) became the first grand master of the Valley of Mexico Grand Lodge as well as first sovereign grand commander of the Supreme Council, Ancient and Accepted Scottish Rite. Like all orthodox grand lodges, the one established in Mexico City in 1868 claimed exclusive authority over the first three degrees (those awarded in the blue lodges or *logias azules*) granted in symbolic lodges located within a circumscribed territorial region. It is interesting to note that only one of the three charter lodges forming the Valley of Mexico Grand Lodge conducted their rituals in Spanish; the second chose French, and the third German.

The exclusive jurisdiction claimed by the new grand lodge ran counter to claims of other organs, but this did not seriously impede its membership growth. Other grand lodges and schismatic Masonic movements arose in subsequent decades to challenge the broad jusisdiction of the Valley of Mexico, but today, after a century of life, this same grand lodge is bigger than ever. The appellation "Valley of Mexico" may be misleading, for while the grand lodge has its central temple in Mexico City, its jurisdiction encompasses a wide area—the Federal District, plus the states of Aguascalientes, Guanajuato, Guerrero, México, Michoacán, Morelos, Puebla, Tlaxcala, and Zacatecas. Therefore, such disperse lodges as "Renovación No. 72" in Acapulco, "Melchor Ocampo No. 18" in Morelia, "Temoanchán No. 260" in Cuernavaca, and "Ideal Simbólico No. 87" in Tehuacán all come under the same grand lodge.

The Scottish Rite first entered the country in 1860 and 1865, under questionable and conflicting patents enveloped in politics touching upon the Civil War in the United States and the imperial government of Maximilian in Mexico. Scottish Riters had resolved their differences sufficiently by 1868 to set up a Supreme Council with exclusive jurisdiction over all Mexico. Orthodox enough to acquire full recognition from the Supreme Council of Charleston, South Carolina (the original granddaddy of the Scottish Rite), the Supreme Council in Mexico made good use of its authority—so much so that the Ancient and Accepted Scottish Rite, despite its ups and downs and schismatic movements, today enjoys a virtual monopoly over philosophical Freemasonry open to Mexicans. A roster of personalities distinguished with the title of Grand Inspector General in philosophical Freemasonry (that is, those awarded the highest or thirty-third degree) indicates the range and scope of the rite's appeal, and also negates those critics who attack the Scottish Rite as anti-Catholic, anti-Christian, anti-Semitic, or just antireligious. Among the thirty-third degree Masons we find the authoritarian Porfirio Díaz, the positivists Ignacio M. Altamirano and Emilio G. Cantón, the Madero-supporters Manuel Bonilla, José María Pino Suárez, and Federico González Garza, the foreigners Arthur Elian, William B. Richardson (long-time manager of the First National City Bank in Mexico City), and Henry Cain (one-time superintendent of the American School Foundation in Mexico City and founder of Mexico City College), the *callistas* Emilio Portes Gil, Pascual Ortiz Rubio, and Abelardo Rodríguez, such liberal Revolutionaries as Luis Manuel Rojas, Gen. Abel Rodríguez, and Genaro P. García, and former president Miguel Alemán. Although Emperor Maximilian apparently rejected an offer to become a thirty-third degree Freemason, at least two of his palace intimates accepted. Such diversity underscores the real nature of the Scottish Rite in Mexico: Whenever philosophical Freemasonry followed the true landmarks of higher degrees, it could not by its very nature attack the Catholic Church as such or, for that matter, any other institutional religion. The Scottish Rite in Mexico points up another basic element of philosophical Masonry: It opposes fanaticism and religious intolerance wherever and whenever manifested. Hence the basis for judging the Scottish Riters rests in the determination of their beliefs as to what constitutes fanaticism and intolerance.

Freemasonry took a turn for the worse under the regime of Porfirio Díaz. Two of his brethren, grand potentates—grand masters Emilio Cantón and Ignacio Altamirano, ran the show for decades. Soon after the old autocrat entrenched himself in the presidency, the *logias azules* and, with them, the grand lodges became subject to the dictates of a Grand Orient—and a few years later, on February 15, 1890, to the authority of the Grand Scottish Symbolical Diet of Mexico. Both the upstart Diet and Orient were schismatic movements that patterned their ritual and organization after the French model of 1877; the French had removed the requirement of the belief in the "Supreme Architect" in order to accommodate a number of positivists. As in the heyday of the Mexican National Rite, Masonry carried the heavy stamp of politics. Many state governors became Freemasons and headed delegations from grand lodges to the Grand Diet. Meanwhile, Díaz's indifference and lack of sincerity were reflected in the fact that he never once attended a session of the

Grand Diet; all available evidence suggests that after 1895 the old dictator lost complete interest in Freemasonry. Masonically speaking, the
Grand Diet proved a farce within the first year of its life. Yet despite its
irregularities, its general discredit in Mexico, and the autocratic manner
in which Cantón handled lodges outside the Federal District, the Grand
Diet carried out a successful propaganda campaign abroad, based largely
on the false assertion that Díaz really headed Freemasonry. It was true
that he was the nominal head, but he was never more than a very disin-
terested, clearly nominal leader. Cantón's propaganda influenced the
Grand Lodge of Texas to recognize the Grand Diet in 1891; then other
grand lodges in the United States followed suit. Yet measured against
the codes of orthodox Freemasonry set down by the Lausanne Convention of 1875, the Grand Diet hardly fulfilled requirements of "free and
accepted" Masonry. An inspection visit of the grand secretary of the
Grand Lodge of Iowa in the late 1890's typifies the generally uninformed
opinions on the Mexican Masonic movement held by American Freemasons. After visiting several lodges, the grand secretary submitted his
report to brothers back in Iowa. On the basis of an incorrect evaluation of
the Masonic situation in Mexico, he contributed to the recognition of a
discredited wing of Mexican Freemasonry. The over-all decadence of the
Grand Diet was measurable in the fact that of eleven grand lodges affiliated to the Diet in 1895, only four remained faithful in 1897—the
grand lodges Valley of Mexico, State of Jalisco, "Benito Juárez" (in
Piedras Negras), and "Ignacio Ramírez" (in Tampico).

An ironic development of international Freemasonry during the
Díaz epoch was that the procedures of the Grand Orient of France
achieved great prestige in Mexico at the very time when Freemasonry
virtually everywhere else in the world was breaking formal relations with
the Grand Orient of France. How grand lodges in the United States
reconciled their acceptance of the Grand Diet in Mexico, especially after
their rupture of relations with the Grand Orient of France, remains a
mystery—perhaps only traceable to a few "Robber Barons" who came to
Mexico in the 1890's. One thing is certain: In an essentially spiritual
sense, Mexican Masonry divided at its very roots over the issue of natural-
ism versus Christianity. Díaz, under the influence of his Catholic wife,
contributed little to a solution. Anticlerical provisions of the Constitution of 1857 notwithstanding, he dabbled with religion as though it
were a plaything—up with the Catholic Church one day, down with it
the next.

Even the twentieth century was slow to provide satisfaction for
Freemasons who insisted that Mexico should encourage free and accepted Masonry and vest authority over the first three degrees in autonomous grand lodges that would see to it that discussion of politics and institutionalized religions remained outside lodge meetings. First on the

list of "heretical" Freemasons (although there is room to inquire whether Díaz and the existing Masonic councils were not the real heretics) was Gen. Bernardo Reyes. He gathered numerous lodges into a schismatic orient supporting his political ambitions, but nonetheless failed both Masonically and politically. He did, however, inspire lodges into questioning the hold that Díaz maintained and, in some cases, into overt activities against the old order. In this sense, we can accept the contention that the Mexican Revolution had its genesis in part in various Freemasonic corporations. The so-called "Pachuca Civic Group" was nothing less than the local lodge reconstituted. Ambulatory lodges in the Mexican army and lodges of railroad employees and miners did much to inject a fundamental dislike of autocracy into the minds of lodge members. Francisco Madero, Pino Suárez, Filomeno Mata, Manuel Bonilla, Federico González, and other Revolutionaries were Freemasons. At least in two instances, entire lodges down to the last member joined Madero against Díaz.

Yet there is no evidence that Masonry united to oppose Díaz or to favor Madero. On the contrary, too many Porfirians retained high posts in Freemasonry both during and after the overthrow of the old dictator to lend credence to any claim of Masonic unanimity. What Freemasonry did contribute, however, was a not insignificant group of Masons who firmly believed that a privileged caste of positivists had transformed Mexico into a despotic state in which the true landmarks of Freemasonry could never find expression, and that joining in the overthrow of the old despot was therefore a clear moral obligation.

One schism of the early Revolutionary period clearly negates the case for Masonic unanimity. There were two explosions in 1910: the outbreak of the Mexican Revolution, and the rupture of Freemasonry along lines of nationality. It was in 1910 that American, Canadian, and British Freemasons in Mexico took over the Valley of Mexico Grand Lodge and left the Mexicans on the outside. The rupture occurred after months of impassioned debate, which night after night attracted virtually every Freemason in Mexico City to temple headquarters on Donceles Street. That temple had constituted one of the foremost forums where the more educated liberals of Mexico might interchange views on the dictatorship. The Anglo-Saxons first managed to have themselves legitimately installed in key positions of the grand lodge; then they proceeded to ban discussion of political themes in all lodges. The action provoked such tension that the foreigners attempted to bring their Mexican brothers into line with strongly worded accusations of "never really understanding Freemasonry" and of "possessing Latin minds incapable of grasping Freemasonry."

If we accept first-hand accounts of the rupture reported by Mexicans, we are led to believe that the fissure ran much deeper than Freemasonry—that "many foreigners in Mexican lodges saw an imminent threat to their business interests in the prospect of an overtoppling of Díaz." The Anglo-Saxons, said these Mexican reports, wanted no adverse comment on the power elite running Mexico, for they were, after all, part and parcel of that elite. The fissure also ran laterally, into jurisdictions over other grand lodges where English-speaking lodges operated. Joining the Canadians and British of the "Toltec" and "Anahuac" lodges of Mexico City, from which the hard core of anti-Revolution leadership emerged, were lodges from the states of Yucatán, Jalisco, Hidalgo, Guanajuato, San Luis Potosí, and in all the then-existent border states—Sonora, Chihuahua, Coahuila, Nuevo León, and Tamaulipas. In this way, the majority of influential Anglo-Saxons in Mexico served notice on many influential Mexicans that, come what may, Americans, British, and Canadians intended to stick with Díaz.

With the downfall of Díaz and the outbreak of Revolution in 1911, this decision became costly indeed for foreigners in Mexican lodges. As the decade unfolded, English-speaking Masons in Mexico realized that their own obstinacy had opened a chasm that they could bridge only by permitting the Mexicans unquestioned control of Freemasonry organizations. But this action carried the corollary that Mexicans were equal or perhaps even superior to the foreigners. Why, asked the Anglo-Saxons, should Mexicans be permitted to control Freemasonry in Mexico? If they must have power, foreigners argued, then we want no part of it. Let them have their grand lodge. And the Anglo-Saxons had a trump card. They were willing to barter all jurisdiction over the Valley of Mexico Grand Lodge in exchange for the privilege of establishing a new grand lodge, reserved exclusively for English-speaking foreigners. This situation led to the founding of the "York Grand Lodge of Mexico" (the formal title is in English, not Spanish), with its unique feature of conducting rituals in the English language and, unlike the York Rite in the United States, of combining blue lodge and philosophical Freemasonry in one organizational framework.

Orthodox Freemasonry abhors schismatic grand lodges. Either a grand lodge of a given territory possesses exclusive jurisdiction over granting of the first three degrees of Freemasonry or serious trouble arises. There should be one and only one grand lodge. In setting up the York Grand Lodge of Mexico, which ran counter to acceptable Masonic doctrines (in the United States, the York Rite represents philosophical Masonry above the third degree), Americans, Canadians, and Englishmen served notice that Mexicans, Mexicanism, and orthodox Freemasonry meant less to them than winning their point. In their conception, foreigners were to run Freemasonry in Mexico, even if the new York Grand Lodge contradicted orthodox principles. Once definitely split into an autonomous organization, the York Grand Lodge sought recognition from grand lodges in the United States and elsewhere. Of course, grand lodges outside Mexico that recognized the York Grand Lodge relegated the Valley of Mexico Grand Lodge and other grand lodges in Mexico to a schismatic position; a grand lodge extends recognition to one and only one grand lodge per geographical region. The highhandedness of Anglo-Saxons heading the York Grand Lodge provoked a group of English-speaking Freemasons—some disenchanted with the new lodge, others in favor of the Mexican Revolution, and still others who believed that they should place themselves under the jurisdiction of Mexican-directed lodges —to set up during the end of the Carranza administration a "City of Mexico Lodge Number 35" under the old Valley of Mexico Grand Lodge. The "City of Mexico" persists today as the leading blue lodge in Mexico City open to English-speaking residents, Christian or non-Christian, as-piring to Masonic influence within Mexican councils.

But the York Grand Lodge did not recede. On the contrary, it be-came markedly aggressive in seeking recognition from grand lodges in the United States. With affiliated lodges in Mexico City, Tampico, Monte-rrey, Puebla, Guadalajara, and elsewhere in Mexico, the York Grand Lodge began claiming jurisdiction for the entire Mexican republic, not-withstanding the fact that at least 90 per cent of the Freemasons in Mexico fell under the jurisdiction of other grand lodges. Disputes be-tween the York Grand Lodge and other grand lodges intensified when Masonic organizations in the United States announced that they were sending official delegations to investigate the situation in Mexico at first hand. Important for the Valley of Mexico Grand Lodge in particular was the arrival in 1920 of a delegation representing several grand lodges in the United States, including the grand masters of Texas, Louisiana, and California, which sought to discover acceptable solutions to the jurisdic-tional problem confronting Freemasonry in Mexico. On the basis of in-vestigations conducted by this delegation, the grand lodges of Texas and Louisiana soon recognized the Valley of Mexico Grand Lodge, not the York Grand Lodge; other grand lodges under the Southern Jurisdiction of the United States, notably those of Kentucky and New Mexico, followed suit. Grand lodges elsewhere in the world, led by those of Panama and New Zealand, also recognized or confirmed their recognition of the Val-ley of Mexico. Yet, on the whole, the Yorkist Anglo-Saxons fared much better and convinced virtually the entire Northern Jurisdiction of the United States that the York Grand Lodge was the legitimate organiza-tion to recognize. Today, more than fifty years after the Anglo-Saxons first split Freemasonry in Mexico along nationalistic lines, the York Grand Lodge enjoys recognition from more grand lodges in the United States than does the giant Mexican-oriented and Mexican-staffed Valley of Mexico Grand Lodge.

Meanwhile, in the mainstream of Mexican Freemasonry, the tendency to make Freemasonry "free and accepted" and also Mexican-led prospered during the first decade of Revolution. Political activity there was, but orthodox Freemasonic tenets forbidding overt politicking were clearly asserted. Two instances of political "intervention" stand out. First, while World War I was in progress, someone close to Carranza apparently influenced the Valley of Mexico Grand Lodge, by then under Mexican control, to elect a pro–Central Powers German resident to the grand mastership. But whatever Carranza's motives may have been, Herr Krum-Heller seemed to possess little awareness of true Masonic landmarks and produced slight effect on Masonry in Mexico. After this experience, Carranza himself seemed to have but little interest in Freemasonry. The second intervention came amidst the explosive political atmosphere that produced the assassination of Carranza in 1920. Grand Master Ignacio Cortés of the Valley of Mexico Grand Lodge committed the unforgivable error of issuing an official suggestion that all Masons, as citizens of Mexico, should vote for Alvaro Obregón in the July, 1920, presidential election. Despite the triumph of Obregón, the repercussions of using a Masonic post for political ends were so profound that Brother Cortés failed miserably the following year in his attempt at re-election to the grand mastership. For all their political mistakes, neither Carranza nor Obregón, neither one a Freemason, made the mistake that Díaz had committed of using political power to interfere in Masonic affairs.

Nonetheless, Freemasonry and Mexican politics did seem to intermingle significantly. Many delegates to the Querétaro convention that gave birth to the Constitution of 1917 had Masonic affiliation. The convention president, Luis Manuel Rojas, achieved high positions in the Masonic councils of Jalisco and Mexico City both before and after the promulgation of the Constitution. Other Masons who participated in the Constitutional assembly included army generals Esteban Baca Calderón, José Alvarez, Heriberto Jara, and Amado Aguirre, and Dr. Jesús López Lira, José Solórzano, and Alfonso Cravioto. The extent to which the Masonic beliefs of these men influenced the deliberation at Querétaro is a moot point. That the Constitution incorporated measures on freedom of religion, separation of church and state, anticlericalism, and free education can hardly be attributed to Masonic influence alone: Traditional Mexican liberalism and other historical considerations were uppermost influences. Some of these same Conventionalists reappeared on both sides of the Adolfo de la Huerta–Alvaro Obregón clash in 1923, when the ranks of Freemasonry as well as those of the Mexican army were split.

A further bitter division in the higher councils of Freemasonry occurred during the presidency of Calles, when a long-time, Spanish-speaking American resident was selected to serve as grand master of the Valley of Mexico Grand Lodge. The forced renunciation of the office by "Meester" Hirschfeld in 1926 marks the last time any foreigner occupied the top post in Mexico's most influential grand lodge, and it is highly unlikely that a foreigner will ever again be elevated to that post. This affair reopened the whole question of the place of foreigners in Mexican lodges, and that disagreement, along with contests over the content of symbolic and philosophical ritual, characterized Freemasonry in Mexico over the years 1926–45. During that period, however, the most significant development in Mexican Freemasonry was the founding in 1927 of the Mexican Independent Symbolical Grand Lodge, popularly known as the "Cárdenas Lodge," which came to exert far-reaching influences in both Masonry and politics.

There is ample reason to question whether the "Cárdenas Lodge" bore any substantial relationship to true Freemasonry. Being neither "free" nor "accepted" in the orthodox sense of speculative Freemasonry, it did not qualify for full status in Freemasonry. It did not acquire formal recognition of grand lodges in the United States or Great Britain, nor did its leaders particularly seek such recognition. The "Cárdenas Lodge" did emulate certain rituals pursued in Freemasonry, but it added special ingredients of a peculiarly Mexican nature, so that, in general, older Masons looked upon the new group with dismay. Still, a number of "orthodox" Masons of high standing abandoned other grand lodges in favor of what their more conservative brothers held to be a schismatic, illegitimate movement.

However unsavory the "Cárdenas Lodge" was to the taste of regular Masons both inside and outside the country, it enjoyed exceptional popularity among the middle and popular sectors of the population—the soldier, the civil servant, the peasant leader, the railroad worker, the rural teacher, the miner. With its own "Orient" established at Puerto México in the state of Veracruz merely claiming exclusive jurisdiction over the state of Veracruz and the Isthmus of Tehuantepec, the new rite spread over the entire republic, obviously infringing on jurisdictions of other grand lodges.

Especially after December, 1934, when its former grand master Lázaro Cárdenas (1929–31) became President of Mexico, the "Cárdenas Lodge" experienced a vogue unknown in Masonic circles since the early days of national independence. New lodges blossomed, and many existing lodges—particularly in the states of Michoacán, Veracruz, Oaxaca, México, and Hidalgo—placed themselves under the jurisdiction of the "Cárdenas Lodge." Civil servants in various government ministries (notably the treasury, agriculture, and agrarian) either belonged to the new lodge or to none at all. An affiliated lodge was even set up in Los Angeles, California.

Behind the ideology of the Cárdenas lodges was the belief held by Cárdenas and probably shared by others of its leaders—such as Gen. Rafael Sánchez Tapia, José Campistro de Cáceres, Santiago Vázquez

Bueno, Gen. Héctor F. López, Gabino Vázquez, Gen. Cristóbal Rodríguez, and José Domingo Lavín—that the Scottish Rite, the York Rite,
and every grand lodge in the nation were directed by foreigners and subject to the control of foreign powers. The latter charge seems completely
without foundation. Beyond this, however, the "Cárdenas Lodge" held
that the Scottish Rite was surreptitiously directing symbolical lodges and
grand lodges all over Mexico. It was clear that the York Grand Lodge was
foreign-dominated—nobody denied it. In the Scottish Rite itself there was
also a powerful faction that from time to time asserted that the only
interest foreigners had in philosophical Masonry in Mexico was the prestige that accrued to them from recognition of their degrees by supreme
councils in the United States. In fact, a highly interesting document was
prepared on this very subject by the Commission on Foreign Relations of
the Grand Lodge of Massachusetts, dated in Boston, September 13, 1944,
and signed by Claude L. Allen, Melvyn M. Johnson, Roscoe Pound, and
Arthur M. Price. The occasion was a report examining the state of Freemasonry in Mexico, prepared by a special committee of that grand lodge.
Despite the possibility of minor errors occasioned by the translations first
into Spanish, then here back to the original English, the following ex-
cerpts seem pertinent (italics have been added):

> We believe that *the nationals of any country*, whenever they com-
> ply with the Ancient Landmarks and fundamental laws of the Fraternity,
> and their Masonic origin is legitimate, *have the right to rule and govern
> their own Masonry*. As a corollary, we would like to point out that *for-
> eigners are not authorized in any country to claim the right to exclusive
> control of the Masonic organization by noncitizens of that country*, nor
> are they authorized to conduct the business of the Grand Lodge and its
> subordinate organizations in a foreign tongue, instead of the national
> language.
> There is no doubt that *we would not tolerate such a situation in
> our own country*.
> It is obvious that it [the York Grand Lodge of Mexico] is not a
> national Mexican institution, and that it can never be so. If Masonry is
> good for the English-speaking residents of Mexico, it is also good for those
> of native origin and speech. We have adopted an attitude of unwarranted
> superiority, of which we should not be proud, since this has been the
> principal reason why the bulk of American Masonry has obstructed the
> development of Mexican Masonry by refusing help, at the same time
> refusing to recognize the activities and the fraternity in a foreign country
> when conducted by its nationals.

This substantiates, at least to some extent, part of the beliefs of General
Cárdenas regarding foreign influence in Freemasonry in Mexico.

On the other hand, the "Cárdenas Lodge" represented first and foremost an independent, rigidly nationalistic brotherhood composed of peas-

ant, military, and bureaucrat elements. Reaching the popular classes with "Masonic" principles constituted the crusade of this lodge. Without schooling, living on minimal incomes, and in general lacking prestige, the popular elements of Mexico were all too obviously in no position to "obtain invitations" into the regular lodges. Honorable individuals of meager incomes might have heard of Freemasonry, perhaps even witnessed the good works of local lodges, but they could not escape the conclusion that Masonry appeared to be a luxury of and for the elite. Cárdenas and his associates brought a type of Masonry—whatever its shortcomings and omissions—to the most humble of social classes: a creed that emphasized civic responsibility, the condemnation of vice, hypocrisy, and fanaticism, and all in all, the preparation of the Mexican to live a more humanitarian and constructive life based on love, culture, work, and justice.

The strife in symbolical lodges was reflected in the philosophical rites: schisms, illegitimate claims, frequent disorder. Between 1933 and 1945, no less than six new supreme councils appeared on the Mexican scene, in addition to the authentic Supreme Council of the Scottish Rite (recognized by the International Confederation of Supreme Councils) and the authentic "Supreme Council (in exile) for Spain and its Possessions" (which has maintained its official headquarters in Mexico City since February 5, 1943). There was a Supreme Council for the Northern Jurisdiction of Mexico at Monterrey, a Supreme Council for Southeastern Mexico in Yucatán, and a National Supreme Council, corresponding to the higher degrees of the "Cárdenas Lodge." Joining the hodgepodge was a Unifying Supreme Council under the strong Catholic Maximino Ávila Camacho, minister of communications and public works (1940–45) in the government headed by his brother. A unique "Masonic University" embraced the higher degrees of philosophical Masonry. And a rump supreme council was constituted in Mexico City by five sovereign grand inspectors who defected from the authentic supreme council. Not until 1945 could both philosophical and blue-lodge Freemasonry—excluding the York Grand Lodge and York Rite under control of resident foreigners—manage to unite their respective orders under the single authority of one legitimate supreme council and nineteen autonomous grand lodges.

In the face of all this bickering, this atmosphere of claims and counterclaims, could anyone maintain that Freemasonry in Mexico was consistently a tightly knit, unified organization and force?

The tendency toward a stabilized, practicing Freemasonry in recent years is marked. Present jurisdiction over the blue lodges is shared among nineteen grand lodges affiliated to the informal Confederation of Regular Grand Lodges of Mexico. The stabilizing force developed even during the years of turmoil in a series of national congresses (First National Masonic Congress, Monterrey, December 1925; Second, Durango, April 1927; Third, Mexico City, February 1928; Fourth, Tampico, April 1934). A resolution adopted at the Tampico Congress would circumscribe the essential features required of grand lodges in order to enjoy "regular" status. The "essential" features follow basic landmarks of orthodox Freemasonry. Since the Fourth Congress, the Confederation has sought to standardize degree requirements and at the same time avoid the invasion of rights claimed by individual grand lodges. Participating in the Confederation are the Valley of Mexico Grand Lodge, with jurisdiction over the states already noted; the Benito Juárez (Coahuila); Campeche; Cosmos (Chihuahua); Chiapas; El Pacífico (Sinaloa and Sonora); El Potosí (San Luis Potosí); Guadalupe Victoria (Durango); Hidalgo; Nuevo León; Oaxaca; Occidental Mexicana (Jalisco and Nayarit); Oriental Peninsular (Yucatán and Quintana Roo Territory); Querétaro; Restauración (Tabasco); Suroeste (Colima); Tamaulipas; Baja California; and Unida Mexicana (Veracruz).

Despite these efforts at unification, every blue lodge has not been brought under the jurisdiction of some grand lodge. There are holdouts of the old RNM (*Rito Nacional Mexicano*) organization, some dating back to mid-nineteenth century, including RNM lodges in Texas, New Mexico, and Arizona. And there are blue lodges of "Cárdenas Rite" mold that persist in holding aloof from affiliation with a grand lodge.

But the biggest split is not within the lodges, but between the Mexican-led and Mexican-staffed grand lodges, headed by the Valley of Mexico Grand Lodge, and the Anglo-Saxon-led and staffed York Grand Lodge. Whenever promising signs of unification appear, either the foreigners of the York Grand Lodge or the Mexicans of other grand lodges manage to throw a monkey wrench into the negotiations. Yet since 1945, when the majority of Cárdenas lodges united in the Confederation, Freemasonry in Mexico has tended to follow "free and accepted" principles. Administrative conflict and politicking in the lodges have given way to study and ritualism. To the young Mexican aspiring to a solid future in government, business, education, or the military, Freemasonry is not indispensable; but few educated Mexicans, except for militant Catholics, choose the generally slower path of building a career without Masonic affiliation. The lodges are not centers of political maneuvering, but they are sources of liberal instruction where the Mexican can prepare himself to comprehend what the Revolution is about and to lead his nation along acceptable Revolutionary lines.

EIGHT

ECONOMIC PROGRESS: THE BIG LOOK

Mexico of the 1960's offers sharp contrasts to the "philosophy of little things" proposed by Frank Tannenbaum for guiding Mexican economic development after World War II. Tannenbaum, an authority on our southern neighbor, wrote in 1949 that the big-city planners, especially the government brain trust in Mexico City, were so intent on transforming their nation that they "would make big plans, procure large foreign funds, organize great industries, discover some magic in 'industrialization' and have a national economy served by a national market at any cost, even if in their hearts they suspect that it is chiefly a dream, which, because of inadequate resources, cannot be realized." [1] Big plans there have been, and bigger ones still are on the drawing board. Substantial foreign funds, both private and government, have been procured. Large, if not great, industries have blossomed. And the creation of a national economy served by a national market is indicated by the many infant industries that are growing because of government protection, which forces the consumer to buy Mexican-made goods at prices substantially higher than the foreign-made goods that are prohibited from entering the country. But despite government claims to the contrary, the "magic of industrialization" has not entirely relegated the "philosophy of little things" to oblivion. That cannot be accomplished overnight in any underdeveloped nation—not even in Mexico, where rapid capital accumulation is accomplishing some miracles.

Tannenbaum, unlike many who wanted the Mexican immunized from undesirable effects of industrialization, did not oppose economic modernization for sentimental reasons. His logic, tempered by decades of first-hand experience in many regions of Mexico, flowed from the imperatives of the past and the nature of Mexican character and resources. He proposed that it would be infinitely better for Mexico "if it turns its eyes to Switzerland and Denmark rather than to the United States as a model,"

---

[1] Frank Tannenbaum, *Mexico: The Struggle for Peace and Bread* (New York: Alfred A. Knopf, Inc., 1950), p. 244.

and in this fashion find solutions "on a local, parochial basis in thousands of little communities, adapting to them all of what modern science and skill can make available for the needs of the little community without making it increasingly dependent upon a national market." Tannenbaum saw no virtue in creating high-cost domestic industries and forcing little towns to buy inferior factory-made products when the local craftsmen could make most needed goods, "by their own arts, and make them beautiful and strong and serviceable." [2] For Tannenbaum, the "strength and resiliency" of Mexico lay in the rural community, and destroying it contained no virtue whatsoever.

By the 1960's, despite many somber consequences of industrialization, including what Oscar Lewis has identified as the "culture of poverty," the thought of basing the Mexican economy on the rural community had virtually disappeared from writings of economists, anthropologists, and political sociologists. It had not, however, disappeared from the hard facts of Mexican life. In the place of "community economies" now appear such expressions as economic integration, industrialization, agricultural reform, economic growth, public ownership, private initiative, and financial stability—collectively, the planks in the Revolutionary Creed to which the Revolutionary elite running the country seems dedicated today. But tossing aside the Tannenbaum approaches to economic development has not established the neat type of "institutional revolution" described by some observers. The theory of achieving economic progress by opening the official party to "individuals and to organized interest groups previously excluded" and by limiting presidential authority has been examined in previous chapters, where it was applied to realities of recent decades and found lacking. The claims of those who contend that only a minority of the population is now in a lower-class status—claims such as, "in 1960, probably less than half the population is proletarian," or "the middle stratum of Mexican society probably amounts to a third of total population" —seem equally unrealistic. The Revolutionary elite, along with industrialists and merchants, wish that such a high proportion of the population possessed effective purchasing power. Materialization of this dream, however, lies ahead.

Contentions that Mexico has a burgeoning middle class and minority lower class (the terms themselves are extremely elusive) have been popularized by a few scholars in the United States and several Mexican economists, but such claims would horrify directors of the official National Housing Institute and sophisticated Mexican economists. During 1962, Luis Quintanilla and Javier Rondero, president and secretary-general of the Institute, reiterated what they had been saying on housing since early 1959: In 70 per cent of all dwellings in the Federal District, four persons or more occupy one room; 75 per cent of the Mexican population lives in

[2] *Ibid.*, p. 242.

a wretched, highly precarious condition; less than 8 per cent of all dwellings in Mexico consist of more than two rooms; 3.5 million low-cost housing units are needed immediately to house some 14 million people now living in "subhuman" conditions. Sophisticated Mexican economists maintained that in 1963 over one-third of all Mexican families—the average size of the Mexican family is 5.6 members—had monthly incomes of $24 or less, that over 80 per cent of Mexico's families had monthly incomes of $80 or less, and that less than 9 per cent of Mexico's families had a monthly income above $175. These statistics dramatize the truth of the assertion that the generation of workers since the Cárdenas administration has lived and labored to build a bigger and better Mexico, and contributed to doing so for some Mexicans, yet the great majority of workers took a bumpy back seat to stability and rapid capital accumulation.

In over-all terms, however, the Mexican economy of the 1960's is infinitely more dynamic, creative, and healthy than the relatively static, export-oriented, and feudalistic economy of 1910. The Revolution demanded a new social order, one that required basic changes in the economy, and a political elite, the Revolutionary Family, provided the human direction for creating a productive structure in accord with new social principles. Setting in motion one of the profoundest agrarian reforms in history, the Revolutionary elite succeeded not only in breaking up and changing the ownership pattern of agricultural lands, but also in accelerating over-all economic development and bringing about greater labor mobility, a new structure and composition of supply and demand, new patterns of income distribution, different utilization of natural and human resources, a profound impact on capital formation, and, ultimately, new roles for foreign investment.

The human spark driving the economic mechanism forward has been supplied by many men. Some men, like Madero, Zapata, and Obregón, died violent deaths. Some like José Vasconcelos, Emilio Portes Gil, and Vicente Lombardo Toledano, experienced political eclipses. Others, the very heads of the Revolutionary Family, met rejection and public defamation. Still others, private entrepreneurs like William Jenkins, Carlos Trouyet, and the Garza Sada–G. Sada families, made their contributions with little fanfare. And some, like the technical brain trust of the Revolutionary Family today, men such as the Ortiz Mena brothers and Carrillo Flores brothers, continue working away at the big problems. Before World War II, the biggest push at the top came from the three C's: Carranza (the Constitution of 1917), Calles (public works, fiscal and monetary reforms, secular education, professionalization, and confiscation of Church properties), and Cárdenas (agrarian reform, public works, oil expropriation, public-credit institutions, public ownership, public education, and institutionalization of vested economic interests). Since 1940, the big push has focused on the four A's: Ávila Camacho (public educa-

tion, national unity, and capital accumulation), Alemán (industrialization, commercialization, education, private investment, and public works),
and the two Adolfos (agricultural reform, education, industrialization and
commercialization, nationalization of the electric-power industry, public
works, and state distribution of basic commodities).

REVOLUTIONARY ACHIEVEMENTS IN ECONOMIC LIFE

The Mexican economic system centers on the achievements of the
Revolution in the realm of socio-economic life. Some of the achievements,
conceivably all of them, contain shortcomings and contradictions, but they
collectively represent major accomplishments in transforming the society
of 1910 into the society of the 1960's. Attributing these achievements to
the Revolution alone would be a serious error, however; forces outside
Mexico, forces in the international economy and the larger context of
world politics, exerted immeasurable influence on the Revolutionary Family's decisions to apply certain sets of policies and reject others. Once this
is said, the major credit and, whenever in order, blame belong to the Revolutionary elite. Whether it has created a productive structure compatible
with Revolutionary social principles and capable of maintaining and per-
petuating the Revolution is not fully answerable. The following achievements do, however, supply a big part of the answer.

1. Revolution Broke the Vicious Circle of Poverty.   Although Díaz
had initiated the material buildup of Mexico by railroad construction,
mineral exploitation, certain manufacturing establishments, and electric-
power installations, these modifications did little to alter the static agricultural economy that was retarding internal development. Dominated by a
small economic elite of rural land barons, foreigners, and Church interests
committed to semifeudalism and the exploitation of minerals to satisfy the
demand of foreign markets, the economy had little in the way of a national
domestic market. Díaz' policy of "rails and progress" really meant construction of railroads for getting raw materials out of Mexico and, to a
lesser extent, for bringing into Mexico foreign-made goods that ultimately
reached the Mexican consumer at exorbitant prices. The Mexican was
poor, committed to poverty by tradition, the priests, and debt peonage.
The interrelationship of cause-and-effect operated to imprison the Mexican economy in its own shortcomings: low productivity, low saving, low
investment, and low productivity; or looked at in another way, low income,
low consumption, low productivity, and low income. The vicious circle of
poverty, or the "circular constellation of forces tending to act and react
upon one another in such a way as to keep a poor country in a state of
poverty," pointed to a "circular and cumulative process, continuously

pressing levels downward, in which one negative factor is, at the same time, both cause and effect of other negative factors." [3] Hopes of generating a circular and accumulative process leading to sustained growth were nowhere present. The Revolution broke this vicious circle of poverty by tearing down archaic economic structures and releasing human and material resources for the big push, for the "take-off into sustained growth." Though most Mexicans are still impoverished, they are not perpetually sick. They owe everyone, but they are not in debt peonage, owing everything to only one. Some 20 per cent, not 2 per cent of the population, are enjoying the direct, immediate economic benefits of social modernization. The lot of the 80 per cent is often sad, but the Mexican people, tens of millions of them, are no longer forgotten by the political elite running the nation.

2. Economic Development Became Inextricably Bound With a Higher Standard of Living for the Masses. The Constitution of 1917 defined democracy not only as a juridical structure and a desired form of political society but, above all, as a system of life founded on the continuous economic, social, and cultural improvement of the people. Making neat distinctions of "economic" and "political" was impossible. The Revolution had exploded because of blatant economic inequalities and oppression, and the new elite discovered that advocating political equality without giving attention to economic equality was a meaningless and politically risky policy. Mexico thus committed itself to social security, progressive taxation, labor rights, and social justice *before* the country was industrialized. Keeping living standards of the masses low, suppressing strikes, condoning long working hours, ignoring the general health condition of workers and their families—all the deplorable features of the early stages of capitalist development in the United States that conduced to its rapid economic growth—these were prohibited constitutionally in Mexico before that nation industrialized. Economic equality was not a goal of American society during the long decades of industrialization, and there is some doubt whether this became an explicit goal until the New Deal, if even then. Economic equality was made an explicit objective in Mexico in 1917. Economic freedom, as that expression was known to the

[3] The theory has been developed by Ragnar Norkse, *Problems of Capital Formation in Underdeveloped Countries* (London: Oxford University Press, 1953), and Gunnar Myrdal, *Rich Lands and Poor* (New York: Harper & Brothers, 1957). For its relevance to Mexico, see Edmundo Flores, *Tratado de economía agrícola* (Mexico: Fondo de Cultura Económica, 1961). Also, see two recent studies that emphasize the roles of motivation, innovation, and creativity in breaking the "vicious circle of poverty": David McClelland, *The Achieving Society* (Princeton: Van Nostrand, 1961); and Everett Hagen, *On the Theory of Social Change: How Economic Growth Begins* (Homewood, Ill.: Dorsey, 1962).

"Robber Barons," never entered Revolutionary vocabulary. And though Revolutionary policy fostered a sort of capitalism in industry and commerce, the entrepreneur south of the border lacked the relatively unlimited freedom of action enjoyed by early capitalists in the United States. The marriage of politics and economics in Mexico pushed political inequalities into the background by soft-pedaling the political authoritativeness of the Revolutionary Family, but it also raised the goal of economic equality to new importance. Unfortunately, advances toward real economic equality have been uneven, slow, and enveloped in conscious efforts toward breaking the vicious circle of poverty and bringing about growth by forced savings through inflation.

3. *The Traditional Privileged Interests Lost Their Monopolistic Hold on the Mexican Economy.* The favored quadruplets of pre-Revolutionary days—the Catholic Church, high military officers, rural land barons, and imperialistic foreign capitalists—no longer call the plays. The myth of egalitarianism replaced the myth of racial and elite superiority. Calles completed what Gómez Farías and Benito Juárez had begun in the nineteenth century: elimination of property ownership by the Church. Generals Calles, Amaro, and Cárdenas first combined forces to rid the nation of predatory militarism, then Cárdenas and Ávila Camacho introduced the formula for keeping army generals content without periodic resort to armed force. Several Revolutionary leaders, but particularly Zapata, served notice that the hacienda and hacienda life was finished; then, two decades later, Cárdenas made agrarian reform come true. The fourth of the quadruplets, foreign capital, learned its lessons from land expropriation, new forms of diplomacy, new tax structuring, and a series of instructions highlighted by the expropriation of oil properties. Not even the giant foreign oil companies proved capable of overcoming the economic nationalism of the Revolution. Cárdenas dramatically rejuvenated domestic interests by informing the nation that Mexico and the public welfare superseded foreign capital. The oil industry, railroads, agricultural lands, street railways, banking, insurance, and other sectors of the economy became reserved for Mexicans, whether by state, private, cooperative, or communal ownership. Holdings of foreigners are by no means secure from state intervention today. Since World War II, the government has purchased holdings of foreigners whenever it believed an industry was not keeping pace with developmental expectations (the Consolidated Steel mills), or constituted an excessive monopoly (motion-picture distribution companies), or comprised a bottleneck for sustained growth (the electric-power industry). And though the Catholic Church, the military, owners of large agricultural estates, and foreign capital are present in Mexico today, their role in economic life differs radically from what it was in the

days of Díaz. Race, religion, and family background no longer disqualify the Mexican from assuming important roles in economic life.

4. The Revolution Altered the Concept of Private Property and the Function of the State.   The theory of capitalistic equilibrium is neither valid nor attractive for Mexico. To the degree that the exigencies of world markets permit, Mexico seeks a release from the "natural" forces of the market place. The Constitution of Mexico is based on the premise that, without public initiative and control, private enterprise brings disorder and exploitation of the weak by unscrupulous capitalists. Private property is respected within a special social context, yet the "natural forces" of the market place long ago ceased to be the major determinant of Mexican economic life. The "public interest," as that concept is circumscribed by constitutional mandates making property a social function, transcends everything else. The patrimony of the nation, including its lands, waters, and natural resources, belongs to the nation; although the state may transfer title thereover to private individuals for specific utilization, its right to retract such concessions is inalienable. Granting concessions to private interests for the development of resources does not mean that the state passes "ownership" to private parties, but rather that it bestows the privilege of using resources for specific ends approved by the state and always subject to public revision. Primacy of the state over economic life is neither a usurpation, as followers of Adam Smith would have it, nor a panacea, as Marxians would maintain. On the crucial question of ownership and management of the means of production, state intervention draws its legitimacy from the earliest content of Spanish colonial laws carried forward into national independence, as well as from the Constitution of 1917. Even before the Revolution, a private concessionaire who failed to live up to the letter of his grant ran the risk of unilateral abrogation of the concession by the state. No bill of attainder or ex post facto action was involved; the state merely took back what had belonged to it all along.

As good government ceased to be equated with little government, the state moved into the ownership and operation of entire industries—oil, railroads, telegraph, and electric power—and of specific factories on a stock participation or joint stock-operation basis. Revolutionary economists justified state ownership because of the "unattractiveness of an industry to private capital," or because of "the powerful hold that this industry exerts on the economy," or because "the urgencies of economic development required higher productivity than private owners were willing or able to underwrite." The state became responsible for keeping in leash the forces of social change while simultaneously providing an economic infrastructure, and any slowdown in the rate of economic growth thus became attributable primarily to shortcomings in the fiscal, monetary, and investment policies necessary for accelerated development. It was left to the disposition of the state whether emphasis was to be placed on income redistribution or capital accumulation, inflationary or deflationary measures, price controls or demand and supply, industrialization or agricultural reform. Besides its role in a managed economy, including attention to the law of economic saturation, the state also committed itself to provide social services. As a result, despite the insistence of consecutive Revolutionary Family leaders that substantial private initiative is indispensable and that excessive centralization is undesirable, the state has persistently enlarged its role in the ownership and management of productive means, in setting controls, and in providing social services.

5. Agrarian Reform Became an Accomplished Fact, and Agricultural Reform Is Fully Under Way.   Redistribution of agricultural lands was the essence of Zapata's exhortations for "land and liberty." Zapata insisted that land belonged to those who worked and lived on it. He died before any real agrarian-reform program was put into effect. The pace of the agrarian reform, though given its initial momentum by Obregón and Calles, was relatively slow under early presidents. It was stepped up under the short Portes Gil administration, de-emphasized during the remaining years of the Sonoran Dynasty, accelerated greatly under Lázaro Cárdenas, delayed again except for a few dramatic expropriations by Ruiz Cortines (such as those at Cananea and Cloete), then vigorously reasserted in the 1959–64 period by López Mateos. Though the shortcomings of agrarian reform have been many and varied, the imperative before the Revolutionary Family was clear: Redistribute land and kill the hacienda system once and for all. More than anyone else, Cárdenas worked toward this end. It is interesting to note that while he was fulfilling constitutional mandates on agrarian reform, few foreign governments condoned his action; today, advanced industrial nations urging development of backward nations propose agrarian reform as an indispensable requisite, frequently pointing to the Mexican experience as a prime example. One thing is certain: Agrarian reform, whether a success or failure in terms of agricultural output, directly and indirectly helped to break the vicious circle of poverty and set in motion the forces leading to sustained economic growth.

Often subsumed in the topic of agrarian reform, the subject of agricultural reform actually encompasses credit, investment, irrigation, mechanization, crop rotation and diversification, electrification, fertilizers and insecticides, soil conservation, and the whole gamut of measures necessary to efficiency and productivity. Agricultural reform got underway with the rural credit institutions and the works of the national irrigation and national road commissions created by Calles in 1925 and 1926. Cárdenas enlarged the rural credit system, founded a federal electricity commission responsible for rural electrification, and emphasized capacitation of farm workers. With Ávila Camacho and Alemán, the issuance of certificates of "ineffectability" and the constitutional amendment on agrarian reform that enlarged the legal maximum size of holdings brought new incentive to invest in private agriculture, to mechanize, irrigate, and electrify farms, and to diversify crops. The two Adolfos promoted rural credit, investments, mechanization, irrigation, the use of fertilizers, insecticides, better seeds, soil conservation, and crop rotation and diversification. Agricultural reform is the principal means by which Mexico expects to feed her burgeoning population. As we shall observe in Chapter 9, there is reason to believe that she will succeed in this crucial task.

6. *A New Concept of Labor Was Introduced.*   Though many Revolutionary legal concepts on economic matters coincide with colonial and early national doctrines, the Revolutionary theory of labor is a unique product of twentieth-century Mexico. The labor measures put into the Constitution of 1917 were not only harbingers of advanced labor legislation subsequently adopted by industrialized nations, but largely antedated industrialization and commercialization in Mexico itself. These measures dealt with legal recognition of unions, minimum wages, maximum hours, job security, protection of women and children, collective bargaining, the right to strike, social security, participation of labor in profits, and a controlling position for the state on boards of labor conciliation and arbitration. Labor-management relations clearly became subject to state control, even before these sectors of economic life developed in any sustained, dynamic sense. In short, the state set itself up as the arbiter of economic life. Unions became creatures of the state; if the state wanted strong unions, they were strengthened, and if the state wanted weak unions, they were weakened.

Although the law bestows special privileges on labor, in effect ordering that the proletariat be elevated to a favored position in society, the successive Revolutionary regimes decide whether these laws will be implemented and which unions will receive the benefits ordained. Whereas foreign interests owned the major industrial and commercial enterprises during the early years of the twentieth century—a situation which suggested to lawmakers that a way of facilitating government control over foreign capital would be to place the state on the side of labor, today, the productive machine is largely owned by the state and Mexican private capitalists. With only a small portion of industry and commerce in foreign hands, the government-labor alliance has assumed new meanings and new structures. The new theory of labor brought into vogue by the Revolution still stands, but unlike the golden days under the Cárdenas regime, most of Mexican labor is crawling ahead decidedly slower than capital accumulation, favored labor bosses, and inflation. The development of the labor movement points up the fact that labor has become stronger whenever the state wills it, but the state becomes stronger whether labor wishes it or not.

7. Industrial and Commercial Revolutions Are Under Way. Industrialization and commercialization are major components of Mexican economic development. With some Revolutionaries persistently contending that Mexico should avoid full industrialization and that a "philosophy of little things" based on agriculture should prevail, it was not until the post–World War II years that industry managed to acquire a preferential role in economic development. The key question today is not whether Mexico should industrialize—this question was answered affirmatively some years ago—but rather, how rapidly can Mexico industrialize? This second question introduces further considerations, such as how markets can be expanded to sustain industrial expansion, where the government will find finances for building a petrochemical complex, what additional tax concessions and tariff modifications show promise of encouraging industrialization, and a whole series of variables touching on industrialization and commercialization. The industrial and commercial transformation of Mexico is indeed impressive. Quantitatively, 25,000 new factories and almost 60,000 new service establishments came into being between 1950 and 1960, raising the total number of factories to almost 100,000 and service establishments to over 105,000. Qualitatively, technology, management, and widening markets are combining to place better products before the public. Problems concerning industrialization and commercialization abound and become more complex year by year, yet Mexico continues pushing these two realms of economic activity to new heights. (Precisely *how* high forms a central theme of Chapters 10 and 11.)

8. The Revolution Changed the Nature and Attitude of Foreign Investment. The interrelation of foreign investment, traditional vested interests, economic nationalism, and sustained economic growth is vividly exemplified in Mexican economic development. Before 1910, investment was predominantly foreign in the sense that it formed an integral part of the economy of investing nations and did little to contribute directly to the domestic development of Mexico. The belief that foreign capital per se would become the panacea of Mexico's economic ills was disproven, for as long as the vicious circle of poverty shackled the economy, foreign capital tended to perpetuate the *status quo.* Economist Alfredo Navarrete has estimated that by the last years of the Díaz regime, American investments controlled more than half of the national wealth; that is, Americans not only possessed more than other foreigners, but more than other foreigners and all Mexicans combined. Foreign capital completely monopolized certain economic activities, and the entire public debt rested in the hands of foreigners.

Within this context, Revolutionaries understandably turned on foreign capital and promulgated legal provisions that greatly enhanced the power of the state in economic life and prohibited foreign capital from entering certain strategic realms of the economy. The place of foreigners in business management was severely restricted. Only after foreign capital had had its knuckles rapped enough times, did agrarian and agricultural reforms, industrialization and commercialization, healthier patterns of foreign trade, and progressive fiscal reforms begin to attract foreign capital on strictly nationalistic terms. This time, instead of contributing to the entrenchment of a static economy, foreign investments truly accelerated domestic economic development and facilitated the realization of certain national social aspirations without forcing Mexico into application of further collectivist measures.

The treatment of foreign capital in Mexico reflects a nationalistic philosophy typical of many underdeveloped nations. What at first glance may appear to be ambivalence thus becomes a clear-cut policy on foreign capital: Destroy capital that impedes domestic economic growth, exclude foreigners from certain strategic economic activities, then invite foreign capital anew to help accelerate internal economic growth on strictly nationalistic terms. Mexico has not entirely eliminated the traditional type of foreign capital. There are the German coffee barons in southern Mexico, Americans in sulfur and other mineral exploitation, Spaniards in granite, marble, and onyx, plus other traditionalists. Persistently but spasmodically, various Revolutionary elites have confiscated, expropriated, or nationalized the properties of traditional foreign capitalists. Preceding or accompanying direct action have been legal restrictions prohibiting foreign capital from entering certain industries altogether and from owning property in specific regions of the nation. Finally, legal limitations on the size of agricultural lands, too frequently enforced for the comfort of foreigners, make agriculture unattractive to old-style foreign capital.

Reducing the size of traditional-style foreign investment and substantially circumscribing direct foreign investment to prevent its ever again becoming traditional in size, structure, or form has permitted Mexico to invite foreign capital without sacrificing its economic sovereignty. Though it is difficult, if not impossible, to calculate the precise amount of direct investment even today, to say nothing of fifty years ago, the direct foreign investment in 1911 was probably apportioned somewhat as follows: transportation (about 40 per cent), minerals (28 per cent), industry (4 per cent), commerce (10 per cent), and public utilities (18 per cent). By 1960, transportation represented only 2 per cent of foreign investment, mining had declined to 15 per cent, industry had experienced a phenomenal increase, representing 44 per cent of the total direct foreign investment, commerce had risen to 16 per cent, and public services remained at 18 per cent. After nationalization of American & Foreign Power, Mex-Light, and other foreign holdings in the electric-power industry in 1960 and 1961, plus the Mexicanization of American Metal Climax properties in 1961, the proportion of foreign investment in public utilities and mining further declined, so that industry accounts for more than half of the total direct foreign investment. Estimates on the value of direct foreign investment suggest that of the nearly two billion dollars invested in 1921, only $380 million remained in 1940. By 1962, the total had risen to $822 million. Measured in terms of new direct investments into the Mexican economy in 1961 and 1962, Mexican private capital supplied about 50 per cent, the public sector 45 per cent, and foreign capital about 5 per cent.[4]

Change also characterized indirect foreign investment. Today, a majority of the public debt is in Mexican hands—quite a reversal from the days of Díaz when the entire foreign debt was held by foreigners. Assuming an ever-increasing role in the complex of foreign capital are long-term credits extended to the Mexican government by foreign government agencies (such as the Export-Import Bank), international financial institutions (such as the World Bank), and private foreign sources (such as the Prudential Insurance Company and Bank of America). Solely in the form of long-term loans granted by agencies of the U.S. government and international lending agencies, Mexico received $595.8 million in 1961 and the first six months of 1962. From 1949 to March 1963, the World Bank provided Mexico with $386.8 million in credits. This type of foreign capital has permitted a bigger portion of the productive machine to pass into Mexican hands, usually those of the state.

9. *Creation of a Sound National Banking System.*   From a system of exclusively private banks and multiple sources of currency issuance, Mexican banking has evolved into a system of public and private banking headed by a central bank enjoying exclusive power of issuance. Slowly at first, then in accelerated form during three distinct epochs, the government entered the banking community to become the senior partner in a vast financial complex. The permanent entrance of the state into banking originated in the first two years of the Calles administration with the creation of a National Banking Commission, a central Bank of Mexico, and a National Agricultural Credit Bank. A second period of institutional reform, 1933–38, brought an expansion of the authority and functions of the Bank of Mexico and the establishment of several credit agencies that are playing leading roles in the financial life of the nation today—agencies

[4] Statistics are taken from annual reports of the Banco de México and Nacional Financiera.

such as the National Mortgage Bank, the Industrial Development Bank (Nacional Financiera), agricultural credit banks, and the sugar producers' union. Between this series of reforms and the next additional modifications, the first *financieras* appeared and a number of financial innovations occurred: Mexico created a bank for the development of cooperatives, obtained its first credit from the Export-Import Bank of Washington, and joined the International Monetary Fund and International Bank for Reconstruction and Development. The third period of reform, corresponding to the entire administration of Miguel Alemán and the first year of the Ruiz Cortines regime, introduced additional features into the financial system when the government created (or assigned new functions to) the National Securities Commission, the National Insurance Commission, and separate governmental banks for military personnel, the motion-picture production industry, the sugar industry, transportation, and small and medium-size businesses, plus a national "pawn shop" and a national savings fund. Of immeasurable significance to Mexican economic development and bank relationships with foreign credit institutions were the first loans extended to Mexico by the International Bank. In the decade of the fifties, banking and credit operations, while centering on the Bank of Mexico, Nacional Financiera, other government institutions, and on private banking, insurance, and finance companies, were further modified by new roles assigned existing agencies, particularly the National Warehouse Commission, the stock exchange, and insurance companies, and by the introduction of mutual funds and agricultural insurance. Rapid expansion of the state into the nation's banking is reflected in the fact that government institutions today possess more than one-half of the country's financial resources and supply more than 50 per cent of all financing.

Accompanying the growth of state institutions in banking and credit has been the introduction of sound banking practices. Nobody thinks of a bank failure in Mexico; such a contingency is virtually impossible. The credit, discount, reserve requirements, and open-market operations of the Bank of Mexico parallel Federal Reserve System practices in the United States. Public confidence in paper money, in savings and checking accounts, and in the banking system in general is high. With exclusive currency issuance lodging in the Bank of Mexico, the ageless problem of "worthless paper" has been overcome. The persistent scarcity of short-term capital keeps interest rates relatively high, and lowering them has been a continuing problem for successive administrations, along with inflation and tempering Mexican psychology on the subject of money devaluation. Without exchange controls, Mexicans can take money out of the country whenever they wish, and they tend to do so whenever the threat of devaluation becomes imminent. Suffering four devaluations—in 1931–33, 1938–40, 1948–49, and 1954—and one revaluation (in 1940), the Mexican public is keenly sensitive to money, banking, and credit. Even with these shortcomings in financial structures, the Revolution has nonetheless succeeded in creating a relatively sound banking system in which, by 1964, nineteen major governmental financial institutions and scores of auxiliary state agencies were financing the economy, along with 69 insurance companies and 238 private banking institutions, some with numerous outlets (such as the Banco de Comercio and the Banco Nacional de México, with more than 150 branches each).

   10. Progressive Fiscal Reforms Have Replaced Anachronistic Tax Structures.   The structure of public finance has changed drastically since 1910. From a system in which regressive, indirect taxes supplied virtually all public revenue, the governmental income base has come to rest on a foundation of progressive and direct taxes, indirect taxes, loan placement, returns on investments, operating profits, and fees. As late as 1940, indirect taxes—largely from customs and tax stamps—were supplying nearly 85 per cent of total revenue; by 1963, they were contributing less than 50 per cent. Exports were traditionally duty free, but the Revolution imposed export taxes on many unelaborated raw materials and set up a comprehensive series of protective tariffs on imports. Nonetheless, the Mexican tax coefficient (relation of taxes to gross national product) is about the same today as it was at the time of Díaz, having varied no more than from 6 per cent to 11 per cent of the gross national product during the 1910–60 period. In 1960, the tax coefficient was lower than fifty years ago: With much heavier financial burdens, the Mexican government actually took a lower proportion of the gross national product in 1960 than it did in the years preceding the Revolution. Of course, public revenue is much higher in absolute terms, having exceeded one billion dollars every year since 1961.

   Contributing to the growth of public revenue have been improvements in collection systems, higher tax rates, the introduction of new levies, and the growth of economic activity in general. The major direct taxes are laid on income, excess profits, distributable profits, and capital transfers. The principal indirect taxes come from foreign trade, gross-sales taxes, and federal stamp taxes. There has been a major change in public expenditures, with a shift of emphasis from military spending and public-debt servicing to spending for education, hydraulic resources, and communications. In fact, in 1960, only 27 per cent of public expenditures was absorbed by the military (11 per cent), general administration (8 per cent), and the public debt (8 per cent) combined, and the remainder flowed into public works, education, agriculture, social welfare, and economic promotion. Except for 1953, the year that the Ruiz Cortines administration operated with a public treasury that had been emptied by Alemán and others of his administration, public expenditures have increased annually since 1945. Yet the proportion of government expenditures in the national product has varied slightly from the 9 per cent spent annually by Porfirio Díaz. Specific items in the public budget have changed substantially, however. For example, in 1910, 78 per cent of the service on the public debt consisted of interest payments, while in 1959 payment on principal (loan retirement) represented 87 per cent of public-debt service.

Scrutiny of public finances in the light of over-all economic growth leads an observer to wonder just how the Mexican government has accomplished so much with relatively so little. Part of the answer has been relatively heavy borrowing abroad: Tax exemptions for new industries and on machinery and industrial raw-material imports have tended to keep revenue down, although this condition is rapidly disappearing as exemptions run out. In order to further modernize Mexico's tax system and seek more equitable patterning of income distribution, the López Mateos administration decreed a new tax law in early 1962 that incorporated revised levies on property, surplus profits, earned income, and inheritance and gifts. The government's goal is to increase the number of tax subjects from 1.4 million in 1962 to 4.1 million in 1964.

11. A Socially Responsible Class of Mexican Entrepreneurs Has Come into Being. The human generators of Mexican economic development are primarily a group of Mexican entrepreneurs. Contrary to the contention that foreign capital, foreign management, and foreign technology have built every important business in Mexico, modern Mexico is largely a product of Mexican entrepreneurship. But unlike the United States, where state ownership of the means of production is insignificant, Mexico demanded two sets of men to run business—namely, private businessmen and public "businessmen." Extensive state ownership—of steel, textile, and sugar mills, of the railroads and telegraph system, of the petroleum and electric-power industries, of chemical plants, of banks and auxiliary financial institutions, and of dozens of additional economic activities—created a need and simultaneously an opportunity for competent young men. Twenty-five years of state management of the oil industry and the railroads, for example, has brought into existence a broadly competent clique of "oilmen" and "railroaders." The men at the top of bureaucratic business, including some career politicians who usually last only six years at the very top, contribute substantially more to Mexican economic development than their designation as government employees or bureaucrats connotes. This group of bureaucrats is persistently fighting for new capital, for the right to make, retain, and reinvest earnings, for the application of improved technology, and for just about the same thing a private entrepreneur terms "profits."

Another striking difference between economic developments of the

United States and Mexico over the past fifty years is that Mexico has been busy creating aggressive, individualistic owners and managers, while business in the United States has tended to eliminate this personality type in favor of the "organization man." Getting rid of traditional foreign capital, keeping foreigners out of certain economic activities altogether, and restricting foreign capital to a minority equity position in other realms, yet at the same time avoiding the creation of a collectivist state, required the emergence of a class of Mexican private entrepreneurs. Although little is known about the ambitions and personalities, the politics and religion, or the education, ethics, and achievements of these new entrepreneurs, on the basis of personal associations it is possible to note several typical characteristics: (1) The new entrepreneur enters public office rarely, if at all, although many former politicians enter private business; (2) he exhibits extraordinary drive, energy, and determination in his desire to create a "private empire"; (3) once he is near or at the top of Mexican business, he exerts unusual efforts to build for the future of Mexico; (4) he usually fails several times on his way to the top; (5) he is so self-reliant, self-confident, and self-assertive that the Mexican corporation is far from being the epitome of a democratic business structure; (6) he invests part of his capital in real estate, a tradition among Mexican capitalists that he has not discarded despite his capital accumulation from other economic activities; and (7) he displays tremendous confidence in the future of Mexico.

The majority of the truly big entrepreneurs date the beginning of their fortunes to the 1920's and 1930's—some to even earlier times. Surprisingly few of the top men today were ever in active political life. They are not part of the anti–foreign-capital group of businessmen that Sanford Mosk once labeled the "New Group," who actually comprise the second and lower echelons. Among the men at the top are Raúl Bailleres (finance, mining, breweries, bottling, and real estate), Carlos Trouyet (finance, telephone, manganese steels, cellulose and paper, banking, cement, and a host of other activities), the Garza Sada and G. Sada families (the vast Monterrey industrial and commercial complex of beer, glass, chemicals, banking, insurance, finance), Luis Aguilar (banking, pharmaceuticals, real estate, construction materials, consumer goods, wholesale distribution, manufacturing), Emilio Azcárraga (radio, television, hotels, sports arenas), the García family (sugar and finance), Joel Rocha (chain merchandising, supermarkets, chemicals), Antonio Ruiz Galindo (office equipment, truck bodies, coffee, hotels, aluminum), and Bruno Pagliai (steel pipes, finance, real estate, aluminum). The Mexican private entrepreneur, whether at the top or just beginning with a small factory, is building toward the future of Mexico. His willingness to invest in capital equipment requiring eight or more years to amortize, with only the Mexican domestic market as a sales outlet (which is the case in several large plants now under construction), is a far cry from the habits of Mexican capitalists of earlier years. Private capital, management, and personnel, no less than their counterparts in the public sector, are forcefully building the nation.

12. *New and Healthier Patterns of Foreign Trade Have Materialized.* Exports comprise an important element of economic development. They help pay for imports of machinery and industrial raw materials that sustain Mexican industrialization, and they provide incentive for raising output within Mexico. In recent years, agricultural exports have represented about one-fourth of total domestic agricultural, livestock, and forest production. There is good reason to believe that without prospects of selling abroad, over-all agricultural production would not have reached its present heights. Many farms in the northwest and Apatzingán regions would still be cultivated by poor peasants scratching out a marginal existence by planting corn year after year had not new investments for raising export crops flowed into these farmlands. Exploitation of sulfur, manganese, and fluorspar deposits, as well as the establishment of hormone plants, also anticipated heavy sales in world markets.

Excessive reliance on foreign demand has its pitfalls for a developing nation, since relatively slight fluctuations in world commodity prices can mean the difference between depression and prosperity, deflation and inflation, bad times or good times. Fortunately, export-price fluctuations are having increasingly less effect on the Mexican economy. The safety valve for Mexico is contained in the changing composition of its exports. During the first fifty years of Revolution, the export structure shifted emphasis from precious metals to a diversification of exports. Unlike many another Latin American nation, neither in 1910 nor 1960 did Mexico rely on a single commodity for earning more than half of its export income. The banana and coffee economies to the south of Mexico are still struggling to toss off this shackle. In 1910, three minerals—gold, silver, and copper—accounted for almost three-fifths of Mexican exports. In 1960, the four leading export products—cotton, cattle, coffee, and shrimp, none of them significant in the export picture of 1910—accounted for less than half of total exports. And in 1960 there were eight additional commodities that were considered "major" exports—lead, copper, zinc, tomatoes, sulfur, fuel oil, henequen, and sugar—plus five "minor" exports of some prominence—fresh and refrigerated meats, canned foods, calcium fluoride, hormones, and ixtle fiber. In addition, five other products—drugs, ceramics, shoes, beer, and glass—showed promise of acquiring a strong place in export markets of the future. Total annual Mexican exports since 1960 have constituted about 0.5 per cent of the world's exports. Raising Mexico's share of international markets, a preoccupation of government economists, naturally depends on several variables outside the control of Mexico—

variables such as the pace of economic growth in the United States, the nature and effectiveness of attempts to stabilize world commodity prices, and the opening of new markets, especially in the nascent Latin American Free Trade Area.

Changes in export structure have been accompanied by radical modifications in import patterns. Corn, soap, and luxury goods were the big import items in 1910. Machinery installations, spare parts for machinery, automobiles and automobile parts, mechanically driven machines, and trucks were the largest imports of the 1950's and early 1960's. Except for years of unfavorable weather, such as the drought of 1958, domestic agricultural production generally has kept pace with higher food demands and thus eliminated the need for large-scale imports of foodstuffs. Unfortunately, prices of most goods that Mexico imports have been rising, while world prices of commodities exported by Mexico have tended to remain stationary or decline. This price disequilibrium explains in part why Mexico's trade balance has been unfavorable every year since 1944, and why 1960 imports represented more than 1 per cent of total world imports, while exports accounted for only 0.5 per cent of the world's exports.

Both Mexican export markets and the countries exporting to Mexico have also changed since the Revolution began. Europe figured in this two-way trade substantially more in 1910 than in the 1950's and early 1960's. For example, the proportion of Mexican imports coming from Europe dropped from 43 per cent in 1910 to about 21 per cent in 1960. Exports to Great Britain alone fell from 12 per cent in 1910 to 3 per cent in 1960. On the other hand, imports from the United States rose from 55 per cent to 72 per cent of total Mexican imports, while sales to the United States have been accounting for 70 to 80 per cent of all Mexican exports. The most phenomenal relative increases in import trade must be credited to Japan and Canada, whose percentage of imports has risen to more than six times that of 1910. Transcending all other trade relationships, however, is that with the United States. Despite prosperity and recession, war and peace, high prices and low, the United States has consistently accounted for over 70 per cent of Mexico's trade. Several reasons explain this phenomenon: the geographical proximity of Mexico and the United States, the absence of currency-exchange restrictions, the desire of Mexico to sell into the greatest single market in the world, and the relatively complementary nature of the two economies. But in addition to its importance as a market for Mexican goods, there are other ways in which the United States has figured in the prevention of serious disequilibria in Mexico's balance of payments. Of most importance are revenue from tourists—of which four out of five come from the United States—and remittances by Mexican workers in the United States. The number of tourists visiting Mexico rose from 408,000 in 1950 to 681,000 in 1960. During the 1950's, tourists supplied Mexico with foreign-exchange income in excess of $4 billion, with American tourists alone contributing 90 per cent of the entire tourist income in 1950 and 80 per cent in 1960.

13. Sustained and "Balanced" Economic Growth Have Come to Characterize Mexican Development. Revolutionaries have been interested in more than economic growth as such. They know that population increases are compelling the nation to work ever harder just to preserve the *status quo*. But this is not enough. They seek economic advances that will raise real incomes and levels of living. What they are actually seeking is economic development. Anxious to raise the rate of capital formation above the levels that would normally be attained through voluntary saving and private investment, the Revolutionaries have imposed a series of state interventions, including forced saving. They know that higher real income is impossible unless total output rises faster than population growth. And they also know that if remedies for development bottlenecks are not found and applied, the economy may slide backward.

The relatively phenomenal economic advances of recent years, therefore, are less a result of "natural forces" and accident than of state planning in six-year packages. Decisions as to what and how much to produce, and what percentage of current production to dedicate to capital formation, have comprised a mighty challenge. The Mexicans have met it, albeit with much bureaucratic bungling and many errors. The growth rate of the gross national product, expressed in real terms, was raised from an average annual increase of 2.9 per cent in the period 1895–1910 to 6.6 per cent duing the 1939–50 years, then dropped somewhat to 5 per cent in the decade of the 1950's. In 1960, the gross national product grew 5.7 per cent, the highest rate of annual growth since 1956, but growth in product dropped below 4 per cent in 1961 and advanced less than 5 per cent in 1962. Relating the gross national product to population, the average annual growth of real production per capita between 1939 and 1950 was 3.8 per cent, and between 1951 and 1960, about 2 per cent. The public sector apportioned greater amounts to long-range economic activities that did not show immediate contributions to national product, and a greater percentage of Mexican private capital went into liquid assets and inventories instead of direct production. All in all, real investment declined from an average annual increase of 10.5 per cent during 1939–50 to 5.6 per cent in 1951–60, with the years 1959–60 particularly bleak—largely, according to some investment sources, because of the influence of Castroism. It is too soon to make definitive judgment on whether the decade of the 1940's was an exceptional period of growth or whether that of the 1950's was an exceptional period of adversity, but reflection on the entire period since 1935 indicates some of the causes of the decline and the efficacy of programs designed to accelerate growth.

Desirous of economic development, the Revolutionary elite has placed emphasis on "balanced" growth as well as sustained growth. This double preference explains public attention to the promotion of transport, power, communications, and education, as well as basic industries primordially aiding production and distribution, and to variations in fiscal and monetary policies. Without question, works promoting the economic infrastructure have been vitally beneficial to the entire economy. Without them, agricultural production and industrial output surely could not have risen 223 per cent and 225 per cent between 1939 and 1959, nor could such high average increases have been achieved since 1945 by petroleum, manufactures, and stock-raising. Over the years since 1910, balanced growth in Mexican terms has meant reducing the proportion of the gross national product represented by agriculture, stock-raising, and mining, and increasing that represented by manufactures, transport, petroleum, and electric power. Revolutionary economists properly contend that one of the notable achievements of Mexican economic development is that increases in production have been proportioned among the various sectors of economic activity.

Since 1956, increased public investment has helped compensate for lower private investment, but the over-all investment rate declined nonetheless. After growing 14.2 per cent in 1956, the investment rate plummeted to 1.6 per cent in 1959. Investment structure also changed; a higher proportion went into private construction and a lower proportion entered capital formation. Since capital formation is decisive in sustaining economic growth, the government should be seriously concerned with this twist in Mexican economic development. For simply to have an industrial complex well under way is not enough. The investment rate must reach a level high enough to set in motion forces that assure a relatively autonomous maintenance of new levels of production. To accomplish this, technology, efficiency, and reduced waste and spoilage must be combined with new investment.

Reviewing these several major achievements of economic development has provided us with some insight into the workings of the Mexican economic system. Yet weighing against these and other entries on the asset side of the Revolutionary balance sheet are multiple liabilities. Subsequent chapters, on population and the labor force, on Mexico's problem of feeding her burgeoning population, and on the specifics of industry, agriculture, and commerce, are devoted to discovering the major entries to be made on both sides of the ledger. First, however, we should investigate the issue of capitalism and socialism in Mexico, since it is of such importance to what follows and to Mexican development as such.

CAPITALISM AND SOCIALISM IN MEXICO

The new directions of the revised economic course that Mexico charted about the time President Roosevelt tied the destiny of the United States to Hitler's defeat still persist. The heart of the Cárdenas administration's social, political, and economic reform programs—accelerated land redistribution, labor unionism, political popularism, and emphatic state ownership—gave way to "national unity"; radical change had to await the war's end. But it did not come even then. The United States came out of the world struggle rich and mighty, capable of educating, feeding, clothing, and housing its rapidly increasing population. Mexico, on the other hand, once it had exhausted the dollar reserves it had gained, saw the collapse of its false dream of a self-sustaining economic prosperity. The machinery, mining equipment, and vehicles on hand were obsolescent. Freedom from want had not and obviously could not have materialized in the short span of a few years. Disillusionment in Mexico roughly coincided with the lengthening of the Communist specter over Western Europe. The United States met the latter threat by extending large-scale financial assistance to European nations, backing this up with military support. It chose to rebuild economies in one part of the free world and bypassed the need to build economies in another part. Government aid flowed profusely eastward and, after 1950, westward, but only meager public funds went southward. Until 1959, Washington seemed to believe that the panacea for the economic ills of Mexico and all Latin America was a return to pre–New Deal patterns—to wide-open investment opportunities for private foreign capital. This solution had failed before the New Deal, and it was doomed to fail after World War II. Private foreign capital could, and indeed, did help, but Mexico required more capital than private sources made available.

When they reached the decision to industrialize Mexico as rapidly as possible, the Revolutionary elite controlled a state that already owned large sectors of the economy and that sought foreign capital for activities outside the traditional investment realm of mineral and commodity export. Though the Korean War stimulated investment in manganese, mercury, and other minerals, and though big foreign purchasers of cotton, coffee, and other agricultural commodities found a certain degree of crop financing indispensable for their business operations, subsoil and agrarian-reform legislation (from which the government could not turn without committing political suicide) made mineral exploitation and agriculture only marginally attractive to the foreign investor. The biggest mineral field of all, petroleum, so vitally important to an industrializing economy, had become a government monopoly; again, the Mexican government could not hand this industry over to private capital without risking a full-scale popular uprising. Industrialization required the building of a vast transportation network to facilitate the movement of raw materials, finished goods, and ever-increasing numbers of American tourists, but private capital was ill-disposed toward advancing money for the construction of roads, streets, docks, or airfields. And with the railroads and street-railway systems largely owned and operated by the state, the heavy financial burden in the transportation quarter also fell on the public sector. Three additional sectors of the economy—electric power, the iron and steel industry, and credit institutions—had to be expanded greatly; here, too, the state held a significant ownership stake. Unwilling to divest itself of holdings in these sectors, the Mexican government thus embarked on an industrialization program in which direct foreign investment was virtually shut out of the nation's economic infrastructure and basic industry.

Foreign capital had four investment alternatives: (1) It could, as did many foreign manufacturing concerns, invest directly in building a plant or other business concern, either alone or in partnership with Mexican capitalists or the Mexican government; (2) it could, like the International Bank for Reconstruction & Development, the Export-Import Bank, Prudential Insurance Company of America, Bank of America, and additional public and private financial institutions, lend capital to instrumentalities of the Mexican government; (3) it could, like some flight capital and some tourists, buy securities of governmental and private businesses or deposit funds in Mexican banks; or (4) it could lend to private businesses, which all too few foreign capital sources did. Encouraged to invest in manufacturing and commercial enterprises, many large American corporations set up subsidiaries and affiliates, while smaller foreign investors established thousands of little plants and shops, bringing along precious technological know-how. Though not always in quite as responsible a capacity as the government wished, private capital—foreign and Mexican alike—played a continuing role in economic development.

The private entrepreneur soon learned, however, that commercial credit was scarce and that vital sectors of the economy, including certain government-owned concerns, were incapable of keeping abreast of industrial needs. Private investors also learned that private banks in the United States showed little inclination to extend them credit, preferring indirect investment, largely in the form of loans to Mexican governmental banks. The banks preferred the safety of dollar loans guaranteed by the Mexican government to loans extended to private business concerns in Mexico. The American executive in Mexico properly raised the question of why credit institutions in the United States did not at least match monies loaned to the government with loans to private businesses in Mexico.

Private enterprise also became caught up in the growing socialization of the means of production. The private sector manifested little displeasure with the government's short-run policy of sacrificing of social justice and income redistribution to the prospect of long-range benefits from industrialization. Some of society's underdogs tossed off the shackles of poverty and enlarged the "middle class," but a substantial segment of this new "middle class" lacked the bourgeois philosophy of the American middle class. Indeed, as creatures of government employment—civil servants, teachers, government officials, party politicians, military officers, and doctors, agronomists, accountants, engineers, bankers, and labor rank and file employed in businesses owned by the state, including the powerful petroleum, railroad, and electric-power industries—they had a vested interest in promoting further socialization. This situation did not perceptibly worry private capitalists, however, since the emergence of more "middle-class" consumers, whether employees of the state or not, meant more customers. Private capitalists did become concerned, however, when the state not only spent huge sums on running the railroad and petroleum industry, but also enlarged its holdings in the entire industrial sector: The state expanded, bought into, or set up banking and credit institutions; cellulose and paper, steel, textile, and sugar mills; meat-packing, chemical, fertilizer, insecticide, and electric-power plants; electrical products and auto and truck assembly; shipbuilding, aviation, motion-picture distribution and exhibition, railroad-car manufacture, and wood-products elaboration companies. Mexico probably needed every concern promoted by the state, but private entrepreneurs questioned the wisdom of the state's buying large jet airplanes and investing in theaters while two-thirds of Mexico's people were without electric lights and safe drinking water. The great mass of Mexicans wanted clothing, education, a public market place, a sanitary slaughterhouse—in short, a small place in the sun, one that the government might have given them instead of spending huge sums in concerns attractive to private investment, Mexican and foreign. Aided by taxes and outside financing, the Mexican government pushed deeper and deeper into ownership of Mexico's productive means.

The Revolutionary elite running Mexico asserted that history, social justice, need, and the absence of "responsible private capital" justified the kind of economic system it was creating. They paid little heed to United States claims for the intrinsic advantages of capitalism and the malignancy of state ownership. They noted that despite American condemnation of socialism, Yugoslavia, with its markedly socialistic system, was annually receiving hundreds of millions of dollars from the United States. The Revolution kept converting the Mexican economy from a system of private corporations and large haciendas into one based on state corporations, communal farms, and widely circumscribed private businesses. Foreign ownership gave way to Mexican ownership. Though Mexico accomplished this feat over the frequent objections of private capitalists, Americans should take note that Mexico neither received nor solicited guidance from Soviet Russia. The Constitution of 1917, written before Lenin overthrew Kerensky, and on which Mexican political economists justified economic changes, incorporated Mexican heritages, Mexican practices, and Mexican ideals. And though many Mexicans disagree with the Revolutionary Family on the indispensability of socialization, the ruling clique will encounter no constitutional impediment to yet further socialization.

The Revolutionary Center, in power since 1952, has asserted that state ownership of the principal means of production and communal farms, complemented by private property and free enterprise, correspond best to Mexican needs and aspirations. Accustomed to multiple ownership patterns, to public, private, mixed public and private, cooperative, and communal enterprise, the Mexican is more removed from the credo of "private enterprise" than the American. Only when certain basic services and industries are placed under state ownership and operation, say Revolutionaries, will free enterprise have any chance of flourishing under predominantly Mexican ownership. Free enterprise is in vogue at the secondary level of industry and in commerce, mining, and a part of agriculture, but it is circumscribed on all sides. While capitalists raise the question of how much *should* be done by the state to speed economic growth, Mexican officials, aided by foreign banking institutions, seem more anxious to determine how much *can* be done by the state.

A striking contrast in philosophies on political economy held north and south of the Rio Grande is provided by Nacional Financiera (NAFIN), Mexico's central development bank. Drawing on models of European investment banks and state financing institutions, the Rodríguez administration issued a decree in July, 1934, establishing a government development bank (NAFIN) that would dispense credit needed in building the Mexican economy. Until 1942, when NAFIN obtained its first credit from the Export-Import Bank of Washington, Mexico's development bank amounted to little more than one of many public agencies engaged in vague financial operations assisting economic growth. The Export-Import Bank credit influenced NAFIN operations in two ways: It induced the Mexican government to assign NAFIN specific responsibility for stimulating industrial development, and it opened previously shut doors leading to important financial sources abroad. The loan from Washington bestowed funds, but it also bestowed inestimable international prestige on a Mexican governmental bank now determined to inject the state into quarters previously reserved for private entrepreneurs. Once the government heading the strongest capitalist nation in the world sanctioned NAFIN and its goals, a decision consistently backed up by new Export-Import Bank loans, private capital and public capital elsewhere could hardly be condemned for following suit. Included in the long list of foreign financial institutions that have extended credits to this powerful state agency are Bank of America, Chase Manhattan Bank, Chemical Bank, New York Trust Company, Girard Trust Corn Exchange Bank, First National City Bank of New York, Prudential Insurance Company of America, the Bank of Tokyo, the Institute Mobiliare Italiane, and Barclays Bank, Ltd. Foreign credits now account for more than one-third of NAFIN's total financial resources, to say nothing of the income accruing to NAFIN from investments made with foreign credits since 1942 and now pooled into its over-all financial resources.

In the years since 1942, NAFIN has assumed such a crusading posture on promotion of Mexican industrialization, while steadily enlarging its capital funds, the scope of its industrial operations, and its staff of experts, that this one institution not only controls the most extensive diversified industrial complex in the nation, but enjoys a singular position in determining which industries should receive financial assistance as well as in reserving for itself the final word (of course, in the last instance the President of Mexico may exercise a veto on all NAFIN activities) on all foreign credits solicited by any governmental dependency. NAFIN financing represents about 20 per cent of the total financing conceded by the entire Mexican banking system, private and public, and its stake in industry amounts to almost 30 per cent of total bank financing to industry. Its credits and investments have underwritten the promotion of two new industrial centers—the iron and steel, coal and coke, and petrochemical complex of Monclova (north of the city of Monterrey), and the railroad-car production, automobile and truck assembly, textile machinery and sewing-machine manufacturing complex at Ciudad Sahagún (in the central state of Hidalgo). NAFIN capital has assisted pulp and paper plants in five states, lumber and wood-products elaborators in four states, fishing and food packing and canning in five states, cement plants in six states, sugar growing and refining operations in four states, fertilizer-insecticide plants in four states, and steel mills and steel-products elaborators in five states. No region of Mexico has escaped the financial attention of NAFIN. There is nothing comparable in the United States economy to NAFIN and the transcendent power this state agency exercises over Mexican economic life.

A list of some of the sectors of the Mexican economy that are not privately owned suggests the divergence between the American and Mexican economies:

1. *Subsoils.* The state reserves to itself title to all subsoil rights.
2. *Agriculture.* Over one-fourth of Mexico's entire national territory is in the hands of communal farmers (*ejidatarios*). Communal and co-operative farms account for more than half of the agricultural land under cultivation.
3. *Irrigation.* The state owns eight-ninths of all sources of irrigation outright and theoretically holds title to the remaining one-ninth.
4. *Communications and transportation.* The state possesses sizable per-

centages of ownership in every important realm of communications and transportation: Telegraph—100 per cent; roads, highways, and streets (once built, these automatically form part of the public domain)—100 per cent; maritime transportation (by capacity)—70 per cent; railroads—97 per cent; municipal railways—92 per cent; docks and other port facilities—90 per cent; domestic commercial aviation (passenger miles)—35 per cent; international commercial aviation (by capitalization according to projects pending)—75 per cent; newsprint manufacture by the paper mill in which the state enjoys majority equity interest—100 per cent; newsprint distribution —100 per cent; motion-picture distribution and exhibition—80 per cent; motion-picture production (financing)—50 per cent. While the telephone industry is run by private capital, the state has lent it impressive sums and holds 85 per cent of its equity, preferred included.

5. *Basic industries.* The state holds impressive equity in other basic industries: electric power, installed capacity—90 per cent; electric power, sales to the public—96 per cent; petroleum exploration and ownership of wells, natural gas reserves, oil lines and gaslines—97 per cent; gasoline—100 per cent; petroleum refining—96 per cent; oil, by sales to the public—92 per cent; petrochemicals, by Pemex plants plus an additional three dozen major petrochemical plants owned outright or conjointly with private capital by the government, expressed in terms of total investment in the petrochemical field—85 per cent; iron and steel production of mills in which the state enjoys majority control in relation to total domestic production —40 per cent.

6. *Other industries.* The state also retains a majority or complete interest in the only railroad-car and caboose manufacturing plant; one of the largest automobile and truck assembly plants; two of the nation's biggest textile mills; the sole newsprint manufacturing plant; a large sugar mill; the largest concern manufacturing electrical products; the nation's biggest meat-packing plant; two of the country's important elaborators of wood products; and the country's largest warehouse concern.

7. *Municipal services.* The state owns all slaughterhouses, public market places, municipal street lighting, and municipal waterworks.

8. *Hospital beds.* The state and civil servants' unions combined own hospitals and clinics that contain 85 per cent of Mexico's hospital beds.

9. *Banking and finance.* The state owns 100 per cent or near this percentage in the following banks: the Bank of Mexico and the central industrial development, foreign commerce, private agricultural, *ejidal* agricultural, national transport, sugar producers, sugar financing, motion-picture, cooperatives, army and navy personnel, public works and urban mortgage, and small-commerce banks. It also owns controlling interest in the national pawn shop, national warehouse com-

mission, small-business guarantee bank, the Financiera of León, the Bank of Zamora, and the Provincial Bank of Sinaloa.

10. *Consumer distribution.* Three agencies of the state—the Foreign Commerce Bank, ANDSA, and CONASUPO—effectively control the export-import, domestic purchase, and low-cost distribution of basic agricultural commodities. Civil servants, teachers, and members of the armed forces buy basic consumer goods in special outlets at reduced prices.

11. *Churches.* The Constitution bestows title over church properties, including church buildings proper, on the state.

With so much for the Mexican government to accomplish in such vital areas of the public sector as schools, hospitals, roads, drainage, irrigation, and municipal services, why has the Revolutionary elite led Mexico step by step into state ownership of the principal means of production? Political demagoguery and necessity have certainly had much to do with it: The propaganda value of announcing to the restless, impoverished masses that they, instead of the "rich foreign imperialists," now own the petroleum industry and electric industry is immeasurable. It is certain that the state cannot keep pushing rapid economic growth unless political stability is assured, and expropriation has proven to be an extremely popular device for assuaging the masses with the belief that the state is doing its best to contend with the might of private capitalists, "who are really to blame for Mexico's economic ills." Expropriation also permits a rich politician to speak out of both sides of his mouth. In earlier years, "vindication of Mexico's resources" and breaking the hold of a few land barons and foreign corporations on the economy represented a powerful motive for state ownership. In recent years, however, a foremost component of Mexico's advancement toward welfare-state socialism has been the crusading urge to industrialize rapidly, with an accompanying impatience with private entrepreneurs who seemed unwilling or unable to keep abreast of the developmental expectations of government planners.

A principal reason for continuous steps in the direction of state ownership has been the unwillingness of foreign capital, both public and private, to make sufficient capital available to private business in Mexico. Though the International Bank, the Export-Import Bank, and large private banks abroad have lent hundreds of millions of dollars to the Mexican government, they have not extended adequate credit to the private sector of Mexican business. What happens to private businesses? Needless to say, in an economy where the state plays an overwhelming role as regulator, supplier, and purchaser, the businessman requires unusual forbearance in times of stress. The psychological impact of dramatic removal of a sector of economic life from private hands is particularly profound on the average American investor, unacquainted with the intricacies of the Mexican economy. The direct consequences of one act of state intervention may thus place other private concerns in financial crises from which they can only salvage their investment by selling to the state. At the moment when private business urgently demands more financial help, and this usually includes Mexican and foreign-owned businesses alike, private and public banks too frequently abandon them. Unwilling to run the risks in Mexico that they would at home, large United States banks are underwriting the socialization of Mexico with their capitalist depositors' money.

This brief exploration of the nature of Mexican socialism points up the challenge facing investment capital in Mexico and, for that matter, in much of the underdeveloped world. The government, bankers, and businessmen of the United States have tended to compound revolutionary situations by either opposing them as such, or by assisting the state without simultaneously aiding private businesses, or vice versa. Much of the foreign and domestic private capital now invested in Mexico is not of the traditional imperialistic variety of earlier days. The stockpile of responsible private entrepreneurs has grown, although few of the big private capitalists can hope to match the recent annual performances of NAFIN in earning 10 per cent net profit on total operations. Of business in Mexico, we should no longer think in terms of a weak, passive state at the mercy of private capitalists, nor of a state so powerful that private enterprises have no chance of success.

Another force working in favor of socialization is the existence of an exclusive political elite intent on retaining control of Mexican destinies. Its long entrenchment in public power highlights continuity with the past. Those policies seemingly popular with the masses, such as agrarian reforms, oil expropriation, and antiforeignism, are continually publicized in textbooks, political rallies, and official addresses. Largely left unquestioned are multiple errors, the opportunism of specific Revolutionary leaders, and the wisdom of present policies. The political atmosphere so generated is probably incompatible with a competitive economic system. We must question, therefore, whether the absence of a truly competitive political system can give rise to and sustain a competitive economic system. To no small degree, extensive socialization is one price that Mexico has paid for keeping an entrenched elite in power.

No analysis of capitalism and socialism in Mexico can overlook the impact of the past and the big problems still confronting Mexican leadership. It is easy to underestimate the influence on state intervention and state ownership coming before 1917 from latifundio, peonage, exploitation of natural resources by a small group of foreigners, the nonexistence of individual and social rights, the Spanish and Indian heritages, the great power of the Catholic Church, and inferiority before foreigners. The presence of serious problems may also tend to work on behalf of socialism —and Mexico's problems include ignorance, misery, poverty, disease, and inflation; insufficient development of certain branches of industry; back-wardness of much of agriculture and stock-raising; insufficiency of engi-neers, skilled workers, and scientists; rapid population growth; urbaniza-tion; expensive irrigation works; unfavorable terms of trade; and insufficient credit.

Capitalists, Socialists, or Communists, Europeans or Asians, Ameri-cans or Russians—none holds the absolute power of persuasion over Mex-ico. Complete independence from the United States is unwanted and, under present economic patterns, impossible. The Mexican government prefers public loans to direct private investment, but welcomes humanist capitalism sensitive to Mexican aspirations and institutions. If private capital cannot discover a way to work together with publicly owned con-cerns, then the state undoubtedly will adopt other patterns of ownership. Mexico knows that socialism is not the paradise that the Russians picture. Still, Mexico rejects the notion that socialism is such a social malignancy that preservation of freedom requires its abolition. State ownership in Mexico is not Marxism-Leninism, neither are expropriation and national-ization. These developments are symptomatic of Mexico's evolving ex-pectation, itself a product of national pride and self-confidence—perhaps not so much in what has been done since 1910, but in what can be accom-plished tomorrow. Idiosyncrasies of economics, no less than those of politics, religion, and foreign policy, are really expressions of a deeper truth: The Mexican wants to be master of his own house.

NINE

MEXICO VERSUS MALTHUS

~~~~~~

How many people will be living in Mexico by 1970? By 1985? By 2000? Can Mexico feed its burgeoning population? Create millions of new jobs? Avoid mass unemployment? Enlarge the effective consumer market? What is the status, strength, and promise of the labor movement? Agrarian reform? Agricultural reform? These important questions of Mexican economic development will be discussed in this chapter.

POPULATION TRENDS

The population of Mexico is expanding rapidly. Prior to the census of 1930, the general impression shared by successive governments was that Mexico possessed abundant agricultural land and hence that immigration should be encouraged, especially from European nations. The census findings of 1930 and 1940 converted official thinking to the belief that Mexico lacked sufficient agricultural land for satisfying the natural growth of its existent population. Then, with the 1950 and 1960 censuses, official policy was again revised to incorporate the concept that Mexico had enough land, but clearly not an abundance. Over the years, the appeal of becoming a Mexican citizen has attracted few immigrants and, except for the wave of Spanish refugees who arrived in the 1930's, there has been no instance of large-scale immigration. Population growth in Mexico has been and probably will continue to be almost entirely attributable to higher birth and lower death rates. This phenomenon alone frightens some economists, however, for Mexico is exhibiting one of the highest population growth rates in the world. The 34.6 million inhabitants counted in the census of 1960 represented an increase of 8.8 million over 1950 and 15 million over 1940. Yearly growth during the 1950's averaged 3 per cent; the average since 1940 has been 2.9 per cent. Contrasted with earlier periods, today's growth appears phenomenal. Between 1875 and 1900, population increased only four million, which corresponds to an average annual increase of merely 1.2 per cent. In the first decade of the twentieth century growth was similarly low, and as a consequence of civil war, there was an absolute decline in Mexico's population during the next ten years.

By 1940, population was growing by leaps and bounds, so that the number of inhabitants were more than doubled between 1930 and 1960.

POPULATION OF MEXICO
ACCORDING TO OFFICIAL CENSUSES: 1895–1960

Census	Date	Population
1	Oct. 20, 1895	12,632,427
2	Oct. 27, 1900	13,607,259
3	Oct. 25, 1910	15,160,369
4	Nov. 30, 1921	14,334,780 [a]
5	May 15, 1930	16,552,722
6	March 6, 1940	19,653,552
7	June 6, 1950	25,791,017
8	June 8, 1960	34,625,903 [b]

[a] Former director of the census Gilberto Loyo has asserted the following in respect to the controversial census of 1921: "I estimate that the population in 1921 was 14.8 million inhabitants and not the 14.3 noted in the official census, because in 1927 I had in my hands documents from the old Department of National Statistics indicating deficiencies in that census which permit me to estimate that the official census erred by underestimating the population by at least 500,000 inhabitants." If the average annual increase of the years 1900 to 1910 is applied to the following census period, then the population of Mexico should have reached 16.8 million. "Therefore, it can be estimated that the population from 1910 to 1921 lost two million persons. One part of this two million, the lowest, corresponds to the loss of lives suffered during the armed conflict of the Mexican Revolution, and the other, the highest, to the tremendous mortality caused by the epidemic of grippe called 'Spanish Influenza.'" Gilberto Loyo, *La población de México: estado actual y tendencias, 1950–1980* (México: Investigación Económica, 1960), p. 4.

[b] Preliminary release of Census Bureau.

Presuming that immigration will not increase, that sanitation, better nutrition, and improved living conditions will tend to reduce mortality rates, and that birth-rate trends of the last decade will persist into the immediate decades ahead, then a set of prerequisites exists for estimating future population. Efforts of the United Nations to do precisely this have been somewhat disappointing. In its study on *Los Recursos Humanos de Centroamérica, Panamá y México en 1950–1980*, published in early 1960 on the basis of 1950 census statistics, the United Nations' most optimistic estimates proved too low for the true population counted in the census of 1960. The low and medium estimates of the United Nations' study, based on annual growth rates of 1.98 per cent and 2.45 per cent, underestimated growth by more than two million inhabitants, while the highest estimate fell short of the true mark by more than one million. According to Gilberto Loyo, former director of the Mexican census, projections of the United Nations should be readjusted to incorporate higher birth and lower mortality rates so that the high estimates of the world organization become the new lows and higher projections serve as medians and highs.

On this revised basis, that is to say, if Mexican population grows at the same rate that it did in the 1950's, then Mexico should have a population of 46.6 million in 1970, 62.6 million in 1980, and 113.1 million by the turn of the century. On the other hand, if population follows approximate patterning of the last two decades, increasing every decade at an average yearly rate of 0.1 per cent over the preceding decade, then Mexico will have to provide for 46.8 million in 1970, 64.1 million in 1980, and 123.8 million by the year 2000. Even an annual growth comparable to the decade of the forties would make the Mexican population double roughly every 25 years, quadruple every half-century.

Population trends in Mexico also show a heavy migration to urban centers. At the beginning of this century, an estimated 18.2 per cent lived in communities of 2,500 inhabitants or more, which, according to official census definitions, made them "urban." Ecologists acquainted with rural Mexico have questioned the urbanity of rural communities of 2,500 to 5,000 population whose inhabitants leave for and return from the fields daily; however, if we use the official Mexican census definition of urban, then this sector had grown to 33.5 per cent by 1930 and to 49 per cent by 1960. Employing slightly different norms, the United Nations estimates that Mexican population was 43 per cent urban in 1950 and 50 per cent urban in 1960. Furthermore, the world organization reckoned that Mexico will become 55 per cent urban in 1970 and 62 per cent in 1980. One thing is certain: The population growth of the larger cities is reaching alarming proportions. Between 1930 and 1960, the Federal District nearly quadrupled its inhabitants, and by 1964 this small district probably had almost six million residents. The English economist P. Lamartine Yates recently predicted that unless steps were taken to decentralize industry, the Valley of Mexico, which comprises the Federal District and its environs, would have a population of 15 million inhabitants in 1980. Mexico City, the big metropolis of the Federal District, alone contained 2.3 million residents in 1960. The census of 1960 also confirmed that larger provincial cities had grown rapidly: Guadalajara (736,000), Monterrey (597,000), Ciudad Juárez (261,000), Puebla (289,000), and León (209,000).

Population continues to be distributed unevenly. Nearly half of Mexico's inhabitants live on the 14 per cent of national territory that comprises the central region focusing on the Valley of Mexico. Population density there is 61 inhabitants per square kilometer, considerably above the national average of 18. But the fastest-growing region of all is that of the northern border states. With an average annual growth rate of 8.6 per cent, the state of Baja California doubled its population between 1950 and 1960. In the same period, other northern states manifested increases substantially above the annual national average: Sonora (4.2 per cent), Chihuahua (3.8 per cent), Nuevo León (3.6 per cent), and Tamaulipas

(3.5 per cent). Lowest increases were registered in entities where the indigenous Indian element is heavy—namely, in Hidalgo (1.5 per cent), Oaxaca (1.6 per cent), Yucatán (1.7 per cent), and Puebla (1.9 per cent), as well as in the mining states of Durango (1.8 per cent) and Zacatecas (1.8 per cent). Migration to coastal regions, despite the official promotion of a "march to the sea" policy to encourage migration from the central region to coastal areas, seems negligible. On the other hand, the relatively high population increases of border states occurred without direct governmental promotion.

Higher population density suggests in part why Mexican economists seem justified in advocating a "philosophy of big things." Decades hence, with a potential internal market in excess of 100 million inhabitants, Mexican industry could possess one of the world's best national markets. In terms of absolute numbers of inhabitants, Mexico will probably rank ninth in the world by the year 2000, above France, Italy, Germany, and Great Britain. In fact, the United States, Brazil, and Mexico might be the only non-Asiatic nations (considering Russia with Asia) with populations over 100 million. Yet rapid population increase in Mexico should not frighten us. As demographer Kingsley Davis has pointed out, higher density did not pose an obstacle for industrialization in Japan, since the apparent disadvantage of a large population was converted into a decided advantage: cheap labor. Mexico seems to be working in a similar direction. However, the blessing of a potentially growing internal market introduces some troublesome corollaries: How will the coming population be fed, clothed, and housed? Can the pace of industrialism and over-all capital accumulation be stepped up sufficiently? Will agriculture readjust productivity toward the Mexican domestic market? Can urban regions absorb excessive population from the countryside?

THE LABOR FORCE

Attention to these issues requires consideration of the size and composition of the labor force. Urbanization and rapid population growth imply that dynamic human resources are moving into the labor force and in turn becoming subject to the role that government will play. With its urban market of privileged consumers already saturated, Mexican industry now faces crises perhaps only resolvable by raising labor's real wages, at least temporarily, and working out schemes for a clearer interdependence of Mexican industry and agriculture. Also to be considered are such factors as labor underemployment and the exact number of days laborers actually work. Included in the labor force are at least 1.5 million individuals, and probably as many as 2.5 million, who find work only four or at best five months out of the year. The rest of their time is spent in scratching out a living as well as they can, often by migrating to other

POPULATION OF MEXICO, 1950 and 1960: REGIONS, STATES, RATE OF GROWTH, AND DENSITY [a]

Region and States	Political Capital	Population 1950	Population 1960	Percent of Growth 1950-60	Density 1960 (Inhabs. per Sq. Mile)
REPUBLIC OF MEXICO	México (City)	25,791,017	34,625,903	34.26	45.6
PACIFIC NORTH		1,724,241	2,558,658	48.34	16.1
Baja California	Mexicali	226,965	520,913	129.51	18.7
Baja California Sur	La Paz	60,864	83,433	37.08	3.0
Nayarit	Tepic	290,124	391,970	35.10	37.5
Sinaloa	Culiacán	635,681	790,679	24.38	35.0
Sonora	Hermosillo	510,607	771,663	51.53	11.0
NORTH		5,176,855	6,812,257	31.59	22.1
Chihuahua	Chihuahua	846,414	1,235,891	46.01	13.0
Coahuila	Saltillo	720,619	896,509	24.41	15.4
Durango	Durango	629,874	754,220	19.74	15.8
Nuevo León	Monterrey	740,191	1,063,399	43.67	42.3
San Luis Potosí	San Luis Potosí	856,066	1,054,206	23.15	43.2
Tamaulipas	Ciudad Victoria	718,167	1,009,800	40.61	32.9
Zacatecas	Zacatecas	665,524	798,232	19.94	28.4
CENTER		12,449,201	16,966,452	36.29	159.2
Aguascalientes	Aguascalientes	188,075	236,574	25.79	94.7
Distrito Federal	México (City)	3,050,442	4,829,402	58.32	8,443.0
Guanajuato	Guanajuato	1,328,712	1,728,358	30.08	146.4
Hidalgo	Pachuca	850,394	983,161	15.61	122.0
Jalisco	Guadalajara	1,746,777	2,402,884	37.56	77.2
México	Toluca	1,392,623	1,883,291	35.23	227.9

Michoacán	Morelia	1,422,717	1,862,568	30.92	80.3
Morelos	Cuernavaca	272,842	381,346	39.77	196.9
Puebla	Puebla	1,625,830	1,957,380	20.39	149.2
Querétaro	Querétaro	286,238	354,154	23.73	82.2
Tlaxcala	Tlaxcala	284,551	347,334	22.06	223.5
GULF OF MEXICO		3,068,911	4,049,658	31.96	44.3
Campeche	Campeche	122,098	164,256	34.53	8.4
Quintana Roo	Chetumal	26,967	52,312	93.99	2.7
Tabasco	Villahermosa	362,716	471,808	30.08	48.2
Veracruz	Jalapa	2,040,231	2,749,235	34.75	99.1
Yucatán	Mérida	516,899	612,047	18.41	41.2
PACIFIC SOUTH		3,360,046	4,237,824	26.12	46.1
Chiapas	Tuxtla Gutiérrez	907,026	1,215,475	34.01	42.3
Colima	Colima	112,321	157,338	40.08	78.3
Guerrero	Chilpancingo	919,386	1,189,085	29.33	47.8
Oaxaca	Oaxaca (City)	1,421,313	1,675,926	17.91	46.1
Complementary		11,763	1,054		

a 1960 figures are based on preliminary release of census bureau.

regions. The scope of this problem is recognized in Edmundo Flores' assertion that two million peasants and their families could abandon agriculture "without lowering the volume of production or the rate of growth of production and thus, instead, permit those who remain on the farms to augment their occupation and income level."

Further complicating precise study is the fact that in determining the size of the labor force, the Mexican government employed one set of rules before 1950, another since. In earlier decades, the term "economically active population" was used to designate all persons twelve years of age or above who declared that they had a remunerative job, profession, or occupation, whether they exercised it or not at the time the census was taken. Beginning in 1950, "economically active population" was discarded in favor of a "labor force," defined as persons twelve years of age or older who declared that they had engaged in remunerative activity within the twelve weeks preceding the census. Thus, both before and after 1950, unemployed persons were counted in the labor force. Despite such discrepancies, the censuses do reflect absolute increments to the labor force: from nearly 4.9 million workers in 1921 to almost 5.9 million in 1940, 8.3 million in 1950, and 11.4 million in 1960. These figures indicate that since 1900 the proportion of the total population making up the labor force has varied only slightly, remaining at a fairly constant level of one-third. Using the high projection of the United Nations study mentioned earlier, this would suggest that the labor force should number more than 20 million workers by 1980.

Two additional features of population trends bear on the labor force. The first is that a greater proportion of the population is appearing in the 15–64 age bracket. This grouping, encompassing the highest productive years, will show a remarkable increase in the decades ahead, and both the 0–4 and 5–14 years of age brackets should exhibit relative declines. Structural changes of this sort, accompanied by compulsory public education, suggest that decade by decade, the average age at which the Mexican will begin "economically active work" should rise, and the age at which he will retire should come earlier. These phenomena will in turn introduce a whole series of new problems, because for every hundred Mexicans between the ages of 15 and 69, an estimated 88 other Mexicans will be found in the unproductive age brackets below 15 and above 69. The 1960 census showed that 17 million persons, or 48.6 per cent of Mexico's population, were under 15 or over 69.

A second noteworthy feature is that the proportion of women in the labor force has increased substantially over the last decades, and although millions more women will undoubtedly join the economically active population in the decades ahead, the percentage increase will probably slow up. Between 1940 and 1960, the total number of women in the labor force quadrupled, yet demographers believe that it is unlikely that the next two decades will witness more than a doubling of the female labor force. An important variable that will influence the size of the female working force of the future is the number of girls leaving rural areas to take up domestic chores in cities. Women in Mexico have already proven their willingness to assume jobs in industry, commerce, and government, and their adaptability once employed.

A further demographic factor of importance is the pronounced decline in the proportion of the labor force engaged in agricultural pursuits and the decided increase in the proportion occupied in industry, transportation, commerce, the service industries, and government. About 80 per cent of the labor force was dedicated to agriculture at the outset of the Revolution—a proportion that for most societies indicates gross underdevelopment. Today, Mexico is steadily pushing toward an 85 per cent nonagricultural labor force—a level indicative of advanced industrialization. Agriculture accounted for about 70 per cent of the labor force in 1930. Since then, the percentage has been declining rapidly: to 65 per cent in 1940, to about 58 per cent in 1950, and to 51 per cent in 1960. Although few economists believe that Mexico will reach the high 85:15 ratio of development before the turn of the century, if then, there appears little doubt of its reducing the ratio to 60:40 by 1980. In terms of total population in 1960, of which 67.2 per cent of Mexico's inhabitants were considered economically unproductive—namely, minors under twelve years of age (38 per cent of total population), unemployed housewives (27 per cent), and other groupings (2.2 per cent)—the 32.8 per cent of Mexican population forming the labor force was comprised of workers in agriculture (18 per cent), industry (5.5 per cent), services (2.5 per cent), commerce and finance (2.5 per cent), transportation and communications (1.2 per cent), government employment (1.2 per cent), mining (0.4 per cent), and other sectors (1.5 per cent). Within the nonagricultural labor force, mining is the only major sector that has declined. The 416,000 Mexicans in government service in 1960, in comparison to only 63,000 in 1921—both figures exclude employees in state-owned enterprises such as the railroads —reflects the growing role of the state in all aspects of Mexican life.

An increase of better-educated, healthier, and technically competent workers, technicians, administrative personnel, and entrepreneurs should also characterize the years ahead. Increases in literacy, from 26 per cent in 1910 to 62 per cent in 1960, lend testimony to magnificent achievements in education and, indirectly, to preparation of a labor force capable of higher efficiency. The extension of social security, which in Mexico includes hospitalization and other medical services, has fostered higher levels of health. Yet measured against former decades, though he is relatively better educated, healthier, and technically more competent, the Mexican laborer still receives meager real wages. This condition raises a question of whether the steadily rising rate of literacy in the labor force will not tend to create a more vocal working force—one that will become increasingly critical of the opportunistic union bosses who have acquiesced in a program of economic development that has retained the low real wages for over half of the labor force that they had twenty years ago. The imminent danger to an uninterrupted push in capital accumulation is that labor may turn to nonpacific means for alleviating its plight.

UNIONS AND UNION LEADERS

From the outset of any discussion on the labor force, we should understand that the organized labor movement in Mexico is neither independent nor free, that organized labor comprises a minority segment of the labor force as a whole, that labor unions exaggerate membership statistics, and that the labor force as a whole receives miserably low wages, even though one segment of organized labor has managed to carve out a notch for itself alongside the middle and upper sectors of society. The labor movement has been inextricably tied to the captive official party since the days of Cárdenas. Indeed, as we noted in Chapter 5, the key labor organizations were tied to Revolutionary administrations in the 1920's, even before establishment of the official party. The labor leader carries out the whims of the Revolutionary elite running the nation, or he is "voted out of office." When militant autonomous union leaders attack the government, they are often jailed or given similar rough treatment. With the Revolutionary brain trust pushing capital accumulation in its present form, unions will remain captive in that they will not be able to call strikes that will bring fruitful rewards to the rank and file. No strike of national importance occurs unless the government gives it the green light. Higher real wages constitute the immediate, day-by-day preoccupation of Mexican labor. How to keep labor from achieving this goal constitutes a preoccupation of recent governments. However, nominal wage increases have appeared in the form of biennial restructuring of legal minimum wages on a regional basis. But except for privileged unions periodically blessed with substantial real wage raises, the union boss in Mexico's political economy is more like a policeman than a responsible and responsive leader. The indictment of labor leaders is softened somewhat with the understanding that unionism has been part and parcel of the broader context of Mexican social development.

To ascertain the precise numerical strength of organized labor in Mexico is difficult. Government labor agencies tend to understate union membership. Unions invariably exaggerate membership. Reaching reliable estimates is further complicated by successes of the CTM, Mexico's largest nonagricultural central, in convincing scholars and international organizations that the CTM has two million unionists. Remembering that this central avowedly counted in its ranks more than a million affiliated unionists in the late 1930's, logic might appear to be on the side of CTM bosses asserting that their central, the favorite of successive administrations, has at least as large a membership in 1964 as it did more than twenty years ago. Two facts intervene to negate such reasoning: First, the CTM exaggerated its membership strength in the 1930's no less than it does today; and, second, in its heyday, the CTM included peasants, railroad workers, bank employees, civil servants, miners, and metalworkers who no longer adhere to the big central. Of the strictly nonagricultural labor force of 1940, census data showed a total union membership of slightly over 875,000, probably a fairly reliable count when measured against the total economically active population outside agriculture. Taking into account the membership accountable to other centrals, to autonomous national unions, and to unaffiliated local unions would suggest that the CTM could have enlisted a maximum of 500,000 nonagricultural workers in 1940. Split-offs in the 1940's and 1950's, plus the formation of new centrals and the preference of workers in many plants for company unions, have affected CTM membership adversely. Thus, it is probable that by 1964 the CTM has no more than 600,000 regular members.

Statistics from official censuses and government ministries indicate that approximately one-third of the nonagricultural labor force is unionized. By way of comparison, the same ratio has rarely been reached in the United States. In Mexico, out of a total nonagricultural labor force of 5.1 million in 1960, there were probably 1.3 million workers in conventional trade unions and 315,000 in organized bureaucrat unions. The ratio of one-third, as an absolute maximum, coincides with statistics on job occupation. In the first place, the census category of "domestic services–professionals" accounted for over 865,000 Mexicans, and the real estate category included nearly 520,000. Few persons in these two categories were unionized. Second, owners and managers of industrial and commercial concerns are counted in the over-all labor force, yet few hold union membership. Third, few workers between the ages of twelve and sixteen are unionized, but they are not omitted from the "labor force." Additionally, bank employees are prohibited by law from belonging to regular unions. Moreover, the conventional practice of using day laborers in construction work and similar industries keeps another segment of labor nonunionized. And, finally, a large proportion of office workers, clerks, and similar laborers engaged in commercial activities are unorganized. When all these nonunion elements in the labor force are totaled, it is impossible to believe that more than one-third of the nonagricultural labor force is unionized.

Unionism in Mexico follows the general pattern of syndical organization elsewhere in Western civilization, with one exception: Mexican labor leaders place great emphasis on grouping unions into territorial units corresponding to politico-electoral districts. Local unions affiliate with national unions, which may or may not affiliate with a national central. But local unions, largely for political ends, also belong to local, district, regional, and state federations. Furthermore, some locals affiliate directly with a national central, while others remain autonomous. State federations also affiliate with confederations and centrals. Craft unions are relatively insignificant; industrial unions are clearly in vogue. By 1964, only two centrals and two autonomous national unions could validly claim more than 60,000 members—namely, the CTM and the CROC centrals and the autonomous Railroad Workers' Union and the Mining and Metal Workers' Union.

From the days of Calles, unionization has experienced several fluctuations. In 1930, probably less than 300,000 workers were unionized. The decidedly prolabor policies of Lázaro Cárdenas were a mighty boon to organized labor, and by 1940, nonagricultural unionists, including civil servants, probably numbered slightly over 900,000. Politics inimical to an immediate expansion of unionization, encompassing a clearer demarcation of the jurisdiction of the communal agricultural union over agricultural workers as fostered by Cárdenas, entered with the Ávila Camacho administration. By 1942, nonagricultural union membership dropped, perhaps to less than 700,000. Since then, unionization has exhibited a steady increase, interrupted only by a marked decline in 1947 accountable to Alemán's antilabor crusade during his first year in office. Despite the rapid industrialization and commercialization typifying Alemán's administration, his own roughshod treatment of organized labor contributed to an absolute drop in nonagricultural union membership compared with a decade earlier. Falling to slightly more than 800,000 members, the grand total of nonagricultural unionists was higher than ten years before only because the organized civil servants' union had grown to about 210,000 members. Unionism became popular once again with the advent of Ruiz Cortines, not because the new head of state did anything special on behalf of labor, but rather because the industrialization and commercialization begun by Alemán was consolidated and stepped up notably in terms of actual plant operation. Economic modernization proceeded, and by 1960 the nonagricultural labor force under union banners probably reached about 1.6 million workers in all. Three years later, further unionization, particularly of the independent company-union variety, had probably pushed the total 150,000 workers higher.

These crude figures hide many schisms within organized labor. The communal agricultural organization (CNC)—Mexicans call it a "union" —has virtually nothing in common with conventional trade unions except for the political propaganda associating CNC *ejidatarios* with organized labor in the official party. Grabbing a deputyship or senatorship in an impotent legislature, which is one reward given to CNC leaders for remaining loyal to the Revolutionary brain trust running the nation, accomplishes little for the rank and file of the CNC. In fact, looked at from an economist's viewpoint, agricultural labor and industrial-commercial labor are actually in competition for higher wages. Someone must pay for capital accumulation, and this must be done at least partly by labor. Besides this split, the house of organized labor is itself divided. The "business unionism" accompanying an economic development geared to forced savings and crude exploitation of labor in general has witnessed the creation of a privileged group of unions. The government has granted certain unions periodic pay increases in line with higher costs of living while denying wage increases to others. The privileged labor class in the electric-power, petroleum, telephone, aviation, and motion-picture industries, plus the railroad workers, electricians, civil servants, and workers in several dozen choice factories—together, less than one-seventh of the nonagricultural labor force—keeps fairly abreast of inflationary forces. Meanwhile, the hard core of the total labor force finds itself a captive of government, capital, and inflation.

Whether a union belongs to the Labor Unity Bloc, a basically political instrument utilized by labor bosses for giving banquets and for persuading the Revolutionary elite to award these labor leaders legislative seats, or whether it is dead set against it, has not influenced the status of privileged unionism. A privileged status has been achieved through a complex set of relationships, including presidential favor, dynamic union leadership, and the strategic nature of the industrial activity involved. Some unions in the Bloc are privileged, like the railroad and petroleum workers' unions (though the latter union rejoined the CTM in 1958, it was permitted to retain its separate identity in the Bloc). Others, like the CROM and CGT, are not. Meanwhile, the Central Nacional de Trabajadores (CNT), which was established in 1960 by independent leftist unions, has on occasion been rather outspoken in its disagreements with government policies. Formed by the CROC, SME, STERM, CRT, and four insignificant union organizations, the new CNT represents less than 100,000 unionists, yet wage scales of workers in the SME and STERM are among the highest in organized labor. On the other hand, the Labor Unity Bloc, representing about 1.1 million unionists and organized bureaucrats (the Bloc claims 4 million affiliated members), whose leaders pledge wholehearted support to government, finds among its affiliates unions whose wage scales are on the margin of legal minimum wages. The divide-and-rule policy toward organized labor was reflected in the composition of the 1961–64 national legislature, which saw the Revolutionary elite bestow deputy seats on six CROC leaders, four mining and metalworkers' union leaders, three railroad workers' leaders, and nineteen CTM leaders. Obviously, CNT is not antigovernment. Neither is it anti–United States, despite the fact that one leader of the CNT-affiliated Federación Nacional de Cañareros, a union with less than 2,500 members, is an avowed Communist. His verbal gymnastics may convince the CROC, which accounts for more than two-thirds of CNT membership, to abandon the new political central. Stripped of all window dressing, the CNT represents competition for Labor Unity Bloc leadership, not for the Mexican government.

Raising real wages involves a frustrating enigma. On the one hand, if real wages are not raised, the effective domestic market into which industry and commerce can sell will probably remain at about 20 per cent of the Mexican population. This is roughly the present size of the upper- and middle-class market (if we include in the latter category families of privileged unionists) into which secondary and tertiary industries sell now. On the other hand, if real wages are raised without making substantial changes elsewhere in the economy, capital accumulation will surely slow down. There is no assurance that an adequate graduated tax policy will increase productivity either, at least as far as output from private enterprise is concerned. A small group of privileged unionists within the ranks of organized labor enjoy moderate immediate benefits from the industrialization process, but the vast majority of workers and their families live on relatively low wages and are subjected to continuous inflationary pressures.

During the decade of the 1950's, the legal daily minimum wage in the Federal District fluctuated between $1.00 and $1.25. Most workers in Mexico received less than this amount, however, and the minimum wage was lower in most of the states. Notable exceptions occurred in northern border states where wages were generally higher. But on a nationwide basis, since 1950 a majority of the labor force has probably received less than $36 monthly, and they have been clamoring for higher pay. Since 1958, organized labor in the Federal District has openly pressed for a daily wage of $2.13, but by 1963 the state had sanctioned only a moderate elevation, raising the daily wage level to $1.40. Unless this raise is accompanied by other modifications in the economy, it too will probably be eaten up forthwith by inflationary pressures.

To bridge the gap between low wages with inflation and the fulfillment of constitutional mandates on the rights of labor, the state has advanced certain measures of social justice. Streetcar and bus fares are kept relatively low, social security is extended to cover additional workers, rent controls are moderately enforced, and basic foodstuffs and clothing are sometimes made available at reduced prices. But to expand measures of this sort to a comprehensive national scale that would benefit most of the twelve million persons in the labor force, instead of only a million or at best two million, would require radical changes in fiscal policy, realignments in agricultural and industrial productivity patterns, and perhaps more extensive state ownership of the means of production. In the context of the Mexican economic system, forced savings and higher real wages for the masses are contradictory. The plight of labor thus becomes primarily a question of political economy, not of modifications of basic constitutional mandates. Maximum hours, minimum wages, job security, social security, profit-participation, and the right to organize, bargain collectively, and strike, as well as a host of other rights, have been in the basic law of the land since the Constitution of 1917 and the Labor Code of 1931 became effective. Politically, organized labor must free itself of captive union bosses who carry out the whims of a Revolutionary elite apparently committed to crude exploitation of labor, and must transform the political mechanism of which it forms a nominal part into an organ more responsive to the demands of labor. Economically, Mexico must admit new developmental patterns in order to fulfill the urgency of raising the real income of workers, whether on the farms or in the cities. Social justice, in Revolutionary semantics, should include income redistribution.

FEEDING THE NATION

The Malthusian theory of impending starvation has entered the thinking of many an observer of Mexican development. In broadest terms, the theory contends that food supply grows in arithmetic progression while population grows in geometric progression; hence, population will outdistance food supply and bring on starvation. In applying this theory to Mexico, the philosophers of gloom have variously predicted that "Mexico will be starving by 1980," that "Within a century Mexican territory will only be able to maintain a human population at a very precarious level of subsistence," and that "Birth control offers the only salvation to Mexico's problems." Are these philosophers correct in asserting that Mexico will soon be starving to death? Of course, Mexicans are not eating as well as Americans, nor is there promise of their doing this within decades; but have they ever done so? Furthermore, is there any biological reason why the Mexicans, or, for that matter, future Americans, must consume as much as present-day Americans? The central issue in the Malthusian proposition as it applies to Mexico is whether population will really outdistance the basic food supply and force Mexico into dependence on the outside world for large-scale food imports. As Mexico is now feeding her people, perhaps 7 per cent are eating extremely well, 13 per cent fairly well, and 30 per cent modestly; 40 per cent are eating little more than "beans and tortillas," and 10 per cent are just barely managing to obtain one completely inadequate meal daily. Nevertheless, if present trends in demography and agriculture persist, Mexico should be in a position to keep abreast of population growth and by the year 2000 feed a population in excess of 100 million inhabitants. Let us look at the facts.

Much of Mexico's land is unproductive. With a national territory of 760,373 square miles (485,604,830 acres) Mexico is about one-fourth the size of continental United States. But almost one-half of Mexico's territory, 222.3 million acres, is conducive to little more than grazing, and another one-sixth is in forest lands. A rugged terrain, accented by numerous and often majestic mountain peaks, reduces the amount of level land to less than 50 per cent; almost 30 per cent of Mexico's land is of grades greater than 25 degrees. Adverse climate and low rainfall make 52.13 per cent of the land arid; 30.56 per cent is semiarid, 10.52 per cent semihumid, and 6.79 per cent humid. In terms of cultivability, this means that 390 million acres are usually too dry and 32 million acres are frequently too wet. Besides topographical handicaps and water shortages, agriculture is beset by low soil fertility, erosion, drought, hailstorms on the central plateau, frost in the north and northwest, and hurricanes in the eastern coastal regions. Drawing up a balance sheet of land realities on the basis of the most reliable of recent surveys (none of which, unfortunately, offers us unquestionable statistics) would indicate that only 74 million acres are susceptible to cultivation. Low as the 74-million figure may sound, it represents a considerable increment over the 49.2 million acres estimated by the census of 1950 to have been the amount of land then available for agricultural use. The new estimate is based on present and potentially feasible irrigation, improved farming techniques, different land utilization, and more-careful inventories of the terrain and soils.

AREA UNDER CULTIVATION

Years	Hectáreas [a]	Index
1929–33	5,359,000	100.0
1934–38	5,213,000	99.1
1939–43	5,804,000	108.3
1944–48	6,168,000	115.1
1949–53	7,993,000	149.1
1954–58	10,205,000	190.2
1959–63	12,500,000	233.3

[a] One hectárea equals 2.47 acres.

Fallowing, lack of credit and of farm machinery, adverse climate, irrigation needs, fear of unfavorable governmental action, and other forces combine to restrict the amount of land actually cultivated today to about only 40 per cent of the estimated total of 74 million acres available for agricultural use. But this 40 per cent represents almost 30 million acres placed under cultivation in 1959, 1960, and 1961—50 per cent higher than the nearly 20 million acres cultivated a decade earlier, and double the acreage worked twenty and thirty years ago. Considering the average amount of land under cultivation during consecutive five-year periods, estimates of the Bureau of Agricultural Economy in the Ministry of Agriculture indicate that the area under cultivation has been rising steadily.

There have been marked shifts in the proportion of land devoted to the raising of various crops. Corn and beans, the Siamese twins of the Mexican diet, remain the two basic crops of Mexican agriculture. The area devoted to these crops has more than doubled, although they are slowly consuming a lower percentage of cultivated land: 66 per cent in 1959 against 72 per cent in 1939. Wheat and rice are also gaining acreage, yet, somewhat surprisingly, at a slower rate than either corn or beans. (Between 1939 and 1959, the area planted in corn and beans increased 103 per cent; that in beans alone, 126 per cent; in corn alone, 99 per cent. The area planted in rice and wheat combined increased 72 per cent; in rice alone, 122 per cent; and in wheat alone, 68 per cent.) The greatest relative growth in cultivation has occurred in cotton, tomatoes, and coffee. Twice in the last two decades the area planted in cotton was four times the 1939 acreage. And without exception since 1952, the amount of farm land devoted to tomato-raising has been three times greater than that planted in 1939. The big increases in coffee acreage, now more than twice the 1939 acreage, have taken place since 1957.

AGRICULTURAL LAND UNDER CULTIVATION IN MEXICO, DISTRIBUTED ACCORDING TO PRINCIPAL CROPS, 1939–1959

(thousands of hectáreas)

Year	Total	Corn	Beans	Wheat	Rice	Tomato	Coffee	Cotton	Others
1939	5,429	3,267	632	563	45	20	120	262	520
1942	6,010	3,342	750	600	65	31	130	362	730
1945	6,031	3,451	728	468	59	41	135	366	783
1948	6,692	3,722	788	577	82	50	136	405	932
1951	8,326	4,422	969	673	104	58	166	884	1,030
1954	9,475	5,253	1,108	765	90	63	199	922	1,075
1957	10,083	5,392	1,116	958	117	61	272	916	1,251
1958	11,412	6,348	1,423	840	117	62	281	1,048	1,293
1959	11,804	6,500	1,432	946	100	62	282	754	1,728

The crucial problem in Mexican agriculture is not merely to cultivate additional acreage but also to raise over-all productivity by boosting output per acre. On this measurement, the great increases in agricultural production since 1939, both in absolute terms and in output per acre, have been concentrated in only two major regions of the nation: the far north and the northwest, where a new commercial agriculture based on large plots, irrigation, and mechanization has developed. Minor regions elsewhere have found the raising of sugar cane, tomatoes, cotton, wheat, strawberries, and garlic, to mention but a few of the leaders, conducive to higher output. Between 1939 and 1959, the most striking productivity rise among Mexico's principal crops occurred in wheat acreage, which more than doubled in productiveness, and in cotton land which almost doubled in output per acre. Higher output efficiency was also registered by tomatoes, sugar cane, potatoes, rice, *ajonjolí* (sesame seed, from which cooking oil is made), tobacco, citrus fruits, peanuts, and even by beans and corn. On the other hand, coffee and rice remained relatively stationary in this respect.

The major obstruction to crop diversification is the preference bestowed on the mighty tyrant of Mexican agriculture that antedates the arrival of the Spaniards: corn. Production of corn per acre registered about a 33 per cent growth in the two decades (1940–60) when world market prices were clearly favoring other commodities that Mexico seemed capable of producing with higher efficiency. Annual corn production fluctuated between 5 million and 5.5 million metric tons during the late 1950's and early 1960's. Although this was considerably above the 1.5 million tons produced in 1930, the less than 2 million tons in 1940, or the 3.1 million tons in 1950, it is nonetheless inferior to Mexican needs. The fluctuations also influenced the foreign-trade balance: Mexico imported 104 million dollars' worth of corn in 1957–58 and then, in 1960, swung fully 180 degrees and exported 22 million dollars' worth of corn. Changing the ageless customs of the rural Indian communities of the central plateau region, where almost 50 per cent of the agricultural land is cultivated in corn, remains an unresolved problem of the Revolution. Perhaps 20 per cent, and possibly as high as 50 per cent, of the Mexican people will continue to eat better, regardless of whether the rural masses in central Mexico switch to the growing of other crops. Unfortunately, this prospect is not in store for the lower 50 per cent of Mexican income-earners.

Despite the corn problem, changes elsewhere in the economy have converted Mexico from a country exporting primarily minerals to a country exporting primarily foodstuffs and other agricultural products. Since 1959, agricultural commodities and cattle, meat, seafood, canned food and fish, and textile products (largely of crude henequen and ixtle fibers) have been accounting for more than two-thirds of Mexican exports. The implications of the changing export structure are clear: Mexican agriculture is not only feeding the nation but, assisted by tourist dollars, is paying for the bulk of Mexican imports; thus, agriculture is carrying a very heavy burden in providing the machinery and industrial raw materials that are transforming Mexico's cities into industrial centers. In the second half of the 1950's, raw cotton earned a yearly average of more than 196 million dollars in precious foreign exchange, bringing in 263 million dollars in the record year of 1956. In the decade 1951–60, cotton production averaged 1.75 million bales (of 230 kilos each)—equivalent to a 28 per cent increase over the single year 1951. Mexico produced 2.36 million bales in 1962. Future expansion is intimately linked to the cotton-export policy of the United States, since attempts to increase Mexican cotton export on the Free World market would face vigorous price competition should the

United States choose to regain a larger share of the world cotton market.

Improvement in world coffee prices after World War II intensified the development of Mexico's coffee plantations. Within a decade, coffee acreage doubled, as did the number of sacks of coffee exported, and coffee became Mexico's second-ranking export. The value of coffee exports almost tripled before settling in the 1958–60 period to a yearly average of 1.4 million bags at an annual value in excess of 71 million dollars. The global importance of coffee to the Mexican economy is reflected in the fact that in 1960 coffee accounted for 2.4 per cent of all cultivated lands, 6.3 per cent of the value of total agricultural production, and 9.1 per cent of Mexican export income. Now that Mexico is participating in the multilateral world coffee growers' agreement she seems assured of a steady market for her coffee and Mexico's coffee export quota is likely to remain above 1.3 million bags.

The next earners of export income in the category of foodstuffs and agricultural commodities were (1) cattle on the hoof and fresh and refrigerated meat, (2) shrimp, and (3) tomatoes. In recent years, the stock-raising industry has been growing at a 13 per cent annual rate, representing a high growth indeed in Mexican developmental terms. Improvements in breeding, better forage, elimination of cattle diseases, and government promotion of cattle-raising are the principal reasons why this branch of agriculture is coming into its own. For the period 1957–60, the average yearly income from cattle on the hoof amounted to 33 million dollars, and that of fresh and refrigerated meats accounted for another 8.4 million dollars. A foodstuff, although obviously not agricultural, shrimp held the fourth position in this export category by virtue of average yearly exports of 31.8 million dollars during 1957–60. A luxury for 80 per cent of Mexico's population, shrimp, like the bulk of Mexican foodstuff exports, are primarily shipped to the U.S. Finally, tomatoes comprise a fifth export item in this category, having averaged slightly above 24 million dollars yearly from 1957 through 1960. For 1961–62, rankings in this export category were: cotton, coffee, cattle-meat, sugar, shrimp, and tomatoes.

Sugar is now challenging other commodities, although the annual average of sugar export in 1957–60 fell behind that of commodities mentioned above. Exports of sugar shot up to over 52 million dollars in 1960—39.2 million dollars in refined sugar and 13.7 million dollars in raw or unrefined sugar—some 23 times higher than sugar exports in 1950. Sugar growers are planting more and more land in sugar cane in the expectation of permanently retaining the new sugar quota bestowed on Mexico when Castro's Cuba was cut from the U.S. import quota. But, some cautious growers are asking, is it so certain that Cuba without Castro, or perhaps even with a reformed Castro, will remain permanently outside the U.S. quota? And if Cuban sugar returns to the U.S. market, what will become of Mexican surpluses? In 1961, Mexico exported 566,000 metric tons of sugar—many times more than years in the Fifties and impressively the highest export year up to that time for Mexican sugar. Since 1957, Mexico has been producing in excess of one million tons of sugar annually; in fact, the yearly average for the 1958–62 period exceeded 1.3 million metric tons. Annual increases in sugar output in 1959 and 1960 were 13 per cent and 18.5 per cent over the preceding year's production, much above the 8.5 per cent yearly average achieved in 1951–55 and far above the 3.8 per cent yearly advances of two decades earlier (1931–35). In the single year of 1960, Mexico produced more sugar than in the entire five-year period 1931–35 and almost as much as in the 1936–40 period. Meanwhile, the sugar industry has been taking care of domestic needs, which climbed from 12.4 kilograms per capita in 1930 to 22.7 in 1950 and 29.8 in 1960. If corn production could only match the performance of the sugar industry, Mexico might eliminate its food imports once and for all.

In addition to the commodity market and export markets in general, future advances in agricultural output seem to depend on eight major variables: legal and political action affecting the size of agricultural plots and the direction of agrarian reform; the availability and nature of agricultural credit; the opening of new lands to cultivation; irrigation; mechanization; changes in crops raised and employment of crop rotation; the use of fertilizers, better seeds, insecticides, and fungicides; and improved methods of handling perishable foodstuffs. Let us examine some of these variables in detail.

Many economists believe that the biggest question of all involves ownership patterns and what to do about the millions of minute plots created and protected by the agrarian-reform program. The *ejido* and small private property are the principal forms of land tenure in Mexico. In marked contrast to land-tenure systems common to Anglo-America, the *ejido* is in essence a community or village with communal lands that have been granted it by the federal government and are therefore "inalienable, unattachable, untransmutable, imprescriptible, and indivisible." *Ejido* lands are worked communally or parceled out among the individual *ejidatarios*; except for the cotton-growing areas of the north and the henequen-growing areas of Yucatán, communal exploitation is largely confined to forest and grazing lands. The "small (private) property" is defined by law to be an agricultural holding not exceeding 247 acres of irrigated or otherwise choice land, 494 of temporal rainfall land, 988 of comparatively drought land, or 1,976 of arid or mountainous land. Several exceptions are made in the case of cotton-raising (370.5 acres of irrigated land), the cultivation of bananas, sugar cane, coffee, henequen, rubber, olives, vanilla, cacao, and fruit trees (741 acres), and stock-raising (the amount of land necessary to maintain up to 500 head of major stock or its equivalent in minor stock). A great deal of Mexican land ownership is still illegal, in the sense that the size of many rural estates exceeds legal maximums—as late as September, 1960, one source claimed that there were still some estates of more than a million acres, that 551 haciendas had from 123,500 to 247,000 acres each, and that all in all, 9,600 private landowners possessed a total of over 197 million acres. (Presumably, much of this land is unattractive and nonarable.) Nevertheless, the agrarian reform succeeded in transforming Mexican agriculture on a comprehensive national scale from a land-tenure system composed overwhelmingly of giant haciendas to one consisting predominantly of medium-size and tiny plots.

The fundamental shortcoming of the agrarian-reform program is not that communal land tenure has joined and partly replaced private ownership, although there are naturally some who oppose communal ownership per se. The economist looking at productivity will discover that the larger *ejidos* engaged in commercial agriculture as well as the individual *ejidatario* working a moderate-size plot have already adapted to modern farming methods, or could do so without much difficulty. The real clash on agrarian politics is rather a clash of the communal *ejidatarios*, private farmers who possess too little land or an insufficient amount of good land, and to a certain extent the landless peasants versus those agriculturalists, whether *ejidatarios* or private farmers, who have sufficient land to make farming productive. Up to September 1, 1961, the agrarian-reform program had distributed somewhere between 110,622,702 acres (if we accept the total hectareage of 44,786,519 corresponding to definitive grants registered by the Agrarian Affairs Department) and 124,426,446 acres (if we accept the total hectareage of 50,415,565 of provisional as well as definitive grants issued by successive presidents). Similarly, because of inexactness in definitive and provisional titles, estimates of the number of *ejidatarios* vary between 2,225,000 and 2,300,000, with another million certified as legitimately in line to receive land whenever further distribution takes place. Experts in Mexico favor the lower figures in both cases. Whatever an exact inventory might produce, we can conservatively estimate that about one-fourth of the entire national territory is now in the hands of *ejidatarios*.

A common error of outside observers is assuming that such a vast redistribution program would leave little agricultural land in private hands. The truth is that much land turned over to the peasants is not agricultural land at all, but in reality forest, grazing land, and sometimes completely unproductive areas, with the truncated parcels turning out to be a conglomeration of forest, grazing, agricultural, and unproductive lands. Regardless of who owns the land there are, as we have already noted, only about 74 million acres in the entire nation suited to agricultural use. And though we lack satisfactory information on the amount of this acreage that is communally held (for example, part of the officially listed grazing land is conducive to cultivation), we do know that the 1950 census discovered that more than 27.4 million acres, or about 56 per cent, of the 49 million acres then considered conducive to cultivation were privately owned. Applying this same percentage to the 74 million acres deemed conducive to cultivation today (a fairly safe assumption, since the lands redistributed by Alemán, Ruiz Cortines, and López Mateos have been predominantly grazing, forest, and "mixed" lands), we find that some 33 million acres of "agricultural land" are communal. Even presuming that as much as 37 million acres, or one-half of the land that is conducive to cultivation, might be communal land, we still find that more than two-thirds of the 111 million acres now in the form of *ejidos* is nonarable. In terms of area, therefore, the lion's share of *ejidal* lands rests outside the strictly crop-raising realm.

LAND DISTRIBUTED TO *EJIDOS*, 1915–1961
(expressed in hectárea units)

According to presidential informes (includes definitive and provisional titles)		According to the Agrarian Affairs Department (lands given with definitive title)	
Carranza	224,393	1915–20	172,997
De la Huerta	157,532	1921–24	1,556,983
Obregón	1,677,067	1925–28	3,045,802
Calles	3,195,028	1929	1,749,583
Portes Gil	2,065,847	1930–32	1,520,139
Ortiz Rubio	1,203,737	1933–34	1,924,149
Rodríguez	2,094,637	1935–40	17,609,139
Cárdenas	20,072,957	1941–46	3,335,575
Ávila Camacho	5,327,942	1947–52	3,998,807
Alemán	4,057,993	1953–58	3,198,780
Ruiz Cortines	3,664,379	1959–61 (Sept. 1)	6,674,565 [a]
López Mateos (to Sept. 1, '61)	6,674,053		
	50,415,565		44,786,519

[a] Unverified. By September, 1963, López Mateos claimed that his administration had distributed in excess of 10,000,000 hectáreas.

Here is where the problem of *minifundia* enters. Too many *ejidatarios* are concentrated on too little land; more than half live on less than one-third of all *ejidal* lands. Discounting the choice *ejidal* lands under cultivation in the northwest zone (Baja California, Sonora, and Sinaloa) and those *ejidos* farmed collectively, approximately 1.2 million *ejidatario* families (with an average of 5.5 members per family) are living on an estimated 14.8 million to 19.8 million acres. The deplorably sad state of economic affairs endured by these *ejidatarios* is no worse and perhaps even a little better than that of one million small farmers and their families. On the basis of 1950 census figures, which await revision by publication of 1960 census results, the 1,004,835 small private farms of 12.35 acres or less accounted for only 3,366,114 acres in all; that is to say, that the average size of their plots was a fraction above three acres. Combining these two groups of farmers, and understanding that the plight of the small farmer is worsened by the fact that in the 1950 census figure, uncultivable plots were included along with cultivable ones, we find that 2.2 million farmers and their families (accounting for approximately one-third of Mexico's entire population) are living on plots that are unbelievably uneconomical. Short of large-scale colonization programs, which López Mateos undertook to the modest and inadequate degree of placing about 2 million acres of cultivable agricultural land in the hands of new settlers (*colonos*), or short of provoking armed revolt on the Mexican countryside, no immediate workable solution to this weighty problem of *minifundia* presents itself. It has been possible to keep hundreds of thousands of these families alive through the temporary migration of *braceros* and "wetbacks." Abolition of the United States' farm program favoring Mexican migratory labor carries graver consequences than those intrinsic in the migratory labor program itself. In time, many of these peasants will leave their small plots for the city, permitting those who remain to work larger plots. Meanwhile, feeding this sector of agriculture as well as the urban population will fall to farmers with medium- and large-size extensions, whether they be privately, communally, or cooperatively owned by *colonos*.

The Mexican nation is now relying on these medium- and larger-size plots to win the battle against Malthus. Output per person occupied in agriculture is lowest in those states where traditional, *minifundia*, non-commercial farming dominates—in Tlaxcala, Oaxaca, Puebla, Querétaro, Zacatecas, México, San Luis Potosí, Hidalgo, and Guanajuato—and highest in the states where commercial farming prevails—in Baja California, Sonora, Sinaloa, Coahuila, Chihuahua, Tamaulipas, and Nayarit. Irrigation, mechanization, and virtually every measure geared to higher efficiency will make little difference in the productivity of the more than two million Mexican peasants with tiny plots. Their marginal propensity to save is zero, a point at which it undoubtedly will remain for some time. Fully realizing this undesirable consequence of agrarian reform, President López Mateos centered his stepped-up program of land redistribution, which saw 16,684,911 acres distributed to *ejidatarios* between December 1, 1958, and September 1, 1961, almost exclusively on grazing and pasture lands, while leaving cultivable acreage virtually untouched. But he did assuage pressure from the landless by explicitly asserting in a new Forestry Law of February 1, 1960, that new concessions to exploit national forests will go to *ejidatarios* alone. When relatively good lands entered agrarian politics, López Mateos placed exploitation of them in the hands of *colonos*, so that during the first three years of his regime 72,000 colonizers and their families obtained in excess of two million acres. Settlers on these lands, who favor the cooperative tenure system, are concentrating on the raising of cotton, beans, soybeans, and citrus fruits. Since 1940, therefore, successive presidents have redistributed more or less land in full awareness of the fact that creating more *minifundia* would be certain suicide: Mexico would starve to death. Assuming that future administrations will not excessively split up the medium- and moderate-size cultivable plots (what agrarian legislation now sets as legal limits of "small private" farms) or break up the big collective *ejidos* (except on the sisal hemp lands of Yucatán), and even if future regimes do subdivide the highly productive large haciendas (like that of former president Miguel Alemán in the state of Veracruz), future legal and political action affecting the size and ownership of agricultural lands should not pose additional barriers to higher output.

But higher output will require extensive credit, mechanization, fertilizers, insecticides, fungicides, and above all, irrigation. The answer to how much credit will be needed is simple: as much as possible. For thirty-five years, the government has been financing private and communal farmers alike, and financing private farming is once again gaining vogue among private bankers. The amount of agricultural credit extended by government banks is steadily increasing and, together with the rapidly expanding price guarantee and public commodity-warehouse building programs, should deliver the needed financial impetus. The biggest state credit institutions extending direct financial assistance to agriculture are the National Agricultural Credit Bank & National *Ejidal* Credit Bank, the National Bank of Foreign Commerce, the National Warehouse Commission (ANDSA), the National Sugar Finance Corporation, two subsidiaries of the Bank of Mexico helping small farmers, and the National Popular Subsistence Corporation (CONASUPO). Although agricultural loans amounted to only 5 per cent of total crop value in 1950, this proportion had climbed to 35 per cent by 1960, with private banks supplying between 50 per cent and 55 per cent of agricultural credit and private moneylenders providing another 20 per cent. Unfortunately, both private banks and local moneylenders favor short-term, high-interest loans; some credit operations involve loans with interest rates as high as 1 per cent per day. On the more optimistic side is the fact that since 1945 a consortium of private insurance companies, in partnership with the government, has been issuing agricultural insurance coverage against hail, frost, drought, floods, excessive moisture, hurricanes, fire, and plant pests and diseases. By 1962, insurance of this type—which promises recovery of the total investment ordinarily necessary to obtain a given crop, whether the investment has been made or not—had been issued to cover almost two million acres.

Mechanization is unquestionably contributing immeasurably in keeping the specter of starvation away from Mexico. Mechanization saves time, lowers production costs, provides direct increases in output, reduces underemployment, and results in an over-all strengthening of the Mexican economy. Mechanization is highest in the north and the northwest, where plot size and topography favor commercial farming, and lowest on the two million *minifundia* plots and parcels, where the machete, wooden stick, hoe, and oxen prevail. One farm expert recently estimated that "20 per cent of Mexico's cultivated lands are worked by pre-Hispanic methods of cutting and burning without benefit of plow and oxen." Another submits that "probably 8 per cent of Mexico's cultivated area is being worked without any implements whatsoever." And a third asserts that "less than 1 per cent of the cultivated land is worked with the aid of tractors." The latest published studies of farm mechanization in Mexico employ statistics of 1950, when there were 2.2 million plows, 174,000 cultivators, and 23,000 tractors. On the basis of yearly imports and domestic implement manufactures since then, we can estimate that in 1963 Mexican agriculture had 3 million plows, 270,000 cultivators, and 55,000 tractors. This would mean that, since 1940, the number of plows in use has doubled, the number of cultivators quadrupled, and the number of tractors increased thirteen times. The increased use of tractors implies the steady displacement of animal labor: Almost 96 per cent of agricultural horsepower came from animal labor in 1930, less than 75 per cent in 1950, and probably less than 60 per cent comes from this source today. The heaviest incidence of mechanization occurs where adequate plot size permits, on medium and large tracts. Unfortunately, this means that more than half of the 6.2 million workers in the agricultural labor force of 1960 were denied mechanized methods of cultivation and probably will not be enjoying mechanization a decade or two hence. The impoverished small farmers and small-parcel *ejidatarios* simply cannot modernize when topography and *minifundia* are prohibitive.

Agricultural productivity is also increasing through more extensive use of fertilizers. To what degree output is raised in this fashion is difficult to judge accurately, since application of a given amount of fertilizer does not everywhere bring equal results. The general condition of the soil and the climate, the degree of mechanization, and the kind of crop raised, as well as fertilizers, insecticides, and fungicides, all affect the size of the harvest. Despite the difficulty in determining the proportion of higher yields attributable to the use of fertilizers, fertilizers alone do tend to improve soils, add nutritional value to foodstuffs, and generally increase yields. An estimated 25,000 acres received commercial fertilizers in 1925; twenty-five years later the figure had increased to only 84,000 acres. It is true that before mid-century the government had initiated a modest program of giving fertilizers to *ejidatarios* and had established what was destined to become the government's and the nation's largest fertilizer plant, Guanos y Fertilizantes de México. But production of fertilizers remained extremely low until the 1950's.

Gains since 1950, however, are notably impressive. In one decade, as the above statistics indicate, application of three principal fertilizers increased 26.5 times by tonnage and over 52 times by area fertilized. Additionally, widespread use of animal dung prevails in the central region, and guano and fish are used as fertilizers along coastal regions. Throughout the

COMBINED USE OF NITROGEN, PHOSPHATE, AND POTASSIUM FERTILIZERS IN MEXICAN AGRICULTURE, DECADE OF THE 1950's

Year	Metric tons	Hectáreas fertilized [a]
1950	5,283	33,960
1951	20,956	251,340
1952	28,017	269,420
1953	38,371	285,160
1954	42,248	333,620
1955	39,975	345,760
1956	59,004	579,640
1957	82,292	878,600
1958	88,955	1,350,700
1959	140,175	1,790,080

[a] One hectárea equals 2.47 acres.

decade under examination, the government fought tradition, high costs, inadequate credit, and the absence of distribution equipment to do something about the agronomists' warning that 86 per cent of Mexico's cultivable land was in need of phosphate and 32 per cent needed potassium. (The need for nitrogen per hectárea is placed at 44 kilograms, although some soils require additional kilograms per hectárea.) In 1951, the government underwrote construction of a new plant for Guanos y Fertilizantes de México, a company that up to that time had concentrated on exploitation of guano deposits on Pacific coastal islands, to produce 66,200 tons of ammonium sulfate yearly. By 1960, this company was producing 20 per cent of the nation's nitrogen needs and 60 per cent of its phosphate needs. The government also joined in partnership with French and private Mexican investors in setting up another fertilizer plant, Fertilizantes de Monclova, which in 1961 produced 30,000 metric tons of nitrogen in the form of anhydrous ammonia and ammonium nitrate. Both companies obtain natural gas free of charge from Pemex, in return for which both have obligated themselves to provide fertilizers at 40 per cent less than the cost of imported equivalents. Although this effort to raise domestic fertilizer production is impressive, it is nonetheless inadequate for satisfying present consumption, and importations of fertilizers have increased twentyfold since World War II. To reduce imports and simultaneously meet growing demand, the government is expanding plant capacities at the two plants, as well as building a new fertilizer plant at Cuautitlán in the state of México. Another plant, Fertilizantes del Istmo, located in Minatitlán, Veracruz, began producing fertilizers in 1962. Government and private business alike are now concentrating on devising improved fertilizer distribution systems, including local installation of small mixing units and utilization of individual hand-pushed fertilizing units. Even the *minifundia* plots and parcels can benefit from fertilizers.

Another component of higher agricultural yields, the final one to which we will give detailed attention, is irrigation. Irrigation in Mexico is centuries old; the complicated system of dikes, canals, aqueducts, and dams built by the Aztecs antedated the Spaniards. A cumulative view of irrigation financed by the government and by private sources produces the following picture:

IRRIGATION FINANCED BY GOVERNMENT
AND BY PRIVATE SOURCES

Up to the year of	Government-financed hectareage	Privately financed hectareage	Total hectareage under irrigation
1926	0	1,700,000	1,700,000
1934	148,600	1,700,000	1,848,600
1940	267,095	1,750,000	2,017,095
1946	816,224	1,600,000	2,416,224
1952	1,441,736	1,750,000	3,191,736
1958	2,238,810	1,750,000	3,988,810
1961 (Sept.)	2,363,900	1,765,000 (est.)	4,128,900 (est.)
1964 (est.)	2,739,000 (est.)	1,775,000 (est.)	4,514,000 (est.)

Since 1926, when President Calles founded the National Irrigation Commission and initiated publicly financed irrigation, the Mexican government has devoted an average of 12 per cent of its expenditures to irrigation. The average declined to 5.5 per cent of the federal budget in 1960 and to just under 7 per cent in 1961, dramatizing the fact that the López Mateos administration will bring fewer than 500,000 new hectáreas under irrigation—less than any regime since Cárdenas. Aided by very substantial loans from the World Bank, López Mateos did undertake the rehabilitation of irrigation systems serving in excess of 900,000 hectáreas. The temporary slowdown in new irrigation should be compensated for in future administrations, however, when regional-development projects now receiving heavy financing—in the Grijalva, Pánuco, Balsas, Fuerte, and Tepalcatepec river basins—reach fruition. The preceding statistics on privately financed irrigation substantiate the contention that Mexico cannot depend on private capital for new direct investment in irrigation, although the state has been reimbursed by private farmers for some of its irrigation projects (the going rate for irrigating one additional hectárea is about $425) in accordance with the Irrigation Law of 1947, which provided that "farmers receiving benefits from [state-financed] irrigation must reimburse the government in accord with their capacity to pay." The fact that the National Irrigation Commission was enlarged and given the status of a cabinet ministry, the Ministry of Hydraulic Resources, on January 1, 1947, is another indication of the importance that Revolutionary regimes place on irrigation.

How much is irrigation contributing to higher output? Again, it is difficult to judge, because raising agricultural productivity in this way depends in the first instance on the crop raised; for example, irrigation raises the output of beans and wheat considerably higher than it does either potatoes or corn. In general, the over-all increase in production due to irrigation has been variously estimated to be 200 per cent (economist Luis Yáñez-Pérez in 1957), 250 per cent (former minister of hydraulic resources Orive Alba in 1960), and 300 per cent (Professor Frank Tannenbaum in 1950). Applying the Orive Alba estimate to 1960 yields, when approximately one-third of the twelve million hectáreas under cultivation received irrigation, indicates that the four million hectáreas of irrigated lands were producing more than the entire eight million hectáreas of non-irrigated land: Roughly one-third of Mexico's cultivated land (the irrigated portion) was producing five-ninths of total agricultural output.

Returning to the original contention of this chapter—that Mexico can defeat Malthus—we can see that action in several areas will be necessary.

New Irrigation.   Studies by the ministry of hydraulic resources indicate that by utilizing surface, subterranean, and other waters, another 11 million hectáreas could be irrigated without resorting to unorthodox or grandiose schemes. This official estimate is crudely substantiated by the estimates of four recently published individual surveys: E. Cravioto, 12,197,500 hectáreas (survey made in 1955), Rodríguez L., 14,700,000 hectáreas (1957), L. Tamayo, 11,024,456 hectáreas (1958), and García Quintero, 17,694,146 hectáreas (1959). On the amount of additional agricultural land irrigable by surface waters alone, the four vary in their estimates from 5.9 million to 10 million hectáreas. This all bears out the possibility that beginning in 1964, and based on an average of 1.1 million hectáreas every six years (a projection in line with achievements of the Ruiz Cortines administration and with greater apparent public-expenditure capacity in the years ahead), 5.5 million additional hectáreas of irrigated land could be prepared in five six-year regimes. Added to the 4.5 million hectáreas that should be irrigated by 1964, this new effort would raise the total amount of irrigated lands to 10 million hectáreas. This projection means that only 20 per cent more land (1.1 million hectáreas), would be brought under irrigation during the 1964–84 period than was irrigated during the five six-year regimes since Abelardo Rodríguez—that is, in the period 1934–64. The cost of the new program would amount to about 93 million dollars annually at the current price of $425 per new hectárea placed under irrigation—the equivalent of less than 9 per cent of projected public expenditures during the first years of the new program and even lower percentages in subsequent years. While projections on the future cost of irrigation might prove overly optimistic, higher costs could be absorbed by maintaining the present ratio of Mexico's enlarging annual budgets devoted to irrigation. (The ratio of new investment in irrigation to total public expenditures has averaged 12 per cent since 1926.)

New Croplands. Our southern neighbor possesses 30 million hectáreas of cultivable land, of which 12.5 million are now cultivated and 17.5 million left relatively idle. Some hectareage is unworked because the land is marginal or requires irrigation for months out of the year, or because topography is highly demanding; some is unworked because the peasant is lazy, or without credit, implements, or seeds. But at least 5 million hectáreas of workable agricultural land are relatively idle—uncultivated, poorly cultivated, and grossly underutilized—because the landowner fears expropriation, prefers the role of gentleman *hacendado* without responsibilities, lives off his estate in preference to city life, or places his capital in what appears to be safer investments. The area cultivated increased more than 230 per cent from 1930 to 1960, and the ratio of newly irrigated lands to newly cultivated lands was 1 to 1.5 in the 1930's, 1 to 2.4 in the 1940's, and 1 to 4 in the 1950's. Though this ratio is an uncertain guidepost to the distant future, obviously becoming inapplicable as cultivated areas approach 30 million hectáreas, it does suggest on the record of the 1950's that an additional 11.5 million hectáreas placed under cultivation by 1994 would constitute a reasonable estimate. And if it seems unduly optimistic to believe that this land will be planted in high-yield crops, at least marketable crops of some sort do appear feasible. Added to the estimated 13.5 million hectáreas that will very likely be planted in 1964, the total area cultivated in 1994 would reach 25 million hectáreas, still leaving uncultivated another 5 million hectáreas of agricultural land conducive to cultivation.

Further Mechanization. The marketability of tractors, harrows, cultivators, seeders, plows, and other modern farm implements will undoubtedly grow in keeping apace of agricultural reform. As it does, International Harvester and other companies now manufacturing in Mexico will be joined by new industrial concerns that also possess technical know-how. Some industrialists are already puzzled over why the government holds back state enterprises like Diesel Nacional, which with plant modifications could manufacture farm implements. Whether state or privately owned, domestic farm-implement manufacturing will surely expand. But it is one thing to assert that farm mechanization and domestic farm-implement manufacture will improve, another to extrapolate from higher agricultural yields and say that mechanization will account for a specific amount of increased output. Reaching a final estimate on over-all productivity demands some reasonable prediction, however, so let us apply to the entire 1964–94 period the modest calculation of a 25 per cent increase in output from further mechanization, taking note of the fact that one Mexican economist has estimated that if present horsepower in Mexican agriculture were tripled within a 24-year period, output would increase 800 per cent!

Extensive Use of Fertilizers, Insecticides, and Fungicides. Consumption of three major fertilizers alone, as we noted previously, rose 26.5 times during the 1950's, and by 1960 some 1.8 million hectáreas of farmlands were using commercial fertilizers. Expanded plant capacity, technical education of the peasants, improved distribution systems, and easier credit should combine to multiply the hectareage covered by high-quality fertilizers at least threefold, and perhaps as much as four or five times, by 1994. The new DDT plant at Salamanca and the construction of other insecticide-manufacturing concerns presently on the drawing board should lead to wider application of insecticides without incurring balance-of-trade problems in the process. Crop-dusting, currently employed on bananas, cotton, and additional crops, should also witness a steady growth. Finally, the Institute of Industrial Investigations of the central Bank of Mexico and several autonomous commissions in charge of specific agricultural crops are promoting use of new fungicides and, through other agencies and ministries, the government is fighting crop disease wherever it appears. How will the use of fertilizers, insecticides, and fungicides affect 1964–94 output? Again, leaning on the conservative side, it seems that they should contribute to at least a 25 per cent increase in productivity.

Better Seeds, Crop Rotation, Changes in Crops Raised, and Improved Handling. Obtaining, multiplying, certifying, and distributing better seeds is one function of the governmental National Institute of Agricultural Studies, the successor of earlier commissions originated by Henry Wallace, the Rockefeller Foundation, the Corn Commission, and the Mexican government. Results from this sort of labor are unmeasurable, yet we know that improved wheat seeds are contributing to a 100 per cent increase in yields, corn seeds have helped improve yields as much as 30 per cent, and better seeds in general are producing sturdier plants with greater initial likelihood of reaching a harvest. Additionally, changes in crops presently raised would show immediate comparative advantages, not only on medium and large tracts, but on the unfortunate *minifundia*. This is equally true of crop rotation. Finally, further benefits should come about through new roads, docks, airfields, refrigeration, dehydration, freezing, and other measures geared toward bringing a bigger share of harvests to the market place. The total effect of these forces on raising output in the 1964–94 period? Fifty per cent appears to be a modest enough estimate.

Now let us relate these projections of increased agricultural output to population growth. Between 1964 and 1994, Mexico's population probably will increase from around 39 million inhabitants to somewhere between 89.2 million and 101.3 million inhabitants, depending on whether estimates of low, median, or high rates of growth prove accurate. This will represent a percentage increase of from 229 per cent to 260 per cent. Meanwhile, what will be happening in agriculture? (1) There will probably be 25 million hectáreas under cultivation, an increase of 185 per cent over 1964, made up of 15 million hectáreas of nonirrigated land and 10 million hectáreas of irrigated land. (2) This area will represent over-all additional cultivation of 11.5 million hectáreas—6 million of new nonirrigated land and 5.5 million of new irrigated land. (3) Presuming that a million hectáreas of nonirrigated land produces X dollars and a like quantity of irrigated land (applying the Orive Alba estimate of 1 to 2.5) produces 2.5X dollars, then the value of 1964 output would be $20.25X (9 million hectáreas of nonirrigated output times X, plus 4.5 million hectáreas of irrigated output times 2.5X), and the value of 1994 output would be $40X (15X, plus 10 times 2.5X). Hence, output value would increase 197.5 per cent. (4) But higher output is not the exclusive province of irrigation and new cultivations, for the combined weight of farm mechanization (25 per cent), fertilizers, insecticides, and fungicides (25 per cent), and better seeds, crop rotation, changes in crops raised, and improved handling (50 per cent) should contribute another 100 per cent. (5) Applying this projected increment to the cultivated area of 1994, which should be 1.85 times greater than that of 1964, we discover that these many other improvements should boost output 185 per cent.

To recapitulate: By placing new lands under cultivation and irrigating some of them, taking care that erosion does not render presently cultivable lands unusable for agriculture, Mexico would increase output 197.5 per cent. Then, through the use of mechanization, fertilizers, insecticides, fungicides, better seeds, crop rotation, changes in crops raised, and improved handling, output should increase another 185 per cent. Adding these two percentages together suggests that by 1994 Mexico may expand crop output about 332.5 per cent. Thus, even without taking into consideration the effects of selling lower proportions of agricultural crops abroad and of reorienting output toward the urban quarter, we can see that accomplishing these goals would provide Mexican food production with a comfortable margin over the estimated 229 per cent to 260 per cent growth in population. Sound policies, enforced with renewed and unyielding vigor, should thus stave off starvation and disprove the gloomy philosophers who are predicting inevitable famine in Mexico.

TEN

INDUSTRIAL REVOLUTION

Fervent Revolutionary Leftists contend that the only real revolution since Cárdenas left office has been the industrial revolution. Their evaluation misses the point on many counts, yet nobody can deny that the Mexican government has wholeheartedly encouraged industrialization. The firm establishment of basic industries has become so indispensable in the Revolutionary scheme of things that whenever important factories consistently fall short of development expectations, the state intervenes, sometimes by assuming plant ownership. To the present generation of Mexican planners, possessed with the purpose of achieving over-all economic growth, industrialization is a potent ingredient of a national formula combining natural, human, financial, and cultural resources. To these planners, industrialization is neither autonomous nor in contraposition to other economic activities, but together with commerce, mining, agriculture, and the services forms part of an indivisible, integral, and organic economic development. Whether Mexico should or should not industrialize is no longer the crux of the matter: Mexico has industrialized to such a degree and in such a way that a return to preindustrial patterns is out of the question. The key issue in Mexican economic development, therefore, involves the pace and extent of industrialization. For this reason, and others relating to agriculture, labor, and internal markets, we can join the late Professor Sanford Mosk in asking anew "whether the rate of industrial development should be reduced substantially until the rest of the country has sufficiently developed to support it."

THE EVOLUTION OF MEXICAN INDUSTRIALIZATION

Aspirations to industrialize Mexico long antedate the Revolution. Though voices were raised in favor of industrialization and economic diversification as far back as colonial times, the mercantilist-oriented policies of Spain hardly permitted serious consideration of the industrialization of New Spain; besides, at the time Mexico achieved independence, England was just beginning to gear itself to comprehensive industrial techniques.

Industrial enthusiasts in Mexico soon discovered that nationhood had not reduced the powerful influence exerted on the economy by the rural land barons and the Catholic Church, so that political reform was a prerequisite to economic reform. By the 1830's, Lucas Alamán, one of Mexico's earliest foreign ministers and one usually identified in Mexican history as an advocate of Church and large landowner privileges, joined the industrial chorus, asserting that "as long as Mexico does not become a manufacturing nation, its agriculture will remain reduced to languidness and misery in the midst of potential abundance, and its riches extracted from the bowels of the earth will pass immediately from mine to seaport, serving to demonstrate to nations upon which nature bestowed rich minerals that possessing them is not enough, since those who live in abundance have industry and know how to utilize natural resources and multiply their value through active circulation." Aware of the Mexican penchant for grandiose projects, Alamán cautioned his countrymen that "creating manufacturing industries in a country where they have never existed before is the hardest enterprise which that nation can undertake to execute." (As a footnote to economic history, this same Lucas Alamán initially promoted the Orizaba region of Veracruz as a textile center.) The 1850's and 1860's saw the rise of Benito Juárez, with urban businessmen supporting him against the Church, the *hacendados*, conservatives in general, and of course, against Maximilian. According to some historians, these liberal capitalists hoped that Juárez would tear down prevailing feudal structures, break up Church properties, and thus create new business opportunities and markets. But despite industrialist designs, the Reform did not release the human and material forces indispensable for emulating the industrialism of the nineteenth-century U.S. and Western Europe. When Porfirio Díaz assumed office in 1876, Mexican industrialization consisted of the beginnings of a railroad and telegraph system, some textile, sugar, and flour mills, several match, jewelry, and pottery factories, and small foundries and carriage-repair shops.

It was Díaz who truly began the material buildup of Mexico. Since his economic successes, omissions, and failures have already been pointed out in Chapters 2, 3, and 8, there is no reason to repeat them here. Suffice it to say that by 1910 his "order and progress" policies, despite their adverse effects on society as a whole, had succeeded in establishing a reasonable industrial base upon which the Mexican Revolution could, and to a substantial degree did, build a modern industrial nation. Let us look at a few examples of private industrial concerns existent by 1910, some Mexican-owned, others foreign-owned:

- Since the 1890's, one Mexican, Isaac Garza, in concert with his wife's relatives, the G. Sada family, had been increasing beer production in their Cuauhtémoc brewery in Monterrey and had opened a glass works, unaware that they were laying the groundwork for what would become the giant Garza Sada–G. Sada industrial, commercial, and financial complex, nowadays valued in excess of 700 million dollars.

• A Spanish immigrant, Señor Prieto, and his Mexican colleagues, who included Isaac Garza, with their Compañía Fundidora de Fierro y Acero located in Monterrey, began producing cast iron in 1903, and thereby became the first mill anywhere in Latin America to utilize the coking process.

• An American, Edward L. Doheny, and an Englishman, Weetman D. Pearson, were pioneering the petroleum industry, and by 1910 their companies were on a firm production basis.

• De la Macorra and Lenz had already applied German technology to the San Rafael paper mills, founded in 1894 and destined to become a multimillion-dollar pulp and paper business in Revolutionary Mexico.

• Ernesto Pugibet and Basagoit, Zaldo & Company had begun to manufacture tobacco, and by 1910 their El Buen Tono and La Tabacalera Mexicana factories controlled domestic tobacco production.

• The CIDOSA textile group of Tomás Braniff and French immigrant families had mills in the Orizaba region (among them the infamous Rio Blanco plant where workers called the memorable strike of 1906), backing up factory output through special sales arrangements with dry goods stores in several Mexican cities.

• Other textile mills, such as the old Atoyac plant in Oaxaca, "La Carolina" in Guanajuato, Cía. Industrial de Parras in Coahuila, "Covadonga" in Tlaxcala, "El León" in Puebla, and "Santa Rosa" in Veracruz, had been operating for some years.

• Joel Rocha and Benjamín Salinas had opened a "cottage industry," making beds and small artifacts—a business that the Revolutionary epoch helped convert into the complex of Salinas y Rocha factories, department stores, and affiliated merchandising outlets.

• A cement industry was under way in the form of the Cementos Hidalgo plant in Nuevo León, the Cruz Azul plant in Jasso, Hidalgo, and the Tolteca plant in Tolteca, Hidalgo.

• Mexican Power & Light Company and other public-utility groups were developing the electric-power industry. Telephones, the telegraph, and the railroads had been operating for some decades.

• And there were sugar mills, mineral ore treating foundries, soap and oil factories, match factories, and a minor drug industry.

Then, as now, low consumer purchasing power was a big impediment to economic growth.

Once Díaz was overthrown, industrialization retroceded until civil war had run its course and the Sonoran Dynasty entrenched itself in political power. In fact, the physical volume of manufacturing was lower in 1921 than it had been in any single year from 1903 to 1913. Obregón and Calles promoted industry; the effects of politicians becoming businessmen, the return of pre-Revolution businessmen from exile abroad, the impact of public spending, and political stability came together to move the industrial machine forward. Among the new private entrepreneurs emerging large in the 1920's were William Jenkins, Julio Lacaud & Carlos Trouyet, Harry Wright, and Raúl Bailleres. Jenkins entered the cement, sugar, motion-picture, and textile industries. Lacaud and Trouyet placed decades-old French investments in order, then assumed direction of new financial complexes underwriting industrial development. Wright shook off his Porfirian tastes long enough to promote anew his Consolidated Iron and Equipment Company. And Bailleres set up CREMI for unifying segments of the mining industry and for business promotion in general. Also in the 1920's, the Legorreta family consolidated its position in the Banco Nacional de México, a private financial institution established in 1884, which now began financing a substantial part of Mexican industrialization. Jenkins and his associates in the Banco de Comercio similarly engaged in industrial promotion. Additional impulses to industrialization came, as we have noted in earlier chapters, from the public sector.

In the 1930's, a new set of Mexican industrialists emerged. They were headed by Emilio Azcárraga in the radio, electronics, and motion-picture industry, Romulo O'Farrill and Gastón Azcárraga in automobile assembly, Eloy Vallina in the industrial-minded Banco Comercial Mexicano and in industrial developments in Chihuahua, and Harry Steele (then an American) and Antonio Ruiz Galindo in office-equipment manufacture. The 1930's witnessed the entrance of the state into ownership of such important industries as electric power and petroleum, but contrary to some detractors of Cárdenas, who tried to represent this Revolutionary as a Communist, his economic policies harmed few Mexican industrialists: Garza Sada–G. Sada, Salinas y Rocha, Bailleres, Trouyet, Ruiz Galindo, and others survived and in most cases expanded their industries, while dozens of large and hundreds of medium-size industries of the 1960's date their origin to the Cárdenas epoch. Cárdenas opposed traditional foreign capital shackling Mexico's basic industries, but he did not oppose Mexican industrialists manufacturing for the domestic market or foreign capital of nontraditional types.

Lack of competition from foreign goods, in Mexico as well as in certain accessible markets abroad, stimulated industrial output during World War II. Between 1940 and 1945, industrial output registered increases of 9.4 per cent a year, largely through intensive use of equipment on hand before 1939, while exports of Mexican manufactured goods rose from 1.7 per cent to 6 per cent of total manufacturing production. Outstanding among the new industrialists appearing on the scene were the Swedish exile Axel Wenner-Gren and Antonio Sacristán, a Spanish refugee banker, who with his colleagues formed the financial complex, Sociedad Mexicana de Crédito Industrial, which by 1962 owned more than eighty businesses. War's end also ended the artificial economic world into which Mexican manufacturers had been selling: Foreign producers began satisfying their own domestic needs and recapturing their traditional foreign markets; they also discovered that entering the Mexican market had become easier than before the war, because Mexico's tariff wall had in effect been lowered by reliance on specific duties rather than self-adjusting ad valorem tariffs. Structural bottlenecks within the Mexican economy, such as shortages of materials, electric power, fuel oil, and transportation media, further impeded production.

Since 1945, industry has received high priority in Mexican economic development. The loss of foreign markets, new competition from abroad, and the over-all adverse impact of internal and external factors in the immediate postwar years prompted President Alemán to elevate tariffs, apply import controls, devaluate the peso, improve public services, and introduce other ameliorative devices designed to raise industrial output. By 1948, the industrial pace had stepped up somewhat, registering an 8 per cent increase over 1947; the following years of Alemán's administration were equally good ones for manufacturing, with the volume of industrial output rising 9 per cent in 1949, 14 per cent in 1950, and 18.6 per cent in 1951. In six years of Alemanism, steel production doubled, sulfuric acid output quadrupled, and manufacture of numerous products, including gas stoves, electric washing machines, and refrigerators, was undertaken for the first time in Mexico. At the end of 1952, the index of industrial production by 1945 volumes stood at 131.6 and that of manufacturing industries alone at 126.3 (see accompanying chart).

Contrary to exaggerated popular versions of what Alemán accomplished, industrialization received equal and in some instances greater impetus from Ruiz Cortines. The latter's achievements loom mightily when we recall that he confronted a serious economic crisis in his first year of rule: The end of the Korean War, coupled with Alemán's financial capers, made 1953 a sad year for industrial progress. According to Bank of Mexico indices, over-all industrial output, crude-oil extraction, construction, mining in general, and industrial metal ore, gold, and silver production all experienced absolute declines in 1953, while manufacturing barely managed to equal its 1952 performance. Ruiz Cortines refused to halt industrialization; he economized, devaluated the currency, and punished overt pilfering of public funds. Older industries, like cotton textile manufacturing, were modernized; basic industries were greatly expanded; new industries, among them railroad boxcar construction, TV assembly, and chemical and pharmaceutical manufacture, were established. Between the end of 1952 and beginning of 1959, output of steel and fertilizers more than doubled, caustic soda production tripled, electric generation went up 70 per cent, production of crude oil and petroleum derivatives increased 77 per cent, and manufacturing output as a whole rose 48 per cent. Tens of

INDEX OF INDUSTRIAL PRODUCTION IN MEXICO
(measured by physical volume)

I. BANK OF MEXICO ESTIMATIONS (BASE INDEX OF 1945) [a]

Year	General Index	Electric Generation	Petroleum			Minerals & Metallurgy			Construction	Manufacturing
			Extraction	Refining	Average	Gold, Silver	Ind. Metals	Total		
1945	100.0	100.0	100.0	100.0	100.0	100.0	100.0	100.0	100.0	100.0
1946	100.1	108.1	113.1	109.3	110.0	71.2	75.7	73.8	113.2	102.0
1947	103.2	117.3	129.2	128.9	129.0	85.8	100.3	94.2	93.2	103.0
1948	106.1	129.3	134.4	128.3	129.4	78.3	88.8	84.5	104.9	107.1
1949	111.3	141.1	139.8	141.3	141.0	73.8	90.5	84.9	126.7	111.0
1950	122.7	144.2	166.4	150.5	153.5	76.0	104.2	92.4	154.2	121.4
1951	130.1	160.0	177.5	167.5	169.4	69.9	100.9	87.8	172.6	128.7
1952	131.6	173.9	177.5	185.6	184.1	80.8	104.5	94.5	189.3	126.3
1953	131.4	185.9	166.3	199.3	193.1	79.3	100.3	91.4	177.7	126.6
1954	140.2	204.7	192.1	206.3	203.6	65.6	96.9	83.7	186.8	137.7
1955	155.8	228.2	205.3	241.5	234.7	73.1	103.3	90.6	205.9	152.9
1956	171.3	255.1	208.7	269.1	257.8	71.0	114.5	98.0	231.5	167.9
1957	183.6	275.5	204.4	304.1	285.2	75.5	118.1	101.7	259.7	178.5
1958	192.1	296.5	223.1	350.3	326.1	75.2	111.8	97.3	255.4	187.1
1959	207.1	318.6	234.1	414.7	380.2	70.0	115.0	98.1	266.6	200.9
1960	224.7	349.7	241.1	443.9	405.0	69.8	119.5	101.1	300.4	218.6

II. NACIONAL FINANCIERA ESTIMATIONS (BASE INDEX OF 1950)

	1950	1951	1952	1953	1954	1955	1956	1957	1958	1959	1960
General Index	100.0	109.2	118.1	117.3	123.7	138.3	153.8	168.9	181.2	193.5	214.2
Mining	100.0	93.7	103.8	101.4	95.5	104.3	115.0	108.9	108.6	108.1	110.7
Precious metals	100.0	91.1	105.2	103.4	85.1	96.5	93.7	93.0	93.0	87.1	87.0
Industrial metals	100.0	95.2	103.4	100.9	98.4	106.5	120.8	113.2	112.7	114.0	117.4
Petroleum	100.0	112.6	124.1	133.4	136.5	158.2	174.8	200.0	218.4	257.9	286.5
Crude	100.0	106.7	106.7	100.0	115.5	123.4	127.1	135.0	155.0	165.6	170.4
Derivatives	100.0	113.3	126.3	137.8	139.2	162.7	180.8	209.4	226.0	271.8	319.9
Construction	100.0	110.7	118.2	120.5	127.2	150.3	168.3	181.5	179.9	190.2	222.5
Manufacturing	100.0	111.0	119.4	116.8	125.4	138.4	152.4	171.7	181.7	195.7	213.5
Consumer goods	100.0	107.6	116.4	112.3	116.9	123.1	132.1	143.6	153.1	159.8	179.2
Producer goods	100.0	116.5	124.2	123.8	138.8	162.2	187.2	215.5	224.0	252.2	260.9

[a] By revision of its measurements, Bank of Mexico estimations now indicate that growth in manufacturing, hence the general index as well, was underestimated in the 1950's.

thousands of new small industries cropped up, and a few new big industrialists, like Bruno Pagliai in seamless pipe and Julio Serrano in the
cement and maritime industries, joined the upper elite of Mexican businessmen.

López Mateos emphasized higher output in basic industries and the
establishment of a petrochemical industry. When a steel mill fell behind
expectations, the state took it over, and when private electric-power companies began slowing up, he expropriated virtually the entire industry. He
followed the example of his predecessor in pushing rehabilitation of the
railroads, farm mechanization, intensive use of fertilizers and insecticides,
construction of new plants to eliminate imports of manufactured goods,
and installation of ever-greater capacity in basic industries owned by the
state. Though troubled by a lowering in the private investment rate, an
adversity partly offset by heavier public expenditure, the industrial sector
registered impressive production gains in 1959 and 1960: Increases in
crude oil and petroleum derivatives were 17 per cent and 6.5 per cent
annually; refined sugar, 13 per cent and 18.5 per cent; fertilizers, 23 per
cent and 38 per cent; cement, 6 per cent and 17 per cent; electric-energy
generation, 7 per cent and 10 per cent; steel, 19 per cent and 16 per cent;
and manufacturing in general, 7 per cent and 9 per cent.

National income increased only 3.5 per cent in 1961, barely surpass-
ing population growth. To raise this percentage, accelerate private investment, meet critics of increasing state ownership, and fulfill a host of
additional purposes, the presidential office made public on May 10, 1962,
a list of five hundred new industries in which the Mexican government
desired private capital participation. Called "Plan, 1962–1965," it asserted
that needed investment in these new industries amounted to almost 1.6
billion dollars. It called for plants to function in iron and steel, chemical,
electrical products, food processing, and a multitude of other industries.
The state promised new investors special help in the form of credit facilities, tax concessions, and reduction of red tape. Full implementation of
"Plan, 1962–1965," according to presidential office calculations, would
create an estimated 300,000 new jobs, eliminate many imports, expand
production in many existing factories, and generally increase output. National income rose 4.8 per cent in 1962 and 1963.

In contrast to most countries of Latin America and, for that matter,
of the entire underdeveloped world, Mexico possesses relatively abundant
resources of industrial raw materials. Her power resources are good. Although her coal is neither of highest industrial qualities nor always conveniently located, it is good enough and found in relatively extensive
reserves. Oil and natural-gas resources are sufficiently high to satisfy Mexican demands for many decades, and Pemex is keeping abreast of growing
industrial fuel-oil and natural-gas consumption by laying new pipelines
from its fields on the Gulf coast and in Tabasco. Furthermore, potential

hydroelectric capacity is higher than present electric-power generation suggests. For specific branches of industry, Mexico possesses iron ore, copper, manganese, mercury, gold, silver, lead, zinc, other nonferrous minerals, timber, hard fibers, cotton, seafood, farm animals, natural resins and oils, and innumerable nonmetallic minerals. Mexico's only serious lacks in major raw materials needed for completing a preatomic industrial society are bauxite and natural rubber, and need for the latter can be discounted as soon as the synthetic-rubber manufacturing plant now under construction eliminates heavy imports of raw rubber and new rubber trees planted in southeastern Mexico begin producing. Bauxite for the new joint U.S.–Mexican private venture aluminum plant, however, will be imported. Mexico is indeed fortunate in possessing extensive reserves of industrial minerals, especially of coal, iron ore, and oil, the big three of modern industry.

Mexico also displays other elements required for industrial productivity. There is a sizable labor force, a sufficiently growing stockpile of managerial and technical personnel, a steadily modernizing national transportation and communications network, and a juxtaposition of raw materials, labor, and markets. There is also political stability. Mexican industry really lacks only two major factors: abundant investment capital and widening markets. The forced-savings policy of the Mexican government has brought about remarkable accomplishments in capital formation, but greater investment is needed in order to keep the industrial revolution rolling forward. The state believes that savings may be obtained by further depressing labor's share of output; however, industrialists can expand only to the point where they can continue selling their goods, and then they must await new customers, who in the case of Mexico will appear no sooner than wage levels permit. Thus we return to the critical question in Mexican industrialization and general economic development: Should real wages be raised now, even at the expense of short-run capital accumulation, or kept relatively low in order to underwrite new productive capacity, conspicuous consumption for the few, and modest but satisfactory living levels for about 20 per cent of the population? Presidents Alemán, Ruiz Cortines, and López Mateos preferred the second alternative. This continuing emphasis on higher productive capacity suggests that we should examine what is happening in specific branches of industry.

PETROLEUM INDUSTRY

Petroleum is a precious national resource. It represents such an indispensable element of economic independence that the Constitution itself states that "the direct dominium over petroleum and all solid, liquid, or gaseous hydrocarbons resides in the nation." Every year on March 18, in commemoration of the day in 1938 when President Cárdenas expropriated the oil industry, the nation patriotically celebrates Petroleum Day. Until expropriation, the Mexican petroleum industry concentrated on exportation and probably exercised a relatively negative influence on over-all Mexican domestic growth. The average Mexican knew little about the immediate issues at stake in the 1938 dispute (which were identified in Chapter 4), but he did know that the oil industry was owned by foreigners —perhaps not conventional Spaniards, yet indisputably foreigners—and this fact alone put him on the side of his righteous, unyielding, and stubborn president, who demanded that the great "international imperialists" abide by Mexican laws. To all intents and purposes, Cárdenas, like presidents past and present, was the law, and to challenge him was to challenge the law. Traditional foreign capital died that March day of 1938, giving birth to a new type of foreign capital with healthier attitudes and different expectations about Mexican investment and to a new faith and confidence among Mexican entrepreneurs, who saw in this expropriation an unequivocal expression of Mexicanism.

Expropriation converted the government into the third party to exploit Mexico's black gold. Prior to state management, oil was exploited by individual foreign adventurers who had founded independent companies and, later, by the giant international oil corporations. Decisive among the individual developers were two foreigners who originally left their homelands to work on the Mexican railroads. One adventurer, the American Edward L. Doheny, exploited private lands in the Tamaulipas-Veracruz zone, bringing in his first well in 1901 near Tampico; Doheny organized his operations into the Huasteca Petroleum Company. The other, Weetman D. Pearson, an Englishman subsequently endowed by the British Crown with the title of Lord Cowdray, concentrated his operations on federally owned lands, primarily in the Tehuantepec region, where under the organizational framework of his Eagle Petroleum Company (Compañía Mexicana de Petróleo El Águila), he brought in his first well in 1906. Between 1901 and 1921, the latter date representing an all-time high in oil production that elevated Mexico to the rank of number-two oil producer in the world, there was only one year, 1909, when production failed to rise over the preceding year.

As phase one in the exploitation of Mexican oil ended—dramatized by sales of Pearson's "El Águila" to Royal Dutch in 1923 and of Doheny's interests to Standard Oil of Indiana in 1925, plus the entrance of other foreign oil concerns—the progressive annual increases in output also ended. From 1922 to 1932, output declined year after year. Though tougher governmental policies, world depression, and the appearance of heavy saline deposits in a few major fields indubitably affected production adversely, there is probably some truth in Mexican claims that the new owners favored exploitation of Venezuelan and United States reserves at the expense of Mexican petroleum. On the other hand, it was a large private corporation that discovered and opened the famous Poza Rica fields in 1933. When a balance sheet of the oil industry was drawn up by Mexican economists for 1901–38, it indicated that foreigners had derived profits ten times greater than their investment. Dying hard, the giant oil companies conducted a propaganda campaign that aggravated the alarming flight of capital from Mexico during 1938, 1939, and 1940. Nonetheless, over the years the Mexican government made good its promises to recompense the private companies according to agreements reached with them— Sinclair in 1940, the rest of the U.S. companies in 1942, and English companies in 1947—and, aside from the foreign private concerns that are licensed to conduct limited activities on behalf of the state agency supervising petroleum, the state has tenaciously prohibited foreign influence from entering its oil industry.

Since June 7, 1938, the petroleum industry has been under the direct supervision of the autonomous governmental dependency popularly known as Pemex (an abbreviation for Petróleos Mexicanos). The new agency's responsibilities were crystallized in a constitutional amendment of 1940, which asserted that petroleum not only belonged exclusively to the state, but that the state alone could carry on exploitation. Lacking markets and finance, Pemex found the initial years following expropriation difficult ones indeed. President Alemán attempted to place the industry on a businesslike basis, appointing the competent Antonio Bermúdez as director-general of Pemex. But the excesses of labor, uncontrolled graft, price subsidies, and efforts to supply distant points of the nation with fuel oil and gasoline at the same relatively low prices charged in Mexico City, prevented much progress. Reappointed by Ruiz Cortines for another six-year term, Bermúdez overcame countless obstacles in raising output to levels unknown since the 1920's.

Accompanying López Mateos into office on December 1, 1958, was a new director-general for Pemex, Pascual Gutiérrez Roldán, a government finance expert who came to his new post from the state-owned steel company, Altos Hornos de México. Announcing that the moment had arrived for Pemex to gear prices to production costs and pay its own way, Gutiérrez Roldán raised gasoline prices, removed the cheapest quality gasoline from the market, reshuffled petroleum zone managers, pushed construction of gas and oil pipelines and new refineries, accelerated exploration, and pushed the annual production of crude oil to over 100 million barrels (of 159 liters each). Ending speculation on whether private business would be permitted to own, construct, or manage urgently needed petrochemical industries, the new director-general announced in 1959 that Pemex itself was initiating the construction of eighteen projected plants. First on the construction list of Pemex plants were dodecilbenzene, anhydrous ammonia (plants to be built in Salamanca, Guanajuato, and in Minatitlán, state of Veracruz), extraction of aromatics (Minatitlán), polyethylene (Azcapotzalco, state of México), and a detergent, butadiene, styrene, artificial rubber, and tetraethyl lead complex (Ciudad Madero, state of Tamaulipas). Expenditures of Pemex in 1962 amounted to a record $652,250,000, yet high as this figure may appear, Pemex managed to show a profit, repeating its performance of 1960 and 1961—which had represented the first time that this state-owned industry had shown a profit.

Are the shortcomings of the petroleum industry due to government ownership? Perhaps. Evaluating Pemex is impossible without understanding that it is part and parcel of Mexican economic development, that the presidential office determines the pace of growth in the oil industry by allotment of expenditures, and that the state cannot jeopardize its program of "balanced economic growth" by ignoring other sectors of the economy in favor of Pemex. Considering the political economy climate, the traditional habits of international oil cartels, and the huge financing necessary for oil exploitation, Pemex appears to be keeping pace with Mexican economic development. The majority of present oil production comes from wells discovered since 1938, no mean feat when we consider that private companies had dug some of Mexico's finest wells.

Under Pemex direction, the oil industry has become an integral part of the Mexican economy. Unlike the international oil companies in Mexico before 1938, Pemex cannot think in simple terms of digging wells, transporting crude to seaports, and exporting it. Growing demands of automobiles, trucks, factories, asphalt roads, thermoelectric generators, fertilizer plants, and homes and office buildings require continuous raising of the ratio of refined to crude oil. Pemex is satisfying these domestic needs and simultaneously, through exploitation of gas reserves and sales of crude, making about 20 per cent of its total sales to foreign customers. An importer of natural gas in 1938, Mexico has become an exporter today. Gaslines now connect the Ciudad Pemex fields in Tabasco with Mexico City and Salamanca, and the Gulf fields with Monterrey; the Monterrey line now reaches Torreón, and a new line stretching along the entire northern border will provide border cities of Mexico and the United States with natural gas coming from Gulf fields. Since 1938, Pemex has more than tripled refining capacity, quintupled proven oil reserves, and quadrupled the length of oil lines.

Oil production rose at a yearly average of 13 per cent between 1938 and 1960, amounting to an over-all 280 per cent growth despite four years (1941, 1942, 1953, and 1957) when production suffered absolute declines. By mid-1963, average daily production reached 335,000 barrels. A look at crude-oil production figures for selected years illustrates the four phases through which the industry has passed: steady growth to 1921, persistent decline to 1932, uneven growth to 1957, and regular growth to the present.

Once private ownership of the petroleum industry ended, the state determined the manner in which gasoline, oil, and natural gas were to

OIL PRODUCTION [a]

1901	10,345	1938	38,818,213
1910	3,932,900	1940	44,448,191
1911	12,552,798	1941	43,385,822
1915	32,910,508	1942	35,148,633
1920	157,514,700	1945	43,877,430
1921	193,397,587	1950	73,881,478
1922	182,278,457	1955	91,370,125
1925	115,514,700	1957	92,197,297
1926	90,420,973	1958	100,641,404
1930	39,529,901	1959	105,758,471
1932	32,805,496	1960	108,810,569
1933	34,000,830	1961	116,400,000
1937	46,906,650		

[a] The figures indicate production of 159-liter barrels.

reach the Mexican public. Remembering that expropriation of the oil industry was intended to remove private ownership from this vital lifeline to economic modernity, there is room to question present distribution patterns. First of all, Pemex products are frequently transported by private trucking concerns, usually the property of politicians. Second, when Pemex decided that filling stations should remain "private," attractive locations were acquired by a few Revolutionary opportunists—and absence of competition converted a filling station into an absolute monopoly of given location. Third, distribution of natural gas finds several companies ostensibly "competing" to service households and office buildings, yet all companies somehow arrange to make sizable fortunes. Furthermore, in the case of the few petrochemical plants left to "private" hands, politicians are conspicuous in ownership. A neglected lesson of the Mexican oil expropriation, therefore, is that politicians, not responsible local businessmen, took the place of previously responsible foreign entrepreneurs wherever and whenever possible.

STEEL INDUSTRY

Mexico's (and Latin America's) modern steel industry began on February 7, 1903, when the Fundidora de Fierro y Acero de Monterrey mill succeeded in producing cast iron by the coking process. Promoted, partly owned, and managed by Señor Prieto, a Spanish immigrant who founded the company in 1900, Fundidora continued for almost half a century to be Latin America's largest integrated manufacturer producing iron ore to finished steel products. The second blast furnace in Latin America, one of 600 metric tons capacity, was also installed by the Fundidora Mill in 1943 to supplement its existent 350-ton furnace. This was followed successively by installing a 600-metric-ton furnace for Altos Hornos de México in Monclova, Coahuila, which began operating in 1944, and by inauguration the following year of the Volta Redonda works in Brazil. Aside from Mexico and Brazil, other Latin American nations could not boast of an integrated steel mill until the 1950's—Chile in 1951, Colombia in 1955, Peru in 1957, and Argentina in 1960. Of course, in the meantime there had come into being both in Mexico and elsewhere in Latin America many foundries using scrap, as well as numerous mills employing electric furnaces. In Mexico, this type of steelmaking was evident in such enterprises as the La Consolidada company with installations at Piedras Negras (Coahuila), Lechería (state of México), and Mexico City; the National Artillery Foundry, which began producing steel in 1919; and the Tezuitlán Copper, Hojalata y Lámina, Fundidora de Aceros Tepeyac, Tubos de Acero de México, Aceros Ecatepec, Laminadora Kreimerman, Siderúrgica de Monterrey, and many smaller manufacturers. In 1960, the installed capacity of the steel industry had reached 1,916,000 tons, of which over 70 per cent lodged in the Big Four of Mexican steel: Altos Hornos (600,000 tons), Fundidora (450,000 tons), Hojalata y Lámina (280,000 tons), and La Consolidada (168,000 tons). The latter company has been absorbed by Altos Hornos.

The following estimates on metric tons of steel production, net importation of steel (that is, the difference between imports and exports), and apparent consumption of steel (production plus net importation during a given year) indicate that Mexican production falls short of consumption, while imports of steel, much of it specialty steel, constitute a big item in the over-all satisfaction of demand.

PRODUCTION, NET IMPORTATION, AND APPARENT CONSUMPTION OF STEEL

	Production	Net Importation	Apparent Consumption
1940	149,414	152,353	301,767
1945	229,993	350,219	580,212
1950	390,993	397,651	788,007
1955	725,350	413,574	1,138,924
1960	1,539,537	386,700	1,926,237

Low efficiency, which in some years saw the ratio of output to installed capacity fall to 50 per cent, partly explains the need for imports. In 1960, output achieved the high level of about 80 per cent of capacity, yet certain imports were unavoidable because many specialty steels indispensable for economic development were too costly to produce in Mexico. In addition to normal swings of the business cycle, the steel industry has been subject to a cyclical pattern of decreasing consumption coinciding every six years with changes in the political administration of Mexico. The downward swing appeared earlier than usual in the 1958–64 period, with steel ingot production of 1,603,671 metric tons somewhat below the

1,611,955 of the previous year. The state is a large purchaser of steel, and the last year of one regime and the first of the next invariably reflect insecurity, relatively unsound fiscal policies, and hence, lower purchases.

But shortcomings should not obscure remarkable achievements. Steel production was 2.6 times higher in 1950 than a decade earlier, and almost 4 times higher in 1960 than at midcentury. Calculated in another way, steel output in 1960 was 10 times higher than steel production in 1940. Between 1950 and 1958, the average annual growth of steel output in Mexico was 14 per cent, perceptibly above that in such steel-producing centers as the U.S.S.R. (8.9 per cent), West Germany (8.4 per cent), and France (6.2 per cent). Furthermore, the proportion of steel consumption covered by imports declined from 55.3 per cent and 55.5 per cent in the periods 1940–44 and 1945–49 to 31.1 per cent in 1955–59 and to only about 20 per cent in 1960. And for the entire 1945–59 period, the index of growth of the steel industry (578.2) was higher than that of general manufacturing (200.9), construction (266.6), and electric energy (318.6). Meanwhile, per capita consumption rose from about 32.7 kilograms in 1950 to nearly 56 kilograms a decade later.

In recent years, the state has become the major promoter of the steel industry. Aside from owning majority equity in the largest and third-largest companies, Altos Hornos de México and La Consolidada, which in early 1962 were integrated into one complex bearing the name of the former, the government has extended generous financial assistance to numerous privately owned steel-producing and steel-elaboration concerns. Nacional Financiera has guaranteed repayment of big loans on steelmaking equipment, and the Bank of Mexico has provided invaluable technical assistance. The private sector of the industry has profited from tax concessions. And in laying new pipelines, gaslines, and railroad tracks, in building bridges and public buildings, and in financing public construction in general, the government has become the largest single steel consumer in Mexico. The government is hoping that the steel industry will reach output levels that will permit exports of crude steel, but unless the ratio of output to installed capacity goes up to unprecedented heights, the aspiration of the government on this point is surprisingly unrealistic. Government projections indicate the following company-by-company picture of installed capacity should appear in 1966:

Company	1966 Capacity in Metric Tons
Altos Hornos de México	1,430,000
Fundidora de Fierro y Acero de Monterrey	1,000,000
Hojalata y Lámina	700,000
Tubos de Acero de México	250,000
Aceros Nacionales	135,000
Others	360,000
Estimated total installed capacity in 1966	3,875,000

To accomplish this will require investment of millions of additional dollars, which in turn will depend on the general health of the economy and on Mexico's ability to acquire foreign financing for a large part of the new equipment required.

In order to fulfill what Mexico desires in the steel industry, higher production must come primarily from mills producing steel with iron ore. To plan to reduce steel imports by importing great quantities of scrap hardly represents the kind of financial solution that prompted domestic production in the first place. Fortunately, Mexico possesses sufficient reserves of iron ore, coal, fluorspar, natural gas, oil, manganese, and limestone, the principal raw materials used in making steel. Reserves of iron ore exist in twenty states of the republic and are estimated to be in excess of 500 million metric tons, of which the majority is probably ores containing 60 per cent iron. The positive reserves of four locations—El Mamey (Colima), Cerro de Mercado (Durango), Las Truchas (Michoacán), and La Perla (Chihuahua)—alone amount to more than 200 million tons. By 1960, Mexican mills were consuming over one million tons of iron ore annually. Positive reserves of coal in the Sabinas fields of Coahuila, Nuevo León, and Tamaulipas, the major coal field of Mexico, amounted to over two billion tons, which when added to probable and possible reserves, raise the estimate of coal in this one field alone to thirteen billion tons. Other coal reserves are distributed around the nation. Supplying the steel industry with increasingly higher quantities of domestic manganese, fluorspar, natural gas, and petroleum raises no particular obstacles. This is equally true of firebrick, inasmuch as Mexican producers are already satisfying 90 per cent of the steel industry's requirements on this item. The three major resource problems are (1) the unfavorable composition of most coal, (2) low coke production, and (3) the heavy reliance on imports of scrap iron. The government is attempting to resolve the first two problems by raising output and improving technical processes in two state-owned companies, Carbonífera de Sabinas and Mexicana de Coque y Derivados. Reducing imports of scrap, which since 1955 have been increasing markedly, depends, as previously noted, on reducing production of steel from scrap while simultaneously raising the proportion of steel made from iron ore.

ELECTRIC POWER

Private enterprise monopolized electric-power generation in Mexico from the late 1800's until the 1930's. The first electric-power plants were installed by mining companies and by textile, paper, jute, flour, and sugar mills for purposes of generating enough electricity for their own particular needs and selling excess power to others. In 1889, the Batopilas mining company introduced the first electric-generating plant for treating motors.

In 1892, San Rafael installed its own electric plant for making pulp and paper. In 1897, the CIDOSA textile complex put in its first electric-generating plant. While a Mexican group had formed the first electric-utility company in 1881 for providing a limited section of Mexico City with street lighting, it was the French, German, English, and Belgians who truly promoted generation for public sales. After the Belgian-dominated Mexican Light and Power Company opened its Necaxa plant and dropped prevailing electricity rates 50 per cent, it succeeded in forcing other companies serving Mexico City to sell out. The Belgian company then convinced the Mexican government to grant it the exclusive right to service Mexico City for the 1906–26 period. As Mex-Light contracts were drawing to a close in 1926, the government was considering the idea of public ownership of the electric-power industry, but decided to abandon the scheme. Nonetheless, in January, 1934, the government went on record in favor of the creation of a federally owned electricity commission to generate and distribute electricity, since "private companies had failed, refused, or otherwise proven incapable to keep pace with the growth of Mexico." This action was followed by an amendment of the Constitution empowering the government to legislate on the electric industry. Private monopoly ended definitively in 1937 with the creation of the Federal Electricity Commission, and limitations on foreign owner-ship became explicit the following year when a new Electricity Law declared that henceforth "only Mexicans and Mexican companies may obtain concessions in the electric-power industry," although "foreigners already operating in the country will be allowed to continue and their concessions respected."

When the Federal Electricity Commission began generating and distributing electricity in the late 1930's, the state had assumed a perma-nent place in the electric-power field. FEC operations received a shot in the arm when the government purchased the Compañía Eléctrica Chapala in 1940, and from then forward expansion of state electric installations steadily reduced the proportion of total electric-power generating capacity in private hands. By the 1950's, the big Mex-Light and American & Foreign Power holdings had come under serious government fire. American & Foreign Power, a subsidiary of Electric Bond & Share, had entered Mexico in the 1920's and rapidly moved into electrification of provincial regions, becoming the number-two private utility in the whole industry; mean-while, Mex-Light, the largest electric-power company in Mexico, had continued to center its activities on Mexico City and nearby districts. As early as 1952, Mex-Light's chairman of the board proposed that the state "purchase the existing private systems at a fair price" and undertake their future development, but the Alemán and Ruiz Cortines administrations refused to take over the entire industry. President López Mateos, on the other hand, publicly announced in 1959 that nationalization of the electric-power industry would take place "within my six-year administration." True to his pledge, López Mateos nationalized both American & Foreign Power and Mex-Light properties, the first being transferred to the state on April 22, 1960, and the second on September 27, 1960. Then, in October, 1960, after picking up smaller private utilities, he modified article 27 of the Constitution to prohibit entrance of any newcomers into the electric industry. By 1964, the state owned more than 90 per cent of electric-generation capacity in Mexico.

The evolution of the electric-power industry illustrates the antipathy of Revolutionary regimes toward traditional-type foreign capital. The Constitution of Mexico unquestionably permitted state intervention and, ultimately, state ownership. Equally certain was a growing popular pressure on behalf of nationalization, aroused by persistent government–private company controversies on rate-setting. By the late 1950's, financial shortcomings, undervalued rate bases, regulatory lags, rate inadequacy, continuous invasions of private concessions by the Federal Electricity Commission, and other forces had combined in such fashion that it had become highly dubious whether private companies could have introduced ameliorative measures capable of warding off nationalization. Quite aside from legislation that steadily circumscribed their activities, private companies had been facing several irritating obstacles: State governments had refused to intercede in the consumer nonpayment strikes of the 1930's, which meant that private companies failed to collect many accounts; municipal and state governments as well as federal agencies frequently accrued huge debts for service bills, then coerced the power companies into granting rebates up to 50 per cent; and the National *Ejidal* Credit Bank was particularly notorious in not paying the electric bills of *ejidatarios*. These incidents point up the truth of private-company claims that, unduly beset by government chicanery in bill payment and political demagoguery in general, further large-scale investment seemed too insecure.

Greater growth took place in generation capacity, actual generation, and electricity consumption in the short span of 1957–60 than in the evolution of the electric-power industry during its first seventy years in Mexico. By 1948, almost seven decades after the electric-power industry entered Mexico, installed capacity stood at one million kilowatts. It climbed over the two-million mark eight years later and the four-million kilowatt level in 1963. López Mateos had set five million kilowatts as Mexico's goal before the end of 1964. Between 1934 and 1960, generation increased six times, with remarkable advances registered in the 1950's, when generation shot upward from 4.4 billion kilowatt hours in 1950 to 7 billion KWH in 1955, and to 10.7 billion KWH in 1960. Generation surpassed 12.4 billion KWH in 1962. Per capita consumption tripled between 1934 and 1960 and now exceeds 300 KWH yearly. The record shows that annual electric generation rose 7.5 per cent and consumption of electricity 7.9 per cent during the 25-year period preceding 1960, both figures somewhat below the 8.8 per cent growth in generation and 9.7 per cent increase in consumption achieved in 1960, the year of nationalization; nonetheless, the 1960 performances fell short of yearly averages for the 1950's. Industrialization requires increasingly higher investment in electric-power installations, a demand that the government hopes to satisfy in part by new loans from the World Bank, the Export-Import Bank, and other foreign lending agencies. By 1964, five entities—the Federal District, Puebla, Veracruz, Michoacán, and the state of México—were accounting for more than 50 per cent of Mexico's electric consumption, dramatizing the lack of rural electrification, which since 1937 has been the major responsibility of the Federal Electricity Commission.

An exciting hydroelectric project is under way on the Balsas River at the border of Michoacán and Guerrero, where the construction of a 500-foot dam will create an artificial lake some sixty miles in length. Scheduled for completion in 1964, the Little Hell (Infiernillo) project represents an investment of 640 million dollars, underwritten in part by loans from a large French bank to the Mexican government. When it is finished, the 600,000 kilowatts of electric energy generated annually by Little Hell will make it the largest single hydroelectric installation in all Latin America. The entire output is destined for Mexico City, whose consumption is increasing by 70,000 kilowatt hours per year. Other hydro-electric projects of considerable scope are being developed on the Pánuco River, the Tepalcatepec River, the Grijalva River, in the Papaloapan River valley, and at the Alemán system in the Bravo Valley region of the state of México.

CEMENT INDUSTRY

Conservation policies protecting Mexico's forests and the relatively high prices of steel, aluminum, and glass make the use of cement wide-spread and heavy. Often made of cement are such unexpected items as streetlight posts, telephone poles, highway guard posts, and "board" fences. How many American housewives have ever washed dishes or clothes in cement sinks or cement washbasins? This is a common occurrence in the homes of lower-class Mexicans. Besides employment in conventional con-struction—dams, bridges, public market places, military installations, ware-houses, hospitals, airfields, port facilities, highways, streets, sidewalks, foundations, columns, walls, and floors—cement is playing an increasingly greater role in the manufacture of tile and asbestos products, roofing materials, mosaics, water tanks, and bricks and building blocks. In the latter category alone—which includes pressed brick, common construction brick, refractory brick, drain pipes, flooring and roofing brick, light-weight blocks, hollow bricks, and refractory building blocks—production increased from 42.1 million bricks and blocks in 1955 to 122 million in 1959. As Mexico builds up and out, at the yearly rate of more than 10,000 new private construction projects in the Federal District alone, the heavy burden of supplying construction materials will fall on the cement industry.

Unlike many other basic economic activities in Mexico, such as electric power, petroleum, steel, transportation, and communications, the cement industry has escaped the ownership clutches of the state. Except for two cooperatives running three plants, three additional plants controlled by British capital, and financial assistance given by the government in the form of loans, the industry is owned, financed, and managed by Mexican private entrepreneurs. The reasons why control remains in private hands are found in the evolution, performance, and continuing promise of the industry under private auspices. This subject takes us back to the beginning of the twentieth century and to the pioneering efforts of the American businessman John Brittingham, who in 1906 succeeded in placing into operation the first rotating oven in a modest plant located in Hidalgo, Nuevo León. Later in the same year, the Englishmen Henry Gibbons and George Watson established the "Cruz Azul" cement plant in Jasso, Hidalgo. Near the Jasso site some Americans founded the "Tolteca" plant in 1909, but fearing the exigencies of civil war, they soon thereafter sold out to an English group. The decade 1910–20, an era of extreme political upheaval, was a sad one for the cement industry. Cementos Hidalgo suspended operations for the entire decade. Cruz Azul assumed such heavy losses that it passed into the receivership hands of Banco Nacional de México. And only by assuming heavy debts did Tolteca operate. The fact that the price of cement skyrocketed meant little, for ovens were poorly worked and civil war made collection of bills difficult or impossible. Total production during this first decade amounted to less than daily production today.

The following score of years comprise a period of moderate growth. Cementos Hidalgo renewed operations in 1921. La Tolteca and Cruz Azul expanded output. A new plant under the name of Cementos Landa was established in the city of Puebla by Ignacio and Germán Landa, but it early became the property of the wealthy resident American, William Jenkins. In 1925, Jenkins sold a substantial interest in the Puebla plant to Julio Lacaud and Carlos Trouyet, Mexico City financiers, who forthwith changed the company name to Cementos Atoyac. The Cementos Monterrey plant was also installed in the 1920's on a site near the city of Monterrey by Lorenzo Zambrano and other industrialists of that northern community. The decade of the 1930's gave birth to three additional cement plants. In 1930, investors led by Ignacio Soto set up the Cemento Portland Nacional plant in Hermosillo, Sonora, to satisfy the growing cement needs of the northwest zone. The following year, British investors behind Tolteca established a second plant, this time in Mexico

City under the name of Cemento de Mixcoac. A final plant founded in the 1930's was located in Apasco, state of México, by Gustavo Espinosa and Federico Cuéller and given the name of Compañía Mexicana de Cemento Portland Apasco. By the end of the Cárdenas regime, the capacity of the eight cement plants then operating was already proving inadequate for satisfying both private demand and heavy public needs in the construction of dams and other irrigation projects, roads, sewage systems, schools, hospitals, and public buildings.

When subsequent years saw demand further outstripping supply, new plants were born and existing companies expanded. The demand for cement, augmented by large public construction projects, rose to unprecedented heights during World War II. In 1943, Lacaud and Trouyet established another plant, this time in Estación Majonera, Jalisco, bearing the name of Cementos Guadalajara. These two entrepreneurs promoted yet a third cement plant, the Cementos Veracruz operation in Orizaba, state of Veracruz, which opened in 1945. That same year, Alfonso Rivas Bustamante was instrumental in establishing Cementos Moctezuma in Cuernavaca, Morelos; Cruz Azul, which had become a cooperative, added to its Jasso installation by founding a second plant at Lagunas, Oaxaca; and Julio Serrano and the Banco Nacional de México founded the Cementos Anáhuac plant in Tlalnepantla, just outside Mexico City. Despite the erection of these new plants and expansion in older plants, there was still a shortage of cement in Mexico.

To satisfy this progressively greater demand, nine new cement plants have appeared on the scene since World War II; a tenth is under construction, and several more are projected. In 1946, Ramón Salcido and the Banco Nacional de México founded Cementos del Pacífico in Mármol, Sinaloa. The following year gave birth to three new factories: Cementos del Norte in Monterrey, promoted by long-time industrialists of "Mexico's Pittsburgh"; Cementos Portland del Bajío in León, Guanajuato, set up by the financier Luis Montes de Oca; and Cementos de Chihuahua in Nombre de Dios, Chihuahua, owned by the Vallina banking interests. Of the six remaining plants, three are in the region immediately contiguous to the Valley of Mexico—Cementos Portland Blanco de México, founded in 1954 by Arcadio Hernández and Armando Ibáñez and situated in Vito, Hidalgo; a new Tolteca plant in Atotonilco, Hidalgo, bearing the corporate name of Cemento de Atotonilco, set up in 1961; and Cementos Hércules near Acatlán, Puebla, promoted by Pueblan quarry interests and placed in operation in late 1960, but still struggling in 1963 to solve serious production problems. The rest have been located in outlying sites: Cementos Maya in Mérida, Yucatán, set up in 1950 by José Saborit and Antonio Benavent; Cementos California in Ensenada, Baja California, established in 1958 by Joseph Clark and the Banco Nacional de México; and a final plant, under construction, Cementos del Sur in Acapulco, Guerrero, owned by German interests. Mention should also be made of the plans of two older companies to establish new plants: Cementos Atoyac is in the process of installing a new plant in Puebla, while Cementos Mexicanos presumably will install a second factory at Torreón, Coahuila. Finally, long-range projections include new plants for Los Mochis (Sonora), the city of Zacatecas, Macuspana (Tabasco), and Minatitlán (Veracruz).

What this impressive expansion means in terms of Mexican economic development is that the cement industry is keeping pace with over-all growth—indeed, even going ahead of it. Installed capacity and actual output have increased at phenomenal rates since the end of the war. Taking the 1945–60 period as a whole, that is to say, including the relatively low-output years accompanying transfer and consolidation of presidential power, cement production averaged yearly increases of 8 per cent. In tonnage figures, this meant expansion from 803,318 metric tons in 1945 to 3,086,126 metric tons in 1960. These figures also reflect a big victory for domestic producers in reducing imports to a negligible proportion of Mexican consumption—actually, to less than 1 per cent. Mexican cement producers, though hampered by higher overland transportation costs in comparison to foreigners shipping cement by ocean carriers, even captured markets in the "free zones" that are permitted to buy goods wherever they choose. In recent years, production, imports, exports, and apparent consumption (production plus imports minus exports in a given year), expressed in metric tons, have reached the following levels:

	Production	Importation	Exportation	Apparent Consumption
1940	485,000	10,647	948	494,699
1945	808,318	146,862	—	955,180
1950	1,387,544	29,453	21,325	1,395,672
1955	2,085,652	43,470	46,610	2,079,512
1956	2,276,660	62,830	9,513	2,329,977
1957	2,518,559	65,231	7,445	2,576,345
1958	2,495,848	42,105	6,500	2,531,453
1959	2,637,960	1,476	1,753	2,636,284
1960	3,086,126	1,680	3,539	3,084,267
1961	2,984,069	1,715	3,614	2,982,170
1962	3,266,407	2,420	13,104	3,255,723

This supreme effort in raising output is reflected in the favorable standing of the Mexican cement industry in comparison to per capita cement production of the highly industrialized United States. While per capita output in the U.S. by 1960 was 35 times higher than Mexico in steel, 33 times higher in paper, and 10 times higher in electric energy, it was only 4 times higher in cement. No other basic industrial activity in Mexico approximates the achievement of the cement industry on this score. In world-wide terms, Mexico produces about 1 per cent of total world output, making it fourth in the Western Hemisphere (behind the United States, Canada, and Brazil) and nineteenth in world rankings. Mexican cement production in 1962 reached almost 3.3 million metric tons.

Satisfying demand comprises only one of the major achievements of the cement industry. Competition has helped in raising quality, in leading to standardization, and in introducing a variety of types of cement. Mexico now produces nine major types of cement, four of which are considered basic types and the rest, semibasic. In the basic category are standard gray portland, white portland, puzolanic, and slag-ferrocement. In the semibasic category are high-early-strength portland, low-heat, masonry, hydraulic-pressure-resistant, and oil-well. Most of these cements are produced in negligible quantities, because more than 90 per cent of present cement consumption is satisfied by standard gray portland and puzolanic. Furthermore, the cement industry is making a notable contribution toward building provincial centers and creating meaningful regional economies by locating plants outside the Valley of Mexico and Monterrey areas. In an economy with such a limited market as Mexico now possesses, industrial decentralization and deconcentration carry mixed blessings. While they tend to raise production costs, bring into being marginal high-cost plants, and preclude the rise of "economy to scale" operations, decentralization and deconcentration also lighten population pressures, spread the effects of industrialization, and give impetus to the rise of new industrial and commercial centers. A cement plant installed in a provincial city means an industrial start, employment of labor, and new businesses. Of the 22 cement plants operating in Mexico, half are outside the densely populated central market zone composed of the Federal District, Guerrero, Hidalgo, the state of México, Morelos, Puebla, Tlaxcala, central Veracruz, northern and western Oaxaca, and the southern half of Querétaro and Michoacán. Half of present installed capacity and of the projected number of new plants is also outside this zone. All regions of Mexico have at least one cement plant.

The future of the cement industry looks brighter than that of the economy as a whole. While the exportation of cement to Central America, once an aspiration of Mexican producers, appears highly improbable in light of the new plants being established there, domestic consumption alone should keep the cement industry fully occupied. Projecting the 1946–60 period's average annual growth rate of 8 per cent, consumption should rise to 6,664,000 metric tons in 1970 and 9,762,000 in 1975. This means that cement consumption should double during the 1960's and quadruple by 1975. There is no apparent reason why cement producers cannot meet these demands. On the contrary, the biggest question mark in the cement industry is not whether the cement industry can keep up with economic growth, but rather whether development in general and the construction industry in particular will duplicate the first fifteen years of postwar performance. In this context, the cement industry is successfully challenging the government and other sectors of economic activity.

TEXTILE INDUSTRY

For decades, the textile industry occupied first place in industrial activity in terms of output value and number of employees. Continuously since 1535, when Spaniards established a cotton mill in Puebla, textile manufacturing has attracted private investors. The first "modern" textile factory, the "La Esperanza" mill, was established at Puebla in 1830; later in the century, textile production began to increase rapidly as the industry became integrated vertically, with the same capitalists controlling the business from the opening of the cotton bale to the retailing of the finished product. Between 1900 and 1926, the number of spindles and looms doubled, only to slow down in the 1927–58 period to a 40 per cent increase in spindles and 20 per cent in looms. From 1942 until 1951, Mexican textile exports steadily climbed, with as much as 25 per cent of total annual cotton textile production exported in a single year, and with some 60 countries buying Mexican textiles in 1951; by 1956, the number of foreign clients had dropped to thirty-three and the value of textile exports was almost one-third under 1951 levels, even though textile exports still amounted to 19.4 million dollars in 1956. Obsolescence in textile machinery, reflected in the fact that more than three-fourths of all looms used in 1942 had been installed before 1910, higher production costs, which doubled between 1940 and 1946 and kept climbing while prices plummeted, and competition from synthetic textiles and from advanced industrial nations that re-entered world markets after World War II were the major reasons for Mexico's eclipse in foreign markets. In the meantime, domestic sales of cotton went up from 238,000 bales in 1949–50 to 475,000 bales in 1959–60, about one-fourth of it directly entering the textile industry, while consumption of cotton textiles per capita declined. The invasion of artificial-fiber textiles, spearheaded from 1947 forward by Celanese Mexicana with rayon and other acetate-fiber production, by 1950 succeeded in having 9,286 looms dedicated exclusively to synthetic-fiber weaving. Adding together the entire textile production— in cottons, woolens, other natural fibers, and synthetics—volume and value of output has consistently increased since 1943.

The textile industry has suffered for many decades from two major shortcomings: obsolescence and excess installed productive capacity. One Mexican economist estimated that in 1950 less than 35 per cent of the looms being used in the textile industry were made after 1900. Everyone seems concerned with obsolescence, yet little is being said of the large-scale modernization that has been going on since Ruiz Cortines entered office, purportedly affecting 60 per cent of Mexico's textile machinery. Since 1952, and over the strenuous objections of organized textile workers, every big mill has undertaken plant modernization—Atoyac Textile (founded in 1870 in Oaxaca and moved in 1921 to Puebla), CIDOSA (founded in 1888 in the Orizaba region of Veracruz), Cía. Industrial Veracruzana (founded in 1896 in Tlaxcala), Textiles La Carolina y Reforma (founded as separate mills in Guanajuato and Mexico City in 1908 and 1935), Cía. Industrial de Parras (founded in 1899 in Coahuila), Cía. Industrial de Atentique (founded in 1941 in Jalisco), Textiles Morelos (founded in 1944 in Cuernavaca), Ayotla Textil (founded in 1946 in the state of México), Hilados de México (founded in 1946 in Mexico City), and Zahuapan (founded in 1953 in Tlaxcala). Two wool washing and combing centers in Mexico City also have modernized their installations.

A census of the entire textile industry would probably reveal that much textile machinery is outmoded, but that this factor is less disruptive than the existence of too much textile machinery. Not until 1950 did the Mexican government step in to restrict imports of textile machinery. By 1956, Mexico had 753 wool textile establishments, 300 cotton textile mills, and hundreds of additional concerns elaborating synthetic and other fibers. The same pattern prevails in much raw material supply, in the sense that supplies of raw cotton and certain hard fiber, no less than synthetic fiber, exceed domestic consumption requirements. Shortages of long-staple cotton and raw wool, on the other hand, are made up by imports. In the case of wool, this comprises a growing balance-of-trade deficit item, since wool imports more than doubled in the 1950's and in the single year 1959 climbed 33 per cent in volume and 12 per cent in value over the preceding year.

Another problem involves cotton-mill location. The availability of cheaper labor and proximity to markets are still placed above proximity to cotton fields. The result is a concentration of textile mills in a few centers. In 1960, 77 per cent of cotton textile output came from four centers— Puebla (30 per cent), the Valley of Mexico region (25 per cent), the Orizaba region (16 per cent), and Guadalajara (6 per cent)—all distant from the cotton-raising districts in the north, which produced more than 90 per cent of the nation's cotton. Synthetic and wool textile mills are also heavily concentrated in the Federal District and Puebla regions.

To recapitulate, Mexico's textile industry is changing from an antiquated, unprogressive, and inefficient industry to a modern, progressive, and fairly efficient industry, overcoming labor featherbedding, obsolescence, and raw-material problems (except for quality wools and long-staple cotton), but doing little to decentralize textile-plant location.

PAPER AND PULP INDUSTRY

Further investment is sorely needed in the paper and pulp industry, despite continuous increments in productivity that raised paper capacity to more than a half-million metric tons by 1963. Since World War II, achievements in the paper industry have been impressive: (1) Over-all paper and paperboard output more than doubled in the 1950's, registering a 10.4 per cent yearly average increase during 1955–59 and 16.9 per cent in 1960 alone; (2) utilization of domestic raw materials in pulp manufacturing has intensified, as consumption of wood is slowly giving way to straw, bagasse of sugar cane and bananas, and wastepaper; straw and bagasse of sugar cane show highest proportionate gains and now constitute 25 per cent of all raw materials used in making pulp; (3) pulp made by chemical processes has also risen and at present is accounting for about one-half of national pulp output; (4) new paper mills have been opened, as the total number of Mexico's paper mills grew from 25 in 1952 to 45 in 1962, and older factories were busy modernizing technical phases of production and installing new machinery; and (5) the varieties of papers produced rose steadily, reaching over 400 by 1963, which in effect means that importation of specific paper types has been eliminated. Nonetheless, imports of finished papers accounted for 34 per cent of Mexican national paper consumption in 1960, largely consisting of newsprint and photographic and other special-finish papers, while importation of raw materials used in paper manufacture, though declining markedly during the 1950's, remained uncomfortably high.

Mexico's paper mills are concentrated in the Federal District and state of México region, although notable productive capacity is found elsewhere in the republic. The two biggest paper companies, both of pre-Revolutionary vintage, San Rafael and Peña-Loreto, have two mills each; all four are located in the state of México and Federal District region. Empaques de Cartón Titán, the most important paper-box manufacturer in the nation, founded in 1936 by the Garza Sada financial group, has factories in Monterrey, Mexico City, and Guadalajara. The San Cristóbal plant, owned jointly by the Cusi family and Scott Paper Company and utilizing bagasse of sugar cane for making its pulp, is located in the state of México. The Cía. Industrial de Atentique plant, established by Nacional Financiera in 1941, is situated in Jalisco. Celulosa de Chihuahua, a joint promotion in the 1950's of Mexican private capitalists and Nacional Financiera, in which Kimberley-Clark recently assumed an equity position along with its older technical management contract, has its large mill on the deserts outside Chihuahua city. Finally, of the large mills, Fábricas de Papel Túxtepec, which is owned by Nacional Financiera and foreign interests and which began producing newsprint on a modest scale in 1958, has its installations in Oaxaca. Also worthy of mention are other plants located in the Federal District—Fábrica de Papel Coyoacán, "El Fénix," Kimberley-Clark, Negociación Papelera Mexicana, Kraft (Inc.), Papelera Iruña, Productora de Papel, and Cartonera Covadonga—as well as Papelera Poblana in Puebla, Cía. Veracruzana in Orizaba, and Papelera de Chihuahua in Chihuahua.

Achievements in pulp and paper production are uneven. The Mexican market prefers cheap paper of low quality; this need, especially for semi-kraft paper used in paper cartons and boxes, is being satisfied. The Mexican market does require higher output of good kraft papers used in making paper bags (any housewife buying fruits and vegetables at the market place can attest to the fact that paper bags regularly break apart) in spite of production statistics indicating that the paper industry is completely satisfying paper-bag requirements. Nor are domestic paper manufacturers meeting demands for good-quality writing paper, photographic paper, cigarette paper, and specialized kraft papers. Yet the import value of these products is negligible in comparison to the value of imports of cellulose pulp and newsprint. Wider utilization of bagasse of sugar cane, which normally is burned or left rotting at sugar mills, would reduce cellulose pulp imports substantially. Even now, the value of pulp imports is much below that of newsprint; nearly 90 per cent of Mexico's newsprint is imported, although newsprint production of the Túxtepec mill is increasing rapidly. Mexico no longer lacks capacity in its paper and pulp industry. It does require more efficient utilization of what exists in order to realize higher production levels and the manufacture of improved-quality papers. Hence, future investment should concentrate on technical improvements.

OTHER INDUSTRIES

The mining and metallurgical industry, besides what was observed earlier in relation to the steel industry, is keeping abreast of general industrial progress. Ownership is passing into Mexican hands, aided by a new mining law denying new mining concessions to non-Mexican–controlled concerns. The Mexican investment group of Raúl Bailleres and the government acquired 51 per cent of Peñoles, Mexico's second-largest mining-metallurgical company, from American Metal Climax, and the government has been buying up small mining properties in many regions. Copper production has been varying, in terms of "impure bars or blisters," between 55,000 and 65,000 metric tons annually, sufficiently high to permit Mexico to satisfy most of its domestic needs for electrolytic copper and copper conduit, wire, cable, and pipe. Refined lead and zinc manufactures are rising, as 30 per cent of Mexico's lead output now enters the domestic market; when the new Torreón refining plant is completed, Mexico will raise its zinc-refining capacity to 32 per cent of total zinc output. Production of copper, lead, and zinc today represents almost 54 per cent of total mining output. Gold and silver account for about 18 per cent by value of total mining production, with approximately three million troy ounces of silver being devoted to making silverware, jewelry, and silver products for industrial use. Other industrial minerals, whose combined value represents more than 15 per cent of mining production, are antimony, arsenic, bismuth, cadmium, coal, cobalt, graphite, manganese, mercury, molybdenum, selenium, tin, and tungsten. Among Mexico's important nonmetallic minerals, sulfur deserves special mention; production has exceeded a million metric tons every year since 1956, an output level amounting to from 10 per cent to 11 per cent of total mining output by value, excluding the pure sulfur recovered from gas and used principally in manufacturing fertilizers. Fluorite and barite now account for 3 per cent of total mining production by value.

A final note on a few other industries seems appropriate. During the 1950's, output of sulfuric acid almost quintupled, caustic soda output increased nearly ten times, and ammonium sulfate production rose 35 times. Some fertilizers, insecticides, and other petrochemicals were made in Mexico for the first time. Mexico also became a recognized world leader in the manufacture of hormones. Production of rayon-grade chlorine even exceeded domestic demand. The glass industry, although unsuccessful in discovering domestic sources of silicon sand to replace costly raw-material imports, has also been outproducing market needs. And electric-transformer output, reaching in excess of 100,000 units by 1960, had increased fiftyfold in one decade.

The consumer-goods industry is confronted by serious crises. Almost incredibly, in view of what little effort was dedicated to this industry two short decades ago, the consumer-goods industry needs several million additional paying customers. There is excessive production in virtually every line of package foodstuffs and beverages, articles for the home, and other consumer items. From giant factories, processing plants, bakeries, and breweries down to small "cottage industries," the number of establishments manufacturing consumer goods has mushroomed. Freely competitive capitalism (and, in some instances, monopolistic capitalism) characterizes the consumer-goods industry.[1] (Such freedom of action long since ceased in the producer-goods industry.) There are too many plants, too much productive capacity, and too many trade-marks on the Mexican market. Nationwide redistribution of income, which conceivably might occur in the form of a vast state distribution program, will alone save most small entrepreneurs from bankruptcy. The consumer-goods industry is therefore ahead of the rest of the economy, and waiting for the two to pull even is proving to be a costly affair.

Consumer-goods industries have brought mixed blessings. Tastes of

[1] See section on merchandising in Chapter 11.

the Mexican consumer are changing. Thirty years ago, probably 80 per cent of the people wore no footwear whatsoever; today, 17.2 per cent go barefoot, 22.6 per cent wear *huaraches* or sandals, and 60.2 per cent wear regular shoes. Radio is replacing the village orchestra; the gas stove is making cooking by charcoal and wood obsolete; beer is slowly relegating pulque to a secondary position; and soap, detergents, and to a limited degree, washing machines are lightening laundry chores. Unfortunately, several phenomena intervene to mar this colorful picture. Annual growth in the consumer-goods industry is slowing down. Corporate profits are lower, and companies are trying to squeeze each other out of business. Fourteen out of every fifteen Mexican families are without refrigerators, six out of seven without gas stoves, twenty-four out of twenty-five without washing machines. Moreover, the number of telephones and automobiles, a subject discussed in the next chapter, remains low. To make matters worse, more than 50 per cent of the television sets and refrigerators sold in Mexico are repossessed by creditors; carrying charges and interest on credit sales of household goods are rarely below 24 per cent. Prices on articles for the home and on canned foods are very high compared with prices in the United States: a small refrigerator costs $280 and an 18-inch television set, $240 (not including carrying and interest charges), while a standard-size can of peas costs 36 cents and of beans, 32 cents. At the opposite extreme, poor and rich alike can smoke "black" cigarettes for five cents per pack and drink a bottle of beer for six cents. The quality of consumer goods, though improving, still leaves much to be desired. As late as 1958, for example, the National Health Laboratory discovered that 24 per cent of all *pasteurized* milk sold in the Federal District was adulterated. The hard realities of the Mexican consumer market pose mighty obstacles for manufacturers of refrigerators, television sets, stoves, cosmetics, and canned goods. Having saturated the 15 per cent to 20 per cent of the population in a financial position to buy these goods, producers now must rely on their dealers to squeeze the impoverished masses into buying on long-term, virtually impossible terms. Two books of social anthropologist Oscar Lewis, *Five Families* and *The Children of Sánchez*, pinpoint this crisis dramatically.

CONCLUSIONS

In drawing together the strands of Mexican industrial progress, an observer is struck by both achievements and shortcomings. Raw materials and labor have been combined in such a way as to permit relatively rapid capital accumulation and increases in industrial output. Production from the industrial sector has risen at a substantially higher rate than other sectors of the Mexican economy. No insuperable problem, including the need for ever-greater investment capital, confronts the vitally important power industries. A class of responsible private entrepreneurs has come into being, as has a generally competent team of administrators handling the many state enterprises. And while industrial production has been rising, there has been less inflation in Mexico than in other large Latin American states that have undertaken industrialization. Industrialization has succeeded in transforming Mexico from an overwhelmingly agricultural economy into a nation in which industry, commerce, and agriculture all play strong roles.

Shortcomings and unresolved problems are equally present. Recent policies on political economy involve the dual danger of pushing crude capital formation too fast: First, many industries, in the form in which they are presently evolving, require a larger market, an imperative that is impeded by low wages and in much of agriculture by low productivity; and second, the Mexican masses, awakened to the new Mexico of industrialization, popular education, and commercialization, appear unwilling to accept indefinitely the economic lot cast upon them since 1940. Hence, prolonging rapid industrialization carries with it imminent political as well as economic dangers. Among related shortcomings are the high unit costs of producing many goods, duplication of investments, lack of adequate tax policies, and the virtual absence of public policy on wealth. High protective tariffs are coddling some infant industries that are obviously destined to remain infants with excessively high production costs. Greater investment capital and expanded credit facilities are indispensable, yet the state has been taking over certain sectors of industrial life and in the process discouraged some private investment. Instead of buying productive capacity already installed in Mexico, the state might have facilitated industrial growth better by underwriting new productive capacity. No new capacity was created in merely changing ownership.

ELEVEN

COMMERCIAL REVOLUTION

The industrial and agricultural revolutions cannot raise living standards without the assistance of an extensive commercial apparatus. Transportation, communications, merchandising, and the services feed industry and agriculture, keeping them alive. An adequate distribution system is the *sine qua non* of a modern business community. Lacking commercial counterparts, industry and agriculture stagnate. Some economists contend that underdeveloped commercialization is the major deterrent to accelerating Mexican industrialization. Whether it is the most important single factor is a moot point; in fact, whether the commercial sector is less developed than the industrial sector is also unmeasurable. But one thing is certain: Commerce is indispensable to Mexican growth and development.

This chapter examines selected phases of the commercial revolution unfolding in Mexico. After a look at transportation and communications media—which include the railroads, roads, automobile industry, municipal transit, maritime transportation, aviation, postal services, telegraph and telephone services, radio and television, and motion pictures—we shall focus on the hotel industry and on merchandising. This particular triumvirate of commercial life illustrates an important characteristic of the Mexican economy—its various patterns of ownership. In the transportation and communications sector, the Mexican government is the major owner. The hotel industry, on the other hand, represents a sector almost exclusively reserved for private enterprise. And merchandising is a sector in which the state is just beginning to present a major challenge to private investment.

TRANSPORTATION AND COMMUNICATIONS

Railroads.   Rehabilitation of the Mexican railroad system has demanded serious attention from every Revolutionary regime since Madero's. Before the Revolution, the industry was still in its initial phases of development. As early as 1875, there were 357 miles of railroads, but railroad builders, some of them United States Civil War generals who came to Mexico after 1865 and who were little concerned with the internal economy of the country, duplicated lines in their desire to compete for export business. The Porfirio Díaz government, inspired by its finance minister, José Limantour, interceded in 1898 to put some order into railroad building, then, in 1908, bought a majority interest in the three largest railroad lines, integrating them into a National Railways of Mexico system. By 1910, Mexico had 12,257 miles of railroads—a little less than what it has today!

Under Revolutionary auspices, the railroad industry became one of the very controversial segments of Mexican commercial life. Civil war destroyed much of the rolling stock and was responsible for the tearing up of hundreds of miles of track and the wholesale burning of ties. Pancho Villa frequently boasted of his methodical destruction of the railroads. By 1921, the Obregón regime was claiming that the nation had 13,946 miles of railroads, much of which stood in deplorable condition. By 1938, the Cárdenas regime asserted that Mexico had 13,543 miles of track, a figure that Mexican economists accept as a reliable estimate, which suggests that either Obregón had inflated statistics in 1921 or that successive Revolutionary governments over a seventeen-year period had accomplished absolutely nothing in the way of increasing railroad mileage. Conceivably, both Obregón and Cárdenas submitted correct estimates, since Calles and the callista governments apparently concentrated their efforts on eliminating duplicating lines and laying new tracks to connect formerly isolated regions with Mexico City. The railroad industry experienced two shocks during the 1930's: Cárdenas expropriated that portion of National Railways stock belonging to private stockholders and, even more shocking, the system was placed under a chaotic administration of railroad workers. Although the expropriation was never revoked, the labor management was replaced in 1940 by an autonomous governmental agency that still runs the National Railways.

The state has persistently followed a six-point program in respect to the railroads: (1) replacement of small, uneconomical lines by roads and airfields; (2) substitution of wide-gauge for narrow-gauge track; (3) retirement of old steam locomotives and purchase of new diesel engines; (4) installation of modern railroad stations and railroad repair shops; (5) laying of heavy rails and sturdy ties; and (6) manufacture of boxcars in Mexico to retire those rented from foreign railway companies. Implementation of this program has resulted in a growing proportion of wide-gauge track (from 75 per cent in 1910 to 93 per cent in 1960), the discarding of light rails and light ties, a decline in the number of locomotives (from 1,623 in 1930 to 1,230 in 1960), but a notable increase in the percentage of diesel locomotives, which now constitute about one-half of the total, and the construction of modern passenger terminals and extensive repair shops in Mexico City and San Luis Potosí.

The state has also supported establishment of the government-owned

National Railroad Construction Company, located in Ciudad Sahagún, about 65 miles from Mexico City. Turning out its first boxcar in December, 1954, this state industry manufactured only 858 units in 1955 but a total of over 1,600 units yearly since 1958. By 1964, the railroads were using over 13,000 "made in Mexico" railroad cars. Initially, 82 per cent of the parts entering boxcar manufacture were imported; by 1964, only 20 per cent were imported. Although the plant was originally intended to eliminate an unfavorable item in the balance of payments, since Mexico was paying dearly for rental of U.S. units, plant directors are now looking forward to continuous export sales, following initial foreign sales of fifteen boxcars to Panama and 100 freight cars to Missouri Pacific.

The amount of cargo hauled by rail is steadily increasing, but the number of passengers riding by railroad varied little between 1950 and 1960. Passengers, however, were riding longer distances. Nobody acquainted with Mexican railways can overlook the concrete improvements

CARGO AND PASSENGERS
TRANSPORTED BY RAILROAD, 1950–1960 [a]

Year	Productive cargo (metric tons)	Millions of kilometer-tons of cargo	Paying passengers	Millions of passenger-kilometers
1950	18,992,000	8,904	28,561,000	2,742
1951	18,983,000	9,022	29,084,000	3,016
1952	19,930,000	9,623	26,962,000	2,964
1953	19,310,000	9,137	24,711,000	2,672
1954	20,159,000	9,864	27,486,000	2,990
1955	21,477,000	10,175	31,242,000	3,420
1956	23,192,000	11,465	31,767,000	3,430
1957	25,596,000	12,452	30,182,000	3,398
1958	25,009,000	12,309	26,694,000	3,110
1959	25,627,000	11,713	27,774,000	3,314
1960	28,977,000	13,423	29,885,000	3,756

[a] Source: Banco de México, *Informe Anual*, 1960.

in service. Trains generally leave on time. Food served in dining cars is satisfactory. And ticket-sellers, conductors, and porters are usually courteous and helpful.

To compete more favorably with truck transport and eliminate duplication of costs, it has become imperative for the government to coordinate the railroads under a single administrative organ. Mexico has no less than thirteen different lines, of which the leaders are the National Railways (Ferrocarriles Nacionales de México), which controls more than two-thirds of the entire trackage; the Mexican Railway (Ferrocarril Mexicano); the Pacific Railway (Ferrocarril del Pacífico); the Chihuahua Pacific Railways (Ferrocarriles de Chihuahua al Pacífico), which resulted from the fusion of the old Northwest Railways and the Kansas City,

Mexico, & Orient system; the Southeast Railroad (Ferrocarril del Sureste); and the Sonora–Baja California (Ferrocarril de Sonora–Baja California). Industry gains could be passed on, however, to the greater advantage of the customer. Mergers particularly should bring readjustments of freight rates in favor of the shipper. Railroads should also learn to utilize every inch of freight space instead of leaving with only partial cargoes, as is the case much of the time today.

Automobiles. The automobile industry is another highly controversial business in Mexico. Opinion varies widely, from the extreme of those who would nationalize the industry to the extreme of those who would permit unrestricted, tariff-free importation of fully-assembled foreign makes. Local assembly of automobiles, trucks, and buses suffers from the same obstacle: a market limited by relatively low purchasing power and high unit costs of production. To these barriers should be added the upsetting effects of constantly changing governmental policy on the automotive industry. Nonetheless, expectation of profits, based on the potential of a growing market and the lower costs of some factors of production, has attracted assemblers to Mexico. These newcomers may take comfort in the fact that very few Mexicans own cars; the low number of automobiles places Mexico below the world average in this area.

The evolution of the automotive industry dates from 1908, when the first automobiles arrived on the Mexican scene. Skepticism about the utility of autos was dramatically reduced in 1916 when a general strike in Mexico City halted public transportation facilities and brought private automobile owners to the rescue of stranded passengers. The strike assured the future of the taxi business in Mexico City. By 1925, Henry Ford had initiated a limited assembly operation and a modest truck- and bus-body industry got underway. The 1930's witnessed the inauguration of assembly plants owned by Ford (1932); General Motors (1936); Automotriz O'Farrill, for making Packard and Hillman cars and Mack trucks (1937); and Fábricas Auto-Mex, for producing Chrysler products (1939). Other foreign manufacturers established organizations in Mexico on a scale varying from sales outlets to assembly operations. During the early years after World War II, small truck- and bus-body makers were squeezed out of business by the comparatively large concerns of General Motors, TYCSA, IMBA-MEX, Carrocerías González, and Industrial Metálicas de Monterrey. Simultaneously, an important auxiliary arm of the auto industry, the rubber-tire business, assumed its present structure of manufacture under three companies with U.S. equity capital: Hulera Oxo (Goodyear), Hulera El Popo (General Tire), and Hulera Euzkadi (Goodrich).

Since the 1930's, and particularly since 1950, the Mexican government has stressed the sale of cars assembled with a maximum amount of Mexican-made parts. The state itself entered the auto-assembly business in 1952 by establishing the Diesel Nacional (DINA) plant for making small automobiles and diesel trucks under Fiat patents. After a succession of financial and technical failures, the DINA-Fiat marriage ended in complete divorce, making room in January, 1960, for a DINA partnership with Renault, this time to produce low-price economical automobiles. The first Renaults "made in Mexico," actually reassembled units from France, reached the Mexican public at about $1,500 per car. It is apparent to everyone in Mexico that the government is still undecided about whether it should enter the automobile-assembly business on a large scale. The state was not undecided, however, about prohibiting luxury automobiles from entering the Mexican market or about promoting four-cylinder cars over sixes and eights. In 1960, the López Mateos regime prohibited the importation of certain makes of automobiles, established an official maximum retail sales price of $4,400, reduced tariffs on cars that would reach the Mexican car-buyer at a price of $1,920 or less, offered subsidies and higher quotas to assemblers placing cars on the market at $1,920 or less and those utilizing a high proportion of parts made in Mexico, and, in general, promoted four-cylinder models.

These steps were followed by a deliberate policy paving the way for integration of the automobile industry. The government first reduced the number of makes sold in Mexico, from 44 in 1960 to 22 in 1962. Any assembler that wished to remain after 1962 had to meet stiff investment requirements, including establishment of local production facilities to provide 60 per cent local content by 1965. Approval to assemble locally has been granted to eight firms: Ford, General Motors, DINA (Renault), Fábricas Automex (Chrysler-Fiat), Kaiser (Ramblers and Jeeps), Reo de México (Toyota), Promexa (Volkswagen), and Impulsora Mexicana Automotriz (a Mexican group that bought and shipped to Mexico the German Borgward factory).

How many automobiles are on the road? Official government statistics, based on units assembled and legally imported into Mexico, placed the total number of automobiles, trucks, and buses operating in Mexico as of mid-1960 at 827,017. Automobiles accounted for 483,101 of this total. This estimate was unduly low, however, since unregistered cars and trucks are excluded from official estimates. When, in 1959, the government declared a grace period for registering illegal vehicles without penalty, some 45,414 auto and truck owners came forward. Reliable private sources estimate that there are at least 600,000 cars and 400,000 trucks and buses operating in Mexico, plus about 30,000 cars belonging to resident foreigners. Between 1950 and 1964, the sale of legally imported and assembled automobiles reached an annual rate of between 30,000 and 60,000 units, and that of trucks and buses varied between 22,000 and 40,000 units.

Although automobile parts and spare parts still constitute one of the big problems in the balance-of-payments picture, a problem that is being faced by officials, the value of Mexican-made parts in vehicles assembled in the country reached in 1964 about 35 per cent of total wholesale value. Parts and accessories now made in Mexico include batteries, tires, inner tubes, spark plugs, glass windows, brake linings, cables, seats, mufflers, paint, solvents, abrasives, shock-absorbers, springs, radios, and exhaust pipes. Soon to join the "Made in Mexico" list are piston rings, tire rims, and blocks. As the distribution and quality of gas and oil improve, as spare-parts outlets are extended into all regions, as roads improve, as the price of cars goes down, and as over-all national income rises, only one major change is required to make the auto industry an attractive business in Mexico: higher real purchasing power for more Mexicans.

Roads.   Road construction is keeping up with the expanding demands of automobile, truck, and bus owners. Mexico relied on roads built during the colonial epoch until the Calles administration, when a foreign firm was hired to construct highways between Mexico City and Puebla, Pachuca, and Cuernavaca. With the experience gained in working on these important projects, the government believed that Mexicans had acquired sufficient technical competence to build roads without foreign direction. Since then, roads in Mexico have been surveyed, constructed, and maintained by Mexican engineers. In 1934, the federal government began a grants-in-aid program to help finance arterial roads leading into the national highway system. By 1940, highways had been completed between Mexico City and such distant points as Laredo, Veracruz, Córdoba, Zacatecas, Oaxaca, Guadalajara, and Acapulco. A decade later, with cities on the northern border linked to central Mexico by several routes, autos could proceed as far south as Tuxtla Gutiérrez, near the Guatemalan border. By 1964, Mexico had 33,000 miles of permanent transit highways. Highways connected Mexico City with all state capitals and with Nogales, Ciudad Juárez, Piedras Negras, Nuevo Laredo, Mier, Reynosa, and Matamoros on the U.S. border, with Tapachula and Ciudad Cuauhtémoc on the Guatemalan border, with Tampico, Tuxpan, Veracruz, Coatzacoalcos, and Progreso on the Gulf coast, and with Guaymas, Topolobampo, Mazatlán, Manzanillo, Zihuatanejo, Acapulco, and Salina Cruz on the Pacific coast. Toll roads, administered by the autonomous government agency, Caminos y Puentes Federales de Ingresos, linked Mexico City and Cuernavaca, Cuernavaca and Iguala, Mexico City and Puebla, and Mexico City and Querétaro. To finance road construction, the government has relied partly on a ten-centavo tax levied on every liter of gasoline (a source of forty million dollars in revenue in 1960), partly on direct national and provincial government appropriations, and partly on foreign loans. From 1925 to 1964, the gas tax financed less than 50 per cent of total public expenditures on roads.

The Mexican government has asserted that by 1965 the country will have 35,000 miles of highways. In this projected total are included 2,200 of the 2,700 miles projected for the Pacific-coast highway, 1,000 of the 1,600 miles projected for the U.S. border highway between Matamoros and Tijuana, and the entire 1,400 miles of the new Gulf-coast highway. Also included and scheduled for total completion by 1965 are major highways to link Zacatecas and Saltillo, Ciudad Victoria and San Luis Potosí, Torreón and San Luis Potosí, and Toluca and Naucalpan. The 35,000-mile goal also includes completion of a trunk superhighway around Mexico City and of seven toll superhighways: Puebla-Orizaba-Córdoba, Mexico City–Pachuca, Tijuana-Ensenada, Texmelucan-Tlaxcala, Ciudad Serdán–Esperanza, Tacamaca-Teotihuacán, and an extension of the Cuernavaca superhighway to bypass that city in a direct route to Cuautla. Finally, the projected total also includes the spans of five new toll bridges.

Municipal Transit. Archaic municipal transit systems are impeding the smooth flow of commerce. In many provincial towns, narrow cobblestone streets, holdovers from colonial days, are frequently unattended for decades at a stretch. Where modern paved streets do exist, shortages in public conveyances cancel out a good part of this new asset. Interstate trucking concerns consume countless hours in slowing down for hundreds of little *pueblos* along state and national highways. Once goods reach a city of destination, they may sit in a local warehouse for weeks until delivered to a purchaser. Transportation of people is little better developed than transportation of goods.

A crucial problem in municipal transit involves metropolitan Mexico City. Improvements in widening and opening new streets, in street lighting and general cleanup and beautification of city streets, in safety precautions and vehicle inspection, and in modernizing the bus system have been accelerated since 1952. Yet much is lacking. Officials have rejected plans to intersect the area with an overhead monorail system, and porous soil precludes subway construction. For these reasons, metropolitan Mexico City depends exclusively on surface transit. For the transport of four million passengers riding public conveyances daily there are only 300 streetcars, 150 electric trolley buses, 7,000 gasoline buses, and about 18,000 taxis; approximately 25 per cent of these licensed vehicles are regularly out of service in need of repairs. For the average commuter, these shortages mean waiting an hour in order to board a streetcar or bus that is invariably overcrowded. Meanwhile, the number of commuters keeps rising. While 300,000 private automobile owners and thousands of tourists enjoy relative comfort cruising along Mexico City's 400 modern boulevards in their own cars, the plight of the commuter is overlooked. To alleviate this situation, municipal authorities will have to double the number of public conveyances or otherwise face a serious transportation problem—and hence, a potential political crisis.

Maritime Service. Since 1918, when the henequen regulatory agency bought three ships and formed the Mexican Navigation Company for purposes of transporting hemp to American markets, the merchant marine had grown by 1963 into a fleet of 900 ships with a total tonnage in excess of 300,000 metric tons. Unfortunately, the majority of these vessels are antiquated; only fifty displace significant tonnage. Aside from the steamer shortage, the Mexican maritime industry has been impeded by unfavorable labor laws and inadequate dock and port facilities. The largest single fleet is owned by Pemex, the government oil monopoly, and used in hauling petroleum. The largest private fleet is owned by the Mexican Maritime Transportation Company, which started operations in 1955 under a different name. At the close of 1964, this company possessed nine vessels serving Atlantic and Gulf ports and four vessels serving Pacific ports. Keenly aware of the continuing demand in central Mexico for grains and fresh foods from the northwest, of the demands of the northwest zone for manufactured goods coming from central Mexico, and of the requirements of Mexico's growing foreign trade, the government has been making relatively large investments in dock and port facilities. In the six-year period, 1955–60, the state spent more than 600 million dollars in maritime improvements, concentrating this investment on the three ports of Veracruz, Tampico, and Manzanillo, but also improving facilities at Mazatlán, Guaymas, Salina Cruz, Coatzacoalcos, Progreso, and Topolobampo. Construction of a new port in Acapulco remains in the planning stage.

Aviation. Commercial aviation has grown rapidly since 1950. In 1910, Tomás Braniff piloted the first airplane flown in Mexico, and seven years later the first mail flight took place, between Pachuca and Mexico City. The first truly commercial airline did not materialize until the Pan American Airways affiliate, Mexican Aviation Company (Compañía Mexicana de Aviación), was chartered in 1924 for the "air transport of passengers, mail, and freight within Mexico and to foreign countries." The number of commercial airlines grew slowly until the 1950's: from 11 in 1940, 14 in 1945, 29 in 1950, to a total of 300 in 1960, although only 34 of these lines were offering regularly scheduled flights. By 1964, Mexico had 900 airports, including 13 serving international traffic, which facilitated the movement of the more than two million passengers annually. "Passenger-kilometers" were above one billion every year since 1953 and passed the two-billion mark for the first time in 1960. Income of commercial airlines has been rising, but encumbered by higher salaries, strikes, fuel costs, and landing fees, expenses have been rising faster.

Three Mexican airlines fly international routes: Compañía Mexicana de Aviación, Guest Airlines, and Aeronaves de México. Guest Airlines, purchased by the government in 1962, appeared doomed to extinction through absorption into the bigger state-owned Aeronaves de México organization. Encountering stiff international competition from the outset, Mexican lines have been losing money on their overseas flights. In an effort to save airline charters and promote tourism to Mexico, the Mexican government stepped into the picture with a proposal to unite international operations into one concern in which the government would invest 50 per cent of the equity, CMA 25 per cent, Aeronaves 15 per cent, and Guest 10 per cent. Inasmuch as the state already owns Aeronaves and Guest outright, acceptance of this plan would find the state in immediate control of 75 per cent of the stock. One impediment to integration is that CMA is not favorably disposed toward continuously losing money on overseas flights, whether the state shares its losses or not. The problem is compounded by the presence of nineteen foreign-owned airlines also servicing international traffic to and from Mexico.

Postal Service. Public mails early assumed an important place in Mexican communications. Adoption of the postage stamp in 1856 made construction of post offices indispensable. By 1910, Mexico had 2,709 post offices; fifty years later, the country boasted 4,632. Modern post-office buildings are coming into vogue—Mexico City has more than a hundred of them—and none too soon, since they are urgently needed to facilitate the fifty million additional pieces of mail entering the mails annually, in addition to the billion pieces already being sent each year. Opening new postal routes at the rate of one almost every three days, the Mexican postal service is reaching virtually every little *pueblo* in the nation, and shortening its delivery time as well. Except for burdens imposed by the extraordinary volume of mail in late December, a letter mailed from Mexico City normally reaches a provincial capital within three days. Delivery in Mexico City has been reduced to two days.

Telegraph. Until the civil strife of 1910–20 disrupted normal services, the telegraph enjoyed high prominence among media of communications. In the wake of the first telegraph line, placed in operation between Mexico City and Veracruz in 1852, came rapid expansion, and by 1873 telegraph lineage exceeded 4,300 miles. Of this total distance the federal government controlled 54 per cent, provincial governments controlled 14 per cent, and the private sector owned the rest. When control of the entire telegraph system passed into the hands of the federal government in 1891, the nation had an extensive network of 21,000 miles of telegraph lines, and by the end of 1905, a peak year in the telegraph industry, 34,100 miles of lines were serving the nation. The telegraph subsequently declined in relative importance, partly because many lines and stations destroyed during the second decade of the twentieth century and during the De la Huerta uprisings of 1923–24 were never restored, and partly because telephones, automobiles, airplanes, and in general, new and faster means of transportation and communications reduced the heavy traditional reliance on telegraph. The state dependency supervising the telegraph system itself discovered that in some instances radiotelegraph and radiotelephone were more convenient, even more economical, than regular telegraph. Though many alternatives to the telegraph have entered the communications picture, it remains a basic communications medium in Mexico. With 29,500 miles of lines, actually 13 per cent less than five decades earlier, and with 1,400 telegraph stations, the telegraph system handled in excess of 50 million messages in 1963, or the equivalent of more than one message per adult Mexican.

Telephones. The telephone enjoys a long history in Mexico. In 1879, one year after the first conversation by telephone in Mexico (between Mexico City and its suburb of Tlalpan), the government issued an initial concession for public telephone service. By 1909, the two major companies, Ericsson and Compañía Telefónica y Telegráfica Mexicana, had placed in service a total of 12,491 phones, of which nearly two-thirds were in the Federal District. The same year, the Díaz government promoted an extension of telephone service by permitting telephone companies to string lines on government-owned telegraph posts. Civil war raised havoc with telephone installations: By 1922, the number of telephone centrals in the entire nation numbered only eight. Lack of capital investment further retarded the telephone industry, and it was not until 1947, the year when Ericsson spearheaded an integration of diverse telephone operations into Teléfonos de México, that some order returned to the industry. Three years later, Compañía Telefónica y Telegráfica Mexicana, an IT&T holding, was merged into the new corporation. Even though the telephone industry registered substantial gains after a group of Mexican entrepreneurs, headed by Carlos Trouyet and the late Eloy Vallina, purchased a majority interest in Teléfonos de México in 1957, in the decade of the fifties it fell behind the growing demands imposed by business, government, and other quarters. By 1964, there were only 635,000 telephones installed in the entire republic.

A subject on which Mexicans rarely disagree is their telephone system. Nobody, except perhaps for the telephone company stockholder, is satisfied with telephone service in Mexico. The man in the street inclines toward the opinion that state control of this industry could not result in worse service. Many densely populated sections of large cities and entire counties in the provinces are completely without service. Few public telephone booths have been installed. Equipment is antiquated. Lines become crossed, mixing two or three conversations. Wildcat strikes of telephone workers invariably occur during business hours. And the telephone service in hotels has been criticized by tourists who have been overcharged threefold and more.

Acquiring a telephone is itself a most controversial procedure. Knowing someone high in the telephone company is usually indispensable. Then, before a phone is installed, the lessee must buy $240 worth of telephone company stock and pay an additional $10 for a telephone apparatus, as well as $8 or more to the electricians making the installation. Few Mexicans possess $240 and, although stockbrokers can usually purchase telephone stock at market price (which for years has been at least 15 per cent below par value), the whole procedure is unduly cumbersome. In effect, the telephone company finances a high percentage of its operations by imposing stock purchases on new clients. The net result: Mexico, with one telephone per sixty-one inhabitants, ranks below Argentina, Brazil, Chile, Colombia, Cuba, Panama, Uruguay, and Venezuela. Lagging behind every other major branch of communications in Mexico, the telephone requires much more promotion. Mexico's aim is 1,031,000 by 1968.

Radio and Television. The story of commercial radio in Mexico is largely the success story of Emilio Azcárraga, a poor boy who became czar of the industry. Azcárraga's (and Mexico's) first truly commercial station, the 5,000-watt XEW, went on the air in 1930, just nine years after the first commercial transmission had been made in Mexico and seven years after Azcárraga, with the aid of El Buen Tono tobacco company, had introduced station CYB (known today as XEB). Azcárraga, who earlier pioneered phonograph and radio sales in Mexico, concentrated his entrepreneurial talents on radio-television broadcasting from 1930 forward. In 1934 he replaced the 5,000-watt transmitter at XEW with a 50,000-watt unit capable of reaching distant foreign points. He later brought many stations into his Cadena Radiodifusora Mexicana (Mexican Broadcasting Chain), which used material produced by his Radio Programas de México company. At present, with his ninety affiliated radio stations, including virtually every major station in Mexico, Azcárraga clearly dominates the radio-transmission industry.

The number of radio-broadcasting stations grew from 61 in 1935 to 113 five years later, to 195 in 1950, and to 420 by 1964. Of these 420 stations, 385 were commercial stations, the majority of which possessed relatively weak transmitters. Highly competitive production by American, European, and exclusively Mexican electronics manufacturers is making relatively inexpensive, quality radio sets available to the Mexican consumer. The number of radios in use rose from 750,000 in 1950 and 2.5 million in 1955 to more than 6 million by 1964. This means that there is one radio set for every six persons, placing Mexico in front of other Latin American countries on this score.

Emilio Azcárraga also dominates the television industry. By 1964, his Telesistema Mexicano encompassed 20 of the 22 commercial television stations operating in Mexico. The two stations over which he exercised no control were NBC-affiliated channel 6 in Monterrey and channel 6 in Guadalajara. To insure that his Mexican-produced programs will be rebroadcast in some areas of the U.S. with a high incidence of Spanish-speaking residents, Azcárraga bought an interest in several stations north of the border.

Evolution of the television industry dates back to 1950, when Rómulo O'Farrill, president of the Pan American Highway Commission and publisher of the newspaper *Novedades*, bested Azcárraga in a race to introduce the first television broadcasting station in Mexico. O'Farrill and Azcárraga joined forces shortly thereafter, the former as vice-president and the latter as president of the Mexican Television Network (Telesistema Mexicano) centering on Azcárraga's Television Center (Televicentro) in Mexico City. Today, Center and Network systems rely on three originating channels in Mexico City—channels 2, 4, and 5—and on the repeater transmitters of channels 2 and 4 located in Paso de Cortés, state of Guanajuato, and in Aguascalientes. The systems are reaching an area served by an estimated half-million TV sets and inhabited by nine million people, representing 90 per cent of Mexico's TV receivers and a fourth of the nation's population. Distant stations, such as those in Matamoros, Tijuana, and Mexicali, depend heavily on rebroadcasts. Finally, manufacturers estimate that the number of TV receivers in use should reach 1.1 million by 1966 and 2 million by 1970.

Motion Pictures. The first big reorganization in the short but highly controversial history of the motion-picture industry occurred in 1960. It was then that the governmental National Urban & Public Works Mortgage Bank moved against the monopoly that Mexico's wealthiest resident foreign businessman, the late William Jenkins, had enjoyed over the distribution and exhibition of films since the 1930's. The big money in motion pictures invariably accrued to one or the other of Jenkins' holdings, to the Operadora de Teatros or the Cadena de Oro, which interlocked to control the great majority of exhibition theaters in the nation. The structure of the motion-picture industry rested first of all on the Jenkins' distribution-exhibition monopoly, which over the years, according to nationalist sources in Mexico, had favored foreign-made to Mexican-made pictures; second, on the Mexican movie producers headed by Churubusco, CLASA, and San Ángel Inn studios; and, third, on the government National Motion Picture Bank, which acted as financial intermediary between production and distribution. Preference for foreign-made films is substantiated by statistics for the period 1955–60: theaters of the Federal District, for example, played almost twice as many American-produced movies as Mexican-produced and average runs of the former markedly outdistanced those of the latter. The entire culpability hardly belonged to Jenkins, since his concerns relied on the moviegoer's taste for new and better motion pictures, a preference unsatisfied by Mexican-made films. Mexican producers made less than 600 new films during this six-year period, yet almost 2,400 films were shown in the Federal District alone.

The principal motive advanced by the government for purchasing the Operadora de Teatros and the Cadena de Oro was to break the Jenkins monopoly in order to unite the production, distribution, and exhibition phases of the motion-picture industry. To this end, the Mortgage Bank announced that it intended to make stock in these two concerns available to producers, distributors, and the "general public" so that everyone might share in the exhibition phase. By 1964, people in the trade were still awaiting their opportunity to invest in this new vertical integration of the motion-picture business. It should be added that distribution under Jenkins included the ownership and rental of theaters in the United States, Europe, and South America, as well as his operations within Mexico.

The Mexican avidly attends the motion pictures, partly because the price of admission is kept relatively low (the normal maximum legal admission price in the Federal District is the equivalent of 32 American cents, although after government acquisition of the Jenkins chain, a 25 per cent increase was charged for special, extra-length films, and the equivalent of 96 American cents per auto was charged to enter the sole drive-in theater in the Federal District). Attendance is also encouraged because few Mexicans own television sets and, probably, because high-quality foreign films are shown regularly. In 1962, 77 million people attended movies in Mexico City alone. Other Latin Americans apparently find Mexican motion pictures appealing: Every year since 1955, South America and Central America have accounted for between 70 per cent and 80 per cent of Mexican movie exports. The United States and Canada together have been Mexico's third best customer for films, followed by Europe. As far as the importation of foreign films is concerned, the United States clearly predominates, even though European-produced movies are becoming more popular among Mexicans.

Summary. Looking at the communications industry as a whole, it seems justifiable to assert that postal services, telegraph, radio, and television broadcasting are keeping abreast of demands and general economic development. At the same time, there is an urgent need to expand the telephone system, to improve the administrative workings of the motion-picture industry, to produce more first-class Mexican motion pictures, and to make television available to millions of additional Mexicans. Filling this last need obviously requires more equitable income distribution in order to place greater purchasing power in the hands of a larger segment of the population. Finally, the modernization of communications in commerce, industry, and government will require many more than the 500 telex installations now in operation.

THE HOTEL INDUSTRY

Veteran travelers in Mexico can remember when it required extreme patience and very good luck to discover a clean, secure hotel room at a reasonable rate during peak tourist seasons. When the summer rush ended, the situation temporarily improved in Mexico City, but tourists in the provinces had to learn to live with conditions as they found them. Bottled water, canned food, and disinfectants were indispensable equipment twelve months out of the year. To leave valuable personal effects unguarded in one's room was to invite their loss. Hotel restaurants served unsanitary food, hotel bars watered drinks, and hotel managers committed frequent "mathematical errors" in presenting a guest with his bill and in exchanging pesos for dollars. Suitcases had to be kept in sight or, better, in hand. Tourist guides, in partnership with hotel managers, steered the unwary tourist to shops where prices had been adjusted to provide commissions for guide and manager alike. Why worry about building up a regular clientele, reasoned hotel managers, when thousands of innocent new tourists kept arriving every year. Needless to say, hotel managers succeeded in making themselves the number-one enemy of tourism.

Slowly in the 1940's and decidedly in the 1950's, ameliorative forces began having a constructive effect on Mexican hotelry. The great increase in hotels, motels, and tourist boardinghouses, with a doubling in the number of tourist rooms between 1954 and 1962, introduced healthy competition. By 1962, a total of 120,000 rooms were available in some 4,200 hotels, motels, tourist camps, and tourist boardinghouses. Six federative entities—the Federal District, Veracruz, Jalisco, Guerrero, Tamaulipas, and Morelos—with 36 per cent of Mexico's population, accounted for 55.5 per cent of Mexico's hotels. Almost 23 per cent of Mexico's hotel, motel, and tourist boardinghouses, containing 30 per cent of the rooms available to tourists, are found in the Federal District alone. Fortunately, hotel capacity in Mexico City, Guadalajara, Veracruz, Acapulco, Taxco, and Cuernavaca is sufficient to meet virtually every tourist contingency arising in these specific localities. On the other hand, fourteen of Mexico's 32 federative entities lack adequate tourist facilities, possessing less than fifty hotel establishments each. On a national scale, therefore, even though the Mexican hotel industry by 1963 provided room capacity for about 240,000 guests daily, the bulk of this capacity was concentrated in a few urban centers and favorite resort spots.

A second force working to erase undesirable hotel practices emerges from the sheer magnitude of the tourist trade. In the eleven-year span of 1950–61, more than seven million foreign tourists visited the interior of Mexico, while tens of millions—28 million Americans in 1961 alone—visited outlying towns bordering on the United States or Guatemala. During the same period, an estimated fifty million Mexican tourists stopped at Mexican hotels. The number of foreign tourists entering the interior of Mexico has soared: from 8,000 in 1920 and 92,000 in 1936 to 255,000 in 1946, 636,000 a decade later, and 930,000 in 1963—a ten-times increase in foreign tourists between 1936 and 1963. In 1962 and again in 1963, 80 per cent of the foreign tourist trade came from the United States, representing an 11 per cent drop in the proportion that American tourists bore to all tourists visiting Mexico an earlier decade. The difference was made up by the arrival of larger numbers of Europeans, Canadians, Guatemalans, and Mexicans resident in the United States. The rising tide of tourists from abroad, however, is no match for the rapidly increasing number of Mexican tourists. The weekly average of 100,000 Mexican tourists contrasts sharply with the weekly average of fewer than 18,000 foreign tourists (excluding border tourists).

The amount of money spent annually for hotel services is difficult to calculate, since many hotel owners hide the truth in order to evade taxes. As a rough guide, treasury officials contend that monetary outlays of Mexican tourists are several times higher than total dollar expenditures made by foreign tourists. According to Bank of Mexico estimates, foreign tourists who visited the Mexican interior spent 134.2, 141.8, and 152.2 million dollars in 1958, 1959, and 1960, respectively, while border tourism brought in an additional 407.4, 494.9, and 517.6 million dollars. The Mexican government expects foreign tourists to be spending over one billion dollars annually by 1965. These amounts highlight the fact that for some years now foreign tourist expenditures have been a leading item on the asset side of Mexico's balance of payments, bringing in almost as much foreign exchange as all Mexico's exports.

How much of the money spent by foreign tourists enters the hotel industry? Bank of Mexico economists calculate the figure to be about 19 per cent of the combined outlays made on the border and in the interior. Apportionment of the foreign tourist dollar according to major categories of expenditures produces the following picture: purchases, 26 per cent; restaurants, 25 per cent; hotels, 19 per cent; transportation, 17 per cent; entertainment, 9 per cent; and other expenses (taxis, tips, etc.), 4 per cent. This would mean, therefore, that in both 1959 and 1960, foreign tourists supplied the Mexican hotel industry with more than 125 million dollars. When this figure is multiplied several times to take account of the Mexican tourist, we can understand why the hotel industry has become one of Mexico's vital businesses.

The Mexican hotel industry has also benefited from government supervision and assistance. State direction of tourism resides in an autonomous department of tourism charged with establishing hotel standards, setting room rates, licensing tourist guides, and promoting tourism in general. The department publishes a brochure entitled "Basic Information of Mexico," it subsidizes private tourist guides such as "This Week," "The Gazer," and "Mexico This Month," and it advertises in dozens of newspapers and magazines in the U.S. Other government dependencies are similarly promoting tourism: A special national tourist council, the National Bank of Foreign Commerce, the ministry of communications and transport, the National Institute of Anthropology and History, the National Institute of Fine Arts, and the Mexican National Railways periodically issue propaganda on tourist attractions; the Club de Viajes of Petróleos Mexicanos answers queries of Mexican travelers; the ministry of health establishes regulations on the handling of food and drinks; the Federal Security Commission, ministry of government, Mexican army, and local police officers back up hotel detectives in protecting the life, liberty, and property of the tourist; the Nacional Financiera, the Fund for the Guarantee and Development of Tourism, and the Hotel Credit Agency sometimes extend credit assistance to hotels in financial difficulties; the Material Improvement Boards in border and port cities construct and maintain roads, airfields, public market places, and parking lots; and sixteen state governments have passed laws regulating the tourist business in their respective federative entities. While the Mexican government budget for tourism is still deplorably low in comparison to what many nations spend on promoting tourism, the work of governmental agencies indubitably assists the Mexican hotel industry.

Pressure on behalf of improved hotel service originates in yet another branch of Mexican society—the private groups concerned with tourism. The organized private interests directly engaged in promotion of the Mexican hotel industry are headed by two large national hotel associations: the Mexican Hotel Association (AMHRM), which was founded in 1922 and now numbers more than five hundred members, principally of Class AA and Class A hotels; and the National Confederative Association of Hotels (CNAH), established in 1955 and already possessing seven hundred members from Class B, C, and D hotels. The AMHRM and CNAH advance hotelry in a number of ways, such as publicizing tourism in general and the hotel industry in particular, sponsoring a hotel training school, lobbying before the Mexican government to increase its expenditures on tourism, and making available to their members confidential information on Mexican hotelry. A second category of private associations is represented by the Mexican Automobile Association (AMA), National Automobile Association (ANA), and similar groups that assist member automobile owners with information on the status of hotels, motels, and roads. In addition, the Mexican Association of Travel Agents

issues numerous brochures, pamphlets, and advertisements; the Confederation of National Chambers of Commerce and its local affiliated chambers periodically serve the hotel industry by promoting conventions,
excursions, and hotel luncheons; fraternal organizations such as Rotary
International and the Lions Club provide similar impetus; and the Mexican Restaurant Association publicizes vacations, as do such profit-making
enterprises as the Diner's Club, car-rental companies, airlines, bus lines,
and steamship companies. The North American Pro-Mexico Committee,
formed primarily of U.S. businessmen resident in Mexico, is also promoting tourism by preparing motion pictures, books, pamphlets, and stickers
for distribution in the United States. All in all, private associations are
doing their bit to improve and sustain the Mexican hotel industry.

Responsibility for transforming the hotel industry into a modern,
socially conscious sector of Mexican commercial life falls heaviest on the
hotel owners themselves. As in many Mexican businesses, initial modernizing tendencies in the hotel industry accompanied the intense nationalism
of the 1930's. It was then that President Cárdenas notified the world that
foreign capital unconcerned with domestic economic development was no
longer welcome in Mexico. The same set of rules was to apply equally to
Mexicans, so that all businessmen, whatever their nationality, henceforth
had to take into account the building of Mexico and the general welfare
of Mexicans. The enforcement of laws prohibiting foreigners from owning
property within fifty kilometers of Mexico's borders induced some hotelmen to become Mexican citizens. Also stemming from nationalistic urges
was the enactment of a law prohibiting foreigners from buying hotels,
though foreigners already owning hotels were exempted from its enforcement. Some foreign hotelmen entering the Mexican hotel industry since
World War II have done so by stretching legalities, setting up dummy
corporations, or placing titles in banks or law firms, and they run the
risk of losing their investment in the event of a decision by the Mexican
government to enforce the letter of the law. Foreigners in the hotel
business today are few in number; 95 per cent of the Mexican hotel
industry is Mexican-owned and, in most cases, owned by Mexicans who
reside in Mexico and who are readily accessible to hotel guests.

The change to the new kind of hotel management arrived late on
the Mexican scene. Not a single first-class modern hotel existed in all
Mexico before 1936. There were several good establishments in a few cities
—Mexico City, Monterrey, Cuernavaca, Taxco, Puebla, Oaxaca, Veracruz,
and Acapulco—none of which is today ranked as a Class AA hotel. The
harbinger of the present epoch of Mexican hotelry, based on responsible
management, good food, standard prices, night-club entertainment, correct
accounting, on the philosophy that the tourist and travel agent are the
hotelman's best friends, and on the belief that repeat customers are just

as vital as first callers, was the 1936 opening of Alberto Pani's revolutionary Hotel Reforma. The highly respected Pani, several times finance minister of Mexico, lent considerable prestige to hotelry.

The spark struck by Pani and his Hotel Reforma ignited the industry. Older hotels modernized physical facilities and adopted different management practices. A new crew of businessmen entered the hotel industry—men like Antonio Ruiz Galindo in Veracruz, José Brockman, Pablo Corcuera, and Antonio Rivas in Mexico City, and Gen. Juan Almazán and Arturo Guajardo in Acapulco. Interrupted by World War II, construction of Class AA hotels (those with a minimum daily rate of six dollars per single room) resumed after 1945 and raised the number of AA hotels to 86 by 1963. Besides these excellent hotels, an additional 42 Class AA motels, apartment hotels, and tourist courts appeared. It is from the Class AA hotel that the hotel industry receives its prominence. There are some 23 establishments of this class in Mexico City, 18 in Acapulco, 8 in Taxco, 5 in Cuernavaca, and 4 in Veracruz. Backing up these first-rate hotels are nearly 500 Class A hotels (minimum single room from $2.80 to $6 daily).

In many branches of Mexican industry and commerce, no single business leader has emerged at the top, and guidance has devolved on the Mexican government, on plural executives, or on several entrepreneurs. In the hotel industry, however, one individual stands out. This entrepreneur acquired his prominence in the short span of years since 1958, after the hotel industry had become highly competitive. This man is César Balsa: promoter, part-owner, and dynamo of Nacional Hotelera.

Nonexistent before 1958, Nacional Hotelera now operates ten hotels, four restaurants, and one motel, owning one of the hotels—the El Presidente in Acapulco—and the four restaurants outright while leasing the rest of its charges except for the Prado Alffer, a straight management affair. Seven concerns are in Mexico City and seven in Acapulco; one, the St. Regis Hotel, is in New York City. Balsa has molded together not merely the best combine of hotels in Mexico, but one of the best hotel chains in the Western Hemisphere. When Balsa signed a long-term lease on the St. Regis, one newspaperman described the transaction as "turning imperialism in reverse."

César Balsa belongs to the new group of Mexican entrepreneurs who possess a strong conviction that the promise of Mexico's future is bright. Besides Balsa, we find such men as Antonio Sacristán and Carlos Trouyet in finance; Antonio Ruiz Galindo, the Garza Sada brothers, and Bruno Pagliai in manufacturing; Joel Rocha and Jaime Garza in merchandising; and Emilio Azcárraga in radio and television. Intelligent, alert, personable, trustworthy, ambitious yet not ruthless, these private entrepreneurs balance off the able career bureaucrats in the Mexican government who are also building a greater Mexico.

MERCHANDISING

Merchandising of food and dry goods at the close of World War II varied little from traditional patterns. In the large department and dry goods stores, glass counters covered most sales items; open racks exposing merchandise to public handling were virtually unknown. Store interiors were dark and dull. Credit buying was extremely limited, and imported goods were usually preferred to Mexican-made goods. Meanwhile, the humble popular classes purchased basic necessities from street vendors displaying low-quality items on the narrow streets of slum areas; the privileged classes relied on smuggling or delicatessens for imported canned foods and, like the masses, on the public market for fresh fruits and vegetables. Corn was ground at home, or tortilla mix was bought at small stands. Rich and poor alike visited the *panadería* for bakery goods. Slaughterhouses were dirty, unsanitary, smelly holes treating inferior meats. Milk was adulterated, and fish and fowl were generally unsafe. The Mexican diner feared disease everytime fish, fowl, or meat were not thoroughly cooked or milk boiled. Fixed prices were nonexistent: Bargaining between merchant and customer was an integral part of the merchandising of food, clothing, furniture, drugs, and cosmetics. Fortunately, merchandising policies were changing for the better by 1945.

Modern merchandising methods brought product standardization, quality control, customer credit, and continuous supply. Merchandising and consumer industries as such depend on continuing improvements by the packaging industry in its use of paper, glass, tin cans, cardboard, cellophane, polyethylene, tinfoil, etc. The packaging industry met the challenge in the 1950's, putting production of quality products on a regular basis. Big companies pushed to the forefront in the food and beverage industry: Clemente Jacques and Del Fuerte (canned foods); Ideal and Pan Bimbo (packaged bakery goods); Iberia, Brener, and IDA (cold and processed meats); Industrias 1-2-3, El Fénix, Clavel, and Anderson-Clayton (cooking oils); Nestlé and Café Oro (packaged coffee); Industrias Carrancedo, Chalco, Kraft, and Chihuahua (cheese); Lechería Nacional (pasteurized milk); Carnation and Alpine (evaporated milk); Yom-Yom, Holanda, and Cremelados (ice cream); Mundet, Garci-Crespo, Jarritos, Coca-Cola, Pepsi-Cola, Refrescos Pascual, and Peñafiel (carbonated beverages); and Cuauhtémoc, Modelo, and Moctezuma (beer).

Another set of companies monopolize other sectors of consumer-goods manufacture. La Tabacalera Mexicana and El Águila have become Mexico's major tobacco manufacturers. Nacional de Drogas, Sanborn Hermanos, and the Luis G. Aguilar Company lead drug and cosmetics distributors. Canada Shoes and United Shoe & Leather are foremost in quantity footwear. In the general soap and detergent field, Colgate-Palmolive, La Luz, and Procter & Gamble predominate. The big manufacturers supplying dry goods, department, and furniture needs include Celanese, CIDOSA, and Ayotla (textiles); Briones, Mabe, Salinas y Rocha, and Delher (kitchen and dining-room furniture); Salinas y Rocha and Atlas (beds and mattresses); Delher, IEM-Westinghouse, ACROS, Hoover, Frigidaire, and General Electric (refrigerators and stoves); Industrias Celsa, Oster, General Electric, and ECKO (kitchen appliances); Necchi, Singer, and Toyoda (sewing machines); Luxor, Mohawk, and Armstrong (carpets and rugs); and El Anfora, Nueva San Isidro, Keramos, and La Favorita (porcelain).

Merchandising innovations are traceable to a very few entrepreneurial sources. Leading off is Jaime Garza and his Super Mercados (SUMESA) chain of supermarkets. Garza introduced the self-service food market in Mexico, and from the company's original incorporation in April, 1945, it has grown into a chain of sixteen markets, the maximum number that Federal District officials have permitted SUMESA to operate. Charging reasonable but somewhat higher prices than public market places, government stores, and private discount houses, SUMESA appeals to the middle- and upper-class shopper. Garza proved that traditional commercial patterns could be changed on two major counts: First, that open counters and self-service would not provoke wholesale thievery but instead produce handsome profits (which in recent years have been calculated on annual gross sales in excess of 25 million dollars); and, second, that managers in many separate stores could be counted on to discharge their duties honestly. In testimony to Garza's successes in lodging supervision in professional managers, the National Confederation of Chambers of Commerce selected Heriberto Vidales, general manager of SUMESA, as its president for 1961–62. In the supermarket category with SUMESA are many late-comers, led by Central de Mercados and Minimax.

Private entrepreneurs in the retail-food industry provided two additional sources of merchandising innovation: the giant discount house–supermarket establishment of Aurrerá and the extensive grocery-store complex of Industrias 1-2-3. Handling everything from fresh oysters and strawberries to automatic washing machines and clothing, Aurrerá's nine grand centrals in Mexico City are attracting tens of thousands of customers monthly, mainly from the middle class. The rapid successes of Aurrerá seemingly pointed the way to duplication of this type of merchandising by Comercial Mexicana and Gigante discount houses. On the other hand, despite apparent trends toward horizontal integration in the staple-food industry, Industrias 1-2-3 represents a working example of vertical organizational structure. A big manufacturer of soaps, detergents, and cooking and edible oils, Industrias 1-2-3 sells its products along with standard staple items produced by other manufacturers in its wholly-owned chain of 70 small stores in the Federal District and an equal number of outlets in the provinces. Unlike SUMESA and Aurrerá, Industrias 1-2-3 employs a "neighborhood grocery store" approach and orients retail sales toward the lower middle class.

A fourth entrepreneur introducing revolutionary merchandising practices to Mexico is Sears, Roebuck. Sears entered Mexico in February, 1947, becoming the first department store to utilize modern merchandising methods. Its innovations are perhaps the farthest reaching of any single private company doing business in Mexico. It pioneered night window-shopping by setting up large illuminated window displays. It made merchandise available on open racks and counters. It did away with the traditional bargaining phase of merchandising by placing tags indicating the exact prices to be paid on every article. It encouraged credit buying. It provided shoppers with free parking space. It took full-page advertisements in newspapers. It instituted profit-sharing, retirement, and group life insurance plans for its employees. And it fathered some of today's large manufacturers, as well as hundreds of "cottage industries." Sears now buys more than 90 per cent of its merchandise from Mexican suppliers. In terms of gross sales, net profits, and taxes paid, Sears has become one of the largest private businesses in Mexico. It has five stores in Mexico City, eleven stores in provincial cities, and small retail outlets in Apisaco, Campeche, and Oaxaca. On the basis of performance, Sears has gained a well-deserved reputation over the short span of fifteen years as one of the foremost commercial establishments in Mexico.

A fifth major entrepreneur responsible for changing traditional merchandising methods is the Salinas y Rocha chain of department stores. The largest privately owned merchandising complex in the nation, the whole Salinas y Rocha complex of factories and stores is Mexican owned, managed, financed, and market-oriented. Mexican-made products account for more than 98 per cent of its department-store sales. Every S y R store manager is a Mexican citizen. And, unlike the average merchant and businessman engaged in other commercial pursuits, Salinas y Rocha has established a network of outlets stretching across the entire country. The present S y R company traces its origin to a small metal-bed factory set up in Monterrey at the end of the Díaz epoch. Founded by Benjamín Salinas and Joel Rocha, Sr., both of middle-class families that had lived in the Monterrey vicinity for generations, S y R discovered in the early 1930's that the depression years had eliminated its better clients. Becoming merchants appeared indispensable for remaining industrialists. Under these circumstances, Salinas y Rocha opened its first retail store for direct sales to the general public in 1933. Within a few years, half of the S y R factory output—by now company plants were making beds, mattresses, metal sinks, cabinets, and kitchen furniture—was sold in S y R retail outlets. This proportion of factory sales to S y R retail outlets holds true today, although the manufacturing phase of S y R operations has become secondary to its merchandising phase. S y R department stores presently handle many brands, makes, and models of thousands of different items. Bedroom furniture is no longer an S y R specialty; in fact, the biggest sales today come from stoves, refrigerators, and bicycles.

The company's radical departure from old-style merchandising methods to modern credit, purchasing, sales, personnel, advertising, and management policies dates back to 1952. It was then that two graduates of the Wharton School of Finance & Commerce, Hugo Salinas and Joel Rocha, Jr., sons of the founders and by then the top executives and owners of S y R, completely streamlined the entire company empire. Purchasing, sales, and public-relations policies were centralized, older stores modernized, and new stores built. Henceforth, the merchandise and merchandising of all S y R department stores became geared to middle- and lower-class Mexican tastes. One measure of the wisdom behind this shift is observable in the growth of Salinas y Rocha operations. Today, there are ten S y R department stores in the Valley of Mexico area, six in Monterrey, and twenty-four others distributed throughout the nation, while dozens of stores in Guanajuato, San Luis Potosí, Aguascalientes, and Querétaro maintain an intimate wholesale purchasing relationship with S y R factories and department stores.

Another group of entrepreneurs introducing changes in Mexican merchandising is the "French group" (although Mexico's dynamic businessmen prefer to believe that other entrepreneurs forced this group to change). It is comprised of owners of textile factories and department stores who are descendants of certain French immigrants who entered the textile and merchandising business during the Porfirio Díaz regime. The whole complex is owned by a score of families, headed in the early days by the Braniffs and today by the Signorets, Jeans, Coutolencs, Michels, Spitaliers, and, by virtue of strong financial backing extended by the Banco Nacional de México (a private bank jointly controlled by Frenchmen and Mexicans of French origin), which they direct, the Legorretas. The principal textile mills of the "French group" are those of the Compañía Industrial de Orizaba (or CIDOSA) in Rio Blanco, San Lorenzo, and Cerritos, all located in the state of Veracruz; Textiles La Carolina y Reforma in Mexico City and Salvatierra, Guanajuato; the Compañía Industrial Veracruzana in Santa Rosa, Veracruz; and of Compañía Lanera de México in Mexico City. The major department stores in the "French group" are the Palacio de Hierro, El Puerto de Liverpool, El Puerto de Veracruz, El Correo Francés, La Ciudad de México, and A. Reynaud y Cía.

For decades this combine enjoyed golden merchandising days. Merchants and textile manufacturers could not compete with the powerful vertical integration of the "French group." But comparative advantage brought complacency: looms became antiquated, production costs climbed ever higher, department-store interiors remained unchanged, and merchandising policies failed to adjust to changing demands. With Celanese introducing synthetic fabrics, government-owned and privately owned textile mills producing high-quality cotton fabrics, new merchandising techniques emerging in Sears, Salinas y Rocha, and discount houses, and with large public markets selling textiles at low prices, the "French group" reached the brink of financial disaster. The few Mexicans of French descent willing to build anew met stiff opposition from their fellow Mexican stockholders as well as from French stockholders living abroad who were adamantly opposed to investing additional capital into what now appeared to be a permanent loser. But the minority succeeded in winning one stockholders' battle after another, and in the process the "French group" became less French and more Mexican. Modernization of CIDOSA, whose majority ownership passed out of the hands of the "French group" in June, 1962, and Cía. Industrial Veracruzana factories preceded the purchase, modernization, and consolidation of La Carolina, adoption of new merchandising techniques, refurnishing of department-store buildings, and most impressive of all, construction of a new, super-modern Palacio de Hierro department store in Mexico City, Mexico's largest. In becoming less French, the "French group" now heading factories and stores grew closer together but simultaneously became more competitive with one another. In time, the "French group" hopes to reconquer the high proportion of the consumer market formerly under its sales wing. Meanwhile, the Mexican consumer should enjoy the competitive sales battles that the "French group" will have to fight in order to accomplish its goal.

A final major innovator of new merchandising methods is the Mexican government. State intervention has been instrumental in the building and operation of sanitary, modern slaughterhouses under strict governmental supervision, the elimination of *aftosa* disease, the breakup of the fish monopoly, the creation of a national beef and poultry industry, the enforcement of certain pure food and drug regulations, the establishment of a giant, modern government-owned meat processing and canning plant, and the regulation of basic commodity prices. In carrying out its role as a direct and continuous merchandiser of food and clothing, the state relies primarily on the dependencies known as CEIMSA (Mexican Export-Import Agency) and CONASUPO (National Popular Subsistence Corporation). The two organs are really one, legally speaking, since the latter superseded the former in early 1961; in another sense, they deserve separate identities, since the traditional functions of CEIMSA persist under the old organizational framework and the name of CEIMSA, while new merchandising is promoted as CONASUPO operations. Both CEIMSA and CONASUPO programs, which the state calls "Operation Public Service," typify the Revolutionary urge to bestow "social justice" on the masses.

CEIMSA has been the major state agency buying and distributing food. Through CEIMSA, the state legally exercised its option to buy foodstuffs produced by the nation's farmers and to purchase foodstuffs from abroad. By large-scale purchasing, CEIMSA reduced the influence of local moneylenders, speculators, and political bosses who were squeezing the small farmer and, in effect, controlled retail prices of private stores by entering into competition with them. Paralleling functions of the United States' now defunct Commodity Credit Corporation, CEIMSA went beyond it in selling basic foodstuffs directly to the consumer. Its distribution outlets, which continue under the name of CEIMSA, have taken one of five forms: the typical small supermarket (Mercado CEIMSA), the small grocery store selling everything except fresh meat (Tienda CEIMSA), the store located on communal farms (Ranchero CEIMSA), the small outlets in large public market places (Mercados Locatorios CEIMSA), and the private grocery store, factory store, or government dependency granted a franchise for handling CEIMSA products along with other merchandise (Clientes Libres). By 1962, excluding Clientes Libres, CEIMSA had 367 outlets in metropolitan Mexico City and hundreds of outlets in provincial cities—in effect, enough stores to control prices in most urban centers.

The purpose of CONASUPO, which absorbed the food-buying functions of CEIMSA as well as part of its food-distribution operation, is, according to a speech delivered by President López Mateos when CONASUPO initiated operations in early 1961, "to supply working-class people with every basic consumption need at prices they can afford to pay." CONASUPO began meeting its responsibilities by introducing the ambulatory market on a relatively large scale: A fleet of fifty large red trailers pulled by powerful diesel tractors was ordered to make stops daily except Sunday at every slum neighborhood in the Federal District. Offering powdered milk and sundry grocery items, the fifty "supermarkets on wheels" attracted the masses by selling commodities at a standard price of one peso (eight cents) per product. A second phase of CONASUPO operations began on August 28, 1961, with the introduction of a new fleet of six trucks. These units distributed cut-rate work clothing every day except Thursday along 36 routes covering nearly 650 miles and making stops at 246 workingmen's neighborhoods in the Federal District. A set of work trousers and shirt sold for $2.40 to $3.20, children's trousers for $.85 to $1.25. The "ambulatory department stores" soon added to their lines many types of men's, women's, and children's clothing, shoes, and blankets. By August, 1962, CONASUPO also had established 80 "Tienda Campesina CONASUPO" stores for supplying 250,000 agricultural workers in the Federal District with low-cost foodstuffs and clothing bearing the CEIMSA trademark. Forty additional CONASUPO *campesino stores* were scheduled for opening by 1965. As far as the workingman and his family were concerned, CONASUPO became an immediate success. On the other hand, private merchants began insisting that they could not meet the relatively low prices charged by a state monopoly "blatantly unconcerned with profits." CONASUPO countered this argument by insisting that the state had no intention of competing with private stores in areas where people can afford to pay higher prices.

The three sectors of commercial life just examined—transportation and communications, the hotel industry, and merchandising—typify the general developmental pattern of the Mexican economy. State intervention in economic life, including state ownership of business activities, is pronounced and growing. At the same time, private enterprise is flourishing in certain realms. This seeming contradiction between greater state ownership and the growth of healthy private enterprises leads us to the subject of the next chapter—consideration of United States–Mexican relations in the context of Mexican evolution and world politics.

TWELVE

FOREIGN POLICY
AND INTERNATIONAL AFFAIRS

~~~~~~

Foreign policy is a fascinating aspect of Mexican life. It is naturally the principal Mexican activity that comes to the attention of citizens in other countries, and therefore has a great influence in forming their images of Mexico and the Mexicans. In turn, foreign reactions to Mexican foreign policy account to a high degree for what Mexicans think of other nations and their peoples. Beyond the observations of those who read little more than newspaper headlines, Mexico's foreign policy assumes a fascinating complexity. We might falsely assume that Mexican political geography and its inferiority to the United States in size of national territory and economic and military power would dictate Mexico's foreign policy as well as much of her domestic policy; but we know from previous chapters that in recent decades, when conflicts of interest have arisen between the foreign policies of the United States and Mexico, Washington has abstained from imposing its will. Yet the Mexican Foreign Office cannot rule out the possibility of diplomatic and economic pressure, though this variable usually rests very low on the scale of values motivating Mexican foreign policy. Variables of this sort, multiplied many times by considerations of national security and national self-determination, of economic development and foreign trade, and of treaty commitments and domestic policies, compound the making of foreign policy.

WHO MAKES FOREIGN POLICY IN MEXICO?

The central figure in the formulation and execution of Mexican foreign policy is the President of Mexico. He utters the final word on foreign relations by virtue of powers granted him by the Constitution and laws, by tradition and expectation of the Mexicans, and by his leadership of the Revolutionary elite and political apparatus of the nation. In effect, he bestows and withdraws diplomatic recognition on and from foreign states. He accredits foreign diplomats in Mexico and appoints Mexico's diplomatic and consular agents abroad. With the formality of

318

senatorial concurrence, he or his diplomatic agent signs treaties on behalf of Mexico. He extends or denies asylum to political refugees. He orders the expulsion of undesirable foreigners. He commands the armed forces and, with the consent of congress, issues formal declarations of war. He is the ultimate arbiter on questions of exchange controls and currency devaluation, on compensatory trade agreements, tariff schedules and export duties, tourist regulations, the rights and obligations of foreign investors, international aviation, and migratory labor. The President of Mexico is the alpha and omega of Mexican foreign policy formulation and execution.

Of course, the president cannot carry out all these responsibilities singlehanded. The heavy burden of day-to-day protocol, of gathering facts bearing on policy, of attending to the whims of thousands of diplomatic, consular, and international organization agents accredited to Mexico and, in general, of supplying the services and information that form the substance of foreign policy falls on the ministry of foreign relations. The key official involved is the minister of foreign relations, who usually is selected from career foreign-service ranks, as with Luis Padilla Nervo and Manuel Tello, or from among Mexico's outstanding intellectuals, as with Jaime Torres Bodet. The minister is assisted by a competent staff of career foreign-service officers—special advisors, deputy ministers, bureau chiefs, and Mexico's ambassadors and ministers abroad. The president also turns to the government (*gobernación*) ministry for advice on foreigners, extradition, asylum, and consular intercourse; to the finance ministry, Bank of Mexico, central industrial development bank (Nacional Financiera), and National Bank of Foreign Commerce for counsel on economic and financial matters concerning foreign nations and foreign investment; to the ministry of industry and commerce for tariff scheduling, export duties, and Mexican participation in common markets; to the ministries of defense and marine and to his defense ministry chief of staff for information of a military and strategic nature; to the education ministry (which has a division of international education) and the Institute of Fine Arts for insight into international cultural affairs touching on Mexico and other nations alike; to parliamentary missions of the Mexican congress for advice of a specific nature; and to special presidential envoys, federal security agents, and the small group of presidential aides for minutiae and general counsel. This, then, is the formal apparatus of foreign-policy making and implementation.

Transcending these formal channels are the demands imposed on the President of Mexico by the "liberal Machiavellian" political system he heads. The president cannot forget in making foreign policy that he is the political leader of Mexico, for his actions may raise or lower the prestige of other Revolutionary leaders, to say nothing of his own. Thus, before the president announces a radical change in Mexico's foreign pol-

icy, he will usually elicit opinions of Revolutionary leaders, sometimes selecting one among them to make what will appear to be an off-the-record
speech but in reality is designed to check public and foreign reaction.
Or he may choose a legislative leader, president of the official party, or
opposition spokesman to test opinion publicly. One thing is certain:
Since 1936, a former President of Mexico has rarely, if ever, delivered
a public address on foreign policy without the knowledge and consent
of the incumbent president. The president must also weigh the potential
foreign-policy consequences of jailing political opponents—as Adolfo
López Mateos did to pro-Communists David Siqueiros and Demetrio
Vallejo—or of appointing ambassadors, such as Narciso Bassols to the
Soviet Union and Alejandro Carrillo to the United Arab Republic, who
are ideologically committed to certain outlooks that run counter to traditional Mexican foreign policy. Similarly, a president knows that if he
handles foreign policy by regularly placing confidence in an extraofficial
consultant, or merely seeming to do so, he may give rise to adverse judgment on his own political acumen. This happened in the 1920's by virtue
of the unique relationship between Calles and U.S. Ambassador Dwight
Morrow, and in the 1930's, when Cárdenas relied on Gen. Francisco
Múgica. As chief executive of the nation, the president speaks for Mexico to the outside world, yet even in his conduct of foreign affairs, he is
first and last the spokesman for the Revolutionary elite in control of
Mexico.

THE MAKING OF FOREIGN POLICY:
GUIDING PRINCIPLES

Nations must take a stand on the morality and ethics of war and
peace, human rights and dignity, and self-determination. Mexico is no
exception, for although the conduct of her foreign policy has not always
been in accord with the highest principles of that nation's people or
those of the international community at large, certain identifiable tenets
do emerge from Mexico's evolution. These basic principles guiding Mexican foreign policy overlap and, when injected into the hard realities of
world politics, sometimes contradict one another. They are few in number: national sovereignty, the juridical equality of nations, national self-
determination, nonintervention in the domestic affairs of another
nation, peaceful settlement of international disputes, collective security,
regionalism, universalism, and protection of basic human rights.

Four of these principles, the very cornerstones of Mexico's existence
as an independent state, are closely interrelated. The first principle, the
doctrine of national sovereignty, means that the Mexican state alone has
authority to exercise coercion over its subjects, and that the Mexican
state, as one among scores of nations making up the world community,

possesses no more and no less authority than other sovereign territorial groups. In the present stage of world affairs, the principle of national sovereignty bestows supreme authority over Mexican territory to the Mexican state. A corollary of Mexico's concept of sovereignty is its rejection of colonialism, whether of a political, military, or economic nature. Similarly, in conceiving all nations to be equal in international dealings, the concept of juridical equality of states ignores differences in the economic and military strength and potential of nations. Such differences, it is believed, should be left outside international bargaining tables. Observance of this particular principle, Mexicans claim, is negated by the right of the United States and the Soviet Union to exercise a veto over United Nations deliberations in the Security Council; at least in this instance, the United States and the Soviet Union seem to personify the principle that all nations are equal, but some nations are more equal than others. In accord with the principles of sovereignty and equality of nations, Mexico insists on observance of the additional principle of national self-determination: Mexicans want to establish their own forms and patterns of government and develop their religious, economic, social, and business life in the way they see fit. According to this principle, answers to what is right and workable for the domestic life in any nation are to be supplied solely by the peoples of that nation.

Supporting Mexico's concepts of national sovereignty, juridicial equality, and national self-determination is the fourth cornerstone, the principle of nonintervention in the domestic affairs of another nation. Venustiano Carranza early in the Revolution asserted Mexico's absolutist doctrine on nonintervention: "Any occupation of foreign territory, even when it is inspired by the highest motives, constitutes a hostile invasion and violation of sovereignty." He reiterated this policy in another address: "No country should intervene in any form and for any motive in the internal affairs of other nations. All nations should strictly and without exception respect the universal principle of nonintervention." Verbal or material, political or economic, interference from abroad was to be countered by determined opposition. (At times, Mexico even has equated inaction of a foreign nation, that is to say, abstention from any action whatsoever, with intervention.) The doctrine of nonintervention usually underlies Mexico's insistence in regional and world organizations on an absolute hands-off policy when treating political matters of other nations. The principle is also incorporated in a policy statement formulated by a Mexican diplomat on recognition of new governments, the Estrada Doctrine, which calls for automatic, immediate recognition of new governments. Needless to say, observance of the principle of nonintervention by foreign nations safeguards Mexico's right to develop its Revolution in its own way, unhindered by outside interference.

Over the years, Mexico generally has adhered to two special corollaries of nonintervention: the Calvo Clause of 1863 and the Drago Doctrine of 1902. The Calvo Clause asserts that decisions of a nation's courts on the rights and obligations of foreign nationals should be regarded as final, as beyond appeal to the alien's home government and its diplomatic missions abroad. However, Mexico has conceded the right of aliens to diplomatic appeal when local channels have been exhausted and denial of justice is involved; some foreign nations, including the United States, have never accepted the concept that agreement to a Calvo Clause by their nationals can preclude diplomatic defense. The Drago Doctrine maintains that "the public debt cannot occasion armed intervention or the actual occupation of the territory of American nations." Designed to prevent intervention on the pretext of these specific grounds, the corollaries emphasize the true nature of the principle of nonintervention: It is, according to the Mexican view, an imperative justified by the principles of national sovereignty, the sovereign equality of states, and national self-determination.

Peaceful settlement of international disputes is the fifth principle guiding Mexican foreign policy. Such reliance on the ethical nature of man for discovering amicable means of resolving international controversies also suggests a belief in pacifism and the outlawing of war. Peaceful settlement appeals to law and justice. It negates the notion of might making right. As a small nation, Mexico recognizes that she lacks effective military defense against possible aggression by a strong nation, and that preservation of her national identity depends on the benevolence of the big powers in restraining their might. Whether large, medium-size, or small, all nations, according to this principle, should restrict their foreign relations to peaceful intercourse. Incorporated in approaches of Mexican foreign policy to questions of war and peace, this principle aims at the prevention of conflict by adoption of such nonviolent procedures as negotiation, inquiry, conciliation, mediation, arbitration, and judicial settlement.

But Mexicans know that history provides dramatic lessons on the dangers of adhering to a lofty principle of peaceful settlement without simultaneously recognizing that armed aggression represents a potential instrument of state behavior. Believing that aggression is a clear, if not equally an always present threat, Mexico understandably places faith in yet a sixth principle, that of collective security. Viewed in global terms, a collective-security system depends on effective collective measures of the world community to deal with acts of aggression and other threats to world peace. In the event of such acts or threats, Mexico's adherence to this principle would require the temporary submission of some of her national sovereignty to collective decisions, for, to be effective, collective security would have to be invoked whenever and as soon as aggression occurs, if not earlier. In the light of Mexico's relatively weak economic and military capabilities, collective security offers her a way out of building and maintaining a large military establishment and engaging in costly armaments races, while at the same time promising protection from the big powers and hostile combinations of foreign groups.

International regionalism and universalism are additional principles of Mexican foreign policy. The first is embodied in Mexico's membership, along with other Latin American states and the United States, in the inter-American regional system, the Organization of American States, in her participation with other Latin American nations in the Latin American Free Trade Area, and in her observance of the right of nations to enter into regional arrangements elsewhere in the world. Universalism embraces the idea of one world, of the need for nations to get along in an often perplexing and potentially explosive universe, and of the intrinsic goodness of international economic, political, social, and cultural cooperation. As a principle guiding foreign policy, universalism is advanced through Mexico's membership in and support of the United Nations, International Bank for Reconstruction and Development, UNESCO, International Monetary Fund, International Labor Organization, and the other specialized agencies of the world organization.

A final principle is the protection of basic human rights and fundamental freedoms. Although the Revolutionary elite running Mexico does not always measure its actions within Mexico to conform with this principle, it is nevertheless one of the principles guiding Mexican foreign policy. The heart of this principle is incorporated in the United Nations pledge to promote "universal respect for, and observance of, human rights and fundamental freedoms for all, without distinction as to race, sex, language, or religion." Mexico supports the use of moral pressure in preventing discrimination against a national, ethnic, racial, or religious group. And Mexico believes in protection of minorities, eradication of human oppression, removal of discrimination against women—in short, in the fundamental rights and spiritual values of mankind.

MEXICAN FOREIGN POLICY: OBJECTIVES

The lofty principles guiding Mexican foreign policy assume more mundane proportions once the pulling and hauling involved in actual policy formulation and execution sets in. Dilemmas arise: How far can Mexico go in defending nonintervention in Castro Cuba without jeopardizing foreign investments and foreign grants? Or in maintaining the principle of pacific settlement of international disputes when her own immediate national security is threatened? To what degree can Mexico foster regional arrangements without making a sham of universalism? Should Mexico honor her commitments to collective-security pacts at the risk of losing exports, or in contradiction to the principle of protection of basic rights and freedoms? Every nation faces similar dilemmas. If in the case of Mexico selection of policy alternatives rarely concerns the crucial issue of war and peace, her reaction to world power struggles nonetheless can spell the difference between rapid economic growth and economic stagnation, between domestic political tranquility and political unrest, between keeping the Revolutionary elite in power and conceivably having it overthrown.

Mexico's policy objectives accent foreign trade, aid, and investment. Mexico wishes to sell dear and buy cheap, obtaining high prices for her exports and paying the least possible for imports. She also wants to enlarge markets for her exports and at the same time reduce her imports. In effect, this leads to adoption of policies geared toward obtaining higher world prices and shares in world markets for her basic export commodities, such as cotton, lead, zinc, sugar, and coffee; toward reducing and eliminating tariffs placed on Mexican exports abroad; and toward promoting greater industrial, agricultural, and mining output at home. Mexico seeks lower tariffs abroad while she must set higher tariffs and import prohibitions at home in protection of her own "infant industries." Acquiring preferential treatment in exporting and importing certain products and obtaining assurance of new, continuous markets for some of her goods explains much of Mexico's motivation and expectation in joining the Latin American Free Trade Area (LAFTA). Aimed in part at the promises of LAFTA growth is Mexico's urge to develop a fleet of merchant ships flying the Mexican flag. All in all, Mexico would like a favorable balance of trade—that is, an excess of exports over imports.

Inasmuch as Mexico has been unable to obtain such a favorable balance, partly because since the Korean War prices of her exports have not risen as fast as prices of her imports, she has since the 1954 devaluation preserved her gold reserves and staved off further currency devaluations and excessive inflation by seeking and usually achieving an over-all balance in her international payments. Success in avoiding payment disequilibrium has come about largely by attracting hundreds of thousands of tourists, who together spend hundreds of millions of dollars in Mexico annually. Another "invisible item" providing dollar income for Mexico, though much less than the dollar income from tourists, has been the remittances from Mexican migratory laborers working in the United States. For this reason alone, another foreign-policy objective has been the bargaining for ever higher wages to be paid Mexican workers in the United States. Until Mexico greatly reduces imports in relation to exports, substantially increasing domestic production, promotion of the tourist trade undoubtedly will remain a major objective of Mexican foreign policy. And the logic of Mexico's position suggests that it should not cease to be an objective even then.

It seems proper to state that Mexico's policy on foreign aid and investment is simply to obtain as much as possible on the best terms possible, and to avoid jeopardizing Mexico's political economy in the process. In the years since 1952, the Mexican government has exhibited a clear preference for outright grants with no political strings attached and for long-term, low-interest loans. Though the state prefers grants and loans to direct foreign investment, private capital from abroad has been invited to invest in those enterprises not specifically denied it by Mexican law. In most instances of direct investment, the Mexican government desires majority control of private enterprises to be lodged in Mexican hands. Mexico wants the technology of advanced industrial nations, preferably in the form of reasonable licensing and royalty arrangements that are not injurious to Mexican business and do not run counter to her antimonopoly laws. She not only restricts the number of business administrators and technicians of foreign nationality permitted to work in Mexico, but insists that Mexicans be trained to replace this type of foreigner as quickly as feasible. Because of traditional antipathies of the Mexican people, offers of technical assistance coming from international and regional organizations are more likely to be accepted than similar ones advanced by the United States.

Regarding foreign-policy objectives of a primarily noneconomic nature, enhancement of Mexican prestige and leadership in world and regional organizations looms high. Foreign policy understandably aims at creating favorable images of Mexico: Adverse sides of Mexican life and temperament—the types of hard realities of which Oscar Lewis and Francisco González Pineda have written—are to be omitted from foreign-policy pronouncements in favor of the glowing evaluations of some apologists and historians on Mexico's "democratic" political processes, her "tremendous" economic progress, and her "advanced" social modernity. Similarly, Mexico would not refuse bigger roles in international councils, particularly in specialized agencies of the United Nations. Moreover, growing respect for certain strands of diplomatic independence running through Mexico's traditional foreign policy, plus the size of her national territory and population and her relatively liberal outlook on political and economic themes, combine to promise her broader authority in the inter-American regional system and among informal associations of Spanish-speaking nations and Latin Americans. From Mexico's big-brother relationship to Central America emerge rumors of her desire to capture some of the traditional influence exercised there by the United States, especially in winning markets for Mexican goods in the nascent Central American common market.

A final set of objectives involve four territorial and boundary questions. First, Mexico attempts to uphold a debatable concept of territoriality by maintaining that her territory extends nine miles beyond her coast line, and, accordingly, that unauthorized vessels discovered within the nine-mile limit automatically become subject to Mexican jurisdiction. Although variations will occur in the claims of different nations, the Mexican interpretation clashes directly with the claim of a three-mile limit usually sustained by the United States. Second, Mexican foreign policy for more than half a century has sought to acquire from the United States a disputed tract of land in El Paso, Texas, known as "El Chamizal." Discussions initiated in 1962 between Presidents Kennedy and López Mateos have now led to a satisfactory solution of this ticklish problem. Third, the Mexican foreign office has persistently demanded a voice in discussions involving proposed transfer of British Honduras territory to Guatemala. Finally, Mexican foreign policy backs up farmers in the Mexicali Valley who irrigate their land with waters from the lower Colorado River and clamor for relief from the adverse effects of saline deposits dumped into the Colorado system by Arizona farmers.

MEXICAN FOREIGN POLICY:
LIMITATIONS AND CONTROLS

On the grand chessboard of world politics and the smaller gaming boards of regional affairs, bilateral relations, and Mexican domestic social life itself, Mexico's foreign policy can be checkmated at many points. Some limitations and controls on the implementation of Mexican principles and objectives stem from physical elements of national power. There are, for example, geographical considerations—Mexico's relatively small size, meager river systems, predominantly unfavorable climate and terrain, location alongside the United States and Guatemala, distance from Europe and Asia, and extensive boundaries. There are demographic influences—Mexico's relatively limited number of inhabitants, small labor force, and high rate of illiteracy. There are military restrictions—Mexico's relatively weak over-all military force, a paucity of naval and air forces, an army based largely on reserves trained on weekends, and, in sharp contrast to arsenals of the superpowers, a meager stockpile of outdated armaments. And there are considerations stemming from Mexico's natural resources and technology—an industrialization geared to establish a pre-atomic industrial economy, relatively underdeveloped resources, low industrial capacity, largely unmechanized agriculture, and low national income and per capita income.

Other limitations and controls grow from ideological and political roots. The principles and objectives of Mexican foreign policy enumerated earlier react on one another and also qualify and shape Mexican attitudes on nationalism, patriotism, and antiforeignism. Of course, these attitudes in turn exert a feedback effect on principles and objectives and help determine how far Mexico can proceed in one direction without jeopardizing other policies and the very principles and objectives in the process. Cold

War politics and similar external forces inherent in world power struggles —forces beyond the direct or immediate control of Mexico—also influence Mexican foreign policy. They enter at least implicitly into Mexican calculations of Mexican national interest versus formal international commitments, and together with domestic political considerations, they help to determine whether Mexico will honor her treaties, alliances, regional collective-security pacts, and economic and financial agreements with the outside world. In other words, external forces help determine whether Mexico will follow conventional doctrines on the binding nature of treaties (*pacta sunt servanda*), or whether she will excuse herself from formal pledges on the grounds that new conditions, imposed by natural evolution or abnormalities, justify breaking previous commitments (the doctrine of *clausula rebus sic stantibus*). Again, keeping the Revolutionary regime in power will usually remain the foremost consideration.

An important, perplexing, and generally elusive influence derives from antiforeignism. Nobody acquainted with Mexico and the Mexicans can deny that a deep current of antiforeign sentiment runs through the width and breadth of the Revolution. Mexican history since 1910 is replete with manifestations of xenophobia, chauvinism, and strong nationalism. Mexican laws contain antiforeign, markedly nationalistic provisions. Obviously, intense nationalism and antiforeignism exist in Mexico; the perplexing question is how to measure these sentiments. By opinion surveys of the Mexican elite? By public rallies? By popular reaction to state visits of prominent foreign statesmen? Since infallible measures of opinion cannot be made to gauge the precise degree and nature of antiforeign sentiment among the Mexicans, an unusually heavy burden of judgment falls on the President of Mexico.

Partly for this reason, and keenly aware of the role history and emotions can play, Mexican leadership finds antiforeignism a ready tool for justifying new policies and for repairing breakdowns in communication between itself and the various Mexican publics. Injections of antiforeignism have appeared regularly in Mexican policy. We have been told that antilabor programs have combated "militant Stalinism," while pro-Marxist policies have coincided with "proletarian demands for eliminating foreign imperialism"; that pro-Catholic programs have restrained "creeping religious influences emanating from the Protestant White House in Washington," while anticlerical policies have "undermined Spanish dictator Franco's efforts to subvert Mexican liberalism"; that the promotion of private enterprise "prevented Moscow from gaining further ground in Mexican society," while nationalization of the motion-picture distribution and electric-power industries "removed the stranglehold that foreigners exerted on these basic activities." By rationalizing policy in this way, the President of Mexico may reflect dominant wishes of the Mexicans, or he may merely utilize antiforeignism to justify public policy that is antithetical to prevailing creeds, institutions, or behavior. In the latter event, he is leading the masses down a xenophobic path, and danger of provoking widespread antipathy beyond easy control looms singularly imminent.

Finally, important limitations and controls on Mexican foreign policy stem from primarily economic and financial considerations. In order to sustain and increase domestic economic growth, simultaneously keeping inflation in bounds, preserving currency stability, and protecting national sovereignty and individual freedoms, Mexico cannot afford to overlook foreign-trade patterns in the Free World. Some of the weighty influences of international commerce are found in world commodity oligopolies and near monopolies, in tariff structures permitting most-favored treatment of certain nations and specific goods, and in the practice of placing quotas on imports. The unsophisticated law of demand and supply, the rule of merely locating foreign markets for a nation's surpluses, lost applicability long ago. Mexicans who wish sales abroad usually discover, as exporters interested in the Mexican market also find, that mastery of complicated sets of rules, regulations, and practices becomes essential. Furthermore, Mexico must be prepared for the prospect of new export competition, of sellers and buyers making exclusive trade agreements, and of countries "dumping" commodities on the world market. Mexico herself has signed compensatory-trade agreements with foreign nations and tied automobile imports to cotton exports. Past and present controls and limitations arising from foreign-trade quarters obviously cannot serve as exclusive guides for Mexico's foreign policy; yet these challenges to Mexican foreign commerce must be met or otherwise compensated for, since lack of sufficient foreign exchange restricts importation of foreign-made goods that are vital to economic growth. Unless ready alternatives are available in the form of restricting trade, finding new trade partners, or enlarging some of her trade with existing partners, Mexico knows she must get along with the nations presently involved in her foreign commerce.

Keeping diplomatic friction between Mexico and capital-exporting nations to a minimum has also traditionally represented a golden rule for attracting foreign investment. But consonance between a Western nation's foreign economic policy on Mexico and the interests of its citizens investing in Mexico is by no means taken for granted today, either by the foreign nation, its investors, or other parties, including the Mexican government. In times of diplomatic stress, the private foreign investor may prefer an attractive investment climate to friendly diplomatic ties between Mexico and his own nation. A foreign government bank, such as the Export-Import Bank of Washington, may abstain from making certain loans desired by Mexico during periods of amicable relations, yet turn around in the midst of political crises and offer her precisely these loans and conceivably others in addition, with or without *quid pro quo* political conditions tied in. And international financial institutions, such as the Inter-American Development Bank and the International Bank for Reconstruction and Development, may extend credits to Mexico regardless of the nature of her diplomatic intercourse with individual capital-exporting countries. The truth of the matter is that on a hard dollars-and-cents basis, indirect foreign investment, largely in the form of loans to the Mexican government, has become just as important as direct private investments coming from abroad. In fact, during the period 1959–62, indirect investments accounted for more than two-thirds of total foreign investment made in Mexico. If this trend persists, the indirect form of investment will relegate new direct capital to a relatively minor role in the over-all foreign-investment picture.

What investment patterns mean in terms of foreign-policy controls and limitations becomes an increasingly complex question. It is fairly certain that private foreign investors who must risk their capital in the traditional ways of business will look for a propitious investment climate. Availability of raw materials and product marketability will be judged together with Mexico's policy on ownership, management, royalties, taxation, labor, and profits. As far as this kind of investor is concerned, particularly the potential new investor, Mexico also must take notice of investment conditions in other lands. To attract foreign investors of this type, the Mexican government will have to keep the potential returns on investment high enough in comparison with rewards promised elsewhere. In this view, Mexico's demand for direct private capital from abroad is therefore subjected to the general supply and nature of investment opportunities everywhere, not in Mexico alone. Often a private investor is also subject to legal dispositions placed on export capital by his home government; in the event of a rupture of diplomatic relations, the foreign government might conceivably forbid its citizens and corporations from investing in Mexico altogether. Mexico must also gauge the possibility of voluntary withdrawal of private investments and loss of potential foreign investment resulting from implications read into her foreign policy. While nobody can say with certainty why direct private investment in Mexico by United States citizens dropped in the period 1959–62, some blame might fall on the manner in which investors interpreted Mexico's voting on Castro Cuba in inter-American system meetings. On the other hand, Mexican posture might not have affected investments as much as the mere presence of Castro Cuba and direct reactions of Washington to the "Red Pearl of the Antilles." However we interpret the effects of the Castro debacle, it illustrates the point that another variable confronting foreign-policy makers in Mexico is the way in which Mexican stands on Cold War struggles might affect private foreign investment.

The minds of the best career diplomats are placed under severe tests when indirect investments, foreign grants, direct investments by agents of foreign governments, and even the tourist trade come up in foreign-policy formulation. All types of questions arise: How far and how fast can Mexico push state ownership without losing, or perhaps before gaining, sympathetic response of foreign and international lending sources? To what degree might radical political or economic reforms place the tourist trade in jeopardy? Will private financial institutions in the United States lend large sums to the Mexican government regardless of her policy on direct foreign investment? Or will private U.S. banks and insurance companies identify themselves so closely with other private capitalists that indirect investment will be jeopardized? What are the merits of upholding the "good behavior" provisions implicit in Alliance for Progress programs if larger financial assistance goes out to nations expressing sympathy to hemispheric outcasts like Castro? Will Washington extend credits essential to accelerated economic growth only if Mexico carries out reforms laid down by Alliance for Progress officials? Would these reforms generate sentiment against the Revolutionary leadership, or even anti-American attitudes, among strong vested interests? Precisely how far can Mexico proceed in attempting to realize its foreign-policy principles and objectives without upsetting the foreign-aid applecart? Can the central Bank of Mexico abandon anti-inflationary policies popular with the International Monetary Fund and still obtain financial assistance from international lending agencies? If Mexican–U.S. relations become so disrupted that investment and aid from the United States are virtually shut off, can Mexico depend on Great Britain, Germany, Japan, and other allies of the United States to come to its financial rescue? As these questions indicate, there are indeed limitations and controls imposed on Mexican foreign policy by economic and financial considerations.

MEXICO AND THE UNITED STATES

The American chapter of Mexican foreign policy contains perplexing, controversial, and exciting pages in Mexico's diplomatic history. Its sheer bulk provides many answers to why Mexicans simultaneously appreciate and depreciate the United States, why they admire yet frequently distrust Washington, and why they refuse to join forces with the U.S. on what appear to Americans to be harmless declarations of Free World thinking. The lofty principles of both nations' foreign policies suggest general consensus, though even here the two countries place different emphases on certain principles. Differences of opinion become sharper at the level of policy objectives, where peculiarities in the social, economic, and political outlook, institutions, and customs of the respective nations come into play. These dissimilarities, strengthened by memories of what the United States and some of its more aggressive citizens have done across the years against the Mexican national interest and individual

Mexicans, help to produce equivocal attitudes that can swing policy from that generated primarily by respect, trust, and confidence to that colored by envy, distrust, and hatred. The assets and liabilities, the inspiration and frustrations, of the controls and limitations noted in the preceding sections also complicate the formulation and execution of Mexican foreign policy toward the United States.

A review of the important issues of twentieth-century world politics reveals that Mexico and the United States disagreed much of the time from 1910 to 1940, generally concurred in the 1940's and 1950's, and then split in the first two years of the 1960's on issues involving the Cold War and Castro Cuba. When the United States went to war against Germany in World War I, Mexico's neutralist policy, mildly sympathetic to Germany, constituted a security risk for the Allies. The United States abstained from establishing diplomatic relations with the Soviet Union until Franklin Roosevelt entered office; Mexico recognized Moscow as early as 1924, the first nation in the entire Western Hemisphere to do so, and maintained this relationship until 1930. The United States rejected membership in the League of Nations, a body in which Mexico took a seat in 1933. The United States stubbornly adhered to the Monroe Doctrine and, until 1929–30, to the Roosevelt Corollary as well—policies highly repugnant to Mexico and openly rejected by it. And while Franklin Roosevelt chose a neutralist policy vis-à-vis the Spanish Civil War, Mexico sent arms to the Spanish Republicans, invited war refugees to immigrate into Mexico, and generally did everything in her power to prevent Franco's victory and his political consolidation. Mexico still does not recognize the Franco regime. While Roosevelt was promoting Anglo-American friendship on the eve of World War II, Mexico and Great Britain, as a direct consequence of Mexico's oil expropriation, broke diplomatic relations. Mexico did join forces with the United States and the U.S.S.R. against Germany, Italy, and Japan. She also joined the United Nations and its specialized agencies, voted to strengthen the inter-American system, signed the Rio Treaty of collective regional security and the Bogotá Charter, and backed the "uniting for peace" resolution aimed at supporting South Korea. On the other hand, Mexico has preferred a stronger stand than the United States on the abolition of colonialism, the outlawing of war, support of neutralist nations, and nonintervention. Policy differences on Castro Cuba and the Alliance for Progress, and they do exist, will receive more extensive comment later in this chapter.

Another interesting feature of Mexican–U.S. relations in the twentieth century is the timing and frequency of meetings of heads of state of the two nations. The first meeting of this sort in history did not materialize until October 16, 1909; at that time, William Howard Taft and Porfirio Díaz met on the "neutral" territory of El Chamizal between El Paso, Texas, and Ciudad Juárez, Chihuahua. More revealing is that during the first three decades of the Mexican Revolution, encompassing all presidencies from Francisco Madero through Lázaro Cárdenas, no U.S. president met with his Mexican counterpart. (However, Presidents Coolidge and Calles made telephone contact, and Ortiz Rubio paid a preinaugural visit to Herbert Hoover.) Then, on April 20, 1943, Franklin Delano Roosevelt and Manuel Ávila Camacho met face to face at Monterrey, Nuevo León, to discuss wartime problems, after which the Mexican chief of state accompanied Roosevelt by train to Corpus Christi, Texas. Harry S Truman became the first U.S. president to make an official state visit to the national capital of Mexico, where he conversed with Miguel Alemán on March 3–5, 1947. Alemán shortly reciprocated by meeting with Truman in Washington, on April 29, 1947. The paucity of meetings characteristic of U.S.–Mexican relations was seemingly redressed by Dwight D. Eisenhower; his presence accounted for exactly 50 per cent of all meetings of heads of state of the two nations from the time of their national independence until 1962. He attended five such reunions: the first with Adolfo Ruiz Cortines at the inauguration of the Falcon Dam on the Texas-Mexico border on October 19, 1953; a second with Ruiz Cortines, which Prime Minister John Diefenbaker of Canada also attended, at White Sulphur Springs, West Virginia, March 26–28, 1956; and three meetings with Adolfo López Mateos, at Acapulco, Guerrero, February 19–20, 1959, at Washington, October 9–14, 1959, and at Ciudad Acuña, Coahuila, October 24, 1959. Adolfo López Mateos also met with John F. Kennedy at Mexico City, June 29–July 1, 1962, and with Lyndon B. Johnson at Palm Springs, California, February 21–22, 1964.

The fact that nine of these ten meetings have occurred since 1943 seems to indicate both Washington and Mexico City are finding reliance on this mechanism useful to their respective foreign and domestic policies. Of course, more rapid means of transportation and a general trend toward meetings of heads of state help explain why U.S. and Mexican presidents meet more frequently. Appraisal of precisely what such meetings of the two chief executives accomplish, however, is difficult to express in positive terms. It appears unwarranted to assert that highly constructive results on behalf of both nations necessarily emerge from them. Equally intangible is the importance laid on a great public turnout on behalf of a visiting chief of state. How much should be read into a gala "ticker-tape" reception on lower Broadway in New York or on Massachusetts Avenue in Washington? Did the millions of Mexicans lining Mexico City streets in June, 1962, for a glimpse at President Kennedy and his wife primarily reflect Mexican curiosity, a disciplined Mexican trade-union movement, love for the United States, personal respect for John and Jacqueline Kennedy, or, perhaps, a symbolic rejection of Castro and Moscow? Such questions aside, meetings of chief executives, particularly when crises develop or appear imminent, do suggest the possibility of reaching immediate understandings on their respective positions and the reasons for them. Through this medium, the U.S. president enjoys the advantage of reaching the one official who really counts in Mexico's politics, though the President of Mexico realizes that constitutional limitations and custom seriously circumvent the foreign-policy making powers of the President of the United States.

Top-level meetings, frequent as they have been in recent years, nonetheless appear to have contributed less toward bringing about friendlier U.S.–Mexican relations than have Mexico's own political stability and moderation. Uninterrupted by armed strife or excessive radicalism since the 1930's, Mexico virtually eliminated the causes of earlier sources of friction. Recognition and protection of American property and lives in Mexico, big issues in U.S.–Mexican relations up to the 1930's, have been reduced to procedural questions. Recognition of successive Mexican administrations has become automatic, continuous, and unhindered. Protection of American lives in Mexico, now so intimately connected with promotion of tourism, has become a major assignment of Mexican police, security, and military forces. And protection of American property in Mexico today enters official U.S. policy only minimally, for the United States has come to accept Mexico's right to expropriate whatever properties she chooses as long as the state's action is in fact expropriation (which requires prompt and adequate payment) and not confiscation. In the specific case of expropriation of property owned by Americans, the U.S. embassy in Mexico City normally waits until dispossessed U.S. property owners have exhausted Mexican legal procedures before it will intercede with Mexican officials, if even then. By this formula, the embassy tries to avoid accusations of obtaining preferential treatment for U.S. citizens, since Mexicans who fail to receive prompt and adequate payment for expropriated property have no equivalent recourse. In following this procedure, we might note, the United States is indeed honoring the strictest interpretation of nonintervention.

Reaching harmonious solutions to the big problems that discolored U.S.–Mexican relations during early decades of the Revolution undoubtedly helped to reduce friction on other bilateral issues. It did not, however, eliminate friction. Five major issues of a bilateral nature stand out: Mexican migratory labor, tariffs on lead and zinc, water rights and boundary questions, "pirating" of Mexican fishing banks by American boats, and racial (nationality) discrimination.

Difficulties over migratory labor involve hourly wage rates and unionization, general working conditions, transportation facilities, and discrimination against Mexican laborers. Recruitment, security, and other procedures impinging on the transportation of several hundred thousand Mexicans back and forth across the border annually introduce many problems, although treatment of these procedures has steadily improved. A "wetback" problem remains, but this, too, has been reduced to workable proportions. Hourly pay rates have slowly risen; the Mexican migratory laborer receives more per hour on U.S. farms than he normally earns per day in Mexican agriculture. Yet Mexico naturally seeks higher wages for its nationals and, in particular, would like farmers in the state of Texas to match the pay scales of California farmers. The Mexican government also would prefer better housing, security, and fringe benefits than many U.S. farmers provide. One difference of opinion on Mexican migratory labor involves U.S. labor unions, which desire termination of the migratory program or at least want Mexican labor organized when it enters the United States. Mexico sympathizes with this viewpoint, but farmers in the United States exhibit a preference for keeping Mexican labor unorganized. Obviously, there is little prospect of finding permanent solutions to all problems. As long as farmers north of the Rio Grande wish to employ Mexican laborers and the Mexican and U.S. governments encourage migration, both farmer and laborer will seek comparatively advantageous terms. In this sense, friction is unavoidable and, except for racial discrimination, perhaps healthy.

A second issue, tariff schedules on lead and zinc imports, really constitutes the biggest item in the broader issue of improving Mexico's terms of trade. It rises to the surface whenever the U.S. Congress begins hearings on subsidies paid to American mining concerns or on prevailing tariff rates. Once largely a matter primarily affecting Mexican subsidiaries of U.S. mining companies, particularly American Smelting & Refining and American Metal Climax, purchase of much of the latter's holdings by Mexican capitalists, plus inroads made into the export trade by mining concerns owned by the Mexican government and by small Mexican miners have changed this picture. The periodic threats of raising tariffs immediately evoke a loud clamor from the Mexican press, radio-television, and motion-picture newsreel industries, mining associations, independent miners, mine and smelter unions, and of course from the Mexican government and its ambassador in Washington. Although lead and zinc exports still represent substantial dollar earners, their percentage contribution to Mexico's yearly balance of payments has been steadily declining. Lead and zinc have become marginal metals in advanced industrial economies, and production continues to exceed world demand, forcing lead and zinc prices downward or at best keeping them stationary. Mexico is helping her own cause through higher domestic consumption and by raising domestic lead and zinc refining capacity, but she nonetheless desires at least to hold her share of the American market, an objective to which higher tariff rates and subsidies to American miners would deal a deadly blow. The lead-zinc issue finds rough counterparts in other commodity exports: cotton (Mexico's fear of U.S. dumping of surpluses), coffee (fear of losing its share of the world market), sugar (fear of quotas being returned to

Cuba), and sulfur (fear of world-wide producers price-cutting Mexico out of world markets). Vested interests in both countries also disagree on tariff rates levied on certain specific goods.

A third issue, rights to the waters of the Colorado, Rio Grande, and Tijuana rivers, appeared suitably resolved after the signing of several water-allocation treaties in November, 1945, and by the continuing work of the International Boundary Commission. But whenever a drought hits farms on either side of the border, farmers adversely affected raise a cry for immediate redress and treaty revision. The water-sharing problem is compounded by the dumping of saline deposits in the Gila River by Arizona farmers in the Wellton-Mohawk area. This highly saline water in turn is carried to the Colorado River, from which Mexicali Valley farmers draw water. Foreign Minister Manuel Tello of Mexico reportedly asserted early in 1962 that this Colorado River dispute contained the seed of the worst tension in Mexican–U.S. relations in over two decades. Completion of waterways now under construction and joint projects scheduled for the future show promise of reducing the problem. But these works alone will not eliminate it. Arizona farmers will have to pump less salt into the Gila and schedule pumping in such a way that greater quantities will enter the Colorado at its highest periods. Better drainage in the Mexicali Valley is also in order. Presidents Kennedy and López Mateos agreed at their meetings in mid-1962 to instruct their respective governments to find a rapid solution to this problem.

Boundary problems arise because the U.S.–Mexico border is placed at the middle of the Rio Grande, "following its deepest channels." This cantankerous stream has never been satisfied to follow a regular, permanent course. An International Boundary Commission set up by mutual consent of Mexico and the United States to adjudicate disputes arising out of changes in the Rio Grande's course has settled numerous cases over the span of more than a half-century. The most recent success—in July, 1963—was the reaching of a decision on a small tract (called "El Chamizal") contiguous to El Paso, Texas, and opposite the Mexican town of Ciudad Juárez, Chihuahua. Back in 1911, the two countries agreed to arbitration of the disputed tract, which came into being in the first place because the Rio Grande switched its course, but when an outside arbiter handed down a ruling favoring Mexico, the United States refused to accept it. The "El Chamizal" affair was more complex than it might appear at first glance. It not only involved Mexican nationalism and a public opinion oriented by the belief that the United States mistreated Mexico in 1909 and since, but the interest of private owners of the tract of land, the local sentiment of El Paso and Ciudad Juárez residents, the sovereignty of the state of Texas, and the disposition of the United States and Mexican governments. In July, 1963, a year after Presidents Kennedy and López Mateos pledged their governments to discover a formula acceptable to all interests concerned, representatives of the two nations signed an agreement which evoked glittering praise from the Mexican press.

Mexico's objections to fishing vessels flying the American flag (and flags of other foreign nations) entering Mexican territorial waters date back many years. Complaints have reached serious proportions since World War II, when Mexico began taking a serious interest in exploiting shrimp and other seafoods and building up a fishing fleet of its own. The most widespread "pirating" involves shrimping off the Gulf coast by ships from Texan ports. When the Mexican navy captures an American fishing vessel, it is usually ordered to proceed to a Mexican port, where fines are levied and nets and catch are confiscated. Because Mexico and the United States place different interpretations on how far territorial waters extend from a nation's coastline, however, a U.S. law offers redress to its fishermen picked up beyond three miles but within the nine-mile territorial limit set by Mexico. Under these circumstances, a procedure exists by which U.S. fishermen can recover fines paid to Mexican authorities. U.S. fishing vessels caught within three miles of Mexico's coasts have no redress. Solution of this problem from the Mexican point of view is simple: U.S. fishing vessels should remain outside Mexico's nine-mile limit.

Discrimination, a final issue, unfortunately takes place on both sides of the border. Many American tourists and American residents in Mexico are charged higher prices by merchants, mechanics, professionals, and hotel and restaurant owners merely because they are Americans, and "all Americans are rich." Intolerance on the American side of the border takes another form: Mexican tourists, students, migratory laborers, and visiting professionals are sometimes denied access to hotels, restaurants, apartment houses, and various public centers. The worst discrimination, according to Mexicans, occurs in Texas, although they also raise complaints against treatment in southern California, New Mexico, Arizona, and New Orleans. One of Mexico's truly outstanding intellectuals, now a high government official and senior professor at the national university, admits that his anti-Americanism originally stemmed from refusals of Austin (Texas) landlords to rent to him and his wife "because we do not cater to Mexicans," despite the fact that he had come to this college town for an American education. Isolated cases of this sort can effect incalculable harm. Some observers believe that the strongest deterrent to intolerance resides in the millions of citizens of both nations who have crossed the border since World War II and reached sound, friendly opinions based on personal experiences untainted by discrimination. Although it is true that Mexicans know the United States at first hand better than they know any other foreign land, and that Americans have visited Mexico and Canada more than any other foreign countries, increased contacts do not, it seems, necessarily guarantee deeper understanding and appreciation.

Such, in fact, is their prejudice, that increased contacts may only lead more Americans to sympathize with "those poor, impoverished, uneducated Mexicans" and more Mexicans to envy "those rich, educated, lucky Americans."

Beyond these issues of a bilateral nature, the United States and Mexico also fall short of mutual accord on hemispheric affairs. The essence of Western Hemisphere relations concerning the two nations is tied up with inter-Americanism, the concept of Latin America and the United States allied together in a regional organization. Before Castro negated the notion that the hemisphere could settle its squabbles without the need for expelling a member state, the inter-American system impressed many jurists as a prime example of effective, advanced regionalism. In operation since the first congress of American republics in 1889, the hemispheric organization comprised one of the oldest functioning regional systems. Before the 1930's, its activity was largely restricted to matters of a nonpolitical nature. Conventions signed in the 1930's broadened its scope by providing for the incorporation of principles of collective security —"an attack on any member state from extrahemispheric quarters is considered an attack on all members"—and of nonintervention and pacific settlement of disputes; these principles were backed up by the creation of appropriate institutional machinery, which soon proved extremely useful in confronting the danger of Axis aggression. Subsequent modifications led to the acceptance of a broader definition of collective security to cover "attack from inside or outside the hemisphere" and to the signing of an economic charter and creation of the present organizational machinery of the Organization of American States, which is based on conferences, meetings of foreign ministers, a permanent council of the O.A.S., a secretariat, auxiliary organs, and special assemblies for handling emergency situations. Mexico, along with nineteen other American republics, joined the United States in pledging to preserve the security, advance the economic and social welfare, and respect the national self-determination of all republics in the New World. By 1948, the inter-American system looked fine—on paper.

As Russia and the United States have clashed on the meaning of democracy, Mexico and the United States have read separate interpretations into the terms *security*, *welfare*, *nonintervention*, and *self-determination*. Conceiving that United States intervention represented a danger that was no less and perhaps even more likely than interference from extrahemispheric powers, Mexico tended to assume an absolutist position on intervention and self-determination, condemning specific postwar interferences of Uncle Sam in Bolivia, Guatemala, and Cuba. On the other hand, the inter-American system notwithstanding, the United States generally favored a policy of overt intervention whenever circumstances threatened to convert any nation into a Soviet satellite. This divergence underscored Mexican resistance in the fifties to U.S.-sponsored plans for a permanent inter-American defense committee with broad authority to prevent political subversion. Mexico also disagreed on foreign economic assistance, preferring large-scale, long-run, government-to-government aid to the private-investment ideas of Washington. Perhaps most important, Mexico truly hoped that the U.S. would become a positive force in raising commodity export prices and improving Latin American terms of trade.

Splits over these issues appeared at successive inter-American gatherings. Mexico plugged away at the urgent need for an inter-American development bank and large-scale U.S. financial assistance. After persistently dragging its feet on both proposals, Washington finally acquiesced by sponsoring the Inter-American Development Bank in 1959 and underwriting Kennedy's Alliance for Progress commitments two years later. Divergent opinions on intervention and national self-determination were expressed in the anti-Communist conferences held at Washington (1951), Caracas (1954), Santiago (1959), San José (1960), and Punta del Este (1962). In abstaining from voting on Secretary of State Dulles' anti-Communist resolutions aimed at Guatemala, Mexico contended that such measures contradicted inter-American commitments on nonintervention. Mexico also opposed holding any special meetings aimed at Castro's Cuba and, when overruled by a majority of O.A.S. members who convoked the meeting of foreign ministers at Punta del Este in early 1962, Mexico abstained from voting on a resolution calling for expulsion of Cuba from the O.A.S. and immediate suspension of commerce in arms with that nation. Mexico's foreign minister did declare at Punta del Este, however, that the ideology of Marxism-Leninism was incompatible with membership in the inter-American system; he also deplored Communist offensives in Latin America. His disapproval of expelling Cuba from the O.A.S., according to his own words, rested on Mexico's traditional absolutist policy on nonintervention and on the belief that inadequate juridical provisions existed in inter-American agreements to permit expulsion.

Whether Mexican voting in inter-American meetings was justified by appealing to juridical inadequacies, traditional Mexican foreign policy, or still other reasons, it was in line with Mexico's consistent policy of remaining aloof from Cold War politics as much as possible. Voting on the Castro regime clearly indicated that Mexico was unwilling to vote for sanctions that might have made big headlines in the United States yet, in the Mexican view, would have had no decisive effect on Castro Cuba. Mexico believes her foreign policy should be neither pro–Soviet Union nor anti–United States. She abhors interference by either nation in Mexican domestic affairs. On June 7, 1961, some months before the Punta del Este meeting, President López Mateos reasserted this desire in an address to the Mexican press. He stated:

Nothing is more harmful to Mexico's well-being and the internal peace which has cost her so much effort to consolidate than entanglement in the struggle between diametrically opposed political philosophies now in world conflict and battling to rob the Mexican people of the political thought incorporated in the Constitution of 1917 as a direct product of historical experience of Mexico's own independent life.

This viewpoint, while expressed in part to restrict extremist domestic movements within Mexico, suggests Mexico's wish for remaining free of Soviet intervention while at the same time refusing to open her doors to other foreign interests which advocate that Mexico change her economy in accordance with classical economic doctrines. Again, in the words of López Mateos, Mexico "shall not permit any retrogression that may injure her dignity or her patrimony, her laws or her rights, under pressure of either foreign forces or domestic groups."

In 1961, seemingly grasping the essence of the Mexican position, which coincided with opinions of other Latin American states, and under pressure of an expansion of Sino-Soviet influence, U.S. President John F. Kennedy launched what appeared to be a new inter-American policy. He dramatically stated that U.S. official policy favored comprehensive social reform in Latin America. In asserting on several occasions that the Latin American policy of the United States should coincide with objectives, policies, and realities of the Latin Americans, Kennedy naturally captured the imagination of many Mexicans. Reduced to their barest outlines, the goals of the Alliance for Progress program of Kennedy announced at Punta del Este, Uruguay, in 1961, envisaged attainment of progress, prosperity, and justice through evolutionary means. Aside from the implicit overtones of containing Marxism-Leninism and Castroism, few Mexicans found fault in what Kennedy stated to be the major objectives of his new Latin American policy: (1) to strengthen democratic institutions through national self-determination; (2) to accelerate economic and social development in order to bring about steady increases in per capita income; (3) to carry out rural housing programs; (4) to encourage comprehensive agrarian reforms; (5) to assure fair wages and satisfactory working conditions and establishment of effective systems of labor management and government cooperation and consultation; (6) to wipe out illiteracy; (7) to press forward with health and sanitation programs; (8) to reform tax laws; (9) to maintain monetary and fiscal policies that will avoid disastrous effects of the business cycle and simultaneously protect real purchasing power; (10) to stimulate private enterprise; (11) to find solutions to problems created by excessive price fluctuations in basic exports; and (12) to accelerate Latin American integration in order to stimulate economic and social development. Much of his program, therefore, centered squarely on Latin American initiative.

An examination of U.S. financial commitments for the Alliance for Progress might suggest that Kennedy's policy was really little more than a new label for drawing together the many uncoordinated programs that Washington had been carrying out for some years. While the Alliance placed greater emphasis on comprehensive development planning and social development than before, the differences appeared to some Mexicans to be more in degree than in kind. Moreover, unlike Roosevelt, Kennedy was not fighting big business at home, and Mexicans watchfully awaited any consequences that might flow from this basic difference. The presumption that greater financial expenditures were to enter the new picture also brought some skepticism: Mexicans did not overlook public remarks of Secretary of the Treasury Dillon upon his return from the Punta del Este Conference, when he assured U.S. businessmen that the Export-Import Bank of Washington, Inter-American Development Bank, other instrumentalities in which the U.S. government had invested, and additional sources encompassed in the Alliance for Progress were already extending capital to Latin America in amounts roughly equivalent to Alliance for Progress promises. The Alliance further raised doubts among Mexican private capitalists, who wondered whether Washington would extend capital on such favorable terms to the Mexican government that private entrepreneurs would suffer in competition, since interest rates on private loans would be comparatively disadvantageous. With Castroism and the Alliance for Progress hardly mutually exclusive subjects, Mexicans along with other Latin Americans probably will continue, as they did before Kennedy, to interpret actions of Washington along the traditional lines of nonintervention and national self-determination.

MEXICO TOMORROW

The Revolutionary Family in Mexico possesses ideological assets that ruling elites in emerging countries usually lack. It has sound notions of what the masses and classes truly desire and require. It knows much of the time where it wishes to lead the nation and how to arrive there. And it grasps the essential truths of social reform and economic progress: dedicated leadership, savings, investment, overcoming resistance to change, hard work, sacrifice. Within the Mexican milieu, Revolutionary Family goals for national development mean devotion to propositions in the Revolutionary Creed: constitutionalism and political liberalism; racial, religious, and intellectual tolerance; public education, public health, and social services; over-all economic growth; higher standards of living; industrialization and commercialization; agrarian and agricultural reform; defense of labor rights; and a greater voice in hemispheric and world councils. In giving substance to these objectives, the Mexican elite gears its policy to the exigencies of domestic and global politics and to the prosperity of Mexico and the world at large. So far, the psychological dynamics of the elite, stemming from the coincidence of dedication, friendship, self-interest, fear, and inertia, has paid off in terms of keeping the Revolutionary Family in power, avoiding political instability, advancing objectives in the Revolutionary Creed, and, all in all, elevating Mexico to an exemplary place in the annals of Latin American history.

Whatever else one may say about the Revolutionary Family, it is developing the nation along lines dictated by Mexico's own past and peculiar needs, demands, and aspirations. Roman Catholic, local Catholic, Freemason, Sephardic, and indigenous strains intermix with Revolutionary and universal pragmatic values in shaping Mexican religion and ethics. Indian and Spanish concepts and institutions underlie state ownership, communal agriculture, and authoritarian government. The Spanish language is successfully resisting the onslaught of English. Art, architecture, drama, and literature, for centuries rarely more than weak reflections of foreign cultures, now exhibit deep expressions of Mexicanism. Various ownership patterns—private, public, communal, cooperative, Mexican, foreign, joint venture—represent society's varying demands for economic and social justice no less than manifestations of custom and regional preferences. Mexico's "liberal Machiavellian" political system is consonant with Mexico's past and attuned to the real needs and expectations of its people.

Will glaring discrepancies between Revolutionary promises and practices continue to mark the Mexican political system in the years ahead? The written law still calls for effective suffrage, federalism, a separation of powers into executive, legislative, and judicial branches, and municipal autonomy. In reality, through utilizing rapid communications and transportation, the Revolution is centralizing and concentrating power in the Revolutionary Family head. Independent legislatures and judiciaries represent aspirations as far from fulfillment as they were before 1910. Select individuals move in and out of the inner circle of power, and interest-group leaders are sometimes consulted from above, yet effective federalism and an effective suffrage are absent. Effective suffrage implies the right of political minorities to acquire sufficient power to approach a position from which they might become the majority, but the Revolutionary Family denies opposition this right and, whenever nominations for offices wielding real power and patronage are at stake, restricts even its own official party to a peripheral role in the nomination process. The Revolutionary Family rules and reigns. Mexico and the Mexicans require and expect this state of affairs. Hence, responsibility for the failure to fulfill major statutory provisions concerning political institutions and processes should not be placed solely on Revolutionary regimes of today. Less obvious culprits are the original architects of 1917 who, while judiciously rejecting foreign models for Mexican cultural, social, and economic development, went astray in presuming that merely writing U.S. and French political creeds into basic Mexican law would transform Mexican political tradition and character.

A wide chasm will continue to separate the theory and practice of Mexico's political system as long as its laws are not revised to make room for liberal authoritarian, tutelary democratic patterns. Legal revision seems highly improbable, however, since popular ambivalence—a desire and need for authoritarianism versus an illusory aspiration for democracy—would exert a negative effect, as would the Revolutionary elite's desire to rationalize its conduct to the masses and to the outside world in terms of "democracy." Effective opposition parties hold no promise of working in Mexico. Free, uncontrolled elections are likewise out of the question. Independent legislatures and judiciaries run counter to tradition, need, and in a profound sense, expectation. The "liberal Machiavellian" heading Mexico must be authoritarian and at the same time perform the role of benevolent patriarch. He must preserve political stability, keep unions and the army loyal, insure peaceful transfer of power, and stamp out subversion; he must also accord human rights a fair degree of dignity, advance social justice, elevate living standards, and permit open criticism. Without political parties, free elections, or effective suffrage, the man at the top accordingly must promote fundamental individual freedoms. He obviously must possess the spirit and passion to govern no less than the art of governance. The Revolutionary Family or its successor will not and probably cannot govern according to the written word of present Mexican laws.

Command of Mexican destinies will by no means lodge in the Revolutionary Family automatically. To retain power, it must prove itself capable of resolving recurrent economic problems. Part of its success in this realm will depend on the vitality of the United States and world economies and, unless alternative sources of foreign exchange are discovered, on attracting growing numbers of foreign tourists. Above all, the Revolutionary elite must guide economic development to higher levels of productivity, further rationalization of agriculture, and broader consumer markets. Much has been accomplished through improving stock-raising methods, land utilization, electric power, petroleum, port facilities, foreign-trade structures, irrigation, industry, commerce, and finance. Much remains to be done. Public enterprises in particular must keep pace with Mexican needs. Some plants require expansion; others need new markets. Initiation of new enterprises is an imperative. Private and public enterprises alike must be permitted to accumulate sufficient surpluses to provide for indispensable expansion. Mexican economists sometimes forget that higher production in the private sector requires a willingness to invest and the motivation to reinvest and innovate. Expansion and higher efficiency also will require closer attention to proper financial planning. With formidable assistance from the World Bank, the Export-Import Bank, and other public foreign financial institutions, the Revolutionary elite has admirably attended to "social overhead" needs, especially in the realm of roads, railroads, electricity, and irrigation. Losing the confidence of these foreign sources of investment capital would prove costly by forcing Mexico to divert into these indispensable economic activities heavy amounts of capital destined for other uses.

The Revolutionary crusade for accelerated industrialization and commercialization of Mexico cannot triumph unless the state proves capable of coordinating the multiple economic and social phalanxes needed to lend proper depth to any advances. First of all, dynamic local entrepreneurs will want, indeed demand, a propitious investment climate. This in turn should expand the nucleus of responsible businessmen and attract larger numbers of young men possessing what Professor David McClelland calls "high achievement motivation." Second, further industrialization will require greater rationalization of agriculture—that is, higher output per unit of input—in order to increase industrial raw-material supplies, create new consumer markets, provide surpluses and savings, and stimulate labor mobility. Third, new tax legislation should not exempt businessmen, but it should reward, not penalize, initiative.

The tax law of 1962 contains so many escape clauses that local entrepreneurs often avoid tax payment entirely while foreign-owned enterprises
pay oppressive taxes that penalize them for their investment and initiative.
Fourth, enlargement of the privileged unionism class is desirable, but as
the constitutional amendment of 1962 forewarns, employer resources
should not be drained to pay for relatively heavy social and retirement
benefits that laborers will not enjoy before reaching old age. Greater
worker efficiency naturally will lead to higher real wages, hence to broader
consumer markets. Meanwhile, factory workers and peasants simply must
pay the price of rapid industrialization and commercialization of the
Mexican economy.

Mexico also should look for new markets abroad. By pushing for
conversion of the Latin American Free Trade Area into a true common
market, Mexico will be serving the best interests of its businessmen. In the
long run, Mexico and Brazil probably would enjoy a comparative edge
over other Latin American nations in any true common market. Close
examination of U.S. and European markets for potential new sales of
Mexican-made goods should become a permanent task of Mexican marketing experts. Replanting marginal farmlands, including croplands growing
surplus coffee and other export commodities no longer salable on world
markets, with high-yielding, marketable crops appears to be economically
feasible and a potential source of foreign exchange.

What is the future of private enterprise in Mexico? It has absolutely no ownership future in petroleum, the telegraph, railroads, or electricity, and a dim future in wholly owned operations in petrochemicals,
international aviation, motion pictures, newsprint, and large-scale mineral
exploitation. But even after state pre-emption of these industries and its
entrance into other business activities in competition with the private
sector, much remains for private enterprise. Precisely how much largely
depends on the Mexican government. The Revolutionary Family should
correct the popular, oversimplified notion that its New Conservative wing
stands for creating wealth and its Revolutionary Left wing advocates redistribution of wealth. Without new and greater sources of productivity,
big redistribution at this stage in Mexican growth would involve meager
wealth indeed. Furthermore, the Mexican government should raise again
and again the vital question of how it can strengthen Mexican private
enterprise and maximize its contribution to the country's economic,
political, and social development. It is the man, not the plan, that
innovates and labors.

Short of total state socialism, Mexico will need responsible private
entrepreneurs. Fortunately, a sizable nucleus of responsible entrepreneurs
exists there. The Garza Sadas, Azcárragas, Rochas, Carlos Trouyet, Bruno
Pagliai, Antonio Ruiz Galindo, César Balsa, and many more Mexican
entrepreneurs are progressive, forward-looking businessmen. They are, in

any modern sense of the term, responsible. The Alliance for Progress should not overlook them, any more than it should persist in wishing to make joint ventures out of all foreign investment. Some businesses will succeed best as 100 per cent Mexican concerns, others as 100 per cent foreign-owned concerns, still others as joint ventures. After all, the source of the investment capital is less important than the attitude and behavior of the investor. If foreign companies *think* and *act* Mexican, like Dupont, Sears, and Tolteca, they are more welcome than Mexicans who think and act "foreign" by engaging in crude, irresponsible exploitation and capital flights. Neither the Revolutionary Family nor U.S. public-assistance programs can afford not to stimulate and encourage the many responsible entrepreneurs long resident in Mexico, whether of Mexican, American, German, Japanese, French, Italian, or British nationality.

The future of agriculture was examined in depth in Chapter 9 and requires little additional comment here. Alliance for Progress declarations on the intrinsic value of Latin American agrarian reform perhaps merit a short remark on lessons available from the Mexican experiment. Mexico's agrarian reform accomplished more than its critics admit and less than its apologists contend. On one side, it frightened sound investment capital away from agriculture, created too many unproductive *minifundia* plots, and destroyed modern, efficient farmers along with irresponsible traditionalists. It brought into the countryside widespread corruption and demagoguery, opportunistic officials who preyed on the peasants, and politicians who grabbed highly productive farmlands away from rightful owners; and it placed ruthless, illiterate local bosses in charge of credit, crop sales, and distribution of machinery, fertilizers, and seeds. On another side, the Mexican agrarian reform generated nationalism, social modernism, and economic integration; it helped break the vicious circle of poverty and make many farmlands productive, and it bestowed personal dignity on the peasant. Nobody should study Mexican agrarian reform outside the context of total Mexican economic and political evolution. In some instances, social justice was served by redistribution of land; in other instances, it was abused. Agrarian reform in Mexico was not, and is not, the panacea that outspoken enthusiasts contend. The Revolutionary Family and the rural masses painfully discovered that agrarian reform does not resolve the big problem of daily bread.

Two interrelated agrarian measures heretofore untried in Mexico might help rural and over-all economic development. One is the application of a land tax based on the potential yield of an agricultural plot, which would penalize inefficient farmers and reward efficient producers. A second is the introduction of a decentralized, self-help house-construction program under which impoverished peasants, aided by their children, could build their own dwellings. With several million Mexican peasant families exhibiting no marginal propensity to save or real alternative labor value, such a project would put a presently marginal economic resource to immediate practical use. The proposed new land tax would alone finance the small amount of required building materials (homemade adobe blocks would serve as primary construction material), tools, and outside technical help. Even then, resistance to change, indolence, and apathy would find hundreds of thousands of peasant families wasting away their opportunity.

A brief comment on organized labor: In view of the excesses of labor leaders, the obsequious behavior of labor bosses before Revolutionary Family rulers, and apparent future development burdens to be carried by the rank and file, why not abolish Mexican trade unions? Government economists know that forced savings, inflation, and other forces are combining to keep the relative size of the several occupational classes in Mexico about the same. Organized labor, except for the privileged unionists in the electricians', telephone workers', electric-power, petroleum, and railroad unions, is probably receiving lower real wages today than it did in the 1930's or early 1940's. (The electric-power industry and railroads, both state-owned, have received big outside financing from the World Bank and the Export-Import Bank; relatively high benefits to oil and telephone workers have slowed down the development of these essential industries.) Unless the Revolutionary Left and Independent Left come into leadership of the Revolutionary Family and order immediate adjustments in income distribution, a not-unlikely prospect that temporarily would raise the affluence of organized labor at the probable expense of investment in Mexico's productive machine, the few reasons for keeping the big CTM and other captive unions intact are these: (1) Without them or their equivalent, Revolutionary Family control would tend to become more authoritarian; (2) trade unions perform the useful, though sometimes abuseful, function of enforcing job tenure and security; (3) these unions serve to keep labor rank and file loyal to the Mexican government, and, hence, to its recent policies of forced savings and balanced economic growth; and (4) captive Mexican union leaders loyal to the arduous task of forging an independent nation maintain vigilance against Communist subversive tactics. Unionization and economic backwardness are strange bedfellows.

A concluding word on foreign policy and the Alliance for Progress. For decades now, the Mexican Revolution has implemented a program of evolutionary reform remarkably like that outlined in the Alliance. The Revolution has transformed Mexican society in many respects and has been able to sustain important phases of domestic economic development. An important object lesson for the Alliance is that the making of modern Mexico already has consumed decades and has still not elevated per capita income sufficiently to lift Mexico into the ranks of the developed nations. Handicapped by a century of national independence with meager material growth, while Europe, the United States, and Japan were saving, building, and industrializing, Mexican manpower has been unable to catch up. Authoritarianism, poverty, ignorance, and capital flights are prevalent. If the Mexican experiment is a fitting model for progress elsewhere in Latin America, then let us realize that the Alliance for Progress, backed up by dedicated leadership in Washington and in Latin American capitals, will require at least a generation before its noble objectives begin to find fulfillment in Latin American reality.

A NOTE ON SOURCES

Although this book is a synthesis of various sources—formal interviews; informal discussions; personal experiences; university field research; private collections of papers; business, interest-group, government, and international-agency archival papers; critiques of early drafts of the manuscript; published data—this note is devoted exclusively to published data. Other sources, the reader may remember, are commented on briefly in the Prelude. The selective list of published materials presented here is classified into eight sections: current bibliographical guides; permanent revolution (Chapter 1); before the revolution (2); fifty years of revolution (3, 4); politics and government (5, 6); religion (7); economic development (8, 9, 10, 11); and international affairs (12).

CURRENT BIBLIOGRAPHICAL GUIDES

Keeping abreast of new publications about Mexico is facilitated by several general reference works. An indispensable aid is the annual *Handbook of Latin American Studies* prepared under the direction of the Hispanic Foundation in the Library of Congress and published by the University of Florida Press. Faster contact is made possible by three quarterly bibliographies: *Inter-American Review of Bibliography*, published by the Inter-American Committee on Bibliography of the Pan American Union; *Doors to Latin America*, issued by the Inter-American Bibliographical and Library Association of the University of Florida library; and *Latin America in Periodical Literature*, prepared by the Center of Latin American Studies of the University of California at Los Angeles. Monthly numbers of the *Readers Guide to Periodical Literature* offer a handy source for seeking current periodical literature on Mexico written in English. The reader may also wish to consult the *Boletín Bibliográfico* (Secretaría de Hacienda y Crédito Público), *México en Cultura* (Fondo de Cultura Económica), the weekly *México en la Cultura* (supplement of the Mexico City newspaper *Novedades*), and book review and bibliographical sections of journals listed under notes for later chapters.

THE PROPOSITION AND THE REVOLUTIONARY FAMILY

Philosophers, critics, and literary figures in Mexico have presented ideas of relevance to the broad themes of Mexico and the Mexicans. To mention but a few: Justo Sierra, Francisco Bulnes, Porfirio Parra, and Andrés Molina Enríquez, who wrote on the eve of Revolution; the *Ateneo de la Juventud* group of 1909–11, which counted in its ranks the illustrious Antonio Caso,

Alfonso Reyes, and José Vasconcelos; the "*Nosotros* Group" of 1912–14—
Gregorio López y Fuentes, Francisco González Guerrero, and Rodrigo Torres
Hernández; the "Seven Wise Men," also known as "The Generation of 1915
Group," composed of Alfonso Caso, Antonio Castro Leal, Manuel Gómez
Morín, Vicente Lombardo Toledano, Alberto Vázquez del Mercado, Jesús
Morena Vaca, and Teófilo Olea y Leyva; Pedro Henríquez Urena (a Dominican
by origin); Luis Cabrera; the *Contemporáneos* of the 1920's, which included
in their fold Jaime Torres Bodet and Carlos Pellicer; the *Estridentistas* of the
1920's, led by Manuel Maples Arce and Germán List Arzubide; the "*Taller*
Group" and "*Tierra Nueva* Group" of the late 1930's, headed respectively
by Octavio Paz and by Leopoldo Zea and Alí Chumacero; Samuel Ramos;
José Gaos (a Spaniard); the "Hyperion Group" of the late 1940's and 1950's,
a small group of writers that included Leopoldo Zea, Emilio Uranga, Luis
Villoro, Ricardo Guerra, Jorge Portilla, and Joaquín McGregor; Alejandro
Rossi (an Argentine); Eduardo García Máynez; Francisco Larroyo; Oswaldo
Robles; Gustavo R. Velasco; Santiago Ramírez; Francisco González Pineda;
Daniel Cosío Villegas; Jesús Silva Herzog; Gonzalo Aguirre Beltrán; Lucio
Mendieta y Núñez; Pablo González Casanova; Víctor Urquidi; and José
Moreno Villa, Luis Recasens Siches, José Medina Echevarría, and Ramón
Xirau (all Spanish refugees). Of course, some writers noted as members of a
specific group subsequently made greater contributions writing strictly on their
own. This is particularly true of the Casos, Vasconcelos, Gómez Morín, Lom-
bardo Toledano, Paz, and Zea. Novelists, essayists, and poets of the earlier
generation—men such as Alfonso Reyes, Mariano Azuela, Martín Luis Guzmán, Manuel Gamio, Jaime Torres Bodet, Carlos Pellicer, and Mauricio
Magdaleno—should be balanced today against such contemporary writers as
Octavio Paz, Agustín Yáñez, Ricardo Pozas, Juan Rulfo, Luis Spota, Carlos
Fuentes, Xavier Vargas Pardo, Alí Chumacero, and Juan José Arreola. Many
contemporary writers on economic, social, political, and cultural themes have
been brought together in the comprehensive four-volume *México: 50 años de
revolución* (I. *La economía*, II. *La vida social*, III. *La política*, IV. *La cultura*),
published by the Fondo de Cultura Económica, Mexico, 1960–62, with funds
appropriated by the Mexican government to commemorate the golden anni-
versary of the Revolution.

Analytical interpretations of subjects presented in Chapter 1 have also
appeared in English. Three reviews recently devoted issues to Mexican intellectualism: *Evergreen Review* (No. 7, 1959) offers excellent translations of
some of Mexico's leading young writers; *Texas Quarterly* (Vol. II, 1959)
contains impressions on twentieth-century culture; and *Mexico This Month*
(November, 1960 and Spring Issue, 1962) presents several interpretations of
Mexican intellectualism. A report on the series of studies growing out of
"Hyperion Group" philosophy and edited by Leopoldo Zea is available in
John L. Phelan, "México y lo Mexicano," *Hispanic American Historical
Review* (XXXVI, 1956). Carl O. Sauer interprets Mexico from a geographer's
outlook in "The Personality of Mexico," *Geographical Review* (XXXI, 1941).
Harold E. Davis, *Latin American Social Thought: The History of Its Develop-
ment Since Independence, with Selected Readings* (Washington, 1961),
appraises important trends in social thinking and includes translations of
Justo Sierra, José Vasconcelos, and Antonio Caso. A skillful effort to relate
Mexican development to a "need for achievement" ethic is found in David C.
McClelland, *The Achieving Society* (Princeton, 1961). A fascinating attempt
to place Mexico in proper world ideological currents, although questionable
in results, is made by F. S. C. Northrup, *The Meeting of East and West* (New

York, 1946). Patrick Romanell, *Making of the Mexican Mind: A Study in Recent Mexican Thought* (Lincoln, 1952), presents a good synopsis of Spanish-refugee thought but omits major contributions of Mexican intellectuals to the "making of the Mexican mind." Frank Tannenbaum, *Mexico: The Struggle for Peace and Bread* (New York, 1950), is an analytical expression of Mexican thought up to about 1950 on theories of land, labor, property, education, and foreign policy. Charles H. Haight, *The Contemporary Mexican Revolution as Viewed by Mexican Intellectuals* (Ph.D. thesis, Stanford Univ., 1956), contains worthwhile material on the intellectuals, little on the "contemporary revolution." Ralph L. Beals and Norman D. Humphrey, *No Frontier to Learning: The Mexican Student in the United States* (Minneapolis, 1957), includes an interesting analysis of the general cultural milieu in which most Mexican students coming to the U.S. were raised. W. Rex Crawford, *A Century of Latin American Thought* (Cambridge, 1961), devotes one section to Mexican thought. John A. Crow, *Mexico Today* (New York, 1957), offers colorful impressions of Mexican character. Oscar Lewis, *Five Families: Mexican Case Studies in the Culture of Poverty* (New York, 1959) and *The Children of Sánchez: Autobiography of a Mexican Family* (New York, 1961) are pioneering studies of a social anthropologist who attempts to capture Mexican values through the hard realities of daily family life. Other works in English consulted in writing this chapter are entered below under sections where they bore a more direct relationship.

BEFORE THE REVOLUTION

Although an abundance of scholarly works are available for most periods and themes of Spanish colonial rule, few can be found that deal adequately with the pre-Conquest and 1810–1910 period. For the pre-Conquest epoch, new discoveries, primarily by Mexicans and Americans, are making several formerly reliable studies unreliable. Recent studies, bringing to light many new finds, accent various subjects. Eric R. Wolf, *Sons of the Shaking Earth* (Chicago, 1959), emphasizes man-land relationships. Frederick A. Peterson, *Ancient Mexico* (London, 1959), primarily a study of the Aztecs, is broader on other pre-Conquest peoples and in general more reliable than the older George Vaillant, *The Aztecs of Mexico*. Carmen Cook de Leonard, ed., *Esplendor del México antiguo* (2 vols., México, 1959), contains summaries by leading authorities on pre-Conquest times. John Paddock, *Tomorrow in Ancient Mesoamerica* (Editorial Pax-México, in press), updates and enlarges his overview of ancient Mesoamerica presented earlier in *Texas Quarterly* (Vol. II, 1959). Miguel León Portilla, *Aztec Thought and Culture* (Norman, Oklahoma, 1963), introduces fascinating themes on Aztec civilization. Michael Coe, *Ancient Peoples and Places: Mexico* (Praeger, 1962), offers readers an up-to-date treatment of ancient Mesoamerica. The erudite Alfonso Caso, *The Aztecs: People of the Sun* (Norman, Oklahoma, 1958), is a good survey of Aztec religion. Deserving inclusion with these recent titles are the earlier works by Miguel Covarrubias, *Indian Art of Mexico and Central America* (New York, 1957), whose scope is much broader than its title suggests, and Eric Thompson, *The Rise and Fall of Maya Civilization* (Norman, Oklahoma, 1954), an excellent nontechnical presentation of Mayan culture. The reader desirous of pursuing pre-Conquest themes in depth is referred to the exhaustive, monumental bibliography published in 1962 and compiled by the noted Mexican anthropologist, Ignacio Bernal—30,000 entries on the ethnology and archeology of Mesoamerica.

For fuller treatment of themes touched upon in the Conquest and colonial epochs, the reader should consult several noteworthy works. Space unfortunately will not permit mention of more than a highly selective few. Hernán Cortés, *Letters to the Emperor* (various editions), incorporates the conqueror's official communications to the King of Spain. William H. Prescott, *History of the Conquest of Mexico* (various editions), is a prodigious, highly readable, though not always reliable account of the Conquest. Arthur Aiton, *Antonio de Mendoza, First Viceroy of New Spain* (Durham, 1927), is helpful in understanding establishment of Spanish governance patterns in New Spain. Clarence A. Haring, *The Spanish Empire in America* (New York, 1947), is the standard definitive work on Spanish colonial rule. Silvio A. Zavala, *New Viewpoints on the Spanish Colonization of America* (Philadelphia, 1943), is a scholarly appraisal by an outstanding Mexican authority. Bernardino de Sahagún, *A General History of the Things of New Spain* (5 vols., Santa Fe, New Mexico, 1950–54), is a translation of original writings by an outstanding Spanish prelate of the early colonial epoch. Lesley B. Simpson, *The Encomienda in New Spain: The Beginning of Spanish Mexico* (Berkeley, 1950), analyzes Spanish policies on Indian labor. Lewis Hanke, *The Spanish Struggle for Justice in the Conquest of America* (Philadelphia, 1949), stands as the classical work on Spanish policy toward the Indians. Philip W. Powell, *Soldiers, Indians, and Silver: The Northward Advance of New Spain, 1550–1600* (Berkeley, 1952), does remarkably good justice to the title chosen. Arthur P. Whitaker, *Latin America and the Enlightenment* (Ithaca, 1961), analyzes cultural influences of the Enlightenment on Spain, Portugal, and their New World colonies in the eighteenth century; Clement Motten, *Mexican Silver and the Enlightenment* (Philadelphia, 1950), is a remarkable little volume on science and intellectual currents of the eighteenth century. Alexander von Humboldt, *Political Essay on the Kingdom of New Spain* (4 vols., various editions), presents valuable impressions on the status of New Spain on the eve of Mexican independence.

Entering the period 1810–1910, the number of quality works by both Mexicans and foreigners declines. Solid interpretations of the transition from colony to nation-state are found in Lillian E. Fisher, *The Background of the Revolution for Mexican Independence* (Boston, 1934), John B. Rydjord, *Foreign Interest in the Independence of New Spain* (Durham, 1935), and Arthur P. Whitaker, *The United States and the Independence of Latin America, 1800-1830* (Baltimore, 1941). An outstanding Mexican conservative's approach to problems of the first decades of the nineteenth century is found in Lucas Alamán, *Historia de México, 1808-1849* (5 vols., México, 1849–52). A scholarly treatment of Morelos is available in Alfonso Teja Zabre, *Vida de Morelos, nueva versión* (México, 1959). An extremely valuable guide to the principal writings on the 1821-1910 period of Mexican history, as well as on the entire national period up to 1960, is Robert A. Potash, "Historiography of Mexico Since 1821," *Hispanic American Historical Review* (Vol. XL, 1960). Evaluations of the status of scholarship in the epoch are also presented by Robert A. Naylor, "Research Opportunities in Modern Latin America: I. Mexico and Central America," *The Americas* (Vol. XVIII, 1962), and by Edmundo O'Gorman, "La historiografía," *México: 50 años de revolución, Vol. IV: La cultura* (México, 1962). With the Potash article readily accessible to most readers desirous of pursuing themes treated in the 1821-1910 section of my Chapter 2, and since I personally agree with most of Professor Potash's comments, I shall first of all merely mention the names of authors whose works in Spanish I have consulted across the years and believe to be representative, referring the reader to the Potash article for full titles and evaluations: Lucas Alamán, Vito Alessio Robles, Ignacio Altamirano, Arturo Arnáiz y Freg, Gabino Barreda, Carlos Bosch García, José Bravo Ugarte, Francisco Bulnes, Alberto María Carreño, José R. del Castillo, Luis Chávez Orozco, Daniel Cosío Villegas, Mariano Cuevas, Francisco G. Cosmes, Genaro García, Ricardo García Granados, Andrés Molina Enríquez, José María Luis Mora, Melchor Ocampo, Porfirio Parra, Francisco Paula de Arrangoiz, Carlos Pereyra, Robert A. Potash ("El banco de avio de México. El fomento de la industria, 1821-1846"), Emilio Rabasa, Jesús Reyes Heroles, Vicente Riva Palacio, Justo Sierra, Alfonso Teja Zabre, Servando Teresa de Mier, José C. Valadés, Francisco Zarco, and Leopoldo Zea. A special note seems appropriate on the progress of the scholarly endeavor being carried on by Daniel Cosío Villegas and his group of historians at the Colegio de México. Entitled *Historia moderna de México* and published by Editorial Hermes, five volumes in this prodigious work had appeared by 1963: 3 volumes on "La República Restaurada"—I. *La vida política*, II. *La vida económica*, and III. *La vida social*—and 2 volumes on "El Porfiriato"—IV. *La vida social* and V. *Vida política exterior*. I should like to add to the Potash balance sheet a recent volume by Jesús Silva Herzog, *Breve historia de la revolución mexicana: los antecedentes y la etapa maderista* (Fondo de Cultura Económica, 1960). Other works consulted and published since 1960 are listed under subsequent chapter headings.

In arbitrarily restricting works on the 1810-1910 period written by foreigners and available in English, my preferential list of fifteen authors would include, in addition to the monumental studies of Hubert H. Bancroft, *History of Mexico* (6 vols., San Francisco, 1883–88) and *History of the North Mexican States and Texas* (2 vols., San Francisco, 1884–89), the following: Carleton Beals, *Porfirio Díaz, Dictator of Mexico* (Philadelphia, 1932), not always precise on facts, yet it remains a colorful and devastating account of the old autocrat; Harry Bernstein, *Modern and Contemporary Latin America* (Philadelphia, 1952), of which Chapters 4–6 are especially outstanding on Mexican regionalism and intellectual history; Frances E. Calderón de la Barca, *Life in Mexico During a Residence of Two Years in That Country* (London, 1843), presents the author's eyewitness account of life in early independent Mexico; Wilfred H. Callcott, *Santa Anna: The Story of an Enigma Who Once Was Mexico* (Norman, 1936), leaves much to be desired but still represents the best available biography of Santa Anna; Egon Corti, *Maximilian and Charlotte of Mexico* (2 vols., New York, 1947), is a respectable accounting of the second empire; Thomas E. Cotner, ed., *Essays in Mexican History* (Austin, 1958), of which Chapters 5–13 present a scholarly treatment of select themes relevant to the period; Charles M. Flandrau, *Viva México!* (New York, 1908), submits eyewitness descriptions of Mexican life at a moment when the Díaz regime is nearly finished; David Pletcher, *Rails, Mines, and Progress: Seven American Promoters in Mexico, 1867-1911* (Ithaca, 1958), is a superb study of foreign entrepreneurial talents at work in the period after Maximilian's demise; J. Fred Rippy, *The United States and Mexico* (New York, 1931), seems to be the best among several studies by U.S. scholars of nineteenth century U.S.–Mexican relations; William S. Robertson, *Iturbide of Mexico* (Durham, 1952), though now requiring revision in the light of recent Mexican studies on the subject, stands as the best biography of Iturbide; Ralph Roeder, *Juárez and His Mexico* (2 vols., New York, 1947), while void of documentation, is the best work available on Mexico's great nineteenth-century liberal; Walter V. Scholes, *Mexican Politics During the Juárez Regime, 1855-1872* (Columbia, Mo., 1957), is a highly readable account of factional politics during the "Age of Reform"; Lesley B. Simpson, *Many Mexicos* (Berkeley, 1952), of which Chapters 20–23 contain provocative interpretations of the 1821-1910 period; Alfred P. Tischendorf, *Great Britain and Mexico in the Era of Porfirio Díaz* (Durham, 1961), is a balanced account of British investments in the Mexico of Díaz; and Henry Ward, *Mexico in 1827* (2 vols., London, 1823), is an eyewitness account of events during the first decade of Mexican national independence.

To keep abreast of new research on epochs before the Revolution, see the earlier note on "current bibliographical guides," and additionally consult the following journals: *América Indígena* and *Anuario Indigenista* (Inter-American Indian Institute); *Ánales* (Instituto Nacional de Antropología e Historia); *Boletín Bibliográfico de Antropología Americana* (Pan American Institute of Geography and History); *Ciencias Políticas y Sociales* (UNAM); *Filosofía y Letras* (UNAM); *Hispanic American Historical Review* (Conference on Latin American History, American Historical Association); *Historia Mexicana* and *Foro Internacional* (El Colegio de México); *Memorias* (Instituto Nacional de Antropología e Historia); *Revista de Historia de América* (Commission on History, Pan American Institute of Geography and History); *Revista Mexicana de Estudios Antropológicos* (Sociedad Mexicana de Antropología); and *The Americas* (Academy of American Franciscan History).

FIFTY YEARS OF REVOLUTION

With new archival material made public yearly, particularly files of organized interest groups and cabinet ministries, intellectual doors are opening to the historian of contemporary Mexico. Research needs and suggestions on procedure—excluding, however, several important themes and references to archival materials—have been offered by Professor Naylor (see third paragraph of notes for Chapter 2). In the last decade alone, four valuable bibliographical studies have appeared: Howard F. Cline, "Mexican Community Studies," *Hispanic American Historical Review* (XXXII, 1952), a comprehensive annotated bibliography of the subject; Luis González González and others, *Fuentes de la historia contemporánea de México* (México, 1961–62), a three-volume compilation of some 24,078 entries on the 1910-1940 period; Robert A. Potash, "Historiography of Mexico Since 1821," *Hispanic American Historical Review* (XL, 1960), an unsurpassed critical commentary on historiography since national independence; and Stanley R. Ross, "Bibliography of Sources for Contemporary Mexican History," *Hispanic American Historical Review* (XXXIX, 1959), a short critique of Mexican bibliographies, plus a description of the Colegio de México's *Historia moderna de México* project. In addition to these sources, the reader interested in pursuing themes presented in Chapters 3 and 4 should consult Roberto Ramos, *Bibliografía de la revolución mexicana* (3 vols., México, 1931, 1935, 1940; vols. 1 and 2 re-edition in 1958), John T. Vance and Helen Clagett, *A Guide to the Law and Legal Literature of Mexico* (Washington, 1945), and the indispensable *Handbook of Latin American Studies* and other bibliographical sources mentioned earlier under "current bibliographical guides."

The reader may profit from knowing the titles of the publications I found most useful in writing Chapters 3 and 4. I defer to later sections those publications bearing directly on the post–World War II epoch—specifically, the period after Cardenas–Ávila Camacho; this seemed a judicious allocation for properly citing specific themes of interest groups, political publics, political processes, religion, education, economic life, and foreign policy, although these

354 A NOTE ON SOURCES

works of course proved helpful in writing Chapters 3 and 4 as well. Limited here by considerations of space, I refer the reader for evaluations of the works listed to bibliographies of González González, the *Handbook of Latin American Studies*, Potash, and Ramos. Publications cited below are grouped into categories of (I) works of a general topical nature encompassing broad periods of the Revolution without focusing on a specific Revolutionary Family phase, and (II-V) studies relevant to a specific Revolutionary Family epoch. Unless otherwise indicated, volumes were published in Mexico.

I. General Works. Miguel Alessio Robles, *Historia política de la revolución* (1946); *México: 50 años de revolución* (4 vols., 1960–62); Harry Bernstein, *Modern and Contemporary Latin America* (Philadelphia, 1952); Blas Urrea, *Veinte años después* (1938); Anita Brenner, *The Wind That Swept Mexico: The History of the Mexican Revolution, 1910-1942* (New York, 1943); Tomme C. Call, *The Mexican Venture* (New York, 1953); Wilfred H. Callcott, *Liberalism in Mexico, 1857-1929* (Palo Alto, Calif., 1931); Agustín Casasola, *Historia gráfica de la revolución mexicana 1900-1960* (4 vols., 1960); Howard F. Cline, *Mexico, Revolution to Evolution, 1940-1960* (London, 1962); Alberto María Carreño, *Páginas de historia mexicana* (1936); Manuel Gamio, *Hacia un México nuevo* (1937); Ernest H. Gruening, *Mexico and Its Heritage* (New York, 1928); Frank L. Kluckholn, *The Mexican Challenge* (New York, 1939); Oscar Lewis, "Mexico Since Cárdenas," in Lyman Bryson, ed., *Social Change in Latin America Today* (New York, 1960); José Mancisidor, *Historia de la revolución mexicana* (1958); Francisco Naranjo, *Diccionario biográfico revolucionario* (1935); Henry B. Parkes, *A History of Mexico* (Boston, 1960); Herbert I. Priestly, *The Mexican Nation* (New York, 1930); Selden Rodman, *Mexican Journal* (1958); Jesús Romero Flores, *Anales históricos de la revolución mexicana* (4 vols., 1939); Lesley B. Simpson, *Many Mexicos* (Berkeley, 1952); Frank Tannenbaum, *Peace by Revolution: An Interpretation of Mexico* (New York, 1933) and *Mexico: The Struggle for Peace and Bread* (New York, 1950); Alfonso Taracena, *La verdadera revolución mexicana* (8 vols., 19?–1962); José Vasconcelos, *Breve historia de México* (1937); Jorge Vera Estañol, *La revolución mexicana, orígines y resultados* (1957).

II. Madero Phase. Luis Cabrera, *Obras políticas del Lic. Blas Urrea, 1909-1912* (1921); Manuel Calero, *Un decenio de política mexicana* (New York, 1920); Charles C. Cumberland, *The Mexican Revolution: Genesis Under Madero* (Austin, 1952); Ricardo Flores Magón, *Epistolario revolucionario íntimo* (3 vols., 1924–25); Manuel González Ramírez, ed., *Fuentes para la historia de la revolución mexicana* (series of studies being published by the Patronato de la Historia de Sonora); Juan Gualberto Amaya, *Madero y los auténticos revolucionarios de 1910* (1946); Manuel Márquez Sterling, *Los últimos días del presidente Madero* (Havana, 1917, and Mexico, 1958); Stanley R. Ross, *Francisco I. Madero, Apostle of Mexican Democracy* (New York, 1955); Jesús Silva Herzog, *Breve historia de la revolución mexicana: los antecedentes y la etapa maderista* (1960); Alfonso Taracena, *Madero: vida del hombre y del político* (1937); Francisco Vázquez Gómez, *Memorias políticas, 1909-1913* (1933).

III. Carranza, Obregón, Zapata, and Villa, 1913-1919. Juan B. Barragán Rodríguez, *Historia del ejército y de la revolución constitucionalista* (1946); Clarence C. Clendenen, *The United States and Pancho Villa: A*

Study in Unconventional Diplomacy (Ithaca, 1961); Antonio Díaz Soto y Gama, La revolución agraria del sur y Emiliano Zapata su caudillo (1960); Juan Gualberto Amaya, Venustiano Carranza (1947); Victoriano Huerta, Memorias de Victoriano Huerta (1957); Gildardo Magaña, Emiliano Zapata y el agrarismo en México (5 vols., 1951–52); Antonio Manero, Qué es la revolución (1915); Luis Melgarejo and J. Fernández Rojas, El congreso constituyente de 1916-1917 (1917); Bernardino Mena Brito, Carranza, sus amigos, sus énemigos (1935); Querido Moheno, Mi actuación política después de la decena trágica (1939); Álvaro Obregón, Ocho mil kilómetros en campaña (1917 and 1959); Félix F. Palaviani, Mi vida revolucionaria (1937) and Historia del congreso constituyente de 1917 (2 vols., 1948); Edgcumb Pinchon, Zapata the Unconquerable (New York, 1941); Robert E. Quirk, The Mexican Revolution, 1914-1915 (Bloomington, Ind., 1960); Pastor Rouaix, Génesis de los artículos 27 y 123 de la constitución política de 1917 (1959); Miguel Sánchez Lamego, Historia militar de la revolución constitucionalista (4 vols., 1956–57); William L. Sherman and Richard E. Greenleaf, Victoriano Huerta: A Reappraisal (1960); Jesús Silva Herzog, Breve historia de la revolución mexicana: la etapa constitucionalista y la lucha de facciones (1960); Jesús Sotelo Inclán, Raíz y razón de Zapata (1943); and Francisco L. Urquizo, Páginas de la revolución (1956).

IV. Northern Dynasty, 1919-1935. Vito Alessio Robles, Los tratados de Bucareli (1937); Alonso Capetillo, La rebelión sin cabeza (1925): Adolfo de la Huerta, Memorias (1957); John W. F. Dulles, Yesterday in Mexico (Austin, 1961); Javier J. Gaxiola, Jr., El presidente Rodríguez, 1932-1934 (1938); Juan Gualberto Amaya, Los gobiernos de Obregón, Calles, y regímenes "peleles" derivados del callismo (1947); Hubert Herring and Herbert Weinstock, ed., Renascent Mexico (New York, 1935); Froylan C. Manjarrez, La jornada institucional (2 vols., 1930); A. C. Matamoros and Gilberto Valenzuela, Sonora y Carranza (1921); Harold Nicolson, Dwight Morrow; Alberto Pani, Apuntes autobiográficos (1943) and Mi contribución al nuevo régimen (1936); Partido Nacional Revolucionario, Plan Sexenal del P.N.R. (1934); Partido Nacional Revolucionario, La jira del general Lázaro Cárdenas: síntesis ideológica (1934); Emilio Portes Gil, Quince años de política mexicana (1941); Stanley R. Ross, "Dwight Morrow and the Mexican Revolution," Hispanic American Historical Review (XXXVIII, 1958); Alfonso Taracena, Mi vida en el vértigo de la revolución (1936); José Vasconcelos, four-volume work entitled (1) Ulises criollo, (2) La tormenta, (3) El desastre, and (4) El proconsulado (1936–38).

V. Cárdenas and Ávila Camacho. Luis Amendolla, La revolución comienze a los cuarenta (1948); Manuel Ávila Camacho, Seis años de actividad nacional (1946); Ramón Beteta, Pensamiento y dinámica de la revolución mexicana (1951) and The Mexican Revolution, A Defense (1937); Gilberto Bosques, The National Revolutionary Party of Mexico and the Six-Year Plan (1937); Lázaro Cárdenas, Seis años de gobierno al servicio de México (1940); Confederación de Trabajadores de México, CTM, 1936-1941 (1941); Eduardo Correa, El balance de cardenismo (1941); David E. Cronon, Josephus Daniels in Mexico (Madison, Wisc., 1960); Josephus Daniels, Shirt-Sleeve Diplomat (Chapel Hill, 1947); Betty Kirk, Covering the Mexican Front: The Battle of Europe versus America (Norman, 1942); PRM, Segundo Plan Sexenal 1940-1946 (1939), Ávila Camacho y su ideologia: la revolución en marcha; jira electoral (1940), and 33 meses al servicio de la revolución: memoria del par-

tido de la revolución mexicana (1943); PNR, *Partido Nacional Revoluciona-rio y el Plan Sexenal* (1937); Virginia Prewett, *Reportage on Mexico* (New York, 1941); Jesús Silva Herzog, *La revolución mexicana en crisis* (1944); W. C. Townsend, *Lázaro Cárdenas: Mexican Democrat* (Ann Arbor, 1952); Nathaniel and Sylvia Weyl, *The Reconquest of Mexico: The Years of Lázaro Cárdenas* (New York, 1939); Arthur P. Whitaker, ed., "Mexico Today," *Annals of the American Academy of Political and Social Science* (March, 1940).

POLITICS AND GOVERNMENT

Several bibliographical sources, unmentioned previously, are helpful in undertaking a study of Mexico's political system. There are the review sections in *Ciencias Políticas y Sociales, Revista Mexicana de Sociología, Foro Interna-cional,* and the *American Political Science Review.* There are the two articles by José Bullejos, "Fuentes para el estudio político y social de América Latina," and Frank R. Brandenburg, "Estudios de gobierno y política sobre América Latina realizados por intelectuales de los Estados Unidos," *Ciencias Políticas y Sociales* (VI, 1960). There are the bibliographical sections of six unpublished doctoral dissertations—Eugene M. Braderman, *A Study of Political Parties and Politics in Mexico Since 1890* (Illinois, 1938); Frank R. Brandenburg, *Mexico: An Experiment in One-Party Democracy* (Pennsylvania, 1955); Stephen E. Goodspeed, *The Role of the Chief Executive in Mexico: Politics, Power and Administration* (California, 1947); Leon Vincent Padgett, *Popular Participation in the Mexican One Party System* (Northwestern, 1955); Wendell K. G. Schaeffer, *National Administration in Mexico: Its Development and Present Status* (California, 1949); and Robert E. Scott, *Some Aspects of Mexican Federalism, 1917-1948* (Wisconsin, 1949). And there are the bibliographical notes in Frank R. Brandenburg, *Partidos políticos* (mimeo., Mexico, 1957), William P. Tucker, *The Mexican Government Today* (Minneapolis, 1957), and Robert E. Scott, *Mexican Government in Transition* (Urbana, 1959).

Perhaps the single major difference among U.S. intellectuals who analyze Mexico's political system centers on the role of the official party. Until a decade ago, except for popular-front enthusiasts who read much more into official-party functions than actually existed, scholars generally agreed that the party represented little more than an appendage of the presidential office, *gobernación* ministry, and governors and *caciques* in the states. Representative of this view were J. Lloyd Mecham, "Mexican Federalism—Fact or Fiction," *Annals of the American Academy of Political and Social Science* (208, 1940); "An Appraisal of the Mexican Revolution" in A. Curtis Wilgus, *The Carib-bean at Mid-Century* (Gainesville, 1951); and Frank Tannenbaum, "Personal Government in Latin America," *Foreign Affairs* (XXVII, 1948), and *Mexico: The Struggle for Peace and Bread* (New York, 1950). Then, in 1953, Howard F. Cline, *The United States and Mexico* (Cambridge, 1953), presented a qualified version of the popular-front notion emphasizing the concept of "intraparty democracy" and of political power centralized in official-party organization instead of in the President of Mexico, state governors, and local chieftains. Modified aspects of the Cline analysis were employed in the studies noted above by Brandenburg (1955 and 1957), Padgett (1955), and Tucker (1957). These three studies in turn were modified further by Padgett, "Mexico's One-Party System: A Re-evaluation," *American Political Science*

Review (LI, 1957), and Brandenburg, "Political Parties and Elections," in Harold E. Davis, ed., *Government and Politics in Latin America* (New York, 1958). Synthesizing concepts of the Cline, Brandenburg, Padgett, and Tucker studies, but inflating the degree and nature of power exercised by the official party proper as well as the membership statistics reached through direct field research and presented earlier in the Davis book (pp. 208–9), Professor Scott (1959 study) saw Mexico's political system run by a "democratic official party." This view by and large was presented anew in Howard F. Cline, *Mexico: Revolution to Evolution, 1940–1960* (London, 1962). Meanwhile, Philip B. Taylor, Jr., "The Mexican Elections of 1958: Affirmation of Authoritarianism," *Western Political Quarterly* (XIII, 1960), contended that the concept of Mexico's political system centering in the official party was erroneous and that interests outside the party and the political elite above the party exercised transcendent influence. Salvador Madariaga, *The Eagle and the Bear* (New York, 1962), reasserted the concept of personal government. The version presented in Chapters 3–7 of the present volume, by placing the official party in the larger context of the Mexican political system and advancing the idea of the Revolutionary Family, comes nearest to the Madariaga, Mecham, Tannenbaum, and Taylor concepts, and in doing so challenges popular-front, intraparty democracy notions, including the major assumptions of my own previous studies (1955 and 1958).

In addition to the studies already mentioned, plus those listed under sources for "Fifty Years of Revolution" by Dulles, Gruening, Kirk, Prewett, and Tannenbaum, several works in English on themes other than or broader than the respective political publics highlighted in Chapter 5 contain useful material: Harold E. Davis, ed., *Government and Politics in Latin America;* John J. Johnson, *The Military and Society in Latin America* (Stanford, 1964), ed., *The Role of the Military in Underdeveloped Countries* (Princeton, 1962), and *Political Change in Latin America: The Emergence of the Middle Sectors* (Stanford, 1958); Orrin E. Klapp and L. Vincent Padgett, "Power Structure and Decision-Making in a Mexico Border City," *American Journal of Sociology* (LXV, 1960); Oscar Lewis, *Life in a Mexican Village: Tepoztlán Restudied* (Urbana, 1951); Edwin Lieuwen, *Arms and Politics in Latin America* (New York, 1961); Austin F. Macdonald, *Latin American Politics and Government* (New York, 1954); W. W. Pierson and Federico Gil, *Governments of Latin America* (New York, 1957); Robert E. Scott, "Budget Making in Mexico," *Inter-American Economic Affairs* (IX, 1955); Eyler Simpson, *The Ejido: Mexico's Way Out* (Chapel Hill, 1934); William Stokes, *Latin American Politics* (New York, 1958); Frank Tannenbaum, "Reflections on the Mexican Revolution," *Journal of International Affairs* (IX, 1955); and Nathan Whetten, *Rural Mexico* (Chicago, 1948) and "The Rise of the Middle Class in Mexico," in *Materiales para el estudio de la clase media en América* (Vol. II, Washington, 1950).

In the same context, a number of studies published in Mexico merit recognition: Gonzalo Aguirre Beltrán, *El proceso de aculturación* (1957) and *Formas de gobierno indígena* (1953); Víctor Alba, *Las ideas sociales contemporáneas en México* (1960); Frank R. Brandenburg, "Capitalismo, socialismo y empresa: el caso de México," *Ciencias Políticas y Sociales* (VIII, 1962); Alberto Bremauntz, *La batalla ideológica en México* (1962); Luis Cabrera, *Obras políticas del Lic. Blas Urrea, 1909-1912* (1921) and *Veinte años después* (1938); Alberto María Carreño, "Las clases sociales en México," *Revista Mexicana de Sociología* (XII, 1950); José R. Colín, *Hacia dónde vamos* (1948); Rafael Corrales Ayala, "Características del estado mexicano,"

Mario de la Cueva, "La constitución política," Vicente Fuentes Díaz, "Partidos y corrientes políticas," and Pablo González Casanova, "La opinión pública," all in *México: 50 años de revolución*. Vol. III, *La política* (1961); Vicente Fuentes Díaz, *Los partidos políticos en México* (2 vols., 1956); Francisco González Pineda, *El mexicano: su dinámica psicosocial* (1959); José Iturriaga, "Los presidentes y las elecciones en México," *Ciencias Políticas y Sociales* (IV, 1958) and *La estructura social y cultural de México* (1951); Lucio Mendieta y Núñez, "La clase media en México," *Revista Mexicana de Sociología* (XVII, 1955), *Las clases sociales* (1947), and *Los partidos políticos* (1947); Julio Ochoa Durán, *Población* (1955); Alberto J. Pani, ed., *Una encuestra sobre la cuestión democrática en México* (1948) and *El problema supremo de México* (1955); Emilio Rabasa, *La constitución y la dictadura* (1956); Hugo Rangel Couto, *Socioplaneación de México* (1958); Guadalupe Salas Ortega, *Directorio de asociaciones y institutos científicos y culturales de la república mexicana* (1959); Rosendo Salazar, *Historia de las luchas proletarias de México* (1956); Andrés Serra Rojos, *Los partidos políticos: reflexiones sobre sus plataformas y programas* (1958) and *La estructura del estado mexicano* (1948); Felipe Tena Ramírez, *Leyes fundamentales de México, 1808-1957* (1957); Gutierre Tibón, *México 1950* (1950); Leopoldo Zea, "La revolución, el gobierno y la democracia," *Ciencias Políticas y Sociales* (V, 1959); and Juan F. Zorilla, *El régimen jurídico mexicano y la cuestión social* (1954).

Among the many written sources focusing on the specific political publics identified in Chapter 5, several deserve listing. RADICAL LEFT: The journals *La voz de México, Liberación*, and *Política;* Victor Alba, *Esquema histórico del comunismo en Iberoamérica* (1960); Robert Alexander, *Communism in Latin America* (New Brunswick, N.J., 1957); Rodrigo García Treviño, *La ingerencia rusa en México y Sudamérica, pruebas y testimonio* (1959); Harry Bernstein, "Marxismo en México, 1917-1925," *Historia Mexicana* (1958); Jorge Carrión, *El PRI: Poco pan y mucho circo* (1955); Dionisio Encinas, *Posición del partido comunista mexicano frente a la sucesión presidencial* (1958), *Plataforma electoral del partido comunista mexicano* (1958), and "38 años de lucha del PCM: La posición del PCM frente al problema de la sucesión presidencial," *Liberación* (VII, 1957); José G. Escobedo y Rosendo Salazar, *Las pugnas de la gleba, 1907-1922: Historia del movimiento social mexicano* (1922); William Z. Foster, *Outline Political History of the Americas* (New York, 1951); Manuel Marcué Pardiñas, *Sólo el gobierno puede hacer política? La concentración del poder político en México* (1955); Enrique Ramírez y Ramírez, *Qué haya diputados de verdad* (1955); Rosendo Salazar, *La Casa del Obrero Mundial* (1962), *Historia de las luchas proletarias de México* (1956), and *Líderes y sindicatos* (1953); and Leandro A. Sánchez Salazar, *Murder in Mexico: The Assassination of Leon Trotsky* (London, 1950). INDEPENDENT LEFT: Annual reports of the Partido Popular Socialista, CROC, CRT, and CNT, the journals *Ciencias políticas y sociales, Política, Problemas de México, Cuadernos Americanos*, and *Trimestre Económica*, and the newspaper *El Popular;* Confederación de Trabajadores de México, *Confederación de Trabajadores de México, 1936-1941* (1941); Partido Popular, *Tésis sobre México* (1957), *La situación política de México* (1957), and *Razon histórica, principios, programa y estatutos del partido popular* (1948); and Vicente Lombardo Toledano, *La filosofía y el proletariado* (1962) and *Teoría y práctica del movimiento sindical mexicano* (1961). TRADITIONAL AND REACTIONARY CONSERVATIVES: The journals *La Nación* and *Órden;* the newspapers *El Norte* (Monterrey) and *El Occi-*

dental (Monterrey); publications of the Instituto de Investigaciones Sociales y Económicas; Francisco Banegas Galván, *El porqué del Partido Católico Nacional* (1960); Frank R. Brandenburg, "Organized Business in Mexico," *Inter-American Economic Affairs* (XII, 1958); Mario Gil, *Sinarquismo, su origen, su esencia, su misión* (1944); Manuel Gómez Morín, *La nación y el régimen* (1940); Efraín González Luna, *El hombre y el estado* (1940); Merle Kling, *A Mexican Interest Group in Action* (Englewood Cliffs, 1961); Alfonso López Aparicio, *El movimiento obrero en México* (1952); Bernardino Mena Brito, *El PRUN, Almazán y el desastre final* (1941); Partido de Acción Nacional, *Principios, programa y estatutos del PAN* (1961), *Discursos en la campaña presidencial de 1958* (1958), *Plataforma electoral del Partido de Acción Nacional* (1957), *Programa mínimo de acción política* (1952), and *Acción Nacional* (1939); Partido Nacionalista de México, *Ante una nueva actitud política* (1952); and Gustavo R. Velasco, *Libertad y abundancia* (1958). REVOLUTIONARY PUBLICS: The journals *Ceteme, CNC, Cooperativismo, Dinámica Social, El Regional, FSTSE, La República, Mexicanas, Rumbos Democráticos* (1950-52), and *Tiempo*; the newspapers *El Nacional* and *Novedades*; annual *informes* of the President of Mexico, minister of gobernación, state governors, and central executive committee of the official party; all publications of the PNR, PRM, and PRI; José Barrales, ed., *Pensamiento político de Adolfo López Mateos* (1958); Gilberto Bosques, *The National Revolutionary Party of Mexico and the Six-Year Plan* (1937); Carlos Chico Alatorre, *Cauce y horizontes de la revolución mexicana* (1953); Luis Chico Goerne, *Ruta política* (1946); Rodrigo de Llano, *México y las elecciones de 1958* (1957); Carlos Denegri, *29 estados de ánimo: periplo de una campaña presidencial* (1960); Juan Espinosa, *Presente y futuro de México* (1958); Partido Auténtico de la Revolución Mexicana, *Programa mínimo de gobierno* (1957); Salvador Pineda, *El presidente Ruiz Cortines* (1952); Bernardo Ponce, *Adolfo Ruiz Cortines* (1953); Rosendo Salazar, *La CTM: Su historia, su significado* (1956); and Rodolfo Seller Rodríguez, *La crisis del Partido Revolucionario Institucional* (1956).

RELIGION

Themes presented in Chapter 7 come from various sources. Reference to entries made under the "Before the Revolution" section is suggested. Reference to other printed materials, some of the most useful of which are listed below, served as a guide to informed interviews with scores of individuals. Over the decade 1953-62, indispensable source material was supplied by a dozen individuals high in the councils of Freemasonry, an equal number of dynamic lay Catholics, and members of several old Jewish Catholic Freemason families. By their request, these individuals remain anonymous. I wish to express my deep appreciation to all of them, however, for without their soul-searching replies to my many queries, the writing of this chapter in the form in which it appears would have been impossible. On the content of religion and religious beliefs in Mexico, the following studies are suggestive: Luis Fernández Amaya, "Indigenismo e hispanismo en México: Su génesis y proyección en la conciencia nacional," *Ciencias Políticas y Sociales* (II, 1956); José Gómez Robleda and María Luis Rodríguez Sala, "Como juzgan los adolescentes a sus padres," *Ciencias Políticas y Sociales* (IV, 1960); Francisco González Pineda, *El mexicano: Su dinámica psicosocial* (Mexico, 1959); Santiago Ramírez, *El mexicano: Psicología de sus motivaciones* (Mexico, 1958); and

Francisco Rojas González, "La institución del compradazgo entre las indígenas de México" *Revista Mexicana de Sociología* (V, 1943). Among many studies touching upon Catholicism and Church-State relations, only a few can be listed here. For a pro-Catholic outlook, see Mariano Cuevas, *Historia de la iglesia en Méjico* (5 vols., Tlalpan, Mexico, and El Paso, Texas, 1921–28); F. C. Kelley, *Blood-Drenched Altars* (Milwaukee, 1935), and Félix Navarrete, *De Cabarrús a Carranza: La legislación anticatólica en México* (Mexico, 1957). Two scholarly studies are presented by E. D. Cronon, "American Catholics and Mexican Anticlericalism," *The Mississippi Valley Historical Review* (VL, 1958), and Robert E. Quirk, *The Mexican Revolution and the Catholic Church, 1910-1929, An Ideological Study* (Ph.D. diss., Harvard, 1950). A Protestant approach is available in C. S. Macfarland, *Chaos in Mexico: The Conflict of Church and State* (New York, 1935), and in the more scholarly J. Lloyd Mecham, *Church and State in Latin America* (Chapel Hill, 1934). The history of Freemasonry in Mexico is so relevant a theme that one wonders why historians have not devoted greater attention to it. The account presented in Chapter 7 draws heavily from private records unavailable to the historian and from personal recollections of Mexicans and resident foreigners intimately associated with the movement. Three studies available to the scholar are: J. Mateos, *La masonería en México* (2 vols., Mexico, 1887); Luis J. Zalce y Rodríguez, *Apuntes para la historia de la masonería en México* (2 vols., Mexico, 1950); and Félix Navarrete, *La masonería en la historia y en las leyes de México* (Mexico, 1957). A sizable quantity of literature is available on education in Mexico. Annual reports and special publications of the Secretaría de Educación Pública and the biweekly *Gaceta de la Universidad* (U.N.A.M.) contain useful material. Several interpretative studies in Spanish, all published in Mexico, are still valuable: Manuel Gamio, *Forjando Patria* (1916) and *Hacia un México nuevo* (1935); Antonio Grompone, *Universidad oficial y universidad viva* (1954); Francisco Larroyo, *Historia comparada de la educación en México* (1947); Vicente Lombardo Toledano, *Análisis filosófico del artículo 3 de la constitución* (1959); Jaime Torres Bodet, *Educación mexicana* (1944). In English, earlier studies by Irma Wilson, George Kneller, and George I. Sanchez have been synthesized admirably by Marjorie C. Johnson, *Education in Mexico* (Washington, 1956). Needed in English is a comprehensive study of the quality and various types of education now offered at all levels as well as a thorough evaluation of the Torres Bodet projections for the next decade.

ECONOMIC DEVELOPMENT

Economists will observe that Chapters 8–11 present much previously unpublished material. Access to new sources arose from my assumption of various identities. My consultant work with Mexican and foreign business concerns uncovered facts of Mexico's economic system not available in published and, in some instances, publishable form. My earlier research on labor and agrarian politics and on interest groups, including organized business, led to an accumulation of valuable data. My seminars on Latin American entrepreneurs, the Mexican economic system, labor in Latin America, Latin American economic problems, and the economics of development provided opportunities for concentrated field research on select topics. Supervision of theses and direction of a doctoral research project also contributed useful data. Officials of private business concerns, the Mexican government, ECLA,

CEMLA, trade unions, business chambers, and embassy staffs supplied information from their files. Above all, the four chapters probably reflect my personal involvement in Mexico's economic development during a decade of great material advances and equally great political tension.

A rapidly growing amount of published literature also eased immeasurably the task of presenting my case on Mexican economic life. Recent interpretative studies on the developing areas that I found especially helpful in presenting the Mexican case included: Gabriel A. Almond and James S. Coleman, eds., *The Politics of the Developing Areas* (Princeton, 1960); Robert E. Asher and others, *Development of the Emerging Countries: An Agenda for Research* (Washington, 1962); Horace Belshaw, *Agricultural Credit in Economically Underdeveloped Countries* (Rome, 1959); Ralph Braibanti and Joseph J. Spengler, eds., *Tradition, Values, and Socio-Economic Development* (Durham, 1961); John K. Galbraith, *Economic Development in Perspective* (Cambridge, 1962); Everett E. Hagen, *On the Theory of Social Change: How Economic Growth Begins* (Homewood, Ill., 1962); Frederick H. Harbison and Charles A. Myers, *Management in the Industrial World: An International Analysis* (New York, 1959); Albert O. Hirschman, *The Strategy of Economic Development* (New Haven, 1958); Bert F. Hoselitz, *Sociological Aspects of Economic Growth* (Glencoe, Ill., 1960); International Labour Organization, *Employment Objectives in Economic Development: Report of a Meeting of Experts* (Geneva, 1961); David C. McClelland, *The Achieving Society* (Princeton, 1961); and Eugene Staley, *The Future of Underdeveloped Countries: Political Implications of Economic Development* (New York, 1961).

Among recent studies focusing on Latin American economic matters, I found the following especially helpful: Agency for International Development, *Report Prepared by the Government of the United States of America for the Second Annual Meetings of the Inter-American Economic and Social Council at the Expert and Ministerial Levels, São Paulo, Brazil, October–November, 1963* (Washington 1963); F. C. Benham and H. A. Holley, *A Short Introduction to the Economy of Latin America* (London, 1960); Frank R. Brandenburg, *Latin American Private Enterprise* (Washington, in press); Committee for Economic Development, *Cooperation for Progress in Latin America* (New York, 1961); John P. Powelson, *Latin America: Today's Economic and Social Revolution* (New York, 1964); H. S. Ellis and H. C. Wallich, eds., *Economic Development for Latin America* (New York, 1961); Edmundo Flores, *Tratado de economía agrícola* (Mexico, 1961); Horacio Flores de la Peña, *Los obstáculos al desarrollo económico: el desequilibrio fundamental* (Mexico, 1955); Albert O. Hirschman, ed., *Latin American Issues: Essays and Comments* (New York, 1961) and his *Journeys Toward Progress: Studies of Economic Policy-Making in Latin America* (New York, 1963); International Bank for Reconstruction and Development, *The World Bank in Latin America* (Washington, 1960) and *The World Bank Group in the Americas* (Washington, 1963); National Planning Association, *The Future of Latin American Exports to the United States: 1965 and 1970* (Washington, 1960) and *Technical Cooperation in Latin America: Recommendations for the Future* (Washington, 1956); Pan American Union, *Planning for Economic and Social Development for Latin America* (Washington, 1961); Pan American Union and Agency for International Development, *Alianza Para El Progreso: The Record of Punta del Este* (Washington, 1962); Theodore W. Schultz, *The Economic Test in Latin America* (Ithaca, 1956); Arnold Toynbee, *The Economy of the Western Hemisphere* (London, 1963); U. S. Department of Commerce, *Proposals to Improve the Flow of U.S. Private*

Investment in Latin America (Washington, 1963); United States Senate, *United States–Latin American Relations* (Washington, 1960); and Víctor Urquidi, *Free Trade and Economic Integration in Latin America* (Berkeley and Los Angeles, 1962) and *Viabilidad económica de la América Latina* (Mexico, 1962).

Current source material on Mexican economic development is found in a growing list of publications. There are the annual publications: *Statistical Yearbook and Economic Survey of Latin America* (United Nations); *Aspectos monetarios de las economias latinoamericanas* (CEMLA); yearly reports of the OAS, IMF, IBRD, and the Inter-American Development Bank; *Informe anual* (President of Mexico); *Memoria anual* (Comisión Nacional de Valores); *Anuario Financiero de México* (Mexican Bankers Association); *Anuario Estadístico* and *Anuario Estadístico del Comercio Exterior de los Estados Unidos Mexicanos* (Dirección General de Estadístico); *Informe anual* (Nacional Financiera); *Informe anual* (Banco de México); the annual reports of the ministries of finance and public credit, industry and commerce, communications and transport, public works, agriculture and stock-raising, hydraulic resources, national patrimony, and labor and social welfare; the annual reports of the private Mexican credit institutions—Banco Nacional de México, Banco de Comercio, Banco Internacional, Sociedad Mexicana de Crédito Industrial, Banco de Londres y México, and Banco Comercial Mexicano; and the annual reports of the Confederación de Cámaras Nacionales de Comercio and Confederación de Cámaras Industriales business chambers. There is the biannual *Boletín Económico de América Latina* (ECLA), the triannual *Económia Latinoamericana* (Pan American Union), and the irregular *Problemas Agrícolas e Industriales* (private). There are the quarterlies: *Latin American Business Highlights* (Chase Manhattan Bank); *El Trimestre Económico* (Fondo de Cultura Económica); *Revista de Administración Pública* (Instituto de Administración Pública); and *Inter-American Economic Affairs* (private). There are the monthlies: *Suplemento Mensual* (CEMLA); *Boletín Mensual* (Dirección de Economía Rural, Secretaría de Agricultura y Ganadería); *Comercio Exterior* (Banco Nacional de Comercio Exterior); *Noticias Latino-Americanas* (Latin-American News Institute Associates); *Economic Panorama* (Banco de Comercio); *International Financial Statistics* (IMF); *Review of the Economic Situation of Mexico* (Banco Nacional de México); *Industria* (Confederación de Cámaras Industriales); *Mexican-American Review* (American Chamber of Commerce of Mexico); *Reseña económica y tecnológica* (Banco de México); *Espejo* (Instituto de Investigaciones Sociales y Económicas); *Comercio Mexicano* (Confederación de Cámaras Nacionales de Comercio); *Comercio Mundial* (ANIERM); *Monthly Bulletin of Statistics* (United Nations); *Noticiero obrero interamericano* (ORIT); and the trade journals *Mexico This Month, Mexican Life, Boletín Financiero y Minero en México, Industria Química, Agricultura y Ganadería, Revista Minera, Revista Industrial, Precios de Mercado, Construcción Moderna.* There are the biweeklies: *Boletín Quincenal* (CEMLA), *Boletín Quincenal* (Cámara Nacional de Comercio de la Ciudad de México); and *Actividad económica en Latinoamérica* (private). And there are the weeklies: *El Mercado de Valores* (Nacional Financiera); *Alliance for Progress Weekly Newsletter* (Alliance for Progress Information Team, Pan American Union); *Noticias* (Council of Inter-American Cooperation–National Foreign Trade Council); and the privately published *Business International, Mañana, Tiempo, Todo, Visión,* and *Mexletter.*

Additional published data was drawn upon for the various subjects of Chapters 8–11. This data is perhaps best listable under three headings: Chapters 8 and 10 (on selective economic themes and industrialization), Chapter 9 (on population, agriculture, and labor), and Chapter 11 (on commerce).

Chapters 8 and 10. For the years preceding 1910, I found useful information in Diego López Rosado, *Ensayo sobre historia económica de México* (México, 1957), and studies listed under notes for "Before the Revolution" by H. H. Bancroft, Daniel Cosío Villegas, Andrés Molina Enríquez, David Pletcher, Richard Potash, Vicente Riva Palacios, Justo Sierra (three-volume work), Jesús Silva Herzog, and Paul Tischendorf. For the Revolutionary epoch, the following studies, all published in Mexico unless otherwise indicated, proved to be constructive: Banco de México, *Tendencias de crecimiento de la industria de transformación en México, 1950-1958, versión preliminar* (1961); Banco Nacional de Comercio Exterior, *México 1963* (1963); Banco Nacional Hipotecario Urbano y de Obras Públicas, *Obras y Servicios Públicos,* a series of monographs on individual federative entity economies (1959–60); W. P. Glade, Jr., and C. W. Anderson, *The Political Economy of Mexico* (Madison, 1963); Frank Brandenburg, "A Contribution to the Theory of Entrepreneurship and Economic Development: The Case of Mexico," *Inter-American Economic Affairs* (XVI, 3, 1962); Antonio Carrillo Flores, "El desarrollo económico de México," *Cuadernos Americanos* (XLI, 1948); Combined Mexican Working Party, *The Economic Development of Mexico* (Baltimore, 1953); Dirección General de Estadística, industrial censuses and population censuses; Manuel Germán Parra, *La industrialización de México* (1954); Henry J. Gumpel and Hugo B. Margain, *Taxation in Mexico* (Boston and Toronto, 1957); Institute of Latin American Studies, *Basic Industries in Texas and Northern Mexico* (Austin, 1950); Daniel James, *How to Invest and Live in Mexico* (1960); George Kalmanoff and Benjamín Rétchkiman, *Joint International Business Ventures in Mexico* (1959); Arthur D. Little, Inc., *Survey of the Institutional and Financial Requirements of Medium and Small Industry in Mexico* (1963); Adolfo López Mateos, *El desarrollo económico de México durante un cuarto de siglo, 1934-1959* (1959) and *Plan México* (1958); Ifigenia M. de Navarrete, *La distribución del ingreso y el desarrollo económico de México* (1960); Antonio Manero, *La revolución bancaria en México, 1865-1955* (1957); Alejandro Marroquín, "Introducción al mercado indígena mexicana," *Ciencias Políticas y Sociales* (III, 1957); *México: 50 años de revolución* (Vols. 1–2, 1960–61); Sanford Mosk, *Industrial Revolution in Mexico* (Berkeley and Los Angeles, 1950); Government of Mexico, *Plan de Acción Inmediata* (1962); Marynka Olizar, *A Guide to the Mexican Markets* (1961); Pan American Union, *Statements of the Laws of Latin America on Matters Affecting Business: Mexico* (Washington, 1956); Stanford G. Ross and John B. Christensen, *Tax Incentives for Industry in Mexico* (Cambridge, 1959); John M. Ryan, *Handbook for the Foreign Investor in Mexico* (1959); Barry N. Siegel, *Inflación y desarrollo, experiencias en México* (1960); Jesús Silva Herzog, *El pensamiento económico en México* (1947); United States Department of Commerce, *Investment in Mexico: Conditions and Outlook for United States Investors* (Washington, 1953); Raymond Vernon, *The Dilemma of Mexico's Development. The Roles of the Private and Public Sectors* (Cambridge, 1963); and P. Lamartine Yates, *Regional Development in Mexico and the Decentralization of Industry* (1960).

On the specific industries described in Chapter 10, several sources, beyond those listed above, merit enumeration. PETROLEUM: Annual reports on Petróleos Mexicanos; Francisco Arellano Belloc, *La exclusividad del estado en el manejo de sus recursos petroleros* (1958); Antonio Bermúdez,

Díez años al servicio de la industria petrolera mexicana (1960); Escuela Nacional de Economía, *La industria petrolera mexicana* (1958); Wendell C. Gordon, *The Expropriation of Foreign-Owned Property in Mexico* (Washington, 1941); José Domingo Lavín, *Petróleo* (1950); and Richard J. Powell, *The Mexican Petroleum Industry, 1938-1950* (Berkeley, 1956). CEMENT: Annual reports of the Cámara Nacional de Cemento; Rachel P. Brandenburg, *The Cement Industry: A Case Study in Mexican Economic Growth* (M.A. thesis, University of the Americas, 1961); Federico Sánchez Fogarty, *Medio siglo de cemento en México* (1957). STEEL: Annual reports of the Cámara Nacional de la Industria del Hierro y del Acero, of Altos Hornos de México, and of Cía. Fundidora de Fierro y Acero de Monterrey; Banco Nacional de Comercio Exterior, *La industria siderúrgica* (1954); Carlos Prieto, *Notas acerca de la industria siderúrgica en México* (1960); and "Proyecciones... 1963–1970," *El Mercado de Valores* (July 3, 1963). ELECTRIC POWER: Annual reports of the Comisión Federal de Electricidad, Nueva Compañía Hidroeléctrica de Chapala, Compañía Mexicana de Luz y Fuerza Motriz (up to 1960), Cía. Impulsora de Empresas Eléctricas (up to 1960); David F. Cavers and James R. Nelson, *Electric Power Regulation in Latin America* (Baltimore, 1959); Ernesto Galarza, *La industria eléctrica de México* (1941); Cristóbal Lara Beautell, *La industria de energía eléctrica* (1953); and Luis Yañez-Pérez, "La nacionalización de la industria eléctrica en México," *Actividad Económica en Latinoamerica* (March 15, 1961). TEXTILES: Annual reports of the Cámara Textil de México, Celanese Mexicana, and Cía. Industrial de Orizaba; Emilio Alanís Patiño, "La productividad de la industria textil algodonera de México," *Investigaciónes Económicas* (1952); Javier Barajas Manzano, *Aspectos de la industria textil de algodón en México* (1959); Banco de México, *Situación presente de la industria textil algodonera en México* (1953); United Nations, *Productividad de la mano de obra en la industria textil algodonera de cinco países latinoamericanos* (1951); *El Mercado de Valores* (December 5, 1960); and "The Cotton Textile Industry in Mexico, A Macro-Study in Industrial Location," in Richard M. Highsmith, Jr., ed., *Case Studies in World Geography, Occupance and Economy Types* (Englewood Cliffs, 1961). PAPER AND PULP: Annual reports of Cía. de las Fábricas de Papel San Rafael y Anexas, and Banco Nacional de Comercio Exterior; "Grupo Asesor en Papel y Celulosa para América Latina," *Comercio Exterior* (December, 1960); and ECLA, *Posibilidades de desarrollo de la industria de papel y celulosa en América Latina* (1952). OTHER INDUSTRIES: Annual reports of business chambers corresponding to industries described and, in the case of the consumer goods industry, sources listed below for notes on Chapter 11.

Chapter 9.   Published material found useful in preparing this chapter and not cited previously includes: annual volumes of the FAO, ILO, Banco Nacional de Crédito Agrícola, Banco Nacional de Crédito Ejidal, Departamento Agrario y Colonización, Instituto Mexicano de Seguro Social, Guanos y Fertilizantes de México, Confederación Nacional Campesina, and Confederación de Trabajadores de México; agricultural censuses conducted by the Dirección General de Estadística; the following studies published in Mexico by the Fondo de Cultura Económica—Julio Durán Ochoa, *Población* (1955); Ramón Fernández y Fernández and Ricardo Acosta, *Política agrícola* (1961); Armando González Santos, *La agricultura; estructura y utilización de los recursos* (1957); José E. Iturriaga, *La estructura social y cultural en México* (1951); Adolfo Orive Alba, *La política de irrigación* (1960); Guadelupé

Rivera Marín, *El mercado de trabajo: Relaciones oberopatronales* (1955); Jesús Silva Herzog, *El agrarismo mexicano y la reforma agraria* (1959)—and, even omitting articles, a substantial number of other publications, both in English and Spanish.

First of all, the publications in English: Robert Alexander, *Communism in Latin America* (New Brunswick, 1957); Odilo Blanco, *Public Housing in Mexico* (M.A. thesis, University of the Americas, 1962); Marjorie Clark, *Organized Labor in Mexico* (Chapel Hill, 1934); Tom Gill, *Land Hunger in Mexico* (Washington, 1951); Henrik F. Infield and Koka Freir, *People in Ejidos* (New York, 1954); John J. Johnson, *Political Change in Latin America: The Emergence of the Middle Sectors* (Stanford, 1958); Oscar Lewis, *The Children of Sánchez* (New York, 1961), *Five Families: Mexican Case Studies in the Culture of Poverty* (1959), *Life in a Mexican Village: Tepotzlán Revisited* (Urbana, 1951); George M. McBride, *The Land Systems of Mexico* (New York, 1923); Wilbert Moore, *Industrialization and Labor* (Ithaca, 1951); Paul Price, *An Investigation into Mexico's Ability to Feed Itself in the Future* (M.A. thesis, University of the Americas, 1961); Eyler N. Simpson, *The Ejido: Mexico's Way Out* (Chapel Hill, 1937); Frank Tannenbaum, *The Mexican Agrarian Revolution* (Washington, 1930) and *Mexico: The Struggle for Peace and Bread* (New York, 1950); United Nations, *Progress in Land Reform* (New York, 1954); United States Department of Labor, *Labor in Mexico* (Washington, 1957); William Vogt, *Road to Survival* (New York, 1948); and Nathan Whetten, *Rural Mexico* (Chicago, 1948).

Finally, the book-length studies in Spanish, all published in Mexico: American Chamber of Commerce of Mexico, *Encuesta de salarios y prestaciones entre compañías manufactureras y de servicios* (1962); Raúl Benítez Zenteno, *Análisis demográfico de México* (1961); María Elvira Bermúdez, *La vida familiar del mexicano* (1955); Ángel Caso, *Derecho agrario: historia, derecho positivo, ontología* (1950); Jacques Chonchol, *Los distritos de riego del Noroeste: teniencia y aprovechamiento de la tierra* (1957); ECLA, *Los recursos humanos de Centroamérica, Panamá y México en 1950-1980 y sus relaciones con algunos aspectos del desarrollo económico* (1960); Ana María Flores, *La magnitud del hambre en México* (1961); Miguel García Cruz, *Evolución mexicana del ideario de la seguridad social* (1962); José Gómez Robleda and Ada d'Aloja, *La familia y la casa* (1959); Miguel Huerta Maldonado, *El nivel de vida en México* (1959); Gilberto Loyo, *La población de México; estado actual y tendencias, 1950-1980* (1960), *La presión demográfica* (1949), and *La política demográfica de México* (1935); Andrés Molina Enríquez, *La revolución agraria de México* (1937); Lucio Mendieta y Núñez, *El problema agrario de México* (1959); Manuel Moreno Sánchez and others, *Política ejidal* (1960); Jorge L. Tamayo, *El aprovechamiento del agua y del suelo en México* (1959); Universidad Veracruzana, *Proyecto de solución integral a los problemas de la industria azucarera en México* (1962); Jorge A. Vivó, *La conquista de nuestro suelo; estudio sobre los recursos naturales de México* (1958); and Luis Yáñez-Pérez, *La mecanización de la agricultura mexicana* (1957).

Chapter 11.   Previously uncited sources were consulted in writing on the three branches of commerce described in this chapter. TRANSPORTATION AND COMMUNICATIONS: Annual reports of the Banco Nacional Cinematográfica, Banco Nacional de Transportes, Cámara Nacional de la Industria Cinematográfica, Cámara Nacional de la Industria de Radiodifusión, Cámara Nacional de Transportes y Comunicaciones, Compañía Mexicana de

Aviación, Constructora Nacional de Carros de Ferrocarril, Diesel Nacional, Ferrocarriles Nacionales de México, Secretaría de Marina, and Teléfonos de México; monthly numbers of the journal *Tráfico*; Dirección General de Estadística, *Tercer Censo General de Transportes de los Estados Unidos Mexicanos* (1957); and Carlos Villafuerte, *Ferrocarriles* (1959). HOTEL INDUSTRY: Annual reports of the Department of Tourism and Nacional Hotelera; special studies by the Mexican Hotel Association (AMHRM), National Confederative Association of Hotels (CNAH), Secretaría de Salubridad y Asistencia Pública, Mexican Automobile Association (AMA), North American Pro-Mexico Committee, Mexican Association of Travel Agents (AMAV), and National Tourist Council. MERCHANDISING: Annual reports of the national business chambers of oil, greases and soap, of electrical products, of the bakery industry, of beauty products, and of the clothing industry, of the Asociación Nacional de Fabricantes de Aparatos Domésticos, CONASUPO, Sociedad Mexicana de Crédito Industrial, Banco Nacional de México, Sanborn Hermanos, Super Mercados, Cuauhtémoc, Cervecería Moctezuma, La Tabacalera Mexicana, and Celanese Mexicana; Robert J. Donnay, *The Mexican Consumer Market: A Marketing Research Analysis* (M.A. thesis, University of the Americas, 1960); Frank M. Dunbaugh, *Marketing in Latin America* (New York, 1960); John Fayerweather, *Management of International Operations* (New York, 1960); and National Planning Association, *Sears, Roebuck de Mexico, S.A.* (Washington, 1953).

INTERNATIONAL AFFAIRS

Although the stockpile of studies on Mexican diplomatic history written from a Mexican point of view is growing notably, surprisingly little has appeared on the formulation and administration of Mexican foreign policy. In the latter category, valuable exceptions are the two chapters by Luis Quintanilla in Philip W. Buck and Martin Travis, Jr., eds., *Control of Foreign Relations in Modern Nations* (New York, 1957). In the former category, the series of studies under the general editorship of Daniel Cosío Villegas, referred to in the notes on Chapter 1, should be consulted for the 1855-1910 period; also, see his *Estados Unidos contra Porfirio Díaz* (Mexico, 1956) and his *Change in Latin America: The Mexican and Cuban Revolutions* (Lincoln, 1961). Other works of merit, published in Mexico unless otherwise indicated, include: Jorge Castañeda, "Pan Americanism and Regionalism: A Mexican View," *International Organization* (X, 1956), and *Mexico and the United Nations* (New York, 1958); Isidro Fabela, *Historia diplomática de la revolución mexicana* (2 vols., 1958–59); Francisco Cuevas Cancino, "The Foreign Policy of Mexico," in J. E. Black and K. W. Thompson, *Foreign Policies in a World of Change* (New York, 1963); Adolfo López Mateos, *México en América* (1960); Aarón Sáenz, *La política internacional de la revolución* (1960); and the monumental Secretaría de Relaciones Exteriores, *Archivo histórico diplomático mexicano* (48 vols., 1923–36, 1943–50).

Scholars outside Mexico have been interested for more than a century in U.S.–Mexican relations. The reader is first of all referred to studies listed under notes to Chapters 2–5, and to foreign economic policies in Chapters 8–11. Including a few exceptional studies cited previously, a selective list of works could not ignore the following: J. M. Callahan, *American Foreign Policy in Mexican Relations* (New York, 1932); Clarence C. Clendenen, *The United States and Pancho Villa: A Study in Unconventional Diplomacy* (Ithaca, 1961); Howard F. Cline, *The United States and Mexico* (Cambridge, 1963);

David E. Cronon, *Josephus Daniels in Mexico* (Madison, Wisc., 1960); Josephus Daniels, *Shirt-Sleeve Diplomat* (Chapel Hill, 1947); Charles W. Hackett, *The Mexican Revolution and the United States, 1910-1926* (Boston, 1926); Harold Nicolson, *Dwight Morrow* (New York, 1935); J. Fred Rippy, *The United States and Mexico* (New York, 1931) and *Joel Poinsett, Versatile American* (Durham, 1935); George L. Rives, *United States and Mexico, 1821-1848* (New York, 1913); Justin Smith, *The War with Mexico* (2 vols., New York, 1919); and Frank Tannenbaum, *Mexico: The Struggle for Peace and Bread* (New York, 1950). Indispensable in studying bilateral relations of the United States and Mexico are the official records presented in U.S. Department of State volumes on the *Foreign Relations of the United States.*

The nature of Mexico's relationships to intra–Latin American and inter-American affairs as well as to over-all United States policy on Latin America is served by reference to the set of writings on broader hemispheric themes. Among the superior studies are: Samuel F. Bemis, *The Latin American Policy of the United States* (New York, 1943); Adolph A. Berle, Jr., *Latin America: Diplomacy and Reality* (New York, 1962); Alexander DeConde, *Herbert Hoover's Latin American Policy* (Stanford, 1951); Donald M. Dozer, *Are We Good Neighbors?* (Gainesville, 1959); John C. Dreier, ed., *Alliance for Progress* (Baltimore, 1962); Laurence Duggan, *The Americas: the Search for Hemisphere Security* (New York, 1949); William Manger, *The Alliance For Progress: A Critical Appraisal* (Washington, 1963); Herbert Matthews, ed., *The United States and Latin America* (New York, 1959); J. Lloyd Mecham, *The United States and Inter-American Security, 1889-1960* (Austin, 1961); Dexter Perkins, *A History of the Monroe Doctrine* (Boston, 1955); Kalman H. Silvert, *The Conflict Society: Reaction and Revolution in Latin America* (New Orleans, 1961); Graham H. Stuart, *Latin America and the United States* (New York, 1955); Frank Tannenbaum, *Ten Keys to Latin America* (New York, 1962); U.S. Senate, *United States–Latin American Relations* (Washington, 1960); Arthur P. Whitaker, *The Western Hemisphere Idea: Its Rise and Decline* (Ithaca, 1954); and Bryce Wood, *The Making of the Good Neighbor Policy* (New York, 1961).

INDEX

Acapulco:
   resort and tourism, 161, 306, 309, 310, 332
   trade and industry, 26, 283, 298, 300
   religion, 194
Agrarian reform:
   significance, 10, 11, 212-213, 339, 341, 345
   in period up to Cárdenas, 28, 38-39, 46, 49, 53, 57, 58, 60, 63, 66, 68, 69, 74, 75, 77
   since Cárdenas presidency, 85-86, 91-95, 105-106, 115, 117, 122, 127, 129, 131, 134, 137, 185, 207, 210, 212-213, 214, 225, 247-263, 339, 341, 345
   tables on land distributed under, 254
Agriculture:
   significance, 10, 11, 15-16, 210-213, 214, 222-224
   credit, fertilizer, mechanization, 75, 104, 109, 110, 133, 139, 212, 227, 229, 230, 248, 256-263, 274, 316, 345
   cultivable land and size of plot, 16, 55, 66, 69, 116, 248-258, 344, 345-346
   irrigation of, 110, 116, 139, 163, 212, 229, 230, 233, 248, 259-261, 263, 326, 335, 343
   labor force in, 16, 19-21, 105-106, 208-213, 224, 244, 334
   productivity and ownership, 15-16, 19-21, 26-27, 39-40, 69, 110, 112, 117, 127-128, 129, 136,

139, 188-189, 205-207, 208, 210-213, 214, 215, 221-222, 224-225, 241, 247-263, 341, 343, 345-346, 364-365
Alamán, Lucas, 34, 188, 265, 351
Alemán, Miguel:
   background to 1945, 64, 101, 145, 146, 147
   as head of the Revolutionary Family, 6, 7, 79, 100-107, 108, 109, 110, 141n, 144, 151, 152, 158, 170, 208, 213, 217, 218, 244, 254, 256, 258, 268, 271, 279, 332
   role in Mexican publics, 112, 131-140
Allende, Ignacio, 33
Alliance for Progress, 330, 331, 338, 339-340, 345, 346-347
Almazán, Juan Andreu, 62, 63, 65, 78, 80, 90, 91, 93, 310
Álvarez, Juan, 34, 183
Amaro, Joaquín, 63, 64-65, 66, 75, 92, 210
Anarchism, 47, 83, 119-125, 129
Argentina, 17-18, 276, 303
Armed forces, military groups:
   before the Revolution, 20, 23, 27, 31-32, 33-37, 44, 45
   role in Revolutionary Family, 3-7, 210
   in the 1910-1945 period, 46, 47-48, 50-51, 52-54, 58-59, 60-66, 67, 74, 77, 79, 81, 91-92, 97, 101, 102, 103, 107, 113
   in Mexican political and security system, 101, 103, 107, 113, 131,

133, 142, 144-145, 149, 150, 152, 155, 158, 159-160, 161, 163-164, 227, 308, 342
in foreign policy, 318-320, 321, 322, 326
in religious associations, 170, 181, 193, 200, 204
Automobile industry, 109, 117, 133, 227, 274, 291
Aviation, 15, 104, 118, 136, 226, 227, 230, 245, 281, 300-301, 308, 319, 344
Ávila Camacho, Manuel:
as head of the Revolutionary Family, 6, 79-100, 101, 103, 106, 110, 144, 145, 146, 147, 170, 207, 210, 213, 244, 254, 332, 355-356
role in Mexican publics, 131-140
Azcárraga family, 220, 267, 303-304, 310, 344

Bailleres, Raúl, 135, 200, 220, 267
Baja California:
economic development, 15, 238, 254, 255, 283, 296, 299, 304, 326
freemasonry, 204
politics, 47, 53, 65, 102, 110, 111, 129, 151
Balance of payments, significance and composition, 17, 103, 216, 222-223, 250-252, 287, 297, 307, 324, 334
Balsa, César, 135, 310, 344
Banco de México, 76, 104, 113, 216, 217, 230, 256, 262, 268, 269, 277, 307, 330
Banking system:
significance and achievements, 15, 17, 216-218
role in economic development, 75, 96, 128, 133, 136, 148, 158-159, 163, 207, 220, 227, 228, 229, 230-231, 243, 256, 259, 267, 277, 280, 281, 304, 314, 319, 323, 329, 330, 340, 343
Brazil, 2, 64, 122, 237, 276, 285, 303, 344

Cabinet (ministries):
composition and role up to 1934,

44, 48, 61, 64-65, 66, 72-75
in the Cárdenas—Ávila Camacho period, 76-78, 79-80, 101, 102, 104, 108, 112
of Alemán, 101, 102, 104, 135
of Ruiz Cortines, 108, 112
of López Mateos, 113-114
selection process, 145-146, 147, 149-150, 153, 157, 158-160, 162
Cabrera, Luis, 14, 50, 110, 349
California (U.S. state of), 199, 201, 332, 334, 336
Calles, Plutarco Elías:
as head of the Revolutionary Family, 4-7, 58-78, 80, 81, 82, 85, 88, 96, 101, 135, 142-143, 145, 146, 320, 332, 355
policies on religion, 170, 179, 186-187, 190, 200-201
and economic development, 207, 210, 212, 216, 244, 254, 259, 266, 294, 298
Calvo Clause, 322
Canada, 197, 222, 285, 305, 307
Cárdenas, Lázaro:
background to 1934, 58, 62, 63, 64, 65, 68, 69, 73, 75, 76-78
importance in Mexican proposition, 8-9, 13, 16
as head of the Revolutionary Family, 6, 7, 78-100, 101, 102, 103, 106, 107, 112, 115, 116, 117, 320, 332, 355-356
role in Mexican publics, 131-134, 137, 142-143, 144, 145, 146, 151, 152
policies on religion, 170, 177, 201, 202-203
and economic development, 207, 210, 212, 213, 225, 242, 244, 254, 264, 267, 271, 272, 283, 294, 309
Carranza, Venustiano, 5, 6, 7, 51, 52-59, 61, 62, 72, 81, 83, 120, 146, 170, 179, 200, 207, 254, 321, 354-355
Caso, Alfonso and Antonio, 14, 42, 70, 348-349
Castro, Fidel, 114-115, 123, 133, 251, 323, 329, 331, 332, 337, 338, 340
Cedillo, Saturnino, 6, 62, 63, 65, 78, 80, 82, 90, 92

CEIMSA foodstuff distributor, 315-316

Cement industry, 15, 40, 41, 98, 105, 220, 266, 267, 270, 281-286

Central America, 23, 42, 285, 305, 325

CGT labor union, 120, 121, 245

Chihuahua:
  economic development, 118, 238, 255, 278, 283, 288, 289, 295, 311
  politics, 46, 49, 52, 53, 54, 58, 81, 109, 129, 331
  religion, 173, 188, 198, 204

China (Red), 2, 18, 133, 339

Ciudad Juárez, 47, 48, 236, 298, 331

Civil service, bureaucrats:
  organized, 84, 86
  role in political system and selection, 91, 133, 134, 135, 137, 145, 158-162, 164
  performance, 16, 48, 54, 67, 68, 75, 104, 106, 107, 201, 227, 230, 241, 243, 244, 245

CNC communal agriculture confederation:
  founded, 85-86
  as interest group, 90, 92, 93, 101, 131, 147, 155, 159, 245-246

Coffee, 311, 324, 334, 344

Cold War (*See* Castro, Communism, Foreign policy, Russia, United States.)

Commercial revolution:
  significance, 14-17, 205-208, 214, 341, 343, 344
  origins and evolution, 26, 27, 42, 68, 88-90, 97-98, 105, 110, 116, 210, 215, 220-221, 225-233, 265-268, 293-317, 365-366

Communication and transportation:
  significance, 15, 215, 217, 224, 226, 229-230, 241, 332, 333, 342
  general development of, 41, 74, 98, 105, 110, 113, 133, 262, 266-267, 278-281, 282, 293-306, 307, 317, 365-366
  (*See* specific sectors of communication and transportation.)

Communism:
  in politics and economics, 73-74, 80, 82-83, 84-85, 86, 90, 92, 93, 94, 95, 97, 102, 112, 113,

  114-115, 116, 119-124, 125, 128-131, 135, 227-228, 246
  and recent Mexican foreign policy, 2, 18, 114-115, 116, 320, 321, 323, 327, 329, 330, 331, 337-340, 346

CONASUPO foodstuff distributor, 117, 136, 256, 315-317

CONCAMIN business association, 88-90, 94, 109, 309

CONCANACO business association, 88-90, 94, 109, 309

Constitutionalism:
  significance, 10-11, 333, 341
  evolution, 64, 68-70, 76, 98, 107, 111, 127, 145, 164, 246

Constitutions:
  before 1917, 33, 34, 37, 38, 43, 55, 185, 186, 188, 194
  of 1917, 8, 10-11, 28, 54-56, 57, 59, 62, 66, 70, 71, 72-76, 100, 105, 117, 120, 127, 128, 170, 175, 186, 187, 188, 189-190, 200, 209, 211, 213, 227-228, 231, 247, 279, 280, 333, 339, 342, 344

Consumer goods, 15, 110, 117, 136, 230, 290-291, 311-317

Cooperatives:
  legality and evolution, 10, 15, 66, 74, 117, 217, 228, 229, 255
  as interest group, 60, 61, 87-88, 94, 132, 142, 152

Corn, 21, 39, 106, 110, 222, 249-250, 252, 311

Corona del Rosal, Alfonso, 114, 151

Cortés, Hernán, 19-28, 70, 351

Cosío Villegas, Daniel, *cited*, 349, 352

Cotton, 221, 225, 249, 250, 252, 286, 287, 324, 328, 334

CROC labor union, 126, 244, 245, 246

CROM labor union, 58, 63, 68, 82-83, 154, 245

CTM labor union:
  founded, 82-85
  membership and organization, 242-247
  in politics, 90-93, 101, 107, 124, 131, 147, 151, 154, 159
  significance today, 346

Cuauhtémoc, 9

Cuba, 35, 114, 115, 133, 192, 251, 303, 323, 329, 330, 331, 337, 338-340
Cuernavaca, 62, 161, 173, 194, 239, 283, 298, 299, 306, 309, 310

Defense (*Consult* Armed forces, Foreign policy, War, Communism, Russia, Castro, United States Inter-American system, Security.)
de la Huerta, Adolfo, 61, 62, 63, 67, 88, 200, 254, 301
Díaz, Félix, 50-51
Díaz, Porfirio, 30, 37-48, 74, 86, 118, 120, 131, 178, 186, 189, 195-198, 200, 208, 214, 216, 218, 219, 265, 266, 294, 302, 313, 314, 331, 351-353
Díaz Ordaz, Gustavo, 113, 118, 145
Drago Doctrine, 322

Economic development:
significance, 14-17, 208-224
before 1910, 19-20, 26-28, 30, 37, 38-42
provisions for in Constitution of 1917, 55-56, 57
evolution in Revolution, 55-58, 96-100, 103, 108, 115-118, 128, 135-137, 205-317, 318, 324, 326, 330, 338, 341, 343-347, 360-366
(*See* Agrarian reform, Agriculture, Balance of payments, Banking, Communication and transportation, Electric power, Entrepreneurship, Food supply, Foreign aid, Policy, Investment, and Trade, Labor, Industry, Petroleum, Property ownership, Taxation.)
Education:
history of, 29, 40, 42, 43, 55, 57, 68, 69, 70-72, 90, 95-96, 101, 114, 129, 177-183, 193, 208, 224
principles and objectives, 8, 9, 10, 14, 55, 57, 118, 166, 170, 177-179
literacy and schools, 2, 79, 96, 104, 109, 122, 159, 178-183, 231, 326, 347

teachers, 81, 84, 86-87, 107, 114, 122, 124, 131, 133-134, 144, 158, 179, 181, 204, 226, 231
students, 122, 124, 175-176, 180-181, 182, 336, 350
Eisenhower, Dwight D., 115, 133, 332
Ejido, ejidatario:
evolution, 50, 55, 69, 87, 96, 103, 105-106, 107, 110, 112, 114, 117, 212-213, 227-228, 229, 230, 244-245, 252-258, 280, 341
table on lands received, 254
as interest group, 56, 85-86, 91-93, 122, 128, 133, 139, 142, 146, 152, 153, 156
Elections:
significance, 3-7, 12, 142-165, 185, 243, 342-343
held, 25, 38, 43, 44-45, 48, 49, 56, 58, 60-66, 67, 76, 90-95, 101-102, 106-107, 110, 111, 112-113, 115
Electric power, 15, 16, 40, 41, 50, 68, 74, 76, 96-97, 104, 115, 116, 122, 123, 133, 136, 139, 163, 208, 210, 211, 216, 219, 227, 230, 231, 245, 277, 278-281, 282, 343, 344, 346
Entrepreneurship:
significance and role, 14, 75, 97-99, 104-105, 125, 134-136, 207-208, 210, 219-221, 225-233, 340, 343-345
in industry, 41, 89-90, 116, 264-268, 272-273, 275-276, 278-279, 282-284, 286-287, 290
in commerce, 41, 88-89, 293, 296-297, 300, 301, 302, 303, 309-310, 311-315, 317
Estrada Doctrine, 321
Europe, 2, 24, 31, 35, 38, 305, 307, 326, 344, 347

Farmers (small independent):
organized, 105-106, 107
productivity and problems, 87, 94, 244, 252-258, 345-346
Flores, Edmundo, *cited*, 209n, 240
Flores Magón brothers, 43, 44, 47, 55, 120
Food supply:
and population growth, 234-263

Food supply (*cont.*)
  problems and distribution, 44, 128,
    213, 300, 311, 315-317
Foreign assistance, Mexican views on,
    118, 139-140, 225, 298, 321-
    325, 328-330, 338-340, 345-346
Foreign investment:
  current policy on, 15-16, 116, 125,
    133, 137, 139, 214-216, 225-
    233, 322, 323, 324-325, 327-
    329, 330, 334, 335, 338, 341
  in Díaz period, 38, 40-42, 43
  evolution, 52, 54, 59, 66, 68, 72-
    73, 75, 89, 97-100, 105, 109,
    120, 127, 128, 130, 134-136,
    148, 188, 210-218
  in industry and commerce, 266-
    267, 279-280, 281, 282-284,
    286, 288-289, 296, 301, 302,
    304, 305, 309, 311-312, 314-315
Foreign policy (Mexican):
  objectives, formulation, administra-
    tion, 17-18, 139-140, 148, 158,
    163, 318-340, 343, 344, 346-
    347, 366, 367
  and the United States (before
    1911), 2, 9, 19, 34-36, 38, 40-42,
    44, 45, 47, 293, 331
  and the United States (1911-
    1961), 50-51, 53, 57, 58, 66,
    68, 72-74, 75, 77, 90, 92, 94,
    96, 97-99, 103, 104, 109, 114,
    115, 116, 330-340
  on Communism, Castro, cold war,
    2, 18, 19, 73-74, 82-83, 120-123,
    126, 129, 329-330, 331, 334,
    337-339
  and the inter-American system, Al-
    liance for Progress, 328, 329,
    330, 337-340, 345, 346-347, 367
  attitudes of Mexican publics on,
    121-123, 124, 125, 126, 127,
    129, 131, 133, 134, 137, 139-
    140
Foreign trade:
  composition of and current policies
    on, 221-223, 233, 250-252, 276,
    277, 278, 287, 289, 318, 323,
    324, 328, 334-335, 336, 338,
    343, 345
  evolution, 26-28, 268, 284, 286,
    288, 290, 296, 297, 300, 305,
    339

France:
  investment and trade, 40, 237,
    258, 266, 277, 279, 281, 297,
    314-315, 345
  foreign policy, intervention and in-
    fluence, 29, 36-37, 53, 192, 193,
    194, 195-196, 342
FSTSE civil servants union, 86, 131,
    147, 159, 161

Garrido Canabal, Tomás, 6, 65, 77,
    80
Garza, Jaime, 310, 312
Garza Sada family, 98, 105, 207, 220,
    265-266, 267, 288, 310, 344
Generation of 1915 group, 349
Germany:
  foreign policy, 53, 57, 59, 90, 121,
    129, 131, 169, 330, 331
  investment and trade, 40, 99, 215,
    225, 237, 266, 277, 279, 284,
    297, 345
  freemasonry, 194, 200
Gómez, Marte R., 80, 151
Gómez Farías, Valentín, 33-34, 178,
    210
Gómez Morín, Manuel, 145, 349
González Pineda, Francisco, *cited*,
    171, 175, 325
Governors:
  election of, 110, 143, 144, 146,
    148, 150-152, 153, 155, 158
  importance and practices of, 4, 38,
    42, 44, 48, 49, 52, 71, 72, 75,
    80, 92, 96, 101, 106, 107, 131,
    141, 142, 159, 163, 164, 170,
    185, 190, 194, 280
  removal of, 81, 103, 111, 115
Great Britain:
  foreign policy and trade, 29, 90,
    98, 222, 330, 331
  investments, 36, 40, 98, 229, 237,
    264, 266, 272, 279, 282, 345
  freemasonry, 43, 50, 197, 198, 201
Greenleaf, Richard, *cited*, 172
Grijalva basin, 15, 118
Guadalajara, 15, 129, 173, 199, 236,
    238, 283, 287, 288, 298, 304,
    306
Guanajuato:
  economic development, population,
    238, 255, 273, 283, 287, 304,
    311

politics, religion, 33, 81, 114, 129, 130, 146, 194, 198
Guatemala, 133, 298, 307, 326, 337
Guerrero (state of):
   economic development, population, 281, 283, 285, 306, 332
   politics, religion, 53, 81, 103, 110, 111, 115, 151, 156, 194
Guerrero, Vicente, 33, 34, 35, 183, 192

Hacienda:
   in colonial epoch, 26-29
   in Díaz period, 38-39, 49, 50
   significance, extensiveness, 96, 128, 148, 208-213, 233, 253-257, 265
Haring, Clarence, *cited*, 24
Henríquez Guzmán, Miguel, 107, 111, 125
Herring, Hubert, *cited*, 24, 172
Hidalgo, Miguel Costilla, 5, 9, 31-32, 33, 192
Hotel Association (Mexican), 308, 366
Hotel industry, 15, 161, 206, 293, 302, 306-310, 336, 366
Housing, 11, 39, 69, 79, 161, 206, 334, 339, 345
Huerta, Victoriano, 9, 48, 50-51, 52, 146, 186
Hyperion group, 349

Indian:
   in conquest and colonial epoch, 19-30, 166, 172, 173, 350-351
   in national period, 12, 30-32, 33, 128, 191, 193, 232, 250, 259, 341
Industry:
   significance, 14-15, 16-17, 144, 148, 205-244, 245-246, 264, 305-306, 324, 326, 341, 343
   evolution, 26-27, 41-42, 56, 84, 88-90, 97, 109-110, 114, 115-116, 127, 119-126, 135-136, 264-271
   specific sectors of, 271-292, 296-298, 305-316
   table on indexes of, 269
Inter-American Development Bank, 329, 338

Inter-American system, 100, 115, 322-325, 329-331, 337-340, 345-347, 367
Interest groups in political system, 2, 3, 66-68, 83-90, 94, 106, 109, 119-164, 308-309, 342
International affairs (*See* Foreign policy.)
International Bank for Reconstruction and Development, 280, 329, 343, 346
International Labor Organization, 323
International Monetary Fund, 323, 330
Iturbide, Agustín, 33, 34-35, 352

Japan:
   foreign policy, 137, 330, 331, 345, 347
   investment, trade, 109, 222, 229, 297
Jenkins, William O.:
   entrepreneurship, 116, 135, 207, 267, 282, 304-305
   foreign policy incident, 58
Johnson, Lyndon B., 115, 137, 332
Juárez, Benito:
   significance, 5, 13
   policies and presidency, 31-32, 34, 36, 37, 178, 183, 188-189, 204, 210, 265, 351-353
Judiciary, judicial processes:
   significance, 10, 11, 131, 141, 158-159, 163, 342
   evolution, 25, 38, 49, 53, 56, 78, 98, 332

Kennedy, John F., 115, 134, 326, 332, 335, 338, 339, 340
Korean War, 324

Labor:
   before the revolution, 20-21, 22, 25, 26-28, 30, 38, 39, 40-41, 43-44
   force, 69, 208-210, 213-214, 224, 237-242, 291, 326
   migratory, 17, 18, 103, 109, 114, 134, 324, 333-334, 336
   movement and unions, 4, 9, 10, 11, 16-17, 52, 53-54, 56, 58, 60, 63-64, 66, 68, 72, 74, 78, 79, 82-87, 90-95, 98, 102-103,

Labor *(cont.)*
  movement and unions *(cont.)*
    114-115, 117, 119-140, 143,
    144, 151, 153-156, 159-160,
    162, 213, 225, 242-247, 294,
    300, 341, 342, 346, 364-365
Latin America:
  free trade area, 118, 222, 324, 344
  economic development, foreign af-
    fairs, 17, 18, 42, 54, 118, 122,
    125, 140, 221, 275, 281, 292,
    303, 305, 323, 325, 337-339
  lessons for 3, 53, 341-347
Lead, zinc, 289-290, 324, 333-335
League of Nations, 331
Legislatures, legislators,
  before 1910, 28, 31, 34, 38, 45,
    185
  of Madero, 48, 49-50
  of Sonoran dynasty, 60-61, 67, 77,
    84
  of 1937, 91-92, 154
  selection of, 94, 131, 148-149, 150,
    153-156, 158, 245-246
  prestige and significance, 55, 56,
    57, 141, 142, 158-159, 163,
    164, 190, 244-245, 342
  in foreign policy process, 319, 320
Legorreta family, 98, 105, 267, 314
Lewis, Oscar, *cited*, 206, 291, 325,
  350
Leyva Velásquez, Gabriel, 108, 111,
  151
Local government:
  objectives and election of, 11, 55,
    91, 92, 109, 130, 152, 162, 342
  prestige, 158-159
  practices, 21, 25, 38, 39, 230,
    280
Lombardo Toledano, Vicente, 6, 80,
  82-85, 87, 90, 92, 93, 107, 125,
  132, 148, 207
López Mateos, Adolfo:
  as head of the Revolutionary
    Family, 2, 3-6, 7, 79, 96, 111,
    112, 113-118, 151, 170, 182,
    183
  role in Mexican publics, 108, 132,
    138, 146, 147
  foreign policies, 320, 326, 332, 335,
    338, 339
  and economic development, 70,
    96, 208, 213, 219, 254, 255,

259, 270, 271, 273, 279-280,
  297, 316
Loyo, Gilberto:
  cabinet officer, 108
  cited, 305

Madero, Francisco:
  in presidential succession of 1910,
    43-48, 197
  as head of the Revolutionary
    Family, 5, 6, 7, 13, 48-55, 57,
    62, 77, 146, 186, 195, 207, 332,
    354
Malthus, 234, 247, 255, 260
Maritime transport, 15, 324, 325-326,
  336
Maximilian, 9, 34, 36-37, 188, 189,
  352
McClelland, David, *cited*, 209n, 349
Mecham, J. Lloyd, *cited*, 171
Mercantilism, 26-27
Merchandising, 15, 110, 117, 136,
  230, 290-291, 293, 311-317,
  366
Mexican proposition (*See* Revolutionary Creed.)
Mexicanism, nationalism, patriotism:
  in Revolutionary Creed, 8-10
  evolution, 44, 68-70, 96-100, 111,
    114, 121, 115-125, 128, 163,
    193, 198, 214, 225-233, 272,
    309, 320, 327-340, 345
Mexico City, Valley of Mexico, Federal District:
  economic development, 18, 42, 59,
    109, 110, 206, 246, 273, 274,
    276, 279, 281, 282-283, 285,
    287, 288, 289, 291, 294, 295,
    298, 299, 301, 302, 304, 305,
    306, 309, 310, 312, 313, 314,
    315, 316
  politics, 20, 21, 23, 30, 35, 36, 45,
    47, 48, 50, 51, 53, 54, 60, 66,
    77, 81, 102, 107, 108, 112, 113,
    129, 147, 150, 151, 152, 153,
    154, 155, 156, 161, 332, 333
  population, 146, 236, 238, 239
  religion, 174, 180, 192, 193, 194,
    195, 196, 197, 198, 199, 200,
    203, 204
Michoacán:
  economic development, population,
    239, 278, 281, 285

politics, religion, 20, 53, 60, 62, 64, 80, 81, 102, 111, 129, 130, 134, 146, 151, 174, 194, 201

Mining:
before 1910, 26, 40, 41, 42, 43-44, 208
development, ownership, 14, 15, 50, 53, 56, 60, 68, 84, 88, 105, 107, 110, 124, 133, 154, 215, 220, 224, 228, 241, 243, 245, 266, 267, 334, 344

Moctezuma, 21, 23

Molina Enríquez, Andrés, 13-14, 43, 55, 348, 352

Monterrey:
economic development, 109, 182, 220, 229, 236, 265, 266, 274, 275, 276, 277, 282, 283, 288, 296, 304, 309, 313, 314
politics, religion, 129, 173, 199, 203, 332

Mora, José María Luis, 178, 193-194, 352

Morelos, José María, 5, 9, 31-32, 33, 34, 192

Morelos (state of):
economic development, population, 15, 239, 283, 285, 287, 298, 299
politics, religion, 53, 54, 57-58, 115, 194

Moreno Sánchez, Manuel, 3, 114

Morones, Luis, 62, 63, 68, 81, 82, 84, 154

Morrow, Dwight, 71, 73, 320

Mosk, Sanford, *cited*, 137, 220, 264

Motion picture industry, 116, 210, 230, 245, 266, 267, 304-305, 344

Múgica, Francisco, 80, 82, 92, 93, 110, 320

Nacional Financiera, 76, 102, 104, 113, 116, 139, 149, 217, 228-229, 232, 269, 277, 288, 308, 319

Navarette, Alfredo, *cited*, 138, 214

Negro, 12, 29, 33, 34

Nonintervention, principle of, 18, 321-322, 340

Oaxaca:
economic development, population,

146, 237, 239, 255, 285-287, 288, 298, 300, 309, 313
politics, religion, 20, 81, 103, 111, 129, 151, 156, 174, 201, 204

Obregón, Álvaro:
significance, 5, 6, 7, 9, 13
as head of the Revolutionary Family, 51, 52-74, 81, 83, 84, 85, 88, 146, 170, 179, 200, 207, 212, 254, 266, 294, 354-355

Organization of American States, 323, 337, 338

Orozco, Pascual, 46, 47, 49, 50, 51, 55

Ortiz Rubio, Pascual, 5-6, 64-65, 67, 69, 78, 146, 195, 254, 332

Pagliai, Bruno, 135, 200, 220, 270, 310, 344

Panama, 42, 303

Papaloapan, 15, 104, 281

Paper industry, 15, 105, 220, 227, 266, 278, 288-289, 311

Pershing, General John, 9, 54

Petróleos Mexicanos (PEMEX), 104, 114, 133, 149, 230, 258, 270, 273-275, 300, 308

Petroleum industry:
in Creed, 10, 15
evolution, 40, 41, 42, 50, 56, 68, 72, 84, 98-99, 104, 109, 114, 117, 122, 123, 131, 136, 154, 210, 211, 219, 224, 227, 231, 245, 266, 268, 270, 278, 282, 343, 344, 346
case study of, 271-275

Plan of:
Hidalgo, 30
Morelos, 32
Ayulta, 34
San Luis, 45-46
Tacubaya, 48-49
Ayala, 49
Orozco, 49
Agua Prieta, 59
PNR, 76, 77
Mexican Liberal Party, 43, 44, 45
11-year education program, 118, 182-183
economic development in 1960's, 118, 205-207, 270, 340, 343

Political parties:
evolution to 1929, 1, 30, 31, 35, 37, 43, 45-46, 49-50, 54, 56-57, 60-

Political parties (*cont.*)
  evolution to 1929 (*cont.*)
    61, 63, 87-88, 101, 120-122, 194
  as part of political publics, 119-140,
    327
  official party, 4, 5, 11, 12, 63, 80,
    83-90, 90-95, 101, 106, 111,
    114, 131-140, 142-165, 177,
    245-246, 320, 341-346
  Communist, 2, 64, 73-74, 80, 82-
    83, 84-85, 86, 90, 92, 93, 94,
    95, 97, 102, 112, 113, 114-115,
    116, 119-124, 125, 128-131,
    135, 227-228, 246
  Sinarquista, 102-103, 129-131
  Trotskyite, 119-124, 125
  PAN, 112, 128, 131, 143
  PNR, 63-67, 69, 76, 77, 80, 81,
    85, 91, 142, 146
  PPS(PP), 103, 112, 125
  PRI, 101-102, 108, 111, 112, 113,
    114, 146
  PRM, 91-95, 131
Political (Mexican) publics:
  identified, 119, 140, 141
  radical left, 83-86, 114, 115, 119-
    124, 129, 141, 358
  independent left, 107, 124-126,
    129, 135, 141, 182, 346, 358
  traditional conservatives, 127-129,
    130, 135, 141, 143, 358-359
  reactionary conservatives, 107, 129-
    131, 135, 141, 358-359
  revolutionary, 103, 114, 115, 131-
    140, 141, 341-346, 356-358,
    359
Population:
  compared, 17-18
  evolution, 20-21, 27-28, 29, 30, 79,
    138, 146, 153, 206, 209, 213,
    223, 225, 233, 304, 306, 326,
    364-365
Portes Gil, Emilio:
  president, 63, 64, 65, 67, 69, 146,
    195, 207, 212, 254
  under Cárdenas, 77, 80, 81, 82, 90
  influence in Tamaulipas, 151
Postal service, 301, 305
Presidency:
  role in Family and Creed, 1-18, 314-
    347
  evolution, 19-118
  relationship to Mexican publics,

    119-140
  powers and election processes, 141-
    165
  in foreign policy, 318-340
Press, 11, 99, 119, 129, 163, 230, 304,
    308, 344
Private enterprise:
  and socialism, 225-233
  (*See* Entrepreneurship, Property
    ownership)
Property ownership:
  in Creed, 2, 8, 11, 15-16, 210-212,
    341, 343-345
  accounting of, 225-233
  evolution, 24, 26, 28, 30, 37, 42,
    55, 56, 57, 58, 66, 68, 74, 75,
    79, 97, 98-100, 103-104, 105,
    107, 109, 115-116, 122, 124,
    127, 170, 188-190, 193
  in industry, 264-268, 272-273, 275-
    276, 278-279, 282-284, 286-287,
    290-292
  in agriculture, 252-256
  in commerce, 293-306, 311-312,
    314, 315
  concept in foreign policy, 322, 323,
    324-325, 327, 329, 330, 334,
    335, 338
Public opinion:
  expressed in Mexican publics, 119-
    140, 164
  and foreign policy, 327-328, 334-
    336
Puebla:
  economic development, population,
    15, 236, 237, 239, 255, 266,
    281, 282, 283, 284, 285, 286,
    287, 298, 299, 309
  politics, religion, 36, 46, 53, 58, 66,
    102, 111, 114, 129, 130, 146,
    151, 156, 169, 173, 191, 192,
    194, 199

Querétaro, 15, 37, 54, 55, 76, 109,
    129, 130, 200, 204, 239, 255,
    285, 298, 314
Quintana Roo, 15, 44, 117, 151, 239

Race, 12, 13, 22, 28-29, 30, 70, 95,
    111, 178, 210, 334
Radio and television, 15, 105, 163,
    220, 268, 291, 303-304, 305,
    310

Railroads, 10, 15, 40, 41, 50, 53, 84,
98, 104, 108, 114, 118, 122,
123, 131, 133, 136, 154, 208,
210, 211, 219, 227, 230, 241,
243, 265, 268, 293-296, 308,
343, 344, 346
Ramos Arizpe, Miguel, 33
Regions, regionalism, 14-15, 19-21, 38,
56, 65, 67, 102, 107, 118, 147,
150-151, 153, 155, 163, 173,
236, 238-239, 244, 259, 304,
320, 322, 323, 324, 325, 326,
337-340, 341
Religion:
church and state, 9, 24, 32-33, 37,
41, 58, 66, 70-72, 90, 93, 95-96,
101, 127-129, 137, 163, 166,
168-191, 207, 210, 230, 359-360
Catholicism, 9, 10, 11, 12, 13, 20,
21, 22, 23-24, 30, 31, 32, 34,
36, 37, 38, 41, 43, 57, 58, 67,
70-72, 75, 114, 129-130, 146-
147, 152, 166-204, 208, 210,
232, 327, 341
freemasonry, 3, 30, 31, 32, 33, 34,
41, 43, 50, 80, 81-82, 95-96,
129, 146, 152, 166, 170, 176,
178, 185, 187, 191-204, 341
Judaism, 13, 166, 168-169, 171,
176, 177, 195
Protestantism, 13, 129, 166-168,
171, 176, 177, 184, 327
Revolutionary Creed:
identified, 3-18, 348-350
historical bases and evolution, 19-
46, 47-347 *passim*
Revolutionary Family:
identified, 3-18, 31, 348-350
evolution, 47-347 *passim*
Reyes, Alfonso, 14, 70
Rivera, Diego, 12, 43, 70, 110, 124,
179
Roads, 15, 74, 104, 163, 226, 230,
274, 308
Rocha, Joel, 98, 105, 135, 220, 266,
267, 310, 312, 313-314
Rodríguez, Abelardo, 65, 67, 73, 102,
111, 135, 146, 151, 195, 254,
260
Rojo Gómez, Javier, 80, 101, 151, 344
Roosevelt, Franklin D., 73, 74, 77,
90, 133, 225, 331, 332, 340

Ruiz Cortines, Adolfo:
as head of Revolutionary Family,
6, 7, 70, 79, 103, 107-113, 114,
144, 145, 146, 147, 151, 152,
170, 332
role in Mexican publics, 138
and economic development, 208,
212, 213, 217, 218, 244, 254,
260, 268, 271, 273, 279, 287
Ruiz Galindo, Antonio, 98, 102, 105,
109, 220, 267, 310, 344
Russia, 2, 18, 56, 73-74, 94, 101, 114,
121-124, 129, 227, 233, 237,
277, 320, 321, 327, 331, 332,
337, 338-340

Sacristán, Antonio, 267, 310
Sánchez Madarriaga, Alfonso, 154
Sánchez Taboada, Rodolfo, 80, 108,
110
San Luis Potosí:
economic development, population,
238, 299, 314
politics, religion, 53, 65, 80, 102,
111, 115, 129, 130, 151, 198,
204
Santa Anna, Antonio López de, 31,
33, 34-36, 178, 352
Scott, Robert, *cited*, 144n
Scott, Winfield, 9, 34-36
Sears, Roebuck, 313
Security:
internal, 162-164, 308
national, 318, 323, 333, 334, 337
Serrano, Julio, 270, 283
Sierra, Justo, 43, 348, 352
Silva Herzog, Jesús, *cited*, 14, 40, 183
Social justice:
component of Revolutionary Creed,
11, 17, 209-210, 212-214
under Sonoran dynasty, 68-70
judgment on, 342, 345
Social order and interest groups, 52,
66-68
Social security, 69, 112, 113, 247
Sonora:
economic development, population,
21, 43-44, 106, 236, 238, 254,
255, 282, 284, 296, 300
politics, religion, 53, 58, 78, 81,
87, 88, 100, 102, 115, 129, 146,
151, 198, 204

Spain:
  colonial rule, 19-35, 128, 166, 167, 168, 192, 211, 232, 259, 264, 286, 350-352
  foreign policy and influence, 36, 90, 99, 127, 129, 131, 133, 174, 180, 203, 234, 327, 331
  investment and trade, 215, 266, 275
State government (*See* Governors.)
Steel industry, 15, 41, 89, 104, 105, 109, 133, 139, 210, 219, 220, 227, 229, 230, 266, 270, 275-278, 281, 282
Steele, Harry, 135, 267
Strikes, 125, 128, 266, 280, 296, 302
Sugar industry, 27, 98, 105, 106, 115, 217, 219, 220, 221, 230, 245, 249-250, 251-252, 278, 288, 324, 334
Supermarkets, 312-313, 315-317

Tabasco:
  economic development, population, 15, 239, 271, 274, 284
  politics, religion, 65, 81, 185, 190, 204
Tamaulipas:
  economic development, population, 239, 272, 274, 278, 304
  politics, religion, 53, 60, 63, 80, 81, 103, 151, 196, 198, 199, 203, 204
Tannenbaum, Frank, *cited*, 137, 179, 205-206, 260
Taxation:
  achievement in economic life, 209, 210, 212, 214, 218-219
  evolution, 27, 28, 56, 74, 103, 117, 118, 129, 133, 136, 270, 298
  projection on, 339, 343, 344, 345, 346
Taylor, Zachary, 35
Teachers (*See* Education.)
Telephone, telegraph, 10, 15, 122, 123, 136, 211, 230, 245, 265, 281, 291, 301-303, 305, 344, 346
Texas, 35, 36, 45, 81, 171, 196, 199, 204, 326, 332, 334, 335, 336
Textile industry, 15, 41, 44, 98, 105, 110, 219, 227, 230, 250, 265,

266, 278, 286-287, 312, 314, 363-364
Torres Bodet, Jaime, 70, 80, 102, 113, 145, 177-178, 180, 182, 319, 349
Tourism, 1, 18, 103, 109, 113, 139, 160, 222-223, 226, 300, 302, 306-310, 330, 333, 336, 343
Transportation (*See* Communication and transportation.)
Trotsky, Leon, 82, 84, 85, 90, 111, 123-124
Trouyet, Carlos, 207, 220, 266, 282, 283, 302, 310, 344
Truman, Harry, 332

UNAM (National University), 70, 108, 133, 179, 180-181
UNESCO, 70, 178, 323
United Nations, 100, 133, 235, 240, 321, 323, 325, 331
United States:
  relations before 1911, 9, 34-36, 38, 40-42, 44, 45, 47, 293, 331
  foreign policy 1911-1927, 50-51, 53, 57, 58, 68, 72, 73-74, 330, 332
  Morrow and Daniels missions, 66, 68, 71, 73-74, 75, 77, 90, 133, 320, 330, 332
  and communism, cold war, Castro, 2, 18, 19, 73-74, 122, 126, 129, 133, 134, 329-330, 331, 334, 337-339
  and religion, 167, 180, 181, 188, 191, 193, 194, 198, 199, 201, 202, 204, 327
  boundary problems, 117-118, 326, 333, 335-336
  case study of relations, 330-340
  compared, 2, 141-142, 148, 166, 205, 209, 210, 217, 219, 220, 237, 248, 265, 284-285, 291, 316
  Eximbank, 99, 138, 228, 231, 281, 328, 340, 343, 346
  inter-American system, Alliance for Progress, 328, 329, 330, 337-340, 345, 346-347, 367
  meetings of presidents, 115, 331-333
  migratory labor, 18, 114, 134, 255, 319, 324, 333-334

tourists, 18, 161, 307, 308, 309, 310, 333, 336-337
trade and investment, 18, 19, 54, 97-99, 116, 118, 136, 137, 210, 215, 216, 222, 225, 232, 233, 250-251, 266, 272-273, 279-280, 282, 288-289, 295, 296, 297, 302, 303, 304, 305, 310, 311-312, 313, 322, 328, 333, 334, 344

Vasconcelos, José, 12, 14, 42, 45, 62, 64, 69, 70, 179, 207, 349
Velásquez, Fidel, 80, 93, 154
Veracruz:
economic development, population, 42, 239, 256, 258, 265, 266, 272, 273, 281, 284, 285, 287, 289, 298, 300, 301, 306, 309, 310, 314, 315
politics, religion, 36, 44, 51, 53, 59, 60, 62, 65, 81, 101, 111, 146, 151, 169, 182, 191, 192, 201, 204
Villa, Pancho:
significance, 5, 6, 9
role in period 1910-1923, 46, 47, 50, 51, 52-55, 57, 58, 59, 61-62, 81, 294, 354-355

Virgin of Guadalupe, 13, 31, 167, 172-173, 176

War, concepts of, preparedness for, 319, 321-323, 324, 330, 337-339
Western Hemisphere, 2, 115, 285, 310, 330, 331, 337, 341
Wilson, Henry Lane, 50-51
Wilson, Woodrow, 42, 51, 53, 54
Women, 94, 110, 174-176, 184, 240-241, 323
World War I, 57, 331, 332
World War II, 82-83, 90, 93, 96, 99, 100, 296, 310, 331, 336

Yáñez, Agustín, 111
Yucatán:
economic development, population, 237, 239, 252, 256, 283, 300
politics, religion, 23, 60, 61, 81, 103, 111, 134, 151, 192, 198, 203, 204

Zapata, Emiliano:
insurgency, 47, 48, 49, 50, 51, 52-55, 57-58, 62, 81, 207, 354-355
significance, 5, 6, 9, 212
Zavala, Silvio, *cited*, 27